A TEXT BOOK OF

# FLUID MECHANICS

FOR

SEMESTER - I

## SECOND YEAR DEGREE COURSE IN MECHANICAL AND AUTOMOBILE ENGINEERING

ACCORDING TO NEW REVISED SYLLABUS OF

NORTH MAHARASHTRA UNIVERSITY, JALGAON

EFFECTIVE FROM JUNE 2013 - 2014

**PV Shrotri**
B. Sc. (Gen.), M.E. (Civil)
Formerly Professor of Civil Engineering
Maharashtra Institute of Technology,
Pune.

N3007

**FLUID MECHANICS (MECHANICAL) (NMU)**　　　　ISBN 978-93-83525-05-8

First Edition : September 2013

© : Author

The text of this publication, or any part thereof, should not be reproduced or transmitted in any form or stored in any computer storage system or device for distribution including photocopy, recording, taping or information retrieval system or reproduced on any disc, tape, perforated media or other information storage device etc., without the written permission of Author with whom the rights are reserved. Breach of this condition is liable for legal action.

Every effort has been made to avoid errors or omissions in this publication. In spite of this, errors may have crept in. Any mistake, error or discrepancy so noted and shall be brought to our notice shall be taken care of in the next edition. It is notified that neither the publisher nor the author or seller shall be responsible for any damage or loss of action to any one, of any kind, in any manner, therefrom.

---

Published By :　　　　　　　　　　　　　　　　　　　　　　　　　　Printed at
**NIRALI PRAKASHAN**　　　　　　　　　　　　　　　　　Repro Knowledgecast Limited
Abhyudaya Pragati, 1312, Shivaji Nagar,　　　　　　　　　　　　　　　　　India
Off J.M. Road, PUNE – 411005
Tel - (020) 25512336/37/39, Fax - (020) 25511379
Email : niralipune@pragationline.com

---

## DISTRIBUTION CENTRES

**PUNE**
*Nirali Prakashan*
119, Budhwar Peth, Jogeshwari Mandir Lane
Pune 411002, Maharashtra
Tel : (020) 2445 2044, 66022708
Fax : (020) 2445 1538
Email : bookorder@pragationline.com

**MUMBAI**
*Nirali Prakashan*
385, S.V.P. Road, Rasdhara Co-op. Hsg. Society Ltd.,
Girgaum, Mumbai 400004, Maharashtra
Tel : (022) 2385 6339 / 2386 9976,
Fax : (022) 2386 9976
Email : niralimumbai@pragationline.com

## DISTRIBUTION BRANCHES

**NAGPUR**
*Pratibha Book Distributors*
Above Maratha Mandir, Shop No. 3, First Floor,
Rani Jhanshi Square, Sitabuldi, Nagpur 440012,
Maharashtra, Tel : (0712) 254 7129

**JALGAON**
*Nirali Prakashan*
34, V. V. Golani Market, Navi Peth, Jalgaon 425001,
Maharashtra, Tel : (0257) 222 0395
Mob : 94234 91860

**BENGALURU**
*Pragati Book House*
House No. 1,Sanjeevappa Lane, Avenue Road Cross,
Opp. Rice Church, Bengaluru – 560002.
Tel : (080) 64513344, 64513355,
Mob : 9880582331, 9845021552
Email:bharatsavla@yahoo.com

**KOLHAPUR**
*Nirali Prakashan*
New Mahadvar Road,
Kedar Plaza, 1st Floor Opp. IDBI Bank
Kolhapur 416 012, Maharashtra. Mob : 9855046155

**CHENNAI**
*Pragati Books*
9/1, Montieth Road, Behind Taas Mahal, Egmore,
Chennai 600008 Tamil Nadu, Tel : (044) 6518 3535,
Mob : 94440 01782 / 98450 21552 / 98805 82331
Email : bharatsavla@yahoo.com

## RETAIL OUTLETS
### PUNE

*Pragati Book Centre*
157, Budhwar Peth, Opp. Ratan Talkies,
Pune 411002, Maharashtra
Tel : (020) 2445 8887 / 6602 2707, Fax : (020) 2445 8887

*Pragati Book Centre*
676/B, Budhwar Peth, Opp. Jogeshwari Mandir,
Pune 411002, Maharashtra
Tel : (020) 6601 7784 / 6602 0855
Email : pbcpune@pragationline.com

*Pragati Book Centre*
Amber Chamber, 28/A, Budhwar Peth,
Appa Balwant Chowk, Pune : 411002, Maharashtra,
Tel : (020) 20240335 / 66281669
Email : pbcpune@pragationline.com

*Pragati Book Centre*
917/22, Sai Complex, F.C. Road, Opp. Hotel Roopali,
Shivajinagar, Pune 411004, Maharashtra
Tel : (020) 2566 3372 / 6602 2728

*PBC Book Sellers & Stationers*
152, Budhwar Peth, Pune 411002, Maharashtra
Tel : (020) 2445 2254 / 6609 2463

### MUMBAI
*Pragati Book Corner*
Indira Niwas, 111 - A, Bhavani Shankar Road, Dadar (W), Mumbai 400028, Maharashtra
Tel : (022) 2422 3526 / 6662 5254
Email : pbcmumbai@pragationline.com

---

www.pragationline.com　　　　　　　　　　　　　　　　　　　　info@pragationline.com

# PREFACE

I am extremely happy to present this book on **"Fluid Mechanics"** as per the New Revised Syllabus of North Maharashtra University, Jalgoan.

This book uses simple language to explain fundamentals of this subject. This book provides logical method of explaining various complicated concepts and stepwise methods to explain the important topics. All chapters are arranged in a proper sequence that permits each topic to build upon earlier studies. Each chapter is well supported with necessary illustrations and neat diagrams.

This book covers the entire subject, that makes the understanding of this subject more clear and makes it more interesting. This book will be very useful not only to the students but also to the subject teachers.

I wish to express my thanks to all those who helped us directly, indirectly in making this book in a reality. I wish to thanks the Publisher, Shri. Dineshbhai Furia, Shri. Jignesh Furia and Shri. M. P. Munde who have taken immense effort to get this book in the time with quality printing. I am also thankful to Mr. Akbar Shaikh (for DTP), Mrs. Anjali Mule (for Figures drawn), Mrs. Roshan Shaikh (for Proof reading) and Mr. Ubhe Kaka for their help.

At the last but not the least, we are also thankful to the reader. Any suggestion for the improvement of this book will be acknowledged and well appreciated.

26th **August 2013**

**Pune**                                                                                           **PV Shrotri**

# SYLLABUS

## UNIT - 1

1. **Fluid Properties and Hydrostatic**            (No. of Lectures : 12, Marks : 16)

   (a) Fluid Properties and its Definitions, Definition of Fluid, Viscosity, Bulk Modulus of Elasticity, Vapour pressure, Surface tension, Capillarity, Manometers (No Numerical on Manometers)

   (b) Pascal's law, Hydrostatic law, Its derivation.

   (c) Total Pressure and Centre of pressure on Vertical, Horizontal, Inclined, Curved Surface, its derivation.

   (d) Concept of Buoyancy and Flotation, Meta Centre, Metacentric height, its derivation. Stability, Unstability, Equilibrium of floating and Submerged body.

## UNIT - 2

2. **Fluid Kinematics and Dynamics**            (No. of Lectures : 08, Marks : 16)

   (a) Types of Flow, Definition of Steady, Unsteady, Uniform, Non-uniform, Laminar, Turbulent, Compressible, Incompressible, Rotational, Irrotational flow, 1D-2D flows, Stream line, Streak line, Path line, Concept of Velocity, Potential and Stream Function Flow Net (No Numerical treatment).

   (b) Continuity equation for Steady, Unsteady, Uniform, Non-uniform, Compressible, Incompressible, 2D Euler's equation, Bernoulli's equation along a Stream line for Incompressible flow.

   (c) Practical applications of Bernoulli's equation - Pitot tube, Venturimeter, Orifice meter.

## UNIT - 3

3. **Viscous and Boundary Layer Flow**            (No. of Lectures : 08, Marks : 16)

   (a) Introduction to Flow of viscous fluid through circular pipes, Two parallel plates derivation.

   (b) Kinetic and momentum energy correction factor (only theory no numerical).

   (c) Power absorbed in Viscous flow, Viscous resistance to journal bearing, Footstep bearing, Collar bearing.

   (d) Introduction to Boundary layer flow, Laminar and turbulent boundary layer, Laminar sub layer, Boundary layer thickness, Displacement thickness, Momentum thickness, Separation of boundary layer. (No numerical treatment).

## UNIT - 4

**4. Dimensional Analysis and Flow through Pipes**      (No. of Lectures : 07, Marks : 16)

(a) Introduction to dimensional analysis, Dimensional homogeneity, Methods of Dimensional analysis - Rayleigh's method, Buckingham's π-theorem, Dimensionless numbers. (No numerical treatment).

(b) Loss of energy in pipes, Loss of energy due to friction, Minor energy losses, Concept of HGL and TEL, Flow through siphon, Flow through pipes in series or Compound pipes, Equivalent pipe, Parallel pipes, branched pipes.

(c) Power transmission through pipes, Water hammer phenomenon (No numerical on Water hammer).

## UNIT - 5

**5. Centrifugal and Reciprocating Pump**      (No. of Lectures : 07, Marks : 16)

(a) Introduction to main parts of Centrifugal pump, Working and Construction of centrifugal pump, Types of impellers, Types of casing, Priming.

(b) Work done on centrifugal pump, Various heads and efficiencies of centrifugal pump, Minimum starting speed of a centrifugal pump, Multistage centrifugal pump, Principles of similarity applied to centrifugal pump.

(c) Specific speed, NPSH, Cavitations in pumps.

(d) Introduction to main parts of reciprocating pump, Construction and Working of reciprocating pump, Classification of reciprocating pump, Slip of reciprocating pump, Air vessels. (No numerical on reciprocating pump).

■■■

# CONTENTS

1. **FLUID PROPERTIES AND HYDROSTATIC**      1.1 – 1.120

2. **FLUID KINEMATICS AND DYNAMICS**      2.1 – 2.66

3. **VISCOUS AND BOUNDARY LAYER FLOW**      3.1 – 3.68

4. **DIMENSIONAL ANALYSIS AND FLOW THROUGH PIPES**      4.1 – 4.72

5. **CENTRIFUGAL AND RECIPROCATING PUMP**      5.1 – 5.60

■■■

# Unit 1

# FLUID PROPERTIES AND HYDROSTATIC

## PART A - FLUID PROPERTIES

## 1.1 Introduction

Fluid is a substance which is capable of flowing. Matter can be classified as (1) solids and (2) fluids. It is the difference in the behaviour of solids and fluids to the application of shear stress which separates them from each other. When a shear stress is applied to solids, within elastic limit, the strain (deformation) is proportional to stress and the strain is recovered as soon as the stress is removed.

On the other hand when a shear stress is applied to fluids, deformation is continuous till the shear stress exists. Further, even if the stress is removed, the strain is not recovered. Thus, the fluids are incapable of resisting any shear stress. It is this inability of fluids to resist any shear stress which makes them capable of flowing.

*'Thus fluid may also be defined as the substance which deforms continuously under the action of shear stress, howsoever small the shear stress may be.'*

**Ideal fluid:** Fluid which does not offer any resistance to deformation under the action of shear stress is called an ideal fluid.

Ideal fluid is supposed to have no viscosity, surface tension and is supposed to be incompressible. Although no ideal fluid exists in nature, the concept of ideal fluid is used to simplify mathematical analysis.

**Practical fluid or Real fluid:** Fluid existing in nature does offer resistance to motion. It has viscosity, surface tension as well as it is compressible. Such a fluid is called practical or real fluid.

Water and air which have very low viscosity are generally treated as ideal fluids.

Fluids are classified as (1) Liquids and (2) Gases. Main difference between them can be given as below.

| Liquids | Gases |
|---|---|
| 1. Have a free surface. | 1. Do not have a free surface. |
| 2. Occupy a definite volume in a container. | 2. Occupy the complete volume of the container and take the shape of the container. |
| 3. Are incompressible (as compared to gases). | 3. Are highly compressible. |
| 4. Properties are not largely affected due to changes in temperature. | 4. Properties are largely affected due to changes in temperature. |

**Fluid mechanics and its branches:**

Fluid mechanics is similar to mechanics of solids and deals with the study of behaviour of fluids either in the state of rest or in motion.

The study of fluids at rest is called fluid statics.

The study of fluids in motion without any reference to the forces acting on fluids and energies possessed by them is called fluid kinematics.

If further, forces and energies are also taken into account, the branch is called fluid dynamics.

## 1.2 Properties of Fluids

The properties of fluids which are important in the study of fluid mechanics are as follows.

### 1.2.1 Mass

Quantitative measure of matter contained in a substance is called mass.

Dimension of mass – [M]

Unit of mass in S. I. system – kg (kilogram)

### 1.2.2 Mass Density

*Mass density or density of a fluid is defined as mass per unit volume of the fluid.* It is denoted by the symbol 'ρ' (rho).

$$\rho = \frac{\text{Mass of fluid}}{\text{Volume of fluid}}$$

$$\text{Dimension of '}\rho\text{'} = \frac{\text{Mass}}{\text{volume}} = \left[\frac{M}{L^3}\right] = [ML^{-3}]$$

Unit of 'ρ' is $kg/m^3$.

At standard temperature of 20° C and under standard pressure of 1 atmosphere, density of water is 998 $kg/m^3$ ($\approx$ 1000 $kg/m^3$). Density of air under similar conditions is 1.205 $kg/m^3$.

### 1.2.3 Specific Weight

*Specific weight or Unit weight or Weight density of a fluid is defined as weight of the fluid per unit volume.* It is denoted by 'γ' (gamma).

$$\gamma = \frac{\text{Weight of fluid}}{\text{Volume of fluid}}$$

$$\text{Dimensions of '}\gamma\text{'} = \frac{\text{Weight}}{\text{Volume}} = \frac{\text{Force}}{\text{Volume}}$$

$$= \frac{[MLT^{-2}]}{[L^3]} = [ML^{-2}T^{-2}]$$

Unit of "γ" is $N/m^3$ or $kN/m^3$.

Further,

$$\text{Weight} = \text{Mass} \times \text{Acceleration due to gravity}$$

∴ $\quad\text{Weight} = \text{Mass} \times g$

∴ $\quad\dfrac{\text{Weight}}{\text{Volume}} = \dfrac{\text{Mass}}{\text{Volume}} \times g$

∴ $\quad\boxed{\gamma = \rho g}$ ... (1.1)

Thus, specific weight of water at 20° C and under atmospheric pressure is

$$998 \times 9.81 = 9790 \text{ N/m}^3$$
$$(\approx 1000 \times 9.81 = 9810 \text{ N/m}^3 \text{ or } 9.81 \text{ kN/m}^3)$$

[**Note:** Unless otherwise stated, γ of water is taken as 9810 N/m³ or 9.81 kN/m³ in this book.]

Specific weight of air under similar conditions is 11.81 N/m³.

## 1.2.4 Specific Volume

The specific volume is defined as volume per unit weight of a fluid. It is denoted by '$V_s$'.

$$V_s = \dfrac{\text{Volume}}{\text{Weight}} = \dfrac{1}{\gamma}$$

$$\text{Dimensions of } V_s = \left[\dfrac{1}{ML^{-2}T^{-2}}\right] = [M^{-1}L^2T^2]$$

Unit of $V_s$ is m³/N.

In thermodynamics, specific volume is defined as volume per unit mass of a fluid.

Thus, $\quad V_s = \dfrac{1}{\rho}$

Dimensions of $V_s$ in this case $= [M^{-1} L^3]$

Unit of $V_s$ in this case is m³/kg.

## 1.2.5 Specific Gravity or Relative Density

Specific gravity is defined as the ratio of specific weight (or mass density) of a fluid to the specific weight (or mass density) of a standard fluid at standard conditions. Specific gravity (sp. gr.) is denoted by 'S'.

$$S = \dfrac{\text{Specific weight of fluid}}{\text{Specific weight of standard fluid}}$$

$$= \dfrac{\text{Mass density of fluid}}{\text{Mass density of standard fluid}}$$

In case of liquids, water at 4° C is taken as standard fluid, while for gases, either air free of carbon dioxide or pure hydrogen at some standard temperature and pressure is taken as standard fluid. Specific gravity is the ratio of two similar quantities and hence is a pure number and has no dimensions.

Specific gravity of water is generally taken as 1.0 and that of mercury is taken as 13.6.

## 1.2.6 Viscosity

One of the very important properties of a fluid is viscosity. Viscosity is very important in study of flow of fluids.

*Viscosity is the property of a fluid by virtue of which the fluid offers resistance to deformation under the action of shear stress.*

In case of *liquids*, viscosity is due to *cohesion* (molecular attraction between liquid molecules) while in case of *gases* it is due to *molecular momentum exchange*.

Consider two parallel plates placed small distance 'Y' apart. The space between them is filled with fluid. Let the lower plate be stationary. Let the upper plate be moved with velocity 'U' by application of force 'F' as shown in Fig. 1.1. Let 'A' be the area of upper plate in contact with the fluid.

Due to viscosity, fluid adheres to the boundary. Thus, there is no relative motion or 'slip' between the boundary and the fluid. This is known as 'no slip condition'.

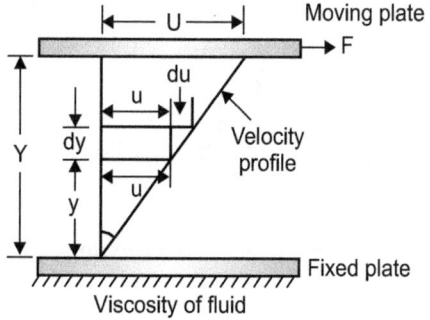
Viscosity of fluid
**Fig. 1.1**

Thus, if the distance 'Y' is sufficiently small and velocity U is sufficiently low, the velocity of fluid will vary linearly from zero at the lower plate to 'U' at the upper plate.

It has been observed that the force 'F' varies directly with the area of contact 'A' and the velocity 'U' and inversely with distance 'Y' between the plates.

$$\therefore \quad F \propto \frac{AU}{Y}$$

$$\therefore \quad \frac{F}{A} \propto \frac{U}{Y}$$

But from similar triangles, $\quad \frac{U}{Y} = \frac{du}{dy}$

$$\therefore \quad \frac{F}{A} \propto \frac{du}{dy}$$

F/A is the shear stress and is denoted by 'τ' (Greek letter 'tau').

$$\tau \propto \frac{du}{dy}$$

∴ We can write

$$\tau = \mu \frac{du}{dy} \quad \ldots (1.2)$$

This equation is called "Newton's law of viscosity".

The constant of proportionality 'μ' (Greek 'mu') is called "Dynamic viscosity" or "Absolute viscosity" or "Coefficient of viscosity" or simply "Viscosity" of fluid. But $\frac{du}{dy}$ represents velocity gradient, or rate of angular deformation.

∴ $$\mu = \frac{\tau}{du/dy}$$

∴ Viscosity of fluid can be defined as the shear stress required to produce unit rate of angular deformation.

[**Note:** Since 'μ' involves force, it is called dynamic viscosity.]

Dimensions of viscosity

$$[\mu] = \frac{[\text{stress}]}{[du/dy]} = \frac{[\text{Force/Area}]}{[\text{Velocity/Length}]}$$

$$= \frac{[F/L^2]}{[LT^{-1}/L]}$$

∴ $$[\mu] = \left[\frac{FT}{L^2}\right] = [FL^{-2}T]$$

If the dimensions of force are substituted as $[MLT^{-2}]$, dimensions of 'μ' work out as

$$[\mu] = \left[\frac{FT}{L^2}\right] = \left[\frac{MLT^{-2} \cdot T}{L^2}\right]$$

or $$[\mu] = [ML^{-1}T^{-1}]$$

Unit of viscosity is $\frac{\text{N-s}}{m^2}$ or Pas, ∵ 1 N/m² = 1 Pa.

Based on dimensions of $[ML^{-1}T^{-1}]$, unit of viscosity is kg/ms.

In C.G.S. system, unit of viscosity is $\frac{1 \text{ dyne-sec}}{cm^2}$ called "Poise".

We have $\frac{1 \text{ N-s}}{m^2}$ = 10 Poise or 1 Poise = $\frac{1}{10} \frac{\text{N-s}}{m^2}$

A smaller unit of viscosity is $\frac{1}{100}$ th of Poise and is called "Centipoise".

In fluid statics, u = 0, $\frac{du}{dy}$ = 0, therefore, viscosity does not play any role.

## Variation of viscosity with temperature:

Viscosity of both liquids and gases varies with temperature but in different manner.

In case of liquids, viscosity is due to cohesion. With rise in temperature, volume of liquid increases, the distance between molecules increases, thus decreasing the cohesion. Therefore, the *viscosity of liquids decreases with rise in temperature.*

In case of gases, viscosity is due to molecular momentum exchange. With rise in temperature of gas, kinetic energy of molecules increases, thus increasing the molecular momentum exchange. Therefore, *the viscosity of gases increases with rise in temperature.*

Under ordinary conditions, viscosity of either liquid or gas is hardly affected by changes in pressure.

## Newtonian and Non-Newtonian fluids

The equation $\tau = \mu \dfrac{du}{dy}$ is called Newton's equation of viscosity.

### Newtonian Fluid:

A fluid for which '$\mu$' is constant is called Newtonian fluid.

Thus, $\tau = \mu \dfrac{du}{dy}$, for a Newtonian fluid.

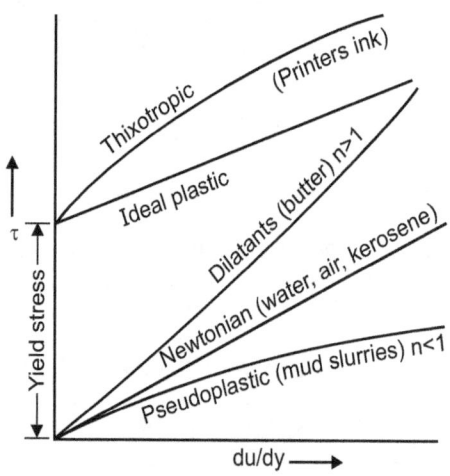

**Fig. 1.2: Rheological definitions of fluids**

Relation between shear stress and rate of deformation is straight line as shown in Fig. 1.2. Slope of this line gives viscosity of fluid. Most common fluids such as air, water, kerosene, glycerine, gasoline etc. are Newtonian fluids.

### Non-Newtonian Fluid:

A fluid for which relationship between shear stress and rate of angular deformation is not linear is called Non-Newtonian fluid. In this case, $\tau = \mu \left(\dfrac{du}{dy}\right)^n$. Some examples of Non-Newtonian fluids are blood, mud slurries, paints, sludges, etc.

If the index 'n' is greater than 1, the fluids are called 'Dilatants.' Butter, quicksand are examples of dilatants.

If the index 'n' is less than 1, the fluids are called 'Pseudoplastics'. Paper pulp, milk, polymer solution are examples of pseudoplastics.

**Ideal Plastic or Bingham Plastic:**

A fluid having a definite yield stress and thereafter a constant linear relation between shear stress and rate of angular deformation is called an ideal plastic. In this case,

$$\tau = \text{Constant} + \mu \left(\frac{du}{dy}\right)$$

Tooth paste, drilling mud, sewage sludge are some examples of Ideal plastics.

**Thixotropic fluid:**

A fluid having a definite yield stress and thereafter non-linear relation between shear stress and rate of angular deformation is called thixotropic fluid.

Thus, $\tau = \text{Constant} + \mu \left(\frac{du}{dy}\right)^n$. Printers ink, lipstick, certain paints and enamels are examples of thixotropic fluid.

The 'X' axis represents an ideal fluid. Since ideal fluid has no viscosity, therefore $\tau = 0$ for any value of $\frac{du}{dy}$. 'Y' axis represents elastic solid.

Fluid mechanics mainly deals only with Newtonian fluids. Non-Newtonian fluids are studied under the head of "Rheology".

## 1.2.7 Kinematic Viscosity

In the analysis of many fluid flow problems, we come across a term dynamic viscosity divided by mass density of fluid. *This ratio of dynamic viscosity to mass density of fluid is called Kinematic viscosity.* It is denoted by Greek letter 'υ' (nu).

$$\upsilon = \frac{\text{Dynamic viscosity}}{\text{Mass density}} = \frac{\mu}{\rho}$$

Dimensions of kinematic viscosity

$$[\upsilon] = \frac{[\mu]}{[\rho]} = \frac{[ML^{-1}T^{-1}]}{[ML^{-3}]}$$

$\therefore \qquad [\upsilon] = [L^2 T^{-1}]$

Since the dimensions of 'υ' involve only length and time and not force dimension, 'υ' is called kinematic viscosity.

Unit of 'υ' is m²/s.

In C.G.S. system, the unit of kinematic viscosity is cm²/s and is called "stoke".

We have 1 m²/s =10⁴ stokes or 1 stoke = 10⁻⁴ m²/s.

A smaller unit which is frequently used is 1/100th of stoke and is called "centistoke".

## 1.2.8 Compressibility - Bulk Modulus of Elasticity

All fluids may be compressed by the application of external force. Such compressed fluids expand to their original volume when the external force is removed.

Compressibility of fluid is expressed quantitatively as inverse of bulk modulus of elasticity 'K' of the fluid.

**Bulk modulus of elasticity** of fluid is defined as

$$\boxed{K = -\frac{dP}{dV/V}} \quad \ldots (1.3)$$

where dP is change in pressure which causes change in volume dV in original volume V. −ve sign indicates decrease in volume with increase in pressure.

$$\text{Dimensions of K} = -\frac{dP}{dV/V} \quad \ldots (1.4)$$

dV/V being ratio of similar quantities is dimensionless. Therefore, K has dimensions of pressure dP which is force per unit area.

$$[K] = \frac{[\text{Force}]}{[\text{Area}]} = \frac{[MLT^{-2}]}{[L^2]}$$

$$\therefore \quad [K] = [ML^{-1}T^{-2}]$$

Unit of K is $N/m^2$ or $kN/m^2$.

Since $-\frac{dV}{V} = \frac{d\rho}{\rho}$, the above equation can also be written as

$$K = \frac{dP}{d\rho/\rho} \quad \ldots (1.5)$$

This equation is mainly used for gases.

At NTP (normal temperature and pressure)

$$\text{K for water} = 2.07 \times 10^6 \text{ kPa (kN/m}^2\text{)}$$

$$\text{K for air} = 101.3 \text{ kPa}$$

which shows that air is approximately 20,000 times more compressible than water.

Further, $\quad$ K for mild steel $= 2.07 \times 10^8$ kPa

which shows that water is about 100 times more compressible than mild steel.

In most of the fluid flow problems involving water, (liquid) compressibility of water is neglected. However, in study of water hammer, wherein water is subjected to sudden changes in pressure of high magnitude, water is treated as compressible fluid and effects of compressibility are taken into account.

Compressibility plays very important role in modern aeronautics.

## 1.2.8.1 Velocity of Sound

Sound is propagated in a fluid due to compressibility of the fluid.

Velocity with which a small pressure disturbance travels through the medium is called velocity of sound in that medium.

Velocity of sound in a medium (like air) i. e. sonic velocity is given by

$$C = \sqrt{\frac{K}{\rho}}$$

The ratio of actual velocity V to sonic velocity C is dimensionless number called Mach number.

$$M = \frac{V}{C} = \frac{V}{\sqrt{K/\rho}}$$

Depending on the magnitude of Mach number, flows of compressible fluids can be classified as follows:

$M < 0.4$ - Incompressible flow
$0.4 < M < 1$ - Subsonic flow
$M \approx 1$ - Transonic flow
$M = 1$ - Sonic flow
$1 < M < 6$ - Supersonic flow
$M > 6$ - Hypersonic flow

## 1.2.9 Vapour Pressure

All liquids vaporize or evaporate. This is due to the molecules escaping from the free surface. If the liquid is contained in a closed container, after some time, an equilibrium stage is reached when the number of molecules escaping from the surface is equal to number of molecules entering the liquid through the surface. *Partial pressure exerted by the vapour molecules on the liquid surface is called vapour pressure.*

$$\text{Dimensions of vapour pressure} = \frac{[\text{Force}]}{[\text{Area}]} = [ML^{-1} T^{-2}]$$

Units of vapour pressure = $N/m^2$ or $kN/m^2$ (Pa or kPa).

If the pressure on the liquid is equal to or less than vapour pressure, it starts boiling, e.g. vapour pressure of water at 100° C is about one atmosphere, therefore, water under atmospheric pressure boils at 100° C.

Higher the vapour pressure more volatile is the liquid. e.g. vapour pressure of petrol at 20° C is 30.4 kN/m² while that of water is 2.345 kN/m², hence petrol vaporizes faster than water.

With rise in temperature, vapour pressure also increases.

Mercury has very low vapour pressure and high density. Therefore, it is used in manometers.

Vapour pressure plays very important role in phenomenon called 'Cavitation.'

## 1.2.10 Cohesion, Adhesion, Surface Tension and Capillarity

### Cohesion:
Molecular attraction between similar type (of the same liquid) of molecules is called cohesion.

### Adhesion:
Molecular attraction between dissimilar type (e.g. water molecules and glass molecules) of molecules is called adhesion.

Surface tension and Capillarity are due to such molecular attractions.

### Surface tension:

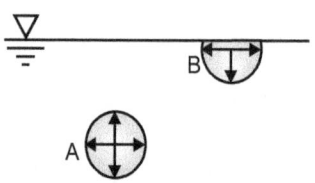

**Fig. 1.3: Forces on the molecules**

As shown in Fig. 1.3, the molecule 'A' inside the liquid is subjected to equal pull on all sides, since it is surrounded by molecules of the same liquid on all the sides. On the other hand, molecule 'B' at the surface of contact (interface between liquid and gas or between two immiscible liquids) is subjected to unbalanced downward pull. All the molecules on the surface are subjected to a downward pull. Due to this the surface of liquid acts like a thin film which is in tension. *This property of surface of liquid to exert tension is called surface tension.*

Surface tension can also be defined as:

*The tendency of liquid surface to contract to acquire minimum surface energy is called surface tension.*

Droplets and bubbles are spherical due to surface tension. Similarly some small insects can walk on water surface due to surface tension.

Surface tension is denoted by 'σ' (Greek letter sigma). It is a line force and is expressed as force per unit length.

$$\text{Dimensions of } [\sigma] = \frac{[\text{Force}]}{[\text{Length}]} = \frac{[MLT^{-2}]}{[L]}$$

$$[\sigma] = [MT^{-2}]$$

Unit of 'σ' is N/m.

Surface tension of water at 20° C is 0.0736 N/m and that of mercury is 0.51 N/m, both in contact with air. Surface tension is important in the study of bubbles, droplets, small models, capillary flows, etc.

Pressure intensity inside the droplet, bubble as well as jet of liquid is increased as compared to outside, due to surface tension forces acting on the surface.

## (i) Pressure intensity inside a droplet:

Consider a spherical droplet of diameter 'd' as shown in Fig. 1.4.

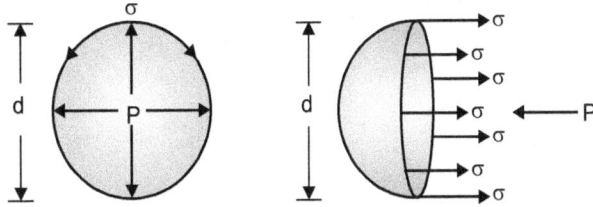

**Fig. 1.4: Forces on droplet of water**

Let intensity of pressure inside the droplet be 'p' in excess of outside of the droplet. Let the droplet be cut into two halves. Forces acting on one half will be (1) due to pressure intensity 'p' acting on projected area and (2) due to surface tension 'σ' acting on the circumference. These two forces must be equal and opposite for equilibrium. Therefore,

$$\text{Force due to pressure} = p \cdot \frac{\pi}{4} \cdot d^2$$

$$\text{Force due to surface tension} = \sigma \pi d$$

Equating,
$$p \cdot \frac{\pi}{4} \cdot d^2 = \sigma \pi d$$

Thus for droplet,
$$\boxed{p = \frac{4\sigma}{d}} \qquad \ldots (1.6)$$

Pressure intensity inside a droplet varies inversely with the diameter of droplet.

## (ii) Pressure intensity inside a bubble:

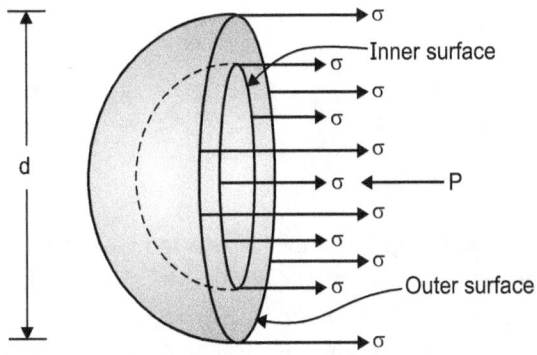

**Fig. 1.5: Forces on bubble**

As can be seen from Fig. 1.5, a bubble has two surfaces in contact with air, one inside and other outside. Thus in this case, surface tension force is double in comparison to a droplet.

| | |
|---|---|
| Force due to pressure | $= p \cdot \dfrac{\pi}{4} \cdot d^2$ |
| Force due to surface tension | $= 2\sigma \cdot \pi \cdot d$ |
| Equating, these two forces, $p \cdot \dfrac{\pi}{4} \cdot d^2$ | $= 2\sigma \cdot \pi d$ |
| Thus for a bubble, | $\boxed{p = \dfrac{8\sigma}{d}}$ ... (1.7) |

**(iii) Pressure inside a liquid jet:**

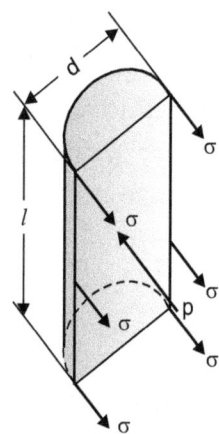

**Fig. 1.6: Forces on jet of liquid**

Consider a jet of diameter 'd' and consider length '*l*' of the jet. Let 'p' be the inside pressure intensity in excess of outside. Let the jet be cut in two halves. Forces acting on one half will be (1) due to pressure intensity 'p' acting on projected area and (2) due to surface tension 'σ' acting along the two edges of the half.

| | |
|---|---|
| Force due to pressure | $= p \cdot d \cdot l$ |
| Force due to surface tension | $= \sigma \cdot 2l$ |
| Equating these two forces, $p \cdot d \cdot l$ | $= \sigma \cdot 2l$ |

Thus for a liquid jet, $\boxed{p = \dfrac{2\sigma}{d}}$  ... (1.8)

## Capillarity:

When a tube of small bore (capillary tube) is inserted vertically into a pool of liquid, the liquid level in the tube either rises or falls relative to the liquid level in the pool. *This phenomenon of rise or fall of liquid level in the capillary tube is called "Capillarity."*

Capillarity is due to cohesion and adhesion. If adhesion between molecules of liquid and tube is more than cohesion between liquid molecules, liquid wets the surface of tube and there is capillary rise. (e.g. water wets glass and rises in the capillary.) (See Fig. 1.7 (a)). Angle of contact 'θ' is less than 90° and the meniscus (liquid surface in the tube) is concave upwards.

On the other hand if cohesion between liquid molecules is more than adhesion between molecules of liquid and molecules of the tube, liquid does not wet the surface and there is capillary depression. (e.g. Mercury does not wet glass and falls in the tube.) (See Fig. 1.7 (b)). Here, angle of contact '$\theta$' is more than 90° and the meniscus is convex upwards.

Rise of sap in a tree, rise of water in soil is due to capillary action.

**Expression for Capillary rise:**

In case of a glass tube inserted in water, if angle of contact is '$\theta$', the water in the glass tube will continue to rise until the vertical component of surface tension i.e. $\sigma \cos \theta$ acting over the wetted length (circumference of the tube) at the free surface equals the weight of water column in the tube above the pool level. (See Fig. 1.7 (a)).

Surface tension force in upward direction

$$= \pi \cdot d \cdot \sigma \cos \theta$$

Weight of liquid in the tube in downward direction

$$= \gamma \left( \frac{\pi d^2}{4} \cdot h \right)$$

Equating,  $\gamma \left( \frac{\pi d^2}{4} \cdot h \right) = \pi \cdot d \cdot \sigma \cos \theta$

Therefore,  $\boxed{h = \frac{4 \sigma \cos \theta}{\gamma d}}$  ... (1.9)

**Expression for Capillary Depression (Fall):**

In case of a glass tube inserted in a pool of mercury, the level of mercury in the tube will be lower than the mercury level in the pool or there will be capillary depression [See Fig. 1.7 (b)].

Let $h$ = height of depression in the tube

When there is equilibrium, two forces acting on the mercury in the tube are:

(i) Surface tension force acting in downward direction = $\pi \cdot d \cdot \sigma \cos \theta$ and

(ii) Hydrostatic force acting in upward direction due to intensity of pressure at a depth of '$h$' below free mercury surface

$$= p \times \text{Area}$$

$p$ = intensity of pressure at depth of h below mercury surface in the pool

$$= p \cdot \left( \frac{\pi}{4} \times d^2 \right)$$

$$= \gamma h \cdot \left( \frac{\pi}{4} \times d^2 \right)$$

Equating these two forces we get

$$\pi \cdot d \cdot \sigma \cos \theta = \gamma h \cdot \frac{\pi}{4} \cdot d^2$$

or  $\boxed{h = \frac{4 \sigma \cos \theta}{\gamma d}}$  ... (1.9 (a))

For pure water in contact with clean glass and air, θ = 0°. In case of mercury and glass, θ is approximately 140°.

Glass tubes are generally used for pressure measurement. To avoid errors due to capillarity, the diameter of the tube should not be less than 10 mm.

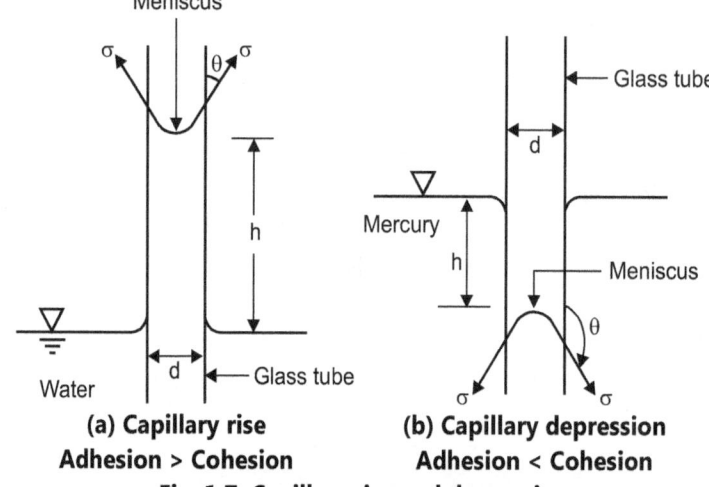

(a) Capillary rise  
Adhesion > Cohesion

(b) Capillary depression  
Adhesion < Cohesion

**Fig. 1.7: Capillary rise and depression**

## ILLUSTRATIVE EXAMPLES

**Example 1.1:**
Five litres of oil weighs 61.80 N. Calculate (1) specific weight (2) specific mass (3) specific volume and (4) relative density.

**Solution:**
All the quantities asked in the example relate to 1 m³ of oil. Further 1 m³/s = 1000 litres.

(1) Specific weight $\gamma_{oil}$ = $\dfrac{61.80}{5} \times 1000$

$= \boxed{12{,}360 \text{ N/m}^3 \text{ or } 12.36 \text{ kN/m}^3}$

(2) Specific mass = mass density, $\rho'_{oil}$

$= \dfrac{\text{Specific weight}}{g}$

$= \dfrac{12360}{9.81}$

$= \boxed{1259.94 \text{ kg/m}^3}$ \qquad (∵ γ = ρ g)

(3) Specific volume $V_s = \dfrac{1}{\gamma_{oil}} = \dfrac{1}{12360} = \boxed{8.09 \times 10^{-5} \text{ m}^3/\text{N}}$

or $V_s = \dfrac{1}{\rho_{oil}} = \dfrac{1}{1259.94} = \boxed{7.936 \times 10^{-4} \text{ m}^3/\text{kg}}$

(4)      Relative density = Specific gravity = $S = \dfrac{\gamma_{oil}}{\gamma_{water}}$

$$= \dfrac{12360}{9810} = \boxed{1.26} \quad \left( \text{or } \dfrac{\rho_{oil}}{\rho_{water}} = \dfrac{1259.94}{1000} = 1.26 \right)$$

### Example 1.2:

Ten litres of a liquid of specific gravity 1.3 is mixed with eight litres of a liquid of specific gravity 0.8. If the bulk of the liquid shrinks by one percent on mixing, calculate specific gravity, the volume and the weight of the mixture.

### Solution:

(i)    Weight of 10 litres of liquid of specific gravity 1.3

$$= 1.3 \times 9810 \times \dfrac{10}{1000} = 127.53 \text{ N}$$

(ii)    Weight of 8 litres of liquid of specific gravity 0.8

$$= 0.8 \times 9810 \times \dfrac{8}{1000}$$

$$= 62.78 \text{ N}$$

(iii)    Weight of mixture

$$= 127.53 + 62.784 = 190.314 \text{ N}$$

∴    $\boxed{\text{Weight of mixture} = 190.314 \text{ N}}$

(iv)    Total volume of liquid before mixing

$$= 10 + 8 = 18 \text{ litres}$$

After mixing volume shrinks by 1%

∴    Total volume after mixing

$$= 0.99 \times \dfrac{18}{1000}$$

$$= 0.01782 \text{ m}^3$$

∴    $\boxed{\text{Volume of mixture} = 0.01782 \text{ m}^3}$

(v)    Now, Specific weight of mixture

$$= \dfrac{\text{Weight of mixture}}{\text{Volume of mixture}}$$

$$= \dfrac{190.314}{0.01782} = 10{,}860 \text{ N/m}^3$$

∴    Specific gravity of mixture

$$= \dfrac{\text{Specific weight of mixture}}{\text{Specific weight of water}} = \dfrac{10860}{9810}$$

$$= 1.089$$

∴    $\boxed{\text{Specific gravity of mixture} = 1.089}$

# FLUID PROPERTIES AND HYDROSTATIC

## Example 1.3:

If density of a liquid is 837 kg/m³, find its specific weight, specific gravity and specific volume. If kinematic viscosity of this liquid is 1.73 cm²/s, obtain its dynamic viscosity.

**Solution:**

(1) Specific weight $\gamma = \rho \cdot g = 837 \times 9.81 = \boxed{8210.97 \text{ N/m}^3}$

(2) Specific gravity $S = \dfrac{\rho_{liquid}}{\rho_{water}} = \dfrac{837}{1000} = 0.837$

or $S = \dfrac{\gamma_{liquid}}{\gamma_{water}} = \dfrac{8210.97}{9810} = \boxed{0.837}$

(3) Specific volume $V_s = \dfrac{1}{\gamma} = \dfrac{1}{8210.97} = \boxed{1.218 \times 10^{-4} \text{ m}^3/\text{N}}$

or $V_s = \dfrac{1}{\rho} = \dfrac{1}{837} = \boxed{1.19 \times 10^{-3} \text{ m}^3/\text{kg}}$

(4) Kinematic viscosity $\upsilon = \dfrac{\mu}{\rho}$   $\therefore \mu = \rho \cdot \upsilon$   $1.73 \text{ cm}^2/\text{s} = 1.73 \times 10^{-4} \text{ m}^2/\text{s}$

$\therefore \mu = 837 \times 1.73 \times 10^{-4} = \boxed{0.1448 \text{ N-s/m}^2}$

## Example 1.4:

A 300 mm wide shaft sleeve moves along a 100 mm diameter shaft at a speed of 0.5 m/s under the application of a force of 250 N in the direction of its motion. If the clearance between the shaft and its sleeve is 0.075 mm, determine the viscosity of lubricating oil filled in the gap.

If a force of 1500 N is applied to the sleeve, what will be the speed of the sleeve?

**Solution:**

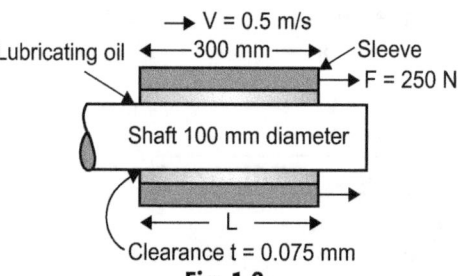

Fig. 1.8

Force F, required to move sleeve = Shear resistance between sleeve and shaft
= $\tau \times$ Area of moving surface in contact with oil
= $\tau \times \pi DL$

$\tau = \mu \cdot \dfrac{du}{dy} = \mu \cdot \dfrac{\text{Velocity of sleeve 'V'}}{\text{Clearance 't'}}$   (Since 't' is very small the velocity variation can be assumed to be linear)

$F = \mu \cdot \dfrac{V}{t} \cdot \pi D L$, $\quad \therefore \mu = \dfrac{250 \times 0.075 \times 10^{-3}}{0.5 \times \pi \times (100 + 0.15) \times 10^{-3} \times 0.3}$

$$\therefore \boxed{\mu = 0.3973 \text{ Ns/m}^2}$$

$F = \mu \cdot \dfrac{V}{t} \cdot \pi D L$, $\quad \therefore \dfrac{F_1}{F_2} = \dfrac{V_1}{V_2}$

$$\therefore \dfrac{250}{1500} = \dfrac{0.5}{V_2}$$

$$\boxed{V_2 = \dfrac{0.5 \times 1500}{250} = 3 \text{ m/s}}$$

## Example 1.5:

Determine the torque and power required to turn a 10 cm long, 5 cm diameter shaft at 500 r.p.m. in a 5.1 cm diameter concentric bearing flooded with a lubricating oil of viscosity 100 centipoise.

### Solution:

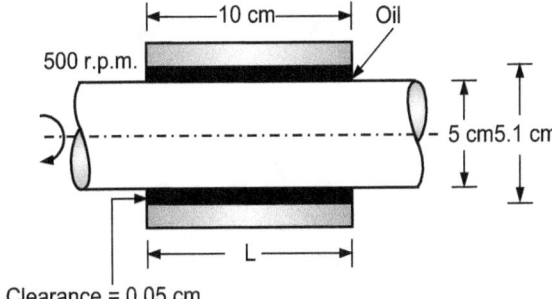

Clearance = 0.05 cm

**Fig. 1.9**

Energy loss is due to power consumed in overcoming the viscous drag resistance at the surface of the rotating shaft.

Tangential velocity of the shaft = $V = \dfrac{\pi D N}{60}$

$$= \pi \times \dfrac{5}{100} \times \dfrac{500}{60}$$

$$V = 1.31 \text{ m/s}$$

∴ Velocity gradient across clearance

$$\dfrac{du}{dy} = \dfrac{V}{t}$$

$$= \dfrac{1.31}{0.05 \times 10^{-2}}$$

$$= 2620 \text{ s}^{-1}$$

∴ Shear stress on the surface of the shaft

$$\tau = \mu \cdot \frac{du}{dy} = 0.1 \times 2620$$

100 centipoise = 1 poise

1 poise = $0.1 \frac{N\text{-}s}{m^2}$

∴ $\tau = 262 \text{ N/m}^2$

∴ Shear force on the shaft $F = \tau \times \pi \times D \times L$

$$F = 262 \times \pi \times \frac{5}{100} \times \frac{10}{100}$$

$$F = 4.115 \text{ N}$$

Torque required to turn the shaft = F × radius of shaft

$$= 4.115 \times \frac{2.5}{100} = 0.103 \text{ N-m}$$

∴ **Torque required to turn the shaft = 0.103 N-m**

∴ Power required to turn the shaft

$$P = F \times V = 4.115 \times 1.31 = 5.39 \text{ watts}$$

∴ **Power required to turn the shaft = 5.39 watts**

### Example 1.6:

A circular disc of diameter 'd' is slowly rotated in a liquid of large viscosity 'µ' at a small distance 'h' from a fixed surface. Derive an expression for torque 'T' necessary to maintain an angular velocity of 'ω' in the form

$$T = \frac{\pi \mu \omega d^4}{32 h}$$

**Solution:**

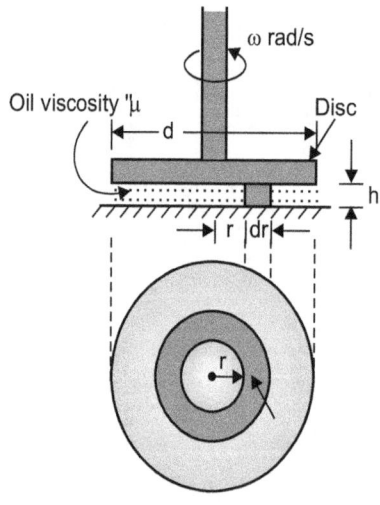

Fig. 1.10

Since the tangential velocity of the disc (du) varies from centre to the outer radius, shear stress $\mu \frac{du}{dy}$ also goes on varying.

Therefore, total torque is found out by integrating torque on elementary area in the form of an elementary annular ring.

Consider an annular ring with width 'dr' at radius 'r'.

Velocity variation in the gap is assumed to be linear.

Then, velocity at radius 'r' from centre

$$= u = r\omega$$

∴ Shear stress on the ring = $\tau = \mu \cdot \dfrac{du}{dy} = \mu \cdot \dfrac{u}{h} = \dfrac{\mu \cdot r\omega}{h}$

∴ Force on ring = $F = \tau \cdot$ Area of contact $= \dfrac{\mu \, r\omega}{h} \times 2\pi r \, dr = \dfrac{2\mu\omega\pi}{h} \cdot r^2 \, dr$

∴ Torque on the ring, $dT = F \cdot r = \dfrac{2\pi\mu\omega}{h} \cdot r^2 \cdot dr \cdot r = \dfrac{2\pi\mu\omega}{h} \cdot r^3 \, dr$

∴ Total torque on disc $= \displaystyle\int_{0}^{d/2} \dfrac{2\pi\mu\omega}{h} \cdot r^3 \, dr = \dfrac{2\pi\mu\omega}{h} \left[\dfrac{r^4}{4}\right]_0^{d/2}$

$$\boxed{\text{Torque} = \dfrac{\pi\mu\omega d^4}{32\,h}}$$

### Example 1.7:
A cube of 0.3 m sides and mass 30 kg slides down a plane inclined at 30° to the horizontal and covered by a thin film of viscosity $2.3 \times 10^{-3}$ N-s/m². If the thickness of the film is 0.03 mm, determine the speed of the block.

**Solution:**

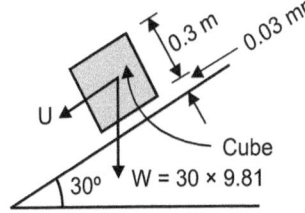

Fig. 1.11

Since the block is moving with constant velocity, the force on the block in the direction of motion must be equal to force in the opposite direction.

Force in the direction of motion = Component of weight of block
= 30 × 9.81 × sin 30° = 147.15 N

Force against the direction of motion = Frictional resistance between block and inclined plane
= $\tau \times$ Area of contact
= $\mu \cdot \dfrac{U}{t} \times 0.3 \times 0.3$   (U = velocity of block)

∴ Equating, $147.15 = 2.3 \times 10^{-3} \times \dfrac{U}{0.03 \times 10^{-3}} \times 0.3 \times 0.3$

$$\boxed{U = 21.33 \text{ m/s}}$$

### Example 1.8:
Water flows between two plates separated by 15 mm. The velocity of water is given by $u = \dfrac{3}{2}(1 - 10^4 y^2)$, where u is in m/s and y in meters measured from the centre. Viscosity of water is 0.1 N-s/m². Draw shear stress diagram and find shear force on each plate if area of each plate is 4 m².

**Solution:**

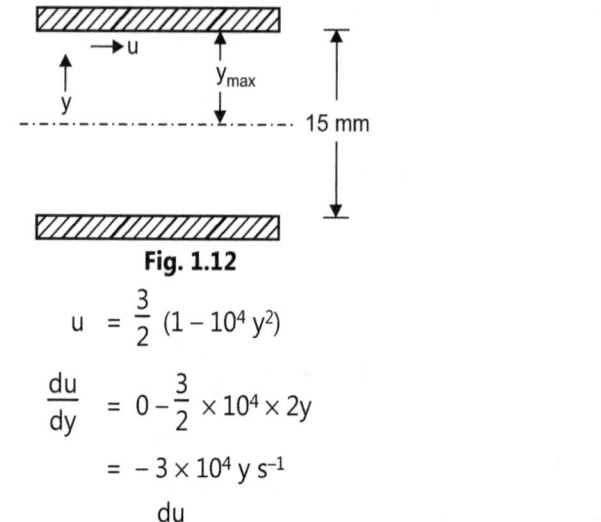

Fig. 1.12

Now $\quad u = \dfrac{3}{2}(1 - 10^4 y^2)$

$\dfrac{du}{dy} = 0 - \dfrac{3}{2} \times 10^4 \times 2y$

$= -3 \times 10^4 \, y \, s^{-1}$

∴ Shear stress $= \mu \dfrac{du}{dy} = 0.1 \times (-3 \times 10^4 \, y) = (-3000 \, y) \, N/m^2$

∴ Shear stress at the plates i.e. when $y = y_{max}$

$= \dfrac{15}{2} \times 10^{-3}$ m, is given by

$\tau_o = (-3000) \times \left(\dfrac{15}{2} \times 10^{-3}\right) = -22.5 \, N/m^2$

∴ **Shear force on each plate** $= -22.5 \times 4 = -90 \, N$

Negative sign indicates force against the direction of flow.

Shear stress diagram:

$\quad\quad\quad$ at $y_0 = 0, \tau = 0$
$\quad\quad\quad$ at $y = 7.5 \times 10^{-3}, \tau_{max} = 22.5 \, N/m^2$

Shear stress varies linearly with $y$ ($\tau = -3000 \, y$)

∴ Shear stress varies linearly from 0 at centre upto 22.5 N/m² upto the plates. Diagram for shear stress is as shown in Fig. 1.13.

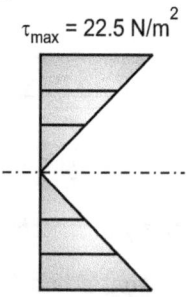

$\tau_{max} = 22.5 \, N/m^2$

Fig. 1.13

## Example 1.9:

The velocity distribution of fluid flow over plate is given by:

$$u = \frac{2}{3}y - y^2$$

where, $u$ is the velocity in m/s at distance '$y$' metre above plate. Determine the shear stress at $y = 0, 0.1$ and $0.2$ m. Take $\mu = 6$ Poise.

### Solution:

We have
$$y = \frac{2}{3}y - y^2$$

∴ $$\frac{du}{dy} = \frac{2}{3} - 2y$$

∴ Shear stress
$$\tau = \mu \frac{du}{dy}$$

$$\tau = 0.6\left(\frac{2}{3} - 2y\right) \quad \mu = \sigma \text{ Poise} = 0.6 \frac{N\text{-}s}{m^2}$$

or $$\tau = 0.4 - 1.2\, y$$

(i) At $y = 0$, $\tau = 0.4 - 1.2 \times 0 = \boxed{0.4 \text{ N/m}^2}$

(ii) At $y = 0.1$ m, $\tau = 0.4 - 1.2 \times 0.1 = \boxed{0.28 \text{ N/m}^2}$

(iii) At $y = 0.2$ m, $\tau = 0.4 - 1.2 \times 0.2 = \boxed{0.16 \text{ N/m}^2}$

## Example 1.10:

If the velocity profile of a fluid over a plate is parabolic with the vertex 20 cm from the plate, where the velocity is 120 cm/s. Calculate the velocity gradients and shear stresses at a distance of 0 cm and 10 cm from the plate. Take viscosity of the fluid as 0.85 Ns/m².

### Solution:

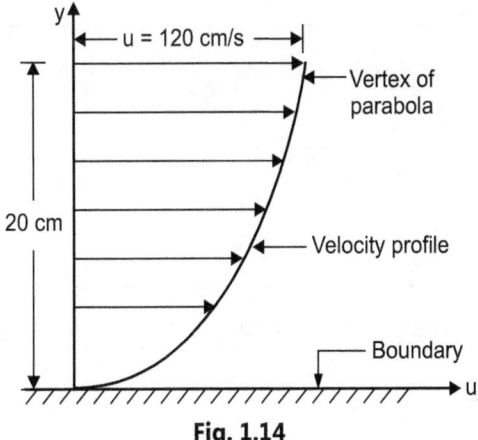

Fig. 1.14

We have $\mu = 0.85$ Ns/m²
Let the parabolic velocity profile be
$$u = ay^2 + by + c \qquad \ldots (i)$$
then,
$$\frac{du}{dy} = 2ay + b \qquad \ldots (ii)$$

The constants a, b and c can be obtained by applying the following boundary conditions:
1. at $y = 0$     $u = 0$
2. at $y = 20$ cm     $u = 120$ cm/s
3. at $y = 20$ cm     $\frac{du}{dy} = 0$     $\left[\because \frac{du}{dy} = 0 \text{ at vertex}\right]$

Substituting the above conditions in eq. (i) and (ii), we get

$0 = c$     or $c = 0$
$120 = a \times (20)^2 + b(20)$

or     $6 = 20a + b$     ... (iii)
and     $0 = 2a \times (20) + b$
or     $0 = 40a + b$     ... (iv)

Solving for a and b, we get
$b = -40a$    and    $6 = 20a - 40a$
$\therefore$     $\boxed{a = -0.3}$    and    $\boxed{b = 12}$

Therefore, the velocity profile can be written as
$$u = -0.3y^2 + 12y \qquad \ldots (v)$$
and
$$\frac{du}{dy} = -0.6y + 12 \qquad \ldots (vi)$$

It may be noted that the above equations are valid only when velocity is in cm/sec and distance y in cm.

Velocity gradients and shear stresses at $y = 0$ and $y = 10$ cm are tabulated in the following table.

| Location from plate | Velocity gradient $\frac{du}{dy}$ | Shear stress |
|---|---|---|
| (i) $y = 0$ cm | $\left(\frac{du}{dy}\right)_{y=0} = (-0.6 \times 0) + 12$ | $\tau_0 = \mu \left(\frac{du}{dy}\right)_{y=0}$ |
| | $\therefore \left(\frac{du}{dy}\right)_{y=0} = 12\ s^{-1}$ | $= 0.85 \times 12$ |
| | | $\therefore \tau_0 = 10.2$ N/m² |
| (ii) $y = 10$ cm | $\left(\frac{du}{dy}\right)_{y=10} = (-0.6 \times 10) + 12$ | $\tau_{10} = \mu \left(\frac{du}{dy}\right)_{y=10}$ |
| | $\therefore \left(\frac{du}{dy}\right)_{y=10} = 6\ s^{-1}$ | $= 0.85 \times 6$ |
| | | $\therefore \tau_{10} = 5.1$ N/m² |

## Example 1.11:

A vertical gap 1.2 cm wide of infinite extent contains fluid of viscosity 1 N-s/m$^2$ and specific gravity 0.9. A metallic plate 1 m × 1 m × 0.2 cm is lifted up with a constant velocity of 0.2 m/s through the gap. If the plate is at a distance of 0.4 cm from one of the plane surfaces of the gap, find the vertical force required. Weight of the plate is 50 N.

### Solution:

1. Force required to lift the plate = Submerged weight of plate + Viscous shear force on the two faces of the plate.

$$= W_s + F_L + F_R \text{ where } F_L = \text{Force on the left face of plate}$$
$$F_R = \text{Force on the right face of plate}$$

$W_s$ = Weight − Weight of liquid displaced by plate
  = 50 − (Vol. of liquid displaced × Sp. weight of fluid)
  = 50 − [(1 × 1 × 0.2 × 10$^{-2}$) (0.9 × 9810)]

$$\boxed{W_s = 32.34 \text{ N}}$$

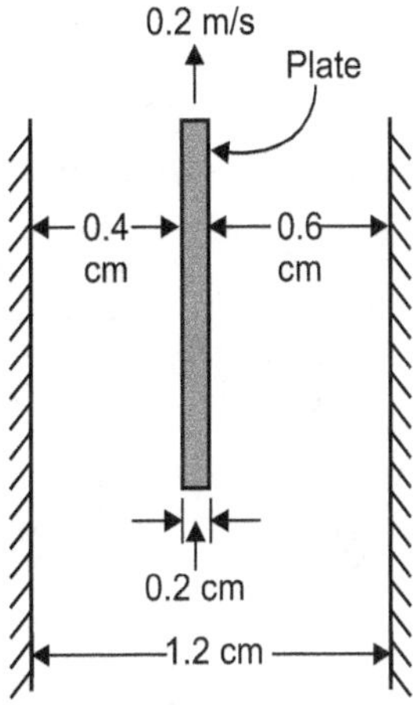

**Fig. 1.15**

2. $\quad F_L = \left(\mu \cdot \dfrac{du}{dy}\right)_L \cdot \text{Area of contact}$

$$= \left(1 \times \dfrac{0.2}{0.4 \times 10^{-2}}\right) \times 1 \times 1$$

$\therefore \quad \boxed{F_L = 50 \text{ N}}$

3. $\quad F_R = \left(\mu \cdot \dfrac{du}{dy}\right)_r \cdot \text{Area of contact} = \left(1 \times \dfrac{0.2}{0.6 \times 10^{-2}}\right) \times 1 \times 1$

$\therefore \quad \boxed{F_R = 33.33 \text{ N}}$

$\therefore \quad \boxed{\text{Total force required} = 32.34 + 50 + 33.33 = 115.67 \text{ N}}$

## Example 1.12:

For the truncated cone as shown in Fig. 1.16, calculate the torque required if the cone is to rotate at 200 r.p.m. Viscosity of oil in the 2 mm gap between the cone and the housing is 2P. Derive the formula if used any.

### Solution:

**Derivation:** Consider the truncated cone as shown in Fig. 1.16. Let $R_t$ and $R_b$ be the radii at top and bottom of the cone '$2\theta$', the vertex angle and t – the gap between cone and housing filled with liquid of viscosity $\mu$. Let the cone rotate at speed of $\omega$ rad/s.

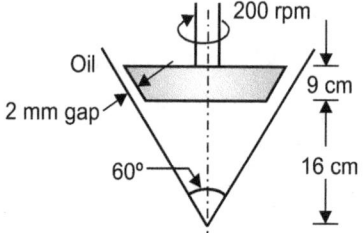

**Fig. 1.16**

Consider an elementary strip of the cone with radius 'r' less than $R_t$ but more than $R_b$.

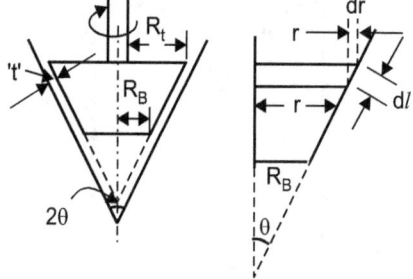

**Fig. 1.17**

Shear stress on the sloping wall of the strip is given by

$$\tau = \mu \cdot \frac{du}{dy} = \mu \cdot \frac{u}{t} = \mu \cdot \frac{r\omega}{t}$$

Area of sloping wall of strip $= 2\pi r \cdot dl = 2\pi r \cdot \dfrac{dr}{\sin\theta}$

∴ Shear force on the strip $= \tau \cdot$ Area

$$= \mu \cdot \frac{r\omega}{t} \cdot 2\pi r \frac{dr}{\sin\theta} = \frac{2\pi\mu\omega}{t\sin\theta} \cdot r^2 \cdot dr$$

∴ Torque on strip $=$ Shear force . r

$$= \frac{2\pi\mu\omega}{t\sin\theta} \cdot r^3 \cdot dr$$

$$\therefore \quad \text{Total torque} = T = \int_{R_b}^{R_t} \frac{2\pi\mu\omega}{t\sin\theta} \cdot r^3 \cdot dr$$

$$= \frac{2\pi\mu\omega}{t\sin\theta} \left[\frac{r^4}{4}\right]_{R_b}^{R_t}$$

$$\boxed{T = \frac{\pi\mu\omega}{2t\sin\theta}\left[R_t^4 - R_b^4\right]}$$

$R_t = 0.25 \tan 30°$, $R_b = 0.16 \tan 30°$

$\mu = 2P = \frac{2}{10} = 0.2$ N-s/m², $t = 2$ mm $= 2 \times 10^{-3}$ m,

$\theta = 30°$, $\omega = \frac{2\pi N}{60} = \frac{2\pi \times 200}{60} = 20.94$ rad/s

$$T = \frac{\pi \times 0.2 \times 20.94}{2 \times 2 \times 10^{-3} \times \sin 30°}\left[(0.25\tan 30°)^4 - (0.16\tan 30°)^4\right]$$

$$\boxed{T = 2.376 \text{ N-m}}$$

### Example 1.13:

A thin square plate 1 m × 1 m is placed horizontally and centrally in a horizontal gap of height 2 cm filled with oil of viscosity 10 P and pulled at a constant velocity 0.1 m/s. Find the force on the plate.

The gap is now filled with another oil. When the plate is placed at a distance of 0.5 cm from one of the surfaces of the gap and pulled with the same velocity, the force on the plate remains same as before. Find viscosity of new oil.

**Solution: Case I:** Force on side of plate:

$$= \mu \cdot \frac{du}{dy} \times \text{Area}$$

$$= 1 \times \frac{0.1}{1 \times 10^{-2}} \times 1 = 10 \text{ N}$$

$$\left(\mu = 10 \text{ P} = \frac{10}{10} = 1 \text{ N-s/m}^2\right)$$

$\therefore$ $\boxed{\text{Force on plate} = 20 \text{ N}}$ ... (I)

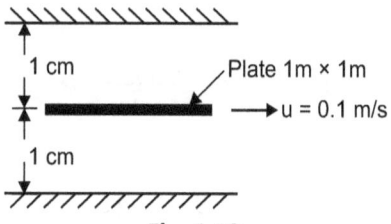

Fig. 1.18

**Case II:**

Force on top of plate $= \mu \left(\dfrac{du}{dy}\right)_{top} \times \text{Area} = \mu \times \dfrac{0.1}{1.5 \times 10^{-2}} \times 1 = \dfrac{20}{3} \mu N$

Force on bottom of plate $= \mu \left(\dfrac{du}{dy}\right)_{bottom} \times \text{Area} = \mu \times \dfrac{0.1}{0.5 \times 10^{-2}} \times 1 = 20 \mu N$

∴ Total force in case II $= \dfrac{20}{3} \mu + 20 \mu = \dfrac{80}{3} \mu N$ ... (II)

Equating (I) and (II), $\dfrac{80}{3} \mu = 20$

∴ $\mu = \dfrac{3}{4} \text{ N-s/m}^2$

∴ $\boxed{\mu = 0.75 \text{ N-s/m}^2}$

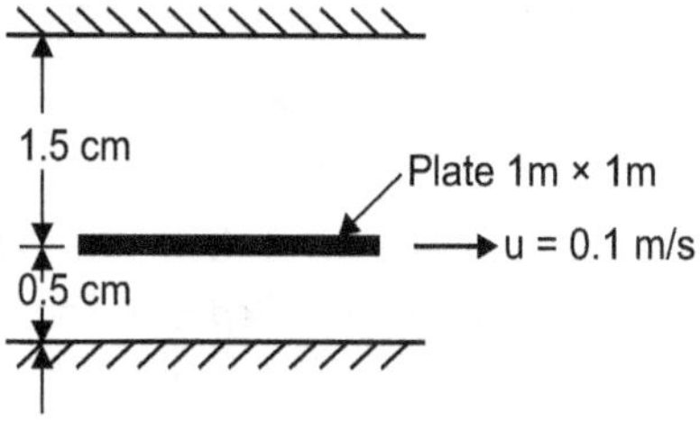

Fig. 1.19

### Example 1.14:

For $K = 2.2 \times 10^9$ Pa (bulk modulus of elasticity) of water, what pressure is required to reduce its volume by 0.5%?

**Solution:**

$\left(-\dfrac{dV}{V}\right) = \dfrac{0.5}{100}$

We know $K = \dfrac{dp}{\left(-\dfrac{dV}{V}\right)}$

∴ $2.2 \times 10^9 = \dfrac{dp}{(0.5 \times 10^{-2})}$

∴ $\boxed{dp = 11 \text{ MPa}}$

# FLUID PROPERTIES AND HYDROSTATIC

**Example 1.15:**

At a depth of 2 km in the ocean pressure is 840 BAR. Assume specific weight at surface as 10,250 N/m³ and average bulk modulus of elasticity as $2.4 \times 10^6$ kN per square meter for that pressure range.

(i) What will be the change in specific volumes between that at the surface and at that depth?

(ii) What will be specific volume at the depth?

(iii) What will be specific weight at that depth?

**Solution:**

In this example, the value of specific weight at sea level is given and values of various quantities at 2 km depth are to be found out.

Due to self weight of sea water, it is compressed due to which the specific volume reduces and specific weight increases.

Now, change in pressure at a depth of 2 km

$$dp = 840 \text{ Bar} = 840 \times 10^5 \text{ N/m}^2$$
$$= (840 \times 100) \times 10^3 \text{ N/m}^2$$

or $dp = (8.4 \times 10^4) \text{ kN/m}^2$

Bulk modulus given,

$$K = 2.4 \times 10^6 \text{ kN/m}^2$$

By definition of bulk modulus:

$$K = \frac{dp}{dV/V}$$

or

$$\frac{dV_s}{V_s} = \frac{dp}{K} = \frac{8.4 \times 10^4}{2.4 \times 10^6} \quad \text{[where } V_s = \text{Specific volume]}$$

$$\therefore \frac{dV_s}{V_s} = 3.5 \times 10^{-2} \quad \text{... (i)}$$

Further, using the definition of specific volume $V_s = \frac{1}{\gamma}$, the specific volume at surface

$$V_s = \frac{1}{\gamma} = \frac{1}{10.25} = 9.756 \times 10^{-2} \text{ m}^3/\text{kN} \quad \text{... (ii)}$$

Substituting value of '$V_s$' from (ii) and (i) we get,

(i) Change in specific volume:

$$dV_s = 3.5 \times 10^{-2} \times 9.756 \times 10^{-2}$$

∴ **Change in specific volume = $34.146 \times 10^4$ m³/kN**

(ii) Specific volume at a depth of 2 km

= Specific volume at surface − Change in specific volume

∴  $V_s = 9.756 \times 10^{-2} - 34.146 \times 10^{-4}$

∴ $V_s$ at 2 km depth = $9.415 \times 10^{-2}$ m³/kN

(iii) Specific weight $= \dfrac{1}{\text{Specific volume}}$

$= \dfrac{1}{9.415 \times 10^{-2}}$

∴ Specific weight at 2 km depth = 10.622 kN/m³

### Example 1.16:

Calculate the pressure in excess of outside pressure in case of (a) a droplet of water 3 mm in diameter and (b) a jet of water 3 mm in diameter. $\sigma_{water} = 0.073$ N/m.

**Solution:**

(a) For droplet, $p = \dfrac{4\sigma}{d} = \dfrac{4 \times 0.073}{3 \times 10^{-3}} = 97.33$ N/m²

∴  $p = 97.33$ N/m²

(b) For jet, $p = \dfrac{2\sigma}{d} = \dfrac{2 \times 0.073}{3 \times 10^{-3}} = 48.67$ N/m²

∴  $p = 48.67$ N/m²

### Example 1.17:

Calculate the pressure inside a soap bubble of 50 mm diameter. Take surface tension at the soap–air interface as 0.1 N/m.

**Solution:**

In case of soap bubble

$p = \dfrac{8\sigma}{d} = \dfrac{8 \times 0.1}{50 \times 10^{-3}} = 16$ N/m²

∴  $p = 16$ N/m² above local atmospheric pressure

### Example 1.18:

A glass tube of internal diameter 2 mm is partially dipped in glycerine with it's lower end 20 mm deep below surface. Air is blown in the tube so as to form an air bubble at it's bottom end of the diameter of the tube. If specific weight and surface tension of glycerine are 12.356 kN/m² and 0.0637 N/m, find the pressure of air blown.

## Solution:

Pressure in the bubble will be sum of the pressure due to 20 mm of glycerine and pressure required to overcome the force due to surface tension.

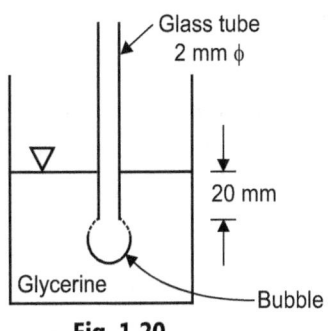

Fig. 1.20

Pressure due to 20 mm of glycerine
$$= \gamma h = 12356 \times 20 \times 10^{-3} = 247.12 \text{ N/m}^2$$

Pressure required to overcome surface tension (bubble has only one surface in this case)
$$= \frac{4\sigma}{d} = \frac{4 \times 0.0637}{2 \times 10^{-3}} = 127.4 \text{ N/m}^2$$

∴ Total pressure inside the bubble
$$= 247.12 + 127.4 = 374.52 \text{ N/m}^2$$

∴ **Total pressure inside the bubble = 374.52 N/m²**

### Example 1.19:

*Calculate the capillary effect in mm in a glass tube 1 mm in diameter when it is immersed in water. Take surface tension of water as 0.08 N/m and angle of contact as zero.*

*If the same tube is now immersed in mercury of specific gravity 13.6 and surface tension of 0.5 N/m, angle of contact between glass and mercury 140°, what will be rise/depression in the level in the tube?*

## Solution:

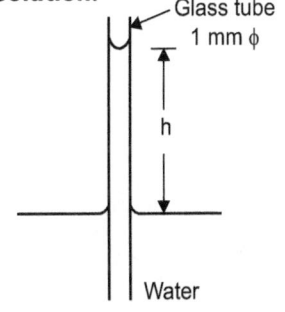

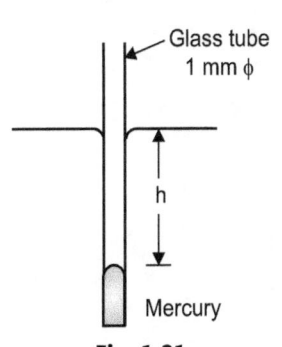

Fig. 1.21

We have

$$\text{Capillary rise 'h'} = \frac{4\sigma \cos\theta}{\gamma d}$$

$$= \frac{4 \times 0.08 \times \cos 0°}{9810 \times 1 \times 10^{-3}}$$

∴ **h = 0.0326 m or 32.6 mm**

In case of mercury, $\theta = 40°$ and $\gamma = 13.6 \times 9810$

$$h = \frac{4\sigma \cos\theta}{\gamma d}$$

$$= \frac{4 \times 0.5 \times \cos 140°}{13.6 \times 9810 \times 1 \times 10^{-3}}$$

∴ **h = – 0.01148 m or –11.48 mm**

Negative sign indicates depression in the level in the tube.

## Example 1.20:

A 'U' tube is made of two capillary tubes; one 2 mm in diameter and other 4 mm in diameter. The tube is vertical and partially filled with water of surface tension 0.0736 N/m and zero angle of contact. Calculate the difference of levels in the tubes.

**Solution:**

The difference in the levels will be due to difference in the capillary rise in the two tubes. 2 mm diameter tube will have more capillary rise as compared to 4 mm diameter tube.

(i) Capillary rise in 2 mm tube

$$h_1 = \frac{4\sigma \cos\theta}{\gamma d}$$

$$= \frac{4 \times 0.0736}{9810 \times 2 \times 10^{-3}}$$

$$= 0.015 \text{ m} \qquad (\because \cos\theta = 1)$$

$$\therefore h_1 = 15 \text{ mm}$$

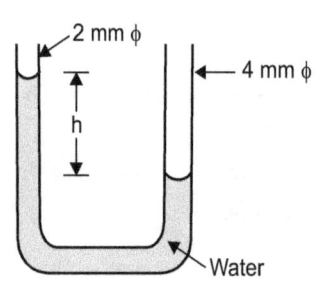

Fig. 1.22

(ii) Capillary rise in 4 mm tube:

$$h = \frac{4\sigma \cos\theta}{\gamma d}$$

$$= \frac{4 \times 0.0736}{9810 \times 4 \times 10^{-3}}$$

$$= 0.0075 \text{ m}$$

$$= 7.5 \text{ mm}$$

∴ Difference in the levels in the tubes

$$h = h_1 - h_2$$

$$= 15 - 7.5$$

$$= 7.5 \text{ mm}$$

∴ $\boxed{h = 7.5 \text{ mm}}$

# THEORETICAL QUESTIONS

1. Define fluid. What do you understand by ideal fluid and real fluid? Give one example of each. What is the difference between real and ideal fluids?
2. Distinguish between gas and liquid.
3. Define the following fluid properties and state their units:
   (i) Specific weight
   (ii) Dynamic viscosity
   (iii) Surface tension
   (iv) Bulk modulus of elasticity.
4. Define following properties and state their units:
   (i) Specific mass
   (ii) Specific weight
   (iii) Specific volume
   (iv) Specific gravity.
5. Write short notes on the following:
   (i) Velocity of sound and mach number
   (ii) Capillarity
   (iii) Surface tension
   (iv) Vapour pressure
   (v) Compressibility
   (vi) Viscosity
6. Explain the following terms:
   (i) Compressibility
   (ii) Surface tension
7. State and explain Newton's Law of viscosity.
8. What is Newtonian and Non–Newtonian fluid? Give examples of each.
9. Draw the stress-strain relationship of the following fluids in one diagram and discuss the behaviour of each fluid under an external shear force:
   (i) An ideal fluid
   (ii) A Newtonian fluid
   (iii) A Pseudoplastic fluid
   (iv) A dilatent fluid
   (v) A bingham fluid
   (vii) A plastic.
10. Identify the following substances as fluids or solids and if fluids, classify them further. The values are obtained from isothermal tests.

| Substance A | $du/dy$ = | 0 | 0 | 0 | 0 | 0 |
|---|---|---|---|---|---|---|
|  | $\tau$ = | 0 | 0.5 | 1 | 1.5 | 2 |
| Substance B | $du/dy$ = | 0 | 1 | 2 | 3 | 4 |
|  | $\tau$ = | 0 | 0 | 0 | 0 | 0 |
| Substance C | $du/dy$ = | 0 | 1 | 2 | 3 | 4 |
|  | $\tau$ = | 0 | 2 | 4 | 6 | 8 |
| Substance D | $du/dy$ = | 0 | 0.5 | 1 | 1.5 | 2 |
|  | $\tau$ = | 0 | 1 | 2.5 | 4 | 6 |

[**Ans.:** Ideal solid, Ideal fluid, Newtonian fluid, Non-Newtonian fluid]

11. What is viscosity of fluid? How and why does it vary with temperature? What are it's units and dimensions?
12. What is kinematic viscosity? Why is it so called? Give it's units and dimensions.
13. Explain why the viscosity does not contribute to hydrostatic law.
14. Explain why viscosity of liquids decreases while that of gases increases with rise in temperature.
15. Explain capillarity.

16. Derive an expression for height of capillary rise.
17. Derive an expression for capillary fall.
18. Define Adhesion, Cohesion, Surface Tension and Capillarity. Prove that Capillary rise or depression 'h' of a liquid of mass density 'ρ' and surface tension 'σ' in a tube of diameter 'd' varies inversely with 'd'.

$$\left[\text{Hint: Prove } h = \frac{4\sigma \cos\theta}{\rho g d}\right]$$

19. Explain Vapour pressure.
20. Explain the property: Vapour pressure. Give it's significance in engineering.
21. Derive an expression between gauge pressure 'p' inside a free jet of liquid and surface tension 'σ'.
22. Derive expressions for pressure 'p' inside the soap bubble, droplet and surface tension 'σ'.
23. What are the characteristic fluid properties involved in the following phenomena:
    1. Rise of sap in tree
    2. Spherical shape of a liquid drop
    3. Cavitation
    4. Water hammer.
    Some more phenomena:
    5. Use of mercury in manometers
    6. A small steel needle can be made to float on water surface
    7. Use of different grade oils in winter and summer in automobiles.
    8. Lubrication
    9. Cavitation
    10. Increase of density of seawater in depth.
24. What is Mach Number and what is it's significance?

## NUMERICAL PROBLEMS

1. One litre of oil weighs 8 N. Calculate it's specific weight, specific volume, mass density and relative density.

    **[Ans.:** 8000 N/m$^3$, 1.226 × 10$^{-3}$ m$^3$/kg or 1.25 × 10$^{-4}$ m$^3$/N, 815.5 kg/m$^3$, 0.8155**]**

2. Density of liquid is 850 kg/m$^3$. Determine relative density and weight density of the liquid. With reason, state whether the liquid will float on water or not.

    **[Ans.:** 0.85, 8338.5 N/m$^3$ S is less than 1, liquid will float on water.**]**

3. A Newtonian liquid of kinematic viscosity 2.528 Stokes flows over a flat horizontal plate of surface area 0.8 m$^2$. Velocity at y meters from plate is given as $u = 2y - 2y^3$ in m/s. If shear force on plate is 0.352 N, find specific weight and specific gravity of liquid.

    **[Hint:** Refer example 1.8.

    $u = 2y - 2y^3, \therefore \frac{du}{dy} = 2 - 6y^2$, At the plate y = 0 $\frac{du}{dy} = 2 \text{ s}^{-1}$,

    Shear stress = $\mu \frac{du}{dy} \cdot A = \rho v \cdot \frac{du}{dy} \cdot A \therefore 0.352 = \rho \times 2.528 \times 10^{-4} \times 2 \times 0.8$ find ρ etc.**]**

    **[Ans.:** 8537.18 N/m$^3$, 0.87**]**

4. The velocity distribution in the flow of a thin film of oil down an inclined channel is given by:

$$u = \frac{\gamma}{2\mu}(d^2 - y^2)\sin\alpha$$

where d-depth of flow, α-angle of inclination of the channel with horizontal, u-velocity at a depth y below the free surface, γ-unit weight of oil and μ-dynamic viscosity of oil. Calculate the shear stress:

(i) On the bottom of the channel
(ii) At mid depth and
(iii) At the free surface

$$\left[\text{Hint: } \tau = \mu\frac{du}{dy} = \mu\left(\frac{\gamma}{2\mu}\sin\alpha\times(-2y)\right) = -\gamma\sin\alpha\cdot y \text{ etc.}\right]$$

$$\left[\text{Ans.: } -\gamma d\sin\alpha, -\frac{\gamma d\sin\alpha}{2}, 0\right]$$

5. A metal disc 400 mm diameter slides down on inclined plane covered with a thin oil film 0.5 mm thick. The plane is inclined at 40° with horizontal. Viscosity of oil is 2.449 Poise. If the speed of the disc is 0.5 m/s, determine weight of disc.

[**Hint:** Refer example 1.7]

[**Ans.:** 47.87 N]

6. A shaft rotating at 180 r.p.m. has a diameter of 400 mm. It rotates inside a sleeve of internal diameter 404 mm with uniform clearance. If the length of the sleeve is 200 mm and power required to rotate the shaft is 892.98 watts, find the viscosity of lubricant filled in the clearance.

[**Hint:** Refer example 1.5]

[**Ans.:** 0.5 N-s/m$^2$]

7. A 400 mm diameter shaft is rotating at 200 r.p.m. in a bearing of length 120 mm. If the thickness of oil film is 1.5 mm and the dynamic viscosity of the oil is 0.7 N.s/m$^2$, determine:

(i) Torque required to overcome the friction in bearing.
(ii) Power utilized in overcoming viscous resistance.

Assume a linear velocity profile.

[**Hint:** Refer example 1.5]

[**Ans.:** 58.954 N-m, 1.235 kW]

8. A piston 100 mm diameter, 125 mm in length moves in a vertical cylinder of 100.4 mm diameter. The annual space between the piston of the cylinder is filled with lubricating oil of dynamic viscosity equal to 0.08 PaS. If the weight of the piston is 30 N, at what velocity the piston would slide.

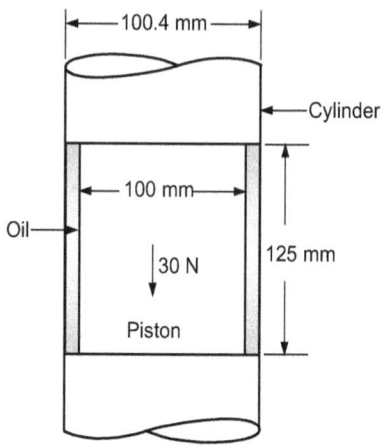

Fig. 1.23

[**Hint:** Piston will attain constant velocity when weight of the piston is balanced by the viscous force on the area of contact between piston and oil.

$$\text{Viscous force} = \mu \cdot \frac{du}{dy} \cdot A = \mu \times \frac{du}{dy} \times \pi \times D \times L$$

$$= 0.08 \times \frac{du}{0.2 \times 10^{-3}} \times \pi \times 0.1 \times 0.125$$

But this is equal to 30 N

∴ $\quad 30 = 0.08 \times \dfrac{du}{0.2 \times 10^{-3}} \times \pi \times 0.1 \times 0.125$ etc.

[**Ans.:** 1.91 m/s]

9. The radar weighing 10 kN is supported on a circular pad of radius 1 m. The pad is supported on oil of dynamic viscosity 0.1 Pa-s and the distance of separation of the pad from the base plate is 0.5 mm. Calculate the minimum oil pressure to support the radar and torque required to rotate it at a uniform speed of 1 r.p.m.
[**Hint:** Refer exmaple 1.6].
[**Ans.:** 3.183 kN/m², 32.90 N-m].

10. A skater weighing 1000 N attains speed of 72 km/hour on ice, average skating area being 10 cm². The dynamic coefficient of friction between skater and ice may be taken as 0.015. Determine the average thickness of water layer existing between the skater and the skating surface. Viscosity of water at 0°C may be taken as $1 \times 10^{-3}$ N-s/m².

[**Hint:** Friction force F = coeff. of friction W = 0.015 × 1000 = 15 N

$$du = \frac{72 \times 1000}{3600} = 20 \text{ m/s}$$

∴ $\quad F = \tau \cdot A$

find dy]

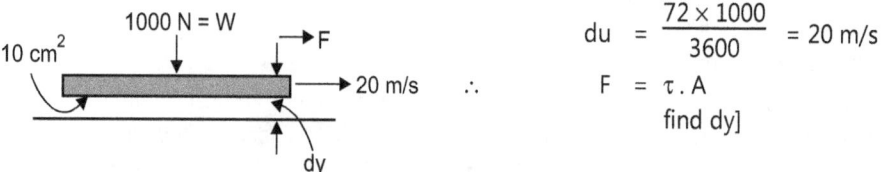

Fig. 1.24

[**Ans.:** 1.33 × 10⁻⁶ m]

11. Through a narrow gap of height 'h', a thin plate of very large extent is pulled at a velocity of 10 cm/s. On one side of the plate is oil of some viscosity and on the other side is oil of three times the viscosity of the previous oil. Find the position of the plate for minimum drag force on the plate. Neglect thickness of the plate.

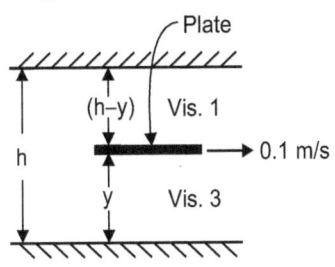

[Hint: Force on the top side $= 1 \times \dfrac{0.1}{(h-y)} \cdot$ Area

Force on the bottom side $= 3 \times \dfrac{0.1}{y} \times$ Area

Total Force, $F = \left[ \dfrac{0.1}{(h-y)} + \dfrac{0.3}{y} \right]$ Area

For F to be minimum $\dfrac{dF}{dy} = 0$ .... etc.]

**Fig. 1.25**

[**Ans.:** y = 0.634 h]

12. Two large plane surfaces are 2.4 cm apart. The space between the surfaces is filled with an oil with dynamic viscosity of $8.10 \times 10^{-1}$ N-s/m$^2$. What force is required to drag a very thin plate of surface area 0.5 m$^2$ between the two large plane surfaces at a speed of 0.6 m/s if:
    (i) the thin plate is in the middle of the two plane surfaces.
    (ii) the thin plate is at a distance of 0.8 cm from one of the plane surfaces.
    [**Ans.:** 40.5 N, 45.56 N]

13. A space of 2.5 cm width, between two large plane surfaces is filled with glycerin. What force is required to drag a very thin plate 0.75 sq. metres between the surfaces at a speed of 0.5 m/s:
    (i) If the plate remains equidistant from the two surfaces.
    (ii) If it is at a distance of 1 cm from one of the surfaces.
    Take dynamic viscosity = 0.705 N-s/m$^2$.
    [**Hint:** Refer example 1.13]
    [**Ans.:** 42.3 N, 44.063 N]

14. A cube of size 300 mm is pushed on a level surface and then allowed to slide down on an inclined plane of its own. Slope of the inclined plane is 0.6 V to 1 H. Both level surface and inclined plane are covered by a thin layer (2 mm thick) of oil. The force required to push the cube is 10 N. If a constant velocity of the cube on plane and terminal velocity on inclined plane are same, what is the weight of the cube?
    [**Ans.:** 19.44 N]

15. The velocity distribution for flow over a flat plate is given by $u = \dfrac{3}{2}y - y^{3/2}$, where u is velocity at a point at a distance y metre above the plate in metres/second. Determine the shear stress at y = 9 cm.
    Assume: μ = 8 poise.
    $\left[ \text{Hint: } \tau = \mu \dfrac{du}{dy}, \dfrac{du}{dy} = \dfrac{3}{2} - \dfrac{3}{2} y^{1/2}. \text{ Calculate } \dfrac{du}{dy} \text{ at 9 cm and hence the shear stress} \right]$
    [**Ans.:** 0.84 N/m$^2$]

16. A rectangular plate of size 0.5 m × 0.5 m dimensions slides down an inclined plane making 30° angle with the horizontal. The velocity distribution in the gap of 2 mm between the plate and inclined plane which is filled by oil of viscosity 1.142 Ns/m$^2$ is given by $u = 5y - 2y^3$. Find weight of the plate sliding down the inclined plane.

[Hint: Find $\dfrac{du}{dy}$ and shear stress at the plate. Calculate shear force on plate and equate to W sin θ]

[Ans.: 2.855 N]

17. A small circular jet of water of 0.5 mm diameter issues from a nozzle. What is the pressure difference between inside and outside of the jet? Assume surface tension between water and air as 0.0718 N/m.

[Hint: Pressure difference for jet = $\dfrac{2\sigma}{d}$]

[Ans.: 287.2 N/m²]

18. Calculate internal pressure of a 25 mm diameter soap bubble if the tension in the film is 0.5 N/m.

[Hint: Refer example 1.17]

[Ans.: 160 N/m²]

19. Determine the diameter of a droplet of water in mm if the pressure inside is to be greater than that outside by 130 N/m². Take σ for water as $7.26 \times 10^{-2}$ N/m.

[Ans.: 2.23 mm]

20. Two wide clean glass plates are hold parallel with a gap of 't' between them. What will be the capillary rise of liquid level between them when dipped in the liquid? 'σ', surface tension of liquid and 'θ' angle of contact.

[Ans.: $\dfrac{2\sigma \cos \theta}{\gamma t}$]

21. State the minimum diameter of glass tube to be immersed in water, for which capillary effects are to be limited upto 2.98 mm. Take surface tension of water in contact with air as 0.073 N/m.

[Ans.: 9.98 mm say 10 mm]

22. A U tube has two limbs of internal diameter 6 mm and 12 mm respectively and contains some water. Calculate the difference in the water levels in the two limbs. Take surface tension of water = 0.0725 N/m.

[Hint: Refer example 1.20]

[Ans.: $2.463 \times 10^{-3}$ m or 2.463 mm]

23. If bulk modulus of elasticity of water is $2.2 \times 10^9$ Pa, what pressure is required to reduce the volume of water by 6%?

[Hint: Refer example 1.14].

[Ans.: $132 \times 10^6$ Pa or 132 MPa].

24. At a depth of 9 km in the ocean, the pressure is $9.5 \times 10^4$ kN/m². The specific weight of the ocean water at the surface is 10.2 kN/m³ and it's average bulk modulus is $2.4 \times 10^6$ kN/m². Determine:
   (i) The change in specific volume,
   (ii) The specific volume at 9 km depth; and
   (iii) The specific weight at 9 km depth.

[Ans.: $3.881 \times 10^{-3}$ m³/kN, $9.416 \times 10^{-2}$ m³/kN, 10.62 kN/m³]

## PART B - PASCALS LAW, HYDROSTATIC LAW

## 1.3 Introduction

When the fluid is at rest, there is no relative motion between adjacent layers and hence shear stresses are absent. Only forces which are important are normal forces.

In this chapter, pressure at a point in fluid, principles and instruments for measurement of pressure are discussed.

## 1.4 Pressure at a Point

**Intensity of Pressure (or Pressure):** It is defined as *pressure force acting on unit area* and is denoted by 'p'. If dF is the force acting on area dA, then

$$p = \lim_{dA \to 0} \frac{dF}{dA}$$

If however, pressure is uniform over the complete area,

$$p = \frac{F}{A}$$

where 'F' is total pressure force acting on area 'A'.

**Dimensions of 'p'**

$$p = \frac{\text{Force}}{\text{Area}} = \frac{[MLT^{-2}]}{[L^2]} = [ML^{-1}T^{-2}]$$

**Units of 'p'**

$$p = \frac{\text{Force}}{\text{Area}}$$

∴ Units of 'p' are $\frac{N}{m^2}$ or $\frac{kN}{m^2}$

$N/m^2$ is Pascal (Pa) and $kN/m^2$ is kilo Pascal (kPa). Sometimes, it is also expressed in bars, where 1 bar = $10^5$ N/m² = $10^5$ Pa.

(**Note:** Pressure force P on area 'A' is given by P = p · A = Intensity of pressure × Area)

## 1.5 Pascal's Law

Pascal's law states that *at a point in a fluid at rest, intensity of pressure acts equally in all directions.*

**Proof:** Pascal's law can be proved by considering a wedge shaped element of fluid as shown in Fig. 1.26. Let 'dx', 'dy' and 'dz' be the dimensions of element along x, y and z directions respectively and 'ds' be the length of the sloping side. Let $p_x$ and $p_y$ be the intensities of pressure along x, y directions and $p_s$ be the intensity of pressure normal to the sloping face. Let $p_s$ make any angle α with the horizontal. Forces acting on the element are as shown in the figure. Since the fluid is at rest, shear forces are absent and hence forces on faces parallel to plane of the paper need not be considered.

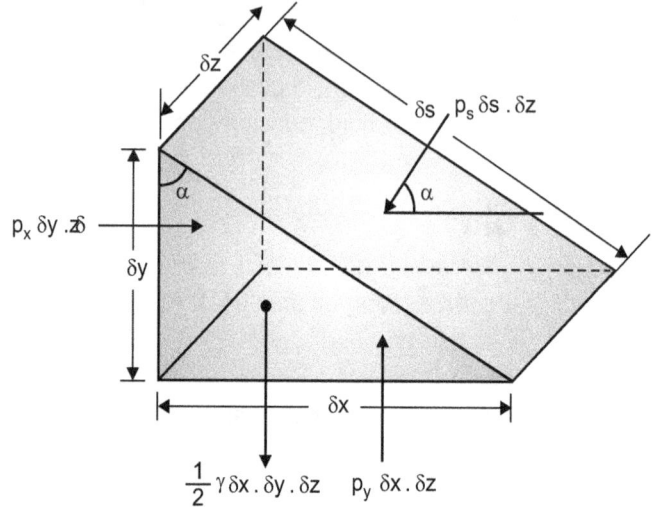

**Fig. 1.26: Forces on element in fluid at rest**

The element is in equilibrium under the action of pressure forces and the weight of fluid in the element. Therefore, sum of the components of these forces in any direction must be zero.

∴ In x direction, $\Sigma F_x = 0$

∴ $p_x \cdot \delta y \cdot \delta z - p_s \cos \alpha \cdot \delta s \cdot \delta z = 0$

but $\delta s \cos \alpha = \delta y$

∴ $p_x \cdot \delta y \cdot \delta z - p_s \cdot \delta y \cdot \delta z = 0$

∴ $p_x = p_y$ ... (1.10)

Similarly, $\Sigma F_y = 0$

∴ $p_y \cdot \delta x \cdot \delta z - p_s \sin \alpha \cdot \delta s \cdot \delta z - \frac{1}{2} \gamma \delta x \cdot \delta y \cdot \delta z = 0$

But $\delta s \sin \alpha = \delta x$ and the third term being of higher order than the other two terms, can be neglected.

∴ $p_y \cdot \delta x \cdot \delta z - p_s \cdot \delta x \cdot \delta z = 0$

or $p_y = p_s$ ... (1.11)

From equations (1.10) & (1.11) $\boxed{p_x = p_y = p_s}$ ... (1.2)

Since α is any arbitrary angle, the above relation proves that at a point in fluid at rest the intensity of pressure acts equally in all directions.

Hydraulic press, hydraulic jack, hydraulic lift, hydraulic crane etc. are some of the machines which make use of Pascal's law to develop large forces by application of very small forces.

## 1.6 Variation of Pressure in a Static Fluid-Hydrostatic Law

Consider an elementary element of mass of static fluid in the form of a parallelopiped with sides δx, δy and δz as shown in Fig. 1.27.

The forces acting on the element are the weight of fluid in the element and the pressure forces on the faces of the element. Let 'p' be the intensity of pressure at the centroid 'O' of the element.

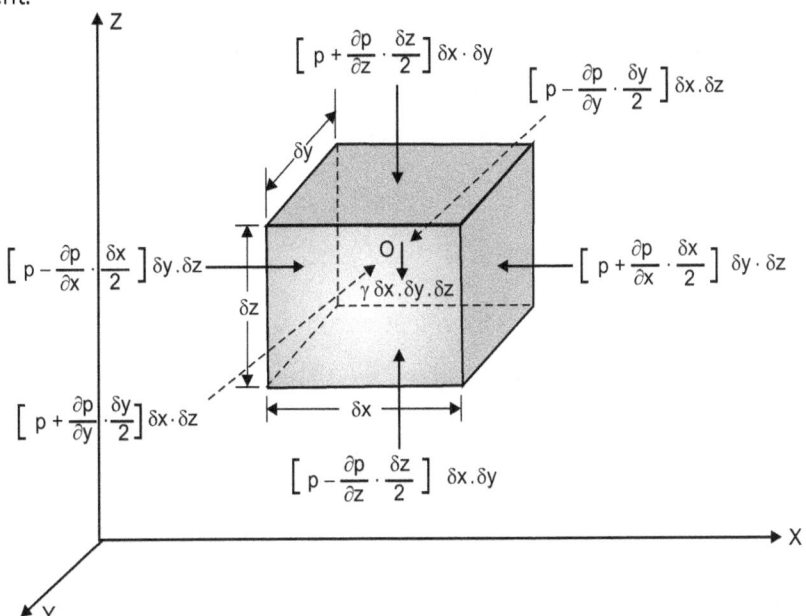

**Fig. 1.27: Forces on static fluid element**

The intensity of pressure on the left face of the element will be $\left[p - \left(\frac{\partial p}{\partial x}\right)\frac{\delta x}{2}\right]$ and the force on this face will be $\left[p - \left(\frac{\partial p}{\partial x}\right)\frac{\delta x}{2}\right] \cdot \delta y \cdot \delta z$. Similarly, intensity of pressure on right face of element will be $\left[p + \left(\frac{\partial p}{\partial x}\right)\frac{\delta x}{2}\right]$ and the pressure force there will be $\left[p + \left(\frac{\partial p}{\partial x}\right)\frac{\delta x}{2}\right] \cdot \delta y \cdot \delta z$.

Similarly, forces on the other faces can be obtained as shown in Fig. 1.27. All these forces will be acting normal to respective faces through the centres of faces. The weight of fluid (γ δx . δy . δz) will be acting vertically downwards through centroid O.

Since, the element is in equilibrium under the action of these forces, sum of the forces acting in any direction must be zero.

∴ For x direction, we can write $\Sigma F_x = 0$.

∴ $\left[p - \frac{\partial p}{\partial x} \cdot \frac{\delta x}{2}\right] \cdot \delta y \cdot \delta z - \left[p + \frac{\partial p}{\partial x} \cdot \frac{\delta x}{2}\right] \cdot \delta y \cdot \delta z = 0$ or $\frac{\partial p}{\partial x} = 0$

For y direction, $\Sigma F_y = 0$

$$\left[p - \frac{\partial p}{\partial y} \cdot \frac{\delta y}{2}\right] \cdot \delta x \cdot \delta z - \left[p + \frac{\partial p}{\partial y} \cdot \frac{\delta y}{2}\right] \cdot \delta x \cdot \delta z = 0$$

or $\dfrac{\partial p}{\partial y} = 0$

For z direction, $\Sigma F_z = 0$

$$\left[p - \frac{\partial p}{\partial z} \cdot \frac{\delta z}{2}\right] \cdot \delta x \cdot \delta y - \left[p + \frac{\partial p}{\partial z} \cdot \frac{\delta z}{2}\right] \cdot \delta x \cdot \delta y - (\gamma \cdot \delta x \cdot \delta y \cdot \delta z) = 0$$

or $\left[-\dfrac{\partial p}{\partial z} \cdot \delta x \cdot \delta y \cdot \delta z\right] - (\gamma \cdot \delta x \cdot \delta y \cdot \delta z) = 0$

or $\boxed{\dfrac{\partial p}{\partial z} = -\gamma}$

The relations $\dfrac{\partial p}{\partial x} = 0$ and $\dfrac{\partial p}{\partial y} = 0$ show that pressure does not vary in x and y directions but varies only in 'z' direction or *in a fluid at rest pressure does not vary in horizontal direction but varies only in vertical direction.*

Since $\dfrac{\partial p}{\partial x} = 0$ and $\dfrac{\partial p}{\partial y} = 0$, partial derivative $\dfrac{\partial p}{\partial z}$ can be replaced by total derivative $\dfrac{dp}{dz}$.

∴ $\boxed{\dfrac{dp}{dz} = -\gamma}$ ... (1.13)

Above equation is called *equation of fluid statics* and holds good for compressible as well as incompressible fluids.

In case of incompressible fluid '$\gamma$' is constant and therefore, integrating above equation between any two points, we get

$$\int_{p_1}^{p_2} dp = -\int_{z_1}^{z_2} \gamma \, dz$$

or $p_2 - p_1 = -\gamma(z_2 - z_1)$

or $\dfrac{p_2}{\gamma} + z_2 = \dfrac{p_1}{\gamma} + z_1$

The expression ($p/\gamma + z$) is called piezometric head. Thus, *in a static fluid, piezometric head is constant at all points.*

Further equation $\dfrac{\partial p}{\partial z} = -\gamma$ can be integrated to give

$$p = -\gamma z + c$$

where c is constant.

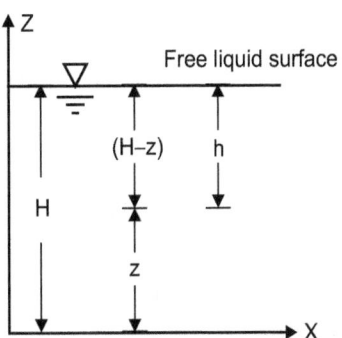

**Fig. 1.28: Pressure at a point**

Referring to Fig. 1.28, at $z = H$, $p = p_a$ (atmospheric pressure)

∴ $p_a = -\gamma H + c$ ∴ $c = p_a + \gamma H$

∴ $p = p_a + \gamma(H - z)$

Now if distances are measured from liquid surface + ve vertically downwards and denoted by 'h', we have $(H - z) = h$.

∴ $\boxed{p = p_a + \gamma h}$ ... (1.14)

If pressure only due to liquid is required, $p_a$ can be neglected and hence pressure due to liquid is given by

$\boxed{p = \gamma h}$ ... (1.15)

This is known as **law of hydrostatics.**

Thus, intensity of pressure at any point in a liquid varies directly with the depth of the point below the free liquid surface (or the height of free liquid surface above the point).

The pressure at a point can thus be expressed in two ways:

(i) As intensity of pressure 'p' in N/m² or kN/m².

or (ii) As an equivalent column of liquid, $h = \dfrac{p}{\gamma}$ in m, standing above a point.

The relation $p = \gamma h$ can be used for conversion. *Height of free liquid surface above any point is called 'Static Head' at that point.*

## 1.7 Measurement of Pressure

Pressure is measured either

1. By taking local atmospheric pressure as zero pressure or reference pressure or datum pressure, or
2. By taking absolute zero (complete vacuum) as zero pressure, or reference pressure or datum pressure.

### 1.7.1 Atmospheric Pressure, Gauge Pressure, Absolute Pressure

**Atmospheric Pressure**

Air which is combination of gases and vapours exerts pressure on the surface of earth due to its weight. Pressure exerted by atmosphere is called *atmospheric pressure*. It is determined by balancing it against a column of mercury with the help of a barometer. Average height of mercury column balanced by standard atmosphere (at sea level) is 760 mm of mercury.

∴ Atmospheric pressure = 760 mm of Hg = 76 cm of Hg
or = 76 × 13.6 = 1033 cm of water
or = 10.33 m of water

When expressed as intensity of pressure,

Atmospheric pressure p = $\gamma h$ = 9.81 × 10.33 = 101.33 kN/m² or kPa.

Atmospheric pressure is also called *barometric pressure*.

## Gauge Pressure

*The pressure of a fluid measured with respect to local atmospheric pressure as zero pressure or reference pressure is called Gauge Pressure.*

Most instruments, generally called gauges, measure pressure in this manner and hence the name.

If the pressure is above atmospheric pressure, it is called *Positive Pressure*.

If the pressure is below atmospheric pressure, it is called *Vacuum Pressure* or *Negative Pressure*.

## Absolute Pressure

*The pressure of a fluid measured with respect to absolute zero or complete vacuum as zero pressure or reference pressure is called Absolute Pressure.*

[**Note:** Thus, atmospheric pressure is zero gauge or one atmosphere absolute]

Following relations can be used for conversion from one system to other system.

For + ve pressure,

Absolute pressure = Atmospheric Pressure + Gauge Pressure

For – ve pressure,

Absolute pressure = Atmospheric Pressure – Vacuum Pressure

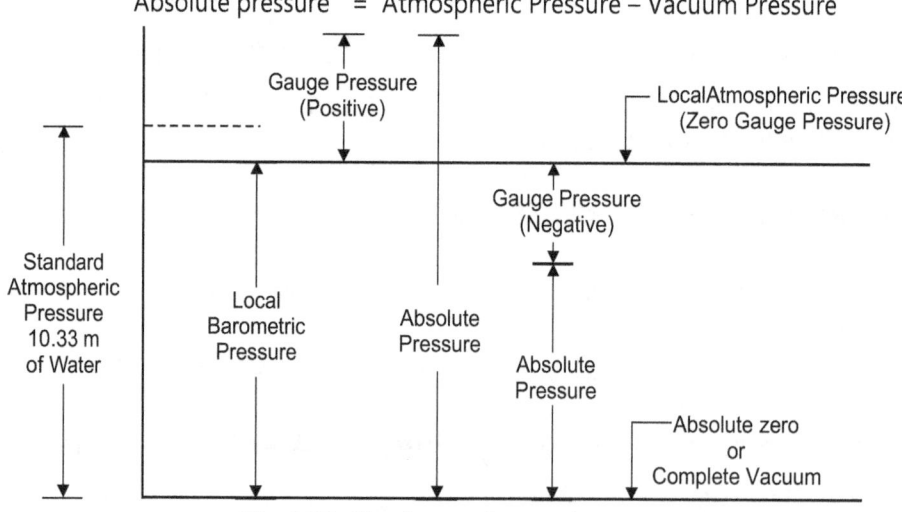

**Fig. 1.29: Absolute and gauge pressure**

Fig. 1.29 illustrates the relationship between the two systems.

## 1.7.2 Pressure Measuring Devices

There are two types of devices used for measurement of pressure:
1. Manometers
2. Mechanical gauges.

**Manometers:** measure the unknown pressure by balancing it against the column of same or different liquid.

**Mechanical Gauges:** measure the unknown pressure by balancing it against a mechanical element like, dead weight, a spring or a diaphragm etc.

| Manometers | Mechanical gauges |
|---|---|
| 1. Bulky, delicate and cannot be transported easily. | 1. Strong, sturdy and can be transported easily. |
| 2. Can be used for low pressure measurement. High pressures cannot be measured. Can be used for limited range. | 2. Can be used for high pressure measurement. Not suitable for low pressure measurement. Can be used for wide range. |
| 3. Accurate throughout the range. | 3. Accurate mainly at the centre of the range. |
| 4. Sensitivity (reading for the same pressure) can be adjusted by proper choice of liquids used. | 4. Sensitivity cannot be adjusted. |

## 1.8 Manometers

Manometers are broadly classified as:
1. Simple manometers and
2. Differential manometers

**Simple manometer:** It measures the pressure at a point and consists of a simple tube, (generally glass tube). It's one end is open to atmosphere while the other is connected to the point where the pressure is to be measured.

**Differential Manometer:** It measures only the pressure difference between two points. It also consists of a simple glass tube. Two ends of the tube are connected to the two points, the difference of pressure between which is to be measured. It does not give the magnitude of pressure at either of the points.

### 1. Simple Manometers

**(a) Piezometer:** The simplest type of simple manometer is piezometer shown in Fig. 1.30. It consists of a glass tube whose one end is open to atmosphere while the other is connected to pressure tapping on a vessel or a pipe where the pressure is to be measured. Liquid rises in the tube till the equilibrium is reached. The pressure is given by the vertical distance 'h' from the meniscus (liquid level in the tube) and the point where the pressure is to be measured. In order to minimize the capillary effect, tube size should not be less than 10 mm.

Since, the surface in the tube is subjected to atmosphere, piezometer will give only gauge pressure.

The pressure at point 'M', the centre of pipe is equal to $h_m$ metres of liquid of sp. gr. 's'. or $s \cdot h_m$ metres of water.

If '$\gamma$' is the unit weight of liquid the pressure at M can be written as:
$$p_m = \gamma h_m \ (N/m^2)$$

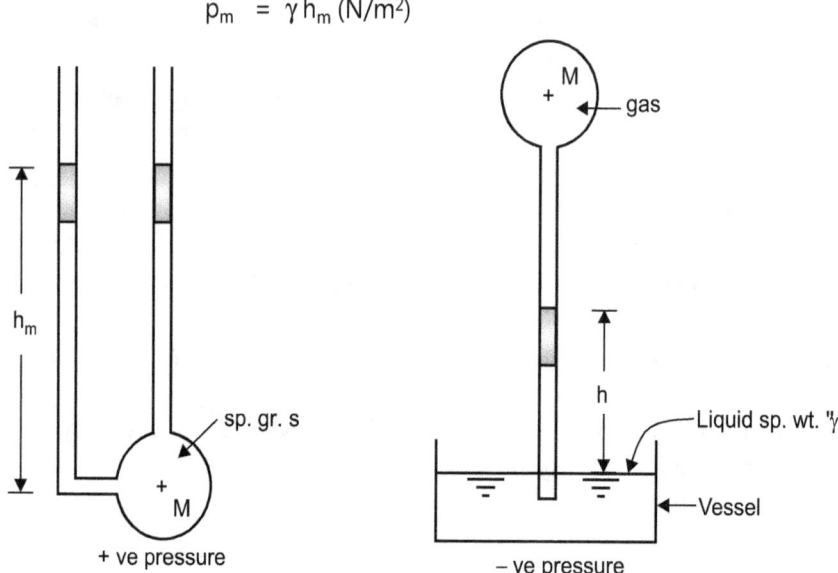

Fig. 1.30: Piezometer

As shown in Fig. 1.30, a piezometer can be used to measure negative pressure. Pressure in this case is

– h metres of liquid in the vessel

or $p_m = -\gamma h$, where '$\gamma$' is specific weight of liquid in the vessel.

The limitations of piezometer viz.

1. It cannot be used for measurement of high pressures and
2. Gas pressure cannot be measured, lead us to another simple manometer, the U-tube manometer.

**(b) U-tube Manometer:** The tube is bent in the shape of English letter 'U', as shown in Fig. 1.31. If the same liquid (in which pressure is to be measured) is used, small – ve or + ve pressure can be measured with such an arrangement. The rise or fall in the tube above or below 'M' gives the + ve or – ve pressure at M.

To measure larger positive or negative pressures, the 'U' portion of the tube is filled with heavier liquid like mercury, immiscible with the first liquid.

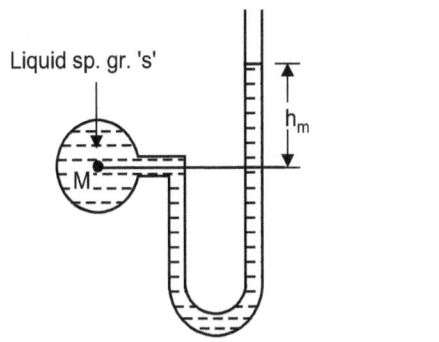
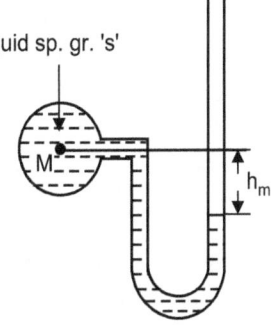

(a) Small + ve pressure
Pressure at M = s . $h_m$ m of water

(b) Small – ve pressure
Pressure at M = – s . $h_m$ m of water

Fig. 1.31

Since, the pressure is measured in terms of column of heavier liquid, higher pressures can be measured with 'U' tubes of moderate size. Fig. 1.32.

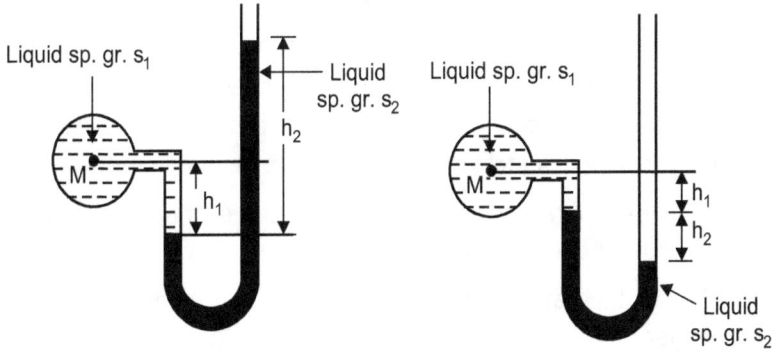

$h_m = s_2 h_2 - s_1 h_1$ m of water
(+ ve pressure)

$h_m = - s_2 h_2 - s_1 h_1$ m of water
(– ve pressure)

Fig. 1.32

## 2. Differential Manometers

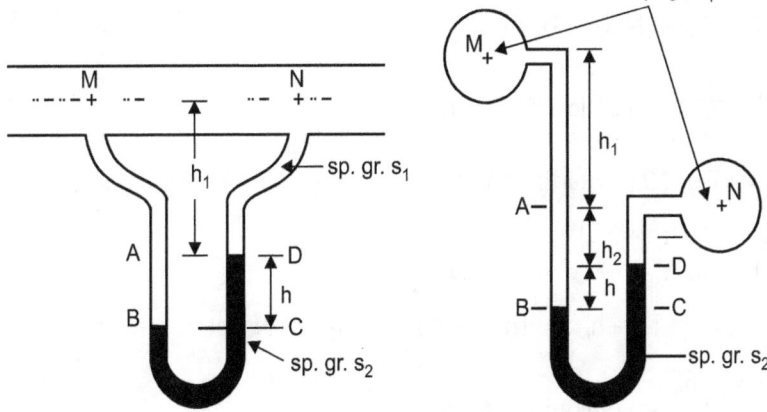

Fig. 1.33: Differential manometer

It measures only the pressure difference between two points. The two limbs of the 'U' tube are connected to two points, the difference of pressure between which is to be measured. The two points may be on the same pipe (carrying same fluid) or two different pipes (carrying different fluids). The choice of manometric liquid depends upon the range of pressures to be measured. For large pressure differences, heavy liquid like mercury is used. For small pressure differences liquids like carbon tetrachloride can be used.

In case of either a simple manometer or a differential manometer, it is easier to come across the unknown pressure or difference of pressure respectively by using the following procedure:

1. Draw a neat sketch of the system.

2. Demarcate the different liquid levels so that we can go from one end to the other via the manometer e.g. levels ABCD in Fig. 1.33 (a) and (b).

3. Starting from known end e.g. atmospheric pressure end in case of simple manometer or from one end, say 'M' in differential manometer, go from level to level. For decrease in elevation add pressure head and for increase in elevation subtract the pressure head taking into account sp. gr. of different liquids.

4. Express all heads in terms of water head and then at the end convert the head in terms of any other desired units.

For example in Fig. 1.33 (a) starting from M and writing manometric equation, going along MABCDN we get

$$\underset{\text{at M}}{h_m} + \underset{\text{at A}}{s_1 h_1} + \underset{\text{at B = at C}}{s_1 h} - \underset{\text{at D}}{s_2 h} - \underset{\text{at N}}{s_1 h_1} = h_n$$

(all the heads are expressed in terms of column of water e.g. $h_m$ is pressure head at M in terms of water column.)

$$\therefore \quad h_m - h_n = [h(s_2 - s_1)] \text{ m of water}$$

or $\left[\dfrac{h_m - h_n}{s_1}\right]$ m of liquid of sp. gr. '$s_1$'

Similarly for Fig. 2.9 (b) starting from M and going along MABCDN we get,

$$\underset{\text{at M}}{h_m} + \underset{\text{at A}}{s_1 h_1} + \underset{\text{at B = C}}{s_1(h_2 + h)} - \underset{\text{at D}}{s_2 h} - \underset{\text{at N}}{s_1 h_2} = h_n$$

$$\therefore \quad h_m - h_n = [h(s_2 - s_1) - s_1 h_1] \text{ m of water}$$

or $\left[\dfrac{h_m - h_n}{s_1}\right]$ m of liquid of sp. gr. '$s_1$'.

## Inverted 'U'-tube Manometer

For small difference of pressure an inverted U-tube manometer as shown in Fig. 1.34 is used. An immiscible lighter fluid, e.g. some oil or air, is used as manometric fluid. Since pressure difference is measured in terms of lighter fluid, a large deflection can be obtained even for small difference of pressure.

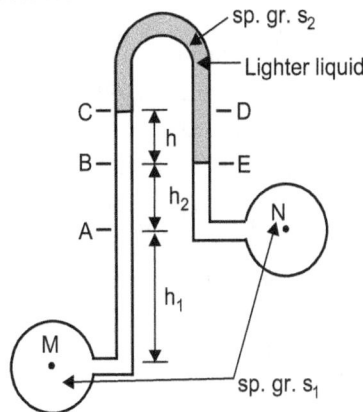

Fig. 1.34: Inverted U-tube Manometer

Using the same procedure as in the previous case, starting from M and going along MABCDEN we can write;

$$h_m \underset{\text{at M}}{} - \underset{\text{at A}}{s_1 h_1} - \underset{\text{at B}}{s_1 h_2} - \underset{\text{at C = at D}}{s_1 h} + \underset{\text{at E}}{s_2 h} + \underset{\text{at N}}{s_1 h_2} = h_n$$

$$\therefore \quad h_m - h_n = \left[h(s_1 - s_2) + s_1 h_1\right] \text{ m of water}$$

or $\left[\dfrac{h_m - h_n}{s_1}\right]$ m of liquid of sp. gr. '$s_1$'

[**Note:** Even if the sp. gr. of liquids in the pipes are different, the same *procedure* can be adopted.]

### 1.8.1 Sensitive Manometers

For the same pressure (in case of simple manometer) or for the same difference of pressure (in case of differential manometer) more the deflection shown by manometer more sensitive is the manometer.

**(a) Inclined Tube Manometer**

If the measuring limb of the manometer is inclined at some angle 'θ' with horizontal, the deflection shown will be more than that shown by the vertical limb as shown in Fig. 1.35 and hence pressure can be measured more accurately.

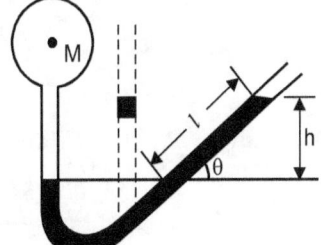

Fig. 1.35: Inclined Tube Manometer

We have $l = \dfrac{h}{\sin \theta}$, sin θ being less than 1, '*l*' is greater than 'h'.

## (b) Single Tube Manometer

It is a modified form of U-tube manometer. A large reservoir whose area is about 100 times the area of the tube is introduced in one of its limbs and is then connected to the pressure tapping as shown in Fig. 1.36.

Variation in the liquid level in the reservoir is small and may be neglected. Reading of deflection only on the other limb will indicate the pressure. Since, reading is taken only on one limb, it is also called *single tube manometer*.

If the liquid level in the reservoir falls by a small distance $\Delta h$ due to application of a small pressure, the volume of liquid displaced from reservoir will be $A.\Delta h$ where A is cross-sectional area of reservoir. This volume will go in the tube (right limb) and increase the level there by '$h_2$' such that $A.\Delta h = a \cdot h_2$ or $h_2 = \frac{A}{a} \cdot \Delta h$, where 'a' is area of tube. Since $\frac{A}{a}$ is very large, deflection '$h_2$' is very large (even for a small pressure) making the manometer, a sensitive manometer.

If $\Delta h$ is the fall in reservoir level and $h_2$ rise of liquid level in the tube, then neglecting $\Delta h$, we can write

$$h_m = s_2 h_2 - s_1 h_1$$

If $\Delta h$ has to be taken into account, starting from open end and going along ABCDEM, we can write:

$$0 + s_2 h_2 + s_2 \Delta h - s_1 \Delta h - s_1 h_1 = h_m$$
at A at B at C = at D at E at M

∴ $\quad h_m = s_2 h_2 + (s_2 - s_1) \cdot \Delta h - s_1 h_1$

but $\quad A . \Delta h = a . h_2$

∴ $\quad \Delta h = \dfrac{a}{A} \cdot h_2$

∴ $\quad h_m = s_2 h_2 + (s_2 - s_1) \cdot h_2 \cdot \dfrac{a}{A} - s_1 h_1$

∴ $\quad h_m = \left[ s_2 + (s_2 - s_1) \dfrac{a}{A} \right] h_2 - s_1 h_1$ m of water.

Further, this manometer can be made more sensitive by making the tube inclined.

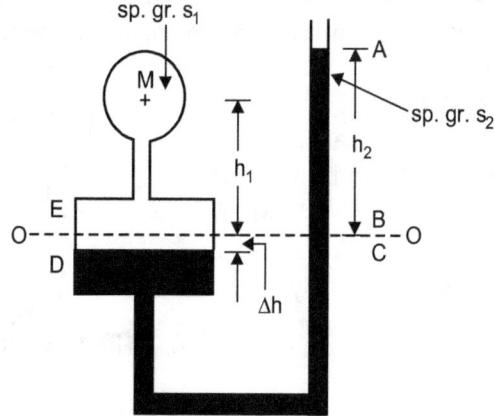

**Fig. 1.36: Single Tube manometer**

## (c) Micromanometers

Micromanometers are used to measure small differences of pressure with high precision. Micromanometers either (1) magnify the readings and/or (2) increase the accuracy of observation.

One such micromanometer is as shown in Fig. 1.37. It makes use of two manometric liquids which are immiscible with each other and also with the fluid whose pressure difference is to be measured. Similar to single tube manometer, it consists of a U–tube which is connected to two large reservoirs (area 100 times the area of tube) which in turn are connected to pressure tappings.

Initially, lower part of U tube is filled with heavier liquid upto O – O and then lighter liquid is filled on both sides upto level X – X. The fluid (liquid or gas) whose pressure is to be measured, fills the space above X – X.

When pressure in bulb 'A' is higher greater than that in 'B', liquid levels will be as shown in Fig. 1.37. Volume of liquid displaced in each tank is equal to volume of liquid displaced in the tube. If 'a' is the area of tube and 'A' that of the tank, then

$$a \cdot \frac{h}{2} = A \cdot \Delta h$$

[ liquid will go down by $\frac{h}{2}$ in the left limb and

or $$\Delta h = \frac{a}{A} \cdot \frac{h}{2}$$

go up by $\frac{h}{2}$ in the right limb, thus giving

$$2 \Delta h = \frac{a}{A} \cdot h$$

reading 'h' of manometer ].

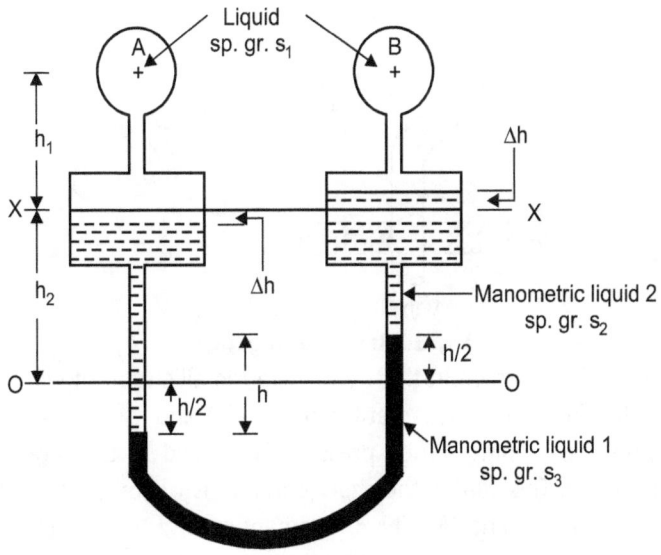

Fig. 1.37

Starting from 'A' and going along manometer, we can write manometric equation as

$$h_A + s_1(h_1 + \Delta h) + s_2\left(h_2 - \Delta h + \frac{h}{2}\right) - s_3 h - s_2\left(h_2 + \Delta h - \frac{h}{2}\right) - s_1(h_1 - \Delta h) = h_B$$

$$\therefore \quad h_A + s_1 h_1 + s_1 \Delta h + s_2 h_2 - s_2 \Delta h + s_2 \frac{h}{2} - s_3 h - s_2 h_2 - s_2 \Delta h + s_2 \frac{h}{2} - s_1 h_1 + s_1 \Delta h = h_B$$

$$\therefore \quad h_A + s_1(2\Delta h) - s_2(2\Delta h) + s_2 h - s_3 h = h_B$$

$$\therefore \quad h_A - h_B = s_3 h - s_2 h + (s_2 - s_1)\frac{a}{A}\cdot h$$

$$\therefore \quad h_A - h_B = h\left\{s_3 - s_2\left(1 - \frac{a}{A}\right) - s_1\cdot\frac{a}{A}\right\} \text{ m of water}$$

If $\frac{a}{A}$ is small, $h_A - h_B = h(s_3 - s_2)$ and hence a large deflection 'h' can be obtained if $s_2$ and $s_3$ are very near to each other.

For measurement of very small differences of pressure, an inverted differential micromanometer can be used.

## 1.8.2 Mechanical Gauges

Out of all mechanical gauges, Bourdon gauge shown in Fig. 1.38 is very widely used since (1) it is very compact (2) it is very robust and (3) it is simple to use, although, it does not give very precise readings.

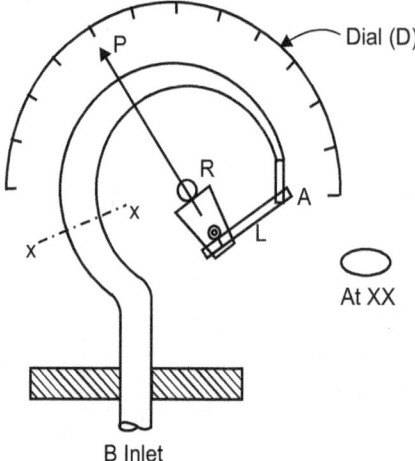

**Fig. 1.38: Bourdon gauge**

The pressure sensitive element in this gauge is a metallic tube of elliptical cross section in the form of question mark. It is closed at the free end A and its other end B, which is fixed, is connected to pressure tapping. When pressure is applied to the tube, its cross-section tends to become circular. This causes the change in radius of curvature of the tube, making the movement of the closed end 'A'. This movement of end A, is connected by link 'L' to mechanical rack and pinion arrangement 'R' which causes the movement of the pointer P, on the calibrated dial D. Pointer indicates zero when the pressures inside and outside of tube are equal. This type of gauge can be used for measurement of positive as well as negative pressure. (Such a gauge is called compound gauge). For different pressure ranges, tubes of different stiffness are used. Since the gauge works on the elastic property of the tube, it requires periodical check–up. The gauge is calibrated in N/m² or mm of Hg or m of water.

Other types of mechanical gauges are:
1. Bellow gauge
2. Diaphragm gauge and
3. Dead weight gauge.

## ILLUSTRATIVE EXAMPLES

**Example 1.21:**
Obtain equivalent head of kerosene (S = 0.8) and mercury (S = 13.6) for a 4 m head of water.

**Solution:**
Heights of columns of different liquids which produce the same pressure are called 'equivalent columns'.

$$p = \gamma_w h_w = \gamma_{ker} \cdot h_{ker}$$

$$h_{ker} = \frac{\gamma_w}{\gamma_{ker}} \cdot h_w = \frac{h_w}{S_{ker}} = \frac{4}{0.8} = 5 \text{ m}$$

$$p = \gamma_w h_w = \gamma_{Hg} \cdot h_{Hg}$$

$$h_{Hg} = \frac{\gamma_w}{\gamma_{Hg}} \cdot h_w = \frac{h_w}{S_{Hg}} = \frac{4}{13.6} = 0.294 \text{ m}$$

**Example 1.22:**
Standard atmospheric pressure in terms of column of liquid of specific gravity 0.83 is ... metres.

**Solution:**
$$\frac{10.33}{0.83} = \boxed{12.45 \text{ metres}}$$

**Example 1.23:**
Barometric reading at a place is 75 cm of Hg. Express the pressure intensity of 10 N per cm² in:
(i) m of water
(ii) mm of mercury
(iii) $\frac{kN}{m^2}$ abs

**Solution:**
Given pressure intensity
$$p_{gauge} = 10 \text{ N/cm}^2 = 10 \times 10^4 \text{ N/m}^2$$
$$\therefore \quad p_{gauge} = 10^5 \text{ N/m}^2 = 100 \text{ kN/m}^2$$

(i) $p_{gauge} = \gamma_w \cdot h_w$

∴ $h_w = \dfrac{p_{gauge}}{\gamma_w} = \dfrac{10^5}{9810} = 10.194$ m of water

$\boxed{\text{metres of water} = 10.194 \text{ m}}$

(ii) Metres of mercury $= \dfrac{10.194}{13.6} = 0.749$ m

∴ $\boxed{\text{mm of mercury} = 749 \text{ mm}}$

(iii) Now, barometric reading is 75 cm of Hg.

∴ $h_{atm} = 75$ cm of Hg
$= 75 \times 13.6 = 1020$ cm of water

or $h_{atm} = 10.2$ m of water

or $p_{atm} = 9.81 \times 10.2 = 100.062$ kN/m²

∴ $p_{abs} = p_{gauge} + p_{atm} = 100 + 100.062$

∴ $\boxed{p_{abs} = 200.062 \text{ kN/m}^2}$

### Example 1.24:

The diameters of the ram and plunger of a hydraulic press are 30 cm and 6 cm respectively. The plunger has a stroke of 30 cm and it makes 120 strokes per minute. Find
(i) Force required on the plunger to lift the load of 20 kN.
(ii) The height through which the load will be lifted per minute.
(iii) Power required in driving the plunger.
Neglect all losses due to friction.

**Solution:**

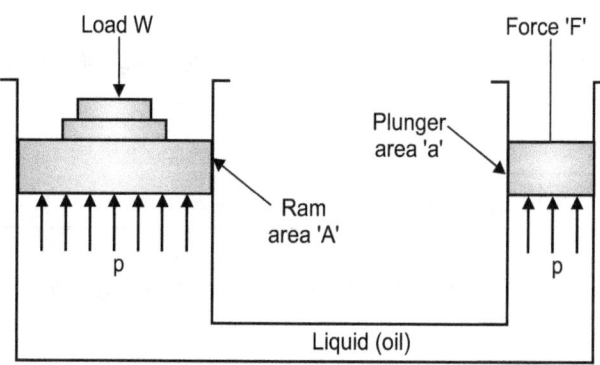

Fig. 1.39: Hydraulic Press

The hydraulic press shown in Fig. 1.39 is used to lift heavy loads using small forces. It works on Pascal's law which states that the intensity of pressure is transmitted equally in all directions in the mass of fluid at rest.

Hydraulic press consists of two cylinders connected at the bottom by a pipe. The cylinders and the pipe are filled by some oil. The ram with area 'A' can move in the larger cylinder while a plunger with area 'a' can move in the smaller cylinder.

When a small force 'F' is applied to the plunger, an intensity of pressure 'p' is exerted on the liquid below it. This intensity 'p' is transmitted equally in all directions through liquid. Thus, the ram also is subjected to the same intensity of pressure 'p'.

Now, Intensity of pressure at the ram
= Intensity of pressure at the plunger

∴ $\dfrac{W}{A} = \dfrac{F}{a}$,  where W is the load to be lifted by the ram.

or  $\boxed{W = F \cdot \left(\dfrac{A}{a}\right)}$

The above equation shows that by application of small force 'F' on the plunger, a large load 'W' can be lifted by the ram. $\dfrac{W}{F} = \dfrac{A}{a}$ is the 'Mechanical advantage of the ram'.

Now for the given example,

(i) Force required on the plunger

$$F = W \cdot \dfrac{a}{A}$$

$$= 20{,}000 \; \dfrac{\frac{\pi}{4} \times d^2}{\frac{\pi}{4} \times D^2} \quad \text{where} \quad \begin{array}{l} d = \text{diameter of plunger} \\ D = \text{diameter of ram} \end{array}$$

or  $F = 20{,}000 \left(\dfrac{d}{D}\right)^2 = 20{,}000 \left(\dfrac{6}{30}\right)^2 = 800 \text{ N}$

∴ $\boxed{\text{Force required on the plunger} = 800 \text{ N}}$

(ii) Now,
Volume of liquid displaced by plunger per stroke
= $S_p$ × Area of plunger      where  $S_p$ = Stroke of plunger

= $30 \times \dfrac{\pi}{4} \times (6)^2$ cm³    ... (1)

This liquid will go to ram and occupy the volume
= $S_R$ × Area of ram    where  $S_R$ = Stroke of ram or the distance through which load is lifted per stroke of the plunger

= $S_R \times \dfrac{\pi}{4} \times (30)^2$    ... (2)

Equating (1) and (2) we get,

$$30 \times \dfrac{\pi}{4} \times (6)^2 = S_R \times \dfrac{\pi}{4} \times (30)^2$$

or  $S_R = 30 \times \left(\dfrac{6}{30}\right)^2 = 1.2$ cm

∴ Height through which load will be lifted per minute
$$= S_R \times \text{Number of strokes per minute}$$
$$= 1.2 \times 120 = 144 \text{ cm/minute}$$
$$= 1.44 \text{ m/minute}$$

∴ **Height through which load will be lifted per minute = 1.44 m**

(iii) Work done in lifting 20 kN through 1.44 m
$$= 20{,}000 \times 1.44 \text{ N-m/minute}$$

∴ Power required in driving the plunger
$$= \text{Work done/second}$$
$$= \frac{20{,}000 \times 1.44}{60}$$
$$= 480 \text{ watts}$$

∴ **Power required in driving the plunger = 480 watts**

[**Note:** Power can also be found out from the plunger side
$$\text{Power} = F \times S_p \times \frac{\text{Number of strokes}}{\text{Second}}$$
$$= 800 \times 0.30 \times \frac{120}{60} = 480 \text{ watts}]$$

### Example 1.25:

The diameters of a small piston and a large piston of a hydraulic jack are 3 cm and 10 cm respectively. A force of 80 N is applied on the small piston. Find the load lifted by the large piston when:

(i) The pistons are at the same level.

(ii) Small piston is 40 cm above the large piston.

Assume the liquid in the jack as water.

**Solution:**

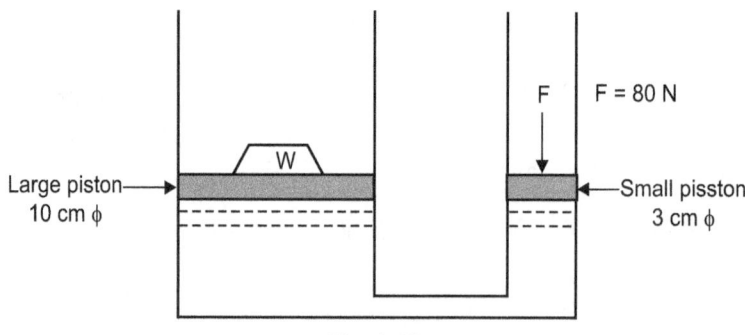

Fig. 1.40

(i) When the pistons are at the same level

$$W = F \cdot \left(\frac{\text{Area of large piston}}{\text{Area of small piston}}\right) = 80 \times \frac{\frac{\pi}{4} \times D^2}{\frac{\pi}{4} \times d^2}$$

$$W = 80 \times \left(\frac{10}{3}\right)^2 = 888.89 \text{ N}$$

∴ **Load lifted by the large piston = 888.89 N**

(ii)

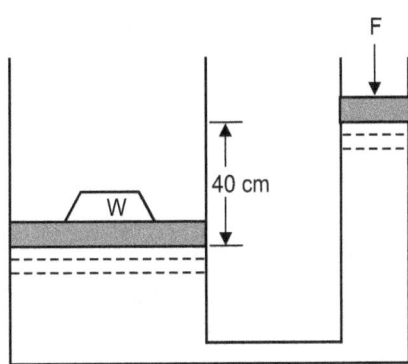

Fig. 1.41

In this case in addition to 80 N, additional force due to weight of water column of height 40 cm acts on the small piston side.

∴ The total force on small piston side

$$= 80 + \frac{\pi}{4} \times \left(\frac{3}{100}\right)^2 \times \left(\frac{40}{100}\right) \times 9810$$

$$= 82.77 \text{ N}$$

∴ $W = 82.77 \times \left(\frac{10}{3}\right)^2$

$$= 919.67 \text{ N}$$

∴ **Load lifted by the large piston = 919.67 N**

## THEORETICAL QUESTIONS

1. Define 'Pressure' and 'Intensity of Pressure'.
2. Define and explain Pascal's law.
3. State and prove Pascal's law.
4. With the help of a neat diagram define the terms: Absolute pressure, Gauge pressure and Vacuum pressure. What is the relation between absolute pressure and gauge pressure?
5. What are absolute pressures? Explain with a neat suitable diagram.
6. Define gauge pressure, vacuum pressure and absolute pressure. Indicate their relative positions on a chart.

7. State and prove hydrostatic law.
8. Distinguish between simple manometer and differential manometer.
9. What is a piezometer? What are its limitations?
10. Explain the construction and use of micromanometer.
11. Write note on 'Bourdon Gauge.'

# PART C

## 1.9 Pressure on Plane Surface

### 1.9.1 Total Pressure and Centre of Surface

**Total Pressure:** *When static fluid comes in contact with either plane or curved surface, the force exerted by the fluid on the surface is called total pressure.*

In case of fluid at rest, no tangential (shear) force exists. Therefore, total pressure acts normal to the surface.

**Centre of Pressure:** *The point of application of total pressure on the surface is called centre of pressure.*

### 1.9.2 Total Pressure on a Plane Surface

Consider a plane surface of arbitrary shape and total area A, completely submerged in a static mass of liquid of specific weight '$\gamma$'. It is held inclined making an angle '$\theta$' with the liquid surface as shown in Fig. 1.42.

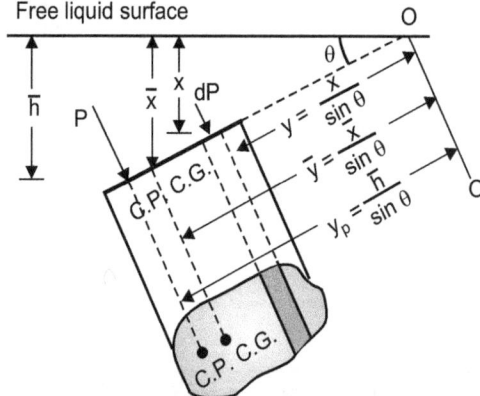

**Fig. 1.42: Total pressure on inclined plane surface**

If the plane of the lamina (surface) is extended till it intersects the free liquid surface, an axis passing through 'O' and perpendicular to plane of paper is obtained. This axis is denoted as 'OO' in Fig. 1.42.

Let,  $\bar{x}$ = Depth of centroid of plane surface vertically below free liquid surface.

$\bar{y}$ = Inclined distance of centroid from OO along the inclined plane.

$\bar{h}$ = Depth of centre of pressure vertically below free liquid surface.

$y_p$ = Inclined distance of centre of pressure from OO.

Consider an elementary strip of area 'dA' on the plane surface. Let it be situated at a vertical distance of 'x' from free surface and let its distance from 'OO' be y. Since the thickness of the strip is very small, intensity of pressure may be assumed to be constant for this strip.

Intensity of pressure for strip $= p = \gamma x$   $[\because p = \gamma h]$

∴ Total pressure on strip = Intensity of pressure × Area of strip

$$dP = \gamma x \cdot (dA)$$

or $\quad dP = \gamma \cdot y \sin\theta \cdot dA$   $[\because x = y \sin\theta]$

Integrating the above expression, the total pressure on the entire surface is given by

$$P = \int dP = \int \gamma \cdot y \sin\theta \cdot dA$$

or $\quad P = \gamma \sin\theta \int dA \cdot y$

but $\quad dA \cdot y = $ First moment of area 'dA' about OO

∴ $\int dA \cdot y = $ Sum of the first moments of areas of elementary strips about axis OO.

$$= \text{Total area 'A'} \times \begin{bmatrix} \text{Distance of centroid of surface} \\ \text{from axis OO} \end{bmatrix}$$

∴ $\quad \int dA \cdot y = A \cdot \bar{y}$

∴ $\quad P = \gamma \sin\theta \cdot A\bar{y}$

∴ $\quad \boxed{P = \gamma A \bar{x}}$   $[\because \bar{x} = \bar{y}\sin\theta]$   ... (1.16)

Above relation shows that *the magnitude of total pressure on plane surface is independent of the inclination 'θ' of the surface.* Thus, for a lamina of given area 'A' and constant value of $\bar{x}$, total pressure will remain same even if the lamina (surface) is turned in any manner. The relation can also be used for horizontal and vertical surfaces.

Further, $\quad P = \gamma A \bar{x} = (\gamma \bar{x}) \cdot A$

but $\gamma \bar{x}$ is the intensity of pressure at C.G. of lamina.

∴ $\quad P = $ Intensity of pressure at centroid × Area of the surface

## Depth of Centre of Pressure ($\bar{h}$):

If the surface is divided into number of elementary strips, the forces on the elementary strips i.e. all dP's, being normal to the surface, will form a system of parallel forces and centre of pressure is the point of application of the resultant P of this system of parallel forces. Therefore, moment of P about the axis OO must be equal to sum of the moments of all dP's about the axis OO.

Moment of P about OO $= P \cdot y_p$

We have $dP = \gamma \cdot y \cdot \sin\theta \cdot dA$

Moment of dP about OO $= dP \cdot y = (\gamma \cdot y \cdot \sin\theta \cdot dA) y$

∴ Sum of moments of forces on all elementary strips about OO $= \int \gamma \cdot y^2 \cdot \sin\theta \cdot dA$

∴ Equating $P \cdot y_p = \int \gamma \cdot y^2 \cdot \sin\theta \cdot dA$

$$y_p = \frac{\int \gamma y^2 \sin\theta \cdot dA}{P} \quad \text{but } P = \int \gamma y \sin\theta \cdot dA$$

$$= \frac{\int \gamma y^2 \sin\theta \cdot dA}{\int \gamma y \sin\theta \cdot dA}$$

or $$y_p = \frac{\int dA \cdot y^2}{\int dA \cdot y} = \frac{2^{nd} \text{ moment of area}}{1^{st} \text{ moment of area}}$$

But $\int dA \cdot y^2$ = Moment of inertia of the plane surface about axis OO = $I_o$

and $\int dA \cdot y = A\bar{y}$

∴ $$y_p = \frac{I_o}{A\bar{y}}$$

But by Parallel axis theorem for moments of inertia,

$$I_o = I_G + A\bar{y}^2$$

∴ $$y_p = \frac{I_G + A\bar{y}^2}{A\bar{y}} = \bar{y} + \frac{I_G}{A\bar{y}} \quad \text{but } y_p = \frac{\bar{h}}{\sin\theta}, \bar{y} = \frac{\bar{x}}{\sin\theta}$$

∴ $$\frac{\bar{h}}{\sin\theta} = \frac{\bar{x}}{\sin\theta} + \frac{I_G \sin\theta}{A\bar{x}}$$

∴ $$\boxed{\bar{h} = \bar{x} + \frac{I_G \sin^2\theta}{A\bar{x}}} \quad \ldots (1.17)$$

$\bar{h}$ is the depth of centre of pressure vertically below free liquid surface.

Further, $$\bar{h} - \bar{x} = \frac{I_G \sin^2\theta}{A\bar{x}}$$

all the terms on right hand side of this equation are always positive and hence $\bar{h} - \bar{x}$ is always positive or $\bar{h}$ is always greater than $\bar{x}$. Thus, *centre of pressure will always lie below centre of gravity of the lamina.*

As the lamina is submerged deeper and deeper, $\bar{x}$ goes on increasing, $\bar{h} - \bar{x}$ i.e. vertical distance between C.P. and C.G. goes on decreasing. Centre of pressure goes on approaching centre of gravity.

If $\bar{x}$ is infinite, C.P. and C.G. will coincide. This is not practically possible and hence C.G. and C. P. will never coincide, the exception being the case of a lamina submerged horizontally.

The position of centre of pressure is independent of liquid in which the lamina is submerged.

Two typical cases are of importance (1) Lamina submerged vertically (2) Lamina submerged horizontally.

(1) For lamina submerged vertically,
$\theta = 90°$, $\sin \theta = 1$, $\sin^2 \theta = 1$

Therefore,
$$\boxed{\bar{h} = \bar{x} + \frac{I_G}{A \bar{x}}}$$

(2) For lamina submerged horizontally,
$\theta = 0°$, $\sin \theta = 0$, $\sin^2 \theta = 0$ and

Therefore, $\bar{h} = \bar{x}$ = depth of lamina vertically below free liquid surface.

Table 1.1 gives the moments of inertia and other geometric properties of various surfaces.

**Table 1.1: Moment of Inertia and other Geometric Properties of plane surfaces**

| Plane Surface | | Area | Moment of inertia of area about axis GG through centroid |
|---|---|---|---|
| Rectangle | (rectangle with width b, height d, centroid G at d/2) | $bd$ | $\dfrac{bd^3}{12}$ |
| Triangle | (triangle with base b, height h, centroid G at h/3 from base) | $\dfrac{bh}{2}$ | $\dfrac{bh^3}{36}$ $\left[ I_{O-O} = \dfrac{bh^3}{12} \right]$ |
| Circle | (circle with diameter D) | $\dfrac{\pi D^2}{4}$ | $\dfrac{\pi D^4}{64}$ |

| Shape | Figure | Area | $I_{xx}$ |
|---|---|---|---|
| Semi-circle | $y = \dfrac{4R}{3\pi} = 0.425\,R$ | $\dfrac{\pi R^2}{2}$ | $\left[\dfrac{\pi}{8} - \dfrac{8}{9\pi}\right] R^4 = 0.11 R^4$ $\left[I_{O-O} = \dfrac{\pi R^4}{8}\right]$ |
| Trapezium | $y = \left(\dfrac{2a+b}{a+b} \times \dfrac{h}{3}\right)$ | $\dfrac{1}{2}(a+b)\,h$ | $\left[\dfrac{a^2 + 4ab + b^2}{36(a+b)}\right] h^3$ |
| Quarter circle | $\dfrac{4R}{3\pi}$, $\dfrac{4R}{3\pi}$ | $\dfrac{\pi R^2}{4}$ | $\left[\dfrac{\pi}{16} - \dfrac{4}{9\pi}\right] R^4 = 0.055 R^4$ $\left[I_{O-O} = \dfrac{\pi R^4}{16}\right]$ |

### 1.9.3 Pressure Diagram

*A pressure diagram is a graphical representation of variation of intensity of pressure over a surface.* A pressure diagram may be constructed by plotting intensities of pressure at various points on the surface to some convenient scale. Pressure diagram is useful in finding out the total pressure and position of centre of pressure on plane surfaces. It has limited application to rectangular surfaces.

Pressure diagrams for horizontal, vertical and inclined surfaces are as shown in Fig. 1.43.

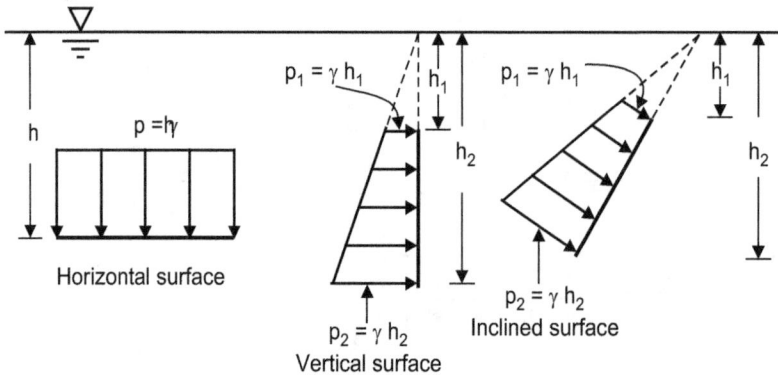

**Fig. 1.43: Pressure diagrams for various surfaces**

Consider a rectangular lamina submerged vertically as shown in Fig. 1.44. Intensity of pressure at the top will be zero and at the base of lamina will be γ h. Thus, Δ abc represents the pressure diagram for the lamina.

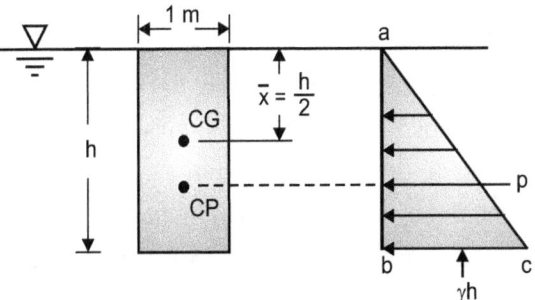

Fig. 1.44

Total pressure on lamina $P = \gamma A \bar{x} = \gamma \times h \cdot 1 \times \dfrac{h}{2}$

$$P = \dfrac{1}{2}(\gamma h) \cdot h$$

which is the area of pressure diagram abc.

∴ *Area of pressure diagram represents the total pressure per unit length of the rectangular surface.*

Further, depth of centre of pressure is given by

$$\bar{h} = \bar{x} + \left(\dfrac{I_G}{A\bar{x}}\right) = \dfrac{h}{2} + \dfrac{1 \times h^3}{12} \times \dfrac{1}{(h \times 1) \times \dfrac{h}{2}}$$

∴ $\quad \bar{h} = \dfrac{h}{2} + \dfrac{h}{6} = \dfrac{2}{3}h$

which is the depth of centre of gravity of pressure diagram abc vertically below free liquid surface.

∴ *The line of action of total pressure must pass through the centre of gravity of pressure diagram.*

[In case of a rectangular surface, with width 'B', total pressure is given by the volume of pressure prism and the line of action of total pressure must pass through the centre of gravity of pressure prism as shown in Fig. 1.45]

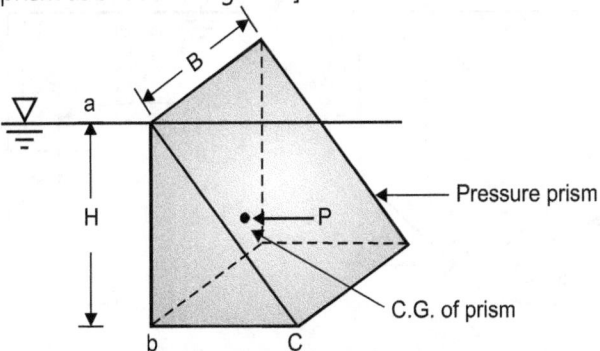

Fig. 1.45: Pressure prism

Although above relations are proved by a special simple case, they are applicable to pressure diagram (pressure prism) for any rectangular surface.

## 1.10 Pressure on Curved Surfaces

In case of a plane surface, total pressure can be found out by summation of total pressures on elementary strips. This is possible only because, the forces on all the elementary strips, being normal to the surface, form a system of parallel forces and hence their resultant can be found out by integration (summation).

On the other hand, in case of a curved surface the elementary forces do not form a system of parallel forces and hence the procedure used in case of plane surface cannot be used in case of curved surface. (See Fig. 1.46 (a)).

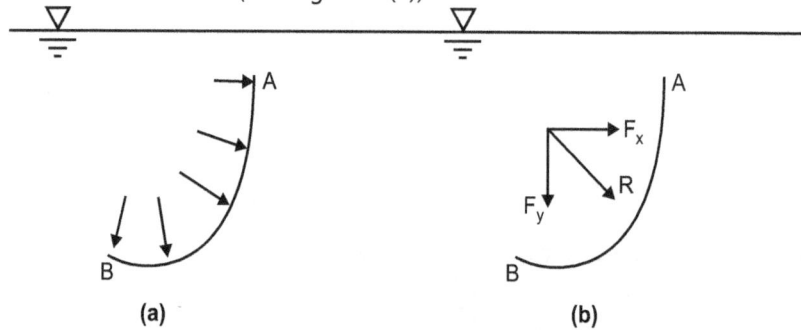

Fig. 1.46: Pressure on curved surface

As shown in Fig. 1.46 (b), resultant force R, acting on a curved surface is found out by finding its components $F_x$ and $F_y$ in horizontal and vertical directions respectively and combining them vectorially.

### (a) $F_x$ – Horizontal component of liquid pressure:

Consider a curved surface completely submerged in a liquid of specific weight 'γ'. Curved surface AB extends in the direction normal to plane of paper. Consider an elementary area 'dA' situated at depth 'h' below free liquid surface. See Fig. 1.47 (a).

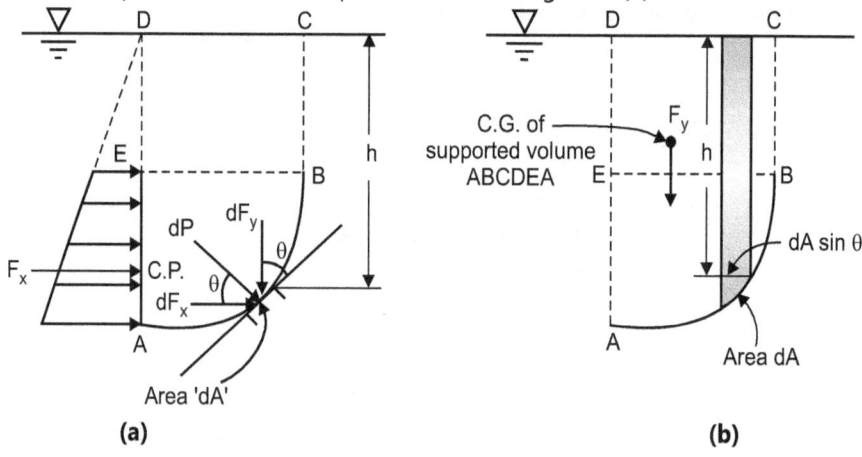

Fig. 1.47: Components of pressure on curved surface

Total pressure acting on area 'dA' = dP = p · dA, where p is the intensity of pressure on area dA. dP will be acting normal to area dA.

The component of dP in horizontal direction

$$dF_x = dP \cos \theta,$$  where '$\theta$' is angle made by dA with vertical
$$= p \cdot dA \cos \theta$$
$$dF_x = \gamma h \cdot dA \cos \theta \qquad [\because p = \gamma h]$$

Integrating,
$$F_x = \int \gamma h \cdot dA \cdot \cos \theta$$
$$= \int (\gamma h)(dA \cos \theta)$$

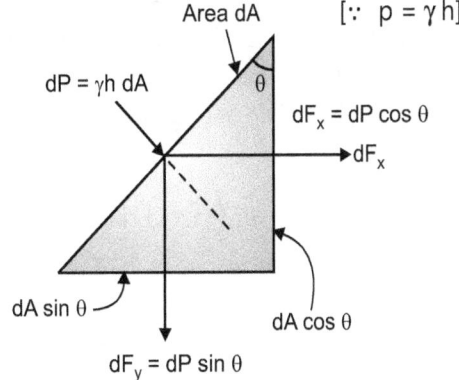

Fig. 1.48

But dA cos θ is the projection of curved surface dA on a vertical plane. Therefore,
$\gamma h \cdot dA \cdot \cos \theta$ = Total pressure on projection of 'dA' on vertical plane.

∴ $\quad F_x = \int \gamma h \cdot dA \cos \theta$

= Total pressure on the projection of curved surface 'AB' on a vertical plane. (See Fig. 1.47)

Therefore, $\boxed{F_x = \gamma A \bar{x}}$ ... (1.18)

where γ = Specific weight of fluid
A = Area of projection of curved surface on a vertical plane
$\bar{x}$ = Depth of C.G. of the projected area vertically below free liquid surface.

$F_x$ will be acting in horizontal direction through the *centre of pressure of the projected area*.

Thus, while calculating $F_x$, we are not concerned with the curved surface but only with its projection on vertical plane.

**(b) $F_y$ - Vertical component of liquid pressure:**

$$dF_y = dP \cdot \sin \theta = \gamma h \cdot dA \cdot \sin \theta$$
∴ $$F_y = \int \gamma h \cdot dA \cdot \sin \theta$$

But as can be seen from Fig. 1.48, dA sin θ is the projection of curved surface dA on horizontal plane and from Fig. 1.47 (b), (dA sin θ · h) represents the volume of liquid supported vertically by curved surface dA, shown hatched in the figure. γ (dA sin θ·h) is the weight of this supported liquid.

Therefore,  $F_y$ = Weight of liquid (either real or imaginary) supported vertically by the curved surface 'AB'. i.e. weight of liquid in the portion ABCDEA [ See Fig. 1.47 (b) ]

∴ $\boxed{F_y = \text{Weight of liquid either real or imaginary supported vertically by the curved surface}}$ ... (1.19)

$F_y$ will be acting through *the centre of gravity of supported liquid*. If supported liquid is real, $F_y$ will be acting in vertically downward direction and if the supported liquid is imaginary, $F_y$ will be acting in vertically upward direction.

Then,

$$\boxed{R = \sqrt{F_x^2 + F_y^2}}$$ ... (1.20)

$$\boxed{\theta = \tan^{-1} \frac{F_y}{F_x}}$$ ... (1.21)

where θ is the angle made by R with horizontal

## ILLUSTRATIVE EXAMPLES

**Example 1.26:**

A circular plate 2m diameter is immersed in water completely and vertically, such that one of the ends of its vertical diameter is 0.6 m below water surface. In a neat sketch, show the total water pressure on one side of the plate and position of centre of pressure.

**Solution:**

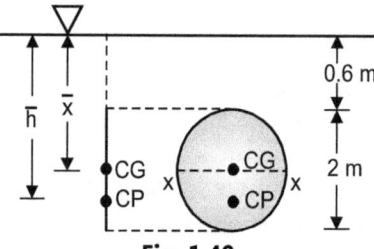

Fig. 1.49

Total pressure on one face of the surface

$$P = \gamma A \bar{x} = 9.81 \times \left(\frac{\pi}{4} \times 4\right) \times (0.6 + 1)$$

∴ $\boxed{P = 49.31 \text{ kN}}$

Depth of C.P. vertically below liquid surface

$$\bar{h} = \bar{x} + \frac{I_G \sin^2 \theta}{A \bar{x}} \qquad \because \theta = 90°, \sin \theta = 1$$

∴ $$\bar{h} = \bar{x} + \frac{I_G}{A \bar{x}}$$

**[Note:** The selection of the axis passing through C. G. about which we find out moment of inertia of the lamina $I_G$ is very important. Procedure is as follows: Extend the plane of the lamina till it meets liquid surface in line passing through 'O' and perpendicular to plane of Fig. 1.50 in the end view (or left figure) or liquid surface in front view (right figure). Then a line is drawn parallel to this line and passing through C.G. of lamina. Here it is line 'XX'. $I_G$ is the moment of inertia of the lamina about this axis].

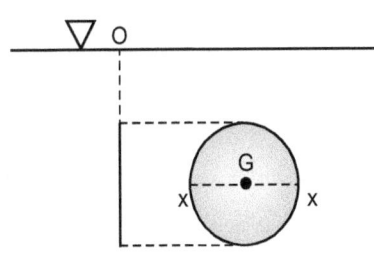

Fig. 1.50

$$\bar{h} = \bar{x} + \frac{I_G}{A\bar{x}}, \text{ For circular plate, } I_G = \frac{\pi d^4}{64} = \frac{\pi \times 2^4}{64} = \frac{\pi}{4} m^4$$

$$= 1.6 + \frac{\pi}{4} \times \frac{1}{\pi \times 1.6} = 1.6 + 0.156$$

∴ $\boxed{\bar{h} = 1.756 \text{ m vertically below free water surface}}$

### Example 1.27:
A circular plate 2 m in diameter is submerged in water such that its greatest and least depths below the free surface are 3.5 m and 2 m respectively. Find the total pressure on one face of the plate and depth of centre of pressure.

**Solution:**

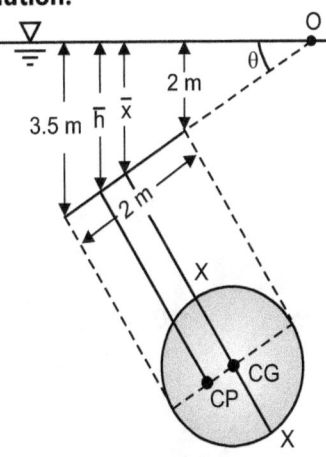

Fig. 1.51

Area of plate $= \frac{\pi}{4} \times 2^2 = \pi \, m^2$

Depth of C.G. vertically below free water surface

$$\bar{x} = \frac{2 + 3.5}{2} = 2.75 \text{ m}$$

Let θ be the angle of inclination of plate with water surface then

$$\sin \theta = \frac{3.5 - 2}{2} = \frac{1.5}{2} = 0.75 \text{ m}$$

Total pressure $P = \gamma A \bar{x}$
$= (9.81) \times \pi \times 2.75$

∴ $\boxed{P = 84.75 \text{ kN}}$

Depth of C. P. vertically below free liquid surface

$$\bar{h} = \bar{x} + \frac{I_G \sin^2 \theta}{A\bar{x}}$$

[Axis about which moment of inertia is taken is axis 'XX'. Refer note in Ex. 1.26]

$$I_G = \frac{\pi \times 2^4}{64} = \frac{\pi}{4} m^4 \qquad \sin \theta = \frac{1.5}{2} = \frac{3}{4}$$

$$\bar{h} = 2.75 + \frac{\pi}{4} \times \left(\frac{3}{4}\right)^2 \times \frac{1}{\pi \times 2.75} = 2.75 + \frac{9}{64 \times 2.75}$$

∴ $\boxed{\bar{h} = 2.8 \text{ m}}$

### Example 1.28:

An equilateral triangle 2 m side is immersed vertically in water with one of its axis of symmetry parallel to water surface and at a depth of 2 m below water surface. Determine total pressure and position of centre of pressure.

**Solution:**

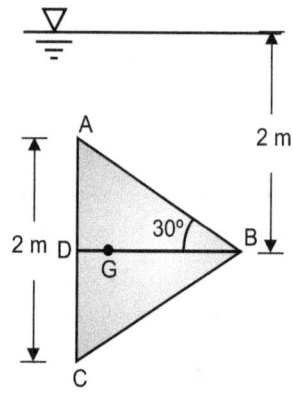

Fig. 1.52

Area of Δ ABC = $\frac{1}{2}$ AC × DB,    DB = $\sqrt{3}$ = 1.732 m

= $\frac{1}{2}$ × 2 × 1.732 = 1.732 m²

P = γ A $\bar{x}$ = 9.81 × 1.732 × 2 = 33.98 kN

$\boxed{P = 33.98 \text{ kN}}$

$\bar{h} = \bar{x} + \dfrac{I_G \sin^2 \theta}{A \bar{x}}$  ∵ θ = 90°   ∴ sin θ = 1

h = $\bar{x} + \dfrac{I_G}{A \bar{x}}$

Now, $I_G$ = Moment of inertia of Δ ABC about DB
= 2 × [Moment of inertia of Δ ABC (or Δ CBD) about DB]
= $2 \times \left[\dfrac{DB \times (AD)^3}{12}\right] = 2 \times \left[\dfrac{1.732 \times 1^3}{12}\right]$
= 0.289 m⁴

$$\therefore \quad \bar{h} = 2 + \frac{0.289}{1.732 \times 2}$$

$$= 2.083 \text{ m}$$

$\boxed{\bar{h} = 2.083 \text{ m below free water surface}}$

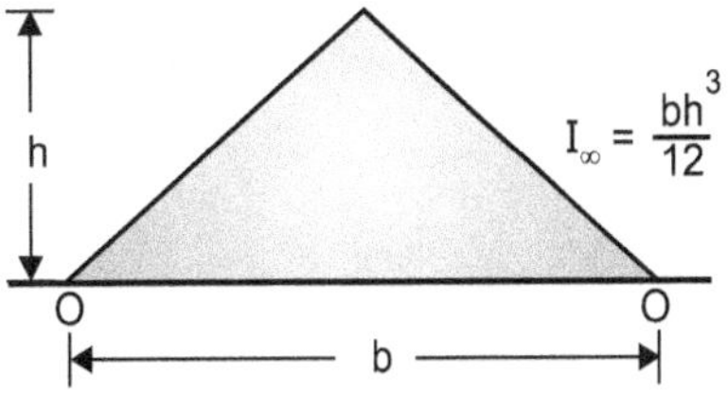

$$I_\infty = \frac{bh^3}{12}$$

**Fig. 1.53**

### Example 1.29:

A square plate 4m × 4m with a hole 1m × 1m cut in it is placed in liquid of specific gravity 0.8 as shown in Fig. 1.54. Determine the total pressure on one face of plate and position of centre of pressure.

**Solution:**

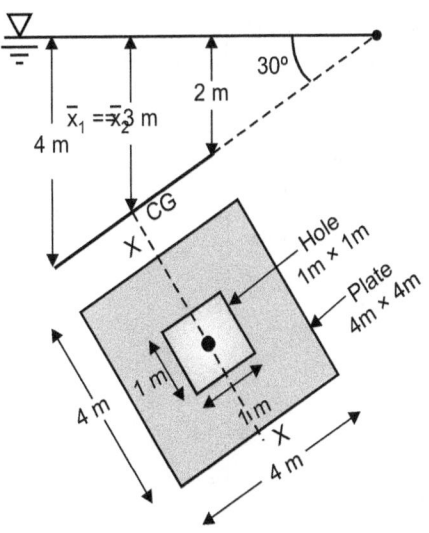

**Fig. 1.54**

$P_1$ = Force acting on the plate 4m × 4m without a hole cut in it

$$= \gamma A_1 \bar{x}_1$$

$$= (9.81 \times 0.8) \times (4 \times 4) \times 3$$

$$= 376.70 \text{ kN}$$

$\bar{h}_1$ = depth of point of application of $P_1$ vertically below free liquid surface

$$\therefore \quad \bar{h}_1 = \bar{x}_1 + \frac{I_{G_1} \sin^2 \theta}{A_1 \bar{x}_1}, \quad \theta = 30°, \sin \theta = \frac{1}{2}$$

$$= 3 + \frac{4 \times 4^3}{12} \times \frac{1}{4} \times \frac{1}{4 \times 4 \times 3}$$

$$= 3 + \frac{1}{9}$$

$$= \frac{28}{9} \text{ m}$$

$$= 3.11 \text{ m below free liquid surface.}$$

$P_2$ = Pressure force acting on plate 1m × 1m placed in the position of the hole

$$= \gamma_2 A_2 \bar{x}_2 = (0.8 \times 9.81) \times (1 \times 1) \times 3 = 23.54 \text{ kN}$$

$$\bar{h}_2 = \bar{x}_2 + \frac{I_{G_2} \sin^2 \theta}{A_2 \bar{x}_2}$$

$$= 3 + \frac{1 \times 1^3}{12} \cdot \frac{1}{4} \cdot \frac{1}{1 \times 1 \times 3} = 3 + \frac{1}{144} = 3.007 \text{ m}$$

$$\boxed{P = P_1 - P_2 = 353.16 \text{ kN}}$$

∴ Taking moments about liquid surface

$$P_1 \cdot \bar{h}_1 - P_2 \cdot \bar{h}_2 = P \cdot \bar{h}$$

∴ $$\bar{h} = \frac{376.70 \times 3.11 - 23.54 \times 3.007}{353.16}$$ ∴ $$\boxed{\bar{h} = 3.117 \text{ m}}$$

### Example 1.30:
A square plate of diagonal 1.5 m is immersed in water with it's diagonal vertical and upper corner 0.5 m below the free surface of water. Find the hydrostatic force on the plate and the depth of centre of pressure from free surface of water.

**Solution:**

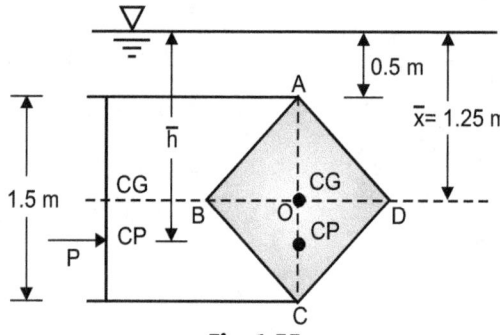

Fig. 1.55

The plate is placed in water as shown in Fig. 1.55.

Now, length of side of square = $\sqrt{(0.75)^2 + (0.75)^2}$ = 1.06 m

$$\bar{x} = 1.25 \text{ m}$$
$$A = 1.06 \times 1.06 = 1.125 \text{ m}^2$$

$$P = \gamma A \bar{x} = 9.81 \times 1.125 \times 1.25 \therefore \boxed{P = 13.8 \text{ kN}}$$

Depth of centre of pressure vertically below free water surface

$$\bar{h} = \bar{x} + \frac{I_G \sin^2 \theta}{A \bar{x}}$$    ∵ $\theta = 90°$   $\sin \theta = 1$

∴ $$\bar{h} = 1.25 + \frac{0.1055}{1.125 \times 1.25}$$

[$I_G$ – Moment of inertia of square ABCD about BD
= 2 × [Moment of inertia of Δ ABD (or Δ CBD) about BD]
$$= 2 \times \frac{(BD)(OA)^3}{12} = 2 \times \frac{1.5 \times (0.75)^3}{12} = 0.1055 \text{ m}^4$$

∴ $$\boxed{\bar{h} = 1.325 \text{ m below free liquid surface}}$$

## Example 1.31:

A vertical square area 1 m × 1 m is submerged in water with upper edge horizontal and 0.5 m below water surface. Locate a horizontal line on the surface such that the force on the upper portion equals the force on the lower portion.

**Solution:**

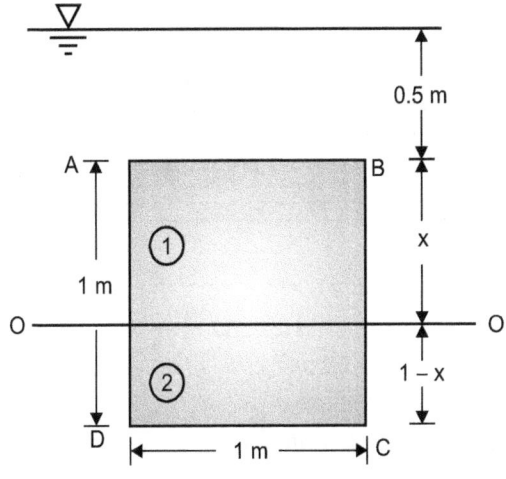

Fig. 1.56

The area ABCD is as shown in Fig. 1.56. Let OO be the required line.

Now,    Force on area (1) = Force on area (2)

Or    Force on area (1) = 1/2 the force on area ABCD

Force on area ABCD = $\gamma \cdot (1 \times 1) \cdot 1 = \gamma$

∴    Force on area (1) = $1/2 \cdot \gamma$      ... (I)

But force on area (1) is also given by

$$P_1 = \gamma \cdot A_1 \bar{x}_1$$

$$= \gamma \cdot (1 \times x) \left(0.5 + \frac{x}{2}\right) \quad \ldots \text{(II)}$$

Equating (I) and (II), we get,

$$\frac{\gamma}{2} = \gamma \cdot x \cdot \left(0.5 + \frac{x}{2}\right)$$

Or    $x^2 + x - 1 = 0$

$$\boxed{x = 0.618 \text{ m}}$$

The line should be drawn at a distance of 0.618 m from the upper edge.

## Example 1.32:

Fig. 1.57 shows a tank with water in it. Water rises in the tube EF as shown. Neglecting the weight of tank and riser tube, determine:

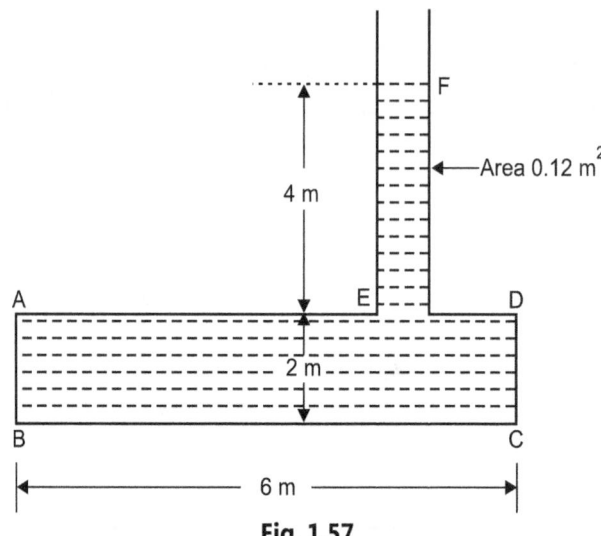

**Fig. 1.57**

(i) Resultant force acting on area AB and its location. AB is 3 m wide.

(ii) Total force on the bottom of the tank.

(iii) Compare total weight of water in tank with result of (ii) and comment on the difference.

**Solution:**

(i) Force on area AB = $\gamma \cdot A \cdot \bar{x}$ = 9.81 × (3 × 2) × 5 = 294.3 kN

∴ $\boxed{\text{Force on area AB} = 294.30 \text{ kN}}$

(ii) Total force on bottom of the tank

= Intensity of pressure on bottom × Area of bottom
= $\gamma \cdot H \cdot$ area
= 9.81 × 6 × (6 × 3) = 1059.48 kN

∴ $\boxed{\text{Total force on bottom of the tank} = 1059.48 \text{ kN}}$

(iii) Weight of water in the tank

W = $\gamma$ × (Volume of water in the tank)
= 9.81 × [(6 × 3 × 2) + 0.12 × 4]
= 357.87 kN

∴ $\boxed{\text{Weight of water in the tank} = 357.87 \text{ kN}}$

It can be seen that total pressure force on the bottom of tank is greater than the weight of total volume of water contained in the arrangement. This is known as 'hydrostatic paradox or Pascal's paradox.)

The hydrostatic paradox can be explained as follows:

Total force on bottom of the tank = $\boxed{1059.48 \text{ kN} (\downarrow)}$

Upward force on face AD, the roof of the tank
= Intensity of pressure at a depth of 4 m below free water surface in the tube × Area of top
= 9.81 × 4 × (6 × 3 – 0.12)
= **701.61 kN (↑)**

∴ Net downward force exerted by water
1059.48 – 701.61 = **357.87 kN**

which equals the weight of water in the tank and pipe.

### Example 1.33:
Gate 'AB' shown in Fig. 1.58 is 3m wide. It is hinged at its bottom and is held in position against water pressure with the help of rod AC, rope and concrete sphere. Find the diameter of sphere if specific gravity of concrete is 2.4.

**Solution:**

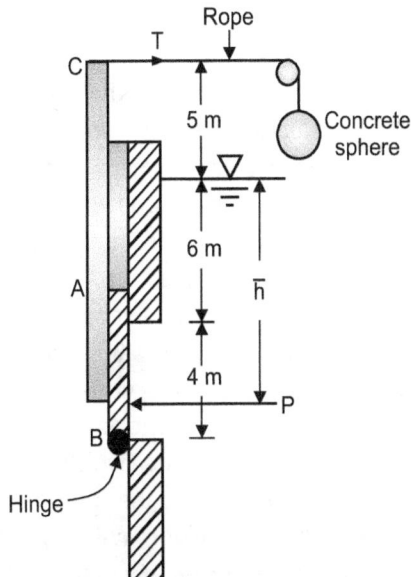

Fig. 1.58

Water pressure will create a force P on the gate from right to left. This will create anticlockwise moment about hinge 'B'. This has to be balanced by moment caused by clockwise moment due to tension in the rope. This tension will be equal to the weight of the sphere from which diameter can be found out

$$P = \gamma A \bar{x} = 9.81 \times (4 \times 3) \times 8$$
$$= 941.76 \text{ kN}$$

$$\bar{h} = \bar{x} + \frac{I_G \sin^2 \theta}{A \bar{x}} \qquad \because \theta = 90°, \sin \theta = 1$$

$$= 8 + \frac{3 \times 4^3}{12} \times \frac{1}{3 \times 4 \times 8}$$

$$= 8 + \frac{1}{6} = 8.167 \text{ m}$$

∴ Distance of P from hinge B = 10 – 8.167 = 1.833 m
Let T be the tension in the rope.

Taking moments about B

$$T \times 15 = 941.76 \times 1.833$$
$$T = 115.08 \text{ kN}$$

∴ Wt. of sphere = $115.08$ = $\gamma_{sphere} \times$ Volume of sphere

∴ $(2.4 \times 9.81) \times \dfrac{\pi D^3}{6} = 115.08$

$$\boxed{D = 2.1 \text{ m.}}$$

## Example 1.34:

A circular opening 2.5 m in diameter in the sloping wall of a reservoir is closed by a disc valve as shown in Fig. 1.59. When there is no water behind the valve, weight of 75 kN is just sufficient to keep the valve closed. Find the additional weight which will be required to be placed on the arm, 2 m from the hinge, in order to keep the valve closed till water level rises to 3 m above the centre of the valve.

### Solution:

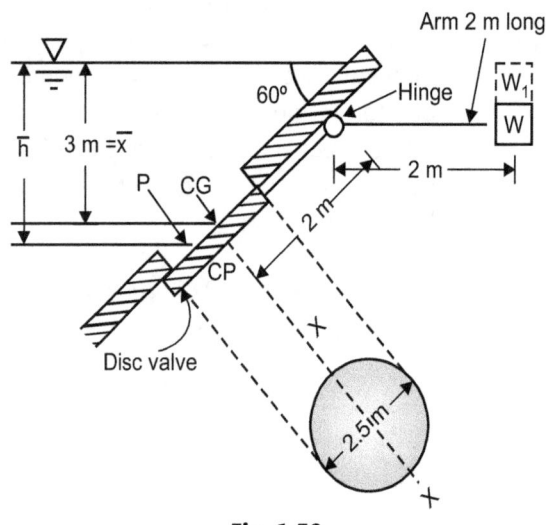

Fig. 1.59

Weight 75 kN, holds the valve closed when there is no water behind the valve. i.e. moment of the weight of the valve about the hinge is balanced by the moment of the weight 75 kN about the hinge. i.e. weight of the gate need not be taken into account. Now when water rises to 3 m above the centre of the valve, it creates anticlockwise moment about the hinge which is to be balanced by the moment of additional weight '$W_1$' to be placed on the arm at 2m from the hinge.

$$P = \gamma A \bar{x} = 9.81 \times \dfrac{\pi}{4} \times (2.5)^2 \times 3$$

∴ $\boxed{P = 144.46 \text{ kN}}$

This will be acting normal to the valve through C.P. To find the lever arm of P from hinge, we find distance between C.P. and C.G. along the slope.

Now the vertical distance between C.P. and C.G. is

$$\bar{h} - \bar{x} = \dfrac{I_G \sin^2 \theta}{A \bar{x}} \qquad \because \theta = 60°, \sin \theta = 0.866$$

$$= \frac{\pi \times (2.5)^4}{64} \times \frac{(0.866)^2}{\frac{\pi}{4} \times (2.5)^2 \times 3} \qquad \left[ I_G = \frac{\pi \times (2.5)^4}{64} \right]$$

$[I_G$ = Moment of inertia of disc valve surface exposed to water pressure about 'XX' axis$]$

$$= \frac{(2.5)^2 \times (0.866)^2}{16 \times 3} = 0.0977 \text{ m}$$

∴ Distance between C.P. and C.G. along the slope

$$= \frac{0.0977}{\sin 60°} = 0.1128 \text{ m}$$

But distance from hinge upto C.G. along the slope is 2m.
Therefore, distance of 'P' from hinge along slope

$$= 2 + 0.1128 = 2.1128 \text{ m}$$

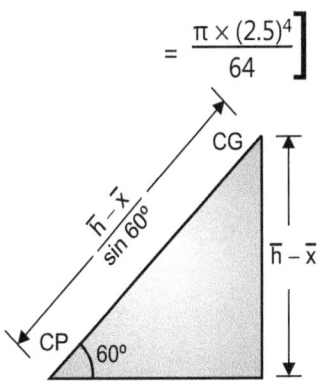

**Fig. 1.60**

∴ Taking moments about hinge

$$P (2.1128) = W_1 \times 2$$

∴ $\qquad 144.46 \times 2.1128 = W_1 \times 2$

Additional weight $\boxed{W_1 = 152.60 \text{ kN}}$

### Example 1.35:

*The gate AB shown in Fig. 1.61 is 1.5 m wide. What vertical force applied at the centre of gravity of the gate will keep it in equilibrium? Weight of the gate 19.62 kN.*

**Solution:**

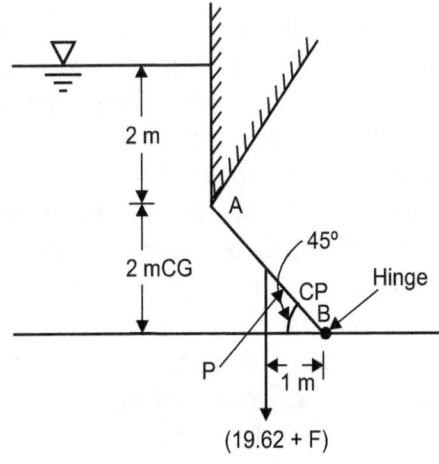

**Fig. 1.61**

Length of the gate AB

$$= 2\sqrt{2} = 2.828 \text{ m}$$

Area of the gate

$$= 1.5 \times 2.828$$
$$= 4.243 \text{ m}^2$$

Water pressure on the gate

$$P = \gamma A \bar{x}$$
$$= 9.81 \times 4.243 \times 3$$
$$= 124.87 \text{ kN}$$

Distance between C.P. and C.G. taken vertically

$$\bar{h} - \bar{x} = \frac{I_G \sin^2 \theta}{A\bar{x}}$$

$$= \frac{1.5 \times (2.828)^3}{12} \times \frac{1}{2} \times \frac{1}{4.243 \times 3}$$

$$= 0.111 \text{ m}$$

∴ Distance between C.P. and C.G. along AB

$$= \frac{0.111}{\sin 45°} = 0.157 \text{ m}$$

∴ Distance between B and CP along the gate

$$= \frac{AB}{2} - 0.157$$

$$= \frac{2.828}{2} - 0.157$$

$$= 1.257 \text{ m}$$

Let F be the additional vertical force applied at C.G.
Therefore, taking moments about hinge 'B'

$$P \times (1.257) = (W + F) \times 1$$
$$124.87 \times 1.257 = (19.62 + F) \times 1$$

∴  $\boxed{F = 137.34 \text{ kN}}$

### Example 1.36:
Find the depth of water 'h' for the flash board as shown in Fig. 1.62 when the board is about to tip. Also find the compressive force on the strut. Assume width of the board as 1m.

**Solution:**

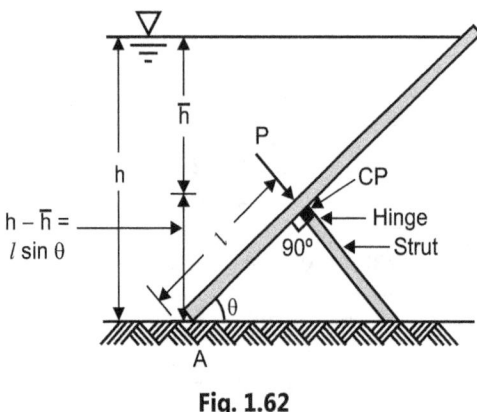

Fig. 1.62

Water pressure force 'P' will act normal to the board. As the level of water is increased, P will move from A in the direction of hinge. In this zone, P will have an anticlockwise moment about the hinge and the board will not tip. When P reaches the hinge, it will have no moment about the hinge. If water level is further increased, line of action of P will move further away from hinge causing clockwise moment. This will tip the board. Therefore, when line of action of 'P' passes through hinge as shown in Fig. 1.62, the board is about to tip. This means the C.P. must coincide with the hinge.

Let 'h' be the height of water when the board is about to tip.

Distance of hinge from base along the board = $l$

∴ Height of hinge i.e. C.P. from the base = $l \sin \theta$

or $\quad h - \bar{h} = l \sin \theta \quad \ldots (I)$

Now, length of board = $\dfrac{h}{\sin \theta}$, area of board $A = \dfrac{h}{\sin \theta}$, $\bar{x} = \dfrac{h}{2}$

∴ $\bar{h} = \bar{x} + \dfrac{I_G \sin^2 \theta}{A \bar{x}} = \dfrac{h}{2} + \dfrac{1 \times \left(\dfrac{h}{\sin \theta}\right)^3}{12} \times \dfrac{\sin^2 \theta}{\left(\dfrac{h}{\sin \theta}\right) \cdot \dfrac{h}{2}} = \dfrac{h}{2} + \dfrac{h}{6} = \dfrac{2}{3} h$

∴ $h - \bar{h} = h - \dfrac{2}{3} h = \dfrac{1}{3} h \quad \ldots (II)$

From (I) and (II), $\dfrac{1}{3} h = l \sin \theta$

∴ $\boxed{h = 3 l \sin \theta}$

Force on strut = $P = \gamma A \bar{x} = \gamma \cdot \dfrac{h}{\sin \theta} \cdot \dfrac{h}{2} = \dfrac{\gamma}{\sin \theta} \cdot \dfrac{1}{2} \cdot (9l^2 \sin^2 \theta)$

∴ $\boxed{P = (4.5) \cdot (\gamma \cdot l^2 \cdot \sin \theta)}$

### Example 1.37:

A 3.6 m by 1.5 m wide rectangular gate is vertical and is hinged at point 0.15 m below the centre of gravity of the gate. The total depth of water is 10 cm. What horizontal force must be applied at the bottom of the gate to keep the gate closed?

**Solution:**

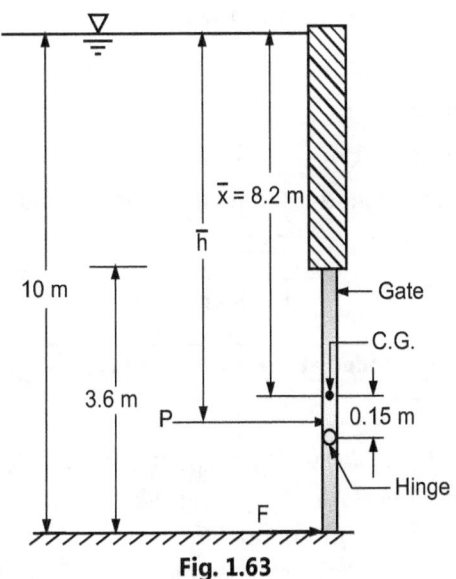

Fig. 1.63

Total pressure P acting on the gate is

$$P = \gamma \cdot A \cdot \bar{x} \qquad A = (3.6 \times 1.5) = 5.4 \text{ m}^2$$
$$= 9.81 \times 5.4 \times 8.2 \qquad \bar{x} = 10 - 1.8 = 8.2 \text{ m}$$

$$\boxed{P = 434.39 \text{ kN}}$$

The depth of centre of pressure below water surface is given by

$$\bar{h} = \bar{x} + \frac{I_G}{A\bar{x}} \qquad I_G = \frac{1.5 \times (3.6)^3}{12}$$

$$= 8.2 + \frac{1.5 \times (3.6)^3}{12} \times \frac{1}{(1.5 \times 3.6) \times 8.2} = 8.2 + 0.132$$

∴ $\boxed{\bar{h} = 8.332 \text{ m}}$

Distance of hinge from water surface

$$= 8.2 + 0.15$$
$$= 8.35 \text{ m}$$

∵ $\bar{h} = 8.332$ m is less than 8.35 m line of action of P is above the hinge. Moment of P about hinge is in clockwise direction.

Moment of P about the hinge

$$= 434.39 \, (8.35 - 8.332)$$
$$= 434.39 \times 0.018$$
$$= 7.819 \text{ kN-m}$$

Let F be the force required to be applied at the bottom of the gate to keep it closed.
Moment of F about hinge

$$F \times (1.8 - 0.15) = (1.65 \, F) \text{ kN-m}$$

Moment of P about hinge = Moment of F about hinge

∴ $\quad 1.65 \, F = 7.819$

∴ $\boxed{F = 4.739 \text{ kN}}$

∴ $\boxed{\text{Force required to be applied at the bottom to keep the gate closed, F = 4.739 kN}}$

### Example 1.38:
A vessel shown in Fig. 1.64 is filled with gasoline (specific gr. 0.8) upto the top of the tube:
(i) Find total forces on surfaces AB, BC, CD and DA,
(ii) Locate the centre of pressure for surface BC,
(iii) Draw pressure distribution diagram for surfaces AB, BC, CD and DA.

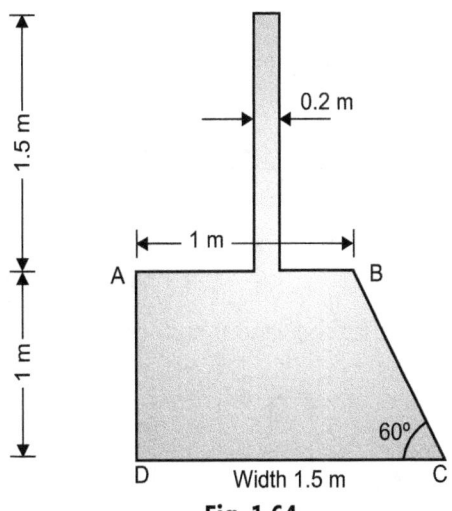

**Fig. 1.64**

**Solution:**

(1) Total force on AB = $\gamma A \cdot \bar{x}$ = $(0.8 \times 9.81) \cdot [1 \times 1.5 - \dfrac{\pi}{4} \times (0.2)^2] \cdot 1.5$

= $\boxed{17.288 \text{ kN}}$

(2) Total force on BC = $\gamma \cdot A \bar{x}$ = $(0.8 \times 9.81) \cdot (BC \times 1.5)(1.5 + 0.5)$

= $(0.8 \times 9.81)(1.155 \times 1.5) \times 2 = \boxed{27.193 \text{ kN}}$

Total force on CD = $\gamma A \bar{x}$ = $(0.8 \times 9.81)[(1 + 0.5775) \times 1.5] \cdot (2.5)$

= $\boxed{46.425 \text{ kN}}$

Total force on DA = $\gamma A \bar{x}$ = $(0.8 \times 9.81)(1 \times 1.5)(1.5 + 0.5)$ = $\boxed{23.544 \text{ kN}}$

(3) Position of centre of pressure for surface BC.

$$\bar{h} = \bar{x} + \dfrac{I_G \sin^2 \theta}{A \bar{x}} \quad \text{For surface BC, } \bar{x} = 2m,$$

$A = (1.155 \times 1.5), \because \theta = 60°, \sin \theta = \dfrac{\sqrt{3}}{2}$

∴ $\bar{h} = 2 + \dfrac{(1.5)(1.155)^3}{12} \times \left(\dfrac{\sqrt{3}}{2}\right)^2 \times \dfrac{1}{(1.5 \times 1.155) \cdot 2}$

∴ $\bar{h} = 2 + \dfrac{(1.155)^2}{12} \times \dfrac{3}{4} \times \dfrac{1}{2}$

$\boxed{\bar{h} = 2 + 0.042 = 2.042 \text{ m}}$

∴ Centre of pressure of BC will be at a distance 2.04 m below free liquid surface.

(4) Pressure diagram is constructed by plotting to some convenient scale, the pressure intensities over the surface. So we will find out intensities of pressure at A (and B) as well as at D (and C).

Intensity of pressure at A = Intensity of pressure at B = $\gamma h$ = (0.8 × 9.81) (1.5)
= $\boxed{11.77 \text{ kN/m}^2}$

Similarly, intensity of pressure at C and D
= $\gamma h$ = (0.8 × 9.81) (2.5) = $\boxed{19.62 \text{ kN/m}^2}$

Therefore, pressure diagrams for the various surfaces will be as shown below.

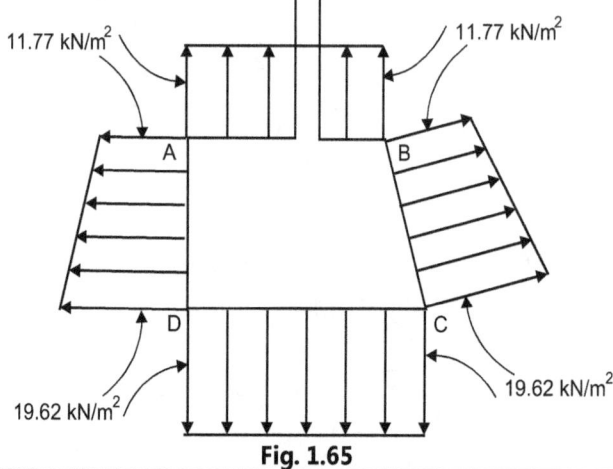

Fig. 1.65

### Example 1.39:

A square tank with 2 m sides and 1.5 m high contains water to a depth of 1m and a lighter liquid of specific gravity 0.8 on the water to a depth of 0.5 m. Find the magnitude and location of pressure force on one of the vertical faces of the tank.

### Solution:

The problem will be solved using a pressure diagram.

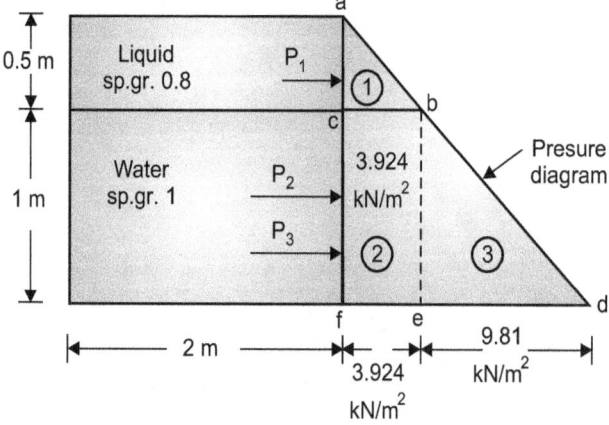

Fig. 1.66

Intensity of pressure at a depth of 0.5 m in liquid of specific gravity 0.8
$$p_1 = \gamma_1 h_1 = (0.8 \times 9.81) \times 0.5 = 3.924 \text{ kN/m}^2$$
Intensity of pressure at a depth of 1m in water
$$p_2 = \gamma_2 h_2 = 9.81 \times 1 = 9.81 \text{ kN/m}^2$$

Now draw line cb perpendicular to the side. Let cb represent the intensity of pressure '$p_1$' i.e. 3.924 kN/m². Join ab. Then, Δ abc represents pressure diagram for upper 0.5 m of the side. This will be transmitted upto base. Thus, fe = cb = 3.924 kN/m². Now draw ed = 9.81 kN/m² representing additional intensity of pressure due to water. Now join bd. Thus, area 'abdfa' represents the pressure diagram for the vertical side.

Area of pressure diagram represents the pressure force acting on 1m width of the side. The total force on side having 2 m width will be volume of pressure prism ['abdfa' × 2 m]. The complete prism is split up in 3 parts.

$$P_1 = \text{Pressure force represented by pressure prism abc}$$
$$= \text{area of } \Delta \text{ abc} \times 2$$
$$= \left(\frac{1}{2} \times 3.924 \times 0.5\right) \times 2 = 1.962 \text{ kN}$$

$P_1$ acts through the centroid of the pressure prism (here through centre of gravity of triangle 'abc').

∴ $$\bar{h}_1 = \frac{2}{3} \times 0.5 = \frac{1}{3} \text{ m from point 'a'}$$

Similarly
$$P_2 = \text{area of rectangle cbef} \times 2$$
$$= 3.924 \times 1 \times 2 = 7.848 \text{ kN}$$

$P_2 = 7.848$ kN, acting at $\bar{h}_2 = 1$m from point 'a'
$$P_3 = \text{area of triangle 'bde'} \times 2$$
$$= \left(\frac{1}{2} \times 9.81 \times 1\right) \times 2$$

$$P_3 = 9.81 \text{ kN, acting at } \bar{h}_3 = \frac{1}{2} + \frac{2}{3} = 1.167 \text{ m from point 'a'}.$$

∴ Total force on the side, P = $P_1 + P_2 + P_3$
$$P = 1.962 + 7.848 + 9.81$$
∴ $$\boxed{P = 19.62 \text{ kN}}$$

To find the position of 'P' taking moments about 'a'
$$P \cdot \bar{h} = P_1 \cdot \bar{h}_1 + P_2 \cdot \bar{h}_2 + P_3 \cdot \bar{h}_3$$
$$19.62 \times \bar{h} = 1.962 \times \frac{1}{3} + 7.848 \times 1 + 9.81 \times 1.167$$

∴ $$\boxed{\bar{h} = 1.02 \text{ m below 'a' or from top of tank.}}$$

## Example 1.40:

A 8 m high closed tank of 2 m × 1.5 m cross section is filled with water upto a depth of 4m and with an oil of relative density 0.9 of 3m depth. The remaining space contains air at a pressure of 120 kN/m². Determine: (i) the pressure at the bottom of the tank and (ii) the magnitude and location of the force on the vertical face of 2 m side of the tank.

**Solution:**

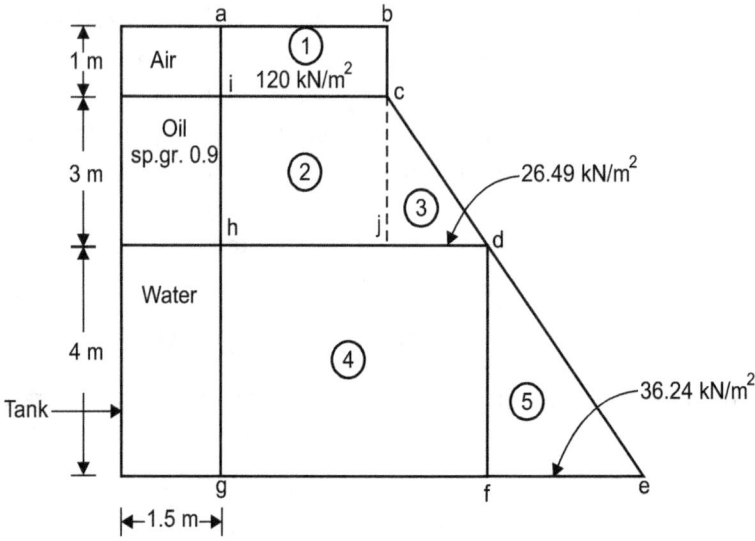

**Fig. 1.67**

(1) Intensity of pressure due to air $p_1$ = 120 kN/m²

(2) Intensity of pressure due to 3 m of oil of specific gravity 0.9
$$p_2 = 0.9 \times 9.81 \times 3 = 26.49 \text{ kN/m}^2$$

(3) Intensity of pressure due to 4 m of water
$$p_3 = 9.81 \times 4 = 39.24 \text{ kN/m}^2$$

(i) Total intensity of pressure on base
$$p = p_1 + p_2 + p_3 = 120 + 26.49 + 39.24$$
$$= \boxed{185.73 \text{ kN/m}^2}$$

(ii) To determine magnitude and location of force on vertical face of 2 m side, we will make use of pressure prism. (Pressure diagram is self illustrative).

In Fig. 1.67 'abcdega' represents pressure diagram for this side.

Pressure prism will have volume = (area 'abcdega') × 2

Pressure prism will be split up in 5 parts.

Now,　　　　　$P_1$ = area 'abci' × 2 = 120 × 1 × 2

∴　　　　　　$P_1$ = 240 kN　　　　　　acting at $\bar{h}_1$ = 0.5 m from 'a'

Similarly,　　$P_2$ = area 'icjh' × 2 = 120 × 3 × 2

∴     $P_2 = 720$ kN     acting at $\bar{h}_2 = 2.5$ m from 'a'

$P_3 = $ area 'cdj' $\times 2 = \dfrac{1}{2} \times 26.49 \times 3 \times 2$

∴     $P_3 = 79.48$ kN     acting at $\bar{h}_3 = \left(1 + \dfrac{2}{3} \times 3\right) = 3$ m from 'a'

$P_4 = $ area 'dfgh' $\times 2 = (120 + 26.49) \times 4 \times 2$

∴     $P_4 = 1171.92$ kN     acting at $\bar{h}_4 = 6$ m from point 'a'

$P_5 = $ area 'def' $\times 2 = \dfrac{1}{2} \times 39.24 \times 4 \times 2$

∴     $P_5 = 156.96$ kN     acting at $\bar{h}_5 = \left(4 + \dfrac{2}{3} \cdot 4\right) = 6.67$ m from point 'a'

∴ Total force on the side $P = P_1 + P_2 + P_3 + P_4 + P_5$

∴     $P = 240 + 720 + 79.48 + 1171.92 + 156.96$

∴     $\boxed{P = 2368.36 \text{ kN}}$

Taking moments about 'a', we get

$$P \cdot \bar{h} = P_1 \cdot \bar{h}_1 + P_2 \cdot \bar{h}_2 + P_3 \cdot \bar{h}_3 + P_4 \cdot \bar{h}_4 + P_5 \cdot \bar{h}_5$$

∴     $\bar{h} = \dfrac{240 \times 0.5 + 720 \times 2.5 + 79.48 \times 3 + 1171.92 \times 6 + 156.96 \times 6.67}{2368.36}$

∴     $\boxed{\bar{h} = 4.322 \text{ m}}$

∴ P will be acting at a distance of 4.322 m from top of the tank.

### Example 1.41:

The radial gate AB as shown in Fig. 1.68 is 5 m long. Find the resultant water pressure on the gate. Also show that the resultant pressure passes through hinge 'O'.

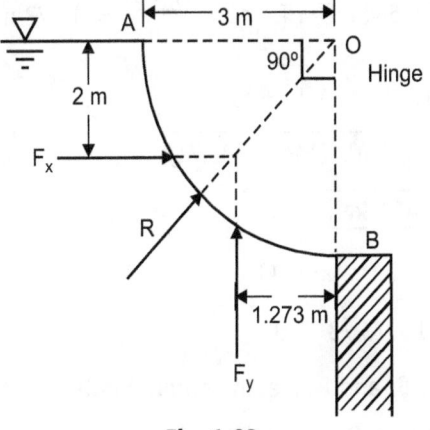

**Fig. 1.68**

## Solution:

Horizontal component of water pressure on the gate

$$F_x = \gamma A \bar{x}$$

∴ $F_x = 9.81 \times 5 \times 3 \times 1.5$

where, $\gamma$ is unit weight of liquid
A is area of projection of curved surface
AB on vertical plane = OB × 5 = (3 × 5) m²

∴ $\boxed{F_x = 220.725 \text{ kN}}$

$\bar{x}$ is distance of centre of gravity of projected area vertically below free liquid surface.

$F_x$ will be acting horizontally from left to right at a distance of 2 m from 'O'.

**[Note:** While calculating '$F_x$' we are concerned only with the projection of curved surface on vertical plane.]

Vertical component of water pressure on the gate

$F_y$ = weight of liquid supported vertically above curved part 'AB'

= $\gamma \times$ Volume of liquid supported vertically by curved part 'AB'

= 9.81 × Area of quadrant 'AOB' × 5

= $9.81 \times \dfrac{1}{4}\pi \cdot 3^2 \times 5$

∴ $\boxed{F_y = 346.71 \text{ kN}}$

Since, the supported liquid is imaginary, $F_y$ will be acting in vertically upward direction. It will be acting through the C.G. of supported liquid i.e. through C.G. of quadrant 'AOB'.

∴ $F_y$ will be acting at a distance of $\dfrac{4r}{3\pi} = \dfrac{4 \times 3}{3\pi} = 1.273$ m from 'O'.

Resultant water pressure, $R = \sqrt{F_x^2 + F_y^2}$

$R = \sqrt{(220.725)^2 + (346.71)^2}$

∴ $\boxed{R = 411 \text{ kN}}$

Taking moments of $F_x$ and $F_y$ about 'O'

$220.725 \times 2 - 346.71 \times 1.273 \approx 0$.

∵ Sum of moments of $F_x$ and $F_y$ (i.e. the components of 'R') about 'O' is zero, moment of R about 'O' is zero. Therefore, R passes through hinge 'O'.

## Example 1.42:

The cylinder of diameter 2 m, as shown in Fig. 1.69 weighs 60 kN and is 2 m long. Find reactions at a and b.

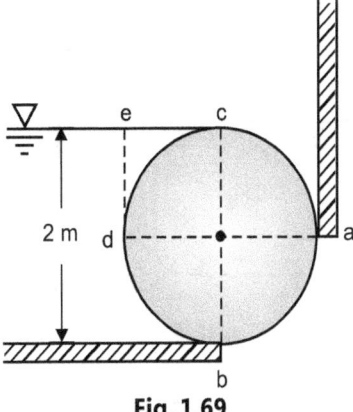

Fig. 1.69

**Solution:**

Reaction at 'a' is due to horizontal component of water pressure acting on the curved part of the cylinder.

$$F_x = \gamma A \bar{x} = 9.81 \times 2 \times 2 \times 1 = 39.24 \text{ kN}$$

∴ $\boxed{R_a = 39.24 \text{ kN from right to left}}$

Reaction at 'b' is due to vectorial sum of the weights, of the cylinder and the net vertical component of water pressure on the curved part 'cdb' exposed to water pressure.

Curved part 'cdb' consists of two parts, (i) part 'db' which supports imaginary liquid and (ii) part 'cd' which supports real liquid.

Upward force on part 'db' = $F_{y_1}(\uparrow)$ = weight of imaginary liquid supported vertically by 'db'

∴ Upward force on part 'db' = $F_{y_1}(\uparrow)$
= 9.81 [Area of quad. 'dbo' + Area of square 'doce'] × 2

Downward force on part 'cd' = $F_{y_2}(\downarrow)$ = Weight of real liquid supported vertically by 'cd'

= 9.81 [Area of square 'doce' – Area of quad. 'doc'] × 2

∴ Net vertical component of water pressure
$F_y(\uparrow) = F_{y_1}(\uparrow) - F_{y_2}(\downarrow)$
= 19.62 [Area of quad. 'dob' + Area of quad. 'doc']
= 19.62 × [Area of semi- circle]

∴ $F_y(\uparrow)$ = 30.82 kN
∴ Reaction at 'b' = 60 – 30.82
$\boxed{R_b = 29.18 \text{ kN}}$

## Example 1.43:

Determine the horizontal and vertical components of the hydrostatic force on the curved area ABCD shown in Fig. 1.70 as well as their location.

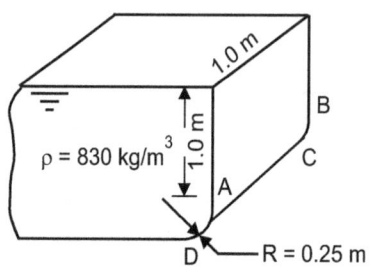

Fig. 1.70

(P. U. 1997)

### Solution:
End view of the surface is shown in Fig. 1.71.

**(1) Horizontal component of liquid pressure curved surface AD**

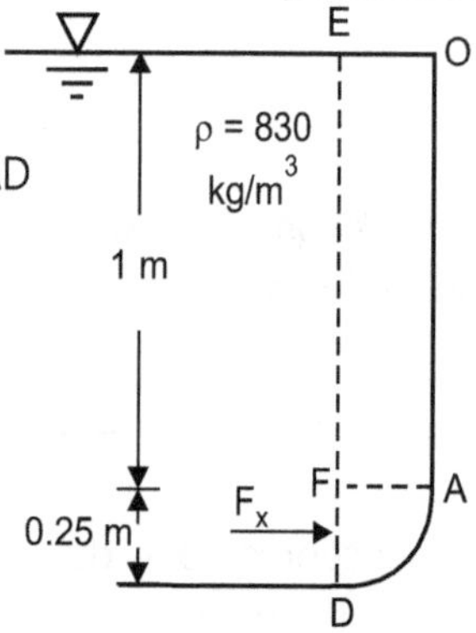

$$F_x = \gamma A \bar{x}$$

$$= (830 \times 9.81)(0.25 \times 1)\left(1 + \frac{0.25}{2}\right)$$

∴ $\boxed{F_x = 2290.02 \text{ N}}$

$F_x$ will be acting from left to right through the centre of pressure of surface (DF × 1)

Fig. 1.71

$$\bar{h} = \bar{x} + \frac{I_G}{A\bar{x}} = 1.125 + \frac{1 \times (0.25)^3}{12} \times \frac{1}{(1 \times 0.25) \times 1.125}$$

∴ $\boxed{\bar{h} = 1.13 \text{ m below free liquid surface.}}$

**(2) Vertical component of liquid pressure**

$F_y$ = weight of liquid supported vertically above the curved surface (represented by AB in end view)

$= \gamma \times [\text{Area 'OADE'} \times 1]$

$= (830 \times 9.81)[\text{Area 'OAFE'} + \text{Area 'ADF'}] \times 1$

$= (830 \times 9.81)\left[(0.25 \times 1) + \frac{1}{4} \times \pi \times (0.25)^2\right] \times 1$

$= (830 \times 9.81)[0.25 + 0.0491]$

∴ $\boxed{F_y = 2435.26 \text{ N}}$

Since the supported liquid is real, $F_y$ will be acting in vertically downward direction.

It will be acting through the centre of gravity of 'OADE'.

Let the distance of centre of gravity of 'OADE' from 'OA' be say 'x'. Then taking moments about 'OA', we get

$$\text{moment of OADE} = \text{moment of OAFE} + \text{moment of ADF}$$

$$\therefore (0.25 + 0.0491) \cdot x = 0.25 \times \frac{0.25}{2} + 0.0491 \left(0.25 - \frac{4 \times 0.25}{3 \times \pi}\right)$$

$$\boxed{x = 0.128 \text{ m}}$$

[Note: Distance of C.G. of quadrant of a circle is at a distance of $\frac{4r}{3\pi}$ from the centre. Refer Table 1.1].

### Example 1.44:

A cylindrical gate is shown in Fig. 1.72. Determine the force 'P' per metre width of the gate, to keep it closed.

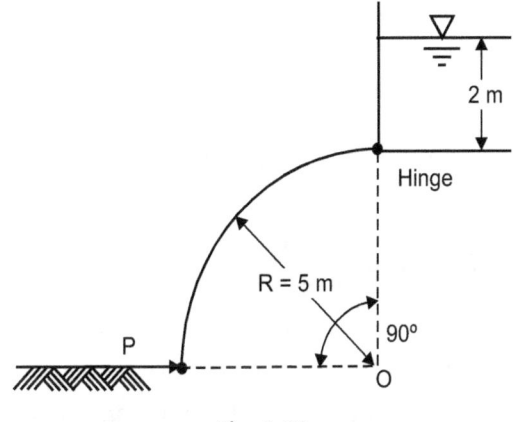

Fig. 1.72

### Solution:

The gate is subjected to horizontal component $F_x$ and vertical component $F_y$. Sum of their moments about hinge must be equal to moment of 'P' about the hinge.

$$F_x = \gamma A \bar{x} = 9.81 \times 5 \times 1 \times 4.5 = 220.725 \text{ kN}.$$

$$\boxed{F_x = 220.725 \text{ kN}}$$

$F_x$ will be acting from right to left through centre of pressure for projection of curved surface on vertical plane i.e. od

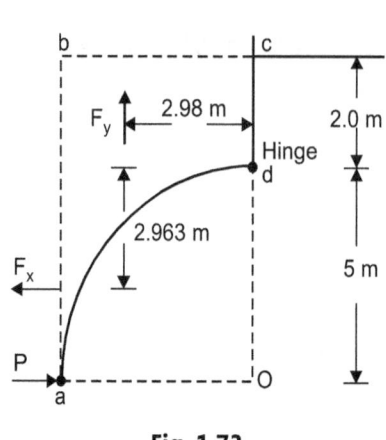

Fig. 1.73

$$\bar{h} = \bar{x} + \frac{I_G}{A\bar{x}}$$

$$= 4.5 + \frac{1 \times 5^3}{12} \times \frac{1}{5 \times 1 \times 4.5}$$

$$\therefore \bar{h} = 4.963 \text{ m from liquid surface}$$

$$\therefore \text{ distance from hinge} = 4.963 - 2.0$$

$$= 2.963 \text{ m}$$

$F_y$ = weight of liquid supported vertically by the curved surface 'ad'

$\therefore \quad F_y = \gamma \times$ Volume of liquid supported

$= 9.81 \times$ Area 'abcda' $\times 1$

$= 9.81 \times$ [Area 'oabc' − Area 'oad']

$= 9.81 \times \left[7 \times 5 - \frac{\pi}{4} \cdot (25)\right]$

$= 9.81 \times [35 - 19.64]$

$= 9.81 \times 15.36$

$\therefore \quad \boxed{F_y = 150.68 \text{ kN}}$

$F_y$ will be acting in vertically upward direction, since the supported liquid is imaginary. It will be acting through centroid of supported liquid i.e. through C.G. of 'abcda'. Let 'z' be the distance of C.G. of 'abcda' from the hinge. Taking moments of areas about hinge, we get,

$$\text{Area 'abcda'} \times z = \text{Area 'oabc'} \times 2.5 - \text{Area 'oad'} \times \frac{4r}{3\pi}$$

$\therefore \quad 15.36 \times z = 35 \times 2.5 - 19.64 \times \frac{4 \times 5}{3 \times \pi}$

$\therefore \quad z = 2.98 \text{ m}$

Taking moments about the hinge, we get

$$P \times 5 = 220.725 \times 2.963 + 150.68 \times 2.98$$

$\therefore \quad \boxed{P = 220.61 \text{ kN}}$

# FLUID MECHANICS (NMU) (S.E. MECHANICAL)        FLUID PROPERTIES AND HYDROSTATIC

## Example 1.45:

A cylinder of diameter 2 m is resting on one of the corners of rectangular tank of length 2m as shown in Fig. 1.74. The tank is full of water under pressure. Find the components of force acting on curved surface ABC of the cylinder. Neglect weight of cylinder and assume it to be empty.

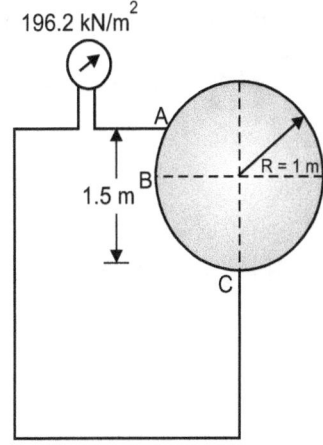

Fig. 1.74

## Solution:

The tank is under pressure of 192.6 kN/m². This can be converted into equivalent head of water.

$$196.2 \text{ kN/m}^2 = \frac{196.2}{9.81} = 20 \text{ m of water}$$

Thus, it is as if the tank is open tank with free liquid surface 20 m above 'HA'. Tank with this additional head is shown in Fig. 1.75. It is as if the free liquid surface is at H'C', 20 m above HA.

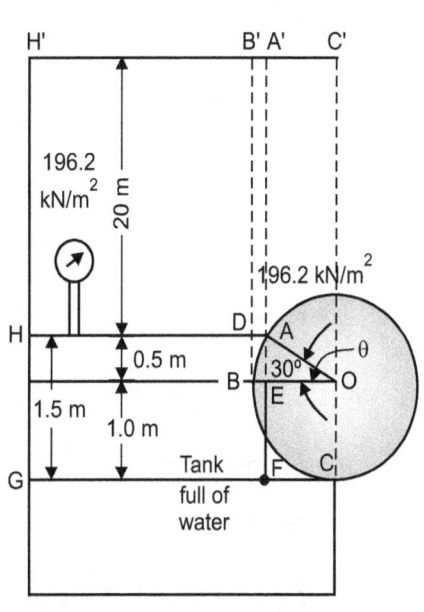

Fig. 1.75: Tank with additional head

**(1) Horizontal component of water pressure on curved surface ABC:**

Let $F_x$ be the horizontal component of water pressure on curved surface ABC.

$$F_x = \gamma A \bar{x}$$
$$= 9.81 \times \text{(projected area)} \times \text{(distance of C.G. of projected area}$$
$$\text{below free liquid surface H'C')}$$
$$= 9.81 \times (AF \times 2) \cdot \left(20 + \frac{AF}{2}\right) = 9.81 \times (1.5 \times 2) \left(20 + \frac{1.5}{2}\right)$$

∴    $\boxed{F_x = 610.67 \text{ kN}}$

**(2) Vertical component of water pressure on curved surface ABC:**

Curved surface 'ABC' is composed of two parts: (1) part CB which supports imaginary liquid and is subjected to upward force $F_{y_1}$ (↑) and (2) part BA which supports real liquid and is subjected to downward force $F_{y_2}$ (↓).

(i) Force acting on part CB

$$F_{y_1} = \text{Weight of water supported vertically by curved part 'CB'}$$
$$= 9.81 \times 2 \times \text{Area BB'C'C}$$
$$= 19.62 \times (\text{Area CBO} + \text{Area BB'C'O})$$
$$= 19.62 \times \left[\left(\frac{1}{4} \cdot \pi \cdot 1^2\right) + 1 \times 20.5\right]$$

∴ $\quad F_{y_1}$ (↑) $= 417.62$ kN.

(ii) Force acting on BA

$$F_{y_2} = \text{Weight of water supported vertically by curved part BA}$$
$$= 9.81 \times 2 \times \text{Area BB'A'A}$$

Now, $\quad$ Area BB'A'A $=$ rectangle DB'A'A + Area BDA $\quad$ ... (a)
Area of rectangle DB'A'A $=$ DA × 20

Now $\quad \sin\theta = \dfrac{AE}{AO} = \dfrac{0.5}{1} = 0.5 \quad$ ∴ $\theta = 30°$

∴ $\quad$ EO $= 1 \cdot \cos 30° = 0.866$ m $\quad$ ∴ DA $=$ BE $=$ BO $-$ EO $= 1 - 0.866$
$$= 0.134 \text{ m}$$

∴ Area of rectangle DB'A'A
$$= 0.134 \times 20 = 2.68 \text{ m}^2 \quad \text{... (b)}$$

Now $\quad$ Area BDA $=$ Area of rectangle BDAE + Area of triangle AEO
$\quad\quad\quad\quad\quad\quad\quad\quad\quad -$ Area of sector AOB $\quad$ ... (c)

Area of rectangle BDAE $= 0.5 \times 0.134 = 0.067$ m²

Area of triangle AEO $= \dfrac{1}{2} \times 0.866 \times 0.5 = 0.2165$ m²

Area of sector AOB $= \dfrac{1}{12} \times \pi \times 1^2 = 0.262$ m²

Substituting the values in equation (c), we get
$\quad\quad$ Area BDA $= 0.067 + 0.2165 - 0.262 = 0.0215$ m² $\quad$ ... (d)

∴ Substituting values from (b) and (d) in (a), we get
$\quad\quad$ Area BB'A'A $= 2.68 + 0.0215$
$\quad\quad\quad\quad\quad\quad\quad = 2.7015$ m²

∴ $\quad F_{y_2}$ (↓) $= 19.62 \times 2.7015 = 53$ kN

∴ Net vertical force on curved surface ABC
$$= F_{y_1} (\uparrow) - F_{y_2} (\downarrow)$$
$$= 417.62 - 53$$

∴ $\quad \boxed{F_y = 364.62 \text{ kN}}$

## Example 1.46:

A dam has a parabolic space: $x = 2\sqrt{y}$. Taking height of water retained by dam as 9 m, calculate the resultant thrust exerted by water per metre length of dam.

**Solution:**

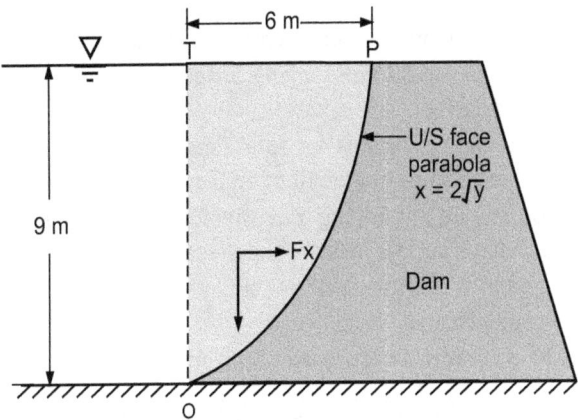

**Fig. 1.76**

Considering 1 m length of the dam (perpendicular to paper).
Horizontal component of water pressure = Force on face OT

$$F_x = \frac{\gamma h^2}{2} = \frac{9.81 \times (9)^2}{2}$$

$$\boxed{F_x = 397.305 \text{ kN}}$$

Now we have, $\quad x = 2\sqrt{y}$

For $y = OT = 9$ m, $x = TP = 2\sqrt{9} = 6$ m.

Vertical component of water pressure

$F_y$ = Weight of water between OT and face of dam
$= \gamma \times 1 \times$ Area of parabola OTP

$$= 9.81 \times \frac{2}{3} \times 9 \times 6$$

$$\boxed{F_y = 353.16 \text{ kN}}$$

Resultant thrust

$$R = \sqrt{F_x^2 + F_y^2}$$

$$= \sqrt{(397.305)^2 + (353.16)^2} = 531.576 \text{ kN}$$

$$\boxed{\text{Resultant thrust} = 531.576}$$

Direction of resultant thrust

$$\theta = \tan^{-1}\frac{F_y}{F_x} = \tan^{-1}\frac{351.576}{397.305} = 41.63°$$

$$\boxed{\theta = 41.63°}$$

# THEORETICAL QUESTIONS

1. Define centre of pressure and total pressure.
2. Derive an expression for total pressure and centre of pressure for an inclined plane surface submerged in static liquid of specific gravity 'w'.
3. Derive expression for total pressure and centre of pressure for vertically immersed surface.
4. Prove that the centre of pressure of a plane surface is always below the centre of gravity when immersed in liquid.
5. From first principles, derive formula for total pressure on a plane surface submerged in the liquid. Also find relation for the point of application of total pressure (C.P.).
6. Why does the procedure of finding out pressure on curved surface defer from the procedure used for plane surface? How is the pressure on a curved surface found?
7. Explain how horizontal and vertical components of the resultant pressure on a submerged curved surface are determined.
8. What is a pressure diagram? What are uses and limitations?

# NUMERICAL PROBLEMS

1. A rectangular plate 3 m long and 1 m wide is immersed vertically in water in such a way that its longer side is parallel to the water surface and 1.5 m below it. Determine the total force on the plate and the position of the centre of pressure.

    **(Ans. P = 58.86 kN, $\bar{h}$ = 2.042 m)**

2. A triangular plate of height 'h' is immersed vertically in a static liquid with apex downward and base horizontal. If the depth of the base below the liquid surface is 'a', find the position of the centre of pressure below the liquid surface.

    **Ans. $\bar{h} = \dfrac{6a^2 + 4ah + h^2}{2(3a + h)}$**

3. A triangular plate of 1 m base and 1.5 m altitude is immersed in water. The plane of the plate is inclined at $30°$ with free water surface and the base is parallel to and at a depth of 2 m from water surface. Find the total pressure on the plate and the position of centre of pressure.

    **(Ans.: 16.554 kN, 2.264 m)**

4. A circular plate of diameter 0.75 m is immersed in a liquid of relative density 0.8 with it's plane making an angle $30°$ with horizontal. The centre of plate is at a depth of 1.5 m from the free surface. Calculate the total pressure on one side of plate and point of application of total pressure.

5. A circular plate 2.5 m diameter is immersed in water. Its greatest and least depth below the free surface being 3.5 m and 1.5 m respectively.
    Find:
    (i) Total pressure on one face of the plate.
    (ii) Position of the centre of pressure.
    **(Ans. 120.39 kN, 2.6 m)**

6. A canal, trapezoidal in section carries silt laden water with a depth of 3 m. If the sides are inclined at 45°, find the total pressure and the centre of pressure per unit width of the side. Specific gravity of silt laden water is 1.08.

   **(Ans. 67.38 kN, 2 m)**

7. A trapezoidal plate having its parallel sides '2a' and 'a' at a distance 'h' apart, is vertically submerged in water with unit weight '$\gamma$', the '2a' side uppermost at a depth 'h' below free surface of the liquid. Find the total pressure and the centre of pressure.

   $$\left(\textbf{Ans. } \frac{13}{6}\gamma a h^2, \frac{3}{2}h\right)$$

8. A circular tank 4 m in diameter and 10 m long rests with its axis horizontal on the bottom of a canal which has water 10 m deep. Calculate the depth of the centre of pressure on each of the flat surface and hydrostatic force resulting on the tank in kN.

   [**Hint:** Resulting hydrostatic force – forces on the two circular faces will cancel each other since they are equal in magnitude but opposite in direction. Therefore, resultant force will be equal to the force acting on the curved surface of cylinder. This will be equal to the buoyant force on the cylinder and will be equal to weight of liquid displaced by cylinder.]

   [**Ans.:** 8.125 m, 1232.76 kN]

9. A rectangular opening in a vertical wall which stores water on one side is closed by a gate of the same size. The sides of the opening are horizontal and vertical. The gate is hinged about a horizontal axis passing through its centre of gravity. If the water level is always above the top of the opening, prove that the moment required to keep the gate closed is independent of the position of water level.

   (Moment = $\gamma \cdot I_G$)

10. Determine the total force 'F' required to keep the gate closed, shown in Fig. 1.77. The gate is 1.6 m wide.

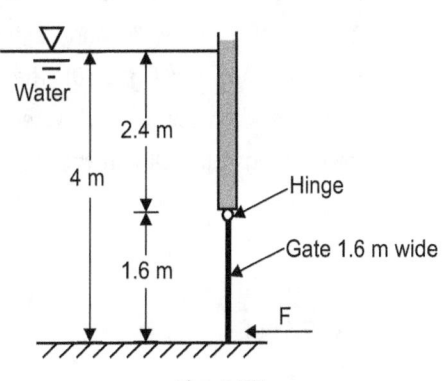

Fig. 1.77

    **(Ans. F = 43.53 kN)**

11. The gate as shown in Fig. 1.78 is 4 m wide. Find the force 'F' required to just lift the gate.

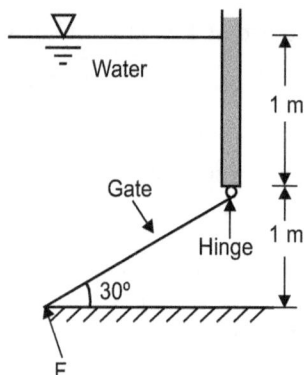

Fig. 1.78

(**Ans.** 65.4 kN)

12. Find the force 'F' to keep the triangular gate closed.

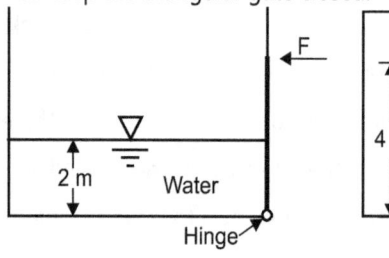

Fig. 1.79

(**Ans.** 4.905 kN)

13. A gate of size 1m × 2m closes an opening of the same size in a vertical wall. It is hinged at its top and held in place by a thin cable, attached to its centre, which pulls it due to buoyancy on a balloon of diameter 'D' and negligible weight (as shown in Fig. 1.80). The gate just opens when the level of water is as shown in Fig. 1.80. Obtain the diameter 'D'.

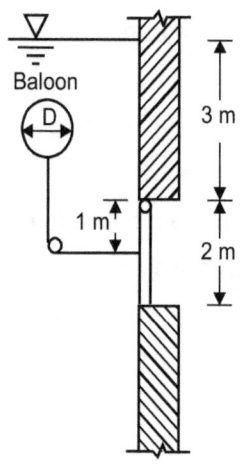

Fig. 1.80

(**Ans.** 2.55 m)

14. Automatic gate ABC shown in Fig. 1.81 is pivoted at 'B'. The gate opens itself when 'H' exceeds 2.5 m. Find length 'L'. Neglect weight of the gate, assume unit width. Draw pressure diagram for the gate.

    (**Ans.** L = 1.67 m)

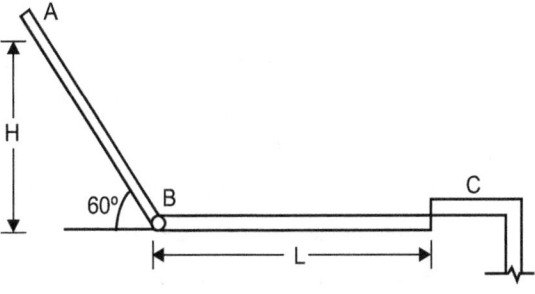

Fig. 1.81

15. A 6 m × 1.5 m rectangular gate is hinged at the base and is inclined at 60° with the horizontal. The upper end of the gate is kept in position by a weight of 5000 N acting at an angle of 90° as shown in Fig. 1.82. Find the level of water when the gate begins to fall. Neglect the weight of the gate.

    (**Ans.** h = 2.093 m)

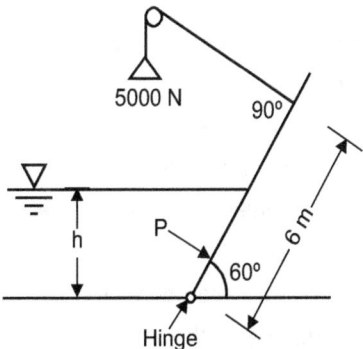

Fig. 1.82

16. For the system shown in Fig. 1.83, find the necessary tension in the chain to just open the gate. The gate size is 1 m × 1 m. Neglect the weight of the gate.

    (**Ans.** 17.882 kN)

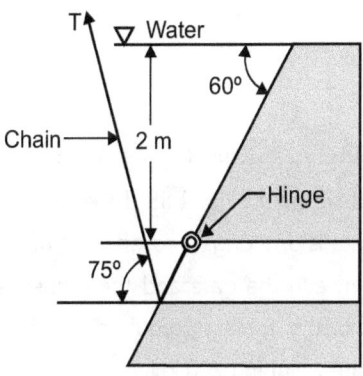

Fig. 1.83

17. A tank with vertical sides contains water to a depth of 1m above which floats liquid of sp. gr. 0.9 to a depth of 1m. Find the total force on the side of the tank which is 5m long and the position of centre of pressure.

    (**Ans.** 90.75 kN, 1.342 m)

18. A closed tank 2m × 2m in plan and 2.5 m high contains oil of sp. gr. 0.8 for a depth of 0.8 m floating on 1.2 m depth of water. The space above oil is filled with air under pressure of 2 N/cm² (gauge). Calculate the total thrust and its location on one of the sides of the tank.
    (Ans. 134.32 kN, 1.407 m)

19. A tank with vertical sides contains 0.9 m of mercury and 5m of water. Find the total force on a square portion of one side, 0.6 m × 0.6 m in area, half of this area being below the surface of the mercury. The sides of the square are horizontal and vertical.
    (Ans. 20.995 kN)

20. Bottom of a 2m diameter cylindrical tank is of the shape of an inverted hemispherical bowl. If the depth of water at the centre is 3m, find the resultant pressure on the bottom of the tank.
    [Hint: Resultant pressure on the base is equal to the weight of water in the vessel]
    (Ans. 102.73 kN)

21. For the radial gate, shown in Fig. 1.84 find out per metre length,
    (i) Horizontal push of water pressure on the gate.
    (ii) Vertical component of water pressure on the gate.
    (iii) Resultant force.
    (iv) Direction of resultant force.

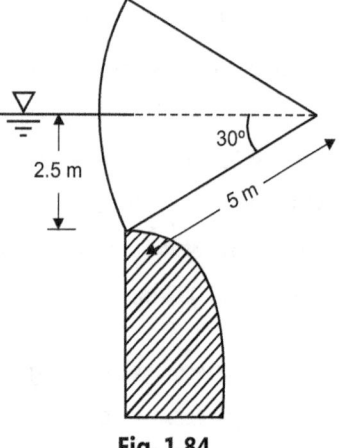

Fig. 1.84

(Ans. $F_x$ = 30.66 kN, $F_y$ = 11.09 kN, R = 32.6 kN, θ = 19° 53' 8")

22. As shown in Fig. 1.85 the 4 m diameter gate is 3m long. If co-efficient of friction between the gate and the guides is 0.1, find the force P required to raise the gate weighing 200 kN.

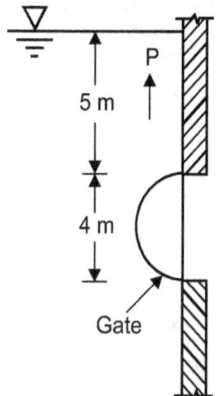

(Ans. 97.5 kN)

Fig. 1.85

23. An opening 1 m wide and 2 m high in the wall of a tank is closed by a gate of the same size hinged at its centre. Water level in the tank is 3 m above the hinge and the gate is held in position by a force F applied at its bottom edge. Find 'F'.
   If the flat gate is replaced by a semi-cylindrical one, as shown in Fig. 1.86, find the reduction in force F, to be applied at bottom edge, to keep the gate in position.

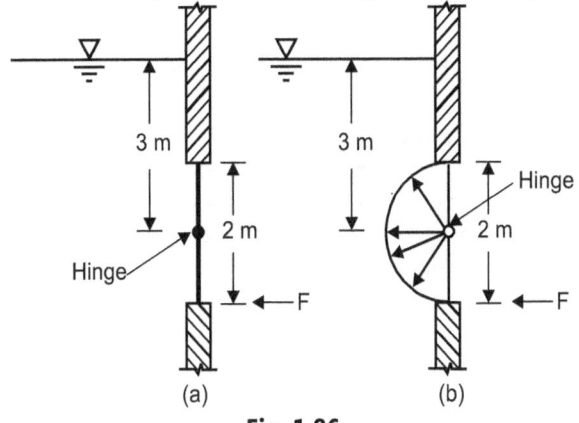

Fig. 1.86

(**Ans.** 6.54 kN, Force required is zero)

## PART D - CONCEPT OF BUOYANCY AND FLOATATION

## 1.11 Buoyancy, Buoyant Force and Centre of Buoyancy

When a body is immersed partially or fully in a fluid, it is subjected to an upward force (due to net vertical component of fluid pressure on the surface of the body). This vertical upward force on a floating or submerged body is known as "*Buoyant force.*" Tendency of submerged body to rise in a fluid due to buoyant force is called "*Buoyancy*". It is the interaction between this buoyant force and the weight of body which is the matter of study in this chapter.

## 1.12 Archimedes Principle

Archimedes principle states that "*when a body is immersed partially or fully it is lifted up or buoyed by a force equal to the weight of fluid displaced by the body.*"
**Proof:**
   Consider a completely submerged body as shown in Fig. 1.87 (a). Consider an elementary horizontal prism MN of the body. Let 'dA' be the area of face of prism at M and N.
   Pressure force in horizontal direction on face M
   $= p_m \cdot dA\ (\rightarrow)$, where $p_m$ is intensity of pressure on face M.
   Pressure force in horizontal direction on face N
   $= p_n \cdot dA\ (\leftarrow)$

∴ Pressure force on prism MN in horizontal direction
$$= (p_m - p_n) \cdot dA$$
∴ Total horizontal force on the body
$$= \int (p_m - p_n) \cdot dA$$

but since M and N are situated at the same depth
$$p_m = p_n$$
∴ Total horizontal force on body = 0.

Thus, there is no horizontal force acting on the body due to fluid pressure. Force due to fluid pressure on the body acts only in vertical direction.

Now consider an elementary vertical prism MN as shown in Fig. 1.87 (b).

Pressure force in vertically upward direction on face M
$$= p_m \cdot dA \;(\uparrow)$$
Pressure force in vertically downward direction on face N
$$= p_n \cdot dA \;(\downarrow)$$
∴ Net force on prism in vertical direction
$$dF = (p_m - p_n) \cdot dA \;(\uparrow)$$

dF will be upward, since $p_m > p_n$    ∵ $h_m > h_n$

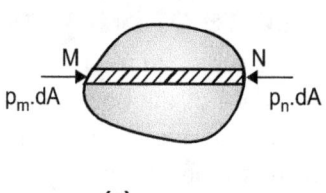

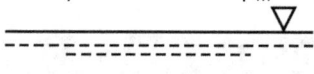

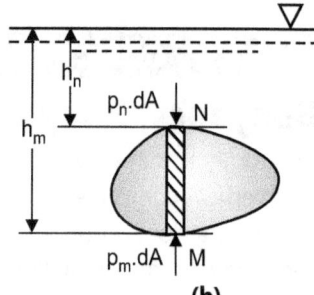

(a)          (b)

**Fig. 1.87**

∴ Total upthrust or buoyant force on the body

$$F = \int dF = \int (p_m - p_n) \cdot dA \qquad \text{But} \quad \begin{aligned} p_m &= \gamma h_m \\ p_n &= \gamma h_n \end{aligned}$$

∴
$$F = \int \gamma (h_m - h_n) \cdot dA$$

but $(h_m - h_n) \cdot dA$ = Volume of prism = $dV$

∴
$$F = \int \gamma \cdot dV \qquad \text{but} \int dV = V = \text{Total volume of the body.}$$

or
$$\boxed{F = \gamma V} \qquad \qquad \text{... (1.22)}$$

V is the volume of body. Therefore, $\gamma V$ is the weight of the fluid displaced by the body. Therefore, buoyant force on the body = weight of fluid displaced by the body, which is nothing but *"Archimedes Principle"*.

Thus, for buoyant force on the body:

1. It is equal to weight of fluid displaced by the body.
2. It acts only in vertically upward direction.
3. Since it is equal to weight of fluid displaced, it acts through the *centre of gravity of displaced fluid.*

The point of application of buoyant force is called *"Centre of Buoyancy."*

## 1.13 Principle of Floatation

Consider a body completely submerged under a liquid surface. Weight of body W will be acting through centre of gravity 'G' in vertically downward direction while buoyant force F will be acting through the centre of buoyancy 'B' in vertically upward direction. ['W' and 'F' will act through the same vertical. Otherwise, they will form a couple and the body will rotate which is not the case.]

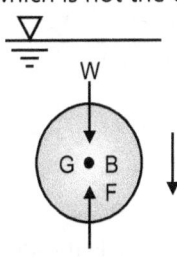

(a)

**Case I:**
If W > F. (Specific gravity of body higher than that of liquid). Body will sink. Fig. 1.88 (a).

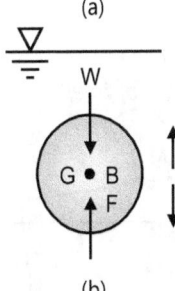

(b)

**Case II:**
If W = F. (Specific gravity of body equal to specific gravity of liquid). Body will remain anywhere inside the liquid surface. [Fig. 1.88 (b)].

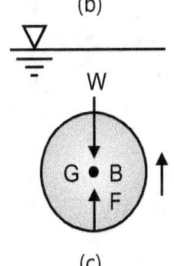

(c)

**Case III:**
If W < F. (Specific gravity of body less than that of liquid). Body will start rising in the liquid. Fig. 1.88 (c).

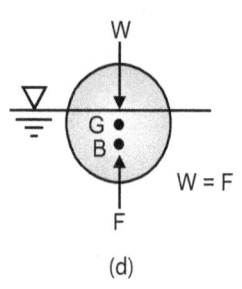

Fig. 1.88

Ultimately, body will start floating Fig. 1.88 (d) in such a way that

When the body is floating,

Weight of the body (W)
- = Buoyant force (F)
- = Weight of liquid displaced by the body.

This is known as "Principle of floatation."

## 1.14 Metacentre and Metacentric height

**(i) Metacentre:** When the body is floating and floats upright in equilibrium as shown in Fig. 1.89 (a) two forces act on the body.
1. The weight of the body, W acts vertically downwards through the centre of gravity 'G'.
2. The buoyant force 'F' acts through the centre of buoyancy 'B', the centre of gravity of displaced liquid (i.e. centre of gravity of submerged portion 'acde' of the body).

'W' and 'F' will be equal in magnitude but opposite in direction and will be acting through the same vertical.

If the body is tilted through a small angle of heel 'θ', the centre of gravity will not change but the centre of buoyancy will shift from B to $B_1$ (centre of gravity of submerged portion $acd_1 e_1$ of the body. Since there is more concentration of area to the right side of the axis, '$B_1$' will be to the right of 'B'). If the vertical line of action of F through '$B_1$' is extended, it will intersect line BG produced at point 'M' called *'Metacentre'*.

Thus, *"Metacentre is the point at which the vertical through the centre of buoyancy intersects the vertical centre line of the section of body, after a small angle of heel"*.

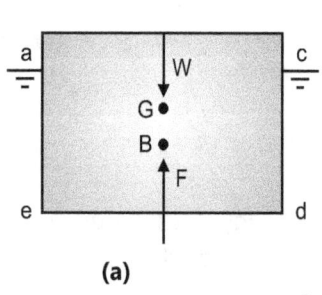
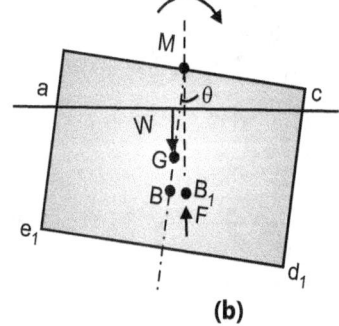

Fig. 1.89: Metacentric height

**(ii) Metacentric height:** The distance between the centre of gravity 'G' of the body and metacentre 'M' i.e. GM is called *"Metacentric height."*

Metacentric height is important in deciding the stability of floating body.

## 1.15 Stability of Submerged and Floating Bodies

Tendency of a submerged or floating body to restore its original upright position, after it is given a slight angular displacement is called stability.

There are three conditions of equilibrium of a submerged or floating body.

1. **Stable Equilibrium:** If the body is given a slight angular displacement after which it comes back to its original position then, the body is said to be in *stable equilibrium*.
2. **Unstable Equilibrium:** If the body is given a slight angular displacement after which it heels further and does **not return to its original position, then the body is said to be in unstable equilibrium.**
3. **Neutral Equilibrium:** If the body after being given a slight angular displacement neither heels further nor restores its original position, but remains at *rest* in new position then the body is said to be in *neutral equilibrium*.

## 1.16 Stability of Submerged Bodies

When a body is completely submerged in a fluid, the positions of centre of gravity 'G' and centre of buoyancy 'B' are fixed. The various relative positions of G and B decide the stability of the submerged body.

(a) **Stable equilibrium:** As shown in Fig. 1.90 (a), centre of gravity 'G' is below the centre of buoyancy 'B'. If the body is given a slight angular displacement (rotation) in clockwise direction a couple called "righting couple" is set up inside the body in counter clockwise direction. This couple tries to restore the body to its original position. The body thus, is in stable equilibrium.

Thus, if 'G' is below 'B' body is stable.

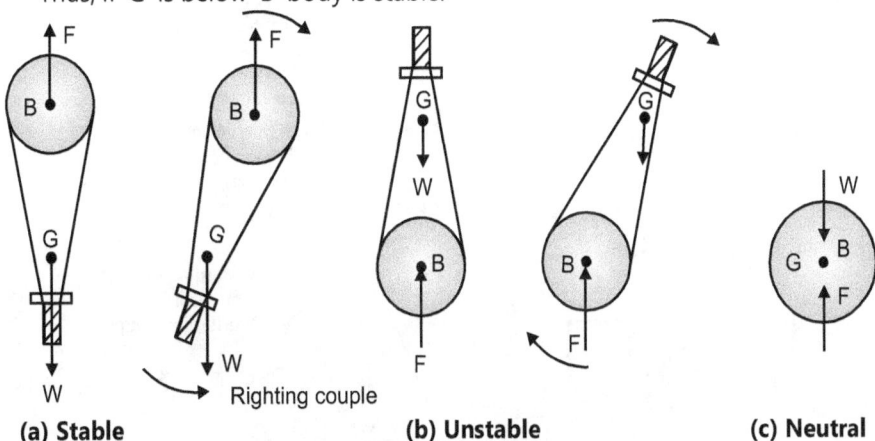

(a) Stable      (b) Unstable      (c) Neutral

**Fig. 1.90: Stability of submerged bodies**

(b) **Unstable equilibrium:** If, however, 'G' is above 'B' as shown in Fig. 1.90 (b), a slight displacement in clockwise direction will set up a couple in the body, in the same direction and body will never restore the original position.

Thus, if 'G' is above 'B', then body is unstable.

(c) **Neutral equilibrium:** If both 'G' and 'B' coincide, Fig. 1.90 (c), then body is in neutral equilibrium.

## 1.17 Stability of Floating Bodies

A floating body, as against submerged body, can be stable even if centre of buoyancy is below centre of gravity. This is because the position of centre of buoyancy generally changes with angular displacement.

It is, therefore, the metacentre 'M' and the metacentric height 'GM' which are very important considerations in deciding the stability of a floating body and design of ships.

(a) **Stable equilibrium:** Consider the body shown in Fig. 1.91 (a). The forces and their positions are as shown in Fig. 1.91 (a). When an overturning moment is applied, the centre of buoyancy shifts from B to $B_1$ although, centre of gravity does not change Fig. 1.91 (b). Now, buoyant force 'F' acts through $B_1$ in vertically upward direction while weight W acts through 'G' in vertically downward direction. Thus, W and F which are equal in magnitude form a couple in anticlockwise direction. This couple restores the position of the body and the body is in stable equilibrium. It can be seen that if the body is in stable equilibrium, metacentre 'M' is above the centre of gravity 'G', BM > BG, or metacentric height GM is + ve.

"Thus, if **M is above G,** or **GM is + ve** or **BM > BG** body is in **stable equilibrium.**"

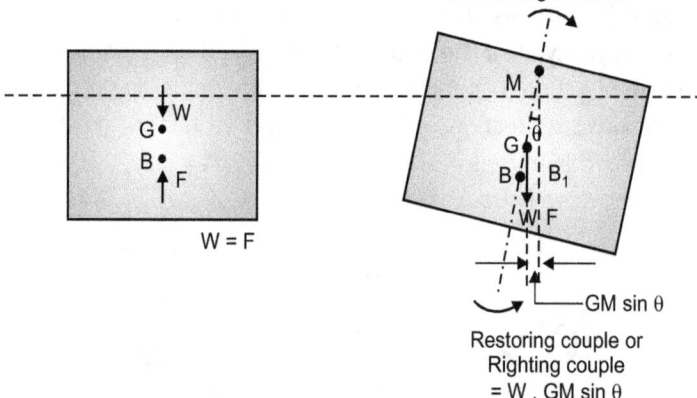

**Fig. 1.91: Stable equilibrium (M above G)**

(b) **Unstable equilibrium**

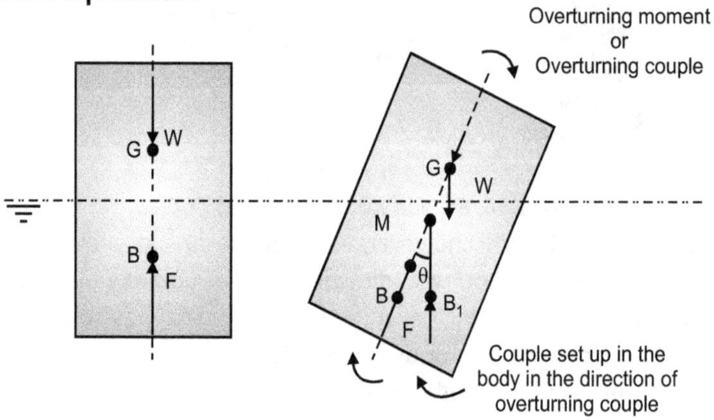

**Fig. 1.92: Unstable equilibrium (M below G)**

Now consider the body as shown in Fig. 1.92 (a). W the weight will act through the centre of gravity 'G' and buoyant force 'F' will act through centre of buoyancy 'B'. When a clockwise overturning moment is applied to the body, the body heels Fig. 1.92 (b). The forces on the body i.e. W and F now form a couple which is also in clockwise direction. Therefore, the body heels (overturns) further and does not restore its position. The body is in unstable equilibrium.

It can be observed that in this case metacentre M is below centre of gravity 'G'.

Thus **"if M is below G or GM is – ve or BM < BG the body is in unstable equilibrium."**

(c) **Neutral equilibrium:** It is clear from the above two cases that

"if **M and G coincide** or **GM = 0** or **BM = BG**, body is in *neutral equilibrium*".

(In this case, no couple is formed, since both W and F pass through same point.)

# 1.18 Determination of Metacentric Height

It is very essential to know the metacentric height of a floating body if the stability condition of the body is to be known. There are two methods of determination of metacentric height.

1. Experimental method 2. Theoretical method

1. **Experimental Method**

Initially, a known weight 'm' is placed at the centre of the deck of a ship. W is the total weight of ship including the small weight m. Initially, ship is in upright position and the deck is horizontal as shown in Fig. 1.93 (a). 'G' is the centre of gravity and 'B' the centre of buoyancy.

The small weight 'm' is then moved across the deck through distance 'x'. This tilts (or heels) the ship through an angle '$\theta$' and ship comes to rest in new position of equilibrium Fig. 1.93 (b). The angle of heel '$\theta$' is measured with the help of a plumb bob, hanging inside the ship from the centre point on the deck. The distance moved 'y' by the plumb bob of length '$l$' on a horizontal graduated scale is measured to get $\tan\theta = \dfrac{y}{l}$ Fig. 1.93 (c). In the new position of equilibrium, the new positions of centre of gravity '$G_1$', and centre of buoyancy '$B_1$' will be in the same vertical.

Moment caused due to shifting weight 'm' through distance 'x' across the deck = m . x.

Moment caused due to shifting of W from G to $G_1$

$$= W.GM.\sin\theta = W.GM.\tan\theta, \text{ if } \theta \text{ is small}$$

Equating the moments, we get

$$m.x = W.GM.\tan\theta$$

or

$$\boxed{GM = \dfrac{m.x}{W.\tan\theta}} \quad \ldots (1.23)$$

and

$$\tan\theta = \dfrac{y}{l}$$

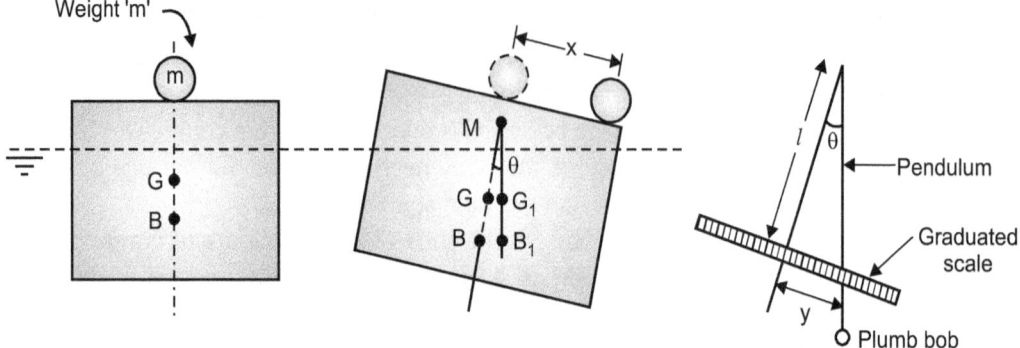

**Fig. 1.93: Experimental determination of metacentric height**

The value of metacentric height corresponding to θ = 0 is determined by plotting graph between values of GM and θ as shown in Fig. 1.94.

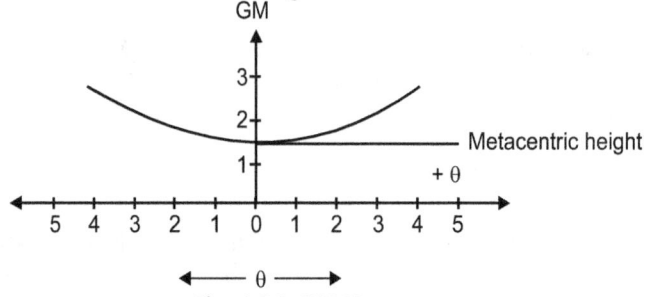

**Fig. 1.94: GM Vs θ curve**

## 2. Theoretical Method

Experimental method can be used only after the ship is constructed. However, while designing a ship or a floating body, it is necessary to know metacentric height eventhough the ship is not constructed. Under such conditions, theoretical method can be used to find the metacentric height.

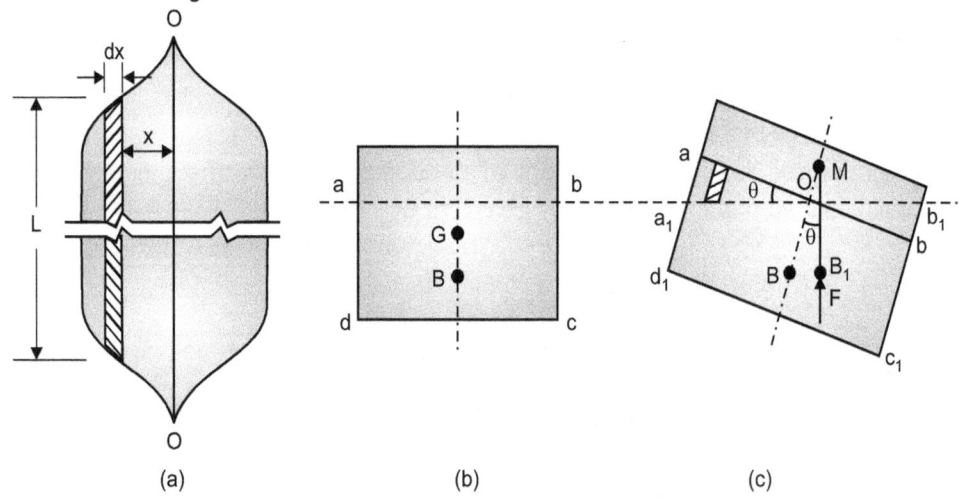

**Fig. 1.95: Determination of Metacentric height – Theoretical method**

The plan view of the ship at water-line and the cross-sections of the ship are shown in Fig. 1.95. The plan view of the ship at water line is shown in Fig. 1.95 (a). G and B are the positions of centre of gravity and centre of buoyancy when the ship is upright and is in equilibrium Fig. 1.95 (b).

Let the ship heel through angle '$\theta$' Fig. 1.95 (c). The effects of heeling of the ship are:
1. the centre of buoyancy has shifted from B to $B_1$ and
2. the immersed portion of ship has changed from abcd to $a_1 \, b_1 \, c_1 \, d_1$. Taking into account these two movements it is possible to get an expression for metacentric height of the ship.

1. The centre of buoyancy has shifted from B to $B_1$ as the volume of displacement has increased on the right hand side. Thus, buoyant force F has been shifted through distance $BB_1$. This causes an anticlockwise moment

$$F \cdot BB_1 = F \cdot BM \cdot \theta$$

2. Wedge shaped portion $aoa_1$ has come out of liquid and wedge shaped portion $bob_1$ has gone inside the liquid. Since weight of ship is same, weight of liquid displaced is same. Therefore, abcd = $a_1 \, b_1 \, c_1 \, d_1$. Therefore, $aoa_1 = bob_1$. Shifting of liquid from $aoa_1$ to new position $bob_1$ causes an overturning couple in clockwise direction. For equilibrium, this couple must be equal to couple caused due to shifting of centre of buoyancy from B to $B_1$.

To evaluate the overturning couple due to wedges, consider two small elementary prisms of wedges at distance 'x' from longitudinal axis (also called fore and aft axis) on either side as shown in Fig. 1.95 (a) and 1.95 (c). If 'L' is length of the prism

$$\text{Volume of prism} = (x \cdot \theta) \cdot dx \cdot L$$

∴ Weight of liquid in the prism

$$= \gamma (x \cdot \theta) \cdot dx \cdot L$$

∴ Moment of the weight about axis oo

$$= \gamma (x \cdot \theta) \cdot dx \cdot L \cdot x$$

∴ Moment of both prisms, one on left side and

$$\text{one on right side} = 2 \cdot \gamma \cdot (x \cdot \theta) \cdot dx \cdot L \cdot x$$

∴ Summation of this moment for the whole wedge

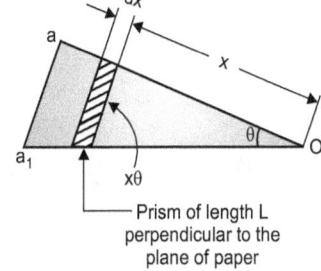

**Fig. 1.96**

$$= \int 2 \cdot \gamma \cdot (x \cdot \theta) \, dx \, L \cdot x = 2 \cdot \gamma \cdot \theta \int (L \cdot dx) \cdot x^2$$

$$= 2 \gamma \theta \int dA \cdot x^2$$

where  $L \cdot dx = dA$,
where, dA is the elemental area of the ship at water line (at water surface). Further,

$2 \int dA \cdot x^2 = I$, the moment of inertia of cross-sectional area of the ship at the liquid surface about the longitudinal axis oo.

∴ Summation of moments of both wedges $= \gamma \cdot \theta \cdot I$
∴ Equating the moments, we get
$$F \cdot BM \cdot \theta = \gamma \cdot \theta \cdot I$$
$$\gamma \cdot V \cdot BM \cdot \theta = \gamma \cdot \theta \cdot I$$

But $F = \gamma \cdot V$, where V is the vol. of liquid displaced by the ship.

∴
$$\boxed{BM = \frac{I}{V}} \quad \ldots (1.21)$$

BM is called metacentric radius.

Then,
$$\boxed{GM = BM \pm BG} \quad \ldots (1.22)$$

```
      . M        . M
      . G        . B
      . B        . G
GM = BM – BG   GM = BM + BG
```

**Fig. 1.97: Metacentric height**

## ILLUSTRATIVE EXAMPLES

### Example 1.47:

*A piece of metal when immersed in water weighs 667.08 N and when immersed in liquid of sp. gr. 0.8 weighs 686.70 N. Determine the volume, sp. gr. and the weight of piece in air.*

**Solution:**

The example is based on Archimedes principle.

1. Let $\forall$ be the volume of the piece and W the weight in air.
   When submerged in water, we have
   
   Weight in water = Weight in air – Weight of water displaced
   ∴ $\quad 667.08 = W - \forall \times 9810$
   or $\quad W = 667.08 + \forall \times 9810 \quad \ldots (I)$

2. Similarly, weight in liquid of sp. gr. 0.8 = W – Weight of liquid displaced
   or $\quad 686.70 = W - \forall \times (0.8 \times 9810)$
   or $\quad W = 686.70 + \forall \times (0.8 \times 9810) \quad \ldots (II)$

Equating (I) and (II)
$$686.70 + \forall (0.8 \times 9810) = 667.08 + \forall \cdot 9810$$
∴ $\quad 686.70 - 667.08 = \forall \cdot 9810 \cdot 0.2$

$$\boxed{\forall = 0.01 \text{ m}^3}$$

From eq. (I), weight of piece in air = 686.7 + 0.01 × 9810

∴ $\boxed{W = 765.18 \text{ N}}$

Weight = Vol. × Specific weight = Vol. × Sp. gr. × 9810
∴ $\quad 765.18 = 0.01 \times S \times 9810$

∴ $\boxed{\text{Sp. gr. } S = 7.8}$ [Metal is steel]

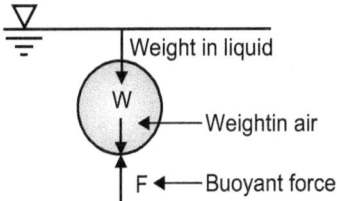

Fig. 1.98

Wt. in any liquid = Wt. in air − Buoyant force

## Example 1.48:

A metallic body floats at the interface of mercury sp. gr. 13.6 and water in such a way that half of its volume is submerged in mercury and half in water. Find the density of the metallic body.

**Solution:**

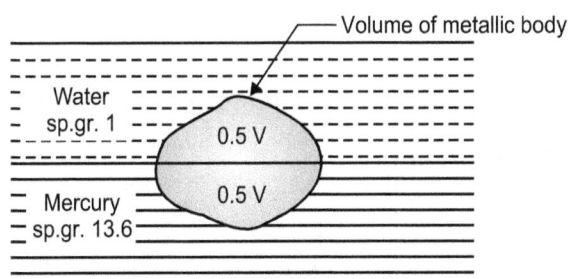

Fig. 1.99

Let the volume of the metallic body = V m³

Volume of body submerged in water = 0.5 V m³

Volume of body submerged in mercury = 0.5 V m³

Let 'S' be the specific gravity of the body.

Now, Weight of body = Volume × Sp. weight of the body

$= V \times S \times 9810$ ... (1)

Weight of water displaced = Volume of water displaced × 1 × 9810

$= (0.5\ V) \times 9810$ ... (2)

Weight of mercury displaced = Volume of mercury displaced × 13.6 × 9810

$= (0.5\ V) \times 13.6 \times 9810$ ... (3)

For equilibrium of the body,

Weight of the body = Weight of water displaced + Weight of mercury displaced.

∴ From (1), (2) and (3), we get,

$$V \times S \times 9810 = (0.5 V)(9810) + (0.5 V)(13.6 \times 9810)$$
$$\therefore S = 0.5 + 13.6 \times 0.5$$
or $$S = 7.3$$
∴ Density of metallic body $= 7.3 \times 1000$

∴ **Density of metallic body = 7300 kg/m³**

### Example 1.49:

A cubical float 1200 mm on side, weighs 1800 N, and is anchored by means of a concrete block weighing 6672 N in air. 230 mm of this float are submerged when the chain connected to the concrete block is taught. What rise in water level will lift the concrete block off the bottom? Concrete weight 25 kN/m³.

### Solution:

Fig. 1.100 shows the various forces when the concrete block is just lifted up.

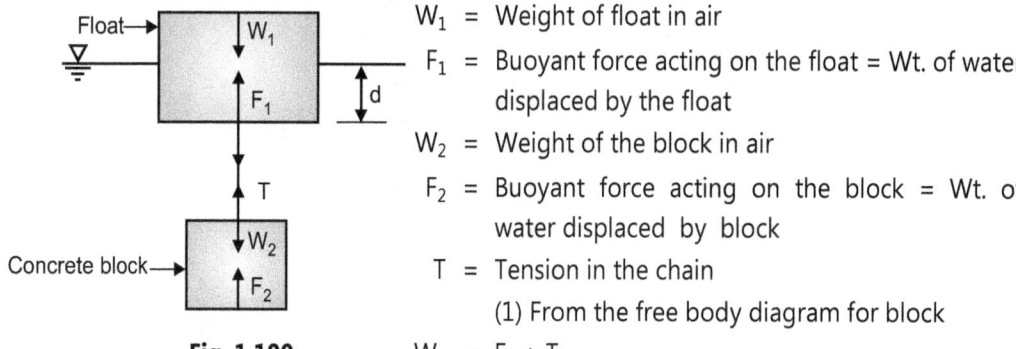

$W_1$ = Weight of float in air
$F_1$ = Buoyant force acting on the float = Wt. of water displaced by the float
$W_2$ = Weight of the block in air
$F_2$ = Buoyant force acting on the block = Wt. of water displaced by block
$T$ = Tension in the chain

(1) From the free body diagram for block

$$W_2 = F_2 + T$$

∴ $F_2$ = Weight of liquid displaced by the block
= Vol. of block × Sp. wt. of water
$$= \frac{\text{Weight of block}}{\text{Sp. gr. of concrete}} \times 9810$$
$$= \frac{6672}{24000} \times 9810 = 2727.18 \text{ N}$$

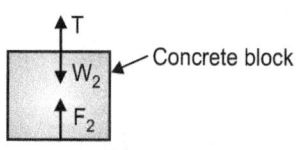

Fig. 1.101: Free body diagram of block

∴ $T = W_2 - F_2 = 6672 - 2727.19 = 3944.82$ N

(2) From the free body diagram of the float

$$F_1 = W_1 + T = 1800 + 3944.82 = 5744.82 \text{ N}$$

but $F_1$ = Weight of water displaced by the float
= Vol. of water displaced × Sp. weight of water

$$\therefore 5744.82 = (1.2 \times 1.2 \times d) \times 9810$$

$$\therefore d = \frac{5744.82}{1.2 \times 1.2 \times 9810} = 0.4067 \text{ m}$$

∴ Additional submergence = 0.4067 − 0.23 = 0.1767 m or

| Additional submergence = 176.7 mm |

**Fig. 1.102: Free body diagram for float**

### Example 1.50:
A slab of wood $1 \times 1 \times 0.25$ m and relative density 0.55 floats in water with 400 N load on it. What is the volume of slab submerged?

**Solution:**
By principle of floatation:

Weight of slab + Additional weight = Weight of liquid displaced

∴ [Volume of slab × Specific weight of the slab + 400] = Specific weight of water × Submerged Vol. of the slab

∴      $\gamma_w$ . Submerged Vol. of the slab = $[(1 \times 1 \times 0.25 \times 0.55 \times 9810) + 400]$

∴      Submerged Vol. of the slab × 9810 = 1748.88

∴      | Submerged Vol. of slab = 0.1783 m³ |

### Example 1.51:
A rectangular pantoon 10 m long, 8 m broad and 3 m deep weighs 980 kN. It carries on its upper deck at boiler 6 m in diameter weighing 588 kN. Longitudinal axis of the boiler is parallel to 10 m side. The centres of gravity of the pantoon and boiler are at the centres of gravity of respective figures and in the same vertical line. Find metacentric height. Take unit weight of water as 9.80 kN/m³.

**Solution:**
In this example, procedure of solving examples relating metacentric height is given step by step.

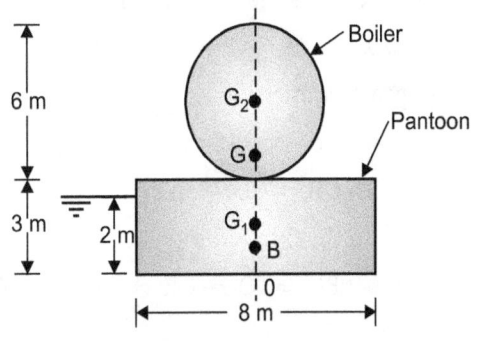

Fig. 1.103

1. Total weight causing displacement

   W = Weight of pantoon ($W_1$) + Weight of boiler ($W_2$)

   = 980 + 588 = **1568 kN**

2. Volume of liquid displaced

   $$V = \frac{W}{\gamma_{Liq.}} = \frac{1568}{9.80} = 160 \text{ m}^3$$

3. Depth of immersion

   $$d = \frac{V}{\text{area in plan}} = \frac{160}{10 \times 8} = 2 \text{ m}$$

4. Distance between point 'O' and centre of buoyancy

$$OB = \frac{d}{2} = 1\text{ m}$$

To find distance between point 'O' and combined centre of gravity 'G' taking moments about 'O'.

$$OG = \frac{W_1 \cdot OG_1 + W_2 \cdot OG_2}{W_1 + W_2} = \frac{980 \times 1.5 + 5.88 \times 6}{1568} = \mathbf{3.1875\text{ m}}$$

5. Distance between centre of buoyancy B and centre of gravity G

$$BG = OG - OB = 3.1875 - 1 = \mathbf{2.1875\text{ m}}$$

6. $BM = \dfrac{I}{V}$    where I is moment of inertia of the area of pantoon at water surface about longitudinal axis.

$$BM = \frac{10 \times 8^3}{12} \times \frac{1}{160} = \frac{bd^3}{12} = \frac{10 \times 8^3}{12} \quad \text{(Fig. 1.104)}$$

$$= \mathbf{2.67\text{ m}}$$

$V = $ Vol. of liq. displaced (Step 2) $= 160\text{ m}^3$

7. $GM = BM - BG$
$= 2.67 - 2.1875$

∴ $\boxed{GM = 0.4825\text{ m}}$

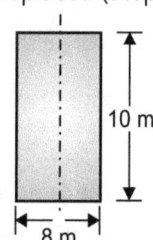

**Fig. 1.104**

### Example 1.52:

A wooden block 50 cm long, 25 cm wide and 18 cm deep has its shorter axis vertical with the depth of immersion 15 cm. Calculate the position of the metacentre and comment on the stability of the block.

**Solution:**

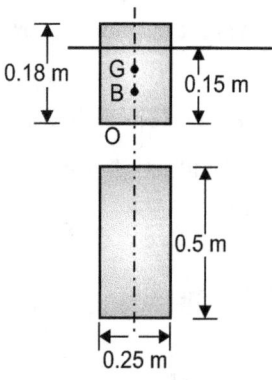

**Fig. 1.105**

The block is shown in Fig. 1.105.

Now we have

depth of immersion

$d = 0.15\text{ m}$

∴ $OB = 0.075\text{ m}$

$OG = 0.09\text{ m}$

∴ $BG = OG - OB = 0.015\text{ m}$

Now,  $I = \dfrac{0.5 \times (0.25)^3}{12}$

$= 6.51 \times 10^{-4} \text{ m}^4$

∴ $BM = \dfrac{I}{V} = \dfrac{6.51 \times 10^{-4}}{0.5 \times 0.25 \times 0.15}$

$= 0.0347 \text{ m}$

$\boxed{GM = BM - BG = 0.0197 \text{ m}}$

∵ GM is + ve block is stable in rolling as well as pitching.

### Example 1.53:

A wooden cylinder of mass density 600 kg/m³ is required to float in a liquid of mass density 800 kg/m³. Find the ratio of diameter 'd' and length 'l' of the cylinder in order that the cylinder can just float with it's longitudinal axis vertical.

**Solution:**

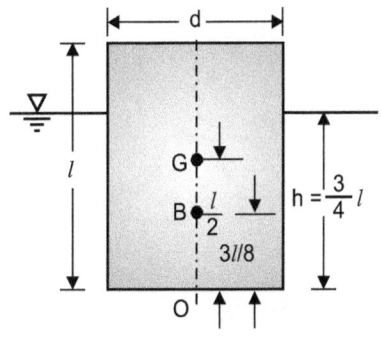

Fig. 1.106

1. Weight causing displacement

   'W' = Weight of cylinder

   W = Volume of cylinder × Specific wt. of cylinder

   ∴ $W = \left[\dfrac{\pi}{4} d^2 \cdot l\right] [600 \cdot (9.81)]$

2. Volume of liquid displaced

   $V = \dfrac{\pi/4 \times d^2 \times l \times 600 \times 9.81}{800 \times 9.81} = \dfrac{\pi d^2}{4} \times \dfrac{3l}{4}$

   [800 × 9.81 = Sp. wt. of liquid]

3. Depth of immersion

   $h = \dfrac{V}{\text{Area in plan}} = \dfrac{\pi d^2}{4} \times \dfrac{3}{4} l \Big/ \dfrac{\pi d^2}{4} = \dfrac{3}{4} l$

4. $OG = \dfrac{l}{2}$, $OB = \dfrac{h}{2} = \dfrac{3}{8} l$

5. $BG = OG - OB = \dfrac{l}{2} - \dfrac{3}{8} l = \dfrac{l}{8}$

6. $BM = \dfrac{I}{V} = \dfrac{\pi d^4}{64} \times \dfrac{1}{\dfrac{\pi d^2}{4} \times \dfrac{3}{4} l} = \dfrac{d^2}{12 l}$

[**Note:** If the cylinder is cut at water level, we get a circle of diameter 'd' and its moment of inertia will be $\dfrac{\pi d^4}{64}$ ].

Cylinder will just float i.e. it will float in neutral equilibrium when M and G coincide or BM = BG.

$$\therefore \quad \frac{d^2}{12l} = \frac{l}{8}$$

or $\boxed{\dfrac{d}{l} = 1.225}$

## Example 1.54:

A solid right triangular prism of equilateral section 1 m side floats in water. Density of prism is 800 kg/m³. Find the maximum length of the prism which will enable the prism to float with its longitudinal axis vertical.

**Solution:**

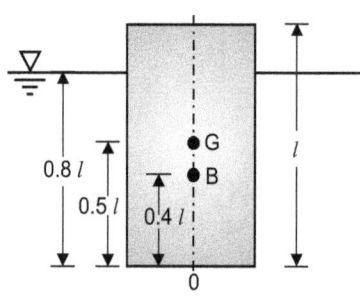

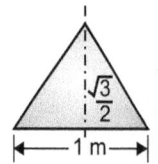

Fig. 1.107

1. Weight causing displacement

   W = Volume of prism × Specific wt.

   $$= \left(\frac{1}{2} \times 1 \times \frac{\sqrt{3}}{2}\right). l . (800 \times 9.81)$$

   where '$l$' is the length of prism.

2. Volume of liquid displaced

   $$V = \frac{W}{\text{Sp. weight of liquid}}$$

   $$= \frac{\frac{\sqrt{3}}{4} \times l \times 800 \times 9.81}{9810} = 0.8 \times \frac{\sqrt{3}}{4} l$$

3. Depth of immersion

   $$d = \frac{V}{\text{Area of triangle}}$$

   $$= \frac{0.8 \times \frac{\sqrt{3}}{4} l}{\frac{\sqrt{3}}{4}}$$

   = 0.8 $l$

4. OB = 0.4 $l$, OG = 0.5 $l$
5. BG = OG − OB = 0.5 $l$ − 0.4 $l$ = 0.1 $l$

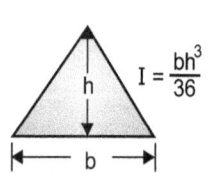

Fig. 1.108

6.  $BM = \dfrac{I}{V}$

$$= \dfrac{1 \times \left(\dfrac{\sqrt{3}}{2}\right)^3}{36} \times \dfrac{1}{\dfrac{\sqrt{3}}{4} \times 0.8 \times l} \qquad I = \dfrac{bh^3}{36}$$

$$= \dfrac{1}{19.2\, l}$$

Length will be maximum when the prism just floats in neutral equilibrium or G and M coincide or BM = BG

∴  $0.1\, l = \dfrac{1}{19.2\, l}$

∴  $l^2 = \dfrac{1}{19.2 \times 0.1}$

∴  $\boxed{l = 0.722 \text{ m}}$

When using $BM = \dfrac{I}{V}$, I is moment of inertia about longitudinal axis. By longitudinal axis, we mean the axis about which the moment of inertia is least.

**Example 1.55:**

A vessel has a length of 60 m, a beam of 10 m and displacement of 13000 kN. A weight of 200 kN moved 6 m across a deck inclines the vessel through 5°. The second moment of area of the load water plane about its fore and aft axis is 60% of the second moment of the circumscribing rectangle. The centre of buoyancy is 2 m below the water line. Find the positions of the metacentre and centre of gravity of the vessel. Density of sea water may be taken as 10 kN/m³.

**Solution:**

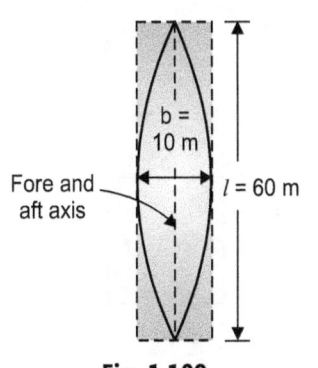

Fig. 1.109

The shape of the vessel is shown in Fig. 1.109.

Beam – Maximum width of the vessel

Displacement – Weight of liquid displaced = Weight of vessel

First we have,

$$GM = \dfrac{m \cdot x}{W \cdot \tan \theta} = \dfrac{200 \times 6}{13000 \times \tan 5°} = 1.055 \text{ m}$$

Further

$$BM = \dfrac{I}{V}$$

I — If the vessel does not have a rectangular shape in plan, it is practice to express the moment of inertia at water line (load water plane) about the longitudinal axis (fore and aft axis) as some percentage of moment of inertia of the circumscribing rectangle $I = k \dfrac{lb^3}{12}$.

$$\therefore \quad I = 0.6 \times \dfrac{60 \times 10^3}{12} = 3000 \text{ m}^4$$

V = Vol. of water displaced

$$= \dfrac{\text{Weight of vessel}}{\text{Sp. Weight of water}} = \dfrac{13000}{10} = 1300 \text{ m}^3$$

$$\therefore \quad BM = \dfrac{I}{V} = \dfrac{3000}{1300} = 2.31 \text{ m}$$

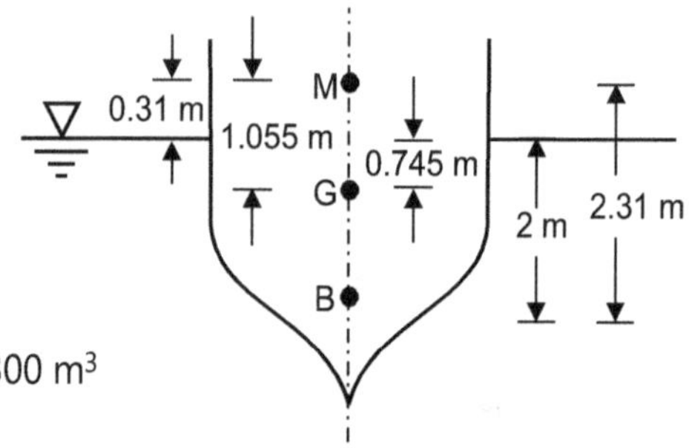

**Fig. 1.110**

∴ M is situated at 2.31 − 2 = 0.31 m above water line. G is situated at 1.055 − 0.31 = 0.745 m below water line (See above Fig. 1.110)

### Example 1.56:

A homogeneous cube of side 100 mm is floating in water. Show that it will float in stable equilibrium with top and bottom faces parallel to water surface and the other faces vertical provided sp. gr. is either less than 0.211 or greater than 0.789.

**Solution:**

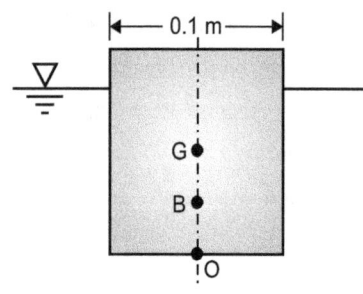

Fig. 1.111

Let 'S' be the specific gravity of cube. The side of the cube = 100 mm = 0.1 m.

1. Weight causing displacement
$$W = \text{Volume of cube} \times \text{Specific wt. of cube}$$
$$= (0.1)^3 \times S \times \gamma_w \qquad \left[\because S = \dfrac{\gamma_{cube}}{\gamma_w}\right]$$

2. Volume of water displaced
$$V = \dfrac{W}{\text{Sp. wt. of liquid}} = \dfrac{(0.1)^3 \times S \times \gamma_w}{\gamma_w} = (0.1)^3 \times S$$

3. Depth of immersion
$$d = \dfrac{V}{\text{Area in plan}} = \dfrac{(0.1)^3 \times S}{(0.1)^2} = 0.1\,S$$

4. $OG = \dfrac{0.1}{2}$; $OB = \dfrac{0.1}{2} \cdot S$

5. $BG = OG - OB = \dfrac{0.1}{2}(1 - S)$

6. $BM = \dfrac{I}{V} = \dfrac{0.1 \times (0.1)^3}{12} \times \dfrac{1}{(0.1)^3\,S} = \dfrac{0.1}{12\,S}$

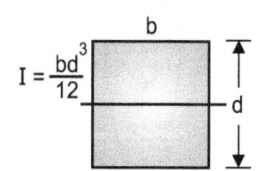

Fig. 1.112

$I = \dfrac{bd^3}{12}$

For stable equilibrium, BM > BG

$$\frac{0.1}{12S} > \frac{0.1}{2}(1-S)$$

∴ $S^2 - S + \frac{1}{6} > 0$

or $(S - 0.789)(S - 0.211) > 0$

or $\boxed{S < 0.211 \text{ or } S > 0.789}$

### Example 1.57:

A ball cock type of float valve, is required to close when 60% of the volume of the spherical float is immersed in water. Diameter of the valve is 10 mm. The fulcrum of the operating level is to be 100 mm from the valve and 400 mm from the centre of the float. If the valve is required to close against the pressure of 160 kN/m² (gauge), find the minimum diameter of the float. Take sp. wt. of water as 10 kN/m³.

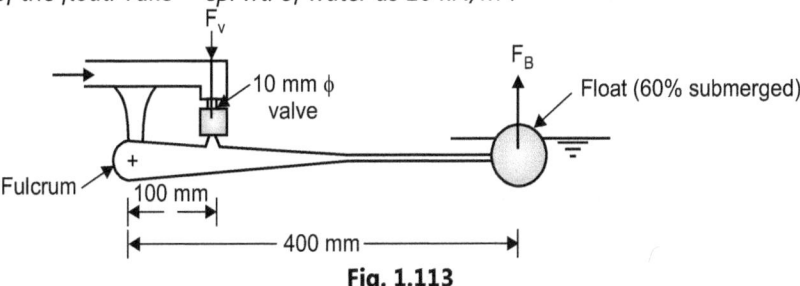

Fig. 1.113

### Solution:

The buoyant force on the float $F_B$ should be able to close the valve against a force on valve '$F_v$'. Thus, the moments of $F_B$ and $F_v$ about fulcrum should be balanced.

Force on the valve = Area of valve × Intensity of pressure

$$= \frac{\pi}{4} \times \left(\frac{10}{1000}\right)^2 \times 160{,}000$$

∴ $F_v = 4\pi$ N

Force on float '$F_B$' = Weight of liquid displaced by the float

$$= 10{,}000 \times 0.6 \times \frac{\pi d^3}{6}$$

$$= 1000 \pi d^3$$

Taking moments about the fulcrum

$$F_v \times 0.1 = F_B \times 0.4$$

∴ $4\pi \times 0.1 = (1{,}000 \pi d^3) \times 0.4$

∴ $d^3 = \frac{1}{1000}$

$d = 0.1$ m or

$\boxed{d = 10 \text{ cm } \phi}$

# Example 1.58:

A right solid cone floats in water with its apex downwards and base horizontal. It has diameter 'd' and height 'h'. If the specific gravity of the cone is 'S', show that for stable equilibrium,

$$h^2 < \frac{1}{4} \frac{d^2 S^{1/3}}{(1 - S^{1/3})}$$

## Solution:

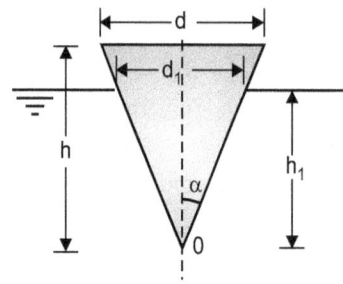

Fig. 1.114

1. Weight causing displacement

   W = Volume of cone × Specific wt. of cone
   
   $= \frac{1}{3}$ [Vol. of circumscribing cylinder] × Sp. wt. of the cone
   
   $= \frac{1}{3} \left[ \frac{\pi}{4} \cdot d^2 \cdot h \right] \cdot S \cdot \gamma_w = \frac{\pi d^2 h}{12} \times S \times \gamma_w$

2. Volume of water displaced

   $$V = \frac{W}{\text{Sp. weight of liquid}}$$
   
   $$= \frac{\frac{\pi d^2 h}{12} \times S \times \gamma_w}{\gamma_w} = \frac{\pi d^2 h}{12} \cdot S$$

3. Depth of immersion

   This example is a typical example of the floating body for which area in plan is not constant. Since area in plan is not constant, the depth of immersion cannot be calculated by the formula, depth of immersion $= \dfrac{\text{Volume of liquid displaced}}{\text{Area in plan}}$.
   
   Here, the volume of liquid displaced as obtained in step (2) is equated to volume of liquid displaced in terms of the dimensions '$d_1$' and $h_1$ of the submerged part.
   
   Volume of submerged part = Volume of submerged cone $= \dfrac{\pi d_1^2 h_1}{12}$
   
   Equating the two volumes
   
   $\dfrac{\pi d_1^2 h_1}{12} = \dfrac{\pi d^2 h}{12} \times S$  or  $d_1^2 h_1 = d^2 h \cdot S$
   
   But from the figure,  $\dfrac{d_1}{d} = \dfrac{h_1}{h}$  or  $d_1 = \dfrac{h_1}{h} \cdot d$
   
   ∴  $\dfrac{h_1^2}{h^2} \cdot h_1 d^2 = d^2 h \cdot S$
   
   or  $h_1^3 = h^3 \cdot S$  or  $h_1 = h \cdot S^{1/3}$

4. $OB = \frac{3}{4}h_1$, $OG = \frac{3}{4}h$ (Centre of gravity of cone is at a distance of $\frac{3}{4}$th height from apex)

5. $BG = OG - OB = \frac{3}{4}(h - h_1) = \frac{3}{4}h(1 - S^{1/3})$ ∵ $h_1 = h.S^{1/3}$

6. $BM = \frac{I}{V}$

   $I$ = moment of inertia of section at water line which will be a circle with diameter '$d_1$' about longitudinal axis $= \frac{\pi d_1^4}{64}$ and $V = \frac{\pi d_1^2 h_1}{12}$

   $= \frac{\pi d_1^4}{64} \times \frac{1 \times 12}{\pi d_1^2 h_1}$

   $= \frac{3}{16} \cdot \frac{d_1^2}{h_1} = \frac{3}{16} \cdot \frac{d_1^2}{h_1^2} \cdot h_1$ ∵ $\frac{d_1}{h_1} = \frac{d}{h}$ and $h_1 = h.S^{1/3}$

   $= \frac{3}{16} \cdot \frac{d^2}{h^2} h.S^{1/3}$

   $= \frac{3}{16} \cdot \frac{d^2}{h} \cdot S^{1/3}$

For stable equilibrium of the cone

$$BM > BG$$

$$\frac{3}{16} \cdot \frac{d^2}{h} \cdot S^{1/3} > \frac{3}{4} h(1 - S^{1/3})$$

or $$\boxed{h^2 < \frac{1}{4} \frac{d^2 S^{1/3}}{(1 - S^{1/3})}}$$

### Example 1.59:
A cylinder of wood of diameter 1 m and length 1 m and specific gravity 0.3 (w.r.t. sea water) is kept in sea water. Show that it will not float with it's axis vertical. Determine what concentrated weight suspended from its bottom will make it float with the axis vertical. Assume that the centre of gravity of the weight is at the bottom of the cylinder and specific weight of sea water is 10 kN/m³.
**Solution:**

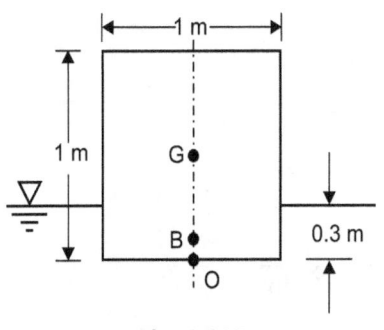

Fig. 1.115

**Without weight**
1. Weight causing displacement
   W = Volume of cylinder × Specific wt. of cylinder
   $= \frac{\pi}{4} \times 1 \times 1 \times 0.3 \times 10 = \frac{3\pi}{4}$ kN

2. Volume of liquid displaced
   $V = \frac{W}{\text{Sp. weight of liquid}}$
   $= \frac{\pi}{4} \times \frac{0.3 \times 10}{10} = 0.3 \times \frac{\pi}{4} m^3$

3. Depth of immersion

$$d = \frac{V}{\text{Area in plan}} = \frac{0.3 \times \pi}{4 \times \frac{\pi}{4}} = 0.3 \text{ m}$$

4. $OB = \frac{d}{2} = 0.15 \text{ m}$,   $OG = 0.5 \text{ m}$

5. $BG = OG - OB = 0.35 \text{ m}$

6. $BM = \frac{I}{V} = \frac{\pi \times 1^4}{64} \times \frac{1 \times 4}{0.3 \times \pi} = 0.208 \text{ m}$

Since BM < BG, metacentre M is below centre of gravity G or GM is – ve

∴ The cylinder will not float with its axis vertical.

## With Weight

In order to bring the centre of gravity down, a weight is attached at the centre of the base with the help of an anchor chain. Let weight (or tension in anchor chain) be say 'T' kN.

Then,

1. Weight causing displacement

$$W' = W + T = \text{say 'm' kN}$$

2. Volume of water displaced

$$V' = \frac{\text{Weight}}{\text{Sp. wt. of liquid}} = \frac{m}{10} \text{ m}^3$$

3. Depth of immersion

$$d' = \frac{V'}{\text{Area in plan}} = \frac{m}{10} \times \frac{4}{\pi} = \frac{2m}{5\pi} \text{ metres}$$

4. $OB' = \frac{d'}{2} = \frac{m}{5\pi} \text{ metres}$

As the additional weight 'T' is increased, the combined centre of gravity G' starts coming down towards new metacentre M'. A stage is reached when G' and M' coincide and the cylinder floats in neutral equilibrium when the combined weight (W + T) acting downwards and buoyant force (W + T) acting upwards pass through same point G' or M' as shown in Fig. 1.116. Taking moments about 'O'

$$W \cdot OG = (W + T) \cdot OG' = m\, OG'$$

$$OG' = \frac{W \times 0.5}{m} = \frac{W}{2m} \text{ metres}$$

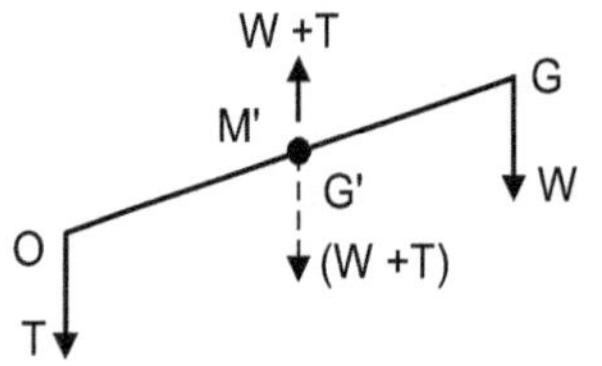

$$\therefore B'G' = OG' - OB' = \frac{W}{2m} - \frac{m}{5\pi} \text{ metres}$$

$$B'M' = \frac{I'}{V'} = \frac{\pi \times 1^4}{64} \times \frac{10}{m} = \frac{5\pi}{32\, m}$$

**Fig. 1.116**

For minimum weight (which will make the cylinder to float just in neutral equilibrium)

$$B'M' = B'G'$$

$$\therefore \quad \frac{W}{2m} - \frac{m}{5\pi} = \frac{5\pi}{32\,m} \quad \text{but } W = \frac{\pi}{4} \times 0.3 \times 10 = \frac{3}{4}\pi \text{ kN}$$

$$\therefore \quad \frac{3\pi}{8m} - \frac{m}{5\pi} = \frac{5\pi}{32m}$$

or $\quad m^2 = \frac{35}{32}\pi^2 \quad m = 3.286 \text{ kN} \quad \therefore \boxed{T = 3.286 - 2.356 = 0.93 \text{ kN}}$

$$\boxed{\therefore \text{ Additional weight } T = 0.93 \text{ kN}}$$

## Example 1.60:

A wooden block of relative density 0.7 has width 15 cm, depth 30 cm and length 150 cm. It floats horizontally on the surface of sea water (density = 1,000 kg/m³). Calculate the volume of water displaced, depth of immersion and the position of centre of buoyancy. Also find the metacentric height.

**Solution:**

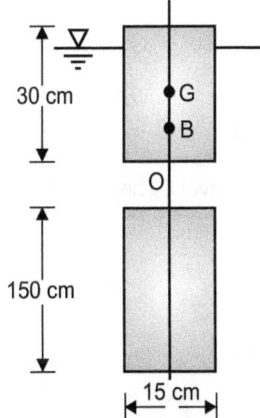

Fig. 1.117

1. Weight causing displacement
$$W = (1.5 \times 0.3 \times 0.15) \times 0.7 \times 9810 = 463.5225 \text{ N}$$

2. Volume of liquid displaced
$$V = \frac{463.5225}{9810} = 0.04725 \text{ m}^3$$

3. Depth of immersion
$$d = \frac{0.04725}{1.5 \times 0.15} = 0.21 \text{ m}$$

4. OB = 0.105 m    OG = 0.15 m
5. BG = OG − OB = 0.15 − 0.105 = 0.045 m
6. BM = $\frac{I}{V}$ = $\frac{1.5 \times (0.15)^3}{12} \times \frac{1}{0.04725}$ = 8.93 × 10⁻³ m⁴
7. GM = BM − BG = 0.00893 − 0.045 = − 0.0360 m

$\therefore$ $\boxed{\text{GM is −ve, since block is in unstable equilibrium}}$

## THEORETICAL QUESTIONS

1. Define 'Buoyancy' and 'Centre of Buoyancy'.
2. Define 'Metacentre and Metacentric Height." How are they important in case of a floating body.
3. Explain the experimental method of determination of metacentric height.
4. Define the following terms:
   (i) Metacentre
   (ii) Metacentric height
   Derive an equation for determination of Metacentric height analytically.
5. With usual notations, prove that $BM = \dfrac{I}{V}$.
6. Explain briefly different types of equilibrium of floating bodies.
7. Describe conditions of equilibrium of a floating body with the help of sketches showing positions of centre of gravity, centre of buoyancy and metacentre.
8. Explain the term metacentre and stability of floating body.
9. What is the significance of metacentric height? For stability is it enough that floating body has as large metacentric height as possible? Explain.
10. Explain with neat sketches, the conditions of equilibrium for floating and submerged bodies.
11. State and prove Archimedes principle.

## NUMERICAL PROBLEMS

1. Find the percent volume of an iceberg above the water surface if it floats in sea water. Assume density of sea water 1010 kg/m$^3$ and density of iceberg 920 kg/m$^3$.
   **[Ans. 8.911%]**
2. Two spheres each of 1.5 m diameter weigh 4.0 and 20 kN respectively. They are connected by a short rope and placed in water reservoir. Find the tension in the rope and the percentage of volume of lighter sphere that will be above water.

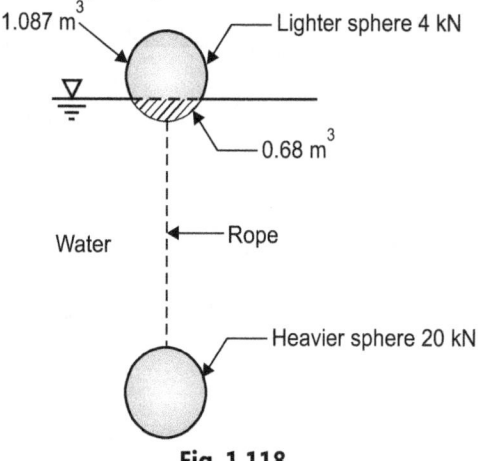

Fig. 1.118

[**Hint:** Volume of sphere = $\frac{4}{3}\pi R^3 = \frac{4}{3}\pi(0.75)^3 = 1.767 \text{ m}^3$

Tension in rope = Submerged weight of heavier sphere
= 20 – 1.767 × 9.81 = **2.666 kN**

For lighter sphere,
Weight causing displacement = 4 + 2.666 = 6.666 kN

∴ Vol. of water displaced by lighter sphere = $\frac{6.666}{9.81}$ = 0.68 m³

∴ % vol. of lighter sphere above water surface = $\frac{1.767 - 0.68}{1.767}$ × 100 = **61.52%** ]

[**Ans.** 2.666 kN, 61.52%]

3. A wooden cone weighing 588.6 N floats with apex downwards in a liquid of specific gravity 0.9. If the specific gravity of the cone is 0.6, find the weight of steel of specific gravity 7.6, suspended from the apex of the cone by a string, will just suffice to just submerge the cone and what would then be tension in the string?
   [**Ans.** 333.83 N, 294.3N]

4. A cargo ship with vertical sides near waterline weighs 40,000 kN and has a draft of 6.7 m in sea water (sp. gr. 1.025). When a weight of 2000 kN is unloaded, the draft reduces to 6.4 m. What would be the draft of the ship in fresh water?
   [**Ans.** 6.5425 m]
   [Note: Draft means depth of submergence]

5. A block of wood (sp. gr. 0.6) is 3 m × 3 m in plan is 2 m deep. It floats in water (3 m × 3 m face horizontal). Find metacentric height.
   [**Ans.** 0.225 m]

6. A wooden cylinder of diameter "d" and length "2d" floats in water with axis vertical. Is the equilibrium stable? Take specific gravity of wood = 0.6.
   [**Ans.** BG = 0.4 d, BM = 0.052 d, BM < BG, unstable)

7. A block of wood of rectangular section is 'b' metre wide and 'd' metre deep. Specific gravity of block is 'S'. Show that for the block to float in stable equilibrium, b > d $\sqrt{6S(1-S)}$.

8. An empty tank rectangular in plan and sides also, is closed at the top. It measures 1200 mm × 700 mm × 900 mm. It is made of steel sheets weighing 370 N/m². If the tank is allowed to float in water with 900 mm edges vertical, prove that the equilibrium is unstable.
   [**Ans.** BG = 0.336 m, BM = 0.1786 m, BM < BG]

9. A closed rectangular box of thin metal sheets measures 300 mm × 150 mm × 100 mm and weighs 10 N. It's centre of gravity coincides with the geometrical centre of the box. It is placed in water with 300 mm × 150 mm sides horizontal. A weight of 30 N is placed on it in a symmetrical manner. The c.g. of the weight is 10 mm above the top face. Determine the metacentric height of the box and its type of equilibrium.
   [**Ans.** GM = – 0.029 m, unstable]

10. A circular cylinder of radius 'R' and height 'H' floats in a liquid with its axis vertical. If $\dfrac{R}{\sqrt{2}}$ > H, prove that the cylinder will float in stable equilibrium for any combination of sp. wt. of liquid and cylinder material (provided the cylinder floats).

$\left[ \text{Ans. } \dfrac{R}{\sqrt{2}} > H \; [S(1-S)] \text{ Hence the result} \right]$

11. A solid cone floats in liquid of specific gravity '$S_l$' with it's apex downwards. It has diameter 'd', height 'h', semi-apex angle '$\alpha$' and specific gravity '$S_c$'. Show that for the cone to float with axis vertical, $\dfrac{S_c}{S_l} \geq \cos^6 \alpha$

$\left[ \textbf{Hint :} \text{ Refer Ex. 1.58, } \tan^2 \alpha = \dfrac{d^2}{4h^2} \right]$

12. A wooden cone of R.D. 0.6 is required to float vertically in water with it's apex downwards. Determine least apex angle so as to make the cone to float in stable equilibrium.
    [**Ans.** $2\alpha = 46°$–37']

13. A cylindrical buoy 2 m in diameter and 2.5 m high weighs 15.71 kN. Show that it will not float in water with it's longitudinal axis vertical. If one end of the buoy is anchored at the centre of the base, find the tension in the chain in order that the buoy will float with its axis vertical.
    [**Ans.** 11.28 kN]

14. A cylindrical buoy weighing 1.8 tonnes is 2 m in diameter and 2.7 m high. Prove that the buoy will be unstable with its vertical axis in sea water of specific gravity 1.02. If one end of a vertical chain is fastened to the centre of the base of the buoy, find the pull on the chain in order that the buoy may just float with its vertical axis.
    [**Hint:** Ref. Illustrative example 1.59]
    [**Ans.** 14.035 kN)

15. A block of wood of sp. gr. 0.8 and size 100 mm × 40 mm × 30 mm floats in water, keeping the surface 100 × 40 mm parallel to the water surface. Determine its metacentric height for its tilt about its longitudinal aixs.
    [**Hint:** Follow standard procedure and find metacentric height]
    [**Ans.** GM = 0.0025 m or 2.5 mm is + ve and hence block floats in stable equilibrium]

16. A ship 48 m long and 12 m wide has displacement of 18 MN. Centre of buoyancy of ship is 1.5 m below the water surface. Second moment of area of plan of the ship of the water surface about its longitudinal axis is 70% of the second moment of area of the circumscribing rectangle about the same axis. Determine the position of metacentre of ship. Take relative density of sea water = 1.025.
    [**Hint:** Refer solved example No. 1.54]
    [**Ans.** M is 1.2 m above water line]

■■■

# Unit 2

# FLUID KINEMATICS AND DYNAMICS

## (A) KINEMATICS OF FLUID FLOW

## 2.1 Introduction

Fluid kinematics is the branch of fluid mechanics which deals with the geometry of motion of fluid without taking into consideration the forces causing the motion.

Only time–space relations like velocity, acceleration etc. are studied in fluid kinematics.

A fluid mass is composed of particles which can have independent movements (as against the particles of solid which move together as a body). Therefore, the velocity and acceleration of a particle may vary with respect to time or space or both.

Therefore, study of motion of fluid starts with the study of motion of an individual particle. There are two methods of analysis of fluid motion.
1. Lagrangian method and
2. Eulerian method.
1. **Lagrangian Method:** In this method a single fluid particle is selected and the path taken by the particle, its velocity, acceleration etc. are studied with respect to time. This method, therefore, describes the motion of single fluid particle.
2. **Eulerian Method:** In this method, a point occupied by fluid is selected and study is made about velocity, acceleration, pressure etc. at that point.
Eulerian approach being simpler is used widely in fluid mechanics.

## 2.2 Velocity of Fluid Particle

A very important characteristic used to describe the motion of fluid is called 'Velocity'. Velocity is a vector quantity having both magnitude and direction.

If 'ds' is the distance travelled by a particle in time 'dt', the velocity 'V' of the fluid particle is given by

$$V = \lim_{dt \to 0} \frac{ds}{dt}$$

If velocity vector V at a point is resolved in three components u, v and w in x, y, z directions respectively and dx, dy and dz are the components of displacement 'ds' in x, y, z directions respectively,

then, $u = \lim_{dt \to 0} \frac{dx}{dt}$, $v = \lim_{dt \to 0} \frac{dy}{dt}$ and $w = \lim_{dt \to 0} \frac{dz}{dt}$

Further, V as well as u, v and w are the functions of space (x, y, z) and time (t) hence we can write $V = f_1(x, y, z, t)$, $u = f_2(x, y, z, t)$, $v = f_3(x, y, z, t)$
and $w = f_4(x, y, z, t)$

In vector form velocity vector can be written as $\boxed{V = ui + vj + wk}$ ... (2.1)

## 2.3 Types of Flow

According to many criteria, fluid flow may be classified as follows:
1. Steady flow and unsteady flow
2. Uniform flow and Non-uniform flow
3. Laminar flow and Turbulent flow
4. Rotational flow and Irrotational flow
5. One dimensional, Two dimensional and Three dimensional flow.
6. Compressible and Incompressible flow.

1. **Steady flow and unsteady flow (Time as criterion)**

**Steady flow:** *If the various characteristics of flow like velocity, pressure, density etc. at **any point** do not change with **respect to time**, the flow is called steady flow.*

**Unsteady flow:** *If any one of the characteristics of flow, like velocity, pressure etc. at any point changes with time, the flow is called unsteady flow.*

**Mathematically,**

$$\frac{\partial V}{\partial t} = 0, \quad \frac{\partial p}{\partial t} = 0, \quad \frac{\partial \rho}{\partial t} = 0 \text{ etc. for steady flow}$$

$$\frac{\partial V}{\partial t} \neq 0, \quad \frac{\partial p}{\partial t} \neq 0, \quad \frac{\partial \rho}{\partial t} \neq 0 \text{ etc. for unsteady flow}$$

Steady flow is simple to analyse than unsteady flow.

**Examples:**

Flow of water with constant discharge through a pipeline is an example of steady flow while flow of water with varying discharge through a pipe is the case of unsteady flow.

Flow through orifice under constant head is steady flow while that under varying (falling or rising) head is unsteady flow.

2. **Uniform flow and Non-uniform flow**

   **(Distance or space as criterion)**

   **Uniform flow:** *If the velocity of flow at a given instant is same in magnitude and direction at different points in the flowing fluid, the flow is called uniform flow.*

   **Non-Uniform flow:** *If the velocity of flow, at a given instant, changes from point to point, the flow is called non-uniform flow.*

**Mathematically,**

$$\frac{\partial V}{\partial s} = 0 \text{ for uniform flow}$$

$$\frac{\partial V}{\partial s} \neq 0 \text{ for non-uniform flow}$$

[**Note:** For convenience, a uniform flow is generally described only in terms of velocity rather than in terms of other variables. Therefore only $\frac{\partial V}{\partial s}$ is considered.]

**Examples:**

Flow through a long straight pipe of uniform diameter is an example of uniform flow.

Flow through a long pipe with varying cross section is an example of non-uniform flow. (Flow through a pipe bend with uniform cross-section is also a non-uniform flow because the velocity changes due to change in direction).

Steadyness means "No change with time" and uniformity means "No change in space", each being independent of the other. Therefore, four combinations of above types of flows are possible:

(i) **Steady uniform flow:**

$$\frac{\partial V}{\partial t} = 0, \quad \frac{\partial V}{\partial s} = 0$$

e.g. flow with constant discharge passing through a straight pipe of constant cross-section.

(ii) **Steady non-uniform flow:**

$$\frac{\partial V}{\partial t} = 0, \quad \frac{\partial V}{\partial s} \neq 0$$

e.g. flow with constant discharge passing through a tapering pipe with varying cross-section.

(iii) **Unsteady uniform flow:**

$$\frac{\partial V}{\partial t} \neq 0, \quad \frac{\partial V}{\partial s} = 0$$

e.g. flow with varying discharge through a straight pipe of uniform cross-section.

(iv) **Unsteady non-uniform:**

$$\frac{\partial V}{\partial t} \neq 0, \quad \frac{\partial V}{\partial s} \neq 0$$

e.g. flow with varying discharge through a tapering pipe.

3. **Laminar flow and Turbulent flow**
   (Behaviour of fluid particles as criterion)

**Laminar flow:**

If velocity of flow is sufficiently low, the characteristic dimension sufficiently small and kinematic viscosity of flowing fluid sufficiently high, particles of fluid behave in systematic or disciplined manner, the flow takes place in number of sheets or laminae gliding over the adjacent laminae and the flow is called 'laminar flow'. Laminar flow is also called viscous flow or stream line flow.

**Turbulent flow:**

If velocity of flow is sufficiently high, the characteristic dimension sufficiently large and the kinematic viscosity of fluid sufficiently low, particles of fluid behave in indisciplined or erratic manner, cross currents or eddies are formed and the flow is called 'turbulent flow'.

The type of flow, Laminar or Turbulent can be decided with the help of a non-dimensional number called "Reynold's Number" which is the ratio of inertia force to viscous force.

Reynold's Number is given by $Re = \dfrac{\rho V l}{\mu}$ or $\dfrac{Vl}{\nu}$

In case of laminar flow, viscous force is stronger than inertial force and hence value of Re is low.

In case of turbulent flow, inertia force is stronger than viscous force and hence Re is high.

For the *flow through a pipe*, Re is less than *2,000* for *laminar flow*. It is *more than 4000* for *turbulent flow*.

For Re *between 2000* and *4000, flow* is called *transitional flow.*

In case of laminar flow, velocity distribution is parabolic in nature.

In case of turbulent flow, velocity distribution in logarithmic in nature.

In case of laminar flow, losses due to friction are directly proportional to velocity ($h_f \propto V$).

In case of turbulent flow, losses due to friction are proportional to $V^n$ ($h_f \propto V^n$). n is generally taken as 2.

**Examples:**

**Laminar flow:** Flow of blood in small veins, flow of oil in bearings, flow in porous media, flow of highly viscous oils in conduits of small diameter etc. are some of the examples of laminar flow.

**Turbulent flow:** In general, flows in nature are turbulent flows. Flow through a river or canal, smoke from chimney, smoke from a cigarette are some examples of turbulent flow.

4. **Rotational flow and Irrotational flow**

**Rotational flow:** *If the fluid particles rotate about their mass centres while moving in the direction of motion, the flow is called rotational flow.*

**Irrotational flow:** *If the fluid particles do not rotate about their mass centres while moving in the direction of motion, the flow is called an irrotational flow.*

**Examples:**

**Rotational flow:** Motion of liquid in a rotating cylinder (called forced vortex) is typical example of rotational flow. Rotating liquid in liquidiser of domestic mixer is another example.

**Irrotational flow:** Flow of liquid in an emptying wash–basin (called free vortex) is a typical example of irrotational flow.

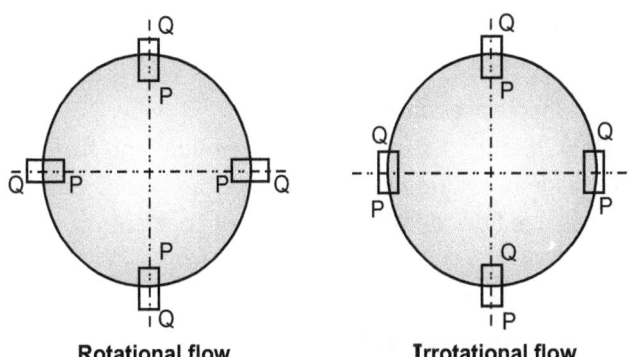

Rotational flow  Irrotational flow

**Fig. 2.1: Rotational and Irrotational flow**

5. **One dimensional, Two dimensional and Three dimensional flows**

   *One Dimensional Flow:* If the characteristics of flow like velocity, pressure, density etc. vary only in one of the three co-ordinate directions, the flow is called one dimensional flow.

   *Two Dimensional Flow:* If the characteristics of flow vary in two of the three co-ordinate directions, the flow is called two dimensional flow.

   *Three Dimensional Flow:* If the characteristics of flow vary in all the three co-ordinate directions, the flow is called three dimensional flow.

   All the above flows can further be unsteady or steady depending upon whether the characteristics are functions of time or not.

**Mathematically,**

| Steady | Unsteady | Type of flow |
|---|---|---|
| $V = f(x)$ | $V = f(x, t)$ | One dimensional |
| $V = f(x, y)$ | $V = f(x, y, t)$ | Two dimensional |
| $V = f(x, y, z)$ | $V = f(x, y, z, t)$ | Three dimensional |

Solution of problems becomes more and more complicated as we go from one dimensional flow to three dimensional flow.

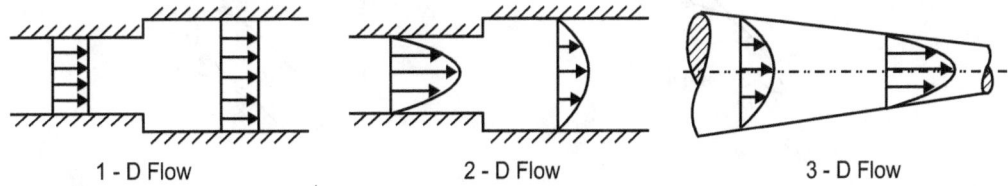

1 - D Flow    2 - D Flow    3 - D Flow

**Fig. 2.2: One, two and three dimensional flows**

**Examples:**

Flow through a pipe may be treated as one dimensional flow.

Flow between parallel plates of large extent, flow in large river, flow over a long spillway, flow below long weirs are examples of two dimensional flow. Flow nets, developed later on in this chapter are useful in solving two dimensional flow problems.

Flow in converging or diverging pipes or open channels are examples of three dimensional flow.

### 6. Compressible and Incompressible flow

**Compressible flow:** If, during the flow, volume of fluid and hence the density of fluid changes due to changes in pressure and temperature, the flow is called compressible flow. Thus, in case of compressible flow, density of fluid is not constant.

**Examples:**
1. Problems involving flight of rockets, aircrafts etc.
2. Flow of air in problems concerned with turbomachines, compressor blades etc.
3. Flow of gases through openings like nozzles.
4. Phenomenon of water hammer in which water has to be treated as compressible fluid.

**Incompressible flow:** If the volume and hence the density of flowing fluid does not change due to changes in pressure and temperature, the flow is called incompressible flow. Thus, the density of fluid remains constant.

**Examples:**
1. Normally problems involving liquids (i.e. hydraulics problems).
2. Flow of gases in machines like fans and blowers.

Generally, flow of gases is compressible flow while flow of liquids is incompressible flow. However, if Mach number is less than 0.4 the effects of compressibility can be neglected and the flow (even of a gas) can be treated as incompressible. (Refer Art. 1.2.8.1)

## 2.4 Path Line, Stream Line, Streak Line

**Path Line:** *It is the actual path traced by a fluid particle over a period of time.*

**Stream Line:** *It is an imaginary line drawn through a flowing mass of fluid such that tangent to it at any point represents the direction of velocity vector at that point* [Fig. 2.3 (a)].

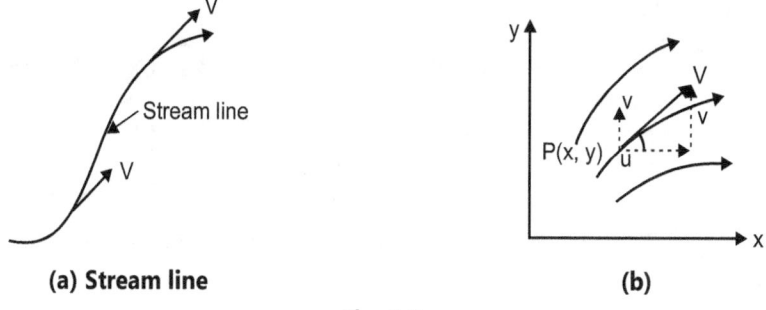

(a) Stream line  (b)

**Fig. 2.3**

Fig. 2.3 (b) shows the stream line pattern for a flow in xy plane. V is the velocity vector at point P (x, y), tangential to the stream line. u and v are the components of V in x and y directions respectively.

Then, we can write

$$\frac{v}{u} = \tan\theta = \frac{dy}{dx}$$

Hence, equation of stream line in two dimensions (xy plane), can be written as:

$$\frac{dx}{u} = \frac{dy}{v}$$

For three dimensional flow, equation of stream line can be written as:

$$\boxed{\frac{dx}{u} = \frac{dy}{v} = \frac{dz}{w}} \qquad \ldots (2.2)$$

Since the stream line is tangential to the velocity vector at every point, there is no component of velocity vector normal to the stream line and hence there can be no flow across the stream line.

**Stream Tube:** *It is a tubular space bounded by a surface consisting of stream lines Fig. 2.4.*

Since the surface of a stream tube consists of stream lines there can be no flow from the surface of a stream tube. Flow can take place only through the end faces of the tube, similar to flow in a closed conduit.

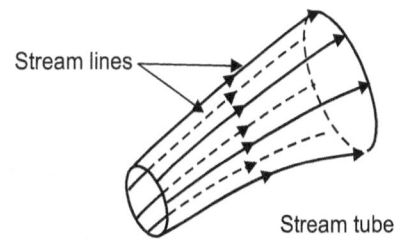

**Fig. 2.4: Stream tube**

**Streak Line:** *It is a line traced by a series of fluid particles passing through a fixed point in the flowing fluid mass.* Sometimes in an experimental work, to trace the motion of fluid particles, a coloured dye or smoke is injected into flowing fluid. The resulting coloured lines are the streak lines.

Similarly, the path traced by particles coming out of a chimney is a good example of streak lines.

For steady flow, path lines, stream lines and streak lines coincide with each other.

## 2.5 Potential Function 'ø' (Phi)

*Velocity Potential is defined as a scalar function of space and time such that it's – ve derivative with respect to any direction gives the fluid velocity in that direction.*

Thus, ø = f (x, y, z, t) for unsteady flow and ø = f (x, y, z) for steady flow. For function 'ø' we have,

$$u = -\frac{\partial\phi}{\partial x}, \quad v = -\frac{\partial\phi}{\partial y} \quad \text{and} \quad w = -\frac{\partial\phi}{\partial z}$$

– ve sign shows that flow takes place in the direction in which 'ø' decreases [or 'ø' goes on decreasing in the direction of flow, similar to electrical potential (voltage)].

Now we will derive some of the properties of potential function.

For three dimensional, steady incompressible flow the continuity equation is given by

$$\frac{\partial u}{\partial x} + \frac{\partial v}{\partial y} + \frac{\partial w}{\partial z} = 0$$

Substituting values of velocity components u, v and w we get

$$\frac{\partial}{\partial x}\left(-\frac{\partial \phi}{\partial x}\right) + \frac{\partial}{\partial y}\left(-\frac{\partial \phi}{\partial y}\right) + \frac{\partial}{\partial z}\left(-\frac{\partial \phi}{\partial z}\right) = 0$$

or

$$\frac{\partial^2 \phi}{\partial x^2} + \frac{\partial^2 \phi}{\partial y^2} + \frac{\partial^2 \phi}{\partial z^2} = 0$$

which is nothing but $\nabla^2 \phi = 0$, the "Laplace Equation".

"*Thus any function, that satisfies Laplace Equation is a possible case of fluid flow*".

Further, consider the components of rotation in x, y and z directions.

$$\omega_x = \frac{1}{2}\left(\frac{\partial w}{\partial y} - \frac{\partial v}{\partial z}\right)$$

$$\omega_y = \frac{1}{2}\left(\frac{\partial u}{\partial z} - \frac{\partial w}{\partial x}\right)$$

$$\omega_z = \frac{1}{2}\left(\frac{\partial v}{\partial x} - \frac{\partial u}{\partial y}\right)$$

Substituting, $u = -\frac{\partial \phi}{\partial x}$, $v = -\frac{\partial \phi}{\partial y}$ and $w = -\frac{\partial \phi}{\partial z}$ we get

$$\omega_x = \frac{1}{2}\left[\frac{\partial}{\partial y}\left(-\frac{\partial \phi}{\partial z}\right) - \frac{\partial}{\partial z}\left(-\frac{\partial \phi}{\partial y}\right)\right] = \frac{1}{2}\left[-\frac{\partial^2 \phi}{\partial y \partial z} + \frac{\partial^2 \phi}{\partial z \partial y}\right]$$

Similarly,

$$\omega_y = \frac{1}{2}\left[-\frac{\partial^2 \phi}{\partial z \partial x} + \frac{\partial^2 \phi}{\partial x \partial z}\right]$$

$$\omega_z = \frac{1}{2}\left[-\frac{\partial^2 \phi}{\partial x \partial y} + \frac{\partial^2 \phi}{\partial y \partial x}\right]$$

But $\phi$ is a continuous function,

$$\therefore \frac{\partial^2 \phi}{\partial y \partial z} = \frac{\partial^2 \phi}{\partial z \partial y}; \frac{\partial^2 \phi}{\partial z \partial x} = \frac{\partial^2 \phi}{\partial x \partial z}; \frac{\partial^2 \phi}{\partial x \partial y} = \frac{\partial^2 \phi}{\partial y \partial x}$$

and hence, $\omega_x = \omega_y = \omega_z = 0$ which shows that the flow is irrotational.

Thus if velocity potential exists the flow is irrotational and vice-versa.

*Thus existence of '$\phi$' which satisfies Laplace equation is a possible case of steady, incompressible, irrotational flow. Such a type of flow is called 'Potential flow'.*

## 2.6 Stream Function 'ψ' (Psi)

Stream function ψ (Greek 'Psi') is defined as scalar function of space and time such that its derivative with respect to any direction gives the velocity component at right angles (in anticlockwise direction) to this direction.

Thus, for the two dimensional fluid flow:

$$\frac{\partial \psi}{\partial x} = v \quad \text{and} \quad \frac{\partial \psi}{\partial y} = -u$$

Now, if values of 'u' and 'v' are substituted in the continuity equation, we get for steady incompressible flow

$$\frac{\partial u}{\partial x} + \frac{\partial v}{\partial y} = 0 \quad \text{or} \quad -\frac{\partial^2 \psi}{\partial x \, \partial y} + \frac{\partial^2 \psi}{\partial y \, \partial x} = 0$$

This is true if ψ is a continuous function. Thus, any function ψ which is continuous is a possible case of flow. However, flow may be rotational or irrotational.

When values of 'u' and 'v' are substituted in rotational component about z axis we get

$$\omega_z = \frac{1}{2}\left(\frac{\partial v}{\partial x} - \frac{\partial u}{\partial y}\right) = \frac{1}{2}\left[\frac{\partial^2 \psi}{\partial x^2} + \frac{\partial^2 \psi}{\partial y^2}\right]$$

The flow is irrotational only if $\omega_z = 0$ or if $\frac{\partial^2 \psi}{\partial x^2} + \frac{\partial^2 \psi}{\partial y^2} = 0$ or if 'ψ' satisfies Laplace equation. Otherwise the flow is rotational.

Hence it may be stated that *any function 'ψ' which is continuous is a possible case of flow since continuity is satisfied. However, flow may be rotational or irrotational. If however, Laplace equation also is satisfied the flow will be irrotational.* The relation between velocity potential 'ø' and stream function 'ψ' can be established as follows:

We have, $\quad \frac{\partial \phi}{\partial x} = -u, \quad \frac{\partial \phi}{\partial y} = -v, \quad \frac{\partial \psi}{\partial x} = v, \quad \frac{\partial \psi}{\partial y} = -u$

and

$$\left[\begin{array}{c} \frac{\partial \phi}{\partial x} = \frac{\partial \psi}{\partial y} \\ -\frac{\partial \phi}{\partial y} = \frac{\partial \psi}{\partial x} \end{array}\right] \qquad \ldots (2.3)$$

These equations are called 'Cauchy–Rieman' conditions and are useful in finding out 'ø' if 'ψ' is known or finding out 'ψ' when 'ø' is known.

## 2.7 Equipotential Line, Stream Line and their Relation

### 2.7.1 Equipotential Line

This is the line along which the velocity potential ø is constant.

∴ For equipotential line,   ø = constant

∴   dø = 0

but ø is function of (x, y)

∴ $d\phi = \dfrac{\partial \phi}{\partial x} \cdot dx + \dfrac{\partial \phi}{\partial y} \cdot dy = 0$, but $\dfrac{\partial \phi}{\partial x} = -u,\ \dfrac{\partial \phi}{\partial y} = -v$

∴   $-u\,dx - v\,dy = 0$

or equation of equipotential line is $\boxed{u\,dx + v\,dy = 0}$

∴ Slope of equipotential line is $\boxed{\dfrac{dy}{dx} = -\dfrac{u}{v}}$, say m ... (i)

### 2.7.2 Stream Line

The line for which stream function 'ψ' is constant is called stream line.

∴ For stream line,  ψ = constant

∴   dψ = 0

but ψ is function of (x, y)

∴ $d\psi = \dfrac{\partial \psi}{\partial x} \cdot dx + \dfrac{\partial \psi}{\partial y} \cdot dy$, but $\dfrac{\partial \psi}{\partial x} = v,\ \dfrac{\partial \psi}{\partial y} = -u$

∴   $v\,dx - u\,dy = 0$

or equation of stream line is

$v\,dx - u\,dy = 0$ or $\boxed{\dfrac{dx}{u} = \dfrac{dy}{v}}$

Slope of stream line is $\boxed{\dfrac{dy}{dx} = \dfrac{v}{u}}$, say m' ... (ii)

It may be noted that numerical difference of 'ψ' values between two stream lines represents the discharge per unit width passing between them.

### 2.7.3 Relation between Equipotential Line and Stream Line

Product of slopes of equipotential line and stream line is [from (i) and (ii) above.]

$$-\dfrac{u}{v} \times \dfrac{v}{u} = -1 \text{ or } mm' = -1$$

If the product of slopes of two lines is minus one (– 1) the lines are orthogonal to each other Fig. 2.5.

Therefore "Stream lines and equipotential lines are orthogonal to each other."

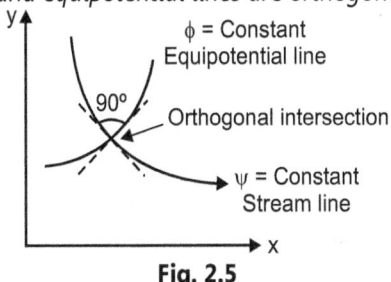

Fig. 2.5

## 2.8 Flow Net

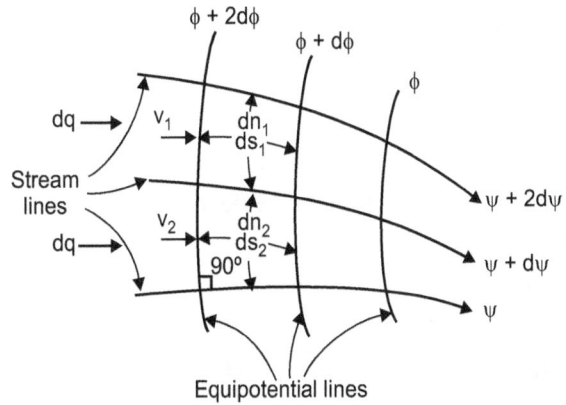

Fig. 2.6: Flow Net

The flow net is the graphical representation of irrotational flow in two dimensions. It is a grid (net) formed by a set of stream lines intersecting orthogonally, a set of equipotential lines.

The stream lines are drawn in such a way that the discharge between the consecutive stream lines is same. The discharge 'dq' is equal to the change in $\psi$ value i.e. $d\psi$ from one stream line to the next. Therefore, stream lines are drawn with equal increment '$d\psi$' between them.

Equipotential lines are drawn normal to stream lines everywhere. They are also drawn with equal spacing '$d\phi$' from one equipotential line to the next equipotential line. Further, both the lines are drawn in such a way that spacing between consecutive stream lines i.e. '$d\psi$' is equal to the spacing between consecutive equipotential lines i.e. '$d\phi$'. Therefore, $d\psi = d\phi$. Therefore, the grid is formed of approximate squares. Fig. 2.6.

Now the discharge between any two stream lines is same. (Width perpendicular to paper is taken as unity).

∴  $\qquad v_1 \, dn_1 = v_2 \, dn_2 = d\psi$ ... (I)

but  $\qquad v_1 = -\dfrac{d\phi}{ds_1}$ and $v_2 = -\dfrac{d\phi}{ds_2}$

∴  $V_1 \, ds_1 = V_2 \, ds_2 = -d\phi = d\phi$ (numerically) ... (II)

Since  $d\psi = d\phi$

From (I) and (II) we can write

$$V_1 \, dn_1 = V_2 \, dn_2 = V_1 \, ds_1 = V_2 \, ds_2$$

or  $\dfrac{V_1}{V_2} = \dfrac{dn_1}{dn_2} = \dfrac{ds_1}{ds_2}$

and  $dn_1 = ds_1$ and $dn_2 = ds_2$

Thus, the flow net grid is made up of number of squares with same or different size. Medians of each square are of the same length. A circle can be drawn in each square to touch all the four sides.

## 2.8.1 Methods of Drawing Flow Net

In order that a flow net can be constructed, the following conditions must be satisfied:
1. The flow should be steady flow.
2. The flow should be irrotational.
3. Gravity force should not govern the flow.

Following methods are used for drawing flow nets:
1. Analytical method
2. Graphical method
3. Experimental analogy method
4. Relaxation method

**1. Analytical Method**

In this method, the expression for $\phi = f(x, y)$ and $\psi = f(x, y)$ are obtained. The flow net is then constructed by plotting values of $\phi$ and $\psi$. The method is applicable only for simple cases.

**2. Graphical Method**

Making use of properties of flow net viz 1. Equipotential lines and stream lines intersect each other orthogonally and 2. The flow grid shall produce squares, a fairly good flow net can be obtained.

First few stream lines are drawn dividing the space between the boundaries (boundaries are stream lines) into few equal number of flow channels. Equipotential lines are then drawn intersecting the stream lines orthogonally and making the flow fields (area between consecutive stream lines and consecutive equipotential lines) approximate square.

By trial and error the net can be perfected. Accuracy of the flow net can be checked by drawing diagonals for the squares. Diagonals should form smooth curves crossing each other orthogonally.

Another check for accuracy of flow net is that the sides of each square should be tangential to a circle drawn inside the square.

## 3. Experimental Analogy Method

Analogy means similarity. Two systems are analogous if they are governed by same law. Thus if various systems are governed by Laplace equation $\nabla^2 \phi = 0$, by conducting experiments in one system, results in the other system can be predicted. Some of the analogies used to draw flow nets are:

1. Electrical Analogy
2. Membrane analogy
3. Viscous flow analogy

Out of these, only first method will be discussed here.

**Electrical Analogy Method:** Both, flow of fluid and the flow of electricity are governed by Laplace equation and hence are analogous. The corresponding (analogous) quantities in the two systems are:

| | Flow of Electricity | Flow of Fluid |
|---|---|---|
| 1. | Electrical potential | Velocity potential ($\phi$) |
| 2. | Electric current | Velocity of fluid flow |
| 3. | Electrical homogeneous conductor | Homogeneous fluid |

**Procedure**

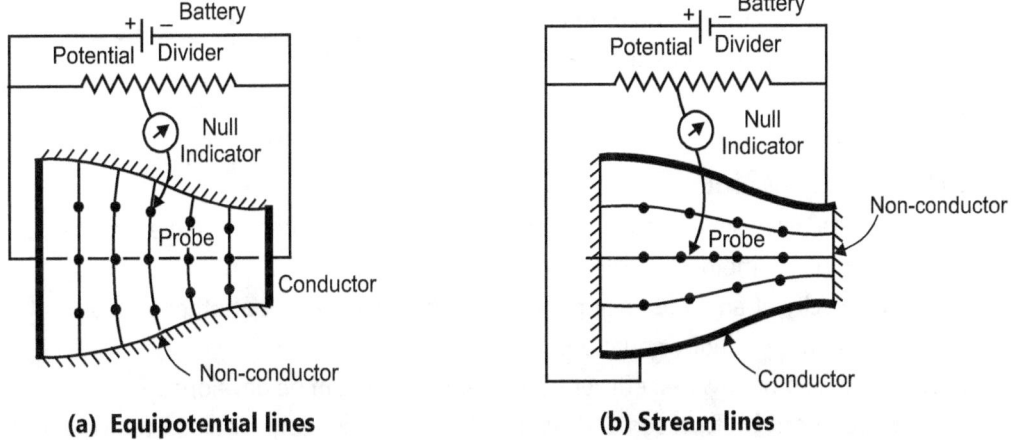

(a) Equipotential lines     (b) Stream lines

Fig. 2.7: Electrical analogy apparatus

First a tray made up of non-conducting material is taken for laying the model. The end equipotential lines are made up of conducting material (generally copper). The fixed boundaries which represent the stream lines are made up of non-conducting material like acrylic sheet. An electrolyte is placed at a uniform depth in the flow space. Electrolyte paper can also be used. Then, voltage is applied between the conducting strips. By means of a voltmeter or a null indicator, in combination with potential divider, lines of constant potential say 90%, 80% ... etc. are traced with the help of moving probe Fig. 2.7 (a). These lines are then plotted. These lines represent equipotential lines. From this pattern of equipotential lines, stream lines are drawn by graphical method. Or otherwise, they can be traced by interchanging the conductors and non-conductors (making fixed boundaries as conducting and the end potential surfaces as non-conducting Fig. 2.7 (b).

Axially symmetrical three dimensional flow problems can also be dealt with by this method.

4. **Relaxation Method**

This method is based on theory of finite differences. First a scale drawing showing the problem is made. The complete flow area is covered by a grid of uniformly spaced points. Fig. 2.8. By proper guess work 'ø' value at different nodes (points of intersection) are then assumed. The relation that should be satisfied by 'ø' values is shown in Fig. 2.8.

$$\phi_1 + \phi_2 + \phi_3 + \phi_4 - 4\phi_0 = 0$$

If the above relation is not satisfied at a given node, the residue is distributed or as it is said "the node is relaxed." (Hence the name "Relaxation Method"). The procedure is continued from node to node till the residues at all the nodes are negligible. From the corrected values of 'ø', equipotential lines and hence the stream lines are drawn to get a flow net.

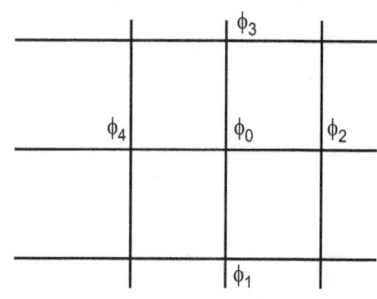

**Fig. 2.8**

## 2.8.2 Uses of Flow Net

1. Since for a given set of boundaries there is only one flow net, the same flow net can be used for geometrically similar boundaries of any size.
2. If the velocity at any reference point is known, the velocities at other points can be found out by continuity equation.
3. With the help of flow net, efficient boundary profiles can be developed.
4. Separation can be foreseen and boundaries can be suitably modified to avoid it or reduce it.
5. The flow net may be used in case of real fluids with sufficient accuracy although it is developed for ideal fluid.
6. Seepage loss in case of hydraulic structures like earthern dams, weirs on permeable foundations etc. can be determined and suitable preventive measures can be designed.
7. Flow net can be effectively used to determine the uplift pressures on hydraulic structures like dams. Further, efficacy of preventive measures can be studied.

## 2.8.3 Limitations of Flow Net

1. The flow net indicates that there is always some velocity at the boundary. However, a real fluid has zero velocity at the boundary due to viscosity. (No-slip condition). Therefore, theory of flow net is not applicable close to the boundary.

2. In case of sharply diverging flow, the flow is very much disturbed due to eddies and reverse flow. As such flow net has limited use in such cases.

3. The flow on upstream side of the solid body is not disturbed while that on the downstream side is highly disturbed due to formation of wake. (zone of disturbance). Therefore, flow net can be used to get correct results on upstream side of the solid body but not on downstream side of the body.

### ILLUSTRATIVE EXAMPLES

**Example 2.1:**

The velocity components of a flow are given by $u = -x$, $v = 2y$ and $w = 5 - z$. Derive the equation of stream line passing through a point (2, 1, 1).

**Solution:**

Equation of stream line is

$$\frac{dx}{u} = \frac{dy}{v} = \frac{dz}{w}$$

Substituting the values of u, v and w, we get

$$\frac{dx}{-x} = \frac{dy}{2y} = \frac{dz}{5-z}$$

Take the first two terms

$$\frac{dx}{-x} = \frac{dy}{2y}$$

Integrating, we get

$$-\log x = \frac{1}{2} \log y + c$$

∴ $\log x + \frac{1}{2} \log y = c_1$

or $x\sqrt{y} = k_1$

when $x = 2$, $y = 1$ ∴ $k_1 = 2$

∴ $\boxed{x\sqrt{y} = 2}$ ... (I)

Taking first and third term

$$\frac{dx}{-x} = \frac{dz}{5-z}$$

Integrating, we get

$$-\log x = -\log(5-z) + c_2$$

or $\dfrac{5-z}{x} = k_2$

when $x = 2$, $z = 1$ ∴ $k_2 = 2$

∴ $\boxed{\dfrac{5-z}{x} = 2}$ ... (II)

Combining (I) and (II), we get the equation of stream line passing through (2, 1, 1) as

$$\boxed{x\sqrt{y} = \dfrac{5-z}{x}}$$

### Example 2.2:

Check whether u, v and w satisfy continuity. $u = x^3 + y^3 - 3z^2 x$, $v = y^3 - 3x^2 y$, $w = z^3 - 3y^2 z + x^3$.

**Solution:**

We have $\dfrac{\partial u}{\partial x} = 3x^2 - 3z^2$, $\dfrac{\partial v}{\partial y} = 3y^2 - 3x^2$, $\dfrac{\partial w}{\partial z} = 3z^2 - 3y^2$

∴ $\dfrac{\partial u}{\partial x} + \dfrac{\partial v}{\partial y} + \dfrac{\partial w}{\partial z} = 0$

∴ $\boxed{u, v \text{ and } w \text{ satisfy continuity}}$

### Example 2.3:

For the flow of an incompressible fluid, the velocity component in the X-direction is $u = ax^2 + by$ and the velocity component in the Z-direction is zero. Find the velocity component v in the Y-direction such that $v = 0$ at $y = 0$.

**Solution:**

$u = ax^2 + by$

∴ $\dfrac{\partial u}{\partial x} = 2ax$

But for continuity $\dfrac{\partial u}{\partial x} + \dfrac{\partial v}{\partial y} + \dfrac{\partial w}{\partial z} = 0$

∴ $\dfrac{\partial u}{\partial x} + \dfrac{\partial v}{\partial y} = 0$, ∵ $w = 0$, given

∴ $2ax + \dfrac{\partial v}{\partial y} = 0$ or $\dfrac{\partial v}{\partial y} = -2ax$

Integrating, we get $v = -2axy + c$

But it is given that when $y = 0$, $v = 0$ ∴ $c = 0$

∴ $\boxed{v = -2axy}$

## Example 2.4:

In a three dimensional fluid flow, two velocity components u and v are $u = 2x^2$ and $v = 2xyz$. Find the third component 'w' such that the continuity equation is satisfied.

### Solution:

$$u = 2x^2 \quad \therefore \quad \frac{\partial u}{\partial x} = 4x, \quad v = 2xyz \quad \therefore \quad \frac{\partial v}{\partial y} = 2xz$$

For continuity
$$\frac{\partial u}{\partial x} + \frac{\partial v}{\partial y} + \frac{\partial w}{\partial z} = 0$$

$$\therefore \quad 4x + 2xz + \frac{\partial w}{\partial z} = 0$$

$$\therefore \quad \frac{\partial w}{\partial z} = -4x - 2xz$$

$$\therefore \quad \boxed{w = -4xz - xz^2 + f(xy)}$$

## THEORETICAL QUESTIONS

1. What do you understand by Kinematics of fluid flow?

2. What is flow of fluid? Which are the methods of analysis of fluid flow?

3. What is the difference between Lagrangian and Eulerian methods of studying a fluid flow?

4. Define: (i) Path line, (ii) Stream line, (iii) Stream tube and (iv) Streak line. What is the special feature of concept of stream tube?

OR

Differentiate between Path line, Streak line and Stream line.

5. Derive equation for stream line, u dy − v dx = 0, for a plane flow in x–y plane.

6. Describe the types of flow bringing out their characteristics.

7. Define the following terms:

    (i) Discharge

    (ii) Mean velocity

    (iii) Stream line

    (iv) Unsteady flow

8. How are the flows classified?

9. Define:
    (i) Steady flow and Unsteady flow
    (ii) Uniform and Non–uniform flow
    What combinations of above flows are possible? Give one example of each such combination.
10. Distinguish between Rotational and Irrotational flow.
11. Define 1 – D, 2 – D and 3 – D flows and give one example of each.
12. Define stream function and velocity potential. Show that the lines of constant stream function and velocity potential must intersect orthogonally.
13. Show that stream lines and equipotential lines always intersect orthogonally from the first principles. What is the significance of this perpendicularity.
14. What is a flow net? What are its uses? What are the methods of drawing a flow net? What are the limitations of flow net?
15. Explain electrical analogy method of drawing a flow net.
16. Distinguish clearly between Laminar flow and Turbulent flow.
17. Classify the following flows as steady, unsteady, uniform and non-uniform.
    (i) Constant discharge through converging pipe under constant temperature.
    (ii) Flow of constant discharge in a long rectangular passage of constant width of wind tunnel.
    (iii) Constant discharge along a long bend.
    [**Ans.:** (i) Steady non–uniform, (ii) Steady uniform, (iii) Steady non–uniform]
18. Identify correct types of flow (state whether steady/unsteady, uniform/non-uniform and compressible/incompressible types clearly).
    (i) Kerosene flowing up through a constant diameter pipe of P.V.C. at constant velocity.
    (ii) Blood circulation through arteries, capillaries.
    (iii) Air flowing from nozzle at the end of pipe with constant rate.
    (iv) Petrol flowing from tank through carburetter of vehicle.
    [**Ans.:** (i) Steady, uniform, incompressible, (ii) Unsteady, non-uniform, incompressible, (iii) Steady, non-uniform, compressible, (iv) Unsteady, non-uniform, incompressible].

# (B) DYNAMICS OF FLUID FLOW

## 2.9 Basic Principles of Fluid Flow Analysis

Basic principles used to analyse motion of solid, are suitably modified so that they can be used to analyse fluid flow. They are as follows:

| Basic Principle | Equivalent fluid flow principle |
|---|---|
| 1. Conservation of mass | 1. Continuity equation |
| 2. Conservation of energy | 2. Energy equation |
| 3. Conservation of momentum | 3. Momentum equation |

Out of these, continuity equation is derived here. Other two will be derived in the next chapter.

## 2.10 Continuity Equation for Three Dimensional Flow in Cartesian Coordinates

Consider an elementary element in the form of a parallelopiped with sides $\delta x$, $\delta y$ and $\delta z$ as shown in Fig. 2.9. Let P (x, y, z) be the centroid of the element. Let u, v and w be the components of velocity vector in x, y and z directions respectively and $\rho$ the mass density of fluid at the centroid.

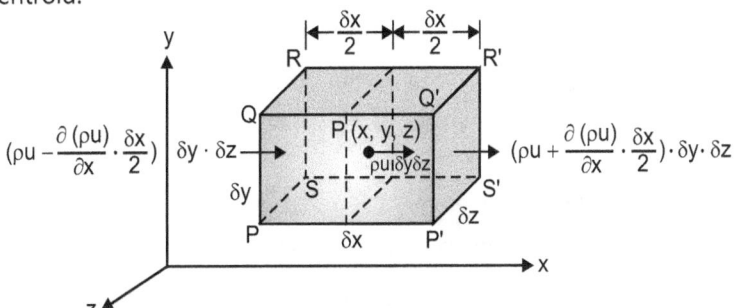

**Fig. 2.9: Continuity Equation - Elementary Parallelopiped**

By conservation of mass principle we can write:

  Rate of inflow of mass in the element = Rate of outflow of mass in the element + Rate of increase of mass in the element

Now consider faces PQRS and P'Q'R'S' perpendicular to x axis.

Rate of inflow of mass in the element through 'PQRS'.

$$\left[\rho u - \frac{\partial(\rho u)}{\partial x} \cdot \frac{\delta x}{2}\right] \delta y \cdot \delta z \quad - \text{(Inflow)}$$

**[Note:** Rate of flow of mass through PQRS = Rate of flow of mass through central section $- \frac{\partial}{\partial x}$ (rate of flow of mass through central section) × (distance between PQRS and central section)

∴ Rate of flow of mass through PQRS $= \rho u \cdot \delta y \cdot \delta z - \dfrac{\partial}{\partial x}(\rho u \cdot \delta y \cdot \delta z) \cdot \dfrac{\delta x}{2}$

$$= \left[\rho u - \dfrac{\partial(\rho u)}{\partial x} \cdot \dfrac{\delta x}{2}\right] \cdot \delta y \cdot \delta z$$

– ve sign is used because PQRS is in – ve 'x' direction from central section.

Similarly, we can write the rate of outflow of mass from the element through face P'Q'R'S'.

$$\left[\rho u + \dfrac{\partial(\rho u)}{\partial x} \cdot \dfrac{\delta x}{2}\right] \delta y \cdot \delta z \quad - \text{(outflow)}$$

Therefore, Net rate of increase of mass in the element through the pair of faces PQRS and P'Q'R'S' is given by

Rate of increase of mass = Inflow – Outflow

$$= -\dfrac{\partial(\rho u)}{\partial x} \cdot \delta x \cdot \delta y \cdot \delta z \quad \ldots \text{(I)}$$

Similarly rate of increase of mass in the element through other two pairs of faces can be written as:

$-\dfrac{\partial(\rho v)}{\partial y} \cdot \delta x \cdot \delta y \cdot \delta z \quad \ldots \text{(II)}$  thro' pair of faces PP'S'S & QQ'R'R

$-\dfrac{\partial(\rho w)}{\partial z} \cdot \delta x \cdot \delta y \cdot \delta z \quad \ldots \text{(III)}$  thro' pair of faces SS'R'R & PP'Q'Q

∴ Net rate of increase of mass in the element is I + II + III i.e.

$$\left[-\dfrac{\partial(\rho u)}{\partial x} - \dfrac{\partial(\rho v)}{\partial y} - \dfrac{\partial(\rho w)}{\partial z}\right] \cdot \delta x \cdot \delta y \cdot \delta z \quad \ldots \text{(IV)}$$

Now the mass of fluid in the element $= \rho \cdot \delta x \cdot \delta y \cdot \delta z$

∴ Rate of increase of mass can also be written as:

$$\dfrac{\partial}{\partial t}(\rho \cdot \delta x \cdot \delta y \cdot \delta z)$$

or $\dfrac{\partial \rho}{\partial t}(\delta x \cdot \delta y \cdot \delta z) \quad \ldots \text{(V)}$

Equating (IV) and (V)

$$\left[-\dfrac{\partial(\rho u)}{\partial x} - \dfrac{\partial(\rho u)}{\partial y} - \dfrac{\partial(\rho w)}{\partial z}\right] \cdot \delta x \cdot \delta y \cdot \delta z = \dfrac{\partial \rho}{\partial t}(\delta x \cdot \delta y \cdot \delta z)$$

or $\boxed{\dfrac{\partial \rho}{\partial t} + \dfrac{\partial(\rho u)}{\partial x} + \dfrac{\partial(\rho v)}{\partial y} + \dfrac{\partial(\rho w)}{\partial z} = 0} \quad \ldots (2.4)$

**This is the continuity equation for three dimensional flow in cartesian co-ordinates. This is the most general form of continuity equation applicable to steady, unsteady, uniform, non-uniform as well as compressible and incompressible flow.**

For steady flow $\quad \dfrac{\partial \rho}{\partial t} = 0$

∴ Continuity equation for steady flow is

$$\boxed{\dfrac{\partial(\rho u)}{\partial x} + \dfrac{\partial(\rho u)}{\partial y} + \dfrac{\partial(\rho w)}{\partial z} = 0} \qquad \text{... (2.5)}$$

For incompressible fluid, ρ is constant

∴ Continuity equation for steady-incompressible flow takes the form

$$\boxed{\dfrac{\partial u}{\partial x} + \dfrac{\partial v}{\partial y} + \dfrac{\partial w}{\partial z} = 0} \quad \text{or} \quad \nabla \cdot V = \text{div } V = 0 \qquad \text{... (2.6)}$$

For two dimensional flow,

$$\boxed{\dfrac{\partial u}{\partial x} + \dfrac{\partial v}{\partial y} = 0} \qquad \text{... (2.7)}$$

## 2.11 Continuity Equation for One Dimensional Flow

In order to derive continuity equation for one dimensional flow, consider an elementary element in the form of a tube shaped volume of fluid along a stream tube as shown in Fig. 2.10. The flow takes place only from the ends of the element and not through the surface of the element. Let A, V and ρ be the area of cross-section, velocity and mass density of fluid at the central section of the element. A, V and ρ are functions of S only. Then following steps, similar to those in three dimensional case we can write.

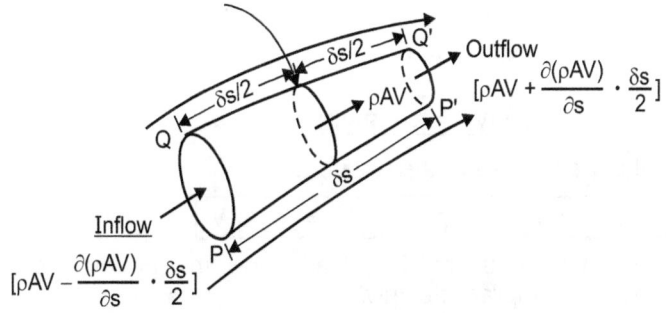

Fig. 2.10: Flow through a stream tube

∴ Rate of inflow of mass in the element through PQ

$$= \left[ \rho AV - \dfrac{\partial(\rho AV)}{\partial s} \cdot \dfrac{\delta s}{2} \right] \qquad \text{... (I)}$$

Rate of outflow of mass from the element through P'Q'

$$= \left[ \rho AV + \dfrac{\partial(\rho AV)}{\partial s} \cdot \dfrac{\delta s}{2} \right] \qquad \text{... (II)}$$

∴ Net rate of increase of mass in the element
$$= \text{Inflow} - \text{Outflow} = I - II$$
$$= -\frac{\partial}{\partial s}(\rho AV) \cdot \delta s \qquad \ldots (III)$$

Now the mass of fluid in the element
$$= \rho \times \text{volume of element}$$
$$= \rho \times \text{Average area at the central section} \times \delta s$$
$$= \rho A \delta s$$

Therefore, the rate of increase of mass in the element can also be written as:
$$\frac{\partial}{\partial t}(\rho A \delta s)$$
$$= \frac{\partial}{\partial t}(\rho A) \cdot \delta s \qquad \ldots (IV)$$

Equating (III) and (IV), we get
$$\frac{\partial}{\partial t}(\rho A) \delta s = -\frac{\partial}{\partial s}(\rho AV) \cdot \delta s$$

Cancelling $\delta s$,
$$\boxed{\frac{\partial (\rho A)}{\partial t} + \frac{\partial}{\partial s}(\rho AV) = 0} \qquad \ldots (2.8)$$

This is the most general form of continuity equation for one dimensional flow and is applicable to steady, unsteady, uniform, non-uniform as well as compressible and incompressible flows.

For steady flow, variation of parameters of flow w.r.t. time is zero. Therefore, for steady flow
$$\frac{\partial(\rho A)}{\partial t} = 0$$

∴
$$\frac{\partial}{\partial s}(\rho AV) = 0$$

or $\boxed{\rho AV = \text{constant}} \qquad \ldots (2.9)$

or for different cross sections of the stream tube
$$\boxed{\rho_1 A_1 V_1 = \rho_2 A_2 V_2 = \rho_3 A_3 V_3 \ldots = \rho_n A_n V_n} \qquad \ldots (2.10)$$

This is the continuity equation for steady flow in one dimension, applicable to compressible as well as incompressible flow.

For incompressible fluid, $\rho$ is constant

∴ Continuity equation for steady, one dimensional flow of an incompressible fluid can be written as
$$\frac{\partial}{\partial s}(AV) = 0$$

or $\boxed{AV = \text{constant}} \qquad \ldots (2.11)$

or $\boxed{A_1 V_1 = A_2 V_2 = A_3 V_3 \ldots = A_n V_n = \text{constant}} \qquad \ldots (2.12)$

## 2.12 Euler's Equation and Bernoulli's Equation

Study of motion of fluid including study of forces causing the motion and corresponding energy changes that take place, is covered under "Dynamics of fluid flow."

As in the case of dynamics of solids, dynamics of fluid flow is also governed by Newton's second law of motion.

Newton's second law of motion states *"The rate of change of momentum is proportional to the impressed force and takes place in the direction of that force."* It can be expressed as

$$\Sigma F = M \cdot a \qquad \ldots (2.13)$$

where
$\Sigma F$ = sum of all external forces in the direction of motion acting on the element of fluid,

M = mass of fluid and a = acceleration.

In three co-ordinate directions, we can write

$$\Sigma F_x = M \cdot a_x$$
$$\Sigma F_y = M \cdot a_y \qquad \ldots (2.14)$$
$$\Sigma F_z = M \cdot a_z$$

where $F_x$, $F_y$ and $F_z$ are components of force in x, y, z directions and $a_x$, $a_y$, $a_z$ the components of 'a' in x, y, z directions respectively.

## 2.13 Important Forces in Fluid Flow

The forces which are generally found to influence the fluid flow are as follows:

1. **Gravity force:** This is due to weight of fluid and is given by M.g. .......................... $F_g$

2. **Pressure force:** The external force due to difference of pressure between two points in the flowing fluid. .......................... $F_p$

3. **Viscous force:** This is due to viscosity of fluid. It always exists in case of real fluids although it does not exist in case of ideal fluids. .......................... $F_v$

4. **Turbulent force:** This is due to turbulence of flow. In turbulent flow, there is continuous momentum exchange between adjacent layers which is responsible for turbulent force. This force is absent in laminar flow. .......................... $F_t$

5. **Surface tension force:** This is due to cohesion between molecules of fluid (liquid). This is important only in case of thin films and when the depth of flow is very small. .......................... $F_s$

6. **Elastic force:** This is due to elastic properties of fluids. This is important when fluid is compressible. It is important in case of incompressible fluids only in some phenomena like water hammer wherein the fluid is subjected to stresses of very high magnitude. .......................... $F_e$

## 2.14 Equations of Motion

(1) Taking into account all the above forces and applying Newton's law of motion, we can write

$$M \cdot a = F_g + F_p + F_v + F_t + F_e + F_s \qquad \ldots (2.15)$$

with proper suffixes equations can be written for x, y, z directions.

(2) In majority of fluid flow problems, $F_e$ is negligible since fluid is incompressible and $F_s$ is negligible since depth of flow is sufficiently large. Therefore, neglecting $F_e$ and $F_s$, the equations of motion may be written as

$$M \cdot a = F_g + F_p + F_v + F_t \qquad \ldots (2.16)$$

and for x, y, z directions

$$\left. \begin{array}{l} M \cdot a_x = F_{gx} + F_{px} + F_{vx} + F_{tx} \\ M \cdot a_y = F_{gy} + F_{py} + F_{vy} + F_{ty} \\ M \cdot a_z = F_{gz} + F_{pz} + F_{vz} + F_{tz} \end{array} \right\} \qquad \ldots (2.17)$$

These equations (2.17) are called "Reynold's Equations" and are applicable to turbulent flow.

(3) If the flow is laminar flow, turbulent forces are also negligible. Therefore, the equations of motion can be written as

$$M \cdot a = F_g + F_p + F_v \qquad \ldots (2.18)$$

and for x, y, z directions

$$\left. \begin{array}{l} M \cdot a_x = F_{gx} + F_{px} + F_{vx} \\ M \cdot a_y = F_{gy} + F_{py} + F_{vy} \\ M \cdot a_z = F_{gz} + F_{pz} + F_{vz} \end{array} \right\} \qquad \ldots (2.19)$$

Equations (2.19) are known as "Navier-Stokes" equations and are applicable to viscous flow.

(4) Further, if fluid is ideal fluid (non-viscous) or real fluid with very low viscosity, viscous forces can be neglected and the equations reduce to

$$M \cdot a = F_g + F_p \qquad \ldots (2.20)$$

and for x, y, z directions

$$\left. \begin{array}{l} M \cdot a_x = F_{gx} + F_{px} \\ M \cdot a_y = F_{gy} + F_{py} \\ M \cdot a_z = F_{gz} + F_{pz} \end{array} \right\} \qquad \ldots (2.21)$$

These equations (2.21) are called "Euler's equations of motion".

## 2.15 2D Euler's Equation of Motion along a Stream Line

Consider steady flow of an incompressible non-viscous fluid (ideal fluid). Consider a cylindrical element of fluid with cross-sectional area '$\delta A$' and length '$\delta s$', moving along a stream line as shown in Fig. 2.11.

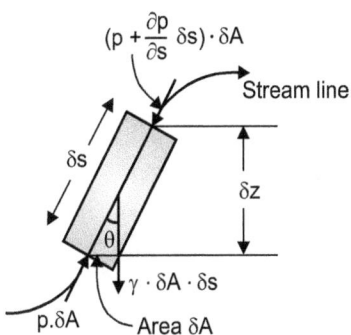

**Fig. 2.11: Euler's equation along a stream line**

Let V be the velocity of the element and '$a_s$' the acceleration. Forces acting on the element are as shown in Fig. 2.11.

(1) Pressure force on the lower face of the element = $p \cdot \delta A$

Pressure forces on the upper face of element = $\left(p + \dfrac{\partial p}{\partial s} \cdot \delta s\right) \cdot \delta A$

Both these forces will act normal to the faces as shown in Fig. 2.11.

∴ Net pressure force on the element in the direction of motion,

$$F_{ps} = p \cdot \delta A - \left(p + \dfrac{\partial p}{\partial s} \cdot \delta s\right) \delta A$$

∴
$$F_{ps} = -\dfrac{\partial p}{\partial s} \cdot \delta A \, \delta s \qquad \ldots (2.22)$$

(2) Weight of the element is $\gamma \, \delta A \, \delta s$ acting through the centre of gravity in vertically downward direction. The component of gravity force (weight) in the direction of motion will be

$$F_{gs} = -\gamma \, \delta A \, \delta s \cos \theta \qquad \ldots (2.23)$$

Now applying Newton's second law of motion, we get

$$\Sigma F_s = M \cdot a_s$$

or
$$F_{gs} + F_{ps} = (\rho \, \delta A \, \delta s) \, a_s$$

Substituting values of $F_{gs}$ and $F_{ps}$, we get

$$-\gamma\, \delta A \delta s \cos\theta - \frac{\partial p}{\partial s} \cdot \delta A \delta s = (\rho\, \delta A\, \delta s)\, a_s$$

(gravity force)   (pressure force)   mass × acc.

Dividing by $\delta A\, \delta s$

$$-\gamma \cos\theta - \frac{\partial p}{\partial s} = \rho \cdot a_s$$

But V is function of s and t [V = f (s, t)], hence

$$a_s = \frac{dV}{dt} = \frac{\partial V}{\partial t} + V \frac{\partial V}{\partial s}$$

Therefore,

$$-\gamma \cos\theta - \frac{\partial p}{\partial s} = \rho \left( \frac{\partial V}{\partial t} + V \frac{\partial V}{\partial s} \right)$$

or

$$\gamma \cdot \frac{\delta Z}{\delta s} + \frac{\partial p}{\partial s} + \rho \left( \frac{\partial V}{\partial t} + V \frac{\partial V}{\partial s} \right) = 0 \qquad \because \cos\theta = \frac{\delta Z}{\delta s}$$

or Dividing by '$\rho$' we get,

$$\boxed{g \cdot \frac{\delta Z}{\delta s} + \frac{1}{\rho} \frac{\partial p}{\partial s} + \left( \frac{\partial V}{\partial t} + V \frac{\partial V}{\partial s} \right) = 0}$$

This is the general form of Euler's equation of motion along a stream line.

If the flow is steady flow, $\frac{\partial V}{\partial t} = 0$

$$\therefore \quad g \cdot \frac{\delta Z}{\delta s} + \frac{1}{\rho} \frac{\partial p}{\partial s} + V \frac{\partial V}{\partial s} = 0$$

Since, all the differentials in the above equation are with respect to 's' only, partial derivatives can be replaced by total derivatives and hence

$$\boxed{g \cdot \frac{dZ}{ds} + \frac{1}{\rho} \frac{dp}{ds} + V \frac{dV}{ds} = 0} \qquad \ldots (2.24)$$

This equation can also be written as

$$\boxed{g \cdot dZ + \frac{dp}{\rho} + V dV = 0} \qquad \ldots (2.25)$$

This is the "Euler's equation" of motion along a stream line and is applicable to steady, compressible as well as incompressible flow of non-viscous fluid.

## 2.16 Bernoulli's Equation

Bernoulli's equation is obtained by integration of Euler's equation along a stream line.
Integrating Euler's equation, along a stream line, we get

$$\boxed{gZ + \int \frac{dp}{\rho} + \frac{V^2}{2} = \text{Constant}} \qquad \ldots (2.26)$$

This equation is "Bernoulli's equation." This can be applied to compressible as well as incompressible fluids.

The term $\int \frac{dp}{\rho}$ can be evaluated only if '$\rho$' is constant (incompressible fluids) or '$\rho$' can be expressed as known function of '$p$' (compressible fluids).

In case of incompressible fluids, $\rho$ is constant and hence Bernoulli's equation can be written as

$$\boxed{gZ + \frac{p}{\rho} + \frac{V^2}{2} = \text{Constant}} \qquad \ldots (2.27)$$

Dividing by '$g$'

$$\boxed{Z + \frac{p}{\gamma} + \frac{V^2}{2g} = \text{Constant}} \qquad \ldots (2.28)$$

This is Bernoulli's equation for incompressible fluids. The constant on the right hand side is called "Bernoulli's" constant. It is constant for a particular stream line but varies from stream line to stream line.

Bernoulli's equation is a very useful equation since it co-relates pressure changes, velocity changes and elevation changes.

### 2.16.1 Assumptions Made in Derivation of Bernoulli's Equation

Following assumptions are made in deriving the Bernoulli's equation in the form of equation (2.28):

(1) Flow is steady flow.
(2) Fluid is incompressible.
(3) Fluid is non-viscous (Inviscid).
(4) Equation is applicable along a stream line.
(5) Only pressure and gravity forces are taken into account.
(6) Velocity is uniform over the cross-section.

## 2.16.2 Significance of Various Terms in Bernoulli's Theorem

(1) Most commonly used form of Bernoulli's equation is

$$Z + \frac{p}{\gamma} + \frac{V^2}{2g} = \text{Constant}$$

**Statement of Bernoulli's Equation:**

*"In a steady flow of an ideal fluid (incompressible and non-viscous), the total head of any particle, is same along a stream line."*

Total head of any particle at a given instant is sum of its (i) datum head, (ii) pressure head and (iii) velocity head.

### (i) Datum Head:

Potential energy possessed by 'W' newton's of fluid when raised through height 'Z' above a datum level is "WZ" (see Fig. 2.12). Therefore, potential energy possessed by one newton of fluid is $\frac{WZ}{W}$ = Z N-m/N or simply 'Z' m. This energy, thus, can be expressed in linear dimensions and is called "Datum head" and denoted by 'Z'. Thus, *"potential energy per newton (unit weight) of fluid is called Datum head."*

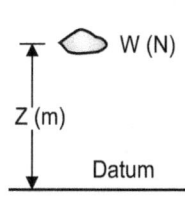

Fig. 2.12: Datum head

(**Note:** Any horizontal plane w.r.t. which energy is recorded is called "datum".)

### (ii) Pressure Head:

Consider a pipe attached to a tank as shown in Fig. 2.13. Let a piston with area 'A' be moved through a distance 'ds' against pressure 'p'. Volume of fluid displaced is A·ds and work done is p·A·ds.

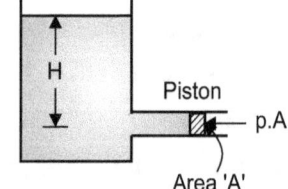

Therefore, work done per newton of fluid is

$$\frac{p \cdot A \cdot ds}{\gamma \cdot A \cdot ds} = \frac{p}{\gamma}$$

Fig. 2.13: Pressure head

This also has a linear dimension $\left(\text{since } \frac{p}{\gamma} = H\right)$. Capacity to do work is energy. Thus, $p/\gamma$ is flow energy per newton of liquid and is called pressure head.

Thus *"flow energy per newton (unit weight) of fluid is called pressure head."*

## (iii) Velocity Head:

W newtons of fluid when moving with velocity 'V' possess kinetic energy $W \cdot \dfrac{V^2}{2g}$.

Therefore, kinetic energy possessed by one newton of fluid when moving with velocity 'V' is

$$\dfrac{W \cdot \dfrac{V^2}{2g}}{W} = \dfrac{V^2}{2g}.$$ This energy also can be expressed in linear dimension $\left(\left[\dfrac{L^2 T^{-2}}{LT^{-2}}\right] = [L]\right)$ and is called velocity head.

*Thus "kinetic energy per newton (unit weight) of fluid is called velocity head."*

∴ Total head = Datum head + Pressure head + Velocity head

$$= Z + \dfrac{p}{\gamma} + \dfrac{V^2}{2g}$$

It may be noted that total head is also the total energy per newton (unit weight) of fluid.

**Other forms of Bernoulli's equation:**

Bernoulli's equation can be written in the following two alternate forms:

(i) Multiplying equation (6.28) by 'g', we get

$$gZ + \dfrac{p}{\rho} + \dfrac{V^2}{2} = \text{Constant} \qquad \text{... (2.29)}$$

Each term in this equation represents energy per unit mass (kg) of fluid.

(ii) Multiplying equation (6.28) by 'γ' we get,

$$\gamma Z + p + \dfrac{\rho V^2}{2} = \text{Constant} \qquad \text{... (2.30)}$$

Each term in this equation represents energy per unit volume of fluid.

Thus, when Bernoulli's equation is applied between two points 1 and 2, we can write

$$Z_1 + \dfrac{p_1}{\gamma} + \dfrac{V_1^2}{2g} = Z_2 + \dfrac{p_2}{\gamma} + \dfrac{V_2^2}{2g} \qquad \text{... (2.31)}$$

Graphical representation of this equation is shown in Fig. 2.14.

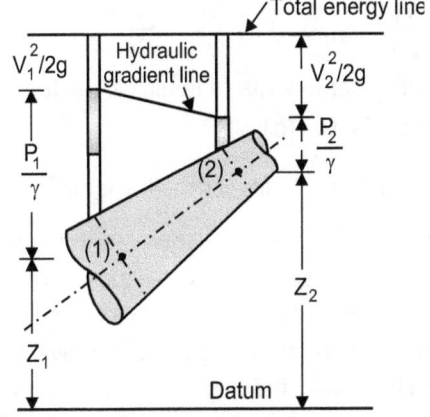

**Fig. 2.14: Bernoulli's equation (Ideal fluid)**

## 2.16.3 Limitations of Bernoulli's Equation

(1) In actual practice, fluid is not ideal fluid. Therefore, due to no slip condition, velocity at the fixed boundary of passage is zero and goes on increasing away from the boundary. Thus, velocity is not uniform across the section as assumed.

(2) In actual practice, some forces like viscous forces are involved in addition to gravity and pressure forces.

(3) Some energy additions or subtractions may take place as fluid passes from one section to the other.

## 2.16.4 Modifications of Bernoulli's Equations

### (i) For loss of head:

If there is loss of energy as the fluid passes from section '1' to section '2', Bernoulli's equation can be modified as follows

$$Z_1 + \frac{p_1}{\gamma} + \frac{V_1^2}{2g} = Z_2 + \frac{p_2}{\gamma} + \frac{V_2^2}{2g} + h_L \qquad \ldots (2.32)$$

(Upstream section)     (Downstream section)

where $h_L$ is loss of head (i.e. loss of energy per newton of fluid). Thus, loss of energy is to be added to the energy of the downstream point (which is reached afterwards in the direction of flow).

### (ii) For addition of head:

If an energy adding device like pump is installed between section '1' and section '2', Bernoulli's equation can be modified as

$$Z_1 + \frac{p_1}{\gamma} + \frac{V_1^2}{2g} + h_p = Z_2 + \frac{p_2}{\gamma} + \frac{V_2^2}{2g} \qquad \ldots (2.33)$$

(Upstream section)     (Downstream section)

where $h_p$ is the head (energy per newton of fluid) supplied by the device.

### (iii) For extraction of energy:

If an energy extracting device like a turbine is installed between section 1 and section 2, Bernoulli's equation can be modified as

$$Z_1 + \frac{p_1}{\gamma} + \frac{V_1^2}{2g} - h_T = Z_2 + \frac{p_2}{\gamma} + \frac{V_2^2}{2g} \qquad \ldots (2.34)$$

where $h_T$ is the head (energy per newton of liquid) extracted by the device.

### (iv) Kinetic energy correction factor ($\alpha$):

While calculating velocity head $\frac{V^2}{2g}$ in Bernoulli's equation, velocity is assumed to be uniform over the cross-section of the passage. However, this is not true in case of real fluids and the velocity varies over the cross section of the passage. Therefore, actual kinetic energy of fluid passing through a section, calculated, taking into account velocity variation is different from the kinetic energy calculated on the basis of average velocity.

Consider Fig. 2.15 which shows the cross-section of passage (pipe) and velocity distribution. Consider elementary area 'dA'. Let 'v' be the local velocity of fluid through area 'dA'.

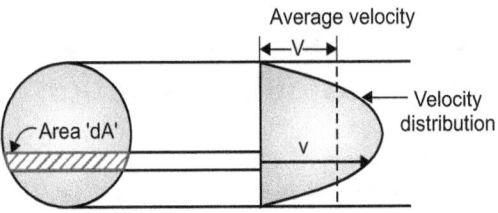

Fig. 2.15: Energy correction factor

Mass of fluid passing through area 'dA' per unit time is $\rho v dA$ and the kinetic energy of this mass will be $(\rho v\, dA)\dfrac{v^2}{2}$. Therefore, total kinetic energy of fluid passing through the entire cross-section A is

$$\int_A \frac{1}{2} \rho v^3\, dA$$

Knowing the velocity profile over the cross section, the actual kinetic energy given by the above integral can be calculated.

But kinetic energy based on the average velocity 'V', passing through the section with area 'A' is

$$\frac{1}{2} \rho V^3 \cdot A$$

In order to compensate for the difference between these two kinetic energies, a coefficient called "*energy correction factor*" denoted by '$\alpha$' is introduced. $\alpha \dfrac{V^2}{2g}$ gives the kinetic energy actually passing a section.

Thus, Kinetic energy correction factor '$\alpha$'

$$= \frac{[\text{Kinetic energy, per second, calculated taking into account actual velocity variation}]}{[\text{Kinetic energy, per second, calculated on the basis of average velocity}]}$$

$$\alpha = \frac{\int_A \frac{1}{2}\rho v^3\, dA}{\frac{1}{2}\rho V^3 A} \qquad \ldots (2.35)$$

or $\boxed{\alpha = \dfrac{1}{A}\int_A \left(\dfrac{v}{V}\right)^3 dA}$  for incompressible fluid, ... (2.36)

For laminar flow through a circular pipe, '$\alpha$' has a value of 2. Since, the velocity is more or less uniform for turbulent flow, '$\alpha$' varies between 1.01 to 1.15 and hence is generally neglected without affecting the results.

Accounting for energy correction factor, Bernoulli's equation can be modified as

$$Z_1 + \frac{p_1}{\gamma} + \alpha_1 \frac{V_1^2}{2g} = Z_2 + \frac{p_2}{\gamma} + \alpha_2 \frac{V_2^2}{2g}$$

$\alpha$ is taken into account only when very accurate results are required.

## (C) APPLICATIONS OF BERNOULLI'S EQUATION

## 2.17 Applications of Bernoulli's Equation

Bernoulli's equation alongwith continuity equation is very widely used in fluid mechanics for solution of wide variety of problems of fluid flow.

Some of the devices based on Bernoulli's equation are described in the following articles.

### 2.17.1 Pitot Tube

Pitot tube is a very simple device based on Bernoulli's theorem and is used for measurement of velocity of flow. If the velocity of flow is reduced to zero at a point called stagnation point, the kinetic energy of fluid and hence velocity head $\frac{V^2}{2g}$ is reduced to zero. But energy can neither be created nor destroyed. Thus, the velocity head is converted in terms of pressure head. By measuring this increase in pressure head, velocity of flow can be determined. Pitot tube named after the inventor Henri de Pitot, a French Engineer, is based on this concept of conversion of velocity head into pressure head.

*2.17.1.1 Measurement of Velocity in Open Channel*

In its simplest form, a pitot tube consists of 'L' shaped glass tube bent at right angles with both ends open. Such a simple tube can be used to measure velocity in an open channel as shown in Fig. 2.16. The tube is placed in a flow in such a way that, the open end of the tube faces the flow (i.e. opposite to flow direction) while other end is vertical and open to atmospheric pressure.

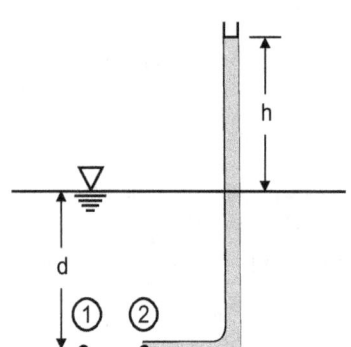

Fig. 2.16: Simple Pitot tube

When the tube is placed in the flow, the liquid enters the tube at the opening (2) until it rises to height 'h' above the liquid level in the channel.

Point (1) is the point in undisturbed flow where velocity of liquid is 'V' and point (2) is the stagnation point where velocity is brought to zero.

Applying Bernoulli's theorem to (1) and (2) taking horizontal through (1) and (2) as datum

$$Z_1 + \frac{p_1}{\gamma} + \frac{V_1^2}{2g} = Z_2 + \frac{p_2}{\gamma} + \frac{V_2^2}{2g} \quad \text{(neglecting losses)}$$

Substituting the values,

$$0 + d + \frac{V^2}{2g} = 0 + (d + h) + 0$$

$$\frac{V^2}{2g} = h$$

or
$$V = \sqrt{2gh} \qquad \ldots (2.37)$$

The total pressure at stagnation point 2 is sum of d, the static head and $\frac{V^2}{2g}$, the dynamic head.

In order to account for the losses, a coefficient is introduced. Therefore, actual velocity is given by

$$V = C\sqrt{2gh} \qquad \ldots (2.38)$$

Value of 'C', the coefficient of Pitot tube, ranges from 0.97 to 1. The practical value may be taken as 0.98.

### 2.17.1.2 Measurement of Velocity in a Pipe

The simple pitot tube can also be used for measurement of velocity in a closed conduit like pipe, which carries liquid under pressure.

(a) If the tube is introduced as shown in Fig. 2.17, it records static head (p/γ) plus the dynamic head $\left(\frac{V^2}{2g} = h\right)$. To find out only $\frac{V^2}{2g} = h$, the static pressure is measured with the help of a simple piezometer which is connected to the pressure tapping on the pipe above the stagnation point.

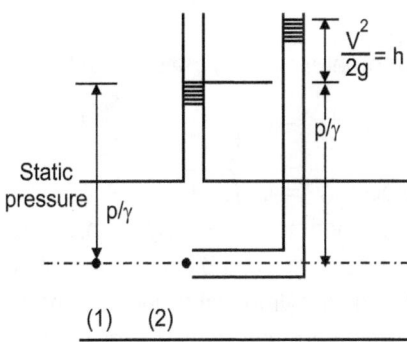

Fig. 2.17: Velocity measurement in pipe with Pitot tube

(b) The above arrangement, however, cannot be used, if (1) static pressure is high and (2) if pipe carries gas. In this case, the dynamic pressure is measured with the help of a differential manometer as shown in Fig. 2.18.

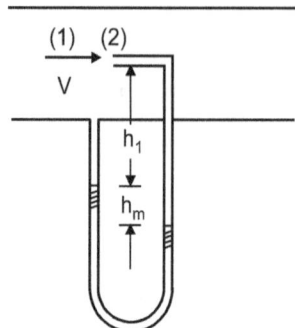

**Fig. 2.18: Velocity measurement with Pitot tube**

Applying Bernoulli's equation between point (1) and stagnation point (2), we get

$$Z_1 + \frac{p_1}{\gamma} + \frac{V_1^2}{2g} = Z_2 + \frac{p_2}{\gamma} + \frac{V_2^2}{2g}$$

The tube is placed such that $Z_1 = Z_2$. Substituting the other values,

$$\frac{V^2}{2g} = \frac{p_2}{\gamma} - \frac{p_1}{\gamma}, \qquad \therefore V_1 = V \text{ and } V_2 = 0 \qquad \ldots \text{(i)}$$

$\frac{p_2}{\gamma} - \frac{p_1}{\gamma}$ can be obtained by writing manometric equation as

$$\frac{p_1}{\gamma} + h_1 + h_m \cdot \frac{S_m}{S_p} - h_m - h_1 = \frac{p_2}{\gamma},$$

$$\therefore \frac{p_2}{\gamma} - \frac{p_1}{\gamma} = h = h_m \left(\frac{S_m}{S_p} - 1\right) \ldots \text{(ii)}$$

where $s_m$ and $s_p$ are the specific gravities of manometric liquid and pipe fluid.

∴ From equations (i) and (ii),
$$\frac{V^2}{2g} = h = h_m \left(\frac{S_m}{S_p} - 1\right) \qquad \ldots (2.39)$$

Actual velocity, $V = C\sqrt{2gh}$

(c) When an inverted manometer is used, the velocity head is given by

$$\frac{V^2}{2g} = h = h_m \left(1 - \frac{S_m}{S_p}\right) \qquad \ldots (2.40)$$

Actual velocity $V = C\sqrt{2gh}$

(d) **Pitot-static tube:** Sometimes, both static pressure measuring tube and the stagnation pressure measuring tube are combined in one device called as Pitot-static tube. (See Fig. 2.19). It consists of a small, cylindrical tube surrounded by a closed outer tube with annular space in between them. The opening at the inner tube records stagnation pressure while the outer tube, with holes drilled on it, measures the static pressure. The pressure head difference (which gives the dynamic pressure $\frac{V^2}{2g}$) can be measured by connecting the outlets from the Pitot-static tube to the ends of a 'U' tube differential manometer.

A Pitot-static tube with specific dimensions is known as Prandtl-Pitot tube.

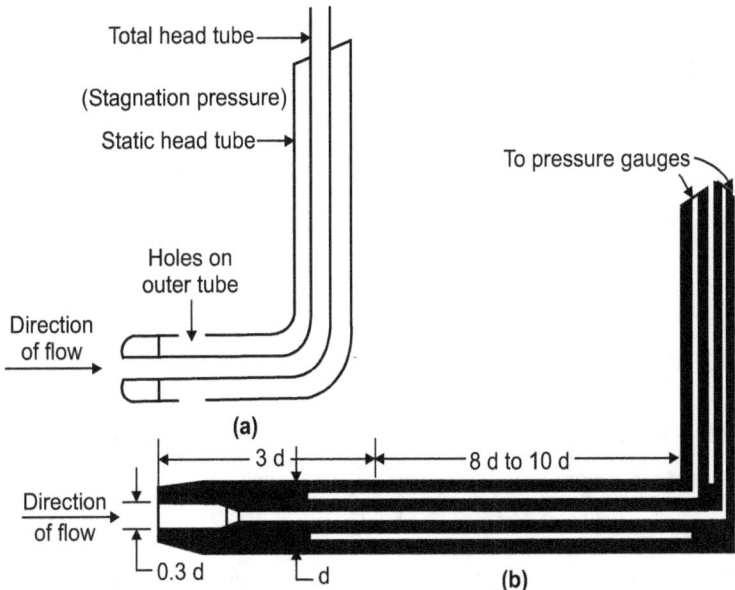

Fig. 2.19: (a) Pitot-static tube, (b) Prandtl-Pitot tube

## 2.17.2 Venturimeter

Venturimeter is a device based on *Bernoulli's equation* and is commonly used for *measurement of flow (discharge) through a pipe line*.

In its simplest form, it consists of a short piece of pipe of a special shape as shown in Fig. 2.20.

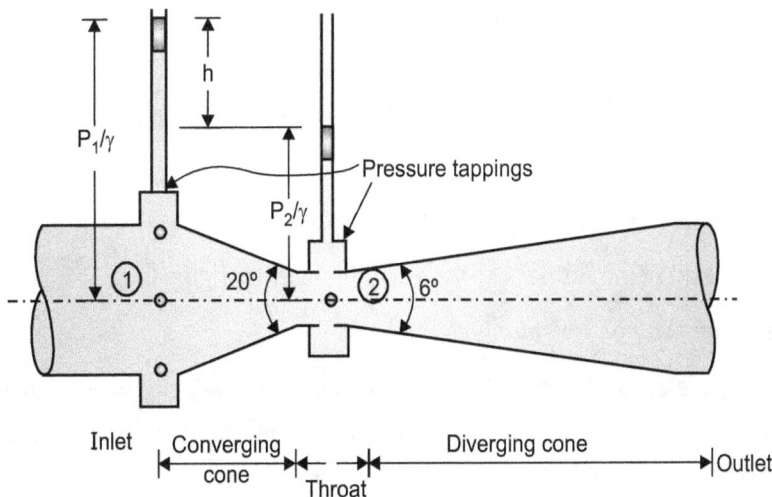

Fig. 2.20: Venturimeter

Venturimeter consists of the following parts:

**(1) Inlet:** It is the starting portion of the venturimeter having the same diameter as that of the pipe. There is a pressure ring provided with a pressure tapping for measurement of average pressure at the inlet.

**(2) Converging Cone:** It is a conical tube converging in the direction of flow. This is used to accelerate the flow. The angle of this cone is about 20°. This angle can be so large because the losses in the accelerating fluid are not appreciable.

**(3) Throat:** It is small tubular portion with uniform cross section. Length of throat is equal to it's diameter. A pressure ring with pressure tapping is provided at the throat.

The diameter of the throat ranges between $\frac{1^{rd}}{3}$ to $\frac{3^{th}}{4}$ of the diameter of inlet. It is generally $\frac{1}{2}$ the diameter of inlet.

**(4) Diverging Cone:** It is a conical tube which diverges gradually in the direction of flow. This is used to convert kinetic energy of flow back into pressure energy and restore pressure as nearly as possible to it's original value.

Angle of this cone is much smaller than converging cone and ranges between 5° to 7°. Commonly used angle is 6°. A smaller angle increases the length of the metre. On the other hand, with a larger angle, the flow tends to separate from the boundary. Due to this, eddies are formed and hence the loss of energy increases. This part is not used for any measurement.

**(5) Outlet:** It is the end portion of venturimeter and has the same diameter as that of the pipe.

For correct results, following points should be noted while installing the venturimeter:

(1) Pipe before (upstream) the venturimeter should be straight and uniform at least upto minimum length of 30 times the diameter of pipe.

(2) There should be no fittings like valves in this length of pipe line.

### 2.17.2.1 Discharge Through a Venturimeter

By reducing the area of throat, the velocity and hence velocity head is increased. This increase in velocity head reduces the pressure head at the throat as compared to that at the inlet. By measuring this artificially created pressure head difference between inlet and throat, it is possible to determine the discharge through the pipe line.

**(a) Horizontal Venturimeter:**

Consider the horizontal venturimeter as shown in Fig. 2.21. Piezometers are used to measure pressure difference between inlet and throat.

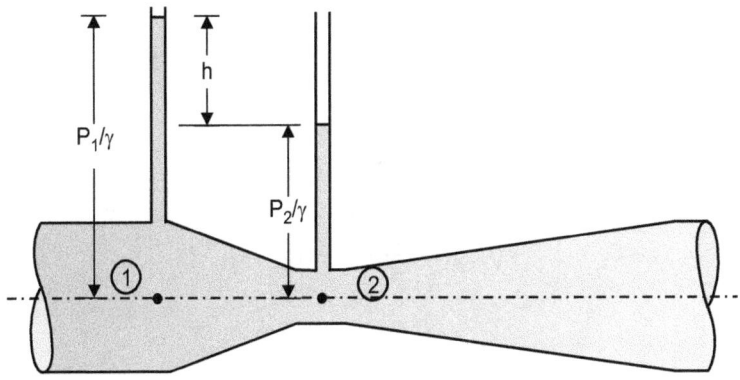

**Fig. 2.21: Horizontal Venturimeter**

Applying Bernoulli's theorem to section 1 - 1 (inlet) and section 2 - 2 (throat), taking centreline of metre as datum, (Quantities with subscript 1 refer to inlet and with subscript 2 refer to throat) we can write

$$Z_1 + \frac{p_1}{\gamma} + \frac{V_1^2}{2g} = Z_2 + \frac{p_2}{\gamma} + \frac{V_2^2}{2g} \quad \text{(neglecting losses)}$$

$$\therefore \frac{V_2^2 - V_1^2}{2g} = \left(Z_1 + \frac{p_1}{\gamma}\right) - \left(Z_2 + \frac{p_2}{\gamma}\right)$$

$\left(Z_1 + \frac{p_1}{\gamma}\right) - \left(Z_2 + \frac{p_2}{\gamma}\right)$ is the piezometric head difference in terms of the column of liquid flowing through the pipe line and is called "Venturi head."

For horizontal venturimeter, $Z_1 = Z_2$

Therefore, 
$$\frac{V_2^2 - V_1^2}{2g} = \frac{p_1}{\gamma} - \frac{p_2}{\gamma} = h \quad \ldots (2.41)$$

But by continuity equation,

$$Q = a_1 V_1 = a_2 V_2$$

$$\therefore V_2 = \frac{a_1}{a_2} \cdot V_1 \quad \ldots (2.42)$$

Substituting value of $V_2$ from (2.41) in equation (2.42),

$$\frac{a_1^2}{a_2^2} \cdot \frac{V_1^2}{2g} - \frac{V_1^2}{2g} = h$$

$$\therefore \quad V_1^2 \left( \frac{a_1^2 - a_2^2}{a_2^2} \right) = 2gh$$

$$\therefore \quad V_1^2 = \left( \frac{a_2^2}{a_1^2 - a_2^2} \right) 2gh$$

$$\therefore \quad V_1 = \frac{a_2}{\sqrt{a_1^2 - a_2^2}} \cdot \sqrt{2g} \cdot \sqrt{h}$$

$$\therefore \quad Q = a_1 V_1$$

$$= \frac{a_1 a_2 \sqrt{2g}}{\sqrt{a_1^2 - a_2^2}} \cdot \sqrt{h}$$

For a given venturimeter $\dfrac{a_1 a_2 \sqrt{2g}}{\sqrt{a_1^2 - a_2^2}}$ is constant and is called as "constant of venturimeter" and is denoted by 'C'.

$$\therefore \quad Q = C\sqrt{h} \quad \quad \ldots (2.43)$$

This is the discharge obtained by neglecting losses between inlet and throat. However, there is always some loss of head between inlet and throat. Due to this, the liquid in the tube at throat rises to lesser height. Hence, observed pressure head difference 'h' is greater than the theoretical pressure head difference. (See Fig. 2.22). To account for this discrepancy, a coefficient 'K' is introduced.

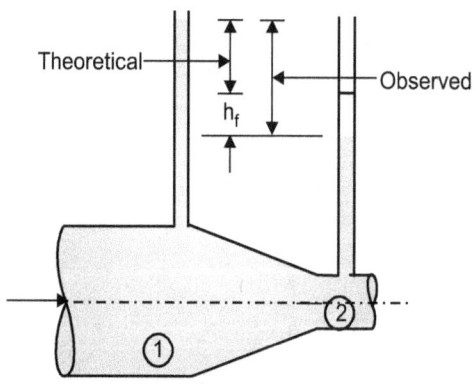

Fig. 2.22

Thus, actual discharge Q is given by

$$\boxed{Q = K \cdot C \cdot \sqrt{h}} \quad \quad \ldots (2.44)$$

The coefficient of meter 'K' is function of Reynold's number and the ratio of $\dfrac{d_2}{d_1}$. Under normal conditions, it has fairly constant value of about 0.98.

## (b) Venturimeter with Differential Manometer:

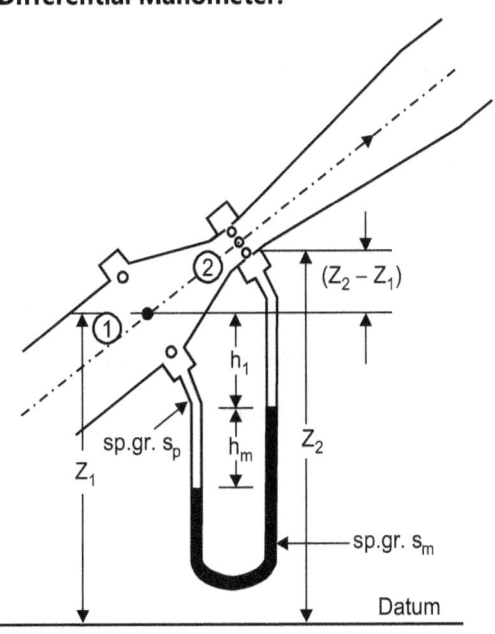

**Fig. 2.23: Inclined Venturimeter with 'U' tube Differential Manometer**

The piezometric head difference between inlet and throat is very often measured with the help of a differential manometer as shown in Fig. 2.23.

Applying Bernoulli's theorem to section 1 and section 2, we can write

$$Z_1 + \frac{p_1}{\gamma} + \frac{V_1^2}{2g} = Z_2 + \frac{p_2}{\gamma} + \frac{V_2^2}{2g}$$

∴
$$\frac{V_2^2 - V_1^2}{2g} = \left(Z_1 + \frac{p_1}{\gamma}\right) - \left(Z_2 + \frac{p_2}{\gamma}\right) = h \qquad \text{... (2.45)}$$

Now, for manometer starting from section 1 and writing manometric equation

$$\frac{p_1}{\gamma} + h_1 + h_m - h_m \cdot \frac{S_m}{S_p} - h_1 - (Z_2 - Z_1) = \frac{p_2}{\gamma} \qquad \text{... (2.46)}$$

where $\gamma$ is the unit weight of pipe liquid and $\frac{S_m}{S_p}$ is the ratio of specific gravity of manometric liquid and specific gravity of liquid in the pipe. $\frac{S_m}{S_p}$ represents the specific gravity of manometric liquid relative to liquid in the pipe.

From equation (2.46)

$$\left(Z_1 + \frac{p_1}{\gamma}\right) - \left(Z_2 + \frac{p_2}{\gamma}\right) = h_m\left(\frac{S_m}{S_p} - 1\right) \quad \ldots (2.47)$$

but $\left(Z_1 + \frac{p_1}{\gamma}\right) - \left(Z_2 + \frac{p_2}{\gamma}\right) = h$ from equation (2.47)

$$\therefore \quad h = h_m\left(\frac{S_m}{S_p} - 1\right) \quad \ldots (2.48)$$

This relation is independent of inclination of venturimeter. Thus, *if a differential manometer is used to measure pressure head difference between inlet and throat, the reading of the manometer is independent of inclination of venturimeter* (whether it is horizontal, inclined at any angle or vertical).

If the pressure head difference is measured with the help of an inverted 'U' tube differential manometer which uses liquid lighter than that in the pipe line as manometric liquid ($S_m < S_p$),

$$h = h_m\left(1 - \frac{S_m}{S_p}\right) \quad \ldots (2.49)$$

The instrument is called venturimeter after the name of inventor Mr. Venturi, an Italian engineer.

## 2.17.3 Orifice Meter

Another simple device used for measurement of flow in a pipe line is orifice meter or orifice plate. It is also based on Bernoulli's equation. It works on the same principle as that of venturimeter.

It consists of a flat circular plate which has a sharp edged circular orifice cut in it and is placed in the pipe such that the orifice is concentric with the pipe line. The orifice diameter 'd' varies from 0.4 to 0.8 times the diameter of the pipe 'D'. Generally, the diameter of the orifice is 0.5 times the diameter of the pipe (d = 0.5 D).

Flow rate in the pipe can be measured by observing the pressure difference between two sections, one on the upstream side of the plate and the other at venacontracta on the downstream side of the orifice plate shown in Fig. 2.24.

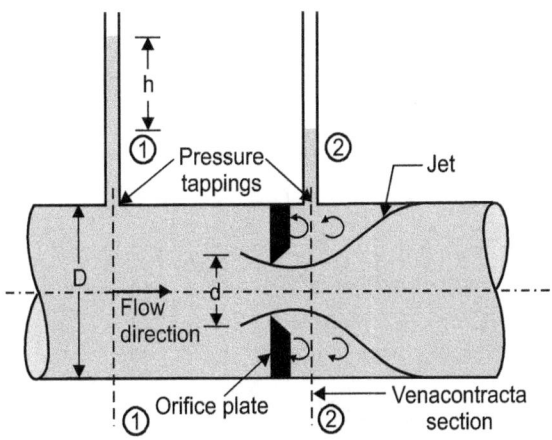

**Fig. 2.24: Orifice meter or Orifice plate**

Applying Bernoulli's theorem to section 1 - 1 and section 2 - 2, we get

$$Z_1 + \frac{p_1}{\gamma} + \frac{V_1^2}{2g} = Z_2 + \frac{p_2}{\gamma} + \frac{V_2^2}{2g} \quad \text{but } Z_1 = Z_2$$

∴
$$\frac{V_2^2 - V_1^2}{2g} = \frac{p_1}{\gamma} - \frac{p_2}{\gamma} = h$$

where 'h' is the pressure head difference between section 1 - 1 and 2 - 2 in terms of column of liquid flowing through the pipe line and can be found out with piezometers or U-tube manometer or inverted U-tube manometer as usual.

[e.g. $\quad h = h_m \left\{ \dfrac{S_m}{S_p} - 1 \right\}$ for U-tube differential manometer

or $\quad h = h_m \left\{ 1 - \dfrac{S_m}{S_p} \right\}$ for U-tube inverted differential manometer etc.]

∴ $\quad V_2^2 - V_1^2 = 2gh$ ... (i)

But by continuity equation, we can write

$$A \cdot V_1 = a_c V_2$$

where, A is the area of pipe and $a_c$ is the area of jet at venacontracta.

But further, $\quad \dfrac{a_c}{a} = C_c,$ the coefficient of contraction for the orifice a is the area of orifice.

∴ $\quad a_c = C_c \cdot a$

∴ $\quad A \cdot V_1 = C_c \cdot a \cdot V_2$

∴ $\quad V_1 = C_c \cdot \dfrac{a}{A} \cdot V_2$

Substituting value of $V_1$ in equation (i), we get

$$V_2^2 - C_c^2 \cdot \left(\frac{a}{A}\right)^2 \cdot V_2^2 = 2gh$$

or
$$V_2 = \sqrt{\frac{2gh}{1 - C_c^2 \left(\frac{a}{A}\right)^2}} \quad \ldots (2.50)$$

This is the theoretical velocity at venacontracta since we have not accounted for losses. To account for losses, we make use of coefficient of velocity '$C_v$' of the orifice

$$C_v = \frac{\text{actual velocity}}{\text{theoretical velocity}}$$

∴ $\quad V_{2\,actual} = C_v \cdot V_{2\,theoretical}$

∴ $\quad V_{2\,actual} = C_v \sqrt{\dfrac{2gh}{1 - C_c^2 \left(\dfrac{a}{A}\right)^2}}$

∴ Actual discharge $Q = C_c \cdot a \cdot V_2$

∴ $\quad Q = \dfrac{C_c\, C_v}{\sqrt{1 - C_c^2 \left(\dfrac{a}{A}\right)^2}} \cdot a \cdot \sqrt{2gh}$

but $C_c \cdot C_v = C_d$, the coefficient of discharge for orifice

∴ $\quad Q = \dfrac{C_d}{\sqrt{1 - C_c^2 \left(\dfrac{a}{A}\right)^2}} \cdot a \cdot \sqrt{2gh} \quad \ldots (2.51)$

but $\quad \left(\dfrac{a}{A}\right)^2 = \left(\dfrac{d}{D}\right)^4$

∴ $\quad Q = \dfrac{C_d \cdot a \sqrt{2gh}}{\sqrt{1 - C_c^2 \left(\dfrac{d}{D}\right)^4}}$

In actual practice, the formula is simplified as

$$Q = \frac{C \cdot a \sqrt{2gh}}{\sqrt{1 - \left(\frac{d}{D}\right)^4}} \qquad \ldots (2.52)$$

where $\dfrac{C_d \cdot a}{\sqrt{1 - C_c^2 \left(\frac{d}{D}\right)^4}}$ is replaced by $\dfrac{C \cdot a}{\sqrt{1 - \left(\frac{d}{D}\right)^4}}$ where C is a coefficient.

The above equation can be written similar to equation for venturimeter in the form

$$Q = K \cdot a \cdot \sqrt{2gh} \qquad \ldots (2.53)$$

where K is $\dfrac{C}{\sqrt{1 - \left(\frac{d}{D}\right)^4}}$ and is known as Orifice meter flow coefficient.

### 2.17.3.1 Comparison between Venturimeter and Orifice meter

| Venturimeter | |
|---|---|
| **Merits** | **Demerits** |
| 1. The losses are very low and hence coefficient of discharge is high of the order of about 0.98. | 1. It is very long and hence requires more space. |
| 2. It is suitable for measurement of higher rates of flow. | 2. It cannot be installed where space is limited. |
| 3. It is preferable for measurement of flow in large pipes. | 3. It is costly for installation and replacement. |
| **Orifice meter** | |
| 1. Since it is a simple plate, it is cheaper. | 1. Losses are more. |
| 2. It requires less space. | 2. Coefficient of discharge has very low value. |
| 3. Replacement is cheaper and easier. | |

It may be noted that $\dfrac{p_1}{\gamma} - \dfrac{p_2}{\gamma} = h$ will depend upon the positions of pressure tappings and hence the coefficient of meter will also depend upon the positions of pressure tappings. Pressure tapping 1 is at (D – d) to 2 (D – d) on the upstream side or 1.5 D to 2 D on the upstream side while pressure tapping is at 0.5 d on the downstream side. Sometimes even corner tappings just on upstream side and just on downstream side of plate are also used. It is, therefore, necessary to calibrate the meter for given pressure tappings before it is used.

# ILLUSTRATIVE EXAMPLES

**Example 2.5:**

A closed tank placed on the ground contains water and air under pressure above it. Water is delivered at the rate of 12.5 l.p.s., from this tank to other tank placed on roof of the building 25 m above the ground. If connecting hose pipe is of 60 mm diameter and the loss of head in the pipe is 3.75 m, find the air pressure in the ground tank.

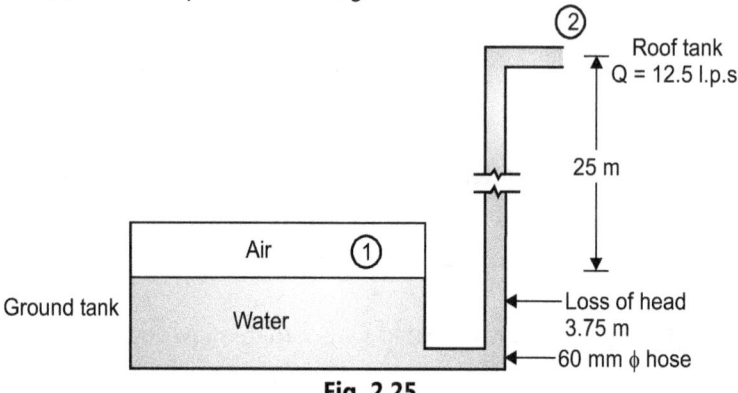

**Fig. 2.25**

**Solution:**

Whenever we apply Bernoulli's equation, we are required to select a datum. Any convenient horizontal plane can be taken as datum. Here we will take liquid level in the tank as datum.

Applying Bernoulli's equation to two points:
1. The water surface in the tank and
2. Outlet of pipe, we get

$$Z_1 + \frac{p_1}{\gamma} + \frac{V_1^2}{2g} = Z_2 + \frac{p_2}{\gamma} + \frac{V_2^2}{2g} + \text{loss} \quad \ldots \text{(i)}$$

Since datum passes through point (1), $Z_1 = 0$, also ground tank velocity is zero.

$$\therefore \quad V_1 = 0$$

$$\therefore \quad 0 + \frac{p_1}{\gamma} + 0 = 25 + 0 + \frac{V_2^2}{2g} + 3.75 \quad \ldots \text{(ii)}$$

Now $V_2$ is the velocity of water in the hose pipe and can be found out by continuity equation.

$$Q = A_2 V_2$$

$$\therefore \quad V_2 = \frac{Q}{A_2} = \frac{12.5 \times 10^{-3}}{\frac{\pi}{4} \times (0.06)^2}$$

$$\therefore \quad V_2 = 4.421 \text{ m/s.}$$

$$\therefore \quad \frac{V_2^2}{2g} = 0.996 \text{ m}$$

Substituting this value in equation (ii), we get

$$\frac{p_1}{\gamma} = 25 + 0.996 + 3.75$$

∴ $$\frac{p_1}{\gamma} = 29.75 \text{ m}$$

∴ **Air pressure in the tank = 291.85 kPa**

[**Note:** The losses are to be added to the energy of that point which is reached afterwards in the direction of flow. Here point (2) is reached afterwards since flow is from (1) to (2).]

### Example 2.6:

Siphon ABCD drains oil of relative density 0.8 from the tank as shown in Fig. 2.26 into the atmosphere. Calculate (i) the velocity of oil through the siphon and (ii) the pressure at B, A and C, (iii) Comment on whether the rate of discharge for water will be different. If different, what will be the rate of discharge, (iv) State the factor controlling the maximum height of B above the level of oil in the tank, (v) State whether the depth of D below oil level in the tank is to be limited or otherwise.

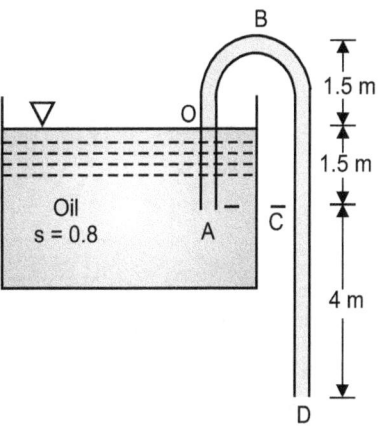

Fig. 2.26

### Solution:

(i) Applying Bernoulli's equation to free liquid surface and point D, taking liquid level in the tank 'O' as datum. (O suffix refers to liquid surface)

$$Z_0 + \frac{p_0}{\gamma} + \frac{V_0^2}{2g} = Z_D + \frac{p_D}{\gamma} + \frac{V_D^2}{2g}$$

but $$\frac{p_0}{\gamma} = \frac{p_D}{\gamma} \text{ and } V_0 = 0$$

$$0 + 0 + 0 = -5.5 + 0 + \frac{V_D^2}{2g}$$

∴ $$\frac{V_D^2}{2g} = 5.5$$

$$V_D = \sqrt{19.62 \times 5.5} = 10.388 \text{ m/s}$$

∴ **Velocity of oil through the syphon = 10.388 m/s.**

(ii) To find the pressure at 'B'.

Applying Bernoulli's equation between liquid surface in the tank and point B, we get,

$$Z_0 + \frac{p_0}{\gamma} + \frac{V_0^2}{2g} = Z_B + \frac{p_B}{\gamma} + \frac{V_B^2}{2g}$$

but

$$\frac{V_B^2}{2g} = \frac{V_D^2}{2g} = 5.5 \text{ m}$$

∴

$$0 + 0 + 0 = 1.5 + \frac{p_B}{\gamma} + 5.5$$

∴

$$\frac{p_B}{\gamma} = -7 \text{ m of oil}$$

or $\boxed{\text{Pressure at B} = -54.936 \text{ kPa (gauge)}}$

Pressure at A = Pressure at C = −4 m of liquid

∴ $\boxed{\text{Pressure at C} = -31.39 \text{ kPa (gauge)}}$

(iii) Discharge depends upon velocity. Velocity depends upon the head i.e. difference of elevation between liquid surface and point D. Since the head remains same, the discharge will be same even if water flows through the syphon.

(iv) If the level of B is raised, the pressure at B reduces. A stage may be reached when the pressure at B is separation pressure. The level of B cannot be further increased. Thus, the controlling factor is the vapour pressure for the oil.

(v) If D is lowered, head causing the flow will increase. Due to this, the velocity in the siphon will increase. This will increase the velocity head at 'B', thus reducing the pressure head at 'B'. If the pressure fall to vapour pressure, the flow will discontinue.

The depth of point 'D', therefore below the level in the tank is limited, depending upon the vapour pressure of oil.

## Example 2.7:

A vertical pipe carrying oil of sp. gr. 0.9 tapers uniformly from 20 cm diameter at the lower section to 10 cm diameter at the upper section. The vertical distance between the sections is 1 m. The pressure gauges installed at the lower and upper sections read 6 N/cm² and 5 N/cm² respectively when the discharge of oil is 30 litres/sec. Calculate the loss of head between the two sections. Determine the direction of flow also.

**Solution:**

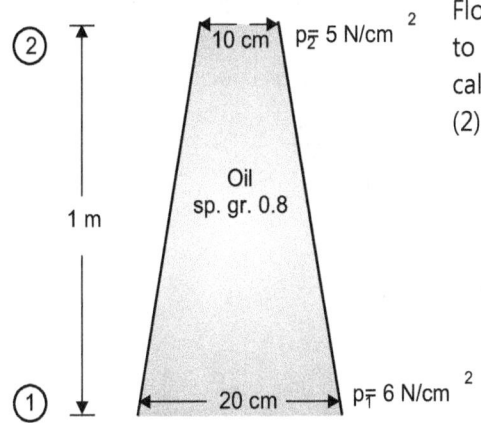

**Fig. 2.27**

Flow always takes place from higher energy level to lower energy level. Therefore, we will first calculate the total heads at section (1) and section (2).

Now, $V_1 = \dfrac{Q}{A_1} = \dfrac{30 \times 10^{-3}}{\dfrac{\pi}{4} \times (0.2)^2} = 0.955$ m/s  $\quad \therefore \dfrac{V_1^2}{2g} = 0.0465$ m

$V_2 = \left(\dfrac{D_1}{D_2}\right)^2 \cdot V_1 = 4V_1 = 3.82$ m/s $\quad \therefore \dfrac{V_2^2}{2g} = 0.744$ m

$\dfrac{p_1}{\gamma} = \dfrac{6 \times 10^4}{0.9 \times 9810} = 6.795$ m

$\dfrac{p_2}{\gamma} = \dfrac{5 \times 10^4}{0.9 \times 9810} = 5.663$ m

Taking horizontal through (1) as datum,

Total head at section (1) = $Z_1 + \dfrac{p_1}{\gamma} + \dfrac{V_1^2}{2g} = 0 + 6.795 + 0.0465$

$= 6.8415$ m

Total head at section (2) = $Z_2 + \dfrac{p_2}{\gamma} + \dfrac{V_2^2}{2g} = 1 + 5.663 + 0.744$

$= 7.407$ m

Since total head at (2) is greater than total head at (1), flow is from (2) to (1) in downward direction.

Loss of head between sections (1) and (2)

= Total head at (2) – Total head at (1)

= 7.407 – 6.8415

∴ $\boxed{\text{Loss} = 0.5655 \text{ m of oil}}$

## Example 2.8:

A pump consuming 7.5 kW power is used to lift water from a sump to an overhead tank. Total lift is 16 m. If efficiency of pump is 85% and the loss of head in the system is 1.5 m of water, find the time required to fill the overhead tank of 22280 litres capacity.

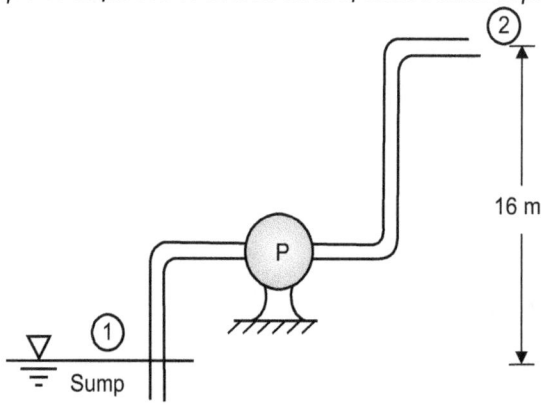

Fig. 2.28

**Solution:**

Applying B.T. between point (1) and point (2) taking liquid level in the sump as datum:

$$Z_1 + \frac{p_1}{\gamma} + \frac{V_1^2}{2g} + h_p = Z_2 + \frac{p_2}{\gamma} + \frac{V_2^2}{2g} + h_L$$

where $h_L$ = loss of head and $h_p$ = head developed by pump, $V_1 = V_2$

$0 + 0 + h_p = 16 + 0 + 1.5$

∴ Head developed by pump = 17.5 m

Now power given to water = $0.85 \times 7.5$ = 6.375 kW

∴  $6.375 = \gamma . Q . h_p = 9.81 \times Q \times 17.5$

∴ Discharge of the pump = 0.0371 m³/s or 37.1 l.p.s.

∴ Time required to fill the tank = $\frac{22280}{37.1}$ = 600 seconds = 10 min.

## Example 2.9:

If a pump imparts 20 kW power to the water being pumped at a rate of 0.10 m³/s, determine the pressure at A and B. (Refer Fig. 2.29).

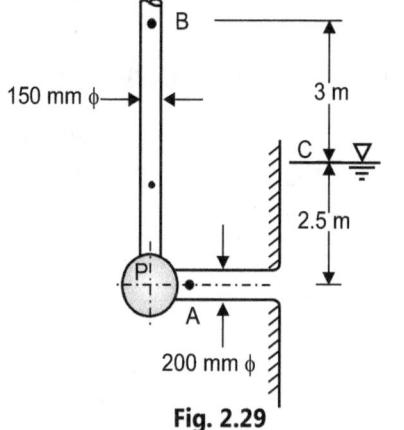

Fig. 2.29

## Solution:

Let 'C' be the point on the liquid surface.

(i) Now, $V_A = \dfrac{0.1}{\dfrac{\pi}{4} \times (0.2)^2} = 3.183 \text{ m}$, $\quad \dfrac{V_A^2}{2g} = \dfrac{(3.183)^2}{19.62} = 0.516 \text{ m}$

$V_B = \dfrac{0.1}{\dfrac{\pi}{4} \times (0.15)^2} = 5.659 \text{ m}$, $\quad \dfrac{V_B^2}{2g} = \dfrac{(5.659)^2}{19.62} = 1.632 \text{ m}$

Applying Bernoulli's equation to C and A taking level at A as datum

$$Z_C + \dfrac{p_C}{\gamma} + \dfrac{V_C^2}{2g} = Z_A + \dfrac{p_A}{\gamma} + \dfrac{V_A^2}{2g}$$

$$2.5 + 0 + 0 = 0 + \dfrac{p_A}{\gamma} + 0.516$$

∴ $\dfrac{p_A}{\gamma} = 1.984$ m of water

$p_A = 1.984 \times 9.81 = 19.463$ kN/m²

∴ **Pressure at A = 19.463 kN/m²**

(ii) Now applying Bernoulli's equation to A and B taking level at 'A' as datum, we get,

$$Z_A + \dfrac{p_A}{\gamma} + \dfrac{V_A^2}{2g} + H_p = Z_B + \dfrac{p_B}{\gamma} + \dfrac{V_B^2}{2g}$$

$0 + 1.984 + 0.516 + H_p = 5.5 + \dfrac{p_B}{\gamma} + 1.632$

Power delivered by pump P $= \gamma Q H_p = 20$ kW

∴ $9.81 \times 0.1 \times H_p = 20$

∴ $H_p = 20.387$ m

Substituting value of $H_p$ in the above equation

$0 + 1.984 + 0.516 + 20.387 = 5.5 + \dfrac{p_B}{\gamma} + 1.632$

$\dfrac{p_B}{\gamma} = 22.887 - 7.132$

or $\dfrac{p_B}{\gamma} = 15.755$ m of water

∴ $p_B = 15.755 \times 9.81$

$p_B = 154.557$ kN/m²

∴ **Pressure at B = 154.557 kN/m²**

## Example 2.10:

A pump draws water from a sump and delivers at the rate of 80 l.p.s. Suction and delivery pipe diameters are 250 mm and 150 mm respectively and their elevations differ by 40 cm delivery pipe above suction. If a differential mercury manometer connected between inlet and outlet to the pump shows 20 cm deflection, find the power delivered by the pump.

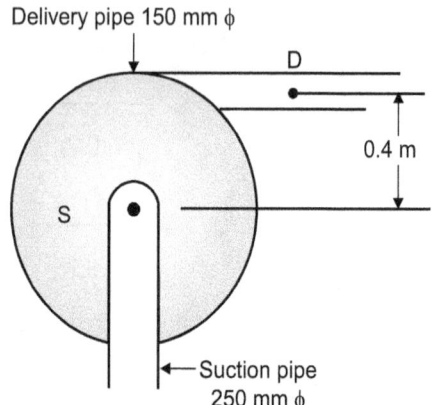

Fig. 2.30

### Solution:
Let S and D represent the points on the suction (inlet) and delivery (outlet) side of the pump.

$$V_s = \text{Velocity in suction pipe} = \frac{Q}{\frac{\pi}{4} \times D_s^2} = \frac{0.08}{\frac{\pi}{4} \times (0.25)^2} = 1.63 \text{ m/s}$$

$$\frac{V_s^2}{2g} = 0.135 \text{ m}$$

$$V_D = \text{Velocity in the delivery pipe} = \left(\frac{250}{150}\right)^2 \times 1.63 = 4.52 \text{ m/s}$$

$$\frac{V_D^2}{2g} = 1.041 \text{ m}$$

Applying Bernoulli's equation to points S and D with horizontal through S as datum

$$Z_s + \frac{p_s}{\gamma} + \frac{V_s^2}{2g} + H_p = Z_D + \frac{p_D}{\gamma} + \frac{V_D^2}{2g}$$

$$0 + \frac{p_s}{\gamma} + 0.135 + H_p = 0.4 + \frac{p_D}{\gamma} + 1.041$$

$$\therefore \quad H_p = \left(\frac{p_D}{\gamma} - \frac{p_s}{\gamma}\right) + 1.041 + 0.4 - 0.135 \quad \text{... (i)}$$

Now see the manometer shown in the figure. Starting from suction S and writing manometric equation we get,

$$\frac{p_s}{\gamma} + h + 0.2 \times 13.6 - 0.2 - h - 0.4 = \frac{p_D}{\gamma}$$

$$\therefore \quad \frac{p_D}{\gamma} - \frac{p_s}{\gamma} = 2.12 \text{ m} \quad \text{... (ii)}$$

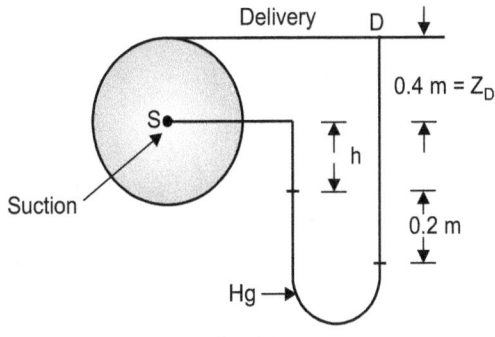

**Fig. 2.31**

Substituting from equation (ii) in equation (i), we can write

Head developed by pump, $H_p = 2.12 + 1.041 + 0.4 - 0.135$

∴ $H_p = 3.426$ m

∴ Power delivered by pump $= \gamma \cdot Q \cdot H_p$

$= 9.81 \times 0.08 \times 3.426$

∴ **Power delivered by pump = 2.69 kW**

[The example can also be solved as

$$Z_s + \frac{p_s}{\gamma} + \frac{V_s^2}{2g} + H_p = Z_D + \frac{p_D}{\gamma} + \frac{V_D^2}{2g}$$

∴ $$H_p = \left(Z_D + \frac{p_D}{\gamma}\right) - \left(Z_s + \frac{p_s}{\gamma}\right) + \frac{V_D^2 - V_s^2}{2g}$$

But $\left(Z_D + \frac{p_D}{\gamma}\right) - \left(Z_s + \frac{p_s}{\gamma}\right) = h_m \left(\frac{S_m}{S_p} - 1\right)$

$= 0.2 \times 12.6 = 2.52$ m

∴ $H_p = 2.52 + 1.041 - 0.135$

$= 3.426$ m

Power $= 9.81 \times 0.08 \times 3.426$

$= $ **2.69 kW** ]

### Example 2.11:

A pump is pumping water at the rate of 7536 lit./min. The pump inlet is 40 cm in diameter and the vacuum pressure over there is 15 cm of Mercury. The pump outlet is 20 cm in diameter and it is 1.2 m above the inlet. The pressure at the outlet is 107.4 kN/m². Estimate the power added by the pump.

**Solution:**

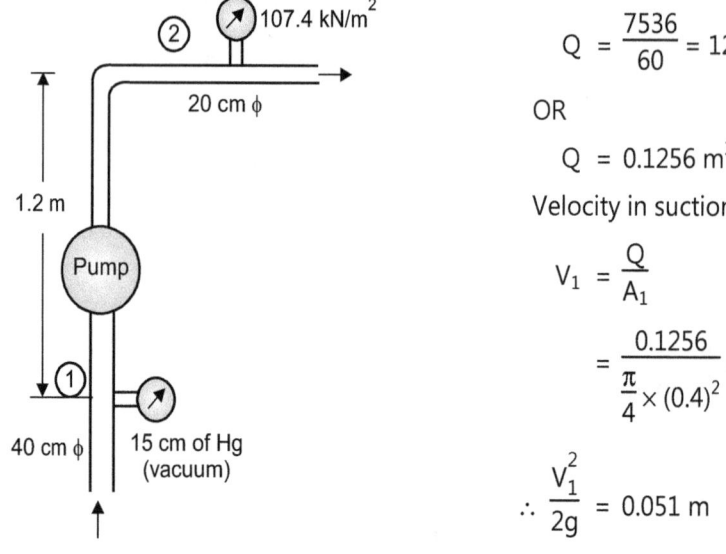

**Fig. 2.32**

$$Q = \frac{7536}{60} = 125.6 \text{ l.p.s.}$$

OR

$$Q = 0.1256 \text{ m}^3/\text{s}$$

Velocity in suction pipe

$$V_1 = \frac{Q}{A_1}$$

$$= \frac{0.1256}{\frac{\pi}{4} \times (0.4)^2} = 1 \text{ m/s}$$

$$\therefore \frac{V_1^2}{2g} = 0.051 \text{ m}$$

Velocity in delivery pipe

$$V_2 = \left(\frac{40}{20}\right)^2 \times 1 = 4 \text{ m/s}$$

$$\therefore \frac{V_2^2}{2g} = 0.8155 \text{ m}$$

Pressure head in suction pipe

$$\frac{p_2}{\gamma} - 15 \text{ cm of mercury}$$

or

$$\frac{p_1}{\gamma} = -0.15 \times 13.6$$

$$\frac{p_1}{\gamma} = -2.04 \text{ m of water}$$

Pressure in delivery pipe

$$\frac{p_2}{\gamma} = \frac{107.4}{9.81} = 10.948 \text{ m of water}$$

Now applying Bernoulli's theorem to section (1) and section (2) taking horizontal passing through (1) as datum, we get

$$Z_1 + \frac{p_1}{\gamma} + \frac{V_1^2}{2g} + h_p = Z_2 + \frac{p_2}{\gamma} + \frac{V_2^2}{2g} \quad \text{where } h_p \text{ is the head supplied by the pump}$$

∴   $0 - 2.04 + 0.051 + h_p = 1.2 + 10.948 + 0.8155$

∴   $h_p = 14.9525$ m

∴ Power added by the pump

$$P = \gamma Q h_p$$
$$= 9.81 \times 0.1256 \times 14.9525$$
$$= 18.42 \text{ kW}$$

∴ **Power added by the pump = 18.42 kW**

### Example 2.12:

Water flows through a turbine at the rate of 0.2 m³/s and the pressures just before and after the turbine are $1.5 \times 10^5$ N/m² and $-0.3 \times 10^5$ N/m². Determine the power delivered by water to the turbine. (Fig. 2.33)

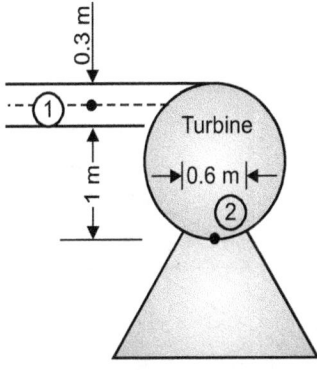

**Fig. 2.33**

### Solution:

Let point (1) be just before the turbine and point (2) just after the turbine.

$$V_1 = \frac{Q}{A_1} = \frac{0.2}{\frac{\pi}{4} \times (0.3)^2} = 2.83 \text{ m/s}; \quad \frac{V_1^2}{2g} = 0.408 \text{ m}$$

$$V_2 = \left(\frac{D_1}{D_2}\right)^2 \cdot V_1 = \frac{1}{4} \cdot V_1 = 0.7075 \text{ m/s}; \quad \frac{V_2^2}{2g} = 0.0255 \text{ m}$$

$$\frac{p_1}{\gamma} = \frac{1.5 \times 10^5}{9810} = 15.29 \text{ m}; \quad \frac{p_2}{\gamma} = \frac{-0.3 \times 10^5}{9810} = -3.058 \text{ m}$$

Applying Bernoulli's theorem to points (1) and (2)

$$Z_1 + \frac{p_1}{\gamma} + \frac{V_1^2}{2g} = Z_2 + \frac{p_2}{\gamma} + \frac{V_2^2}{2g} + H_t$$

$$1.15 + 15.29 + 0.408 = 0 + (-3.058) + 0.0255 + H_t$$

∴ The head extracted by turbine
$$H_t = 19.88 \text{ m}$$
∴ Power delivered by water to the turbine
$$P = \gamma \cdot Q \cdot H_t$$
$$= 9.81 \times 0.2 \times 19.88$$
∴ $\boxed{P = 39 \text{ kW}}$

## Example 2.13:

A drainage pump has a tapered suction pipe and discharges water out of a sump. The diameters of pipe at the inlet and at the upper end are 0.5 m and 0.25 m. The free water surface in the sump is 2 m above the centre of the inlet and the pipe is laid at a slope of 1 (vertical) to 5 (along pipe line). The pressure at the top end of the pipe is 6.6 m (abs) and it is known that the loss of head due to friction between the two sections is $\frac{1}{10}$ of the velocity head at the top section. Compute the discharge in l.p.s. through the pipe if its length is 25 m. Take atmospheric pressure as 10 m.

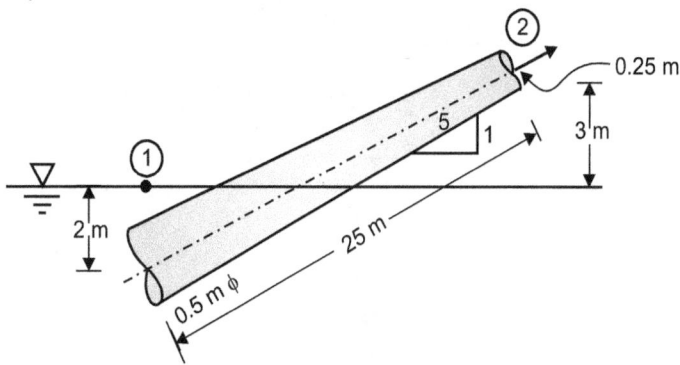

Fig. 2.34

### Solution:

Applying Bernoulli's equation to free liquid surface (1) and upper end (2) with liquid surface in the sump as datum we get:

$$Z_1 + \frac{p_1}{\gamma} + \frac{V_1^2}{2g} = Z_2 + \frac{p_2}{\gamma} + \frac{V_2^2}{2g} + 0.1\frac{V_2^2}{2g} \quad \left[0.1\frac{V_2^2}{2g} \text{ is the loss}\right]$$

$$0 + 10 + 0 = 3 + 6.6 + 1.1\frac{V_2^2}{2g}$$

∴ $V_2 = 2.67$ m/s

$$Q = A_2 V_2 = \frac{\pi}{4} \times (0.25)^2 \times 2.67$$

∴ $\boxed{Q = 0.131 \text{ m}^3/\text{s or 131 l.p.s.}}$

## Example 2.14:
Find out the discharge through a venturimeter with inlet diameter of 10 cm and throat diameter of 5 cm, carrying oil of specific gravity 0.8 when the deflection of oil-mercury manometer is 30 cm. Assume coefficient of the meter as 0.95.

**Solution:**

We have
$$Q = KC\sqrt{h} \qquad K = 0.95$$

$$h = h_m \left(\frac{S_m}{S_p} - 1\right) = 30 \left(\frac{13.6}{0.8} - 1\right) = 480 \text{ cm}$$

$$C = \frac{a_1 a_2 \sqrt{2g}}{\sqrt{a_1^2 - a_2^2}} = \frac{a_1 \sqrt{2g}}{\sqrt{\left(\frac{a_1}{a_2}\right)^2 - 1}} = \frac{a_1 \sqrt{2g}}{\sqrt{\left(\frac{d_1}{d_2}\right)^4 - 1}}$$

$$= \frac{\frac{\pi}{4} \times (10)^2 \times \sqrt{1962}}{\sqrt{\left(\frac{10}{5}\right)^4 - 1}} = 898.24 \text{ cm units}$$

$\therefore \quad Q = 0.95 \times 898.24 \times \sqrt{480}$

$\therefore \quad \boxed{Q = 18695.48 \text{ cm}^3/\text{s} = 18.70 \text{ l.p.s.}}$

## Example 2.15:
A 25 × 12 cm venturimeter is installed in a vertical pipe carrying oil of relative density 0.8. The flow of oil is in upward direction. The difference of levels between the throat and inlet section is 25 cm. The oil-mercury differential manometer gives deflection reading of 35 cm of mercury. Find the discharge of oil. Take coefficient of meter as 0.98.

**Solution:**

Since a "differential manometer" is used, it gives the difference of piezometric heads and hence the elevation difference between inlet and throat is automatically taken care of. The example should, therefore, be solved as if it is a horizontal venturimeter.

$\therefore \quad Q = KC\sqrt{h}$
$\quad K = 0.98$

$$C = \frac{a_1 \sqrt{2g}}{\sqrt{\left(\frac{d_1}{d_2}\right)^4 - 1}} = \frac{\frac{\pi}{4} \times (0.25)^2 \times \sqrt{19.62}}{\sqrt{\left(\frac{25}{12}\right)^4 - 1}}$$

$$= 0.0515 \text{ in metre units}$$

$$h = h_m \left(\frac{S_m}{S_p} - 1\right) = 0.35 \left(\frac{13.6}{0.8} - 1\right) = 5.6 \text{ m of oil}$$

$\therefore \quad Q = 0.98 \times 0.0515 \times \sqrt{5.6}$

$\therefore \quad \boxed{Q = 0.119 \text{ m}^3/\text{s}}$

## Example 2.16:

The inlet and throat diameters of a vertically mounted venturimeter are 30 cm and 10 cm respectively. The throat section is below the inlet section at a distance of 10 cm. The specific gravity of the liquid is 900 kg/m³. The intensity of pressure at inlet is 140 kPa and the throat pressure is 80 kPa. Calculate the flow rate in l.p.s. Assume that 2% of the differential head is lost between inlet and throat and coefficient of discharge 0.97.

**Solution:**

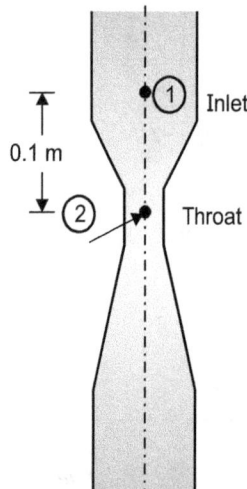

Fig. 2.35

Applying Bernoulli's equation to inlet and throat with throat as datum, we get

$$Z_1 + \frac{p_1}{\gamma} + \frac{V_1^2}{2g} = Z_2 + \frac{p_2}{\gamma} + \frac{V_2^2}{2g} + \text{loss}$$

$$0.1 + \frac{140}{0.9 \times 9.81} + \frac{V_1^2}{2g} = 0 + \frac{80}{0.9 \times 9.81} + \frac{V_2^2}{2g} + \text{loss}$$

but loss is 2% of $\dfrac{p_1 - p_2}{\gamma}$

$$\therefore \quad \frac{V_2^2 - V_1^2}{2g} = \left(\frac{140 - 80}{0.9 \times 9.81}\right) + 0.1 + 0.02 \left(\frac{140 - 80}{0.9 \times 9.81}\right)$$

$$\therefore \quad h = \frac{V_2^2 - V_1^2}{2g} = \left(\frac{140 - 80}{0.9 \times 9.81}\right)(0.98) + 0.1$$

$$\therefore \quad h = 6.76 \text{ m of liquid.}$$

$$C = \frac{a_1 \sqrt{2g}}{\sqrt{\left(\dfrac{d_1}{d_2}\right)^4 - 1}} = \frac{\frac{\pi}{4} \times (0.3)^2 \times \sqrt{19.62}}{\sqrt{\left(\dfrac{30}{10}\right)^4 - 1}}$$

∴ C = 0.035 m units

Now the flow rate Q is given by the formula:

$$Q = K \cdot C \cdot \sqrt{h} = 0.97 \times 0.035 \times \sqrt{6.76}$$

∴ **Q = 0.0883 m³/s**

## Example 2.17:

Water flows through an inclined venturimeter. The inlet and throat diameters are 10 cm and 5 cm respectively and their height difference $(Z_2 - Z_1)$ is 30 cm. A mercury manometer located across the inlet and the throat indicates 10 cm of mercury column at a given flow rate.

Estimate the flow rate, coefficient of discharge and pressure difference between inlet and the throat $(p_1 - p_2)$

(i) neglecting friction,
(ii) when friction loss is 10% of the head indicated by the manometer.

## Solution:

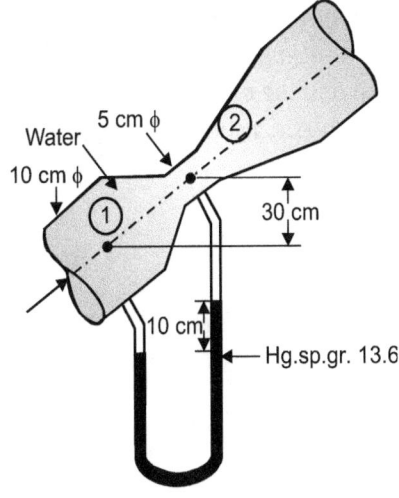

Fig. 2.36

**(i) Neglecting friction**

The differential manometer shows the difference in the piezometric heads between inlet (1) and throat (2).

$$\therefore \left(Z_1 + \frac{p_1}{\gamma}\right) - \left(Z_2 + \frac{p_2}{\gamma}\right) = h_m\left(\frac{S_m}{S_p} - 1\right)$$

$$\therefore \left(\frac{p_1}{\gamma} - \frac{p_2}{\gamma}\right) + (Z_1 - Z_2) = 0.1\,(13.6 - 1)$$

$$\therefore \left(\frac{p_1}{\gamma} - \frac{p_2}{\gamma}\right) - (Z_2 - Z_1) = 1.26$$

$$\therefore \left(\frac{p_1}{\gamma} - \frac{p_2}{\gamma}\right) = 1.26 + 0.3 = 1.56 \text{ m}$$

$$\therefore \boxed{p_1 - p_2 = 1.56 \times 9.81 = 15.30 \text{ kN/m}^2}$$

U – tube differential manometer is used, the inclination of venturimeter does not matter and K = 1

$$Q = KC\sqrt{h} = \frac{a_1\sqrt{2g}}{\sqrt{\left(\frac{a_1}{a_2}\right)^2 - 1}} \cdot \sqrt{1.26}$$

$$= \frac{\frac{\pi}{4} \times (0.1)^2 \times \sqrt{19.62}}{\sqrt{\left(\frac{10}{5}\right)^4 - 1}} \cdot \sqrt{1.26} = 0.01 \text{ m}^3/\text{s} = 10 \text{ l.p.s.}$$

$$\therefore \boxed{Q = 10 \text{ l.p.s.}}$$

**(ii) When the friction loss is 10% of the head indicated by the manometer**

$$K = \sqrt{\frac{h - h_f}{h}}$$

$$= \sqrt{\frac{h - 0.1\,h}{h}} = 0.949$$

$$\therefore Q = 0.949 \times 0.01 = 9.49 \times 10^{-3} \text{ m}^3/\text{s},\ 9.49\ l.p.s.$$

$$\therefore \boxed{Q = 9.49 \text{ l.p.s.}}$$

## Example 2.18:

In an inclined pipeline conveying oil of sp. gr. 0.8, a 300 mm × 150 mm venturimeter is installed. The direction of flow is upwards. The difference of levels between the throat section and the entrance is 1 m. The pressure gauges at the entrance and the throat read 0.17 N/mm² and 0.1 N/mm² respectively. The discharge in the pipe is 0.22 m³/s. Calculate the coefficient of discharge for the meter.

**Solution:**

$$p_1 = 0.17 \text{ N/mm}^2$$

or $$p_1 = \frac{0.17 \times 10^6}{10^3}$$

$$= 170 \text{ kN/m}^2$$

$$\therefore \frac{p_1}{\gamma} = \frac{170}{9.81 \times 0.8}$$

$$= 21.66 \text{ m of oil}$$

$$p_2 = 0.1 \text{ N/mm}^2$$

or $$p_2 = \frac{0.1 \times 10^6}{10^3}$$

$$= 100 \text{ kN/m}^2$$

$$\therefore \frac{p_2}{\gamma} = \frac{100}{9.81 \times 0.8}$$

$$= 12.74 \text{ m of oil}$$

**[Note: K can also be obtained from difference of velocity heads considerations.]**

∴ Piezometric head difference between inlet and throat

$$\therefore h = \left(\frac{p_1}{\gamma} - \frac{p_2}{\gamma}\right) + (z_1 - z_2)$$

$$\therefore h = (21.66 - 12.74) + (0 - 1)$$

$$\therefore h = 7.92 \text{ m}$$

Now $$Q = K.C.\sqrt{h} \qquad [K = C_d]$$

$$0.22 = K \cdot \frac{a_1 a_2 \sqrt{2g}}{\sqrt{a_1^2 - a_2^2}} \cdot \sqrt{h}$$

$$0.22 = K \cdot \frac{a_1 \sqrt{2g}}{\sqrt{\left(\frac{d_1}{d_2}\right)^4 - 1}} \cdot \sqrt{h} \qquad \therefore \left(\frac{a_1^2}{a_2^2}\right) = \left(\frac{d_1}{d_2}\right)^4$$

$$0.22 = K \dfrac{\frac{\pi}{4} \times (0.3)^2 \times \sqrt{19.62}}{\sqrt{\left(\dfrac{0.3}{0.15}\right)^4 - 1}} \cdot \sqrt{7.92}$$

∴ $\quad 0.22 = K \times 0.227$
∴ $\quad K = 0.969$

∴ **Coefficient of discharge for venturimeter = 0.969**

### Example 2.19:

Determine the throat diameter of a venturimeter for installation in a 100 mm diameter pipeline carrying oil of specific gravity 0.87. The maximum range of available oil–mercury differential gauge is 50 cm of mercury deflection. Find the maximum throat diameter which would show full gauge deflection when the flow rate is 20 l.p.s. Assume $C_d = 0.984$.

### Solution:

The maximum deflection of the differential gauge is 50 cm i.e. 0.5 m.

∴ Maximum venturi head that can be recorded in terms of column of oil will be

$$h = 0.5 \left(\dfrac{13.6}{0.87} - 1\right)$$

∴ $\quad h = 7.316$ m of oil.

Now $\quad Q = KC\sqrt{h}$

$$0.02 = 0.984 \times \dfrac{\frac{\pi}{4} \times 0.1^2 \times \sqrt{19.62}}{\sqrt{\left(\dfrac{d_1}{d_2}\right)^4 - 1}} \cdot \sqrt{7.316}$$

∴ $\quad \left(\dfrac{d_1}{d_2}\right)^4 = 22.433$

∴ $\quad \dfrac{d_1}{d_2} = 2.176$

∴ **Diameter of throat = 0.046 m or 46 mm.**

### Example 2.20:

A sub-marine with its axis 15 m below water surface fitted with Pitot tube moves horizontally in sea of specific gravity 1.026 is fitted with mercury U-tube differential manometer giving a deflection of 170 mm. Calculate the speed of sub-marine.

### Solution:

$$V = C\sqrt{2gh} \qquad C = 1, \text{ since value is not given}$$

$$h = h_m \left\{\dfrac{S_m}{S_p} - 1\right\} = \dfrac{170}{1000} \left(\dfrac{13.6}{1.026} - 1\right)$$

∴  h = 2.0834 m of sea water
∴  V = $\sqrt{2gh}$
    = $\sqrt{19.62 \times 2.0834}$
    = 6.393 m/s
    = $6.393 \times \frac{3000}{1000}$ km/hr
∴  V = 23 km/hr.
∴  **Speed of submarine = 23 km/hr**

## Example 2.21:
A Pitot static tube is used to measure velocity of an aeroplane. U-tube differential manometer gives deflection of 5 cm of water. If specific weight of air is 11.75 N/m³ and coefficient of Pitot tube is 0.98, determine speed of aeroplane. Neglect compressibility effects.

**Solution:**
For a Pitot tube:
$$V = C\sqrt{2gh}$$
$$h = h_m \left[\frac{S_m}{S_p} - 1\right]$$
$$= 5 \times 10^{-2} \left[\frac{9810}{11.75} - 1\right]$$
= 41.70 m of air

∴  V = $0.98\sqrt{41.70 \times 19.62}$
∴  **V = 28.03 m/s**

h is the difference between the stagnation pressure head and static pressure head in terms of column of fluid whose velocity is measured.

$$h = \frac{p_s - p_0}{\gamma}.$$

Here manometric liquid is water and fluid flowing is air.

## Example 2.22:
A Pitot tube records a reading of 7.85 kN/m² as the stagnation pressure when it is held at the centre of a pipe of 250 mm diameter conveying water. The static pressure in the pipe is 40 mm of mercury (gauge–vacuum). Calculate the discharge through the pipe assuming that the mean velocity of flow is 0.8 times the maximum velocity. Take $C_d$ = 0.98.

**Solution:**

Stagnation pressure $\frac{p_s}{\gamma} = \frac{7.85}{9.81}$ = 0.8 m of water

Static pressure $\frac{p_0}{\gamma}$ = – 0.04 × 13.6 = – 0.544 m of water

∴  $h = \frac{p_s}{\gamma} - \frac{p_0}{\gamma}$ = 0.8 – (– 0.544)
       = 1.344 m

∴ Velocity at centre line is given by

$$V_c = 0.98 \times \sqrt{2gh} = 0.98 \times \sqrt{19.62 \times 1.344}$$
$$= 5.032 \text{ m/s}$$

∴ $$V_{av} = 0.8 \times 5.032$$
$$= 4.026 \text{ m/s}$$

∴ Discharge through the pipe $= \dfrac{\pi}{4} \times 0.25^2 \times 4.026$
$$= 0.198 \text{ m}^3/\text{s}$$

∴ **Discharge through the pipe = 0.198 m³/s**

## THEORETICAL QUESTIONS

1. What do you understand by dynamics of fluid flow? How does it differ from the kinematics of fluid flow?
2. State the different forces considered in studying the equation of motion of a fluid. State the conditions under which each is significant.
3. Derive Euler's equation of motion along a stream line in the form $\left(\dfrac{dp}{\rho}\right) + gdz + vdv = 0$ and hence establish Bernoulli's equation as an integration of Euler's equation. State assumptions clearly.

**OR**

Derive Bernoulli's equation from Euler's equation along a stream line.

4. Derive Euler's equation along a stream line.
5. State and prove Bernoulli's equation. What are limitations of the Bernoulli's equation?
6. State Bernoulli's theorem. Explain significance of each term in Bernoulli's equation. State the assumptions made clearly.
7. Explain how Bernoulli's equation is applied to the real fluid flow problems.
8. Explain how Bernoulli's theorem, applied to two points in flow, is modified to account for
   1. Loss of head
   2. Installation of pump
   3. Installation of a device like a turbine
   4. Non-uniform velocity variation in the pipe.
9. What do you understand by "Energy correction factor α"? Derive an expression for the same.
10. What is a Pitot tube? How is it used to measure velocity of flow at any point in a pipe or channel?

**OR**

Write a short note on Pitot tube.

11. With a neat sketch describe the working of a Prandtl's-Static Pitot tube.

12. Describe an orifice meter and find an expression for measuring discharge of fluid through a pipe with this device.

13. Draw a neat sketch of Venturimeter, indicate different parts of it, state its governing principle and derive the expression for the discharge through it.

14. Describe a Venturimeter and find an expression for measuring discharge of fluid through a pipe with this device.

15. Compare Venturimeter and Orifice meter.

16. Derive an expression for the discharge passing through an inclined venturimeter.

    For a given flow, show that the reading of differential manometer remains unchanged irrespective of the inclination of venturimeter.

17. Explain, why

    Length of the diverging cone is greater than converging cone in venturimeter.

18. Describe working of any one instrument used for measurement of rate flow in pipes.

## NUMERICAL PROBLEMS

1. At a point in the pipeline where the diameter is 20 cm, the velocity of water is 4 m/s and the pressure is 343.35 kN/m². At a point 15 m downstream, the diameter reduces to 10 cm. Calculate the pressure at this point, if the pipe is:

   (i) Horizontal

   (ii) Vertical with flow downward

   (iii) Vertical with flow upward.

   [**Ans.** 223.37 kN/m², 370.524 kN/m², 76.22 kN/m²]

2. A jet of water coming out from 50 mm diameter rounded nozzle attached to 100 mm diameter pipe is directed vertically downwards. If the pressure in the pipe 20 cm above the nozzle is 200 kN/m² gauge, determine the diameter of jet 5 m below the nozzle level.

   [**Ans.** 47.5 mm]

3. A siphon has circular bore of 75 mm diameter and consists of a bent pipe with its crest (topmost point) 1.8 m above water level in the tank discharging into atmosphere at a level of 3.6 m below water level. Find velocity of flow, the discharge and the absolute pressure at the crest. Take atmospheric pressure as 10 m of water. Neglect losses.

   [**Ans.** 8.4 m/s, 0.03711 m³/s, 45.126 kN/m² (absolute)]

4. For the siphon shown in Fig. 2.37, determine the discharge and the maximum permissible value of 'h'. Water vapour separates below 2 m of w.c. absolute. Assume atmospheric pressure 720 mm Hg. Neglect losses in the siphon.

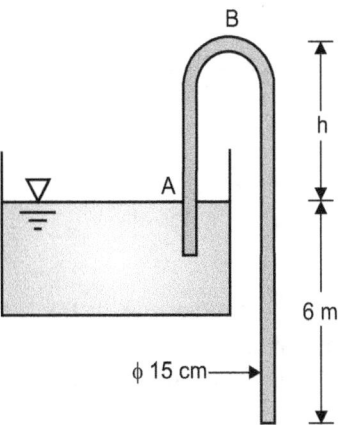

**Fig. 2.37**

[**Hint:** Apply Bernoulli's theorem to liquid level and outlet of siphon to get velocity through the siphon and hence discharge. To get 'h' apply Bernoulli's theorem to liquid level and point B. Putting pressure head at B as 2 m of water (absolute)].

[**Ans.** 191.74 l.p.s., 1.792 m]

5. A nozzle is connected at the end of a horizontal pipe discharging oil from a tank to atmosphere. Estimate the discharge in l.p.m., if the head in the tank is 4 m. Loss in the pipe can be taken as $20 \frac{v^2}{2g}$, where v is the velocity in pipe, and the loss of energy in the nozzle can be assumed as $0.02 \frac{v_n^2}{2g}$, where $v_n$ is the velocity at the nozzle outlet. Also determine the pressure in kPa at the base of the nozzle. Take pipe diameter 100 mm and the nozzle diameter 25 mm. R.D. of oil is 0.8.

[**Ans.** 249 l.p.m., 29.02 kPa]

6. A fire fighting pump draws water from a tank in which water level is 3 m below the axis of the pump and delivers to a nozzle which is 8 m above pump axis. The velocity of water at the nozzle is 25 m/s and the nozzle diameter is 50 mm. The velocity in suction pipe is 4 m/s and delivery to suction pipe ratio is 0.8. If the loss of head on suction side is 2 m and on delivery side is 12 m, find the pressure just before and after the pump. What is the power delivered by the pump to water? Draw total energy and hydraulic grade lines schematically.

[**Ans.** – 5.815 m, 49.87 m, 27.33 kW]

7. A pump takes water from a supply tank and lifts it to another tank. The inlet pipe is 20 cm in diameter and the water level in the supply tank is 2 m above the inlet. The delivery pipe is vertical and 15 cm in diameter. If the pump supplies energy to the flow at the rate of 11 kW when discharging 110 lit./sec., determine the pressure intensities in the inlet pipe just before the pump and the delivery pipe at a height of 5 m above the sump. Neglect losses.

[**Ans.** 13.49 kPa, 31.59 kPa]

8. A conical tube of length 3 m is fixed vertically with its smaller end upwards. The velocity of water at the lower end is 2 m/s and that at upper end is 4 m/s. The pressure head at the lower end is 4.98 m and loss of head in the tube is $0.3 \dfrac{V_1^2 - V_2^2}{2g}$, where $V_1$ and $V_2$ are the velocities at the upper and lower ends respectively. Determine the height to which the jet of water, leaving the upper end, will rise in air.

   [**Ans.** 2 m]

9. Vertical pipe 2 m long has 200 mm diameter at the lower end and 400 mm diameter at upper end. It carries water at 200 l.p.s. If loss in pipe is 1 m of water, find pressure difference in Pa between two ends of pipe. Also find velocities at upper and lower ends of pipe.

   [**Ans.** 10.43 kPa, 1.59 m/s, 6.36 m/s]

10. Fig. 2.38 shows a hydraulic machine M which is a pump or a turbine. Find the power of the machine assuming an efficiency of 85%. Whether it is a pump or a turbine?

    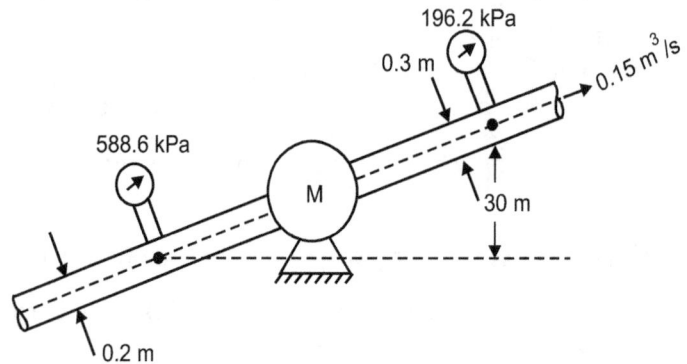

    **Fig. 2.38**

    [**Hint:** Calculate total head before the machine and total head after the machine. If total head after the machine is more than that before the machine, the machine is a pump, and vice–versa.]

    [**Ans.** 13.67 kW, turbine]

11. A horizontal venturimeter is provided in a pipe of 300 mm in diameter carrying water. The throat diameter is 100 mm. If the pressure in the pipe is $14 \times 10^4$ N/m² and vacuum pressure at the throat is 370 mm of mercury, find the discharge in the pipe. Assume that 4% of the differential head is lost between the pipe and throat. Find coefficient of venturimeter.

    [**Ans.** 0.15 m³/s, 0.98]

12. A 15 cm × 7.5 cm venturimeter is installed in a horizontal pipe of 15 cm diameter carrying oil of sp. gr. 0.9. A differential mercury manometer connected between inlet and throat shows a deflection of 20 cm. Calculate the rate of flow in l.p.m. K = 0.98.

    [**Ans.** 1995.37 l.p.m.]

13. A venturimeter has its axis vertical, the inlet and throat areas being 177 cm² and 44 cm² respectively. The throat is 22.5 cm above inlet and coefficient of discharge of meter is 0.96. Petrol of sp. gr. 0.78 flows up through the meter at a rate of 0.029 m³/s. Find the pressure difference between the inlet and the throat.

    [**Ans.** 18.97 kPa]

14. Find maximum discharge of water through a 100 mm × 50 mm venturimeter having coefficient of 0.98. The pressure in the pipe is 8 m (gauge) and separation takes place at 2 m of water absolute. Local barometer shows 10 m of water.

    [**Hint:** The maximum discharge occurs when the pressure at the throat is separation pressure.]

    [**Ans.** 0.0352 m³/s]

15. A flow nozzle of 3 cm throat diameter is to be used to indicate the flow of oil as 20°C (kinematic viscosity = $9 \times 10^{-6}$ m²/s) in a 5 cm diameter pipe. If the measured pressure difference between the taps is 75 mm Hg, determine the oil flow. Take density of oil = 860 kg/m³ and coefficient of discharge = 0.99.

    [**Ans.** 3.618 lps]

16. A Pitot tube is inserted in a pipe of 300 mm diameter. The static pressure in pipe is 100 mm of mercury (vacuum). The stagnation pressure at the centre of the pipe, recorded by the Pitot tube is 0.981 N/cm². Calculate the rate of flow of water through pipe, if the mean velocity of flow is 0.85 times the central velocity. Take $C_v$ = 0.98.

    [**Hint:** Static pressure = – 100 mm of Hg = –1.36 m of water.

    Stagnation pressure = 0.981 N/mm² = $\dfrac{0.981 \times 10^4}{9810}$ = 1 m of water

    ∴ Difference of pressure head, h = 1 – (–1.36) = 2.36 m of water, centre line velocity = 6.668 m/s, average velocity = 5.668 m/s etc.]

    [**Ans.** Q = 0.4 m³/s]

17. A Pitot static tube is used to measure velocity of air passing through a duct. A U–tube manometer connected to Pitot tube connections shows deflection of 8 mm of water. If the coefficient of Pitot tube is 0.98, calculate the velocity of air. Assume specific weight of air as 10 N/m³.

    [**Ans.** 12.15 m/s]

18. A submarine is cruising at a depth of 20 m in ocean water (density 1020 kg/m³). If the forward speed of the submarine is 10 m/s, what readings would be given by Pitot and Static pressure probes? Assume static probe is located to register free stream static pressure.

    [**Ans.** 251.16 kPa, 200.124 kPa]

19. A Pitot static tube is used to measure velocity of air flowing through a wind tunnel. What differential head in mm of water will be registered by an air-water differential manometer when air is flowing with a velocity of 145 km/hr. Assume the mass densities of air and water as 1.208 kg/m$^3$ and 1000 kg/m$^3$ and assume coefficient of pitot static tube as 1.

    [**Ans.** 100 mm]

20. A Pitot tube is mounted on the front end of a car. An air-water differential manometer connected to the Pitot tube shows a deflection of 100 mm of water, when the wind is blowing against the direction of motion of car at the velocity of 15 km/hr. If the density of air is 11.85 N/m$^3$ and that of water is 9810 N/m$^3$, find the velocity of car. Take coefficient of Pitot tube as 1.

    [**Ans.** 130 km/hr]

# Unit 3

# VISCOUS AND BOUNDARY LAYER FLOW

## (A) VISCOUS FLOW

## 3.1 Introduction

It has already been seen that ideal fluids do not have viscosity. Therefore, when such a fluid passes over a boundary it simply slips over the boundary and as such velocity distribution over the boundary is uniform throughout. In case of real fluid, due to viscosity, there is no relative motion between the surface and the fluid just in the vicinity of the boundary. Thus, if the boundary is stationary, the fluid at the boundary has zero velocity. If the boundary is moving, the fluid at the boundary has the same velocity as that of the boundary. This is known as 'no slip condition'. Therefore, in real fluid, with stationary boundary, the velocity is zero at the boundary and goes on increasing as we go away from the boundary. This change in velocity across the flow gives rise to velocity gradient. The velocity gradient in turn gives rise to viscous shear resistance opposing the motion. Due to this, power is required to maintain flow of real fluids (as against the flow of ideal fluids).

In some problems, reasonably satisfactory solutions can be obtained even without taking into account effects of viscosity. But in many problems, even with problems, involving air or water which have very low viscosity, the effect of viscosity near the boundaries cannot be neglected.

## 3.2 Laminar and Turbulent Flow

### 3.2.1 Reynold's Experiments

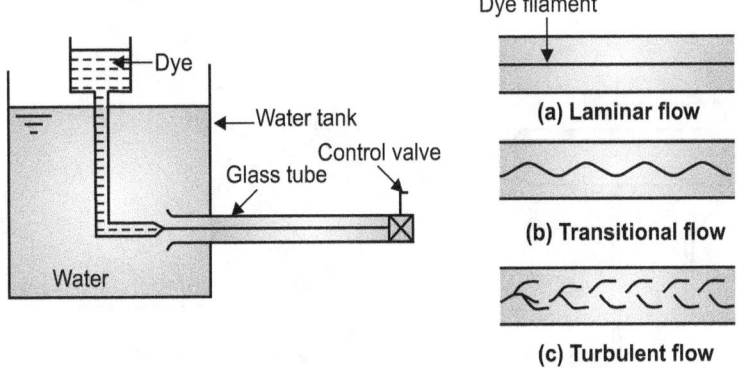

**Fig. 3.1: Reynold's apparatus and types of flow**

It has been observed that depending upon the relative magnitudes of viscous forces and inertial forces, flow can exist in two types, either as laminar flow or turbulent flow. Osborne Reynolds was the first to study the characteristics of flow in this respect. His apparatus

(Fig. 3.1) consisted of (i) a water tank (ii) a glass tube with a bell mouthed entrance inserted into the water tank (iii) a valve at the end of the tube to control the flow in the tube and (iv) an arrangement to inject a fine filament of dye in the glass tube.

The nature of dye filament was observed at different velocities. The results were as follows:

1. At very low velocities, the dye remained in the form of a straight stable filament parallel to the axis of the tube. Fig. 3.1 (a).
2. At higher velocities, dye filament showed irregularities and wavy nature. Fig. 3.1 (b).
3. With further increase in velocity, the filament became more and more irregular and finally dye diffused over the complete cross section. [Fig. 3.1 (c)].

It can be seen that at low velocities the flow takes place in number of sheets or laminae. This flow is called "Laminar flow". At high velocities the flow is disturbed and intermixing of particles takes place. This flow is called "Turbulent flow".

## 3.2.2 Types of Flow and Loss of Head

The existence of two types of flow can also be shown by another experiment. Loss of head '$h_f$' is measured in a pipe of length 'L' for various values of velocity 'V' in the pipe. Fig. 3.2 (a). The graph of $\dfrac{h_f}{L}$ Vs V is plotted on log-log scale. Fig. 3.2 (b).

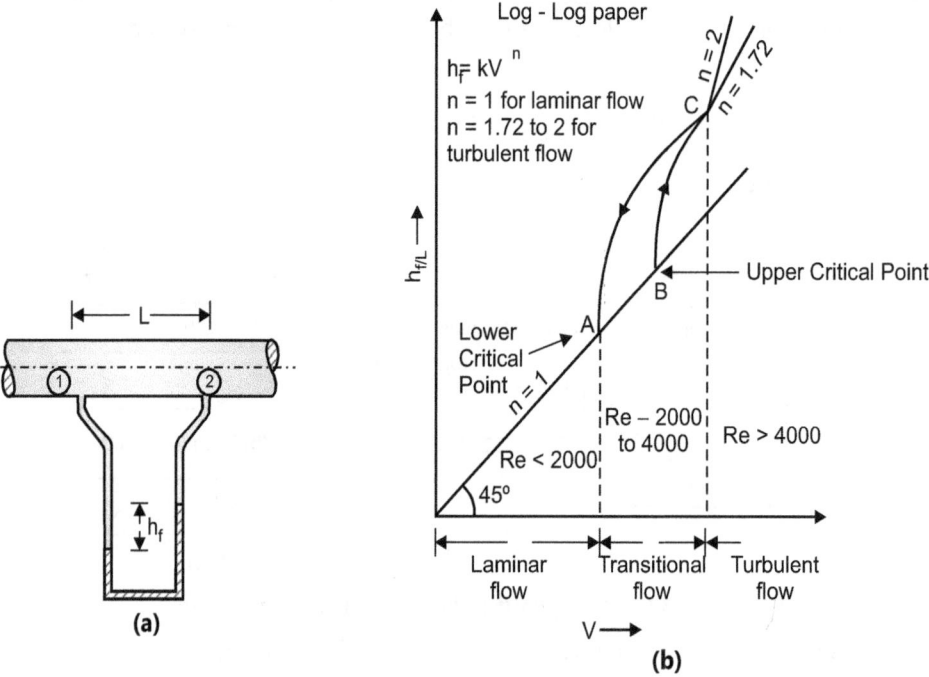

**Fig. 3.2: Types of flow in a pipe**

It can be seen from the graph, that for low velocities, the curve is a straight line with a slope of 1 (line makes an angle of 45°) upto point 'B' indicating that the loss of head is proportional to velocity ($h_f \propto V$) upto point 'B'. Beyond 'B', we can see a transition zone upto point 'C'. After 'C', again the curve obtained is a straight line but with distinctly varying slope varying from 1.72 to 2.

Thus, upto point 'B' it is one type of flow in which $h_f \propto V$. This flow is called laminar flow. Beyond point C, it is another type of flow in which $h_f \propto V^n$, 'n' varying from 1.72 to 2. This flow is called turbulent flow.

However, if velocity is reduced from high value, the line 'BC' is not retraced. Instead, the points lie along curve 'CA'. Point 'B' is called *'higher (or upper) critical point*, and the corresponding velocity is called *'upper critical velocity'*. Point 'A' is called *'lower critical point'*, and the corresponding velocity is called *'Lower critical velocity'*.

However, velocity of flow is not the only deciding factor which determines whether the flow is laminar or turbulent. Reynold's number which is the ratio of inertia force to viscous force is the criterion to decide whether the flow is laminar or turbulent.

Reynold's number is given by $Re = \dfrac{\rho VL}{\mu} = \dfrac{VL}{\nu}$. For pipe flow L = D the diameter of pipe and therefore, for pipe flow $Re = \dfrac{VD}{\nu}$.

The upper critical Reynold's number corresponding to point 'B' of Fig. 3.2 (b) is not definite. It's value depends upon how carefully the initial disturbances affecting the flow are prevented. Normally, upper critical Reynold's number for pipe flow is about 4000. However, laminar flow has been maintained (with proper precautions) upto values of Re as high as 50,000.

The lower critical Reynold's number corresponding to point 'A' of Fig. 3.2 (b) is definite. Lower critical Reynold's number for the flow in straight pipe is 2000. This Reynold's number is the true critical Reynold's number which is the dividing line between laminar flow and turbulent flow.

Thus the Reynold's number below which the flow is definitely laminar (Re = 2000 for pipe flow) is called *'critical Reynold's number'*.

## 3.3 Definition and Characteristics of Laminar Flow

The flow in which the particles of fluid behave in orderly manner without intermixing with each other and the flow takes place in number of sheets, layers or laminae, each sliding over the other is called *'laminar flow'*.

### 3.3.1 Characteristics of Laminar Flow
1. The particles of fluid behave in disciplined manner. There is no intermixing of particles and the flow takes place in layers which glide one over the other.
2. Velocity of flow at a point is nearly constant in magnitude and direction.
3. The viscous force plays an important role (as compared to other forces) in fluid flow.
4. Shear stress is given by Newton's law of viscosity.
5. Any disturbance caused is quickly damped by viscous forces.
6. Due to 'no slip condition' velocity across the section is not uniform (as in case of ideal fluid) but goes on varying. Due to this, velocity gradient and hence shear stress gradient is established at right angles to direction of flow.
7. Loss of head is proportional to velocity of flow.
8. Velocity variation (distribution) is parabolic in nature.

## 3.4 Practical Examples of Laminar Flow
1. Flow of oil in lubricating mechanisms.
2. Flow of oil in measuring instruments.
3. Flow of fluid in capillary tubes.
4. Flow of liquid through filters and sand beds.
5. Flow of blood through veins.
6. Flow of liquid through porous media.
7. Rise of sap in trees.
8. Flow of oil in small tubes of governing mechanisms of prime movers.

## 3.5 Shear and Pressure Gradients in Laminar Flow

The real fluids adhere to the boundary due to viscosity. Due to this there is no relative motion between the boundary and the fluid. This condition is known as 'No slip condition'. Thus in real fluids, the velocity is zero at the stationary boundary and goes on increasing away from the boundary. Thus, the different layers of fluid move over each other with different velocities. The relative motion between the layers gives rise to shear stress. The magnitude of this shear stress varies from layer to layer. It is maximum at the boundary where the velocity gradient is maximum ($\tau = \mu \frac{du}{dy}$, $\frac{du}{dy}$ being maximum, $\tau$ also is maximum) and it's magnitude goes on decreasing with distance from the boundary. Therefore, a shear stress gradient exists across the flow. Along the flow, pressure will vary to maintain the flow and hence pressure gradient will exist along the flow.

A relation between these two gradients can be obtained as follows:

## 3.6 Relation Between Shear and Pressure Gradients in Laminar Flow

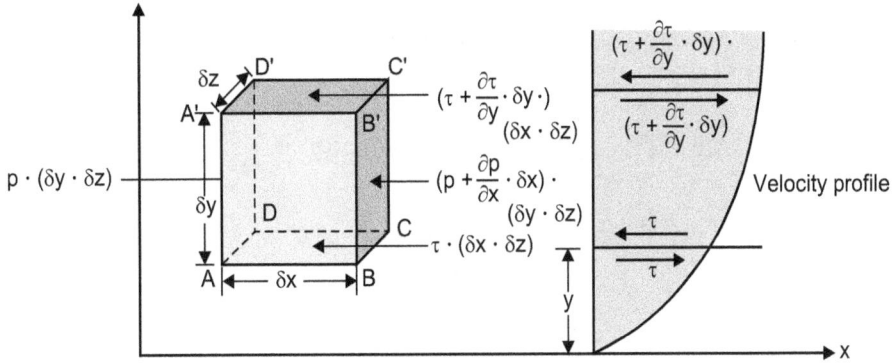

**Fig. 3.3: Forces on fluid element in laminar flow**

Consider a free body of the fluid in the form of a parallelopiped with sides $\delta x$, $\delta y$ and $\delta z$ as shown in Fig. 3.3. It can be seen from the figure that the layer ABCD is moving at higher velocity than the layer below it. Therefore, layer ABCD exerts a shear stress in forward direction (positive 'x' direction) on the lower layer. On the other hand, the lower layer exerts equal and opposite shear stress (in negative x-direction) on the layer 'ABCD'. With similar analysis it can be seen that the layer A'B'C'D' is subjected to a shear stress in the forward direction (positive x direction) due to a faster moving layer above it. Since, the velocity varies in y - direction the shear stress on ABCD and 'A'B'C'D' will be different. Let '$\tau$' be the shear stress acting on face ABCD, then the shear stress on face A'B'C'D' will be $\left(\tau + \dfrac{\partial \tau}{\partial y} \cdot \delta y\right)$.

Further, if 'p' is the intensity of pressure on left face, it will be $\left(p + \dfrac{\partial p}{\partial x} \cdot \delta x\right)$ on the right face of the element.

The various forces acting on the element are as shown in Fig. 3.3. For a two dimensional flow, there will be no forces acting on faces ABB'A' and DCC'D',

Since, the flow is steady uniform flow, there is no acceleration and hence sum of the forces in the direction of motion must be zero. (Forces in positive x - direction are taken to be positive).

$$\therefore \left[p \cdot \delta y\, \delta z - \left(p + \dfrac{\partial p}{\partial x} \cdot \delta x\right) \delta y\, \delta z\right] + \left[\left(\tau + \dfrac{\partial \tau}{\partial y} \delta y\right) \delta x\, \delta z - \tau\, \delta x\, \delta z\right] = 0$$

$$\begin{bmatrix}\text{Pressure force in the}\\ \text{direction of motion}\end{bmatrix} + \begin{bmatrix}\text{Shear force in the}\\ \text{direction of motion}\end{bmatrix}$$

$$\therefore \quad -\dfrac{\partial p}{\partial x} \cdot \delta x \cdot \delta y \cdot \delta z + \dfrac{\partial \tau}{\partial y} \cdot \delta x \cdot \delta y \cdot \delta z = 0$$

Dividing by ($\delta x \cdot \delta y \cdot \delta z$), the volume of the parallelopiped

$$\boxed{\frac{\partial p}{\partial x} = \frac{\partial \tau}{\partial y}} \quad \ldots (3.1)$$

The above relation shows that *for a two dimensional steady uniform laminar flow, the pressure gradient in the direction of flow is equal to the shear stress gradient in the normal direction.*

Further, for this type of flow, $\left(\frac{\partial p}{\partial x}\right)$ is independent of 'y' and $\left(\frac{\partial \tau}{\partial y}\right)$ is independent of 'x'.

According to Newton's law of viscosity $\tau = \mu \frac{\partial u}{\partial y}$

∴
$$\boxed{\frac{\partial p}{\partial x} = \mu \cdot \frac{\partial^2 u}{\partial y^2}} \quad \ldots (3.2)$$

Problems on steady, uniform laminar flow can be analysed by the integration of equation (3.2).

## 3.7 Steady Laminar Flow through a Circular Pipe

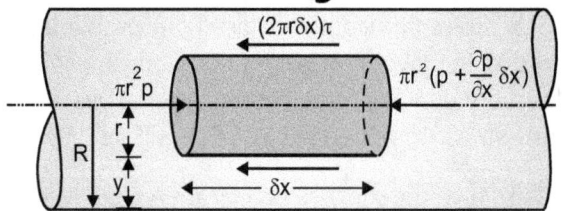

**Fig. 3.4: Laminar flow through a pipe**

Consider steady laminar flow of fluid through a horizontal circular pipe as shown in Fig. 3.4. Consider concentric cylindrical element of fluid having radius 'r' and length '$\delta x$' as shown in Fig. 3.4 Let 'p' be the intensity of pressure on left face of the element and let it increase to $\left(p + \frac{\partial p}{\partial x} \cdot \delta x\right)$ upto the right face of the element. Let '$\tau$' be the shear stress at distance 'r' from the axis of the pipe.

The forces acting on the element are:

(i) the pressure force ($p \cdot \pi r^2$) on left face,

(ii) $\left(p + \frac{\partial p}{\partial x} \cdot \delta x\right) \cdot \pi r^2$ on right face and

(iii) the total shear force ($\tau \cdot 2\pi r \cdot \delta x$) acting on the periphery of the element.

Since the flow is steady uniform flow, there is no acceleration and hence sum of all the forces acting on the element in the direction of motion must be zero.

$$\therefore \quad p \cdot \pi r^2 - \left(p + \frac{\partial p}{\partial x} \cdot \delta x\right) \cdot \pi r^2 - \tau \cdot 2\pi r \cdot \delta x = 0$$

$$\therefore \quad -\frac{\partial p}{\partial x} \cdot \delta x \cdot (\pi r^2) - \tau \cdot (2\pi r) \, \delta x = 0$$

Dividing by $(\pi r^2) \cdot \delta x$, the volume of the element and simplifying, we get,

$$\boxed{\tau = \left(-\frac{\partial p}{\partial x}\right) \cdot \frac{r}{2}} \quad \ldots (3.3)$$

### (i) Shear stress:

Equation (3.3) gives the variation of stress with respect to radius 'r'. The relation shows that shear stress varies linearly (directly) with radius 'r'. At the centre, r = 0, the shear stress also is zero. At the pipe wall, r = R, the shear stress is maximum and its magnitude is given by

$$\boxed{\tau_0 = \left(-\frac{\partial p}{\partial x}\right) \cdot \frac{R}{2}} \quad \ldots (3.4)$$

Shear stress distribution across a section is shown in Fig. 3.5.

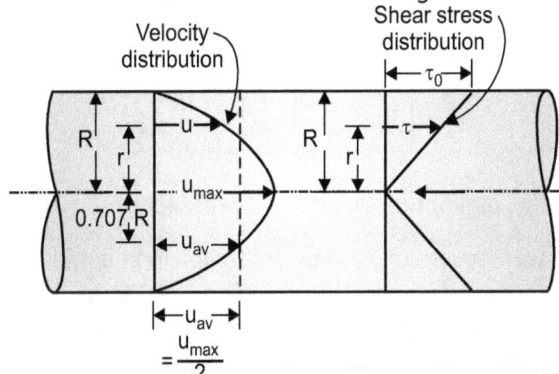

**Fig. 3.5: Velocity and shear stress distribution for laminar flow through a circular pipe**

### (ii) Velocity:

According to Newton's law of viscosity

$$\tau = \mu \cdot \frac{\partial u}{\partial y}, \text{ where y is measured from pipe wall.}$$

But from Fig. 3.4,

$$y = R - r$$
$$\therefore \quad \partial y = -\partial r$$

$$\therefore \quad \tau = \mu \frac{\partial u}{\partial y} = -\mu \left(\frac{\partial u}{\partial r}\right)$$

Therefore, from equation (3.3)

$$\mu\left(-\frac{\partial u}{\partial r}\right) = \left(-\frac{\partial p}{\partial x}\right) \cdot \frac{r}{2}$$

$$\therefore \quad \frac{\partial u}{\partial r} = \frac{1}{2\mu}\left(\frac{\partial p}{\partial x}\right) \cdot r$$

Integrating the above equation w.r.t. 'r' we get,

$$u = \frac{1}{2\mu}\left(\frac{\partial p}{\partial x}\right) \cdot \frac{r^2}{2} + C \qquad \left[\because \frac{\partial p}{\partial x} \text{ is independent of } r\right]$$

or $\qquad u = \frac{1}{4\mu}\left(\frac{\partial p}{\partial x}\right) \cdot r^2 + C \qquad \qquad \ldots (3.5)$

Value of C, the constant of integration, can be obtained from boundary condition, i.e. at r = R, u = 0 (by no-slip condition).

$$\therefore \quad 0 = \frac{1}{4\mu}\left(\frac{\partial p}{\partial x}\right) \cdot R^2 + C$$

or $\qquad C = -\frac{1}{4\mu}\left(\frac{\partial p}{\partial x}\right) \cdot R^2$

Substituting value of C in equation (3.5) we get

$$u = \frac{1}{4\mu}\left(\frac{\partial p}{\partial x}\right) r^2 - \frac{1}{4\mu}\left(\frac{\partial p}{\partial x}\right) \cdot R^2$$

or $\qquad \boxed{u = \frac{1}{4\mu}\left(-\frac{\partial p}{\partial x}\right)(R^2 - r^2)} \qquad \ldots (3.6)$

This relation gives the variation of velocity with respect of radius 'r'. Since $\mu$, $\left(\frac{\partial p}{\partial x}\right)$ and R are constant, 'u' varies with square of 'r'. Thus, *for steady laminar flow through a circular pipe, the velocity variation across the section is parabolic in nature.* The surface of velocity distribution is paraboloid of revolution. At the pipe wall, r = R, velocity is zero and at r = 0 i.e. at centre of pipe velocity is maximum and is given by

$$\boxed{u_{max} = \frac{R^2}{4\mu}\left(-\frac{\partial p}{\partial x}\right)} \qquad \ldots (3.7)$$

From equations (3.6) and (3.7), we can write

$$u = \frac{1}{4\mu}\left(-\frac{\partial p}{\partial x}\right)(R^2 - r^2)$$

or $\qquad u = \frac{R^2}{4\mu}\left(-\frac{\partial p}{\partial x}\right)\left[1 - \left(\frac{r}{R}\right)^2\right] \qquad$ but $\frac{R^2}{4\mu}\left(-\frac{\partial p}{\partial x}\right) = u_{max}$

$$\therefore \quad \boxed{u = u_{max}\left[1 - \left(\frac{r}{R}\right)^2\right]} \qquad \ldots (3.8)$$

Velocity distribution is shown in Fig. 3.5.

## (iii) Discharge and Average Velocity:

**Discharge:** The discharge 'Q' across a section can be found out by integrating the discharge dQ passing through an annular ring of width 'dr' situated at distance 'r' from the axis. Fig. 3.6.

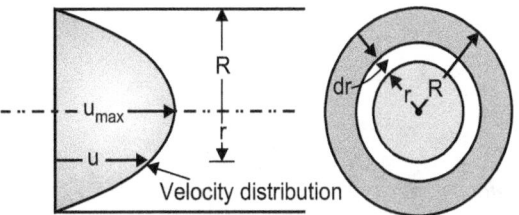

**Fig. 3.6: Discharge through pipe (Laminar flow)**

Discharge through the annular ring dQ = Area of ring × velocity at radius 'r'

∴
$$dQ = (2\pi r \, dr) \cdot \left[\frac{1}{4\mu}\left(-\frac{\partial p}{\partial x}\right)(R^2 - r^2)\right]$$

∴
$$Q = \int dQ = \int_0^R (2\pi r \, dr) \left[\frac{1}{4\mu}\left(-\frac{\partial p}{\partial x}\right)(R^2 - r^2)\right]$$

$$= \frac{1}{4\mu}\left(-\frac{\partial p}{\partial x}\right) 2\pi \int_0^R (R^2 - r^2) \cdot r \, dr$$

$$= \frac{\pi}{2\mu}\left(-\frac{\partial p}{\partial x}\right)\left[\frac{R^2 r^2}{2} - \frac{r^4}{4}\right]_0^R$$

∴
$$= \frac{\pi}{2\mu}\left(-\frac{\partial p}{\partial x}\right)\left[\frac{R^4}{2} - \frac{R^4}{4}\right]$$

∴
$$\boxed{Q = \frac{\pi R^4}{8\mu}\left(-\frac{\partial p}{\partial x}\right)} \quad \ldots (3.9)$$

The average velocity can be found out by dividing the discharge through the section by the area of pipe.

**Average velocity:** $\quad u_{av} = \dfrac{Q}{\text{Area of pipe}} = \dfrac{Q}{\pi R^2}$

Therefore, $\quad u_{av} = \dfrac{\pi R^4}{8\mu}\left(-\dfrac{\partial p}{\partial x}\right) \cdot \dfrac{1}{\pi R^2}$

or $\quad \boxed{u_{av} = \dfrac{R^2}{8\mu}\left(-\dfrac{\partial p}{\partial x}\right)} \quad \ldots (3.10)$

From equations (3.7) and (3.10)

$$\boxed{u_{av} = \frac{u_{max}}{2}} \quad \ldots (3.11)$$

Results of equation (3.11) also follow from the property of paraboloid of revolution.
Thus, *in case of steady laminar flow through a circular pipe, average velocity is half the maximum velocity.*

The point where the spot or local velocity is equal to average velocity can now be found by equating spot or local velocity given by equation (3.8) and average velocity given by equation (3.11).

$$u_{max}\left[1-\left(\frac{r}{R}\right)^2\right] = \frac{u_{max}}{2}$$

$$\therefore \quad \frac{r^2}{R^2} = \frac{1}{2}$$

or $\boxed{r = 0.707\ R}$ ... (3.12)

Thus, the average velocity occurs at a radial distance of (0.707 R), from the centre of the pipe.

### (iv) Pressure drop over a given pipe length:

The pressure drop between two sections (1) and (2) separated by distance 'L' along the pipe line can be found out as follows.

We have, from equation (3.10)

$$u_{av} = \frac{R^2}{8\mu}\left(-\frac{\partial p}{\partial x}\right)$$

Therefore, $\left(-\frac{\partial p}{\partial x}\right) = \frac{8\mu\ u_{av}}{R^2}$

or $-\partial p = \frac{8\mu\ u_{av}}{R^2}\cdot \partial x$

Integrating between sections 1 and 2,

$$\int_{p_1}^{p_2} -\partial p = \int_{x_1}^{x_2} \frac{8\mu\ u_{av}}{R^2}\cdot \partial x$$

$$\therefore \quad p_1 - p_2 = \frac{8\mu\ u_{av}}{R^2}(x_2 - x_1)$$

but $x_2 - x_1 = L$ distance between sections 1 and 2

$$\therefore \quad p_1 - p_2 = \frac{8\mu\ u_{av}\ L}{R^2}$$

or $\boxed{p_1 - p_2 = \frac{32\mu\ u_{av}\ L}{D^2}} \qquad \because R = \frac{D}{2}$ ... (3.13)

Further $u_{av} = \dfrac{Q}{\dfrac{\pi}{4}D^2} = \dfrac{4Q}{\pi D^2}$

Substituting this value of $u_{av}$ in equation (3.13) we get,

$$\boxed{p_1 - p_2 = \frac{128\ \mu\ QL}{\pi D^4}} \qquad \text{... (3.14)}$$

Equation (3.13) (as well as equation 3.14) is called 'Hagen - Poiseuille' equation for steady uniform laminar flow through circular pipe.

## (v) Loss of head:

If $p_1$ and $p_2$ are pressure intensities at sections 1 and 2, the corresponding pressure heads are $\dfrac{p_1}{\gamma}$ and $\dfrac{p_2}{\gamma}$. The difference between these two heads is the loss of head. Fig. 3.7.

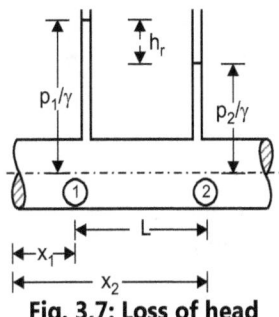

Fig. 3.7: Loss of head

From equation (3.13),

$$p_1 - p_2 = \frac{32\,\mu\,u_{av}\,L}{D^2}$$

$$\therefore \boxed{h_f = \frac{p_1 - p_2}{\gamma} = \frac{32\,\mu\,u_{av}L}{\gamma D^2} = \frac{128\,\mu\,QL}{\pi\,\gamma D^4}} \quad \ldots (3.15)$$

## (vi) Friction Factor 'f':

Loss of head due to friction in pipe is expressed by Darcy-Weisbach equation [Ref. Eq. (3.4)] as

$$h_f = \frac{fL}{D} \cdot \frac{u_{av}^2}{2g} \quad \ldots (3.16)$$

Equating equations (3.16) and (3.15)

$$\frac{fL}{D} \cdot \frac{u_{av}^2}{2g} = \frac{32\,\mu\,u_{av}L}{\gamma D^2}$$

$$\therefore \quad \frac{f\,u_{av}}{2g} = \frac{32\,\mu}{\gamma D} \qquad \because \gamma = \rho \cdot g$$

$$\therefore \quad f = \frac{64\,\mu}{\rho\,u_{av}\,D}$$

$$= \frac{64}{\left(\dfrac{\rho\,u_{av}\,D}{\mu}\right)} \quad \text{but} \quad \frac{\rho\,u_{av}\,D}{\mu} = Re,\ \text{Reynold's number}$$

$$\therefore \quad \boxed{f = \frac{64}{Re}} \quad \ldots (3.17)$$

'f' is called 'friction factor'. *Therefore, value of friction factor for steady laminar flow through circular pipe is* $\left(\dfrac{64}{Re}\right)$.

It may be seen that to maintain the flow through pipe the shear resistance has to be overcome. To overcome this resistance some external power is required. This is generally provided by a pump. The power of the pump required to maintain the flow can be found out as follows,

$$\text{Power} = \text{Rate of doing work}$$
$$= \frac{\text{Force} \times \text{Distance}}{\text{Time}}$$
$$= \text{Force} \times \text{Velocity}$$

The pressure gradient $(-\partial p/\partial x)$ in the direction of flow compensates for the resistance to flow. The pressure gradient represents the force per unit volume of fluid. If A is the area of pipe and L the length, then the total force is given by

$$\text{Force} = \left(-\frac{\partial p}{\partial x}\right) \times A \times L$$

∴ $$\text{Power } P = \left(-\frac{\partial p}{\partial x}\right) (A \times L) \cdot V$$

But $$AV = \text{discharge } Q, \text{ and } \left(-\frac{\partial p}{\partial x}\right) = \frac{p_1 - p_2}{L}$$

∴ $$\boxed{\text{Power } P = (p_1 - p_2) \cdot Q} \qquad \ldots (3.18)$$

Since $\dfrac{p_1 - p_2}{\gamma} = h_f,$  $p_1 - p_2 = \gamma \cdot h_f$

Therefore, formula for power can also be written as

$$\boxed{\text{Power } P = \gamma \cdot Q \cdot h_f} \qquad \ldots (3.19)$$

## 3.7.1 Laminar Flow Through Inclined Pipes

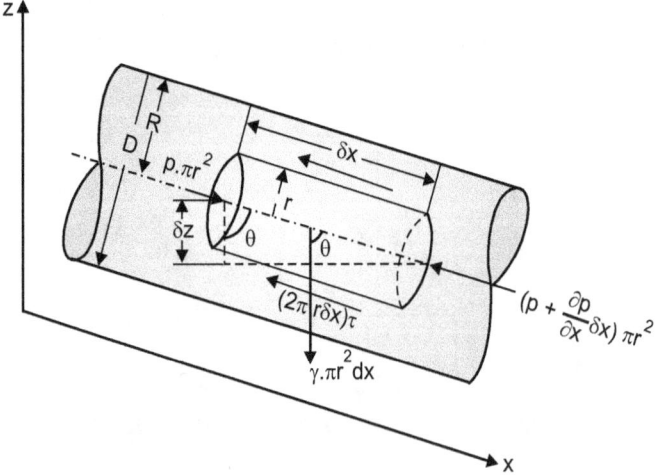

**Fig. 3.8: Laminar flow through an inclined pipe**

Consider a pipe carrying laminar flow of fluid as shown in Fig. 3.8. In this case, gravity forces are also required to be taken into account in addition to viscous shear forces and pressure forces.

Now, consider a small concentric cylindrical element of fluid as shown in Fig. 3.8. The additional force, the weight of the element, is $\gamma \cdot \pi r^2 \cdot \delta x$ acting through C.G. in vertically downward direction. This will have component in the direction of flow $(\gamma \cdot \pi r^2 \cdot \delta x) \cdot \cos \theta$. Thus, the forces on the element are

1. Pressure force $(p \cdot \pi r^2)$ on left face of the element acting in the direction of motion.
2. Pressure force $\left(p + \dfrac{\partial p}{\partial x} \cdot \delta x\right) \cdot \pi r^2$ on the right face of the element acting against the direction of motion.
3. Shear force $(\tau \cdot 2\pi r \cdot \delta x)$ on the periphery of the element acting against the direction of motion.
4. The component of weight $(\gamma \cdot \pi r^2 \cdot \delta x) \cos \theta$ acting in the direction of motion.

   [It may be noted that 'x' is taken along the direction parallel to the centre line of the pipe-line]

Since the flow is steady uniform, there is no acceleration and hence the sum of all forces on the element in the direction of motion must be zero.

$$\therefore \ p \cdot \pi r^2 - \left(p + \dfrac{\partial p}{\partial x} \cdot \delta x\right) \pi r^2 - \tau (2\pi \, \gamma \, \delta x) + \gamma (\pi \, r^2 \, \delta x) \cdot \cos \theta = 0$$

But $\cos \theta = -\dfrac{\delta z}{\delta x}$, where $\delta z$ is the vertical distance between the centres of the faces.

$$\therefore \ -\dfrac{\partial p}{\partial x} \cdot \delta x \cdot \pi r^2 - \tau \cdot 2\pi r \, \delta x - \gamma \pi \, r^2 \cdot \delta x \cdot \dfrac{\delta z}{\delta x} = 0$$

∴ Dividing throughout by $2\pi \, \gamma \, \delta x$ and readjusting the terms, we get,

$$\tau = -\dfrac{\partial (p + \gamma z)}{\partial x} \cdot \dfrac{r}{2} = -\gamma \cdot \dfrac{\partial}{\partial x}\left(\dfrac{p}{\gamma} + z\right) \cdot \dfrac{r}{2}$$

or

$$\tau = -\left(\gamma \cdot \dfrac{\partial h}{\partial x}\right) \cdot \dfrac{r}{2}$$

where, $h = \left(\dfrac{p}{\gamma} + z\right)$, the piezometric head.

It may be seen that in case of inclined pipe the term $\dfrac{\partial p}{\partial x}$ in equation (3.3) is replaced by $\dfrac{\partial (p + \gamma z)}{\partial x}$.

Now τ is also equal to $\mu \dfrac{\partial u}{\partial y}$ or $-\mu \dfrac{\partial u}{\partial r}$ (as seen in Art. 3.7)

∴ $$-\mu \dfrac{\partial u}{\partial r} = -\gamma \left(\dfrac{\partial h}{\partial x}\right) \cdot \dfrac{r}{2}$$

∴ $$\dfrac{\partial u}{\partial r} = \dfrac{\gamma}{\mu}\left(\dfrac{\partial h}{\partial x}\right)\cdot \dfrac{r}{2}$$

Integrating, $$u = \dfrac{\gamma}{\mu}\cdot\left(\dfrac{\partial h}{\partial x}\right)\cdot\dfrac{r^2}{4} + C$$

When r = 0, u = 0

∴ $$C = -\dfrac{1}{4\mu}\cdot\gamma\cdot\left(\dfrac{\partial h}{\partial x}\right)\cdot R^2$$

∴ $$\boxed{u = \dfrac{1}{4\mu}\cdot\gamma\cdot\left(-\dfrac{\partial h}{\partial x}\right)(R^2 - r^2)}$$ ... (3.20)

This is exactly similar to equation (3.6) except that $\dfrac{\partial p}{\partial x}$ in equation (3.6) is replaced by $\left[\gamma \dfrac{\partial h}{\partial x}\right]$. All other expressions can be obtained by replacing $\left(\dfrac{\partial p}{\partial x}\right)$ by $\left[\gamma \cdot \dfrac{\partial h}{\partial x}\right]$ in the expressions for horizontal pipe.

Power P in this case is given by

$$\boxed{P = \gamma Q\,(h_1 - h_2)}$$ ... (3.21)

where $h_1$ and $h_2$ are the piezometric heads at sections 1 and 2 respectively.

With γ in N/m³, Q in m³/s and ($h_1 - h_2$) in m, the power P is in N-m/s or watts. If γ is in kN/m³, power is in kW.

**Note:** Problems on inclined pipe can be solved easily by applying Bernoulli's theorem to the two sections as shown below:

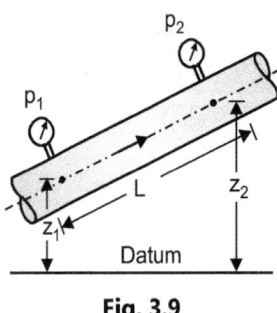

Fig. 3.9

$$z_1 + \dfrac{p_1}{\gamma} + \dfrac{v_1^2}{2g} = z_2 + \dfrac{p_2}{\gamma} + \dfrac{v_2^2}{2g} + h_f$$

For laminar flow through circular pipe

$$h_f = \dfrac{32\,\mu\,u_{av}\,l}{\gamma D^2}$$

∴ $$E_1 = E_2 + \dfrac{32\,\mu\,u_{av}\,L}{\gamma D^2}$$

From this, pressure drop $p_1 - p_2$ can be found out. The power required can then be found out as

$$P = Q\,(p_1 - p_2)$$

## 3.8 Laminar Flow Between Parallel Plates - Both Plates Fixed

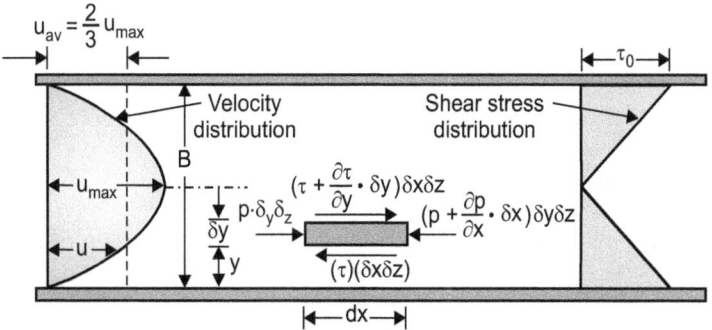

Fig. 3.10: Laminar flow between fixed parallel plates

Consider steady laminar flow of fluid between two fixed parallel plates which are distance 'B' apart as shown in Fig. 3.10. Consider free body in the shape of parallelopiped with sides δx, δy and δz. The lower face of the element is at a distance of 'y' from the lower plate. Forces acting on the element are:

1. Pressure force, $p \cdot \delta y \cdot \delta z$ acting on left face of the element in the direction of flow.
2. Pressure force, $\left(p + \frac{\partial p}{\partial x} \cdot \delta x\right) \delta y \cdot \delta z$ acting on right face of the element, against the direction of flow.
3. Shear force, $\tau \cdot \delta x \cdot \delta z$ acting on lower face of the element, against the direction of motion.
4. Shear force $\left(\tau + \frac{\partial \tau}{\partial y} \cdot \delta y\right) \cdot \delta x \cdot \delta z$ acting on upper face of the element, in the direction of motion.

Since the flow is steady uniform flow, there is no acceleration and hence sum of all these forces in the direction of motion must be zero.

$$p \cdot \delta y \cdot \delta z - \left(p + \frac{\partial p}{\partial x} \cdot \delta x\right) \cdot \delta y \cdot \delta z - \tau \cdot \delta x \cdot \delta z + \left(\tau + \frac{\partial \tau}{\partial y} \cdot \delta y\right) \cdot \delta x \cdot \delta z = 0$$

∴ $$-\frac{\partial p}{\partial x} \cdot \delta x \cdot \delta y \cdot \delta z + \frac{\partial \tau}{\partial y} \cdot \delta x \cdot \delta y \cdot \delta z = 0$$

Dividing by δx δy δz i.e. the volume of the element, we get,

$$\boxed{\frac{\partial p}{\partial x} = \frac{\partial \tau}{\partial y}}$$

which is nothing but equation (3.1).

According to Newton's law of viscosity $\tau = \mu \cdot \dfrac{\partial u}{\partial y}$. Substituting for $\tau$ in the above equation, we get

$$\boxed{\dfrac{\partial p}{\partial x} = \mu \cdot \dfrac{\partial^2 u}{\partial y^2}}$$

which is same as equation (3.2).

Flow between the parallel plates will now be analysed with the help of this equation.

**(i) Velocity:**

We have
$$\dfrac{\partial p}{\partial x} = \mu \dfrac{\partial^2 u}{\partial y^2}$$

or
$$\dfrac{\partial^2 u}{\partial y^2} = \dfrac{1}{\mu}\left(\dfrac{\partial p}{\partial x}\right)$$

Since $\dfrac{\partial p}{\partial x}$ is independent of 'y', integrating the above equation we get

$$\dfrac{\partial u}{\partial y} = \dfrac{1}{\mu}\left(\dfrac{\partial p}{\partial x}\right) y + C_1$$

Integrating once again

$$u = \dfrac{1}{2\mu}\left(\dfrac{\partial p}{\partial x}\right) \cdot y^2 + C_1 y + C_2 \qquad \ldots (3.22)$$

where $C_1$ and $C_2$ are constants of integration. Values of $C_1$ and $C_2$ can be obtained from the boundary conditions.

At $y = 0$ (at the lower plate), $u = 0$
$\therefore \qquad C_2 = 0$
At $y = B$ (at the upper plate), $u = 0$
$\therefore \qquad 0 = \dfrac{1}{2\mu}\left(\dfrac{\partial p}{\partial x}\right) \cdot B^2 + C_1 B$

$\therefore \qquad C_1 = -\dfrac{1}{2\mu}\left(\dfrac{\partial p}{\partial x}\right) \cdot B$

Substituting value of $C_1$ in equation (3.22) we get,

$$\boxed{u = \dfrac{1}{2\mu}\left(-\dfrac{\partial p}{\partial x}\right)(By - y^2)} \qquad \ldots (3.23)$$

Above equation shows that the *velocity distribution for the steady laminar flow between fixed parallel plates is parabolic.* The vertex of the parabola is midway between the plates. Negative sign of $\frac{\partial p}{\partial x}$ indicates that the pressure goes on decreasing in the direction of flow, therefore, $\frac{\partial p}{\partial x}$ is negative and $\left(-\frac{\partial p}{\partial x}\right)$ is a positive quantity.

The maximum velocity will occur midway between the plates and can be obtained by substituting $y = \frac{B}{2}$ in equation (3.23).

$$\therefore \boxed{u_{max} = \frac{B^2}{8\mu}\left(-\frac{\partial p}{\partial x}\right)} \qquad \ldots (3.24)$$

Velocity distribution is shown in Fig. 3.10.

### (ii) Discharge and Average velocity:

### Discharge:

Consider an elementary strip of height 'dy' situated at distance 'y' from the bottom plate as shown in Fig. 3.10. Consider unit width normal to the plane of the paper.

Now area of the strip = $(dy \cdot 1)$

Velocity of fluid passing through the strip = $u = \frac{1}{2\mu}\left(-\frac{\partial p}{\partial x}\right)(By - y^2)$

∴ Discharge through the strip per unit width

$$dq = \text{Area} \times \text{Velocity}$$

$$= (dy \cdot 1)\left[\frac{1}{2\mu}\left(-\frac{\partial p}{\partial x}\right)(By - y^2)\right]$$

∴ Discharge 'q' per metre width of the plates

$$q = \int dq = \int_0^B \left[\frac{1}{2\mu}\left(-\frac{\partial p}{\partial x}\right)(By - y^2)\,dy\right]$$

$$\therefore q = \frac{1}{2\mu}\left(-\frac{\partial p}{\partial x}\right)\left[\frac{By^2}{2} - \frac{y^3}{3}\right]_0^B$$

$$\therefore q = \frac{1}{2\mu}\left(-\frac{\partial p}{\partial x}\right)\left[\frac{B^3}{2} - \frac{B^3}{3}\right]$$

$$\therefore \boxed{q = \frac{B^3}{12\mu}\left(-\frac{\partial p}{\partial x}\right)} \qquad \ldots (3.25)$$

**Average Velocity:**

$$u_{av} = \frac{q}{Area} = \frac{q}{B \times 1}$$

or

$$\boxed{u_{av} = \frac{B^2}{12\mu}\left(-\frac{\partial p}{\partial x}\right)} \quad \ldots (3.26)$$

From equations (3.24) and (3.26)

$$\boxed{u_{av} = \frac{2}{3} u_{max}} \quad \ldots (3.27)$$

This also follows from the property of a parabola. *Thus, in case of steady laminar flow between two fixed parallel plates, average velocity is 2/3 the maximum velocity.*

**(iii) Pressure drop over a given length of plates:**

From equation (3.26), we have,

$$u_{av} = \frac{B^2}{12\mu}\left(-\frac{\partial p}{\partial x}\right)$$

∴

$$(-\partial p) = \frac{12\mu u_{av}}{B^2} \partial x$$

Integrating the above equation between section 1 and section 2, we get

$$\int_{p_1}^{p_2} -\partial p = \int_{x_1}^{x_2} \frac{12\mu u_{av}}{B^2} \cdot \partial x$$

or

$$p_1 - p_2 = \frac{12\mu u_{av}}{B^2}(x_2 - x_1)$$

But $(x_2 - x_1) = L$ the distance (length) between section 1 and section 2.

∴

$$\boxed{p_1 - p_2 = \frac{12\mu u_{av} L}{B^2}} \quad \ldots (3.28)$$

**(iv) Loss of head:**

Loss of head between section 1 and section 2 is given by

$$\boxed{h_f = \frac{p_1 - p_2}{\gamma} = \frac{12\mu u_{av} L}{\gamma B^2}} \quad \ldots (3.29)$$

where '$\gamma$' is the unit weight of flowing fluid.

## (v) Shear stress:

According to Newton's law of viscosity

$$\tau = \mu \frac{\partial u}{\partial y}$$

$$= \mu \frac{\partial}{\partial y}\left[\frac{1}{2\mu}\left(-\frac{\partial p}{\partial x}\right)(By - y^2)\right]$$

or

$$\tau = \mu\left[\frac{1}{2\mu}\left(-\frac{\partial p}{\partial x}\right)(B - 2y)\right]$$

or

$$\boxed{\tau = \left(-\frac{\partial p}{\partial x}\right)\left(\frac{B}{2} - y\right)} \quad \ldots (3.30)$$

Equation (3.30) shows that *shear stress varies linearly with distance 'y'*. It has zero value at $y = \frac{B}{2}$ i.e. midway between the plates.

Shear stress is maximum at the plates i.e. at $y = 0$ or $y = B$ and has a value of

$$\boxed{\tau_o = \left(-\frac{\partial p}{\partial x}\right)\cdot\frac{B}{2}} \quad \ldots (3.31)$$

Shear stress distribution is shown in Fig. 3.10.

## 3.8.1 Laminar Flow Through Inclined Plates

Similar to laminar flow in inclined circular pipe, as seen in section 3.7.1, it can be shown that all the relations in case of inclined plates can be obtained from the relations for horizontal plates simply by replacing $\left(\frac{\partial p}{\partial x}\right)$ by $\left(\gamma\frac{\partial h}{\partial x}\right)$, where $h = \left(z + \frac{p}{\gamma}\right)$, the piezometric head.

For example,

$$u = \frac{1}{2\mu}\left(-\frac{\partial p}{\partial x}\right)(By - y^2) \quad \text{for horizontal plates.}$$

and

$$u = \frac{1}{2\mu}\left(-\gamma\frac{\partial h}{\partial x}\right)(By - y^2) \quad \text{for inclined plates}$$

or

$$= \frac{1}{2\mu}\left[-\gamma\frac{\partial}{\partial x}\left(\frac{p}{\gamma} + z\right)(By - y^2)\right]$$

or

$$= \frac{1}{2\mu}\left[-\frac{\partial}{\partial x}(p + \gamma z)\right](By - y^2)$$

## 3.9 Laminar Flow Between Parallel Plates – One Plate Fixed and other Moving – Couette Flow

Consider the two parallel plates as shown in Fig. 3.11. Let the distance between the plates be 'B'. Let the lower plate be fixed while the upper plate move in the direction of flow with velocity 'U' m/s as shown in the figure. This type of flow is called 'Couette Flow'.

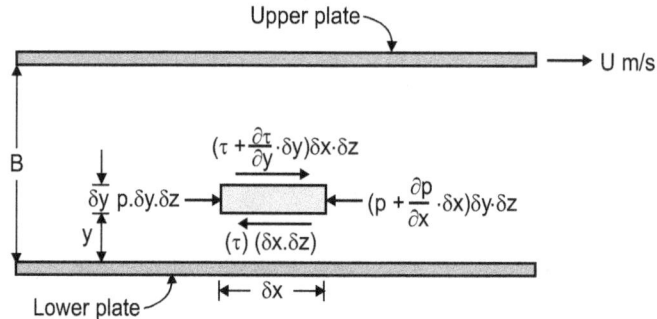

**Fig. 3.11: Couette flow**

By considering the forces on an element in the form of parallelopiped with sides δx, δy and δz as shown in Fig. 3.11 as in the case of fixed plates, we can get the equation:

$$\frac{\partial p}{\partial x} = \mu \frac{\partial^2 u}{\partial y^2}$$

or

$$\frac{\partial^2 u}{\partial y^2} = \frac{1}{\mu}\left(\frac{\partial p}{\partial x}\right)$$

Integrating the above equation, we get

$$\frac{\partial u}{\partial y} = \frac{1}{\mu}\frac{\partial p}{\partial x} \cdot y + C_1$$

Integrating once again

$$u = \frac{1}{2\mu}\left(\frac{\partial p}{\partial x}\right) \cdot y^2 + C_1 y + C_2 \qquad \ldots (3.32)$$

where $C_1$ and $C_2$ are constants of integration. Values of $C_1$ and $C_2$ can be obtained from the boundary conditions.

At $y = 0$ (at the lower plate),  $u = 0$
∴  $C_2 = 0$
At $y = B$ (at the upper plate),  $u = U$
∴  $U = \frac{1}{2\mu}\left(\frac{\partial p}{\partial x}\right) B^2 + C_1 B$
∴  $C_1 = \frac{U}{B} - \frac{1}{2\mu}\left(\frac{\partial p}{\partial x}\right) \cdot B$

Substituting this value of $C_1$ in equation (3.32), we get

$$u = \frac{U}{B} \cdot y - \frac{1}{2\mu}\left(\frac{\partial p}{\partial x}\right)(By - y^2) \quad \ldots(3.33)$$

Above equation gives the velocity distribution in case of Couette flow.

It can be seen from the above equation that the velocity distribution in general Couette flow will depend upon U as well as $\frac{\partial p}{\partial x}$. Here $\frac{\partial p}{\partial x}$ can be negative (– ve), zero or positive (+ ve).

(i) If $\frac{\partial p}{\partial x} = 0$  $\quad u = \frac{U}{B} \cdot y \quad \ldots(3.34)$

Above relation shows that the velocity distribution is linear. This type of flow is called simple Couette flow or plain Couette flow. (In this case, the fluid is simply dragged along by the moving plate). (Refer Art. 1.2.6).

Velocity distribution for simple Couette flow is shown in Fig. 3.12.

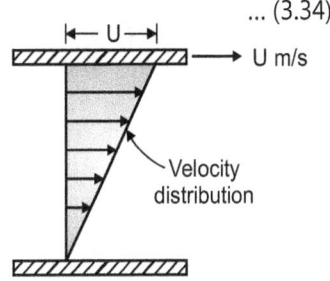

**Fig. 3.12: Simple Couette flow,** $\frac{\partial p}{\partial x} = 0$

(ii) If U = 0, it is the case of flow between two fixed parallel plates and the velocity distribution is given by $u = \frac{1}{2\mu}\left(-\frac{\partial p}{\partial x}\right)(By - y^2)$

which we already know is parabolic in nature. This flow is called Poiseuille flow. (See Eq. 3.23).

It can be seen from the above two cases that the general Couette flow expressed by equation (3.33) is the combination of simple Couette flow and Poiseuille flow.

(iii) If $\frac{\partial p}{\partial x}$ is – ve.

In this case, the flow due to pressure gradient is in the same direction as that of the velocity of upper plate. The combined velocity distribution can be obtained by the superimposition of velocity distributions for case (i) and (ii). Fig. 3.13.

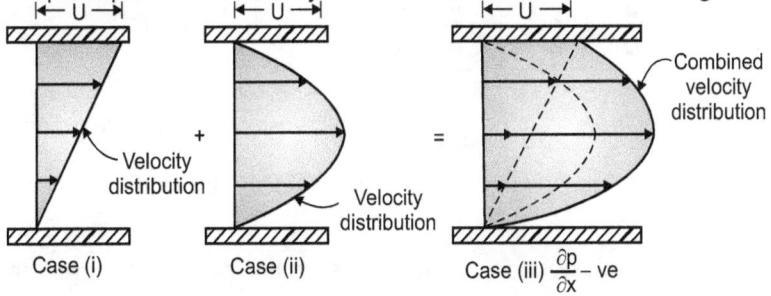

**Fig. 3.13: General Couette flow,** $\frac{\partial p}{\partial x}$ (– ve)

(iv) If $\dfrac{\partial p}{\partial x}$ is + ve.

In this case, the flow due to pressure gradient is in the direction opposite to the direction of motion of upper plate. The combined velocity distribution can be obtained by superimposition as shown in Fig. 3.14.

If the + ve pressure gradient has sufficiently large value, some fluid near the stationary boundary will move in the direction opposite to the direction of motion of upper boundary, thus back flow will take place near the stationary boundary. Fig. 3.14.

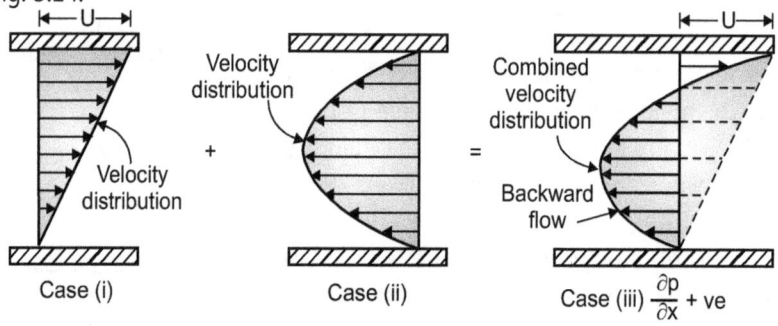

**Fig. 3.14: General Couette flow, $\dfrac{\partial p}{\partial x}$ (+ ve)**

The velocity distribution in case of general Couette flow can be modified as follows:

We have,

$$u = \dfrac{U}{B} \cdot y + \dfrac{1}{2\mu}\left(-\dfrac{\partial p}{\partial x}\right)(By - y^2)$$

Dividing by U

$$\dfrac{u}{U} = \dfrac{y}{B} + \dfrac{1}{2\mu U}\left(-\dfrac{\partial p}{\partial x}\right)(By - y^2)$$

or

$$\dfrac{u}{U} = \dfrac{y}{B} + \dfrac{B^2}{2\mu U}\left(-\dfrac{\partial p}{\partial x}\right)\left(\dfrac{y}{B} - \dfrac{y^2}{B^2}\right)$$

or

$$\boxed{\dfrac{u}{U} = \dfrac{y}{B} + P\left(\dfrac{y}{B} - \dfrac{y^2}{B^2}\right)} \quad \text{... (3.35)}$$

where, $P = \dfrac{B^2}{2\mu U}\left(-\dfrac{\partial p}{\partial x}\right)$, called dimensionless pressure gradient.

Equation (3.35) is the non-dimensional form of velocity distribution for general Couette flow.

A set of velocity distribution curves have been plotted for various values of dimensionless pressure gradient. Fig. 3.15.

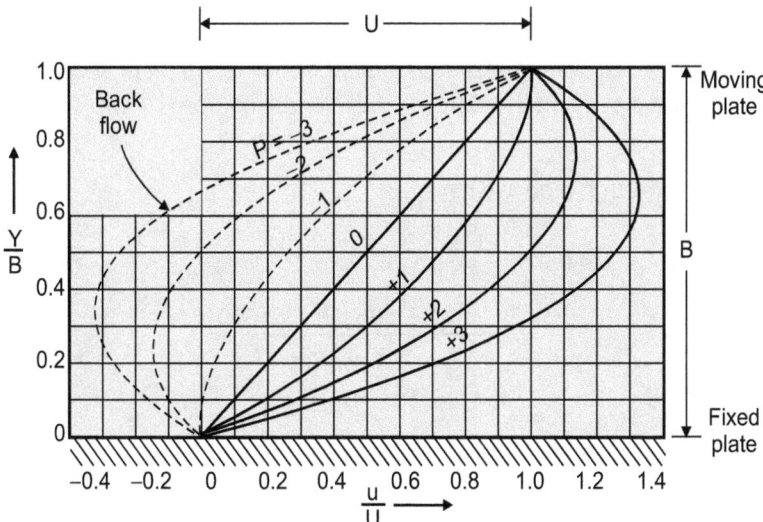

**Fig. 3.15: Non-dimensional velocity distribution curves for Couette flow**

Once the velocity distribution for general Couette flow is known, the other quantities like shear stress, discharge per meter width, average velocity etc. can be obtained by following the same procedure as adopted in case of fixed parallel plates.

General Couette flow finds it's application in hydrodynamic theory of bearing lubrication.

## ILLUSTRATIVE EXAMPLES

**Example 3.1:**

Calculate the loss of head in a pipe having diameter of 15 cm and length of 2 km. It carries laminar flow of oil of specific gravity 0.85 and viscosity of 6 stokes at the rate of 30.48 l. p.s.

**Solution:**

For laminar flow in pipe, we have,

$$h_f = \frac{32\,\mu\,u_{av}\,L}{\gamma D^2} = \frac{128\,\mu\,Q\,L}{\pi\,\gamma\,D^4}$$

$$= \frac{128\,\mu\,Q\,L}{\pi \cdot \rho \cdot g \cdot D^4}, \quad \text{but } \frac{\mu}{\rho} = v = 6 \text{ stokes (cm}^2\text{/s)} = 6 \times 10^{-4}\text{ m}^2\text{/s}$$

$$= \frac{128 \times 6 \times 10^{-4} \times 0.03048 \times 2000}{\pi \times 9.81 \times (0.15)^4}$$

∴  $\boxed{h_f = 300 \text{ m}}$

**Note:** Stokes (cm²/s) or m²/s is the unit of kinematic viscosity and kg/ms or N-s/m² or Poise are the units of absolute viscosity. Thus, from the units given, we can know whether the viscosity given is kinematic (v) or dynamic viscosity (μ).

# FLUID MECHANICS (NMU) (S.E. MECHANICAL) — VISCOUS AND BOUNDARY LAYER FLOW

**Example 3.2:**

Calculate the power required to maintain a laminar flow of an oil of viscosity 10 P through a pipe 100 mm diameter at the rate of 10 l.p.s. if the length of pipe is 1 km.

**Solution:**

For laminar flow through pipe, we have,

$$\Delta p = \frac{128 \, \mu \, Q \, L}{\pi \, D^4} \qquad [1 \text{ N-s/m}^2 = 10 \text{ P}]$$

$$= \frac{128 \times 1 \times 10 \times 10^{-3} \times 1000}{\pi \times (0.1)^4}$$

$$= 4.075 \times 10^6 \text{ N/m}^2$$

∴ Power $= \Delta p \times Q$

$$= 4.075 \times 10^6 \times 10 \times 10^{-3}$$

$$= 40750 \text{ W}$$

or **Power = 40.75 kW**

---

**Example 3.3:**

An oil of viscosity 8 P and specific gravity 1.2 flows through a horizontal pipe 80 mm diameter. If the pressure drop in 100 m length of the pipe is 1500 kN/m², determine

(i) the rate of flow of oil in l.p.m.,

(ii) the maximum velocity,

(iii) the total frictional drag over 100 m length of pipe,

(iv) the power required to maintain the flow,

(v) the velocity gradient at the pipe wall,

(vi) the velocity and shear stress at 10 mm from wall.

**Solution:**

[**Note:** This example deals with almost all aspects of laminar flow through a pipe and hence should be studied thoroughly.]

We have $-\dfrac{\partial p}{\partial x} = \dfrac{1500 \times 1000}{100}$

$$= 15000 \text{ N/m}^2/\text{m}$$

(i) Average velocity, $u_{av} = \dfrac{R^2}{8\mu}\left(-\dfrac{\partial p}{\partial x}\right)$

$$= \dfrac{(0.04)^2}{8 \times 0.8} \times 15000 \qquad \left[\mu = 8P = \dfrac{8}{10} \text{ N-s/m}^2 = 0.8 \text{ N-s/m}^2\right]$$

$$= 3.75 \text{ m/s}$$

Discharge, $Q = \dfrac{\pi}{4} \times D^2 \times u_{av}$

$= \dfrac{\pi}{4} \times (0.08)^2 \times 3.75$

$= 0.01885 \text{ m}^3/\text{s}$

$\boxed{= 18.85 \text{ l.p.s.}}$

or $\boxed{Q = 18.85 \times 60 = 1131 \text{ l.p.m.}}$

(ii) Maximum velocity, $u_{max} = 2\, u_{av}$
(at the centre line) $\boxed{u_{max} = 7.5 \text{ m/s}}$

(iii) Wall shear stress, $\tau_o = \left(-\dfrac{\partial p}{\partial x}\right) \cdot \dfrac{R}{2} = (15000) \times \dfrac{0.04}{2}$

$= 300 \text{ N/m}^2$

∴ Total frictional drag for 100 m length is

$F_D = 300 \times \text{Area of contact}$

$= 300 \times \pi \times D \times L$

$= 300 \times \pi \times 0.08 \times 100$

∴ $\boxed{F_D = 7540 \text{ N} = 7.54 \text{ kN}}$

(iv) Power required to maintain the flow

$P = F_D \times u_{av}$

$= 7.54 \times 3.75$

$= 28.275 \text{ kW}$

Power required can also be obtained as

$P = Q \cdot \Delta p$ where $\Delta p$ is pressure drop in 100 m length of pipe and is given as 1500 kN/m²

$= 0.01885 \times 1500$

∴ $\boxed{P = 28.275 \text{ kW}}$

(v) Now $\tau_o = \mu \left(\dfrac{\partial u}{\partial y}\right)_{y=0}$

∴ Velocity gradient at the pipe wall

$\left(\dfrac{\partial u}{\partial y}\right)_{y=0} = \dfrac{\tau_o}{\mu}$

$= \dfrac{300}{0.8} \text{ s}^{-1}$

∴ $\boxed{\text{Velocity gradient} = 375 \text{ per sec.}}$

(vi) 10 mm from pipe wall means 40 − 10 = 30 mm from centre of pipe or at r = 30 mm

$$\tau_{30} = \tau_o \times \frac{30}{40} = 300 \times \frac{3}{4}$$

∴ $\boxed{\tau_{30} = 225 \text{ N/m}^2}$ $\left[\text{or } \tau_{30} = \frac{30 \times 10^{-3}}{2} \times 15000 = 225 \text{ N/m}^2\right]$

$$u_{30} = u_{max}\left[1 - \left(\frac{r}{R}\right)^2\right]$$

$$= 7.5\left[1 - \left(\frac{30}{40}\right)^2\right]$$

∴ $\boxed{u_{30} = 3.28 \text{ m/s}}$

## Example 3.4:

*A lubricating oil of viscosity of 1 poise and specific gravity 0.9 is pumped through a 30 mm diameter pipe. If the pressure drop per metre length of pipe is 20 kN/m², determine:*
*(1) Mass flow rate in kg/min.*
*(2) Shear stress of pipe wall.*
*(3) Reynold's number of flow.*
*(4) Power required per 50 m length of pipe to maintain flow.*

**Solution:**

(1) We have $\left(-\frac{\partial p}{\partial x}\right) = 20 \text{ kN/m}^2/\text{m}$

$\quad\quad\quad\quad\quad = 20,000 \text{ N/m}^2$ per metre length

Now, $\quad\quad U_{av} = \frac{R^2}{8\mu}\left(-\frac{\partial p}{\partial x}\right)$

$\quad\quad\quad\quad = \frac{(0.015)^2}{8 \times 0.1} \times (20000) \quad$ 1 poise = 0.1 N-s/m²

$\quad\quad\quad\quad = 5.625 \text{ m/s}$

Average velocity of flow, $U_{av} = 5.625 \text{ m/s}$

∴ $\quad\quad$ Discharge Q = Area × Velocity

$\quad\quad\quad\quad = \frac{\pi}{4} \times (0.03)^2 \times 5.625$

$\quad\quad\quad\quad = 0.003976 \text{ m}^3/\text{s}$

∴ $\quad\quad$ Mass flow rate/min. = $\rho \times Q \times 60$

$\quad\quad\quad\quad = 900 \times 0.003976 \times 60$

$\quad\quad\quad\quad = 214.704 \text{ kg}$

∴ $\boxed{\text{Mass flow rate/min.} = 214.704 \text{ kg}}$

(2) Shear stress at pipe wall

$$\tau_0 = \left(-\frac{\partial p}{\partial x}\right) \cdot \frac{R}{2} = (20000) \times \frac{0.015}{2}$$

$$= 150 \text{ N/m}^2$$

∴ **Shear stress at pipe wall = 150 N/m²**

(3) Reynold's number of flow

$$R_e = \frac{\rho \cdot U_{av} \cdot d}{\mu}$$

$$= \frac{900 \times 5.625 \times (0.03)}{0.1}$$

$$= 1518.75$$

∴ **Reynold's number of flow = 1518.75**

(4) Total frictional drag for 50 m length of pipe

$$F_D = \tau_0 \times \text{Area of contact}$$
$$= 150 \times (\pi \times 0.03 \times 50)$$

∴ $F_D = 706.858 \times 5.625$
$$= 3976 \text{ watts}$$

∴ **Power required = 3976 watts or 3.976 kW**

## Example 3.5:

Determine the velocity of flow at a distance 50 mm from the axis of a pipe 150 mm in diameter, when Reynold's number of flow is 1500. Oil of kinematic viscosity $2.4 \times 10^{-6}$ m²/s and mass density 808 kg/m³ flows through the pipe.

**Solution:**

$$Re = \frac{U_{av} D}{\nu}$$

∴ $$1500 = \frac{U_{av} \times 0.15}{2.4 \times 10^{-6}}$$

∴ $U_{av} = 0.024$ m/s

for pipe flow, $U_{max} = 2 U_{av} = 2 \times 0.024 = 0.048$ m/s

Velocity at radius of 50 mm i.e. at r = 50 mm is given by

$$U_{50} = U_{max} \left[1 - \left(\frac{r}{R}\right)^2\right]$$

$$= 0.048 \left[1 - \left(\frac{50}{75}\right)^2\right]$$

$$= 0.0267 \text{ m/s}$$

∴ $U_{50} = 0.0267$ m/s

## Example 3.6:

A 150 mm diameter pipe carries liquid in laminar regime. A Pitot tube placed in the flow at a radial distance of 15 mm from the axis of the pipe indicates velocity of 0.5 m/s. Calculate:
(i) the maximum velocity
(ii) the mean velocity and
(iii) the discharge in the pipe.

### Solution:

For laminar flow through pipe, we have
$$u = u_{max}\left\{1-\left(\frac{r}{R}\right)^2\right\}$$

∴ But at $r = 15$ mm, $u = 0.5$ m/s and $R = 75$ mm

∴ $$0.5 = u_{max}\left\{1-\left(\frac{15}{75}\right)^2\right\}$$

∴ (i) $\boxed{u_{max} = 0.52 \text{ m/s}}$

(ii) $u_{av} = \dfrac{u_{max}}{2} = 0.26$ m/s

∴ $\boxed{u_{av} = 0.26 \text{ m/s}}$

(iii) $Q = \dfrac{\pi}{4} \times D^2 \times u_{av}$

$= \dfrac{\pi}{4} \times (0.15)^2 \times 0.26$

∴ $\boxed{Q = 0.0046 \text{ m}^3\text{/s or } 4.6 \text{ l.p.s.}}$

## Example 3.7:

A 300 mm diameter pipe carries oil of density 950 kg/m³ and dynamic viscosity 1.0 Ns/m². If the length of the pipe is 10 km and the discharge is 150 litres/s, calculate the power required to pump the oil. If the viscosity of the oil changes by a factor of 10 due to increased temperature, compute the new value of power required to pump the oil, other conditions remaining the same. Use the expression $f = \dfrac{0.316}{Re^{0.25}}$ for turbulent flows if required. Note: f is Darcy-Weisbach friction factor.

### Solution:

First checkup whether flow is laminar or not

Average velocity $u_{av} = \dfrac{Q}{A} = \dfrac{Q}{\dfrac{\pi}{4} \times D^2} = \dfrac{4Q}{\pi D^2}$

∴ $= \dfrac{4 \times 0.15}{\pi \times (0.3)^2} = 2.12$ m/s

Now    Re $= \dfrac{\rho \, u_{av} \, D}{\mu}$

$= \dfrac{950 \times 2.12 \times 0.3}{1}$

= 604.2 which is < 2000 ∴ flow is laminar.

Now for laminar flow,  $\Delta p = \dfrac{32 \, \mu \, u_{av} \, L}{D^2}$

$= \dfrac{32 \times 1 \times 2.12 \times 10000}{(0.3)^2}$

= 7537777.8 N/m² or 7537.78 kN/m²

∴  Power required $= \Delta p \cdot Q = 7537.78 \times 0.15$

∴  **Power required = 1130.67 kW**

In the second case, 'µ' changes by 10 times. In case of liquid, viscosity decreases with rise in temperature.

Therefore, µ in second case $= \dfrac{1}{10} = 0.1$ N-s/m²

∴ Re = 6042 which is > 2000  ∴ flow now is turbulent

∴ Friction factor  $f = \dfrac{0.316}{Re^{0.25}} = \dfrac{0.316}{(6042)^{0.25}} = 0.0358$

Now  $h_f = \dfrac{f \, l \, Q^2}{12.1 \, d^5}$

$= \dfrac{0.035 \times 10000 \times (0.15)^2}{12.1 \times (0.3)^5}$

= 273.95 m of oil.

Power $= \gamma \cdot Q \cdot h_f = 950 \times 9.81 \times 0.15 \times 273.95$

= 382961.55 watts

or   **Power required = 382.96 kW**

## Example 3.8:

Oil of dynamic viscosity 1.5 N-s/m² and relative density 0.9 flows through a vertical pipe of diameter 20 mm. Two pressure gauges are fixed 10 m apart on the pipe. The lower gauge reads 25 N/cm² and the higher reads 5 N/cm². Find the direction and the rate of flow through the pipe.

## Solution:

The flow will always take place from higher energy level to lower energy level. Therefore, to find the direction of flow, we will find the total heads at both the points and compare.

Taking the level at lower point A as datum

$$\text{Total head at A} = z_A + \frac{p_A}{\gamma} + \frac{u_A^2}{2g}$$

$$= 0 + \frac{25 \times 10^4}{0.9 \times 9810} + \frac{u_A^2}{2g}$$

$$= 28.32 + \frac{u_A^2}{2g}$$

$$\text{Total head at B} = z_B + \frac{p_B}{\gamma} + \frac{u_B^2}{2g}$$

$$= 10 + \frac{5 \times 10^4}{0.9 \times 9810} + \frac{u_B^2}{2g}$$

$$= 10 + 5.66 + \frac{u_B^2}{2g}$$

$$= 15.66 + \frac{u_B^2}{2g}$$

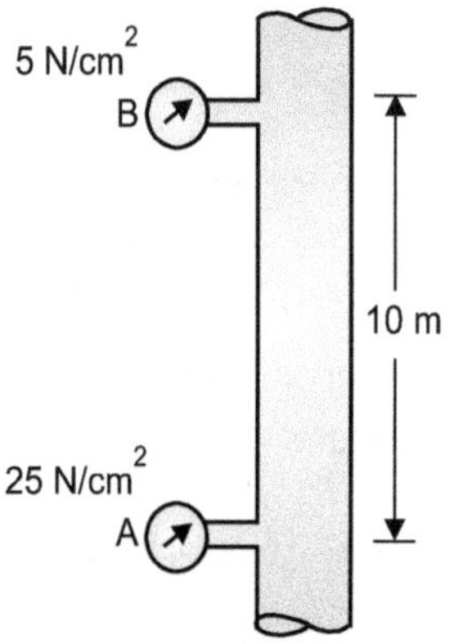

**Fig. 3.16**

But since the pipe is uniform $u_A = u_B$.

Since, the total head at A is greater than that at B, flow is in upward direction. Difference in the total head is due to loss.

∴ $\qquad h_f = 28.32 - 15.66 = 12.66 \text{ m}$

∴ $\qquad 12.66 = \dfrac{32 \times \mu \times u_{av} \times L}{\gamma D^2} = \dfrac{32 \times 1.5 \times u_{av} \times 10}{0.9 \times 9810 \times (0.02)^2}$

∴ $\qquad u_{av} = 0.093 \text{ m/s}$

$$Q = \frac{\pi}{4} \times D^2 \times u_{av} = \frac{\pi}{4} \times (0.02)^2 \times 0.093 = 2.926 \times 10^{-5} \text{ m}^3/\text{s}$$

or $\qquad \boxed{Q = 0.02926 \text{ l.p.s.}}$

## Example 3.9:

A liquid of dynamic viscosity 0.07 Pa-s and relative density 0.86 flows through an inclined pipe of 20 mm diameter. A discharge of 13 lit/min is to be sent through the pipe in such a manner that the pressure along the length is constant. Find the required inclination of the pipe.

## Solution:

Applying Bernoulli's theorem to sections 1 and 2.

$$z_1 + \frac{p_1}{\gamma} + \frac{u_1^2}{2g} = z_2 + \frac{p_2}{\gamma} + \frac{u_2^2}{2g} + h_f$$

But $u_1 = u_2$ and pressure must remain constant

$$\frac{p_1}{\gamma} = \frac{p_2}{\gamma}$$

$$\therefore \quad z_1 - z_2 = h_f = \frac{128 \, \mu \, Q \, L}{\pi \times \gamma \times D^4}$$

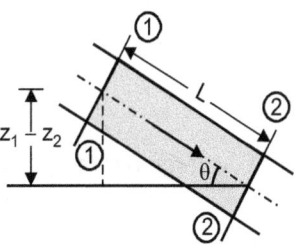

Fig. 3.17

But,

$$Q = \frac{13 \times 10^{-3}}{60} = 2.167 \times 10^{-4} \text{ m}^3/\text{s}$$

$$\therefore \quad \frac{z_1 - z_2}{L} = \frac{128 \times 0.07 \times 2.167 \times 10^{-4}}{\pi \times 0.86 \times 9810 \times (0.02)^4} = 0.458$$

But as can be seen from figure $\frac{z_1 - z_2}{L} = \sin \theta = 0.458 \therefore \theta = 27° - 15' - 30''$

The example can also be solved as follows:

In case of inclined pipes all the relations are same as those of horizontal pipe except that $\left(-\frac{\partial p}{\partial x}\right)$ is to be replaced by $\left[-\frac{\partial (p + \gamma z)}{\partial x}\right]$.

$$Q = 2.167 \times 10^{-4} \text{ m}^3/\text{s}, \quad u_{av} = \frac{2.167 \times 10^{-4}}{\frac{\pi}{4}(0.02)^2} = 0.69 \text{ m/s}$$

Therefore, we can write for inclined pipe

$$u_{av} = \frac{R^2}{8\mu}\left[-\frac{\partial(p + \gamma z)}{\partial x}\right]$$

$$\therefore \quad -\frac{\partial(p + \gamma z)}{\partial x} = \frac{0.69 \times 0.07 \times 8}{(0.01)^2} = 3864$$

$$\therefore \quad \frac{\partial p}{\partial x} + \gamma \frac{\partial z}{\partial x} = 3864 \qquad \text{but p should be constant} \therefore \frac{\partial p}{\partial x} = 0$$

$$\therefore \quad \gamma \frac{\partial z}{\partial x} = 3864$$

$$\frac{\partial z}{\partial x} = \sin \theta$$

$$= \frac{3864}{0.86 \times 9810} = 0.458$$

$$\therefore \quad \boxed{\theta = 27° - 15' - 30''}$$

## Example 3.10:

Oil is pumped in a 200 mm diameter, 1 km long pipe line at the rate of 5300 N/min. The pipe line is laid at an upgrade of 1 : 100. The specific weight of oil is 8833 N/m³ and its viscosity is 20 stokes. Find the power required to pump the oil.

**Solution:**

$$\text{Discharge by weight} = \frac{5300}{60} = 88.33 \text{ N/s}$$

$$\therefore \quad \text{Discharge by volume} = \frac{88.33}{8833} = 0.01 \text{ m}^3/\text{s}$$

$$\therefore \quad u_{av} = \frac{0.01}{\frac{\pi}{4}(0.1)^2} = 0.32 \text{ m/s}$$

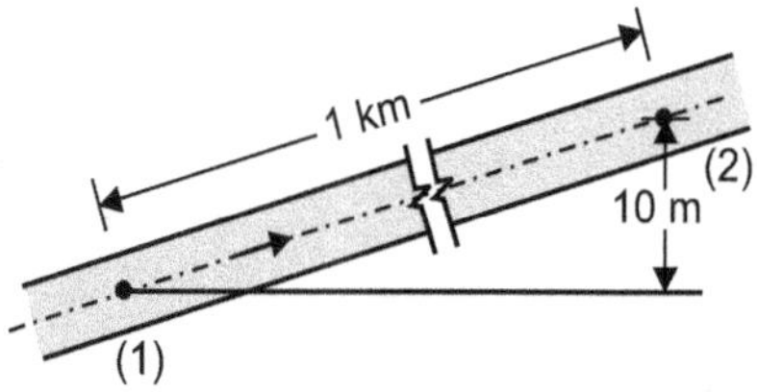

Now viscosity of oil, $\quad \upsilon = 20 \text{ cm}^2/\text{s} = 20 \times 10^{-4} \text{ m}^2/\text{s}$

$$Re = \frac{u_{av} D}{\upsilon} = \frac{0.32 \times 0.20}{20 \times 10^{-4}}$$

$$= 32, \text{ flow is laminar}$$

**Fig. 3.18**

Friction factor 'f' for laminar flow through circular pipe

$$f = \frac{64}{Re} = \frac{64}{32} = 2$$

$$h_f = \frac{fL}{D} \cdot \frac{u_{av}^2}{2g}$$

$$= \frac{2 \times 1000}{0.2} \times \frac{(0.32)^2}{19.62}$$

$$= 52.19 \text{ m}$$

Total head against which the pump will have to work

$$H = 52.19 + 10 = 62.19 \text{ m}$$

$$\therefore \quad \text{Power required} = \gamma \cdot Q \cdot H = 8833 \times 0.01 \times 62.19$$

$$= 5493.24 \text{ watts}$$

$$\therefore \quad \boxed{\text{Power required} = 5.493 \text{ kW}}$$

[Note: Loss can also be found out by the formula

$$h_f = \frac{32 \mu u_{av} L}{\gamma D^2} = \frac{32 (\upsilon \rho) u_{av} L}{\rho g \cdot D^2}$$

$$= \frac{32 \cdot \upsilon \cdot u_{av} \cdot L}{g D^2}$$

$$= \frac{32 \times 20 \times 10^{-4} \times 0.32 \times 1000}{9.81 \times (0.2)^2}$$

$$= 52.19 \text{ m}]$$

## Example 3.11:
A pipe of diameter 20 cm, length $10^4$ m is laid at a slope of 1 in 200. An oil of specific gravity 0.9 and viscosity 1.5 poise is pumped up at the rate of 20 lit./sec. Find the head lost in friction. Also calculate the power required to pump the oil.

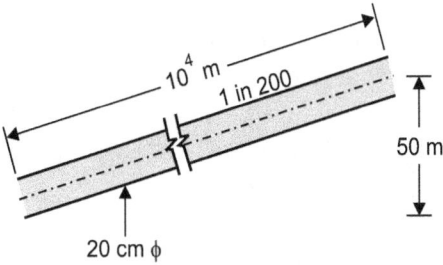

Fig. 3.19

### Solution:

$$\text{Discharge } Q = 20 \text{ l.p.s.} = 20 \times 10^{-3} \text{ m}^3/\text{s}$$

∴ Velocity of flow in the pipe $= \dfrac{Q}{\text{Area of pipe}} = \dfrac{20 \times 10^{-3}}{\dfrac{\pi}{4}(0.2)^2} = 0.637 \text{ m/s}$

∴ Reynold's number $Re = \dfrac{\rho \cdot u_{av} \cdot D}{\mu}$

$$= \dfrac{(0.9 \times 1000) \times 0.637 \times 0.2}{0.15}$$

$$\left[\begin{array}{l} \because 1.5 \text{ poise} \\ = 0.15 \dfrac{\text{N-s}}{\text{m}^2} \end{array}\right]$$

$$Re = 764.4$$

Since Re is less than 2000 flow is laminar.

∴ Loss of head due to friction, $h_f = \dfrac{32 \mu u_{av} L}{\gamma D^2}$

$$= \dfrac{32 \times 0.15 \times 0.637 \times 10^4}{(0.9 \times 9810) \times (0.2)^2}$$

∴ $\boxed{h_f = 86.58 \text{ m}}$

Total head against which the pump will have to work

$$H = h + h_f \qquad\qquad h = \text{head due to elevation}$$
$$= 50 + 86.58 \qquad\qquad = \dfrac{(10)^4}{200} = 50 \text{ m}$$

∴ Power to pump, $H = 136.58 \text{ m}$
$P = \gamma \cdot Q \cdot H$
$= (0.9 \times 9810) \times (20 \times 10^{-3}) \times (136.58)$
$= 24117 \text{ watts}$

$\boxed{P = 24.12 \text{ kW}}$

## Example 3.12:

Oil of relative density 0.92 and dynamic viscosity 1.05 Poise flows between two fixed parallel plates 12 mm apart. If the mean velocity is 1.4 m/s, calculate
(i) the maximum velocity
(ii) velocity and shear stress at a distance of 2 mm from one of the plates
(iii) loss of head over a distance of 25 m.

### Solution:

For laminar flow between parallel plates, we have
$$u_{av} = 1.4 \text{ m/s given}$$

∴ (i) $\boxed{u_{max} = \dfrac{3}{2} u_{av} = 2.1 \text{ m/s}}$

(ii) Velocity at 2 mm from one of the plates
$$u = \dfrac{1}{2\mu}\left(-\dfrac{\partial p}{\partial x}\right)(By - y^2)$$

to get $\left(-\dfrac{\partial p}{\partial x}\right)$ we make use of $u_{av}$ or $u_{max}$

We have
$$u_{av} = \dfrac{B^2}{12\mu}\left(-\dfrac{\partial p}{\partial x}\right)$$

∴
$$1.4 = \dfrac{(12 \times 10^{-3})^2}{12 \times 0.105}\left(-\dfrac{\partial p}{\partial x}\right) \qquad [1.05 \text{ Poise} = 0.105 \text{ N-s/m}^2]$$

∴
$$-\dfrac{\partial p}{\partial x} = 12250 \text{ N/m}^2/\text{m}$$

∴
$$u_{2\text{ mm}} = \dfrac{1}{2 \times 0.105}(12250)\left[(12 \times 10^{-3})(2 \times 10^{-3}) - (2 \times 10^{-3})^2\right]$$

∴ $\boxed{u_{2mm} = 1.167 \text{ m/s}}$

(iii) Loss of head in 25 m length
$$h_f = \dfrac{12\mu\, u_{av}\, L}{\gamma B^2} = \dfrac{12 \times 0.105 \times 1.4 \times 25}{(0.92 \times 9810)(1.2 \times 10^{-3})^2}$$

∴ $\boxed{\text{Loss of head in 25 m length} = 33.933 \text{ m}}$

## Example 3.13:

Two parallel plates kept 100 mm apart have laminar flow of oil between them. The maximum velocity of flow is 1.5 m/s. Calculate
(i) discharge per metre width
(ii) shear stress at the plates
(iii) the pressure difference between two points 20 m apart
(iv) the velocity gradient at the plates and
(v) velocity at 20 mm from the plate.
Take viscosity of oil as 2.45 Pa-s.

**Solution:**

(i) For laminar flow between parallel plates, we have

$$u_{max} = 1.5 \text{ m/s (given)}$$

$$u_{av} = \frac{2}{3} u_{max} = \frac{2}{3} \times 1.5 = 1 \text{ m/s}$$

∴ Discharge per metre width

$$q = (B \times 1) \cdot u_{av} = (100 \times 10^{-3}) \cdot 1$$

∴ $\boxed{q = 0.1 \text{ m}^3/\text{s/meter}}$

(ii) Shear stress at the plates

$$\tau_o = \left(-\frac{\partial p}{\partial x}\right) \cdot \frac{B}{2}$$

$\left(-\dfrac{\partial p}{\partial x}\right)$ can be obtained from $u_{av}$ (or $u_{max}$)

$$u_{av} = \frac{B^2}{12\mu}\left(-\frac{\partial p}{\partial x}\right)$$

∴ $$1 = \frac{(0.1)^2}{12 \times 2.45}\left(-\frac{\partial p}{\partial x}\right)$$    [2.45 Pa-s = 2.45 N-s/m²]

∴ $$\left(-\frac{\partial p}{\partial x}\right) = 2940 \text{ N/m}^2/\text{m}$$

∴ Shear stress at plates,

$$\tau_o = (2940) \cdot \frac{0.1}{2}$$

∴ $\boxed{\tau_o = 147 \text{ N/m}^2}$

(iii) Pressure difference between two points 20 m apart

$$\Delta p = \frac{12\mu \, u_{av} \, L}{B^2}$$

$$= \frac{12 \times 2.45 \times 1 \times 20}{(0.1)^2}$$

∴ $\boxed{\Delta p = 58800 \text{ N/m}^2 \text{ or } 58.8 \text{ kN/m}^2}$

(iv) Velocity gradient at the plates

We have $$\tau_o = \mu \left(\frac{\partial u}{\partial y}\right)_{y=0}$$

∴ $$\left(\frac{\partial u}{\partial y}\right)_{y=0} = \frac{\tau_o}{\mu} = \frac{147}{2.45} = 60 \text{ s}^{-1}$$

∴ $\boxed{\text{Velocity gradient at plates } \left(\frac{\partial u}{\partial y}\right)_{y=0} = 60 \text{ s}^{-1}}$

(v) Velocity at 20 mm from plates

$$u_{20} = \frac{1}{2\mu}\left(\frac{-\partial p}{\partial x}\right)(By - y^2)$$

$$u_{20} = \frac{1}{2 \times 2.45}\left[(2940)\left[(0.1 \times 20 \times 10^{-3}) - (20 \times 10^{-3})^2\right]\right]$$

∴ $\boxed{u_{20} = 0.96 \text{ m/s}}$

## Example 3.14:

Water flows at steady mean velocity of 1.5 m/s through a 50 mm diameter pipe sloping upwards at 45° to the horizontal. At two sections 30 m apart downstream of inlet, the pressure readings are 700 kPa and 462 kPa respectively. Determine the average shear stress at the wall of the pipe and at radius of 10 mm.

### Solution:

It may be noted that all the relations for inclined pipe remain same as in case of horizontal pipe except that the term $\left(-\frac{\partial p}{\partial x}\right)$ in the formulae is to be replaced by $\left[-\gamma \frac{\partial}{\partial x}\left(\frac{p}{\gamma} + z\right)\right]$.

Thus, for the given example, first we will obtain the difference in the piezometric heads at 1 and 2 by applying Bernoulli's theorem.

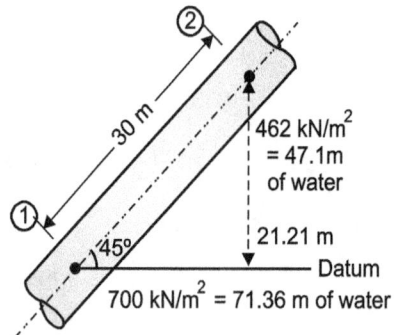

Fig. 3.20

Taking horizontal through 1 as datum, we get

$$z_1 + \frac{p_1}{\gamma} + \frac{u_1^2}{2g} = z_2 + \frac{p_2}{\gamma} + \frac{u_2^2}{2g} + h_L \qquad u_1 = u_2$$

∴ $$0 + \frac{700}{9.81} = 21.21 + \frac{462}{9.81} + h_L$$

$$h_L = \left(\frac{p_1}{\gamma} + z_1\right) - \left(\frac{p_2}{\gamma} + z\right) = 3.05 \text{ m}$$

This change has occurred in distance of 30 m ∴ ∂x = 30 m

∴ $$-\gamma \cdot \frac{\partial}{\partial x}\left(\frac{p}{\gamma} + z\right) = \frac{3.05 \times 9810}{30} = 997.35 \text{ N/m}^2/\text{m}$$

Now formula for boundary shear stress for horizontal pipe is $\tau_o = \left(-\frac{\partial p}{\partial x}\right) \cdot \frac{R}{2}$

∴ formula for inclined pipe will be

$$\tau_o = \left[-\gamma \frac{\partial}{\partial x}\left(\frac{p}{\gamma} + z\right)\right] \cdot \frac{R}{2}$$

$$= (997.35) \cdot \frac{0.025}{2}$$

∴ $\boxed{\tau_o = 12.47 \text{ N/m}^2}$

$$\boxed{\tau_{10} = \tau_o \times \frac{10}{25} = 4.988 \text{ N/m}^2}$$

[Similar procedure can be used for inclined plates as well, with the use of proper formulae.]

### Example 3.15:

A masonry wall of a tank is 0.9 m thick. At the bottom, a crack of thickness 0.3 mm and 600 mm wide has developed and the crack extends the entire thickness of the wall. If the tank contains 4 m of water above the crack and the other end of the crack is at atmospheric pressure, estimate leakage volume per day from the crack (kinematic viscosity of water = 0.01 stokes).

### Solution:

The flow through the crack may be treated as flow between parallel plates. (See Fig. 3.21)

The head of water at the inner end of the crack is 4 m and at the other end is zero. That is the loss of head across the crack is 4 m.

∴ $h_f = 4 \text{ m} = \dfrac{12\,\mu\,u_{av}\,L}{\gamma\,B^2}$ (for parallel plates)

∴ $4 = \dfrac{12 \times 0.001 \times u_{av} \times 0.9}{9810 \times (0.3 \times 10^{-3})^2}$

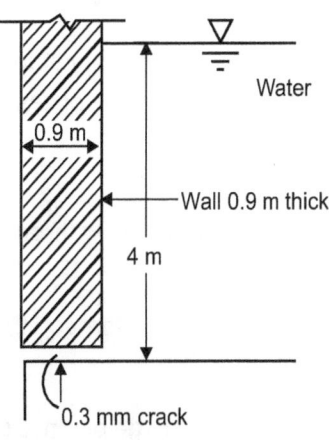

Fig. 3.21

$\upsilon = 0.01$ stokes $= 0.01$ cm²/s $= 0.01 \times 10^{-4}$ m²/s

$\mu = \rho\upsilon = 1000 \times 0.01 \times 10^{-4} = 0.001$ N-s/m²

∴ $u_{av} = 0.327$ m/s

∴ Q = Area of crack × $u_{av}$

∴ Q = $(0.3 \times 10^{-3})(0.6) \times 0.327$

or $= 5.886 \times 10^{-5}$ m³/s

or Q = $5.886 \times 10^{-5} \times 24 \times 3600$

$\boxed{Q = 5.086 \text{ m}^3 \text{ per day}}$

## Example 3.16:

Two parallel horizontal smooth plates of infinite extent are kept at distance 'B' apart and an oil of viscosity 'µ' is filled in the gap. If lower plate is fixed and upper is moved with velocity 'U', show that the pressure gradient for the condition of zero discharge between the plates is given by expression

$$\frac{\partial p}{\partial x} = \frac{6\mu U}{B^2}$$

**Solution:**

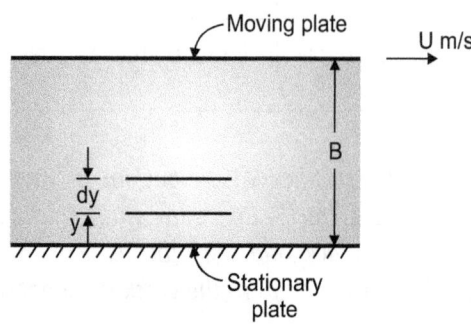

**Fig. 3.22**

Consider an elementary strip of height 'dy' situated at distance 'y' from the fixed plate. Consider unit width of the plates normal to plane of paper.

Now, Area of strip $= (1 \times dy)$

Velocity of flow through the strip $= \frac{U}{B} \cdot y + \frac{1}{2\mu}\left(-\frac{\partial p}{\partial x}\right)(By - y^2)$

∴ Discharge through the strip 'dq' $= (1 \times dy)\left[\frac{U}{B} \cdot y + \frac{1}{2\mu}\left(-\frac{\partial p}{\partial x}\right)(By - y^2)\right]$

∴ Total discharge per metre width between the plates

$$q = \int_0^B \left[\frac{U}{B} \cdot y + \frac{1}{2\mu}\left(-\frac{\partial p}{\partial x}\right)(By - y^2)\right] dy$$

$$= \left[\frac{U}{B} \cdot \frac{y^2}{2} + \frac{1}{2\mu}\left(-\frac{\partial p}{\partial x}\right)\left(B \cdot \frac{y^2}{2} - \frac{y^3}{3}\right)\right]_0^B$$

or

$$\boxed{q = \frac{UB}{2} + \frac{B^3}{12\mu}\left(-\frac{\partial p}{\partial x}\right)}$$

Now we want to find out $\left(\frac{\partial p}{\partial x}\right)$ for condition of zero discharge.

# FLUID MECHANICS (NMU) (S.E. MECHANICAL) — VISCOUS AND BOUNDARY LAYER FLOW

Equating 'q' to zero we get,

$$q = \frac{UB}{2} + \frac{B^3}{12\mu}\left(-\frac{\partial p}{\partial x}\right) = 0$$

$$\therefore \quad \frac{\partial p}{\partial x} = \frac{12\mu\, UB}{2B^3}$$

$$\therefore \quad \frac{\partial p}{\partial x} = \frac{6\mu U}{B^2}$$

$$\therefore \quad \boxed{\text{Pressure gradient for zero discharge} = \frac{6\mu U}{B^2}}$$

### Example 3.17:
Show that the flow rate per unit width for laminar flow between two parallel plates distance 'B' apart, with lower plate held stationary and the upper one moving with a velocity 'U' for condition of zero shear stress over the stationary plate is given by $\frac{UB}{3}$.

### Solution:
In case of general Couette flow, velocity distribution is given by

$$u = \frac{U}{B}\cdot y + \frac{1}{2\mu}\left(-\frac{\partial p}{\partial x}\right)(By - y^2)$$

Now by Newton's law of viscosity

$$\text{Shear stress } \tau = \mu\frac{du}{dy}$$

or 
$$\tau = \mu\left[\frac{d}{dy}\left(\frac{U}{B}\cdot y + \frac{1}{2\mu}\left(-\frac{\partial p}{\partial x}\right)(By - y^2)\right)\right]$$

or 
$$\tau = \mu\left[\frac{U}{B} + \frac{1}{2\mu}\left(-\frac{\partial p}{\partial x}\right)(B - 2y)\right]$$

or 
$$\boxed{\tau = \mu\frac{U}{B} + \left(-\frac{\partial p}{\partial x}\right)\left(\frac{B}{2} - y\right)}$$

Shear stress at the stationary boundary can be obtained by putting y = 0 in the above equation.

∴ Shear stress at the stationary boundary

$$\tau = \mu\frac{U}{B} + \left(-\frac{\partial p}{\partial x}\right)\left(\frac{B}{2}\right)$$

But this stress is required to be zero.

$$\therefore \quad \mu \frac{U}{B} + \left(-\frac{\partial p}{\partial x}\right)\left(\frac{B}{2}\right) = 0$$

$$\therefore \quad \boxed{\frac{\partial p}{\partial x} = \frac{2\mu U}{B^2}}$$

Now discharge per metre width of plates is given by

$$q = \frac{UB}{2} + \frac{B^3}{12\mu}\left(-\frac{\partial p}{\partial x}\right) \quad \text{(See Example 3.16)}$$

Substituting value of $\frac{\partial p}{\partial x}$ for zero shear stress at the boundary, we get

$$q = \frac{UB}{2} + \frac{B^3}{12\mu}\left(-\frac{2\mu U}{B^2}\right)$$

$$\therefore \quad q = \frac{UB}{2} - \frac{UB}{6}$$

$$\therefore \quad q = \frac{UB}{3}$$

$$\therefore \quad \boxed{\text{Discharge per unit width for zero shear stress at stationary boundary, } q = \frac{UB}{3}}$$

### Example 3.18:

Two horizontal plates are placed 10 mm apart. The lower plate is fixed and the upper plate moves with a velocity of 2 m/s. If there is a pressure drop of 100 kN/m² over a length of 250 m, determine the flow rate per metre width of the plates, shear stress along both plates and the maximum velocity of flow.

Take the relative density of the fluid between the plates to be 0.9 and the dynamic viscosity to be 1 Poise.

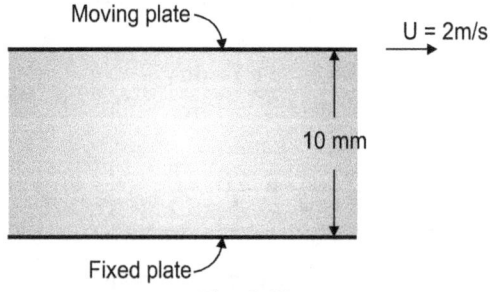

Fig. 3.23

**Solution:**

U = 2 m/s, B = 0.01 m, µ = 1 Poise = 0.1 N-s/m²

$$\frac{\partial p}{\partial x} = \frac{100 \times 1000}{250} = 400 \text{ N/m}^2/\text{m,}$$

R.D. = 0.9

1. Discharge per metre width

$$q = \frac{UB}{2} + \frac{B^3}{12\mu}\left(-\frac{\partial p}{\partial x}\right) \quad \text{(See Example 3.16)}$$

$$= \frac{2 \times 0.01}{2} + \frac{(0.01)^3}{12 \times 0.1}(400)$$

$$= 0.01033 \text{ m}^3/\text{s} \quad \text{or} \quad 10.33 \text{ l.p.s.}$$

∴ **Discharge per meter width = 10.33 l.p.s.**

2. Shear stress

$$\tau = \mu \cdot \frac{U}{B} + \left(-\frac{\partial p}{\partial x}\right)\left(\frac{B}{2} - y\right) \quad \text{(See Example 3.17)}$$

Shear stress at fixed plate can be obtained by putting $y = 0$

∴ $$\tau_f = \mu \cdot \frac{U}{B} + \left(-\frac{\partial p}{\partial x}\right)\left(\frac{B}{2}\right)$$

$$= 0.1 \times \frac{2}{0.01} + (400)\frac{0.01}{2}$$

$$= 20 + 2$$

$$= 22 \text{ N/m}^2$$

∴ **Shear stress at fixed plate = $\tau_f$ = 22 N/m²**

At the moving plate, $y = B$

∴ $$\tau_m = \mu \cdot \frac{U}{B} - \left(-\frac{\partial p}{\partial x}\right) \cdot \frac{B}{2}$$

$$= 0.1 \times \frac{2}{0.01} - (400)\frac{0.01}{2}$$

$$= 20 - 2$$

$$= 18 \text{ N/m}^2$$

∴ **Shear stress at moving plate = $\tau_m$ = 18 N/m²**

3. Maximum velocity of flow will occur when $\frac{du}{dy} = 0$

$$u = \frac{U}{B} \cdot y + \frac{1}{2\mu}\left(-\frac{\partial p}{\partial x}\right)(By - y^2)$$

∴ $$u = \frac{2}{0.01} \cdot y + \frac{1}{2 \times 0.1}(400)(0.01y - y^2)$$

$$\frac{du}{dy} = 200 + 2000(0.01 - 2y) = 0$$

∴ Maximum velocity will occur at
$$y = 0.055 \text{ m}$$
∴ Maximum velocity
$$u_{max} = 200 \times (0.055) + 2000 [0.01 \times 0.055 - (0.055)^2]$$
$$= 6.05 \text{ m/s}$$

**Maximum velocity = 6.05 m/s**

$\left[ \text{It may be noted that} \left(-\dfrac{\partial p}{\partial x}\right) \text{ is a positive quantity since pressure goes on decreasing in the direction of flow. } \dfrac{\partial p}{\partial x} \text{ is negative and hence } \left(-\dfrac{\partial p}{\partial x}\right) \text{ is positive.} \right]$

Now, 
$$u_{av} = \dfrac{q}{\text{Area}} = \dfrac{0.01033}{0.01}$$
$$= 1.033 \text{ m/s}$$

Reynold's number Re $= \dfrac{\rho \, u_{av} \, B}{\mu}$

$$= \dfrac{900 \times 1.033 \times 0.01}{0.1}$$

∴ **Re = 92.97**

Since Re is less than 1000, the critical Reynold's number for parallel plates, flow is laminar.

## THEORETICAL QUESTIONS

1. What do you understand by laminar flow?
2. What do you understand by Reynold's number? How is it connected with type of flow?
3. Explain upper and lower critical Reynold's number with reference to transition from laminar to turbulent flow.
4. Why is the lower critical Reynold's number called the true critical Reynold's number?
5. How is laminar flow characterised? OR Write down important characteristics of laminar flow.
6. State the various applications of laminar flow theory.
7. Show that in case of two dimensional steady uniform laminar flow, shear stress gradient is equal to pressure gradient.
8. Show that for laminar flow through circular pipe, the mean velocity is equal to half the maximum velocity.

OR

For a steady laminar flow through a circular pipe prove that the velocity distribution across the section is parabolic and average velocity is half of the maximum local velocity.

9. Starting from first principles, derive equation for loss of energy for steady laminar flow through pipe.
10. Starting from first principles, derive Hagen-Poiseuille equation for steady laminar flow in pipes.

    State the assumptions made.

    Further, establish relation between Darcy Weisbach friction factor and Reynold's number in laminar flow.
11. Derive an expression for Hagen-Poiseuille's formula with usual notations. Hence derive:

    $$f = \frac{16}{Re}$$

    where      f = Coefficient of friction between fluid and pipe and
                 Re = Reynold's number

    [**Hint:** $f = \frac{16}{Re}$ can be derived if formula $h_f = \frac{4fL}{D} \cdot \frac{u_{av}^2}{2g}$ is used. Otherwise, with formula $h_f = \frac{fL}{D} \cdot \frac{u_{av}^2}{2g}$, $f = \frac{64}{Re}$].

12. Show that for a steady laminar flow through a circular pipe, mean velocity of flow occurs at a radial distance of 0.707 R from the centre of pipe where R is radius of pipe.
13. With usual notations derive an expression for velocity distribution for laminar flow between two fixed parallel plates and show that it parabolic in nature.
14. Starting from first principles, show that for laminar flow between fixed parallel plates, the mean velocity is two-third of maximum velocity.
15. Derive expressions for point velocity and discharge per unit width through a narrow gap between two fixed horizontal plates, when a viscous liquid flows through it.
16. Starting from the first principles, derive the relation between the friction factor 'f' and the Reynold's number $\frac{(\rho \bar{u} B)}{\mu}$ for laminar flow between stationary parallel surfaces. The notations have usual meanings.
17. A liquid flows between two horizontal plates. The flow is fully developed. The x-direction is horizontal and is measured positively from left to right. Derive and sketch the velocity profile and if it is of a simple geometric shape name it in the following three cases:

    (i) The lower plate is at rest, the upper plate moves with a steady velocity in the positive x-direction and $\frac{\partial p}{\partial x}$ is zero.

    (ii) The lower plate is at rest, the upper plate moves with a steady velocity in the positive x-direction and $\frac{\partial p}{\partial x}$ is negative.

(iii) Both plates are at rest and $\frac{\partial p}{\partial x}$ is negative. Assume laminar flow between the plates.

[**Hint:** Refer Art 3.9]

[**Ans.** (i) straight line, (iii) parabola]

18. What do you understand by Couette flow? Where is it useful in study of fluid mechanics?
19. Two horizontal plates are placed distance 'B' apart and the gap between them is filled with liquid of viscosity 'μ'. The lower plate is fixed and the upper is moved with velocity of 'U' m/s. Assuming the flow between the plates as laminar, show with usual notation,

1. $q = \frac{UB}{2} + \frac{B^3}{12\mu}\left(-\frac{\partial p}{\partial x}\right)$

2. $\tau_{fixed} = \mu\frac{U}{B} + \left(-\frac{\partial p}{\partial x}\right)\left(\frac{B}{2}\right)$

3. $\tau_{moving} = \mu\frac{U}{B} - \left(-\frac{\partial p}{\partial x}\right)\left(\frac{B}{2}\right)$

4. $\tau_{centre} = \frac{\mu U}{B}$

5. $\tau = 0$ at $y = \left[\frac{B}{2} + \frac{\mu U}{B}\left(-\frac{1}{\partial p/\partial x}\right)\right]$

## NUMERICAL PROBLEMS

1. A laminar flow is taking in a pipe of diameter 0.2 m. The maximum velocity is 1.5 m/s. Find the mean velocity and the radius at which this occurs. Also calculate the velocity at 0.04 m from the wall of the pipe.
   [**Ans.** 0.75 m/s, 0.0707 m, 0.96 m/s]

2. A liquid with specific gravity 2.8 and viscosity 0.08 Ns/m² flows through a smooth pipe of unknown diameter, resulting in a pressure drop of 800 N/m² in 2 km length of pipe. What is the pipe diameter if the mass flow rate is 2500 kg/hr?

   [**Hint:** $Q = \frac{2500}{3600 \times (2.8 \times 1000)} = 2.48 \times 10^{-4} \, m^3/s$

   $\Delta p = 800 = \frac{128 \, \mu \, QL}{\pi D^4} = \frac{128 \times (0.08) \times (2.48 \times 10^{-4}) \times (2000)}{\pi D^4}$

   $D = 0.212 \, m$]

   [**Ans.** 0.212 m]

3. A viscous liquid of R.D. 0.9 and kinematic viscosity $2.9 \times 10^{-4}$ m²/s flows through a horizontal pipe 100 mm diameter Velocity along the axis is 1.85 m/s. Find:
   (i) Shear stress along the pipe surface in Pa.
   (ii) Discharge in l.p.s. (litres per second)
   (iii) Power required per km length of pipe in kW
   (iv) Whether flow is laminar or not.
   (**Ans.** (i) 19.31 Pa, (ii) 7.265 l.p.s, (iii) P = 5.61 kW, (iv) 319 < 2000, flow is laminar)

4. Crude oil of R.D. 0.9 is pumped through a smooth horizontal pipe 400 m long, 100 mm diameter. Kinematic viscosity of oil is 2.5 stokes. Differential pressure head between two ends of the pipe is 16.31 m of oil. Assuming the flow of oil to be laminar, find:
   (i) Rate of flow of oil through pipe.
   (ii) Power required to maintain the flow.
   Also check whether flow is actually laminar or not.
   **(Ans.** (i) 3.927 l.p.s. (ii) 565.49 watts, Re = 200 < 2000, flow is laminar)

5. What power will be required per km length of pipe-line to overcome viscous resistance to flow of crude oil of viscosity 1.9 poise through a horizontal pipe of 10 cm diameter at the rate of 650 litres per hour? Take specific gravity of oil = 0.85.
   **(Ans.** 2.516 watts)

6. An oil of specific gravity 0.9 and dynamic viscosity of 0.1 N-s/$m^2$ is flowing through a 10 cm diameter pipe. The velocity distribution being parabolic with maximum of 1 m/s. Calculate the shear stress at the pipe wall and within the fluid, 2 cm from the wall.
   **(Ans.** $\tau_0$ = 4 N/$m^2$, 2.4 N/$m^2$)

7. Crude oil of dynamic viscosity of 1.5 poise and relative density of 0.9 flows through a 20 mm diameter vertical pipe. The pressure gauges fixed 20 m apart as shown in Fig. 3.24 show 600 kPa (lower side) and 200 kPa (upper side of pipe) respectively. Find the direction of flow and the rate of flow through the pipe.

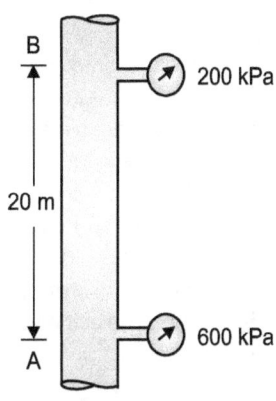

Fig. 3.24

   **(Ans.** Flow from A to B, Q = 0.2925 l.p.s.)

8. The velocity variation in a pipe is expressed as
$$\frac{u}{U} = \left[1 - \left(\frac{r}{R}\right)^2\right]$$
   where, u = Velocity at any point
   U = Velocity at the centre
   r = Distance of any point from centre
   R = Radius of pipe
   Determine the shear stress for ratios of r/R equal to 0, 0.5 and 1 given that u = 10 m/s, $\mu = 2 \times 10^{-4}$ Pa.s and the diameter of the pipe is 1 m.

(**Hint:** $\tau = \mu \dfrac{\partial u}{\partial y}$ but $\dfrac{\partial u}{\partial y} = -\dfrac{\partial u}{\partial r}$. Therefore $\tau = \mu \dfrac{\partial}{\partial r}\left[-U\left\{1-\left(\dfrac{r}{R}\right)^2\right\}\right] = \dfrac{2\mu U}{R}\left(\dfrac{r}{R}\right)$

etc.)

(**Ans.** $0, 4 \times 10^{-3}$ N/m$^2$, $8 \times 10^{-3}$ N/m$^2$)

9. An oil of viscosity 10 P and specific gravity 1.2 flows through a horizontal pipe 80 mm diameter. If the pressure drop in 100 m length of the pipe is 2000 kN/m$^2$, determine:
   (i) The rate of flow of oil.
   (ii) The maximum velocity.
   (iii) The total frictional drag over 100 m length of pipe.
   (iv) The power required to maintain the flow.
   (v) The velocity gradient at the pipe wall.
   (vi) The velocity and shear stress at 10 mm from wall.
   [**Hint:** Refer Illustrative Example 3.3]
   [**Ans.** 20.1 l.p.s, 8 m/s, 10.05 kN, 40.21 kW, 400 s$^{-1}$, 300 s$^{-1}$, 3.5 m/s]

10. Oil of mass density 800 kg/m$^3$ and dynamic viscosity 0.02 Poise flow through 60 mm diameter pipe of length 500 m at the rate of 0.19 l.p.s.
    Determine:
    (i) Reynold's number of flow
    (ii) Centre line velocity
    (iii) Pressure gradient
    (iv) Loss of pressure in 500 m length
    (v) Wall shear stress and
    (vi) Power required to maintain the flow.
    (**Ans.** 1936.32, 0.1936 m/s, 2.478 N/m$^2$, 1239 N/m$^2$/m. 0.235 watts)

11. An oil of viscosity 10 P and specific gravity 0.8 flows through a horizontal pipe of 50 mm diameter. If the pressure drops at the rate of 20 kN/m$^2$ per metre length, determine,
    (i) Rate of flow of oil in lpm
    (ii) The centre line velocity
    (iii) Total friction drag over 1 km of the pipe
    (iv) Power required to maintain the flow in 1 km length of pipe.
    (**Ans.** 184 lpm, 3.125 m/s, 39269.9 N/per km, 61.36 kW)

12. Determine the optimum diameter of the pipe required to carry 69.5 l.p.s. of crude oil maintaining the laminar flow. Also determine the power required for its transport over 2 km. Take mass density of crude oil as 950 kg/m$^3$ and viscosity as $8 \times 10^{-2}$ kg/m-s.
    (**Hint:** Take critical Reynold's number as 2000)
    (**Ans.** 0.525 m, 414.49 watts)

13. A pump of 47 watts is to be used for pumping oil of R.D. 0.9 and kinematic viscosity of 0.08 stokes at the rate of 60 l.p.m., through an inclined pipe of 1 km length. If the pipe is to be laid at a slope of 1: 200, find the diameter of the pipe.
    (**Ans.** 100.7 mm)

14. A laminar flow between two fixed parallel plates 1 m wide, kept at a distance of 200 mm, the pressure drop is 10 N/m$^2$/metre length of plates. If the same discharge is allowed to pass through a circular tube of 200 mm diameter, will the pressure drop increase or decrease? Take µ of liquid as 1.2 Poise.
    (**Ans.** Pressure drop increases to 169.765 N/m$^2$/m)

15. Two parallel plates kept 200 mm apart have laminar flow of oil between them with maximum velocity of 0.6 m/s. Calculate
    (i) discharge per meter width
    (ii) the shear stress at the plates
    (iii) the difference of pressure between two points 30 m apart. Viscosity of oil is 2.5 Pa-s.
    (**Ans.** 0.08 m$^3$/s, 30 N/m$^2$, 9000 N/m$^2$)

16. Oil of viscosity 0.1 N-s/m$^2$ and specific gravity 0.9 is flowing between two parallel plates kept 10 mm apart, with a velocity of 1.5 m/s.
    Determine,
    (i) Maximum velocity
    (ii) Shear stress at the boundary
    (iii) Velocity at a distance of 2.5 mm from the plate
    (iv) Loss of head in a distance of 10 m
    (**Ans.** 2.25 m/s, 90 N/m$^2$, 1.688 m/s, 20.387 m)

17. Two parallel plates kept 0.1 m apart have laminar flow of oil between them with a maximum velocity of 1.5 m/s. Calculate the discharge per meter width, the shear stress at the plates, the difference in pressure in pascals between two points 20 m apart, the velocity gradient at the plates and velocity at 0.02 m from the plate. Take viscosity of oil to be 2.453 Ns/m$^2$.
    [**Hint:** Refer Illustrative Example 3.13. Except the value of '$\mu$' the example is same.]
    [**Ans.** 0.1 m$^3$/s, 147.18 N/m$^2$, 58.872 kN/m$^2$, 60 s$^{-1}$, 0.96 m/s]

18. Shear stress at a point 40 mm from axis of pipe is 28 Pa. Find wall shear stress and rate of flow if pipe diameter is 36 cm and viscosity of flowing liquid is 40 paise. Assume laminar flow through pipe.
    (**Ans.** 126 Pa, 0.144 m$^3$/s)

19. Two horizontal fixed parallel plates are 12 mm apart. Liquid of density 660 kg/m$^3$ flows between the plates. Velocity at a point 4 mm from lower plate is 1.10 m/s. Determine mean velocity and absolute viscosity of liquid assuming laminar flow and head loss of 1.529 per unit length (per metre). Draw neat sketch showing velocity variation.

    [**Hint:** Loss of head/metre = 1.529 m or $\left(-\dfrac{\partial p}{\partial x}\right)$ = (1.529) × (660 × 9.81) = 9900 Pa/m.

    $\therefore$ $\quad 1.1 = \dfrac{1}{2\mu}\left(-\dfrac{\partial p}{\partial x}\right)(By - y^2)$

    $\therefore$ $\quad 1.1 = \dfrac{1}{2\mu}$ (9900) [(12 × 10$^{-3}$) . (4 × 10$^{-3}$) – (4 × 10$^{-3}$)] ... etc.

    (**Ans.** 0.825 m/s, 0.144 Pas)

20. Liquid of specific weight 8000 N/m$^3$ and dynamic viscosity 0.04 Pa-s (N-s/m$^2$) flows between two inclined parallel plates 15 mm apart. If the flow rate is 3 l.p.s per metre width of plate, find the slope of these plates so as to keep the pressure gradient zero.
    (**Hint:** Refer Example 3.9)
    (**Ans.** sin $\theta$ = 0.05331 or $\theta$ = 3° - 3' - 21")

21. A steel ball 1.5 mm in diameter and mass 13.7 mg falls steadily in oil through a vertical distance of 500 mm in 56 seconds. If the oil has a density of 950 kg/m$^3$ and the drum containing oil is large enough to neglect wall effect, what is the viscosity of oil?
    (**Ans.** 0.9342 Pa-s, Re = 0.1111 < 0.2)

## (B) KINETIC ENERGY AND MOMENTUM CORRECTION FACTOR

## 3.10 Kinetic Energy Correction Factor (α)

While calculating velocity head $\frac{V^2}{2g}$ in Bernoulli's equation, velocity is assumed to be uniform over the cross-section of the passage. However, this is not true in case of real fluids and the velocity varies over the cross section of the passage. Therefore, actual kinetic energy of fluid passing through a section, calculated, taking into account velocity variation is different from the kinetic energy calculated on the basis of average velocity.

Consider Fig. 3.25 which shows the cross-section of passage (pipe) and velocity distribution. Consider elementary area 'dA'. Let 'v' be the local velocity of fluid through area 'dA'.

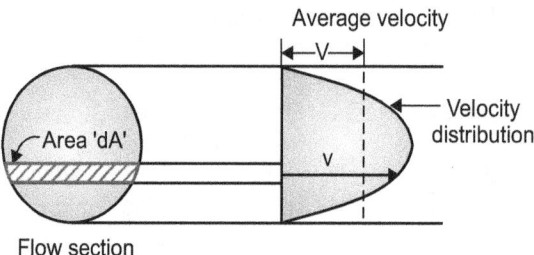

**Fig. 3.25: Energy correction factor**

Mass of fluid passing through area 'dA' per unit time is ρvdA and the kinetic energy of this mass will be $(\rho v\, dA)\frac{v^2}{2}$. Therefore, total kinetic energy of fluid passing through the entire cross-section A is

$$\int_A \frac{1}{2} \rho v^3 \, dA$$

Knowing the velocity profile over the cross section, the actual kinetic energy given by the above integral can be calculated.

But kinetic energy based on the average velocity 'V', passing through the section with area 'A' is

$$\frac{1}{2} \rho V^3 \cdot A$$

In order to compensate for the difference between these two kinetic energies, a coefficient called *"energy correction factor"* denoted by 'α' is introduced. $\alpha \frac{V^2}{2g}$ gives the kinetic energy actually passing a section.

Thus, Kinetic energy correction factor '$\alpha$'

$$= \frac{[\text{Kinetic energy, per second, calculated taking into account actual velocity variation}]}{[\text{Kinetic energy, per second, calculated on the basis of average velocity}]}$$

$$\alpha = \frac{\int_A \frac{1}{2}\rho v^3 \, dA}{\frac{1}{2}\rho V^3 A} \qquad \ldots (3.36)$$

or $\boxed{\alpha = \frac{1}{A}\int_A \left(\frac{v}{V}\right)^3 dA}$ for incompressible fluid, ... (3.37)

For laminar flow through a circular pipe, '$\alpha$' has a value of 2. Since, the velocity is more or less uniform for turbulent flow, '$\alpha$' varies between 1.01 to 1.15 and hence is generally neglected without affecting the results.

Accounting for energy correction factor, Bernoulli's equation can be modified as

$$Z_1 + \frac{p_1}{\gamma} + \alpha_1 \frac{V_1^2}{2g} = Z_2 + \frac{p_2}{\gamma} + \alpha_2 \frac{V_2^2}{2g}$$

$\alpha$ is taken into account only when very accurate results are required.

## 3.11 Momentum Correction Factor ($\beta$)

Momentum theorem as stated is based on the assumption that the velocity of flow is uniform across the cross section. However, in actual practice the velocity is not uniform across the cross section.

Thus, the momentum of fluid at a section of the passage found out on the basis of average velocity of flow at a section is much different from the actual momentum of a fluid passing through the section. This is due to the variation of velocity across the section of the passage.

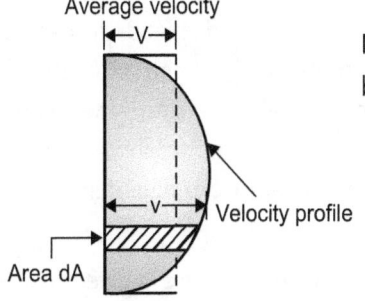

Fig. 3.26

Momentum of fluid passing the cross-section per second based on variation of velocity

$$= \int_A \rho(v \cdot dA) \cdot v = \int_A \rho v^2 \, dA$$

Momentum of fluid passing the section with area 'A' per second based on average velocity 'V' = $\rho A V^2$.

Ratio of these two momentums is called momentum correction factor and is denoted by 'β' (beeta).

∴   β = [Momentum per second calculated taking into account actual velocity variation] / [Momentum per second calculated on the basis of average velocity]

$$\beta = \frac{\int_A \rho v^2 \, dA}{\rho A V^2}$$

∴ $$\boxed{\beta = \frac{1}{A} \int_A \left(\frac{v}{V}\right)^2 \cdot dA}$$

For laminar flow through circular pipe, β = 1.33. Since for turbulent flow, velocity distribution is more or less uniform, 'β' has a value, ranging from 1.01 to 1.05 and hence it is neglected.

## (C) POWER ABSORBED IN VISCOUS FLOW

## 3.12 Power Absorbed in Viscous Flow

An important application of theory of laminar flow of viscous fluids is use of viscous oils in lubrication of various bearings. Although the velocities of the moving parts in the bearing parts are high, the thickness of the film of lubricating oil is very small to give Reynold's number less than critical value and laws of viscous flow are applicable.

The role of lubricating oil is to separate the bearing surfaces with the help of a thin film of oil and prevent direct contact between bearing surfaces. However, the lubricating in itself can create viscous resistance to the motion. If highly viscous oil is used it leads to greater resistance and results in greater power loss. On the other hand, if a light oil (with low viscosity) is used, it may fly out and may not be able to maintain the film between the surfaces and wearing of surfaces will take place. It is therefore, required to choose the oil with proper viscosity which will maintain the film at the same time absorb minimum power due to viscous resistance.

The expressions for power absorbed by different types of bearings are derived in the following articles.

## 3.12.1 Viscous Resistance in Journal Bearing

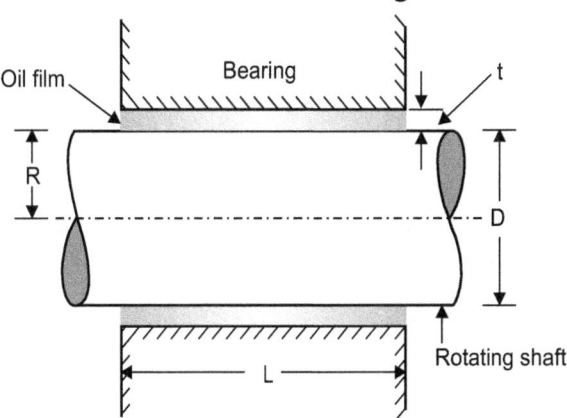

**Fig. 3.27: Journal bearing**

Consider a shaft rotating in a journal bearing as shown in the Fig. 3.27. The clearance (annular space) between the shaft and the journal bearing is filled with viscous oil. According to no slip condition the oil is contact with journal bearing will be stationary while that in contact with moving shaft will have the same velocity as that of the shaft. Thus, a velocity gradient, a viscous shear stress and hence viscous force will be produced. To overcome this force power will be absorbed in the bearing.

Let  
$D$ = Diameter of the shaft  
$N$ = Speed of the shaft in r.p.m.  
$L$ = Length of the bearing  
$t$ = Thickness of the film  

Now, angular speed of the shaft

$$\omega = \frac{2\pi N}{60} \text{ rad/s}$$

∴ Tangential speed of the shaft

$$V = \omega \times R$$

∴ $$V = \frac{2\pi N}{60} \times \frac{D}{2}$$

or $$V = \frac{\pi D N}{60}$$

Now shear stress is given by

$$\tau = \mu \cdot \frac{du}{dy}$$

Since the thickness of the film 't' is a very small, the velocity distribution in the film can be assumed to be linear.

Therefore, $$\frac{du}{dy} = \frac{V-0}{t} = \frac{V}{t} = \frac{\pi D N}{60\, t}$$

Hence, shear stress

$$\tau = \mu \cdot \frac{du}{dy}$$

or

$$\tau = \mu \cdot \frac{\pi DN}{60\, t}$$

∴ Shear force or viscous resistance

$$F = \tau \times \text{Area of surface of shaft in contact with oil}$$

∴ $$F = \tau \times (\pi DL)$$

∴ $$F = \frac{\mu \pi DN}{60\, t} \times (\pi DL)$$

∴ $$F = \frac{\mu \pi^2 D^2 NL}{60\, t}$$

Torque required to overcome the viscous resistance

$$T = \text{Viscous resistance } F \times \frac{D}{2}$$

$$= \frac{\mu \pi^2 D^3 NL}{120\, t}$$

∴ Power absorbed in overcoming the viscous resistance

$$P = T \times \omega = \left(\frac{\mu \pi^2 D^3 NL}{120\, t}\right) \times \left(\frac{2\pi N}{60}\right)$$

∴ $$\boxed{P = \frac{\mu \pi^3 D^3 N^2 L}{3600\, t}}$$ ... (3.38)

## 3.12.2 Viscous Resistance to Foot-Step Bearing

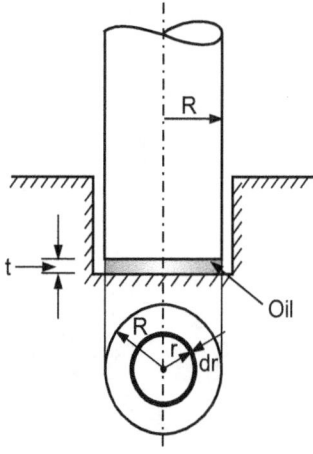

**Fig. 3.28: Foot-Step bearing**

Fig. 3.28 shows the foot step bearing at the end of rotating shaft. An oil film is used between the bottom of the shaft and the bearing for the purpose of reducing the wearing of surfaces.

Since the radius of shaft in contact with oil goes on varying from zero to R, the viscous resistance has to be found out by considering an elementary ring with radius 'r' and with dr.

Let    R = Radius of the shaft
        N = Speed of the shaft
        t = Thickness of oil film

Area of elementary ring = $2\pi\, r\, dr$

The shear stress

$$\tau = \mu \cdot \frac{du}{dy}$$

$$= \mu \cdot \frac{V}{t}$$

where V is the tangential velocity of the shaft at distance 'r' from the axis

$$V = \omega \cdot r = \frac{2\pi N}{60} \times r$$

$$\therefore\quad \tau = \mu \times \frac{2\pi N}{60} \times \frac{r}{t}$$

∴ Shear force on the elementary ring

$$dF = \tau \times \text{Area of the ring}$$

$$= \left(\mu \times \frac{2\pi N}{60} \times \frac{r}{t}\right) \times (2\pi\, r\, dr)$$

$$\therefore\quad dF = \frac{\mu}{15} \times \frac{\pi^2 N r^2}{t} \times dr$$

∴ Torque required to overcome the viscous resistance

$$dT = dF \times r$$

$$\therefore\quad dT = \left(\frac{\mu}{15t} \times \pi^2\, Nr^2\, dr\right) \cdot r$$

$$\therefore\quad dT = \left(\frac{\mu}{15\,t} \times \pi^2 \times N\right) \times r^3\, dr$$

∴ Total torque required to overcome the viscous resistance

$$T = \int_0^R dT = \int_0^R \left(\frac{\mu}{15\,t} \times \pi^2 \times N\right) \cdot r^3\, dr$$

$$= \frac{\mu \pi^2 N}{15\,t} \left[\frac{r^4}{4}\right]_0^R$$

$$\therefore\quad T = \frac{\mu \pi^2 N R^4}{60\,t}$$

∴ Power absorbed in overcoming the viscous resistance

$$P = \text{Torque} \times \omega$$

$$= \frac{\mu \pi^2 N R^4}{60\, t} \times \frac{2\pi N}{60}$$

∴ $$\boxed{P = \frac{\mu \pi^3 N^2 R^4}{1800\, t}}$$ ... (3.39)

## 3.12.3 Viscous Resistance to Collar Bearing

Fig. 3.29 shows the collar bearing used to take the axial thrust of a horizontal shaft. The face of the collar is separated from the surface of the bearing by an oil film of uniform thickness.

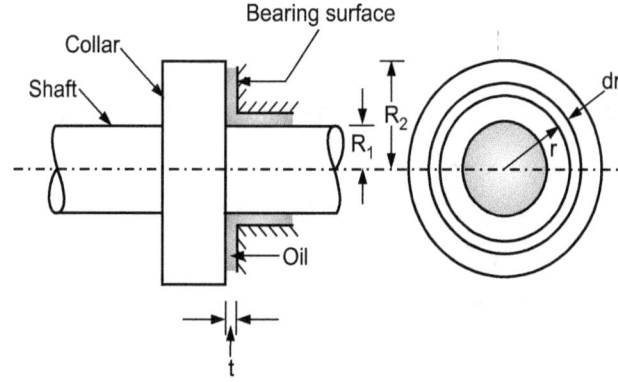

**Fig. 3.29: Collar bearing**

Let      $R_1$ = Internal radius of the collar

$R_2$ = External radius of the collar

$t$ = Thickness of oil film

$N$ = Speed of shaft in r.p.m.

Consider an elementary ring of bearing surface with radius 'r' and width 'dr'.

Now, Area of ring = $2\pi r\, dr$

∴ Shear stress on the ring = $\tau = \mu \cdot \dfrac{du}{dy} = \mu\, \dfrac{2\pi N r}{60\, t}$ (Refer foot-step bearing)

∴ Shear force on the ring

$dF = \tau \times$ Area of the ring

∴ $$dF = \left(\mu \cdot \frac{2\pi N r}{60\, t}\right) \times 2\pi r\, dr$$

∴ $$dF = \frac{\mu \pi^2 N r^2}{15\, t} \cdot dr$$

Torque on the elementary ring

$$d_T = dF \times r$$
$$= \frac{\mu \pi^2 N r^3}{15\,t}\,dr$$

Total torque required to overcome the viscous resistance

$$R = \int_{R_1}^{R_2} dT$$

$$= \int_{R_1}^{R_2} \frac{\mu \pi^2 N}{15\,t} r^3\,dr$$

$$= \frac{\mu \pi^2 N}{15\,t} \left[\frac{R^4}{4}\right]_{R_1}^{R_2}$$

$$= \frac{\mu \pi^2 N}{60\,t}\left[R_2^4 - R_1^4\right]$$

Power absorbed in overcoming the viscous resistance

$$P = T \times \omega = T \times \frac{2\pi N}{60}$$

$$= \frac{\mu \pi^2 N}{60\,t}\left[R_2^4 - R_1^4\right] \times \frac{2\pi N}{60}$$

∴ $$\boxed{P = \frac{\mu \pi^3 N^2}{1800\,t}\left[R_2^4 - R_1^4\right]}$$ ... (3.40)

### Example 3.19:

A shaft having a diameter of 5 cm rotates centrally in a journal bearing having a diameter of 5.1 cm and length of 5 cm. The annual space between shaft and bearing is filled with oil of viscosity 1 P. Determine the power absorbed in the bearing if the speed of rotation is 500 r.p.m.

**Solution:**

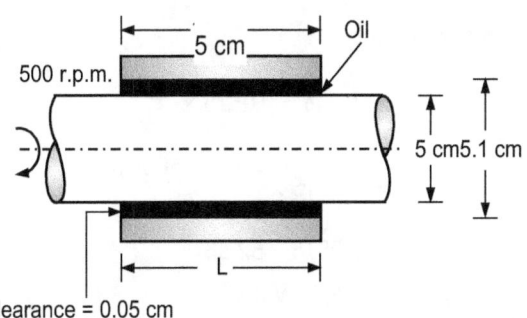

Fig. 3.30

Tangential velocity of shaft $= V = \dfrac{\pi DN}{60}$

$= \pi \times \dfrac{5}{100} \times \dfrac{500}{60}$

$V = 1.31$ m/s

Velocity gradient across the clearance

$\dfrac{du}{dy} = \dfrac{V}{t}$

$= \dfrac{1.31}{0.05 \times 10^{-2}}$

$= 2620 \text{ s}^{-1}$

Shear stress on the surface of the shaft

$\tau = \mu \dfrac{du}{dy} = 0.1 \times 2620$  $\quad \because 1P = 0.1 \dfrac{\text{N-s}}{\text{m}^2}$

$= 262 \text{ N/m}^2$

Shear force on the shaft

$F = \tau \times$ Area of shaft in contact with oil

$= \tau \times \pi \times D \times L$

∴ $\quad F = 262 \times \pi \times \dfrac{5}{100} \times \dfrac{5}{100}$

∴ $\quad F = 2.058$ N

Torque required to run the shaft

$T = F \times$ Radius of the shaft

$= 2.058 \times \dfrac{2.5}{100}$

$T = 0.0515$ N-m

∴ Power absorbed in the bearing

$P = T \times \omega = 0.0515 \times \dfrac{2\pi N}{60}$

$= 0.0515 \times \dfrac{2 \times \pi \times 500}{60}$

$= 0.0515 \times 52.36$

$= 2.697$ Watts

∴ **Power absorbed in the bearing = 2.697 watts**

# FLUID MECHANICS (NMU) (S.E. MECHANICAL) — VISCOUS AND BOUNDARY LAYER FLOW

### Example 3.20:

Find the power required to rotate a vertical shaft of 100 mm diameter at 600 r.p.m. The lower end of the shaft rests in a foot step bearing. The end of the shaft and surface of the bearing are both flat and there is an oil film of 0.5 mm separating them. The viscosity of oil is 2 poise.

**Solution:**

Diameter of shaft, $D = 100$ mm $= 0.1$ m
Speed of shaft $N = 600$ r.p.m.
Viscosity of oil $\mu = 2$ poise $= 0.2$ N-s/m$^2$
Thickness of film $t = 0.5$ mm

The torque required to overcome the viscosity resistance in the foot-step bearing is given by

$$T = \frac{\mu}{60\,t} \times \pi^2 \times N \times R^4 \quad \text{(See text)}$$

$$= \frac{0.2}{60 \times 0.0005} \times \pi^2 \times 600 \times \left(\frac{0.1}{2}\right)^4$$

$\therefore \quad T = 0.2467$ Nm

Power required to rotate the shaft

$$P = T \times \omega = T \times \frac{2\pi N}{60}$$

$$= 0.2467 \times \frac{2 \times \pi \times 600}{60}$$

$$= 15.50 \text{ W}$$

**Power required to rotate the shaft = 15.50 W**

### Example 3.21:

A collar bearing having external and internal diameters of 20 cm and 15 cm respectively is used to take the thrust of a shaft. An oil film of thickness 0.025 cm is maintained between collar surface of the bearing. The shaft rotates at 300 r.p.m. Find the power lost in overcoming the viscous resistance if viscosity oil is 1P.

**Solution:**

External diameter of collar $D_2 = 20$ cm $= 0.2$ m
External radius of collar $R_2 = 0.1$ m
Internal diameter of collar $D_1 = 15$ cm $= 0.15$ m
Internal radius of collar $R_1 = 0.075$ m

Thickness of oil film   t = 0.025 cm = 0.00025 m
Viscosity of oil    $\mu$ = 1 poise = 0.1 Ns/m$^2$
Speed of shaft    N = 300 r.p.m.
Torque required to overcome the viscous resistance

$$T = \frac{\mu}{60\,t} \times \pi^2 \times N \times \left(R_2^4 - R_1^4\right) \text{ (See text)}$$

$$= \frac{0.1}{60 \times 0.00025} \times \pi^2 \times 300 \times \left[(0.1)^4 - (0.075)^4\right] = 1.349 \text{ Nm}$$

Power lost in viscous resistance

$$P = \frac{2\pi NT}{60} = \frac{2 \times \pi \times 300}{60} \times 1.349$$

P = 42.38 W

**Power lost in overcoming viscous resistance = 42.38 W**

# (D) BOUNDARY LAYER FLOW

## 3.13 Introduction

In an ideal fluid flow (potential flow) theory, fluid is assumed to be ideal with zero viscosity and constant density. The analytical results regarding forces on the bodies obtained on the ideal fluid flow theory often do not match with the experimental results. It is quite evident that with ideal fluid, there will be no drag force on body of any shape. However, in practice, bodies like aeroplanes, submarines, cars are subjected to drag forces (drag is the resistance to motion). Further, viscosity of air and water is so low that it is difficult to imagine that such fluids can give rise to shear force on the bodies moving through them.

In practice, fluids adhere to the boundary, and acquire the same velocity as that of the boundary, a condition known as 'No slip condition'. Thus if the boundary is stationary, the velocity of fluid near the boundary is zero and it goes on increasing as we go away from the boundary. This variation in velocity near the boundary gives rise to shear stresses which results in resistance to motion of bodies.

'Boundary Layer Theory' developed by Ludwig Prandtl, in 1904 explained the drag force experienced by the solid body immersed in the flowing fluid which otherwise could not be theoretically explained.

## 3.14 Concept of Boundary Layer

In earlier days it was thought by engineers that when a body is held in flowing mass of fluid, the fluid exerts some shear force on the body due to actual rubbing or friction between the fluid and the surface of the body. However, in 20th century this concept was ruled out since the surface did not show any fatigue or signs of decay due to continuous rubbing action. In 1904, Prandtl put forward a theory called 'Boundary Layer Theory'. According to this theory, the fluid in the vicinity of surface of body may be divided into two portions.

1. A very thin layer of fluid which is in the immediate vicinity of boundary. When a real fluid flows past a solid boundary, there develops a thin layer, very close to the boundary, in which the velocity rapidly increases from zero at the boundary (due to no slip condition) to nearly uniform velocity in the stream. It is in this zone that the effect of viscosity is predominant due to high values of $\dfrac{du}{dy}$ and that most of the energy is lost in this zone due to this viscous shear. "This layer which has had its velocity affected by the boundary shear is called *Boundary Layer.*"

In other words "*A thin layer of fluid, in the vicinity of boundary, whose velocity is affected due to viscous shear is called 'Boundary layer'.*"

2. The remaining portion of fluid outside the boundary layer. In this zone since Reynold's number 'Re' is very high, the viscous effects are negligible and the flow in this zone can be treated as an ideal fluid flow.

## 3.15 Laminar Boundary Layer, Turbulent Boundary Layer and Laminar Sublayer

### 3.15.1 Characteristics of Boundary Layer along a Flat Plate

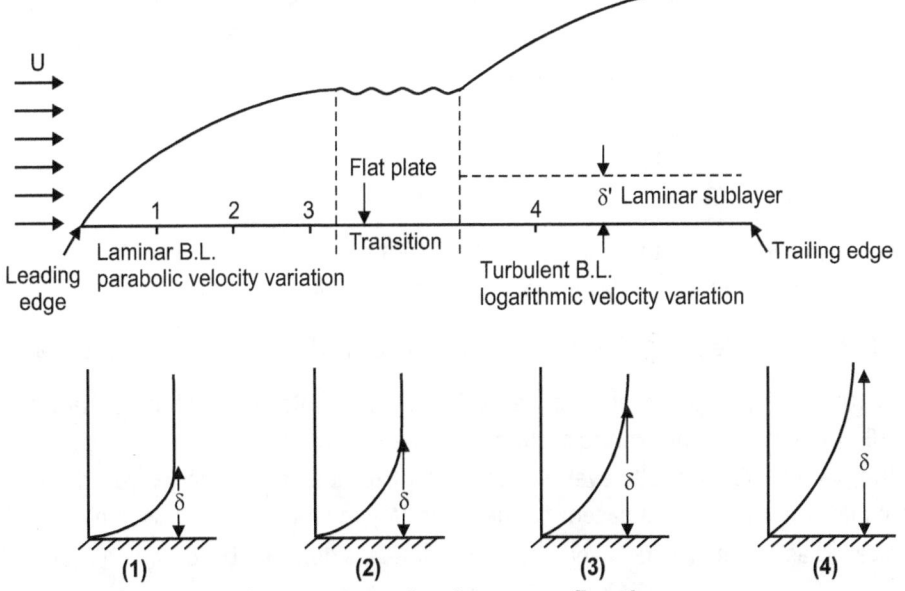

Fig. 3.31: Boundary layer on a flat plate

Consider a thin, long flat plate held steady in a stream of fluid moving with velocity 'U' known as 'Free Stream Velocity' or 'Ambient Velocity' or 'Potential Velocity' [See Fig. 3.31].

At the leading edge the thickness of boundary layer is zero. But on the downstream side as the fluid goes on retarding more and more, the thickness of boundary layer goes on increasing as shown in Fig. 3.31.

Upto a certain portion of the plate from the leading edge, there is a smooth increase in boundary layer and the flow in the boundary layer exhibits all the characteristics of 'Laminar Flow' irrespective of whether the incoming flow is laminar or turbulent. This is known as Laminar Boundary Layer.' In case of laminar boundary layer, the thickness of boundary layer '$\delta$' is given by Blasius as:

$$\boxed{\delta = \frac{5x}{\sqrt{Re_x}}} \qquad \ldots (3.41)$$

where $Re_x$ is Reynold's Number at a distance 'x' from the leading edge given by:

$$Re_x = \frac{Ux}{v} \qquad \therefore \delta = 5\sqrt{\frac{xv}{U}} \qquad \ldots (3.42)$$

Thus, in laminar boundary layer, Newton's law $\tau = \mu \frac{du}{dy}$ is applicable and velocity distribution is parabolic in nature.

If however, the plate is sufficiently long, beyond some distance from the leading edge, the laminar boundary layer becomes unstable and the flow in the boundary layer exhibits characteristics between laminar and turbulent flow. This is known as 'Transitional Region'.

After this zone the thickness of the boundary layer goes on increasing rapidly and flow in the boundary layer exhibits characteristics of turbulent flow. This is known as 'Turbulent Boundary Layer'. In case of turbulent boundary layer, the thickness of boundary layer is given by:

$$\boxed{\delta = \frac{0.377 x}{(Re_x)^{1/5}}} \qquad \ldots (3.43)$$

Velocity profile is logarithmic in case of turbulent boundary layer.

The change of boundary layer from laminar to turbulent depends mainly upon the Reynold's Number, $(Re_x) = \frac{Ux}{v}$. The value of Critical Reynold's Number varies between $3 \times 10^5$ and $6 \times 10^5$ and for all practical purposes, value of Critical Reynold's Number may be taken as $5 \times 10^5$. ('x' is the distance of the section from the leading edge).

If the plate is very smooth, even in the zone of turbulent boundary layer, there exists a very thin layer immediately adjacent to the boundary in which the flow is laminar. This thin layer is called as 'Laminar Sub-Layer' and it's thickness is denoted by '$\delta'$' which is given by:

$$\delta' = \frac{(11.6) v}{\sqrt{\tau_0/\rho}} = \frac{(11.6) v}{u_*} \qquad \ldots (3.44)$$

where $u_* = \sqrt{\frac{\tau_0}{\rho}}$ called shear velocity.

The laminar sub-layer, although very thin, is very important factor in deciding whether a surface is hydrodynamically smooth or rough surface.

## 3.15.2 Factors Affecting the Growth of Boundary Layer

The various factors which influence the growth of boundary layer on a smooth flat plate are as follows:

1. **The distance 'x' from the leading edge:** It varies directly with distance 'x'. More the distance 'x', more is the thickness of boundary layer and vice–versa.
2. **The free stream velocity:** It varies inversely as the free-stream velocity U. If 'U' increases, thickness of boundary layer decreases and vice–versa.
3. **Viscosity of fluid:** It varies directly with viscosity. If viscosity of fluid is more, the thickness of boundary layer is more and vice–versa.
4. **Density of fluid:** It varies inversely with density. For lower denser fluid, thickness is more and vice–versa.

## 3.15.3 Laminar Boundary Layer and Turbulent Boundary Layer

From the study of these two types of boundary layers they can be compared as follows:

| Laminar Boundary Layer | Turbulent Boundary Layer |
|---|---|
| 1. Flow is laminar. | 1. Flow is turbulent. |
| 2. Reynold's number 'Re' is low. | 2. Reynold's number 'Re' is high. |
| 3. Velocity distribution is parabolic. | 3. Velocity variation is logarithmic or follows one-seventh power law. |
| 4. Thickness of layer grows slowly. | 4. Thickness of layer grows rapidly. |
| 5. More prone to separation. | 5. Less prone to separation. |

# 3.16 Thickness of Boundary Layer

The velocity within the boundary layer increases from zero at the boundary to velocity of main stream asymptotically and hence it is not easy to define the thickness of boundary layer. Therefore, many arbitrary definitions of boundary layer thickness are put forward.

1. **Nominal Thickness:** It is defined as that distance from the boundary in which the velocity reaches 99% of the main stream velocity. It is denoted by 'delta'. In other words, when u = 0.99 U, y = δ. [See Fig. 3.32].

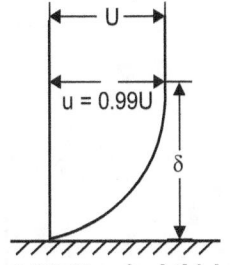

Fig. 3.32: Nominal thickness

2. **Displacement Thickness '$\delta^*$':** It is defined as 'a distance perpendicular to the boundary by which the boundary will have to be displaced outwards so that the actual discharge would be same as that of an ideal fluid past the displaced boundary'.

Consider an elementary strip of thickness 'dy' and at a distance 'y' from the boundary surface, [See Fig. 3.33]. Let 'u' be the velocity of flow through this strip.

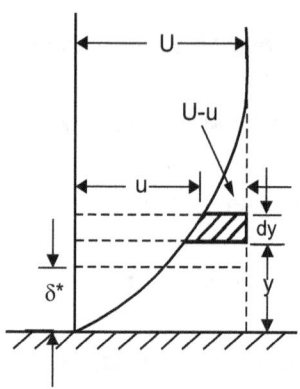

**Fig. 3.33: Displacement thickness**

Now, Area of the strip = b . dy
where 'b' is the width of the strip perpendicular to the plane of the paper.

The rate of flow of mass through this strip
= ρ × area of strip × velocity
= ρ · (b · dy) · u

In the absence of the boundary, the fluid would have moved with a constant velocity equal to the free stream velocity 'U', and the flow rate through the strip would have been
= ρ · (b · dy) · U

∴ Deficit of mass flow rate through the strip due to formation of boundary layer
= ρ · (b · dy) · U − ρ · (b · dy) · u
= ρ · (b · dy) (U − u)

∴ Total deficit of mass flow rate = $\int_0^\delta \rho \cdot (b \cdot dy)(U - u)$

But according to the definition of displacement thickness $\delta^*$, this has also to be equal to

Mass flow rate through $\delta^* = \rho \cdot (b \cdot \delta^*) \cdot U$

∴ $\rho \cdot (b \cdot \delta^*) \cdot U = \int_0^\delta \rho \cdot (b \cdot dy)(U - u)$

∴ $\delta^* \cdot U = \int_0^\delta (U - u) \, dy$ [∵ ρ is constant for incompressible flow]

∴ $\delta^* = \int_0^\delta \left(1 - \frac{u}{U}\right) \cdot dy$

or $\boxed{\delta^* = \int_0^\delta \left(1 - \frac{u}{U}\right) \cdot dy}$ ... (3.45)

**3. Momentum Thickness 'θ':** It is defined as 'the distance measured perpendicular from the actual boundary such that the momentum flux through this distance is equal to the deficit of momentum flux due to boundary layer formation' [See Fig. 3.34].

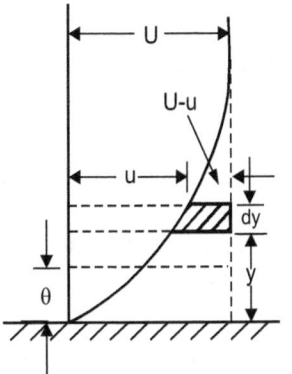

Fig. 3.34: Momentum thickness

Thus, Momentum deficit = ρ (b . dy) (U – u) . u

Total momentum deficit = $\int_0^\delta$ ρ . (b . dy) (U – u) . u

But this is also equal to
(momentum through 'θ') = ρ . b . θ . U²

∴ ρ . b . θ . U² = $\int_0^\delta$ ρ (b . dy) (U – u) . u

∴ θ = $\int_0^\delta \left(1 - \frac{u}{U}\right) \cdot \frac{u}{U} \cdot dy$

$$\boxed{\theta = \int_0^\delta \left(1 - \frac{u}{U}\right) \cdot \frac{u}{U} \cdot dy} \quad \ldots (3.46)$$

**4. Energy Thickness 'δ**':** It is a distance perpendicular to the boundary by which the boundary to be displaced to compensate for reduction in Kinetic Energy of fluid caused due to formation of boundary layer.

$$b . \delta^{**} \cdot U \frac{\rho U^2}{2} = \frac{1}{2} \rho b \int_0^\delta u (U^2 - u^2) \, dy$$

∴ $$\boxed{\delta^{**} = \int_0^\delta \frac{u}{U} \left[1 - \left(\frac{u}{U}\right)^2\right] \cdot dy} \quad \ldots (3.47)$$

It may be noted that δ > δ* > θ

**Shape factor 'H':** It is defined as the ratio of displacement thickness δ* to momentum thickness 'θ'.

∴ $$\boxed{H = \frac{\delta^*}{\theta}}$$

## 3.17 Separation of Boundary Layer

The thickness of the boundary layer is largely affected by the pressure gradient. If the pressure gradient is zero as in the case of flat plate, the boundary layer goes on increasing continuously. With negative pressure gradient i.e. when pressure goes on decreasing in the direction of flow, the pressure forces act in the direction of flow, thus accelerating the flow. This has the effect of accelerating the flow in the boundary layer and hence boundary layer tends to reduce in thickness. With positive pressure gradient or adverse pressure gradient i.e. when the pressure goes on increasing in the direction of flow, the pressure force acts against the direction of flow thus retarding the flow. This has an effect of retarding the flow in the boundary layer and hence thickening the boundary layer more rapidly. This and the boundary shear brings the fluid in the boundary layer to rest and causes back flow. Due to this, the boundary layer no more sticks to the boundary but is shifted away from the boundary. This phenomenon is called 'Boundary Layer Separation'.

Consider the flow over a curved surface as shown in Fig. 3.35. As the fluid flows around the surface, it is accelerated from 'A' to 'C'. At 'C' velocity just outside the boundary is maximum and hence the pressure is minimum. Thus, from 'A' to 'C', $\frac{\partial p}{\partial x}$ is negative and the pressure force acts in the direction of flow on the fluid in the boundary layer. Beyond 'C' pressure increases and hence pressure gradient $\frac{\partial p}{\partial x}$ is positive. The pressure force acts against the direction of flow and hence retards the flow in the boundary layer. At a certain distance from 'C', the liquid in the boundary layer is brought to stand still. At this point 'S', $\frac{\partial u}{\partial y}$ is zero at the boundary. Boundary layer no more sticks to the boundary but starts separating from it. The point where $\frac{\partial u}{\partial y}$ is zero i.e. point 'S' is called 'Separation Point'. On the downstream side of 'S' further retardation of fluid close to the boundary can give rise to a reverse flow as at point 'D'. If all the points with zero velocity are joined by a line, the line is called 'Separation Stream Line'. Between this line and the boundary, due to reverse flow, irregular eddies are formed and lot of energy is dissipated. This region is called 'Wake'.

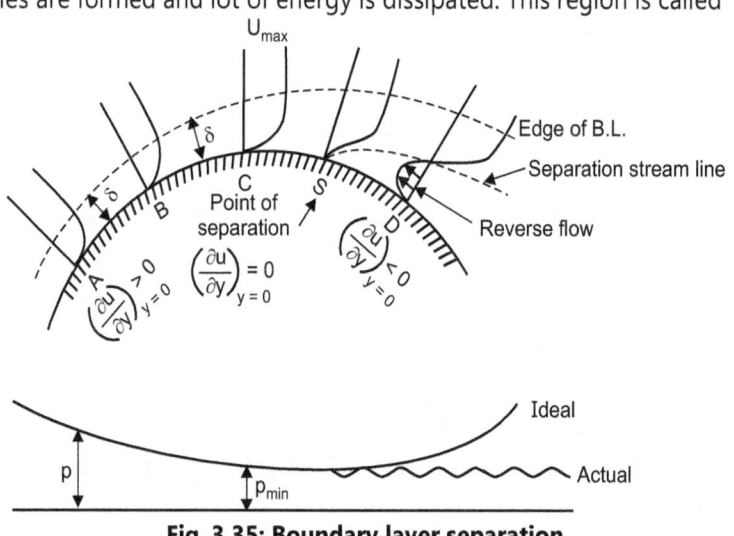

**Fig. 3.35: Boundary layer separation**

The pressure distribution in the wake is quite different from that on the remaining boundary and this gives rise to an additional drag force on the body, called as 'pressure or form drag.' Laminar boundary layers are more prone to separation than the turbulent boundary layers.

## 3.17.1 Effects of Separation

1. Large amount of energy is lost.
2. Bodies are subjected to lateral vibrations which may be harmful.
3. Pressure drag or form drag is increased to very great extent and hence additional resistance to flow or movement of the body is developed.

For these reasons separation should be avoided.

## 3.17.2 Methods for Controlling the Boundary Layer

Bad effects of separation of boundary layer have been studied in Art. 3.9.1. The problem of separation has become very important with high speed vehicles and especially in the field of aeronautical engineering.

Several methods which are used to control or avoid separation are as follows:

1. **Proper design of body:** Designing the body shape which will move the point of separation as much downstream as possible. Due to this, the wake portion is reduced and hence the pressure drag also is reduced. This is known as streamlining the body e.g. bodies like aerofoils. [See Fig. 3.36 (a)].

2. **Delaying the separation of flow in the boundary layer artificially:** This can be done by changing the laminar boundary layer into turbulent boundary layer by providing artificial roughness. (e.g. Golf ball) . [See Fig. 3.36 (b)].

3. **Accelerating the flow by providing slots:** The retarded layer of fluid can be accelerated by providing slots in the wings. [See Fig. 3.36 (c)].

4. **By accelerating the fluid by giving motion:** By giving the motion to the body in the direction of motion, the fluid in the boundary layer can be accelerated and separation can be controlled. But this is practically very difficult.

5. **Suction of the retarded fluid in the boundary layer:** In this method the retarded fluid in the boundary layer is sucked out through suction slots in the boundary surface
[See Fig. 3.36 (d)].

6. **Acceleration of fluid by blowing:** In this method some extra energy is supplied to the retarded fluid in the boundary layer by injecting a high velocity fluid from a blower. This is termed as 'blowing' [See Fig. 3.36 (e)].

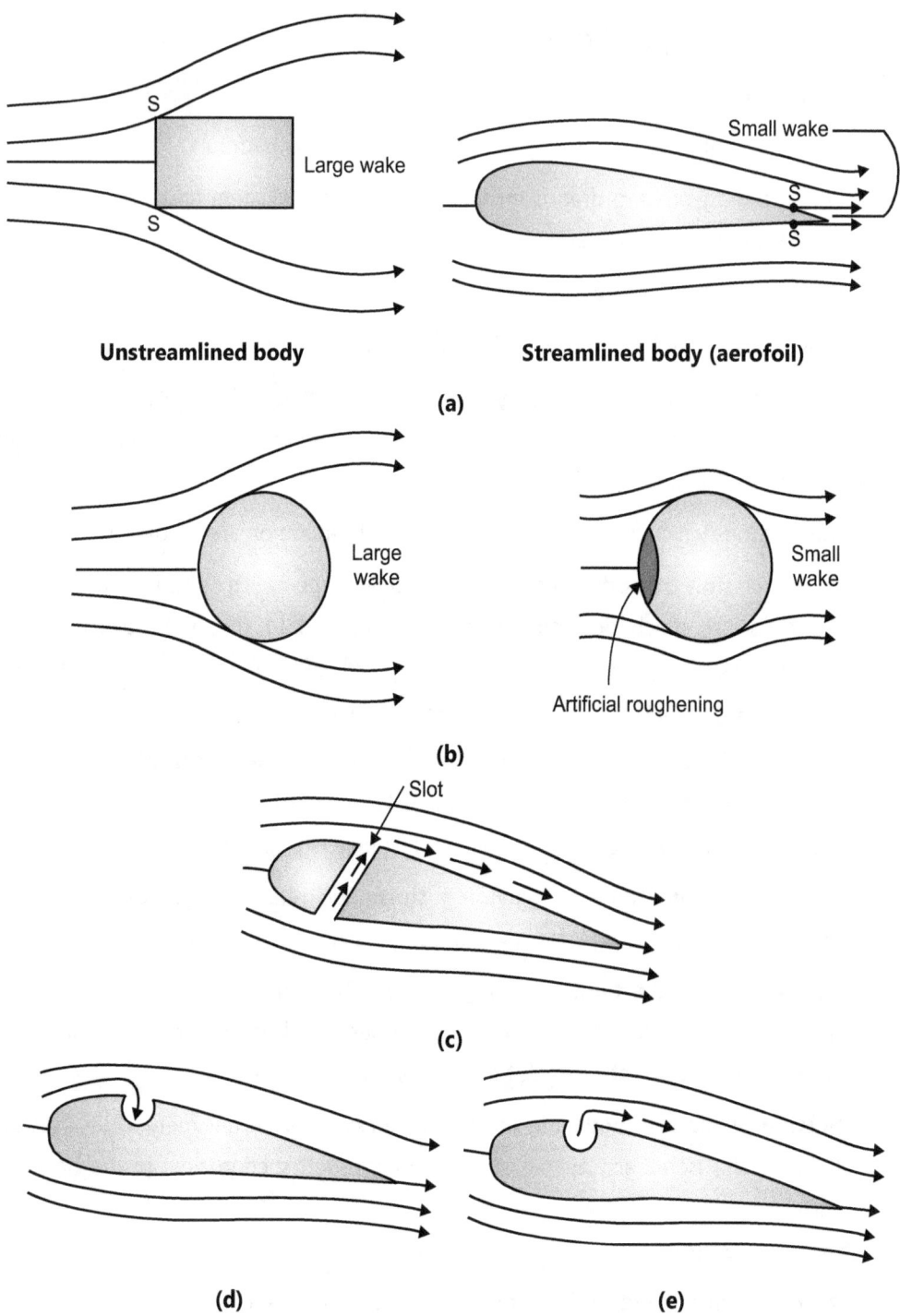

Fig. 3.36: Methods of avoiding separation

## 3.17.3 Location of Separation Point

The separation point 'S' shown in Fig. 3.10 can be located from the condition,

$$\boxed{\left(\frac{\partial u}{\partial y}\right)_{y=0} = 0}$$

If the velocity profile is known, it can be checked from the following conditions whether the boundary has separated, or it is on the verge of separation or will not separate.

1. If $\left(\dfrac{\partial u}{\partial y}\right)_{y=0}$ is **negative**, the flow has separated.

2. If $\left(\dfrac{\partial u}{\partial y}\right)_{y=0} = 0$, the flow is on the verge of separation.

3. If $\left(\dfrac{\partial u}{\partial y}\right)_{y=0}$ is **positive** the flow will not separate or flow will remain attached to the surface.

## THEORETICAL QUESTIONS

1. Explain the concept of boundary layer and state where it is useful.
   What is the importance of boundary layer in fluid flow phenomenon?

2. Define boundary layer and explain the fundamental causes of its existence. Also discuss the various methods of controlling the boundary layer.

3. What is meant by boundary layer? Define nominal thickness and displacement thickness of boundary layer.

4. Define displacement thickness. Derive an expression for displacement thickness.

5. Define:
   (i) Boundary layer thickness,  (ii) Displacement thickness,
   (iii) Momentum thickness and  (iv) Energy thickness.
   Give expression for each.

6. Explain the development of boundary layer over a flat plate held parallel to the direction of flow. State the factors affecting growth of boundary layer.

7. Explain the factors affecting growth of boundary layer.

8. What is a laminar sublayer? How is its existence established? How is a boundary defined depending on laminar sublayer thickness and height of protrusion on the surface?

9. Write a note on laminar sublayer.

10. Explain the terms:
    (i) Laminar boundary layer
    (ii) Turbulent boundary layer and
    (iii) Laminar sublayer.
11. What are the various characteristics of laminar and turbulent boundary layer? Explain.
12. Write a note on separation of boundary layer and methods of controlling it.
13. List out methods of preventing the separating of boundary layer.
14. Explain boundary layer separation clearly with a neat sketch.

■■■

# Unit 4

# DIMENSIONAL ANALYSIS AND FLOW THROUGH PIPES

## (A) DIMENSIONAL ANALYSIS

## 4.1 Introduction

With rapid and vast growth of hydraulic engineering, engineers have to face many new and complicated problems. (This is true for other engineering fields as well). These problems are mainly connected with the design, construction and efficient working of the hydraulic structures and machines.

Some of these problems can be solved by mathematical methods. However, such problems are very few. Majority of problems are complex in nature. They cannot be solved by purely mathematical methods. Under such conditions, experimental methods are necessary. These experiments are carried out on "scale models". The results obtained on models are required to be transformed in terms of results which can be applied to the 'prototype' (the actual full size device). Dimensional analysis is very useful in carrying out such transformations.

## 4.2 Units and Dimensions

**Units**: *Units may be defined as those standards in terms of which physical quantities like area, volume, time, velocity etc. are measured.* For example, unit of length in S.I. system is metre, unit of time is second, unit of mass is kg etc.

**Dimensions:**

Various quantities used to describe a phenomenon can be expressed in terms of a set of quantities which are so to say independent of each other. These quantities are called "*Fundamental Quantities*" or "*Primary Quantities*". These are **mass, length, time** and **temperature** and are represented by M, L, T and θ respectively. [Temperature 'θ' is especially useful in thermodynamics and heat transfer problems.]

All other quantities like, area, volume, velocity etc. can be expressed in terms of fundamental quantities. These are called "Derived Quantities or Secondary Quantities". "*The expression for the derived quantity in terms of fundamental quantities is called "Dimension" of the derived quantity*".

Thus, dimensions of  [Area] = [Length] × [Length] = $[L^2]$

[Velocity] = $\dfrac{[Length]}{[Time]}$ = [L / T] = $[LT^{-1}]$

The rectangular bracket indicates that the dimensions of the quantity are considered and symbol ≡ indicates dimensional equality.

Sometimes, force F is used as fundamental quantity instead of mass M. The system is then denoted as F – L – T system as against M – L – T system.

It may be noted that the dimensions of a quantity remain unchanged in all the systems of units. With the help of dimensions of a quantity, units of the quantity in any system of measurement can be easily found out. e.g. from dimensions of velocity $[LT^{-1}]$, units m/s, cm/s or ft/s can be obtained in SI, CGS and FPS systems.

Table 4.1 gives the dimensions and units (SI system) of various quantities.

### Table 4.1

| Sr. No. | Quantity | Symbol | Dimensions MLT system | Dimensions FLT system | Units of measurement SI system |
|---|---|---|---|---|---|
| **(A)** | **Geometric** | | | | |
| (1) | Length (any linear quantity) | $l$ | L | L | m |
| (2) | Area | a, A | $L^2$ | $L^2$ | $m^2$ |
| (3) | Volume | V | $L^3$ | $L^3$ | $m^3$ |
| (4) | Slope | S | – | – | – |
| (5) | Angle | α θ | – | – | radians or degrees |
| **(B)** | **Kinematic** | | | | |
| (6) | Time | T, t | T | T | sec. |
| (7) | Linear velocity | V, u | $LT^{-1}$ | $LT^{-1}$ | m/s |
| (8) | Angular velocity | ω | $T^{-1}$ | $T^{-1}$ | rad/s |
| (9) | Linear acceleration | a | $LT^{-2}$ | $LT^{-2}$ | $m/s^2$ |
| (10) | Angular acceleration | α | $T^{-2}$ | $T^{-2}$ | $rad/s^2$ |
| (11) | Gravitational acceleration | g | $LT^{-2}$ | $LT^{-2}$ | $m/s^2$ |
| (12) | Discharge | Q | $L^3T^{-1}$ | $L^3T^{-1}$ | $m^3/s$ |
| (13) | Discharge per unit width | q | $L^2T^{-1}$ | $L^2T^{-1}$ | $m^2/s$ ($m^3/s/m$) |
| (14) | Kinematic viscosity | ν | $L^2T^{-1}$ | $L^2T^{-1}$ | $m^2/s$ |
| **(C)** | **Dynamic** | | | | |
| (15) | Mass | M, m | M | $FL^{-1}T^2$ | kg |
| (16) | Force | F | $MLT^{-2}$ | F | N |
| (17) | Weight | W | $MLT^{-2}$ | F | N |
| (18) | Mass density or specific mass | ρ | $ML^{-3}$ | $FL^{-4}T^2$ | $kg/m^3$ |
| (19) | Specific weight | γ | $ML^{-2}T^{-2}$ | $FL^{-3}$ | $N/m^3$ |
| (20) | Specific gravity | S | – | – | – |

*contd. ...*

| (21) | Specific volume | V | $M^{-1}L^3$ | — | m³/kg |
| | | V | $M^{-1}L^2T^2$ | $F^{-1}L^3$ | m³/N |
| (22) | Pressure | p | $ML^{-1}T^{-2}$ | $FL^{-2}$ | N/m² or Pascal (Pa) |
| (23) | Shear stress | $\tau$ | $ML^{-1}T^{-2}$ | $FL^{-2}$ | N/m² |
| (24) | Dynamic viscosity | $\mu$ | $ML^{-1}T^{-1}$ | $FL^{-2}T$ | N-s/m² |
| (25) | Surface Tension | $\sigma$ | $MT^{-2}$ | $FL^{-1}$ | N/m |
| (26) | Modulus of elasticity | K | $ML^{-1}T^{-2}$ | $FL^{-2}$ | N/m² |
| (27) | Moment | M | $ML^2T^{-2}$ | FL | Nm |
| (28) | Momentum Impulse | M I | $MLT^{-1}$ | FT | kg m/s or N/s |
| (29) | Work, Energy | W, E | $ML^2T^{-2}$ | FL | Nm or Joule (J) |
| (30) | Torque | T | $ML^2T^{-2}$ | FL | Nm or Joule |
| (31) | Power | P | $ML^2T^{-3}$ | $FLT^{-1}$ | N-m/s or watt (W) |

Friction factor 'f', energy correction factor 'α', momentum correction factor "β", efficiency 'η' are dimensionless quantities.

## 4.3 Dimensional Homogeneity

Dimensional analysis is based on the principle that the variables in a problem can be arranged to give an equation which is dimensionally homogeneous.

"An equation is said to be dimensionally homogeneous when the dimensions of left hand side (L.H.S.) are same as dimensions of right hand side (R.H.S.).

e.g. Let us check up dimensional homogeneity of the equation for discharge over a triangular notch.

$$Q = \frac{8}{15} C_d \sqrt{2g} \tan \theta/2 \cdot H^{5/2}$$

Dimensions of L.H.S. = $[L^3 T^{-1}]$
Dimensions of R.H.S. = $[LT^{-2}]^{1/2} \cdot [L]^{5/2} = [L^3 T^{-1}]$

Since $\frac{8}{15}$, $C_d$, $\sqrt{2}$, $\tan \frac{\theta}{2}$ are dimensionless quantities.

Dimensions of L.H.S. = Dimensions of R.H.S. Therefore, equation is dimensionally homogeneous.

Now, consider the equation for discharge over a right angled triangular notch in the form

$$Q = 1.417 H^{5/2}$$

Dimensions of L.H.S. = $[L^3 T^{-1}]$
Dimensions of R.H.S. = $[L^{5/2}]$

Dimensions of L.H.S. are not equal to dimensions of R.H.S., therefore equation is dimensionally non-homogeneous. 1.417 although, appears to be constant is not pure number but has dimensions [$L^{1/2}T^{-1}$]. It may be noted that dimensionally homogeneous equations can be used in any system of units of measurement. On the other hand, non-homogeneous equations are valid only for one system of measurement. For example,

$Q = \dfrac{8}{15} C_d \sqrt{2g} \tan \theta/2 \cdot H^{5/2}$ is valid in any system of units of measurement, but

$Q = 1.417 H^{5/2}$ is valid only when H is in metres and Q is in m³/s.

Empirical equations are generally dimensionally non-homogeneous. Chezy's equation, $V = C\sqrt{RS}$ and Manning's equation $V = \dfrac{1}{n} \cdot R^{2/3} \cdot S^{1/2}$ are examples of non-homogeneous equations. Hence, these equations cannot be used in different system of measurement without changing the value of constants. For example, $V = 50\sqrt{RS}$ in SI system changes to $V = 90.5 \sqrt{RS}$ in FPS system.

## 4.4 Dimensional Analysis

Dimensional analysis is a *mathematical process or technique which makes use of dimensions for solution of problems*. Every phenomenon is governed by many variables. Dimensional analysis, with the help of dimensions, helps in arranging these variables in the form of a systematic arrangement (an equation consisting non-dimensional parameters).

## 4.5 Uses of Dimensional Analysis

1. It can be used to check dimensional homogeneity of equations.
2. It is useful in deriving equations for phenomena in terms of non-dimensional parameters like, Froude Number, Reynold's Number etc.
3. It is useful in reducing number of variables in a problem by grouping them in less number of dimensionless groups. This reduces number of tests in model studies.
4. It is useful in arranging the tests in model studies in proper manner. This makes the tests more economical and less time consuming. Results of model studies can be represented in proper manner.

## 4.6 Methods of Dimensional Analysis

There are two methods of dimensional analysis (arranging the variables in a phenomenon in the form of equation consisting of dimensionless parameters).

1. Rayleigh method
2. Buckingham π theorem.

## 4.6.1 Rayleigh Method

In this method, the dependent variable is expressed as a function of independent variables.

Thus,
$$X = f(X_1, X_2, X_3, ..... X_n)$$

where X is dependent variable and $X_1, X_2, .....$ etc. are independent variables.

The above equation can also be written as
$$X = K\left(X_1^a \cdot X_2^b \cdot X_3^c ...... X_n^n\right)$$

where K is a dimensionless number and a, b, c, ..... n are some exponents. First, dimensions of all 'X' terms are substituted. Then, exponents a, b, c, d, .... n are obtained by treating the above equation as dimensionally homogeneous. Then the dimensionless groups are formed by grouping together the variables with like powers.

Following example illustrates Rayleigh method.

Show that the resistance 'R' to the motion of sphere of diameter 'D', moving with uniform velocity 'V' through a fluid of density '$\rho$' and viscosity '$\mu$' is given by

$$R = \rho V^2 D^2 \phi \left(\frac{\mu}{\rho V D}\right)$$

**Solution:**

As can be seen 'R' is dependent variable and D, V, $\rho$ and $\mu$ are independent variables in this phenomenon.

$$R = f(D, V, \rho, \mu)$$

or
$$R = K[D^a \cdot V^b \cdot \rho^c \cdot \mu^d]$$

Substituting dimensions of different variables in the above equation, we get

$$[MLT^{-2}] = [M^0L^0T^0][L]^a[LT^{-1}]^b[ML^{-3}]^c[ML^{-1}T^{-1}]^d$$

Equating powers of M, L and T on L.H.S. and R.H.S. we get,

For M                    $1 = c + d$          ... (1)

For L                     $1 = a + b - 3c - d$          ... (2)

For T                   $-2 = -b - d$          ... (3)

From equation (1), $c = 1 - d$, from equation (3) $b = 2 - d$ and from equation (2)

$$1 = a + (2 - d) - 3(1 - d) - d$$

or          $a = 2 - d$

$\therefore$         $R = K[D^{2-d} \cdot V^{2-d} \cdot \rho^{1-d} \cdot \mu^d]$

$$= \rho V^2 D^2 K \left[\frac{\mu}{\rho V D}\right]^d$$

or          $R = \rho V^2 D^2 \phi \left[\dfrac{\mu}{\rho V D}\right]$

Although Rayleigh's method is simple it has following limitations.
1. This method becomes rather more cumbersome when the number of parameters involved in the problem is large.
2. It does not give information regarding the possible number of dimensionless parameters to be obtained as a result of analysis.
3. It does not give the values of indices explicitly (clearly as say 2, 3, 4 etc.) but gives values only implicitly (indirectly) in terms of other indices.

[See example above a, b, c are obtained only in terms of index 'd' and not in numerical terms.]

Due to the above drawbacks, the method has become obsolete and is not in use. However, it has been mentioned here as a matter of reference only.

## 4.6.2 Buckingham $\pi$ Theorem

**Statement:**

*"The theorem states that if there are 'n' variables involved in a physical phenomenon and if these variables contain 'm' primary dimensions, (e.g. M, L, T) then the variable quantities can be expressed in terms of an equation containing (n – m) dimensionless groups or parameters."*

Buckingham referred to these dimensionless groups as '$\pi$' terms.

Let $A_1, A_2, \ldots$ etc. upto $A_n$ be the quantities such as pressure, velocity, discharge etc. involved in a problem. All these variables are essential (necessary) for solution of the problem and hence some functional relation amongst them must exist. Let the relation be

$$F(A_1, A_2, \ldots A_n) = 0 \text{ or constant}$$

If these variables contain 'm' primary dimensions, according to Buckingham Pi theorem a functional relation, of the type given below must exist amongst them.

$$F_1(\pi_1, \pi_2, \pi_3, \ldots \pi_{n-m}) = 0 \text{ or constant}$$

where $\pi_1, \pi_2, \ldots \pi_{n-m}$ are the dimensionless groups called $\pi$ terms.

The method to get $\pi_1, \pi_2, \pi_3 \ldots \pi_{n-m}$ is as follows.

We select 'm' quantities out of 'A' quantities, with different dimensions but containing all 'm' dimensions and use them as repeating variables. Pi terms are then formed by taking these repeating variables and combining them with remaining variables one after the other.

For example, let $A_1$, $A_2$ and $A_3$ be the repeating variables containing all 'm' dimensions (M, L, T) not necessarily in each one of them but collectively. Then the first $\pi$ parameter is formed as

$$\pi_1 = A_1^{x_1} \cdot A_2^{y_1} \cdot A_3^{z_1} \cdot A_4$$

the second parameter,

$$\pi_2 = A_1^{x_2} \cdot A_2^{y_2} \cdot A_3^{z_2} \cdot A_5 \quad \text{and so on upto}$$

$$\pi_{n-m} = A_1^{x_{n-m}} \cdot A_2^{y_{n-m}} \cdot A_3^{z_{n-m}} \cdot A_n$$

Exponents in the above equations are determined in such a way as to make each Pi term a dimensionless term. Dimensions of all 'A' quantities are substituted and exponents of M, L and T etc. are equated to zero. The equations thus formed are then solved for getting values of $x_1, y_1, z_1$ etc. and hence the different '$\pi$' terms are obtained.

## 4.6.3 Application of Buckingham $\pi$ Theorem

Following steps are helpful in the application of Buckingham $\pi$ theorem:

1. Make a list of all 'n' variables involved in the given problem and write the functional relationship.
2. Identify the dependent variable.
3. Write down the dimensions of all variables and find out number of dimensions 'm' involved. Then determine number of $\pi$ terms which is equal to '(n – m)'.
4. Choose 'm' number of repeating variables. Selection of repeating variables is based on the following guidelines.
    (i) None of the repeating variables should be dimensionless.
    (ii) No two of the repeating variables should have the same dimensions.
    (iii) Repeating variables should not form a dimensionless group or parameter.
    (iv) Repeating variables should contain all 'm' dimensions collectively.
    (v) Dependent variable should not be selected as a repeating variable.
    (vi) In order that we obtain only well known established dimensionless groups like, Reynold's Number, Froude Number, Mach Number etc. the repeating variables are selected in the following manner.
    
    (a) First repeating variable is selected from those variables describing 'Geometry of flow' e.g. length, diameter, height, breadth, chord span etc.
    (b) Second repeating variable is selected from those variables describing 'Kinematics and Dynamics of flow,' e.g. velocity, acceleration, rpm, momentum, force, power etc.
    (c) Third repeating variable is selected from those variables describing fluid property e.g. mass density, viscosity, surface tension, elasticity etc.
    
    **[Note:** In majority of problems in fluid mechanics, mass density '$\rho$', velocity 'V' and length '$l$'/diameter 'd' are taken as repeating variables.
    In case of machinery problems, mass density '$\rho$', rpm 'N', and diameter 'D' are generally taken as repeating variables.**]**
5. Raise the repeating variables to unknown powers and combine them with other variables one after the other to form dimensionless groups.
6. To get the unknown exponents, equate the exponents of M, L and T to zero. Obtain all (n – m) dimensionless groups. Express the final expression in terms of the dimensionless groups obtained.

**[Note:** It may be noted that number of variables are reduced from 'n' to '(n – m)'**]**

Following suggestions are useful to obtain the final expression in the desired form:

(i) A dimensionless variable is a 'π' term e.g. angle 'θ', efficiency 'η' are 'π' terms, by observation.

(ii) Ratio of two variables with same dimensions is a 'π' term. e.g. $\left(\dfrac{L}{D}\right)$ is 'π' term and can be directly written by observation.

(iii) Any 'π' term may be replaced by multiplying it by a numerical constant. e.g. $\pi_1$ may be replaced by $2\pi_1, \dfrac{\pi_1}{2}$, etc.

(iv) Any 'π' term may be replaced by any power of that term. e.g. $\pi_1$ can be replaced by $\pi_1^{3/2}$, or $\dfrac{1}{\pi_1}$ etc.

(v) Any 'π' term can be replaced by multiplying or dividing it by another 'π' term. e.g. $\pi_1$ may be replaced by $(\pi_1 \times \pi_2)$ or $\dfrac{\pi_1}{\pi_2}$ etc.

It can be seen that all the drawbacks of Rayleigh's method are overcome in this method.

Example solved by Rayleigh's method is solved by Buckingham 'π' theorem for illustration of Buckingham 'π' theorem and comparison between the two methods.

*Show that the resistance 'R' to the motion of sphere of diameter 'D', moving with uniform velocity 'V' through a fluid of density 'ρ' and viscosity 'μ' is given by*

$$R = \rho V^2 D^2 \phi \left(\dfrac{\mu}{\rho V D}\right)$$

**Solution:**

$$f(R, D, V, \mu, \rho) = 0 \text{ or constant}$$

Here number of variables, n = 5
Number of dimensions contained in the variables, m = 3
Therefore, number of 'π' terms = n − m = 5 − 3 = 2
Therefore, $f_1(\pi_1, \pi_2) = 0$ or constant
Selecting m = 3 number of variables such that
   1 to represent the geometry of flow − D
   1 to represent the kinematics − V
   1 to represent the fluid property − ρ
The two 'π' terms can be written as

$$\pi_1 = D^{x_1} \cdot V^{y_1} \cdot \rho^{z_1} \cdot R$$

$$\pi_2 = D^{x_2} \cdot V^{y_2} \cdot \rho^{z_2} \cdot \mu$$

Substituting dimensions of the variables

$$\pi_1 = [L]^{x_1} \cdot [LT^{-1}]^{y_1} \cdot [ML^{-3}]^{z_1} \cdot [MLT^{-2}]$$

But '$\pi_1$' has to be dimensionless, therefore sum of indices of M, L and T must be zero.

Thus

For M $\qquad z_1 + 1 = 0 \qquad \therefore z_1 = -1$

For L $\qquad x_1 + y_1 - 3z_1 + 1 = 0$

For T $\qquad -y_1 - 2 = 0 \qquad \therefore y_1 = -2$

Substituting values of $y_1$ and $z_1$ in equation for L,

$$x_1 - 2 + 4 = 0 \qquad \therefore x_1 = -2$$

$\therefore \qquad \pi_1 = D^{-2} \cdot V^{-2} \cdot \rho^{-1} \cdot R$

or $\qquad \pi_1 = \left(\dfrac{R}{\rho V^2 D^2}\right)$

Similarly,

$$\pi_2 = [L]^{x_2} \cdot [LT^{-1}]^{y_2} \cdot [ML^{-3}]^{z_2} \cdot [ML^{-1}T^{-1}]$$

For M $\qquad z_2 + 1 = 0 \qquad \therefore z_2 = -1$

For L $\qquad x_2 + y_2 - 3z_2 - 1 = 0$

For T $\qquad -y_2 - 1 = 0 \qquad \therefore y_2 = -1$

Substituting values of $y_2$ and $z_2$ in equation for L

$$x_2 - 1 + 3 - 1 = 0 \qquad \therefore x_2 = -1$$

$\therefore \qquad \pi_2 = D^{-1} \cdot V^{-1} \cdot \rho^{-1} \cdot \mu$

$$\pi_2 = \left(\dfrac{\mu}{\rho VD}\right)$$

$\therefore \qquad f_1\left(\dfrac{R}{\rho V^2 D^2}, \dfrac{\mu}{\rho VD}\right) = 0$ or constant

or $\qquad \dfrac{R}{\rho V^2 D^2} = \phi\left(\dfrac{\mu}{\rho VD}\right)$

or $\qquad R = \rho V^2 D^2 \, \phi\left(\dfrac{\mu}{\rho VD}\right)$

## 4.7 Important Dimensionless Numbers

Following dimensionless numbers, which are the ratios of forces per unit volume, are very important in analysis of fluid flow. They are also important in representing the experimental data in fluid mechanics.

These numbers are

1. Froude Number $(F_r)$ = $\left(\dfrac{\text{Inertia force}}{\text{Gravity force}}\right)^{1/2}$

2. Reynold's Number (Re) = $\dfrac{\text{Inertia force}}{\text{Viscous force}}$

3. Mach Number (M) = $\left(\dfrac{\text{Inertia force}}{\text{Elastic force}}\right)^{1/2}$

4. Weber Number (W) = $\left(\dfrac{\text{Inertia force}}{\text{Surface tension force}}\right)^{1/2}$

5. Euler Number (E) = $\left(\dfrac{\text{Inertia force}}{\text{Pressure force}}\right)^{1/2}$

### 4.7.1 Froude Number

Inertia force = Mass × Acceleration

$$= \rho \cdot L^3 \times \dfrac{L}{T^2} = \rho L^2 \cdot \dfrac{L^2}{T^2}$$

$\therefore$ $\boxed{\text{Inertia force} = \rho L^2 V^2}$ $\quad \left(\because \dfrac{L}{T} = V\right)$

Gravity force = Mass × Acceleration due to gravity
$$= \rho L^3 \times g$$

$\therefore$ $\dfrac{\text{Inertia force}}{\text{Gravity force}} = \dfrac{\rho L^2 V^2}{\rho L^3 g} = \dfrac{V^2}{gL}$

but Froude Number $F_r = \left(\dfrac{\text{Inertia force}}{\text{Gravity force}}\right)^{1/2}$

$\therefore$ $\boxed{\textbf{Froude Number } F_r = \dfrac{V}{\sqrt{gL}}}$

Froude Number is important in the study of free surface flows e.g. open channel flow, which are dominated by gravity forces.

### 4.7.2 Reynold's Number

Viscous force = Shear stress × Area
$$= \tau \times A$$

but $\tau = \mu \cdot \dfrac{dV}{dy}$ (Newton's law of viscosity)

$$\therefore \quad \text{Viscous force} = \mu \cdot \frac{dV}{dy} \times A = \mu \cdot \left(\frac{V}{L}\right) \times L^2$$

$$\therefore \quad \text{Viscous force} = \mu V L$$

and
$$\text{Inertia force} = \rho L^2 V^2$$

$$\text{but Reynolds Number Re} = \left(\frac{\text{Inertia force}}{\text{Viscous force}}\right) = \frac{\rho VL}{\mu}$$

$$\therefore \quad \boxed{\text{Reynold's Number Re} = \frac{\rho VL}{\mu}}$$

or
$$\boxed{\text{Re} = \frac{VL}{\nu}} \qquad \left(\because \frac{\mu}{\rho} = \nu\right) \text{ (kinematic viscosity)}$$

Reynold's Number is important in pipe flow, motion of completely submerged bodies like submarines, motion of aeroplanes etc. which involve incompressible fluid without any free surface. Viscous forces are important in these phenomena.

### 4.7.3 Mach Number

$$\text{Elastic force} = \text{Bulk Modulus of elasticity} \times \text{Area} = K \cdot A = K \cdot L^2$$

$$\therefore \quad \text{Elastic force} = KL^2$$

$$\therefore \quad \frac{\text{Inertia force}}{\text{Elastic force}} = \frac{\rho L^2 V^2}{KL^2} = \frac{V^2}{K/\rho}$$

$$\text{but Mach Number M} = \left(\frac{\text{Inertia force}}{\text{Elastic force}}\right)^{1/2}$$

$$\therefore \quad \boxed{\text{Mach Number M} = \frac{V}{\sqrt{K/\rho}}}$$

But $\sqrt{K/\rho} = C$, the velocity of sound in the medium (Ref. 1.2.8).

Therefore, $\text{Mach Number M} = \frac{V}{C}$

This number is important in aerodynamics, and in phenomena like water hammer which are concerned with compressible fluids.

### 4.7.4 Weber Number

$$\text{Surface tension force} = \sigma \cdot L$$

$$\therefore \quad \frac{\text{Inertia force}}{\text{Surface tension force}} = \frac{\rho L^2 V^2}{\sigma L} = \frac{V^2}{\sigma/\rho \, L}$$

But
$$\text{Weber Number W} = \left(\frac{\text{Inertia force}}{\text{Surface tension force}}\right)^{1/2}$$

$$\therefore \quad \boxed{\text{Weber Number W} = \frac{V}{\sqrt{\sigma/\rho L}}}$$

This number is important where thin films of liquid or small depths of flow are involved. e.g. study of droplets, capillary flows etc.

## 4.7.5 Euler Number

$$\text{Pressure force} = \text{Intensity of pressure} \times \text{Area}$$
$$= p \cdot A$$
$$= p \cdot L^2$$

$$\therefore \quad \frac{\text{Inertia force}}{\text{Pressure force}} = \frac{\rho L^2 V^2}{p \cdot L^2} = \frac{V^2}{p/\rho}$$

But

$$\text{Euler Number } E = \left(\frac{\text{Inertia force}}{\text{Pressure force}}\right)^{1/2}$$

$$\therefore \quad \boxed{\text{Euler Number } E = \frac{V}{\sqrt{p/\rho}}}$$

This number is important where pressure forces are predominant. It is important in cavitation studies.

All the dimensionless numbers mentioned above are used for model analysis.

## THEORETICAL QUESTIONS

1. What do you understand by (i) Units and (ii) Dimensions?
2. What are fundamental and derived quantities?
3. What is dimensional homogeneity? What do you understand by dimensionally homogeneous equation? Give two examples.
4. What do you understand by dimensional homogeneity? Explain how dimensional analysis is used in analysing fluid flow problems.
5. Check whether following equations are homogeneous or not:

    (i) $V = \sqrt{gH}$  (ii) $Q = A \cdot V$  (iii) $h_f = \frac{fL}{D} \cdot \frac{V^2}{2g}$

    (iv) $V = \frac{1}{n} \cdot R^{2/3} \cdot S^{1/2}$  (v) $N_s = \frac{N\sqrt{P}}{H^{5/4}}$

    **[Ans.** (i), (ii), (iii) - Homogeneous, (iv), (v) - Non-homogeneous]
6. What is dimensional analysis? How is it useful? Explain concept of dimensional analysis.
7. State Buckingham's π theorem and explain procedure for determining the π-groups and their functional relationship.
8. What are repeating variables? How are they selected for dimensional analysis?
9. How can the π - terms be altered without changing their basic character?
10. Write short notes on any three of the following:
    (i) Froude number
    (ii) Reynolds number
    (iii) Weber number
    (iv) Euler number
11. Explain in brief physical significance of (i) Reynold's number, (ii) Froude number, (iii) Mach number.

## (B) FLOW THROUGH PIPES

## 4.8 Introduction

Pipe may be defined *as a passage with a closed perimeter (or a closed conduit) through which the fluid flows under pressure completely filling the cross-sectional area*. If the cross section of pipe is not completely full it is treated as open channel in which liquid will have free surface.

Pipes are widely used for water supply, for supplying water to turbines, in circulating systems, and many other purposes.

Pipe flow problems involve determination of discharge through the pipe under given conditions, design of pipe for given discharge conditions, calculation of power requirement for the flow to be maintained in a system, laying of pipes avoiding undesirable pressure conditions, modifications of old pipe systems with equivalent pipe system etc.

The continuity equation, Bernoulli's theorem and Darcy-Weisbach equation are used for solution of pipe flow problems.

## 4.9 Loss of Energy (Head) in Pipe

When the fluid flows through a pipe, it encounters many resistances due to which losses of head (energy) take place. The various losses which are taken into account in pipe flow are as follows:

(1) Loss of head due to friction (Major loss) — $\dfrac{fl}{d} \cdot \dfrac{V^2}{2g}$

(2) Loss due to pipe fittings like bends, elbows, valves etc. — $K \dfrac{V^2}{2g}$

K is found experimentally

(3) Loss due to sudden enlargement — $\dfrac{(V_1 - V_2)^2}{2g}$

(4) Loss due to sudden contraction — $\left(\dfrac{1}{C_c} - 1\right)^2 \cdot \dfrac{V^2}{2g}$

Generally taken as $0.5 \cdot \dfrac{V^2}{2g}$

(5) Loss due to entry to a pipe — $0.5 \cdot \dfrac{V^2}{2g}$

(6) Loss at exit of the pipe — $\dfrac{V^2}{2g}$

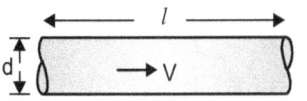

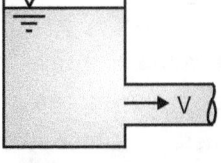
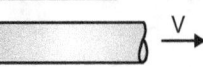

**Long pipe:** If the length of the pipe is more than 500 times the diameter of the pipe, it is called long pipe. (L > 500 D).

**Major loss:** *Loss of head due to friction is called "Major loss."* It has been observed that in case of long pipe, the loss of head due to friction is so large or predominant as compared to all other losses combined together that the results of the problem are not affected even if all other losses except loss due to friction are neglected. Therefore, the loss of head due to friction is called 'Major Loss'. All other losses are called 'Minor Losses'.

## 4.10 Loss of Energy due to Friction

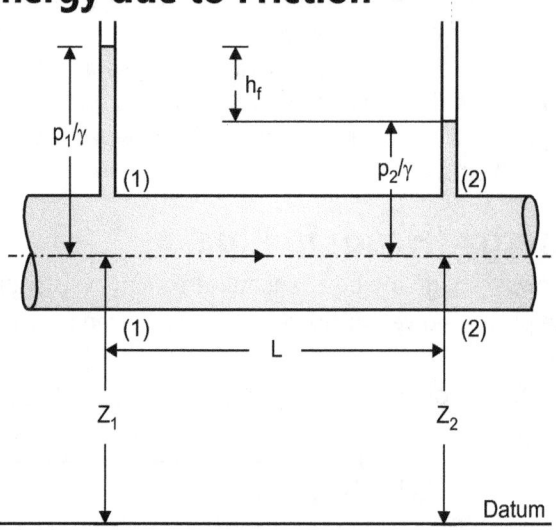

**Fig. 4.1: Loss of head due to friction**

Consider fluid mass between section 1 - 1 and section 2 - 2 as shown in Fig. 4.1. Let 'A' be the area of cross-section of the pipe and 'L' the length of pipe between section 1 - 1 and 2 - 2. Let $p_1$ and $p_2$ be the pressure intensities at the two sections.

For the horizontal pipe as shown in Fig. 4.1, applying Bernoulli's theorem to sections 1 - 1 and 2 - 2, we get

$$Z_1 + \frac{p_1}{\gamma} + \frac{V_1^2}{2g} = Z_2 + \frac{p_2}{\gamma} + \frac{V_2^2}{2g} + h_f$$

but $Z_1 = Z_2$ and $V_1 = V_2$

∴ $$\frac{p_1}{\gamma} - \frac{p_2}{\gamma} = h_f \text{ (as shown in Fig. 4.1)} \quad \ldots(4.1)$$

where $p_1$ and $p_2$ are the pressure intensities at sections 1 - 1 and 2 - 2 respectively.

Now since the velocity of flow is constant from section 1 - 1 to 2 - 2 ($A_1V_1 = A_2V_2$, $A_1 = A_2$ ∴ $V_1 = V_2$), there is neither acceleration nor retardation. Therefore, sum of the forces in the direction of motion must be zero. Or force in the direction of motion must be equal to force against the direction of motion.

Now force in the direction of motion is due to pressure and is given by
$$(p_1 \cdot A - p_2 \cdot A) = (p_1 - p_2) A \quad \ldots (4.2)$$
Experimentally, it was found (by Froude) that the frictional resistance is given by
$$\text{Frictional resistance} = f' \times A \times V^n$$
where, $f'$ = Frictional resistance / unit area / unit velocity
$A$ = Wetted area (area of surface of contact between fluid and pipe)
$V$ = Velocity.

Value of index 'n' is generally taken as 2.
$$\therefore \quad \text{Frictional resistance} = f' \times P \times L \times V^2 \quad \ldots (4.3)$$
where P is the wetted perimeter. i.e. length of line of contact at the section between fluid and pipe. Thus, for pipe running full, $P = \pi D$.

Equating equations (4.2) and (4.3)
$$(p_1 - p_2) \cdot A = f' \times P \times L \times V^2$$
$$\therefore \quad (p_1 - p_2) = f' \times \frac{P}{A} \times L \times V^2$$

Ratio of $\frac{A}{P}$, the area of flow to wetted perimeter is called hydraulic radius and is denoted by R. $\therefore \frac{A}{P} = R$

$$\therefore \quad (p_1 - p_2) = f' \times \frac{1}{R} \times L \times V^2$$

$$\therefore \quad \frac{(p_1 - p_2)}{\gamma} = \frac{f'}{\gamma} \cdot \frac{1}{R} \cdot L \cdot V^2 \ldots\ldots \text{ Dividing both sides by } \gamma$$

but $\dfrac{p_1 - p_2}{\gamma} = h_f$ from equation (4.1)

$$\therefore \quad h_f = \frac{f'}{\gamma} \cdot \frac{1}{R} \cdot L \cdot V^2$$

or $$h_f = \frac{2gf'}{\gamma} \cdot \frac{1}{R} \cdot L \cdot \frac{V^2}{2g}$$

but for pipe running full, $R = \dfrac{A}{P} = \dfrac{\pi D^2}{4 \pi D} = \dfrac{D}{4}$

$$\therefore \quad h_f = \frac{2gf'}{\gamma} \cdot \frac{4}{D} \cdot L \cdot \frac{V^2}{2g}$$

$$\therefore \quad h_f = \left(\frac{8gf'}{\gamma}\right) \cdot \frac{L}{D} \cdot \frac{V^2}{2g}$$

or
$$\boxed{h_f = \frac{fL}{D} \cdot \frac{V^2}{2g}} \quad \ldots (4.4)$$

where $f = \dfrac{8gf'}{\gamma}$, f is a dimensionless factor and is called 'friction factor'. Equation (4.4) is called 'Darcy-Weisbach equation' for loss of head due to friction.

Since $V = \dfrac{Q}{A} = \dfrac{Q}{\frac{\pi}{4}D^2} = \dfrac{4Q}{\pi D^2}$, $\boxed{h_f = \dfrac{fL}{D} \cdot \left(\dfrac{4Q}{\pi D^2}\right)^2 \dfrac{1}{2g} = \dfrac{fLQ^2}{12.1\, D^5}}$

or $\boxed{h_f = \dfrac{fLQ^2}{12.1\, D^5}}$ ... (4.5)

**[Note:** Although the loss is called 'Loss due to friction' for convenience, it is really due to the viscous resistance to the flow. Therefore, the loss can also be found out in terms of boundary shear stress $\tau_0$.]

**Relation between friction factor 'f' and wall shear stress $\tau_0$:**

Consider the free body of fluid mass between sections 1 - 1 and 2 - 2 as shown in Fig. 4.2.

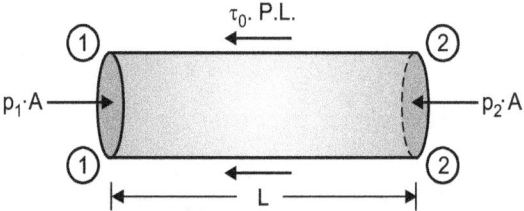

**Fig. 4.2: Forces on cylindrical body of fluid**

Since the velocity of fluid is constant, there is neither acceleration nor retardation. Therefore, force in the direction of motion must be equal to force against direction of motion.

Force in the direction of motion as in the previous case is

$(p_1 - p_2) A$ ... (4.6)

If $\tau_0$ is the shear stress (shear force per unit area) at the boundary (inside surface) of the pipe,

Force opposing the motion $= \tau_0 \times$ Wetted area

$= \tau_0 \cdot P \cdot L$ ... (4.7)

Equating equations (4.6) and (4.7), we get

$(p_1 - p_2) A = \tau_0 \cdot P \cdot L$

∴ $p_1 - p_2 = \tau_0 \cdot \dfrac{P}{A} \cdot L = \tau_0 \cdot \dfrac{1}{R} \cdot L$

∵ $\dfrac{A}{P} = R$ i.e. the hydraulic radius.

∴ $\dfrac{p_1 - p_2}{\gamma} = \dfrac{\tau_0}{\gamma} \cdot \dfrac{1}{R} \cdot L$   $R = \dfrac{\pi/4\, D^2}{\pi D} = \dfrac{D}{4}$ for pipe.

but $\dfrac{p_1 - p_2}{\gamma} = h_f$

∴ $h_f = \dfrac{\tau_0}{\gamma} \cdot \dfrac{4}{D} \cdot L = \dfrac{4\tau_0}{\gamma} \cdot \dfrac{L}{D}$   ∵ $R = \dfrac{D}{4}$

But $\qquad h_f = \dfrac{fL}{D} \cdot \dfrac{V^2}{2g}$ by Darcy-Weisbach equation

$\therefore \qquad f \cdot \dfrac{L}{D} \cdot \dfrac{V^2}{2g} = \dfrac{4\tau_0}{\gamma} \cdot \dfrac{L}{D}$

$\therefore \qquad \dfrac{fV^2}{2g} = \dfrac{4\tau_0}{\gamma}$ but $\gamma = \rho g$

$\therefore \qquad \dfrac{f V^2}{2g} = \dfrac{4\tau_0}{\rho g}$

or $\qquad \boxed{f = \dfrac{8\tau_0}{\rho V^2}}$ ... (4.8)

[Note: $\dfrac{\tau_0}{\rho}$ has dimensions of $\dfrac{[ML^{-1} T^{-2}]}{[ML^{-3}]} = [L^2 T^{-2}]$

$\therefore \sqrt{\dfrac{\tau_0}{\rho}}$ has dimensions of $[LT^{-1}]$ i.e. those of velocity.

$\therefore \sqrt{\dfrac{\tau_0}{\rho}}$ is called shear velocity and is denoted by $V_*$ $\therefore f = 8 \dfrac{V_*^2}{V^2}$ $\therefore \dfrac{V_*}{V} = \sqrt{\dfrac{f}{8}}$.

This relation is frequently used in turbulent flow.]

## 4.11 Minor Energy Losses

### 4.11.1 Loss of Head due to Sudden Expansion

Consider the sudden expansion in the pipe carrying fluid as shown in Fig. 4.3.

Because of sudden change in section of pipe, the flow does not follow the boundary but separates away from the boundary. This gives rise to eddy formation as shown in Fig. 4.3. These eddies are responsible for the loss of head.

Consider the fluid mass between section 1 - 1 before expansion and section 2 - 2 after expansion (at sufficient distance from the junction).

Let $a_1$, $p_1$ and $V_1$ be the area of cross-section, the intensity of pressure and velocity at section 1 - 1. Let $a_2$, $p_2$ and $V_2$ be the corresponding quantities at section 2 - 2.

Now the loss of head due to sudden expansion can be obtained by the application of Bernoulli's theorem, momentum theorem and continuity equation in that order.

Applying Bernoulli's equation to sections 1 - 1 and 2 - 2 taking centreline of pipe as datum, we get

$$Z_1 + \dfrac{p_1}{\gamma} + \dfrac{V_1^2}{2g} = Z_2 + \dfrac{p_2}{\gamma} + \dfrac{V_2^2}{2g} + h_L \qquad h_L \text{ is loss due to expansion}$$

but $Z_1 = Z_2$

Therefore, $h_L = \left(\dfrac{p_1 - p_2}{\gamma}\right) + \left(\dfrac{V_1^2}{2g} - \dfrac{V_2^2}{2g}\right)$ ... (4.9)

Now consider the forces on the liquid mass between section 1 - 1 and section 2 - 2. It may be noted that the curved surface of the liquid mass is subjected to pressure intensity '$p_0$' acting in the direction of flow. This is due to the eddies which try to exert force on the annular ring in the backward direction while the annular ring gives reaction in forward direction (from left to right) as shown in Fig. 4.3.

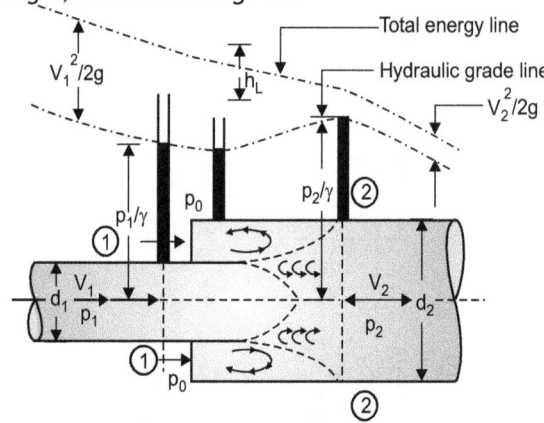

**Fig. 4.3: Sudden expansion**

The net force acting on the liquid mass in the direction of flow
$$= p_1 a_1 + p_0 (a_2 - a_1) - p_2 a_2$$

but it is observed that $p_0 = p_1$.

∴ Net force on the liquid mass between sections 1 - 1 and 2 - 2 is
$$= p_1 a_1 + p_1 (a_2 - a_1) - p_2 a_2$$

∴ Net force $= a_2 (p_1 - p_2)$ ... (4.10)

$$\left\{\begin{array}{c}\text{Now Momentum of fluid}\\\text{passing section 1 - 1 per second}\end{array}\right\} = \left\{\begin{array}{c}\text{mass of fluid passing through}\\\text{section 1 - 1 per second}\end{array}\right\} \times \text{velocity}$$

$$= \frac{\gamma}{g} \cdot a_1 V_1 \cdot V_1 = \frac{\gamma a_1 V_1^2}{g}$$

Similarly momentum of fluid passing section 2 - 2 per second
$$= \frac{\gamma a_2 V_2^2}{g}$$

∴ Rate of change of momentum which takes place between section 1 - 1 and section 2 - 2

$$= \frac{\gamma a_2 V_2^2}{g} - \frac{\gamma a_1 V_1^2}{g} \quad \text{... (4.11)}$$

Applying momentum theorem,

Net force in the flow direction = Rate of change of momentum between sections 1 – 1 and 2 - 2

∴ $$a_2 (p_1 - p_2) = \frac{\gamma a_2 V_2^2}{g} - \frac{\gamma a_1 V_1^2}{g}$$

Now by continuity equation, $a_1 V_1 = a_2 V_2$ ∴ $a_1 V_1^2 = (a_1 V_1) \cdot V_1 = (a_2 V_2 \cdot V_1)$

∴ $$a_2 (p_1 - p_2) = \frac{\gamma a_2 V_2^2}{g} - \frac{\gamma \cdot a_2 V_2 \cdot V_1}{g}$$

∴ $$\frac{p_1 - p_2}{\gamma} = \frac{V_2^2}{g} - \frac{V_2 V_1}{g} \quad \ldots (4.12)$$

Substituting the value of $\frac{p_1 - p_2}{\gamma}$ from equation (4.12) in equation (4.11) we get,

$$h_L = \left(\frac{V_2^2}{g} - \frac{V_2 V_1}{g}\right) + \left(\frac{V_1^2}{2g} - \frac{V_2^2}{2g}\right)$$

$$= \frac{2 V_2^2}{2g} - \frac{2 V_1 V_2}{2g} + \frac{V_1^2}{2g} - \frac{V_2^2}{2g}$$

$$= \frac{V_1^2 - 2 V_1 V_2 + V_2^2}{2g}$$

∴ $$\boxed{h_L = \frac{(V_1 - V_2)^2}{2g}} \quad \ldots (4.13)$$

[Above equation can also be written as

$$h_L = \frac{(V_1 - V_2)^2}{2g} = \left(1 - \frac{a_1}{a_2}\right)^2 \cdot \frac{V_1^2}{2g} = K \frac{V_1^2}{2g}$$

This equation is called Borda Carnot equation.

Values of loss coefficient of expansion 'K' for different values of $\frac{a_1}{a_2}$ are given in Table 4.1.

**Table 4.1: Loss coefficients for sudden expansion**

| $a_1/a_2$ | 0 | 0.1 | 0.2 | 0.3 | 0.4 | 0.5 | 0.6 | 0.7 | 0.8 | 0.9 | 1.0 |
|---|---|---|---|---|---|---|---|---|---|---|---|
| K | 1.0 | 0.81 | 0.64 | 0.49 | 0.36 | 0.25 | 0.16 | 0.09 | 0.04 | 0.01 | 0 |

### 4.11.2 Loss of Head due to Sudden Contraction

Consider a flow through a pipe which suddenly changes in diameter from larger diameter '$d_1$' to a smaller diameter '$d_2$' as shown in Fig. 4.4. The opening at the junction acts somewhat like an orifice. The jet of fluid contracts in area upto a section called 'venacontracta' and then expands, thus filling the cross-section of the smaller pipe at some distance downstream of the junction. In this zone eddies are formed due to which there is loss of energy or head. This is called loss of head due to sudden contraction.

If the energies at section 1 - 1 and venacontracta are compared, they are almost equal. However, if energies at section 1 - 1 and section 2 - 2 are compared, the energy at section 2 - 2 is much less than that at section 1 - 1. This shows that the loss takes place between venacontracta and section 2 - 2.

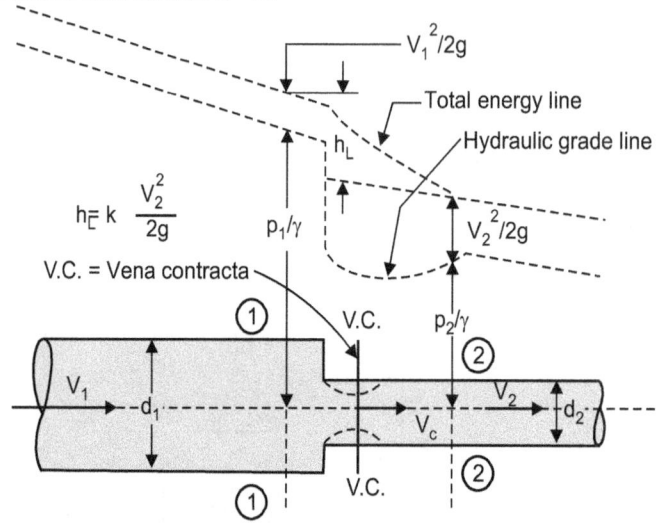

**Fig. 4.4: Sudden contraction**

Thus, *the loss of head due to sudden contraction is really the loss of head due to sudden enlargement which follows the contraction.*

This loss therefore can be written as

$$h_L = \frac{(V_c - V_2)^2}{2g} \quad \begin{bmatrix} \text{i.e. loss due to expansion between} \\ \text{venacontracta and section 2 - 2} \end{bmatrix}$$

where, $V_c$ is the velocity at venacontracta and
$V_2$ is the velocity in the smaller pipe at section 2 - 2.

Now, by continuity equation

$$Q = a_c V_c = a_2 V_2$$

$$\therefore \quad V_c = \frac{a_2 V_2}{a_c} = \frac{V_2}{a_c/a_2}$$

But the ratio $a_c/a_2 = C_c$, the co-efficient of contraction

$$\therefore \quad V_c = \frac{V_2}{C_c}$$

Substituting this value of $V_c$ in the equation for loss of head, we get

$$h_L = \frac{\left(\dfrac{V_2}{C_c} - V_2\right)^2}{2g}$$

or

$$h_L = \left(\frac{1}{C_c} - 1\right)^2 \cdot \frac{V_2^2}{2g}$$

Since the velocity only in the smaller pipe is involved, the formula in general can be written as

$$h_L = \left(\frac{1}{C_c} - 1\right)^2 \cdot \frac{V^2}{2g} \quad \text{where V is the velocity in the smaller pipe} \quad \ldots (4.14)$$

If value of $C_c$ is taken as 0.62, we get,

$$h_L = \left(\frac{1}{0.62} - 1\right)^2 \cdot \frac{V^2}{2g} = 0.375 \frac{V^2}{2g}$$

In practice the loss is taken as

$$h_L = 0.5 \frac{V^2}{2g} \quad \ldots (4.15)$$

If value of $C_c$ is given in the problem, equation (4.14) can be used, however, if $C_c$ is not given, equation (4.15) is used.

**Note:** The loss can be expressed as $K \frac{V^2}{2g}$. Values of K for different values of $\frac{d_2}{d_1}$ ratios are given in Table 4.2

**Table 4.2: Loss coefficients for sudden contraction**

| $d_2/d_1$ | 0 | 0.2 | 0.4 | 0.6 | 0.8 | 1.0 |
|---|---|---|---|---|---|---|
| K | 0.5 | 0.45 | 0.38 | 0.28 | 0.14 | 0 |

### 4.11.3 Loss of Head at the Entrance of a Pipe

This loss is similar to loss due to contraction. The loss is expressed as $K \frac{V^2}{2g}$. Value of K depends upon the type of entrance as shown in Fig. 4.5.

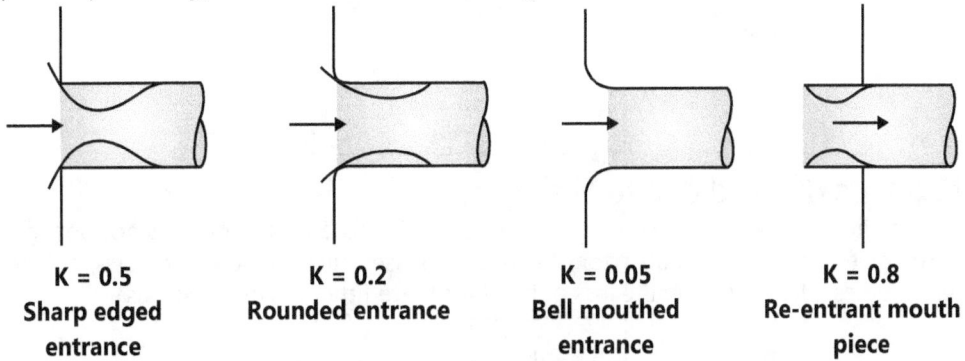

K = 0.5  
Sharp edged entrance

K = 0.2  
Rounded entrance

K = 0.05  
Bell mouthed entrance

K = 0.8  
Re-entrant mouth piece

**Fig. 4.5: Types of entrances**

In practice the loss is taken as $0.5 \frac{V^2}{2g}$ unless the exact nature of entrance is known.

∴ Loss at entrance

$$h_L = 0.5 \frac{V^2}{2g} \quad \ldots (4.16)$$

## 4.11.4 Loss of Head due to Obstruction

Any obstruction like a diaphragm interferes with the flow. This causes formation of eddies and hence loss of energy. An obstruction causes contraction of area of flow which is then followed by an expansion. *The loss of head due to obstruction is really the loss of head due to sudden expansion which follows the contraction due to obstruction.*

Consider a pipe with cross-sectional area 'A' and let an obstruction of area 'a' be placed symmetrically as shown in Fig. 4.6.

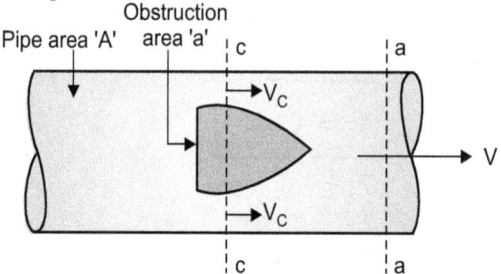

**Fig. 4.6: Loss of head due to obstruction (symmetrical)**

The loss of head due to expansion between section c - c the contracted section and section a - a of pipe is given by

$$h_L = \frac{(V_c - V)^2}{2g}$$

Area of flow section at c - c = $C_c (A - a)$

Also by continuity equation,

$$V_c \cdot C_c \cdot (A - a) = VA$$

∴
$$V_c = \frac{VA}{C_c (A - a)}$$

∴ Loss of head due to obstruction is

$$\boxed{h_L = \left[\frac{A}{C_c (A - a)} - 1\right]^2 \cdot \frac{V^2}{2g}} \qquad \ldots (4.17)$$

## 4.11.5 Loss of Head due to Fittings

All the fittings used in pipe line offer some sort of resistance to flow. It is not possible to obtain exact analytical formulae for the energy losses due to bends, elbows, valves of different types, etc. Therefore, the loss of head for these fittings is expressed as

$$\boxed{h_L = K \frac{V^2}{2g}} \qquad \ldots (4.18)$$

where K is the loss coefficient and V is the average velocity in the pipe in which the fittings are installed. The value of 'K' for the fitting has to be obtained experimentally.

For 90° bend, value of 'K' is taken as 1.

[Specific values of 'K' for different fittings, bends, valves etc. can be obtained from any standard book on piping design.]

## 4.11.6 Loss of Head at the Exit of Pipe

At the end of the pipe, the fluid is discharged with the exit velocity 'V'. Therefore, it has kinetic energy equal to $\frac{V^2}{2g}$. This energy at the exit is taken as loss at exit for the sake of account of energy.

Therefore,

$$\boxed{\text{Loss at exit of pipe} = \frac{V^2}{2g}} \quad \ldots (4.19)$$

# 4.12 Hydraulic Grade Line and Total Energy Line

Concepts of the hydraulic grade line and total energy line are useful in dealing with pipe flow problems.

"Hydraulic grade line (HGL) is the line joining the liquid levels in the piezometers connected along the pipe line." Thus, HGL is the graphical representation of piezometric head $\left(Z + \frac{p}{\gamma}\right)$ at various points along the pipe line, to some selected datum.

Some features of hydraulic grade line are as follows.

In case of a uniform pipe connecting two reservoirs, the HGL is the straight line joining the liquid levels in the two reservoirs. The slope of HGL line is called hydraulic gradient and is given by $h_f/L$. Hydraulic grade line may rise or fall in the direction of flow. If hydraulic grade line is above the centre line of pipe, pressure in the pipe is positive, if otherwise, the pressure in the pipe is negative.

Total energy line (TEL) is the graphical representation, to some selected datum, of the total head $\left(Z + \frac{p}{\gamma} + \frac{V^2}{2g}\right)$ at various points along the pipe line.

By definition, total energy line at any point will be at a vertical distance of $\frac{V^2}{2g}$ above the hydraulic grade line.

Total energy line, in the absence of machines like pumps installed on the pipeline, will always go on dropping downwards in the direction of flow.

Total energy lines and hydraulic grade lines for sudden expansion and sudden contraction have been shown in Fig. 4.3 and Fig. 4.4. respectively.

Further, refer illustrative example 4.10 for actual case of H.G.L. and T.E.L. lines.

# 4.13 Flow Through Siphon

'A pipe line which lifts the liquid to an elevation higher than its free surface and then discharges it at a lower elevation is called siphon.'

Since the liquid is lifted above its free surface, siphon is a pipe line which goes above its hydraulic grade line.

Fig. 4.7 shows a siphon joining reservoir 'A' to reservoir 'B'. It passes over a high level ground or a hill separating the two reservoirs.

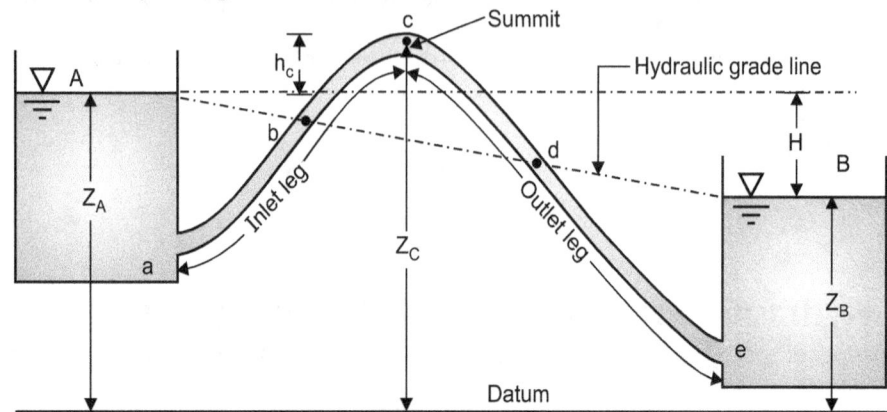

**Fig. 4.7: Flow through siphon**

The short rising length of the system 'ac' is called *'inlet leg'* of the siphon. The falling length 'ce' is called the *outlet leg* of the siphon. The highest point 'c' is called the *'summit'* of the syphon.

Hydraulic gradient for the siphon will be the line joining the liquid levels in the two reservoirs. It may be seen that

(i) In the parts 'ab' and 'de' of the siphon, the pressures are positive since the hydraulic gradient line is above the centre line of the pipe line.

(ii) In the part 'bcd' of the siphon, pressures are negative since the pipe line goes above the hydraulic grade line.

(iii) The maximum negative pressure occurs at the summit 'c' of the siphon. This negative pressure at the summit is the governing pressure for the syphon.

Assuming the siphon to run full throughout it's length and applying Bernoulli's equation to the liquid surfaces in the two reservoirs, we can write

$$Z_A + \frac{p_A}{\gamma} + \frac{V_A^2}{2g} = Z_B + \frac{p_B}{\gamma} + \frac{V_B^2}{2g} + \text{losses}$$

But $\dfrac{p_A}{\gamma} = \dfrac{p_B}{\gamma} = 0$ (atmospheric) and $V_A = V_B = 0$

∴ $Z_A - Z_B$ = losses. But $Z_A - Z_B = H$, (difference of elevation of free surfaces in the two reservoirs)

∴ 
$$H = \text{Losses in the siphon}$$
$$= \begin{bmatrix} \text{Loss of head} \\ \text{at entry} \end{bmatrix} + \begin{bmatrix} \text{Loss of head due to} \\ \text{friction in pipe 'ae'} \end{bmatrix} + \begin{bmatrix} \text{Loss of head} \\ \text{at the exit} \end{bmatrix}$$

$$\therefore \quad H = 0.5\frac{V^2}{2g} + \frac{fL}{D}\cdot\frac{V^2}{2g} + \frac{V^2}{2g}$$

or
$$\boxed{H = \left[1.5 + \frac{fL}{D}\right]\frac{V^2}{2g}} \qquad \ldots (4.20)$$

where f is the friction factor, L the total length (ae), D is the diameter of the siphon and 'V' is the velocity of flow in the siphon.

But the discharge through the siphon is

$$\boxed{Q = aV} \qquad \ldots (4.21)$$

Thus, if 'H' is known, 'Q' can be calculated and if 'Q' is known, 'H' can be calculated by the use of equations (4.20) and (4.21).

Now, applying Bernoulli's theorem to liquid level in the reservoir 'A' and the summit 'c' we get

$$Z_A + \frac{p_A}{\gamma} + \frac{V_A^2}{2g} = Z_c + \frac{p_c}{\gamma} + \frac{V_c^2}{2g} + \text{losses in 'ac'}$$

but $\dfrac{p_A}{\gamma} = 0$, $V_A = 0$, $V_c = V$

$$\therefore \quad Z_A + 0 + 0 = Z_c + \frac{p_c}{\gamma} + \frac{V^2}{2g} + 0.5\frac{V^2}{2g} + \frac{fL_1}{D}\cdot\frac{V^2}{2g}$$

where $L_1$ is the length of inlet leg.

The pressure head at the summit is given by

$$\frac{p_c}{\gamma} = (Z_A - Z_c) - \left(1.5 + \frac{fL_1}{D}\right)\frac{V^2}{2g} \quad \text{but } Z_A - Z_c = -h_c$$

or
$$\boxed{\frac{p_c}{\gamma} = -\left[h_c + \left(1.5 + \frac{fL_1}{D}\right)\cdot\frac{V^2}{2g}\right]} \qquad \ldots (4.22)$$

In equation (4.22), there are three unknowns $p_c/\gamma$ – pressure head at summit, $h_c$ – height of summit above the surface in the higher level reservoir and $L_1$ – the length of the inlet leg. Two of them being known, the third can be obtained.

Thus,

(i) For given values of pressure head $\dfrac{p_c}{\gamma}$ and length of the inlet leg '$L_1$', the maximum height of summit $h_c$ above the liquid level in 'A' can be determined.

(ii) If $p_c/\gamma$ and $h_c$ are known, maximum length of inlet leg '$L_1$' can be obtained.

(iii) If $h_c$ and $L_1$ are known, value of $p_c/\gamma$ can be determined.

Further it may be stressed that the pressure at the summit is always negative and hence there is minimum limit for the pressure at the summit. It can never be allowed to go below vapour pressure of the liquid. If the pressure reaches the vapour pressure of the liquid, the liquid vaporises and the gases dissolved in the liquid are also liberated. The vapour of liquid and the liberated gases get collected at the summit. If sufficient amount of gases are collected, the flow becomes either intermittant or completely stops. Further, there is a possibility of cavitation. A siphon should be designed for cavitation free operation. If the siphon is existing and is prone to cavitation, it can be operated at lower discharge and cavitation can be avoided.

### 4.13.1 Uses of Siphon

Following are the important uses of siphon.
1. Transfer of liquid between two reservoirs at different levels which are separated by high level ground or a hill.
2. To supply water over a ridge separating the two reservoirs.
3. To take out liquid from a tank which is not provided with an outlet.
4. To draw water from a canal which is not provided with outlet device.
5. To connect reservoirs which are separated by a valley.
6. As a spillway in dams. (Siphon spillways).
7. As an inverted siphon to connect two canals.

## 4.14 Flow Through Pipes

### 4.14.1 Pipes in Series or Compound Pipe

When two or more pipes of different diameters and/or roughness are connected one after the other serially to form a single pipe line, the pipes are said to be in series. (See Fig. 4.8).

For pipes in series

(1) The discharge through each pipe is same

$$Q_1 = Q_2 = Q_3 = \ldots$$

(2) The total loss of head is the sum of losses of head in all the pipes

$$H_f = h_{f_1} + h_{f_2} + h_{f_3} + \ldots \text{ for long pipes}$$

or $H_f = h_{f_1}$ + (minor losses in pipe 1) + $h_{f_2}$ + (minor losses in pipe 2 )

$\qquad$ + $h_{f_3}$ + (minor losses in pipe 3) + ..... for short pipes

Consider the two reservoirs A and B connected by three pipes placed in series as shown in Fig. 4.8. Let 'H' be the difference of elevation of the liquid surfaces in the two reservoirs. Let $L_1, L_2, L_3$ be the lengths, $D_1, D_2, D_3$ be the diameters and $f_1, f_2, f_3$ be the friction factors of the pipes. Then we can write

$$H = \left[\frac{f_1 L_1}{D_1} \cdot \frac{V_1^2}{2g} + \text{minor losses in pipe 1}\right] + \left[\frac{f_2 L_2}{D_2} \cdot \frac{V_2^2}{2g} + \text{minor losses in pipe 2}\right]$$

$$+ \left[\frac{f_3 L_3}{D_3} \cdot \frac{V_3^2}{2g} + \text{minor losses in pipe 3}\right]$$

Thus for the pipe shown in Fig. 4.8 (if there are no additional fittings),

$$H = \begin{bmatrix}\text{Loss at the entry}\\ \text{to pipe (1)}\end{bmatrix} + \begin{bmatrix}\text{Loss due to}\\ \text{friction in pipe 1}\end{bmatrix} + \begin{bmatrix}\text{Loss due to sudden}\\ \text{expansion}\end{bmatrix}$$

$$+ \begin{bmatrix}\text{Loss due to}\\ \text{friction in pipe 2}\end{bmatrix} + \begin{bmatrix}\text{Loss due to}\\ \text{sudden contraction}\end{bmatrix} + \begin{bmatrix}\text{Loss due to}\\ \text{friction in pipe 3}\end{bmatrix} + \begin{bmatrix}\text{Loss}\\ \text{at exit}\end{bmatrix}$$

Or

$$H = \left[0.5\frac{V_1^2}{2g} + \frac{f_1 L_1}{D_1} \cdot \frac{V_1^2}{2g} + \frac{(V_1 - V_2)^2}{2g} + \frac{f_2 L_2}{D_2} \cdot \frac{V_2^2}{2g} + 0.5\frac{V_3^2}{2g} + \frac{f_3 L_3}{D_3} \cdot \frac{V_3^2}{2g} + \frac{V_3^2}{2g}\right] \quad \ldots (4.23)$$

Also by continuity, the discharge passing through each pipe, is same

$$\therefore \quad Q = Q_1 = Q_2 = Q_3$$

or

$$Q = \frac{\pi}{4} D_1^2 V_1 = \frac{\pi}{4} D_2^2 V_2 = \frac{\pi}{4} D_3^2 V_3$$

or

$$V_1 D_1^2 = V_2 D_2^2 = V_3 D_3^2 \quad \ldots (4.24)$$

With the help of equations (4.23) and (4.24), the discharge Q can be obtained if 'H' is known, while 'H' can be obtained if Q is known.

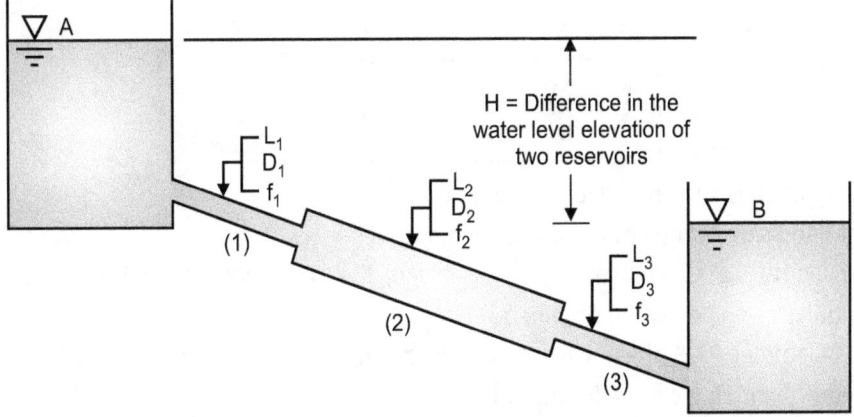

**Fig. 4.8: Pipes in series**

## 4.14.2 Equivalent Pipe-Dupit's Equation

Sometimes a compound pipe line consisting of several pipes with different lengths, different diameters and different frictional factors is replaced by a single uniform pipe. This pipe must pass the same discharge under the same loss of head as in the case of compound pipe line. This pipe is called 'Equivalent pipe."

Thus, equivalent pipe is defined as the pipe of uniform diameter having same loss of head and same discharge as that of the compound pipe.

Let the various pipes specified by ($L_1$, $D_1$, $f_1$), ($L_2$, $D_2$, $f_2$) ....... be connected in series. Let Q be the discharge in the pipes.

Then, the total loss of head in the pipes can be written as

$$h_f = \frac{f_1 L_1 Q_1^2}{12.1 D_1^5} + \frac{f_2 L_2 Q_2^2}{12.1 D_2^5} + \frac{f_3 L_3 Q_3^2}{12.1 D_3^5} + \ldots$$

But since pipes are in series, $Q_1 = Q_2 = Q_3 \ldots = Q$

$$\therefore \quad h_f = \frac{f_1 L_1 Q^2}{12.1 D_1^5} + \frac{f_2 L_2 Q^2}{12.1 D_2^5} + \frac{f_3 L_3 Q^2}{12.1 D_3^5} + \ldots \quad \ldots (4.25)$$

If the system is to be replaced by an equivalent pipe of length $L_e$, diameter $D_e$ and friction factor $f_e$, the loss of head in the equivalent pipe is also $h_f$ for discharge 'Q' by definition.

$$\therefore \quad \frac{f_e L_e Q^2}{12.1 D_e^5} = \frac{f_1 L_1 Q^2}{12.1 D_1^5} + \frac{f_2 L_2 Q^2}{12.1 D_2^5} + \frac{f_3 L_3 Q^2}{12.1 D_3^5} + \ldots$$

or

$$\boxed{\frac{f_e L_e}{D_e^5} = \frac{f_1 L_1}{D_1^5} + \frac{f_2 L_2}{D_2^5} + \frac{f_3 L_3}{D_3^5} + \ldots} \quad \ldots (4.26)$$

If further $f_e = f_1 = f_2 = f_3 = \ldots$

$$\boxed{\frac{L_e}{D_e^5} = \frac{L_1}{D_1^5} + \frac{L_2}{D_2^5} + \frac{L_3}{D_3^5} + \ldots} \quad \ldots (4.27)$$

This equation is known as 'Dupit's Equation.'

Right hand side of the equation is known and hence
1. If length '$L_e$' of equivalent pipe is given, the corresponding diameter '$D_e$' of the equivalent pipe can be obtained.
2. If diameter '$D_e$' of equivalent pipe is given, the corresponding length '$L_e$' of the equivalent pipe can be found out.

[**Note:** Two pipe systems are said to be equivalent when they pass the same discharge for the same loss of head.]

## 4.15 Pipes in Parallel (Looping Pipes)

When two or more pipes are connected as shown in Fig. 4.9, such that they branch out from the same point and afterwards join on the downstream side at the same point to form a single pipe, they are said to be in parallel.

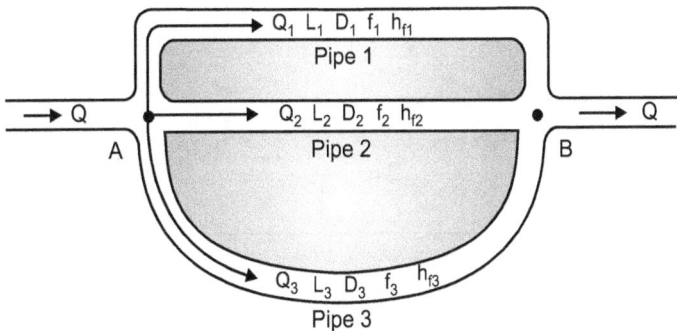

**Fig. 4.9: Pipes in parallel**

[The pipes in parallel, although shown physically parallel in the sketches, need not be physically parallel.]

These pipes in parallel may have same or different characteristics like lengths, diameters and frictional resistances.

For pipes in parallel,

(1) The discharge Q is shared by the pipes.

∴ $Q = Q_1 + Q_2 + Q_3 + \ldots$

(2) The loss of head across each pipe in parallel (i.e. each branch) is same. (Loss of head between points A and B in Fig. 4.9 same for each pipe)

∴ $h_{f_1} = h_{f_2} = h_{f_3} = \ldots$

The parallel arrangement of pipes is used to increase the discharge through the main pipe line.

### 4.15.1 Equivalent Pipe for Pipes in Parallel

A set of pipes specified by $(L_1, D_1, f_1)$, $(L_2, D_2, f_2)$, $(L_3, D_3, f_3)$ .... etc. which are connected in parallel can be replaced by a single uniform pipe which will carry the same total discharge as passing through the system ($Q = Q_1 + Q_2 + Q_3 + \ldots$) for the same loss of head as for the system ($h_{f_1} = h_{f_2} = h_{f_3} \ldots$) across it. Such a pipe is called *equivalent pipe* for system of parallel pipes. The relation between length $L_e$, diameter $D_e$, and friction factor $f_e$ of the equivalent pipe and $(L_1, D_1, f_1)$, $(L_2, D_2, f_2)$, $(L_3, D_3, f_3)$ etc. can be obtained as follows.

We have

$Q = Q_1 + Q_2 + Q_3 + \ldots$  and  $h_f = h_{f_1} = h_{f_2} = h_{f_3} \ldots$

Now we can write

$$h_{f_e} = \frac{f_e L_e Q^2}{12.1 D_e^5}, \quad h_{f_1} = \frac{f_1 L_1 Q_1^2}{12.1 D_1^5}, \quad h_{f_2} = \frac{f_2 L_2 Q_2^2}{12.1 D_2^5} \quad \text{..... etc.}$$

$$\therefore Q = \left(\frac{12.1 D_e^5 h_{f_e}}{f_e L_e}\right)^{1/2}, \quad Q_1 = \left(\frac{12.1 D_1^5 h_{f_1}}{f_1 L_1}\right)^{1/2}, \quad Q_2 = \left(\frac{12.1 D_2^5 h_{f_2}}{f_2 L_2}\right)^{1/2} \quad \text{.... etc.}$$

But $\quad Q = Q_1 + Q_2 + Q_3 \text{......}$

$$\therefore \left(\frac{12.1 D_e^5 h_{f_e}}{f_e L_e}\right)^{1/2} = \left(\frac{12.1 D_1^5 h_{f_1}}{f_1 L_1}\right)^{1/2} + \left(\frac{12.1 D_2^5 h_{f_2}}{f_2 L_2}\right)^{1/2} + \left(\frac{12.1 D_3^5 h_{f_3}}{f_3 L_3}\right)^{1/2} + \text{....}$$

$$\therefore \left(\frac{D_e^5}{f_e L_e}\right)^{1/2} = \left(\frac{D_1^5}{f_1 L_1}\right)^{1/2} + \left(\frac{D_2^5}{f_2 L_2}\right)^{1/2} + \left(\frac{D_3^5}{f_3 L_3}\right)^{1/2} + \text{....} \quad \text{... (4.28)}$$

$$\because h_{f_e} = h_{f_1} = h_{f_2} = h_{f_3} \text{ etc.}$$

## 4.16 Branched Pipes

A pipe system connecting three or more reservoirs having one or more junctions is called branching pipe system.

A typical branched pipe system is a "Three Reservoir Problem". Fig. 4.10.

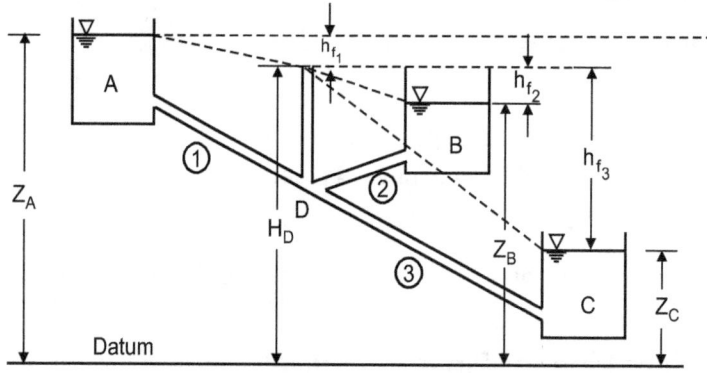

**Fig. 4.10: Three Reservoir Problem**

A, B and C are the three reservoirs connected by pipes 1, 2 and 3 to junction D. It is supposed that all the pipes are sufficiently long so that minor losses and velocity heads can be neglected or they are expressed as equivalent pipe lengths and are included in the pipe lengths. Reservoirs are large so that in steady-state condition the levels in the reservoirs are constant.

Following basic principles are adopted in the solution of such problems:
1. Darcy-Weisbach equation must be satisfied for pipe.
2. At the junction, continuity equation must be satisfied. i.e. inflow to the junction must be equal to outflow from the junction.

It is clear from Fig. 4.10 that flow will take place from reservoir A to reservoir C since C is at very low elevation as compared to A. Whether the flow will take place from reservoir B to junction 'D' or from junction 'D' to reservoir 'B' will depend upon the relative magnitudes of piezometric heads at junction 'D' and reservoir B. If the piezometric head at the junction '$H_D$' is greater than the piezometric head at reservoir 'B' i.e. $H_B$, flow will take place from junction 'D' to reservoir B and $Q_1 = Q_2 + Q_3$. However, if '$H_D$' is less than $Z_B$, flow will take place from reservoir B to the junction and $Q_1 + Q_2 = Q_3$.

Many problems are possible, as can be seen from the figure. However, three such problems are discussed below:

1. Given all pipe lengths and diameters, the surface elevations of reservoirs 'A' and 'B' and discharge in pipe 1, i.e. '$Q_1$', find the water surface elevation of reservoir 'C'.

   In this case from discharge '$Q_1$', loss of head '$h_{f_1}$' can be calculated. Then subtracting $h_{f_1}$ from the elevation of 'A', the piezometric head at the junction $H_D$ can be found out. Knowing $H_D$, $Q_2$ can be found out and knowing $Q_1$ and $Q_2$, $Q_3$ can be found out. From $Q_3$, the loss of head '$h_{f_3}$' can be found out and hence $H_D - h_{f_3}$ gives the elevation of water surface in reservoir 'C'.

2. Given all pipe lengths and diameters, water surface level in reservoirs A and 'C' and discharge '$Q_2$', find the elevation of surface level in reservoir 'B' and '$Q_1$' and '$Q_3$'.

   In this case, we know $h_{f_1} + h_{f_3}$, the difference of surface elevations of reservoirs A and C. If $Q_1$ is the discharge in pipe 1, $Q_3$ will be $Q_3 = Q_1 - Q_2$. Substituting value of $Q_3$ in expression for $h_{f_1} + h_{f_3}$, $Q_1$ can be found out. Knowing $Q_1$ and $Q_2$, $Q_3$ can be found out. From $Q_1$ and $Q_2$, $h_{f_1}$ and $h_{f_2}$ and hence water surface level in reservoir 'B' can be found out.

   This problem can also be solved by trial method. Assuming the level at the junction, the discharges $Q_1$ and $Q_3$ can be found out. $Q_1$, $Q_2$ and $Q_3$ should satisfy continuity equation, i.e. $Q_2 = Q_1 - Q_3$. Compare this value of $Q_2$ with the given value. Repeat the procedure till the two values of $Q_2$ match with each other.

3. Given all lengths, diameters and elevations of liquid surfaces in reservoirs A, B and C to find the discharges $Q_1$, $Q_2$ and $Q_3$.

   In this case, assume discharge $Q_1$ as Q, $Q_2 = mQ$, where m is some fraction, then $Q_3 = (1 - m) Q$. Now write down the equations for '$h_{f_1} + h_{f_2}$' and '$h_{f_1} + h_{f_3}$'. Find value of 'm'. $Q = Q_1$, $mQ = Q_2$ and $(1 - m) Q = Q_3$ can be found out.

   This problem also can be solved by trial method. Assume piezometric head '$H_D$' at the junction 'D'. Find out the values of $Q_1$, $Q_2$ and $Q_3$. Check for continuity i.e., $Q_2 - (Q_1 - Q_3) = 0$. Repeat the process till $Q_2 - (Q_1 - Q_3) = 0$ is satisfied.

   By plotting $Q_2 - (Q_1 - Q_3)$ on x - axis and $H_D$ on y - axis value of $H_D$ corresponding to $Q_2 - (Q_1 - Q_3) = 0$ can be obtained. Knowing the value of $H_D$ and levels in the three reservoirs, $Q_1$, $Q_2$ and $Q_3$ can be obtained.

# (C) POWER TRANSMISSION THROUGH PIPES, WATER HAMMER PHENOMENON

## 4.17 Power Transmission through Pipes

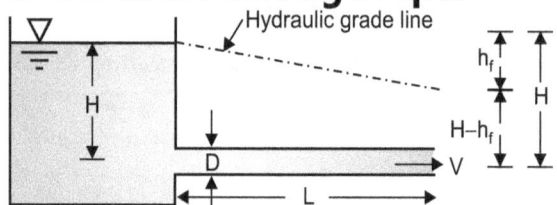

**Fig. 4.11: Transmission of hydraulic power**

Pipes are used for transmitting power from one place to other. For example, transmitting power from dam to turbines in the power house.

As the fluid flows through the pipe, losses due to friction, fittings etc. take place. Thus, if 'H' is the gross head available at the inlet of pipe and $h_f$ is the loss of head due to friction in the pipe, the net head available at the exit of the pipe will be $(H - h_f)$ (neglecting minor losses). (See Fig. 4.11).

Thus, H – Gross head available at the source (inlet of pipe)
$h_f$ – Loss of head due to friction in the pipe line.

∴ Net head available at the outlet $= H - h_f$

∴ Power transmitted by the pipe 'P' $= \gamma \cdot Q (H - h_f)$

But Q is the discharge through the pipe $= A \cdot V$

∴ Power $P = \gamma A V (H - h_f)$

$= \gamma A (HV - V \cdot h_f)$

∴ $P = \gamma A \left( HV - \dfrac{fL}{D} \cdot \dfrac{V^3}{2g} \right)$

Transmitted power will be maximum when $\left( HV - \dfrac{fL}{D} \cdot \dfrac{V^3}{2g} \right)$ is maximum, (because '$\gamma A$' is constant).

$\left( HV - \dfrac{fL}{D} \cdot \dfrac{V^3}{2g} \right)$ will be maximum when $\dfrac{d}{dV} \left( HV - \dfrac{fL}{D} \cdot \dfrac{V^3}{2g} \right) = 0$

or Power 'P' will be maximum when

$H - 3 \dfrac{fL}{D} \cdot \dfrac{V^2}{2g} = 0$ but $\dfrac{fL}{D} \cdot \dfrac{V^2}{2g} = h_f$

or $H - 3 h_f = 0$

∴ $\boxed{h_f = \dfrac{H}{3}}$ ... (4.29)

Thus, power transmitted by a pipe is maximum when loss of head due to friction in the pipe is one third the gross head (head available at the inlet).

Therefore, maximum power transmitted

$$P_{max} = \gamma Q \cdot (H - h_f)$$

$$= \gamma Q \left(H - \frac{H}{3}\right)$$

$$\boxed{P_{max} = \frac{2}{3}\gamma Q H = 2\gamma Q h_f} \qquad \ldots (4.30)$$

Efficiency of transmission = $\dfrac{\text{Power delivered}}{\text{Power available}}$

$$\therefore \quad \eta = \frac{\gamma Q (H - h_f)}{\gamma Q H}$$

$$= \frac{H - h_f}{H}$$

$$= \frac{H - \dfrac{1}{3}H}{H}$$

$$\boxed{h = 0.6667 \text{ or } 66.67\%} \qquad \ldots (4.31)$$

*Thus, when the power transmitted is maximum, efficiency of transmission is 66.67 %.*

It may be noted that when the power transmitted is maximum, the efficiency is not maximum. Efficiency $\eta = \dfrac{H - h_f}{H}$ will go on increasing as $h_f$ goes on decreasing and when $h_f$ is zero, efficiency can be 100% (which is not possible).

## 4.18 Flow Through a Nozzle

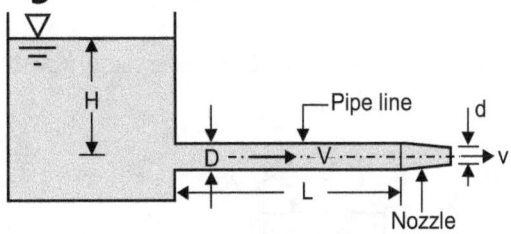

**(a) Flow through a nozzle**

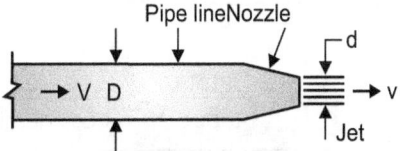

**(b) End of pipe and nozzle**

**Fig. 4.12**

Nozzle is a short tapering piece of pipe, used at the end of the pipe to convert the pressure head into velocity head. For example, such high velocity jet coming out of nozzle is used to derive power from water with the help of Pelton wheel or for extinguishing fire.

Consider the nozzle fitted at the end of the pipe as shown in Fig. 4.12 (a). Let L, D and A be the length, diameter, area of cross-section of the pipe. Let 'V' be the velocity in the pipe. Let 'd' be the diameter, and 'a' the area of cross-section of the jet from the nozzle. Let 'v' be the velocity of the jet from the nozzle.

"Velocity of jet' can be found out as follows.

We have, Net head available $= H - h_f$

But net head available at the outlet is the velocity head at the exit of the jet. Therefore, we can write

$$\frac{v^2}{2g} = H - h_f$$

or

$$H = h_f + \frac{v^2}{2g} = \frac{fL}{D} \cdot \frac{V^2}{2g} + \frac{v^2}{2g}$$

But we have $Q = AV = av$

$\therefore$

$$V = \frac{a}{A} \cdot v$$

$\therefore$

$$H = \frac{fL}{D} \cdot \frac{a^2}{A^2} \cdot \frac{v^2}{2g} + \frac{v^2}{2g}$$

or the velocity of jet

$$\boxed{v = \sqrt{\frac{2gH}{1 + \frac{fL}{D} \cdot \frac{a^2}{A^2}}}} \qquad \ldots (4.32)$$

This is the general expression for a velocity of jet issuing from the nozzle at the end of the pipe.

Power of the jet
$$P = \gamma \cdot Q \cdot \frac{v^2}{2g} \qquad \text{but } Q = a \cdot v$$

$\therefore$
$$\boxed{P = \frac{\gamma a v^3}{2g}} \qquad \ldots (4.33)$$

Efficiency of the jet

$$\eta = \frac{\text{Output}}{\text{Input}} = \frac{\text{Head transmitted}}{\text{Gross head available}}$$

$\therefore$
$$\boxed{\eta = \frac{v^2/2g}{H} = \frac{v^2}{2gH}} \qquad \ldots (4.34)$$

## 4.18.1 Maximum Power Transmission from Nozzle

Power transmitted through nozzle $P = \gamma Q \cdot \dfrac{v^2}{2g}$

but $\dfrac{v^2}{2g} = H - h_f$

$\therefore \quad P = \gamma Q (H - h_f)$

$\therefore \quad P = \gamma \cdot a \cdot v \left[ H - \dfrac{fL}{D} \cdot \dfrac{V^2}{2g} \right]$ but $V = \dfrac{a}{A} \cdot v$

$\quad = \gamma \cdot a \cdot v \left[ H - \dfrac{fL}{D} \cdot \dfrac{a^2}{A^2} \cdot \dfrac{v^2}{2g} \right]$

$\therefore \quad P = \gamma a \left[ H \cdot v - \dfrac{fL}{D} \cdot \dfrac{a^2}{A^2} \cdot \dfrac{v^3}{2g} \right]$

Now the power from the jet will be maximum when

$$\dfrac{dP}{dv} = 0$$

or $\quad \gamma a \cdot \dfrac{d}{dv} \left[ Hv - \dfrac{fL}{D} \cdot \dfrac{a^2}{A^2} \cdot \dfrac{v^3}{2g} \right] = 0$

or $\quad H - 3 \dfrac{fL}{D} \cdot \dfrac{a^2}{A^2} \cdot \dfrac{v^2}{2g} = 0$

or $\quad H - 3 h_f = 0$

or $\quad \boxed{h_f = \dfrac{H}{3}}$ ... (4.35)

This condition is same as expressed by equation (4.35).

Therefore, the power transmitted by the nozzle is maximum when the loss of head due to friction in the pipe is one third the gross head available at the source.

### 4.18.1.1 Diameter for Maximum Power Transmission

The gross head is given by

$$H = h_f + \dfrac{v^2}{2g}$$

but for maximum power transmission

$$H = 3 h_f$$

$\therefore \quad 3 h_f = h_f + \dfrac{v^2}{2g}$

$\therefore \quad 2 h_f = \dfrac{v^2}{2g}$

or $\quad \dfrac{2fL}{D} \cdot \dfrac{V^2}{2g} = \dfrac{v^2}{2g}$ but $V = \dfrac{a}{A} \cdot v$

$$\therefore \quad \frac{2fL}{D} \cdot \frac{a^2}{A^2} \cdot \frac{v^2}{2g} = \frac{v^2}{2g}$$

$$\therefore \quad \frac{2fL}{D} = \frac{A^2}{a^2}$$

$$\therefore \quad \boxed{\frac{A}{a} = \sqrt{\frac{2fL}{D}}} \quad \ldots (4.36)$$

but
$$\frac{A}{a} = \frac{D^2}{d^2}$$

$$\therefore \quad \frac{D^2}{d^2} = \sqrt{\frac{2fL}{D}}$$

$$\therefore \quad \boxed{d = \sqrt[4]{\frac{D^5}{2fL}}} \quad \ldots (4.37)$$

This equation gives the diameter of nozzle for maximum power transmission.

## 4.19 Water Hammer

Under normal circumstances, liquids are considered as incompressible. However, the phenomenon in which the liquids are treated as compressible and their elastic properties are taken into account is the phenomenon of 'Water Hammer'.

When water flowing through a pipeline is suddenly stopped by closing a valve, the kinetic energy (or momentum) of water in the pipeline is suddenly converted into pressure energy. Due to this transformation, a series of positive and negative pressure waves are created. These waves travel forward and backward in the pipeline till they are damped by friction. The pressure waves and vibrations due to it produce noise which is called 'Knocking'.

*This phenomenon of change in pressure above or below the normal pressure in the pipeline due to sudden change in velocity of flow is called 'Water Hammer'.*

Although the name indicates that the phenomenon is concerned with water, it could occur with other liquids as well. The rise in pressure may burst the pipe while drop in pressure may induce cavitation.

A heavy knocking sound is heard and the vibrations of the pipe are felt when a domestic tap is suddenly closed. This is a simple example of water hammer. Penstocks, rising mains, oil transmission lines are prone to water hammer.

The magnitude of pressure developed depends upon:
1. Speed at which the valve is closed - valve closure may be rapid or slow.
2. Velocity of liquid in the pipeline.
3. Length of pipeline.
4. Elastic properties of pipe material and
5. Elastic properties of the flowing liquid.

## 4.19.1 Sequence of Events following Sudden Closure of Valve

Consider the case of sudden closure of a valve at the end 'B' of pipe of uniform diameter and length 'L'. Other end 'A' of the pipe is connected to reservoir. Friction is neglected in this case.

**(i) First Quarter of the Cycle:**

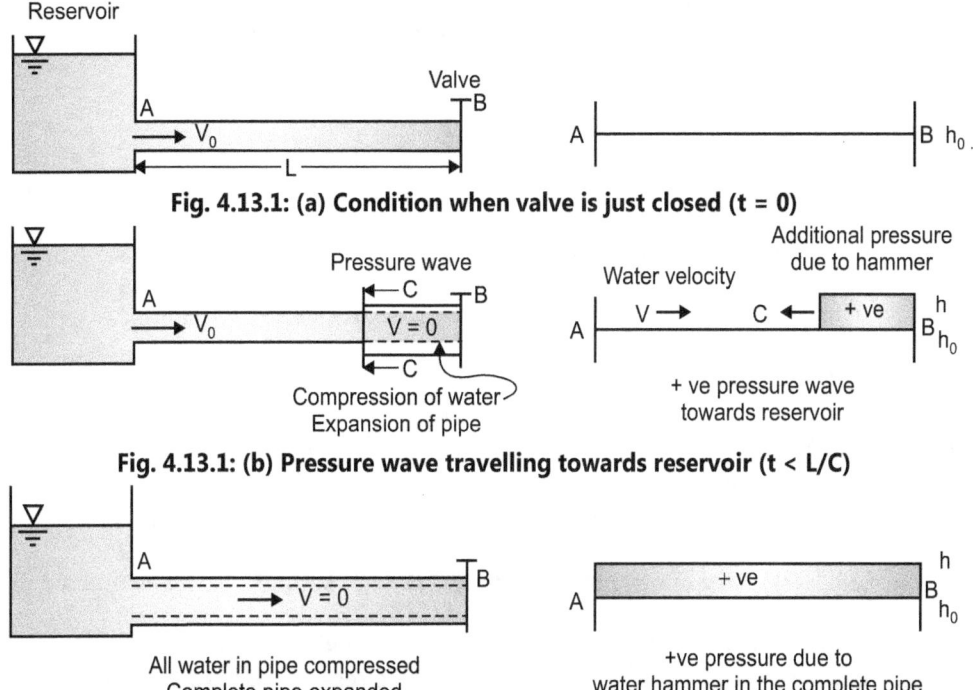

Fig. 4.13.1: (a) Condition when valve is just closed (t = 0)

Fig. 4.13.1: (b) Pressure wave travelling towards reservoir (t < L/C)

Fig. 4.13.1: (c) Pressure wave reaches reservoir (t = L/C) first Quarter completed

At the instant of valve closure i.e. at t = 0, the liquid in the immediate vicinity of the valve is compressed, brought to rest and the pipe there expands (or is stretched). See Fig. 4.13.1 (a). As soon as the first layer is compressed, the process is repeated for the next layer. See Fig. 4.13.1 (b).

The liquid on the upstream side of the compressed section goes on moving with velocity $V_0$ as if nothing has happened to this liquid. The process of compression of successive layers continues till all the liquid in the pipe from 'B' to 'A' is compressed. The high pressure developed travels from 'B' to 'A' as a pressure wave. Liquid in pipe from 'B' to 'A' is brought to rest and the complete wall expands. [See Fig. 4.13.1 (c)]

When the pressure wave reaches the reservoir (point 'A') after time = L/C, where 'C' is the velocity of sound in the liquid, all the liquid is under the extra pressure head 'h' called water hammer pressure, all the momentum has been lost and all the kinetic energy is converted into pressure energy. This completes the first quarter of the cycle.

## (ii) Second Quarter of the Cycle:

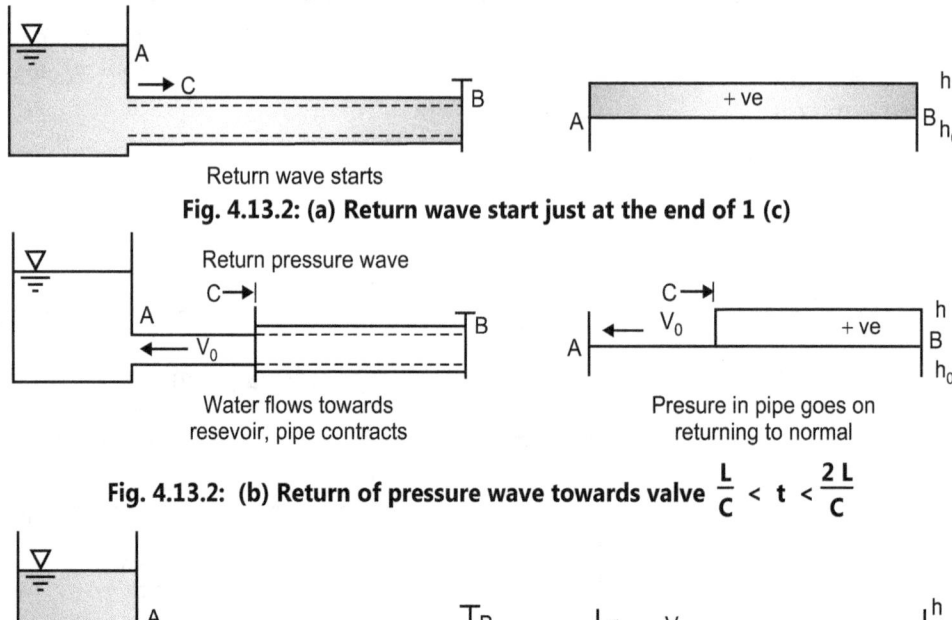

Fig. 4.13.2: (a) Return wave start just at the end of 1 (c)

Fig. 4.13.2: (b) Return of pressure wave towards valve $\dfrac{L}{C} < t < \dfrac{2L}{C}$

Fig. 4.13.2: (c) Pressure wave returns to valve ($t = \dfrac{2L}{C}$) second Quarter completed

Now, when the pressure wave reaches reservoir, there is unbalanced condition, since the pressure in reservoir is not changed (velocity in the reservoir is zero and hence there is no change in velocity and pressure). Pressure in the pipe being more, the flow now starts from pipe into the reservoir at end 'A'. This flow brings the pressure in the pipe to its normal value before the closure. The pipe comes back to its normal size and the liquid moves with velocity $V_0$ in the backward direction. This process travels from 'A' to 'B' at a speed of 'C'. [See Fig. 4.13.2 (b)].

At the instant, t = 2 L/C, the wave reaches 'B', pressure is back to normal all along the pipe. The complete pipe comes to its normal size and liquid moves with velocity $V_0$ in the direction from 'B' to 'A'. This completes the second quarter of the cycle. [See Fig. 4.13.2 (c)]

## (iii) Third Quarter of the Cycle:

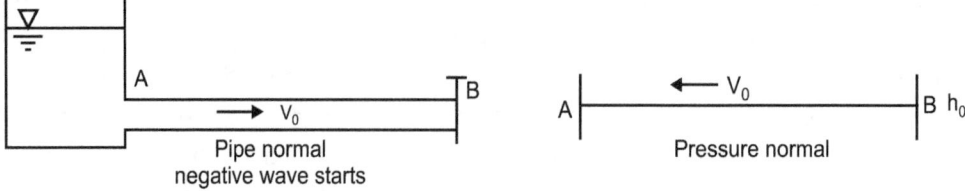

Fig. 4.13.3: (a) Negative wave start just at the end of 2 (c)

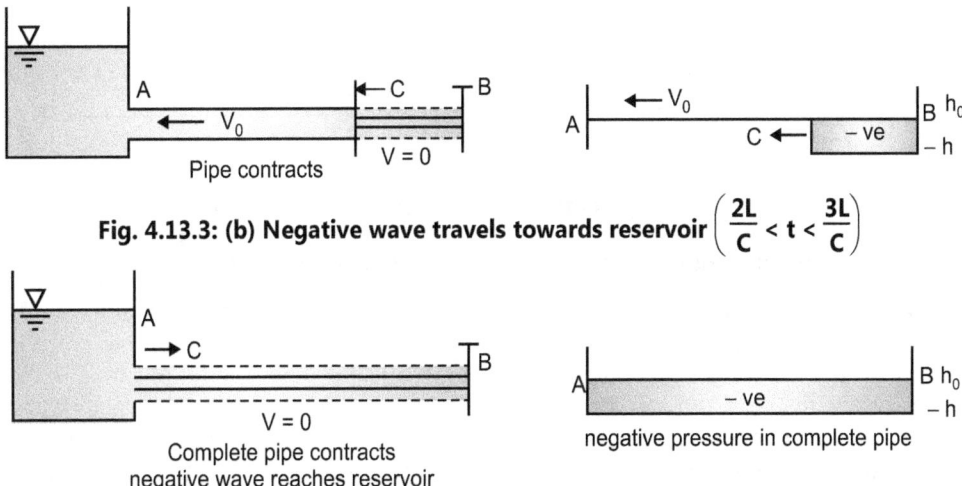

**Fig. 4.13.3: (b) Negative wave travels towards reservoir** $\left(\dfrac{2L}{C} < t < \dfrac{3L}{C}\right)$

**Fig. 4.13.3: (c) Negative wave reaches reservoir** $\left[T = \dfrac{3L}{C}\right]$. **Third quarter completed**

Since the valve is closed, there is no liquid available to maintain the flow when the wave reaches again back to 'B' and hence a negative pressure head 'h' develops in order to bring the liquid to rest. This negative pressure wave travels from 'B' to 'A' at speed of sound 'C' [See Fig. 4.13.3 (b)].

Till it reaches point 'A', all the liquid is brought to rest and all the liquid is subjected to reduced pressure head '– h' below the normal pressure. The complete pipe wall is contracted. This occurs at instant t = 3L/C, after the closure and the third quarter is completed.

### (iv) Fourth Quarter of the Cycle:

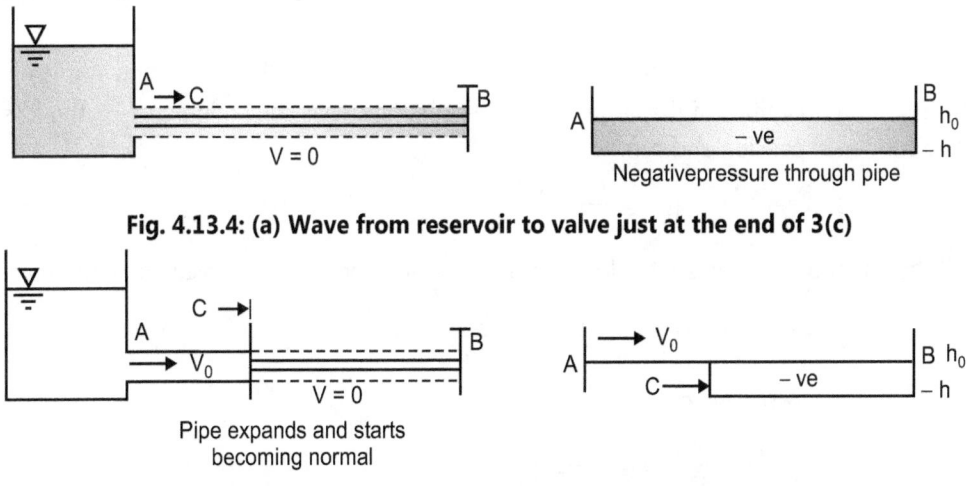

**Fig. 4.13.4: (a) Wave from reservoir to valve just at the end of 3(c)**

**Fig. 4.13.4: (b) Reflex wave travels towards valve** $\left(\dfrac{3L}{C} < t < \dfrac{4L}{C}\right)$

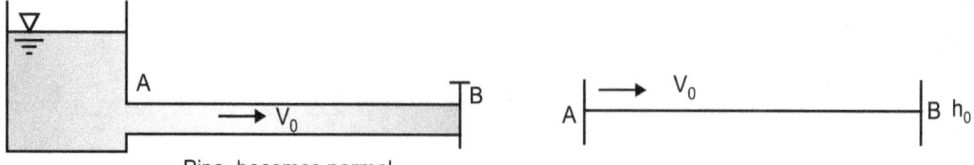

Pipe becomes normal

**Fig. 4.13.4: (c) Reflex pressure wave reaches valve**

**Initial condition reached again one complete cycle** $\left(t = \dfrac{4L}{C}\right)$

Again at the end of third cycle, there is unbalanced condition at the reservoir end 'A'. Pressure in the pipe is less than that in the reservoir. The flow starts from reservoir into pipe with velocity $V_0$ in forward direction. [See Fig. 4.13.4 (b)]

This brings the pipe and the pressure in the pipe to normal conditions, exactly same as before the closure of the valve. Total time taken is $t = 4L/C$ and one cycle is completed.

This process is then repeated every $4L/C$ seconds. However, due to the damping effect of pipe friction, pressure in successive cycles goes on reducing and brings the liquid to rest after some cycles.

## ILLUSTRATIVE EXAMPLES

**Example 4.1:**

The cross-section of a pipe carrying a given discharge is suddenly enlarged. What would be the ratio of the two diameters of the pipe if the magnitude of the loss of head at this change of section is same irrespective of the direction of flow? Assume $C_c = 0.64$.

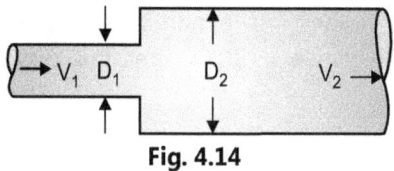

**Fig. 4.14**

**Solution:**

Let $V_1$ and $d_1$ be the velocity and diameter of the smaller pipe and $V_2$, $d_2$ the corresponding quantities of the large pipe. When the flow is as shown in Fig. 4.14, the loss is due to sudden expansion and can be written as

$$h_L = \frac{(V_1 - V_2)^2}{2g}$$

If the direction is reversed, the loss is due to sudden contraction and can be written as

$$h_L = \left(\frac{1}{C_c} - 1\right)^2 \cdot \frac{V_1^2}{2g}$$

Equating the losses, we get

$$\frac{(V_1 - V_2)^2}{2g} = \left(\frac{1}{C_c} - 1\right)^2 \cdot \frac{V_1^2}{2g}$$

But by continuity    $A_1 V_1 = A_2 V_2$    $\therefore V_2 = \dfrac{A_1}{A_2} \cdot V_1$

Substituting value of $V_2$ in the above equation, we get

$$\left[1-\left(\frac{A_1}{A_2}\right)^2\right]\cdot\frac{V_1^2}{2g} = \left(\frac{1}{0.64}-1\right)^2\cdot\frac{V_1^2}{2g}$$

$$\therefore\quad 1-\left(\frac{d_1}{d_2}\right)^2 = 0.5625$$

$$\therefore\quad \frac{d_1}{d_2} = 0.66$$

| Ratio of diameters of the pipe = 0.66 |
|---|

### Example 4.2:

For a sudden expansion in a pipe, determine the optimum ratio between the diameter of the pipe before expansion and the diameter of the pipe after expansion for the pressure rise to be maximum. Also find the maximum rise in pressure head.

**Solution:**

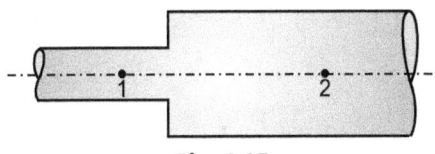

Fig. 4.15

Applying Bernoulli's theorem at points 1 and 2, we get

$$Z_1 + \frac{p_1}{\gamma} + \frac{V_1^2}{2g} = Z_2 + \frac{p_2}{\gamma} + \frac{V_2^2}{2g} + h_L$$

where $h_L$ = loss of head due to expansion.
Further if pipe is horizontal, $Z_1 = Z_2$

$$\therefore\quad \frac{p_1}{\gamma} + \frac{V_1^2}{2g} = \frac{p_2}{\gamma} + \frac{V_2^2}{2g} + \frac{(V_1-V_2)^2}{2g}$$

∴ Rise in pressure head due to expansion

$$\frac{p_2-p_1}{\gamma} = \frac{V_1^2}{2g} - \frac{V_2^2}{2g} - \frac{(V_1-V_2)^2}{2g}$$

$$= \frac{V_1^2}{2g} - \frac{V_2^2}{2g} - \frac{V_1^2}{2g} + \frac{2V_2V_1}{2g} - \frac{V_2^2}{2g} = \frac{2V_1V_2}{2g} - 2\frac{V_2^2}{2g}$$

But by continuity equation, $Q = A_1V_1 = A_2V_2$, $V_2$

$$= \frac{A_1}{A_2}\cdot V_1$$

∴ Pressure rise $= p_2 - p_1 = \gamma\dfrac{2V_1^2}{2g}\left[\dfrac{A_1}{A_2} - \left(\dfrac{A_1}{A_2}\right)^2\right]$

$$\therefore\quad \text{Pressure rise} = K\left[\frac{A_1}{A_2} - \left(\frac{A_1}{A_2}\right)^2\right], \text{ where } K = \gamma\frac{V_1^2}{g}, \text{ constant.}$$

Differentiating above expression with respect to $\left(\dfrac{A_1}{A_2}\right)$ and equation to zero, we get

$$\dfrac{d\left[\dfrac{A_1}{A_2} - \left(\dfrac{A_1}{A_2}\right)^2\right]}{d\left(\dfrac{A_1}{A_2}\right)} = 1 - 2\dfrac{A_1}{A_2} = 0$$

$$\therefore \quad \dfrac{A_1}{A_2} = \dfrac{1}{2} \qquad \therefore \left(\dfrac{D_1}{D_2}\right)^2 = \dfrac{1}{2}$$

$$\dfrac{D_1}{D_2} = \dfrac{1}{\sqrt{2}} = 0.707 \qquad \therefore \boxed{\text{Optimum } \dfrac{D_1}{D_2} = 0.707}$$

Maximum pressure head rise

$$\dfrac{(p_2 - p_1)_{max}}{\gamma} = \dfrac{2V_1^2}{2g}\left[\dfrac{A_1}{A_2} - \left(\dfrac{A_1}{A_2}\right)^2\right]$$

$$= \dfrac{2V_1^2}{2g}\left[\left(\dfrac{D_1}{D_2}\right)^2 - \left(\dfrac{D_1}{D_2}\right)^4\right]$$

$$= \dfrac{2V_1^2}{2g}\left[\left(\dfrac{1}{\sqrt{2}}\right)^2 - \left(\dfrac{1}{\sqrt{2}}\right)^4\right]$$

$$\therefore \boxed{\text{Maximum rise in pressure head} = \dfrac{2V_1^2}{2g}\left[\dfrac{1}{2} - \dfrac{1}{4}\right] = 0.5\dfrac{V_1^2}{2g}}$$

### Example 4.3:
At a sudden enlargement of water main from 0.24 m to 0.48 m diameter, the hydraulic gradient rises by 10 mm. Estimate the rate of flow.

**Solution:**

Area of smaller pipe, $A_1 = \dfrac{\pi}{4}D_1^2 = \dfrac{\pi}{4} \times (0.24)^2 = 0.0452 \text{ m}^2$ (at section 1)

Area of larger pipe, $A_2 = \dfrac{\pi}{4}D_2^2 = \dfrac{\pi}{4} \times (0.48)^2 = 0.181 \text{ m}^2$ (at section 2)

From continuity equation,

$$A_1 V_1 = A_2 V_2$$

$$\therefore \quad V_1 = \dfrac{A_2}{A_1} \cdot V_2$$

$$= \left(\dfrac{D_2}{D_1}\right)^2 \cdot V_2 = \left(\dfrac{0.48}{0.24}\right)^2 \cdot V_2$$

$$\therefore \quad V_1 = 4V_2 \qquad \qquad \ldots \text{(i)}$$

Now loss of head due to enlargement

$$h_L = \frac{(V_1 - V_2)^2}{2g}, \quad \text{But } V_1 = 4V_2$$

$$\therefore \quad h_L = \frac{(4V_2 - V_2)^2}{2g}$$

$$\therefore \quad \boxed{h_L = 9\frac{V_2^2}{2g}} \quad \ldots \text{(ii)}$$

Applying Bernoulli's equation to the sections 1 (before sudden expansion) and 2 (after sudden expansion) we get,

$$Z_1 + \frac{p_1}{\gamma} + \frac{V_1^2}{2g} = Z_2 + \frac{p_2}{\gamma} + \frac{V_2^2}{2g} + h_L \quad \ldots \text{(iii)}$$

Substituting from equation (i) and equation (ii) and rearranging equation (iii) becomes

$$\frac{(4V_2)^2}{2g} - \frac{V_2^2}{2g} - 9\frac{V_2^2}{2g} = \left(Z_2 + \frac{p_2}{\gamma}\right) - \left(Z_1 + \frac{p_1}{\gamma}\right)$$

$$\therefore \quad 6\frac{V_2^2}{2g} = \left(Z_2 + \frac{p_2}{\gamma}\right) - \left(Z_1 + \frac{p_1}{\gamma}\right)$$

But rise in hydraulic gradient

$$= \left(Z_2 + \frac{p_2}{\gamma}\right) - \left(Z_1 + \frac{p_1}{\gamma}\right) = 10 \text{ mm}$$

$$= \frac{1}{100} \text{ m} \quad \text{(given)}$$

$$\therefore \quad 6\frac{V_2^2}{2g} = \frac{1}{100}$$

$$V_2 = \sqrt{\frac{2 \times 9.81}{6 \times 100}}$$

$$V_2 = 0.181 \text{ m/s}$$

$$\therefore \quad \text{Discharge,} \quad Q = A_2 V_2$$

$$= 0.181 \times 0.181$$

$$= 0.03276 \text{ m}^3/\text{s}$$

$$= 32.76 \text{ l.p.s.}$$

$$\boxed{Q = 32.76 \text{ l.p.s.}}$$

## Example 4.4:

What water level 'h' must be maintained in the tank as shown in Fig. 4.16 to deliver a flow rate of $5 \times 10^{-4}$ m³/s through the pipe? Take $f = 0.0295$.

**Solution:**

∵  $L = 25$ m $> 500 \times 0.025$ pipe is long pipe

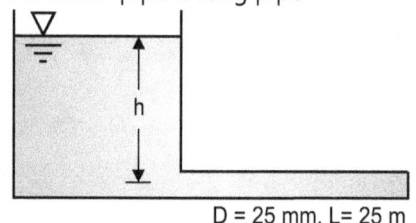

D = 25 mm, L = 25 m

Fig. 4.16

Neglecting minor losses h must be equal to friction loss in the pipe.

∴ $$h = \frac{fLQ^2}{12.1 \, d^5} = \frac{0.0295 \times 25 \times (5 \times 10^{-4})^2}{12.1 \times (0.025)^5} = 1.56 \text{ m}$$

∴ **Water level in the tank is 1.56 m above the centre of pipe.**

## Example 4.5:

The difference in surface elevations in two reservoirs 'A' and 'B' is 10 m and the pressure of air space in 'A' is 50 kN/m². They are connected by a single pipe 200 m long, 20 cm in diameter. If friction factor for the pipe is 0.02, calculate the discharge. (See Fig. 4.17).

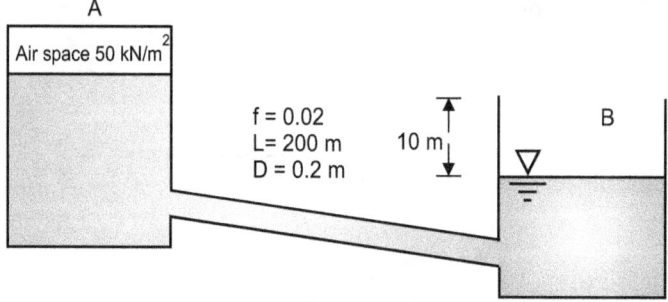

Fig. 4.17

**Solution:**

Flow will take place due to the total head of 10 m plus the head of water equivalent to 50 kN/m².

50 kN/m² is equivalent to $\dfrac{50}{9.81} = 5.1$ m of water

∴ Total head causing flow = $10 + 5.1 = 15.1$ m

Neglecting minor losses, (∵ $L > 500$ D, pipe is long pipe)

$$15.1 = \frac{fLQ^2}{12.1 \, D^5} = \frac{0.02 \times 200 \times Q^2}{12.1 \times (0.2)^5}$$

Therefore, **Q = 0.121 m³/s  or  121 l.p.s.**

## Example 4.6:

Two reservoirs at different elevations are connected with a compound pipe of 1 km total length; consisting of two sections. First section connected to higher level reservoir is 500 m long and 200 mm in diameter. Other half is connected to lower level reservoir and has 100 mm diameter. Darcy-Weisbach friction factors for the pipes are 0.019 and 0.02 respectively. If velocity of flow of water in the second section is 1.5 m/s; find the difference in water levels in the reservoirs considering all losses. Find rate of flow of water also.

Find diameter of a single uniform diameter pipe to replace the above pipe line to carry same discharge.

Take $f = 0.018$ for this pipe.

### Solution:

Considering all the losses, the difference of elevations between the water levels in the reservoirs is

$$H = \text{All the losses} = \text{entry loss} + \text{friction loss in pipe (1)} + \text{loss due to contraction} + \text{friction loss in pipe (2)} + \text{exit loss}$$

We have $A_1 V_1 = A_2 V_2$

$$V_1 = \frac{A_2}{A_1} \cdot V_2 = \left(\frac{D_2}{D_1}\right)^2 \cdot V_2$$

$$= \frac{1}{4} V_2 = \frac{1}{4}(1.5) = 0.375 \text{ m/s}$$

**(1) Loss of head at entrance to pipe (1)**

$$h_e = 0.5 \frac{V_1^2}{2g} = 0.5 \cdot \frac{(0.375)^2}{19.62} = 0.0036 \text{ m} \quad \therefore \boxed{h_e = 0.0036 \text{ m}}$$

**(2) Loss of head due to friction in pipe 1.**

$$h_{f_1} = \frac{f_1 L_1}{D_1} \cdot \frac{V_1^2}{2g}$$

$$= \frac{0.019 \times 500}{0.2} \times \frac{(0.375)^2}{19.62} = 0.340 \text{ m} \quad \therefore \boxed{h_{f_1} = 0.340 \text{ m}}$$

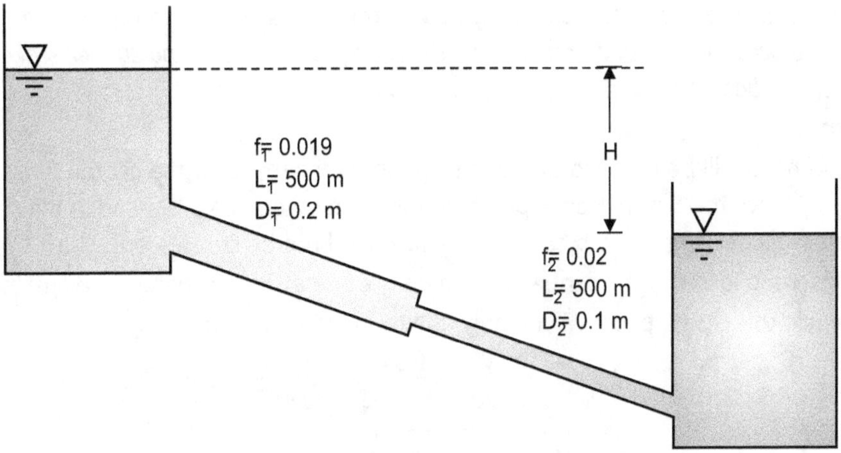

$f_1$ 0.019
$L_1$ 500 m
$D_1$ 0.2 m

$f_2$ 0.02
$L_2$ 500 m
$D_2$ 0.1 m

Fig. 4.18

**(3) Loss at the contraction**

$$h_c = 0.5 \frac{V_2^2}{2g} = 0.5 \times \frac{(1.5)^2}{19.62} = 0.057 \text{ m} \qquad \therefore \boxed{h_c = 0.057 \text{ m}}$$

**(4) Loss of head due to friction in pipe 2**

$$h_{f_2} = \frac{f_2 L_2}{D_2} \cdot \frac{V_2^2}{2g}$$

$$= \frac{0.02 \times 500}{0.1} \cdot \frac{(1.5)^2}{19.62} = 11.468 \text{ m} \qquad \therefore \boxed{h_{f_2} = 11.468 \text{ m}}$$

**(5) Loss of head at the exit**

$$h_{ex} = \frac{V_2^2}{2g} = 0.115 \text{ m} \qquad \therefore \boxed{h_{ex} = 0.115 \text{ m}}$$

$\therefore$ $\boxed{\text{The difference in the water levels} = 11.99 \text{ m} \approx 12 \text{ m}}$ (addition of all losses)

$$\boxed{Q = A_2 V_2 = 11.78 \text{ l.p.s.}}$$

Now for equivalent pipe we have

$$\frac{f_e L_e}{(D_e)^5} = \frac{f_1 L_1}{D_1^5} + \frac{f_2 L_2}{D_2^5} \qquad L_e = L_1 + L_2 = 1000 \text{ m}$$

$\therefore$
$$\frac{(0.018) \times (1000)}{D_e^5} = \frac{0.019 \times 500}{(0.2)^5} + \frac{0.02 \times 500}{(0.1)^5}$$

$$D_e = 0.112 \text{ m}.$$

$\therefore$ $\boxed{\text{Diameter of new pipe} = 0.112 \text{ m}}$

### Example 4.7:

A pipe 50 mm diameter is 6 m long and velocity of flow of water in the pipe is 2.4 m/s. What loss of head and the corresponding power would be saved if the central 2 m length of pipe was replaced by 75 mm diameter pipe, the change of section being sudden. Take $f = 0.04$ for the pipes of both diameters.

**Solution:**

Loss of head will be reduced due to change in the diameter of the central 2 m length of pipe from 50 mm to 75 mm. Hence power also can be saved. [Loss of head in the remaining 4 m of pipe will be same in both cases and hence need not be considered].

Consider the losses in the central section before and after the change in diameter.

**Case I:** In this case the loss will be only due to friction and is given by

$$h_{f_1} = \frac{fL}{D} \cdot \frac{V^2}{2g} = \frac{0.04 \times 2}{0.05} \times \frac{(2.4)^2}{19.62} = 0.47 \text{ m}$$

$$\boxed{h_{f_1} = 0.47 \text{ m}}$$

**Case II:** In this case the losses due to change in diameter of central section will be as follows:

(i) Loss of head due to expansion $= \dfrac{(V_1 - V_2)^2}{2g}$

Now, $V_2 = \left(\dfrac{D_1}{D_2}\right)^2 \cdot V_1 = \left(\dfrac{50}{75}\right)^2 \times 2.4 = 1.07$ m/s

∴ Loss of head due to expansion $= \dfrac{(2.4 - 1.07)^2}{19.62} = 0.09$ m

(ii) Loss of head due to friction in larger pipe

$$= \dfrac{fL}{D} \cdot \dfrac{V^2}{2g}$$

$$= \dfrac{0.04 \times 2}{0.075} \cdot \dfrac{(1.07)^2}{19.62}$$

$$= 0.062 \text{ m}$$

(iii) Loss of head due to sudden contraction

$$= 0.5 \times \dfrac{(\text{Velocity in smaller pipe})^2}{2g}$$

$$= 0.5 \times \dfrac{(2.4)^2}{19.62}$$

$$= 0.147 \text{ m}$$

∴ Total loss of head in the central section due to change in diameter

$$= 0.09 + 0.062 + 0.147$$

$$= \boxed{0.299 \text{ m}}$$

∴ Head saved h $= 0.47 - 0.299 = 0.171$ m

∴ $\boxed{\text{Head saved} = 0.171 \text{ m}}$

Power saved $= \gamma \cdot Q \cdot h \qquad Q = \dfrac{\pi}{4} \times (0.05)^2 \times 2.4 = 4.71 \times 10^{-3}$ m³/s

$= 9810 \times (4.71 \times 10^{-3}) \times 0.171$

$= 7.9$ watts

∴ $\boxed{\text{Power saved} = 7.9 \text{ watts}}$

### Example 4.8:

Water is conveyed from a constant head tank (head of operation 4 m) through a 100 m long horizontal pipe of 100 mm diameter with a valve at its end. With the valve half open, the free flow through the pipe is 12 lps. Obtain the value of loss coefficient for the valve. Take 'f' = 0.026 for pipe and consider all minor losses.

## Solution:

We have $Q = 12$ lps $= 12 \times 10^{-3}$ m³/s

Velocity in the pipe, $V = \dfrac{Q}{A} = \dfrac{12 \times 10^{-3}}{\dfrac{\pi}{4} \times (0.1)^2}$

$V = 1.528$ m/s

Now,

Head of operation = Sum of all the losses in the pipe line
= entry loss + friction loss + loss due to valve + exit loss

$\therefore \quad 4 = 0.5 \dfrac{V^2}{2g} + \dfrac{fL}{D} \cdot \dfrac{V^2}{2g} + K \cdot \dfrac{V^2}{2g} + \dfrac{V^2}{2g}$

$\therefore \quad 4 = \left[1.5 + \dfrac{0.026 \times 100}{0.1} + K\right] \cdot \dfrac{V^2}{2g}$

$\therefore \quad 4 = [1.5 + 26 + K] \cdot \dfrac{(1.528)^2}{19.62}$

$K = 6.11$

$\therefore$ **Loss coefficient for the valve = 6.11**

## Example 4.9:

Water flows through a pipe 100 mm diameter at the rate of 15.71 l.p.s. The straight length of pipe is 50 m and one open globe valve, a 'T' through side outlet and an elbow is provided in it. If the values of 'K' for these fittings are 10, 1.8 and 0.9 respectively, what is the total length of the pipe and total loss of head in it? Take f for pipe 0.022.

### Solution:

It is practice to express minor losses as $K \dfrac{V^2}{2g}$, where K is called the loss co-efficient for the fitting.

Now equivalent length of pipe for minor loss can be obtained by equating $K \dfrac{V^2}{2g}$ to $\dfrac{fL_e}{D} \cdot \dfrac{V^2}{2g}$.

$\therefore \quad \dfrac{fL_e}{D} \cdot \dfrac{V^2}{2g} = K \dfrac{V^2}{2g}$

$\therefore$ Length of pipe equivalent to a minor loss is

$L_e = \dfrac{KD}{f}$

1. Length equivalent to globe valve

$L_{eg} = \dfrac{10 \times 0.1}{0.022} = 45.45$ m

2. Length equivalent to tee

$$L_{et} = \frac{1.8 \times 0.1}{0.022}$$

$$= 8.18 \text{ m}$$

3. Length equivalent to elbow

$$L_{eb} = \frac{0.9 \times 0.1}{0.022}$$

$$= 4.09 \text{ m}$$

∴ Total length of pipe = 50 + 45.45 + 8.18 + 4.09
= 50 + 57.72

∴ Total length of pipe 'L' = 107.72 m

$$\text{Total loss of head} = \frac{fLQ^2}{12.1\,D^5} = \frac{0.022 \times 107.72 \times (15.71 \times 10^{-3})^2}{12.1 \times (0.1)^5}$$

∴ **Total loss of head = 4.834 m**

### Example 4.10:

A compound pipe carries water from a reservoir and discharges in atmosphere. It consists of 30 cm diameter pipe of 150 m length first and 20 cm pipe diameter of 90 m length in latter part. If the discharge is let 45 m below reservoir surface level and 'f' for both pipes is 0.04, compute the discharge. Consider all losses.

If the junction of pipes is 35 m below reservoir water surface, compute the pressures before and after the sudden contraction. Take $C_c = 0.62$. Draw total energy line and hydraulic grade line for the system.

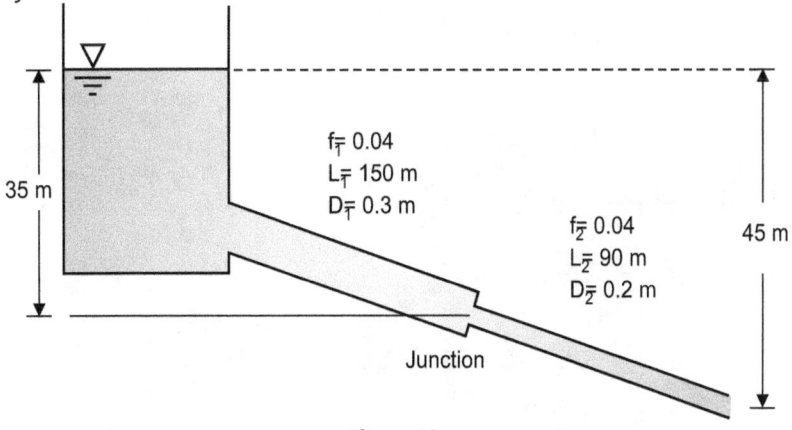

Fig. 4.19

Difference of elevations of reservoir surface level and the outlet of the pipe i.e. 45 m must be equal to all the losses in the pipe.

∴ $45 = h_{entry} + h_{f_1} + h_c + h_{f_2} + h_{exit}$

Now, we will express all the losses in terms of velocity $V_1$ in the first pipe, add them and equate the sum to 45 m.

(1) Loss at the entry to the pipe

$$h_{entry} = 0.5 \frac{V_1^2}{2g}$$

(2) Loss due to friction in pipe 1

$$h_{f_1} = \frac{f_1 L_1}{D_1} \cdot \frac{V_1^2}{2g}$$

$$= \frac{0.04 \times 150}{0.3} \cdot \frac{V_1^2}{2g}$$

$$\therefore \quad h_{f_1} = 20 \frac{V_1^2}{2g}$$

(3) Loss of head at sudden contraction

$$h_c = \left(\frac{1}{C_c} - 1\right)^2 \cdot \frac{V_2^2}{2g} \quad \left[\text{but } A_1 V_1 = A_2 V_2 \text{ or } V_2 = \frac{A_1}{A_2} \cdot V_1 = \left(\frac{D_1}{D_2}\right)^2 \cdot V_1\right.$$

$$= \left(\frac{1}{0.62} - 1\right)^2 \cdot \frac{(2.25 V_1)^2}{2g} \qquad \left.\therefore \ V_2 = 2.25 V_1\right]$$

$$\therefore \quad h_c = 1.9 \frac{V_1^2}{2g}$$

(4) Loss of head due to friction in pipe 2

$$h_{f_2} = \frac{f_2 L_2}{D_2} \cdot \frac{V_2^2}{2g}$$

$$= \frac{0.04 \times 90}{0.2} \cdot \frac{(2.25 V_1)^2}{2g}$$

$$\therefore \quad h_{f_2} = 91.125 \frac{V_1^2}{2g}$$

(5) Loss of head at exit of pipe

$$h_{exit} = \frac{V_2^2}{2g} = 5.063 \frac{V_1^2}{2g}$$

$$\therefore \quad 45 = [0.5 + 20 + 1.9 + 91.125 + 5.063] \cdot \frac{V_1^2}{2g}$$

$$\therefore \quad V_1 = 2.73 \text{ m/s}$$

$$\therefore \quad \text{Discharge } Q = A_1 \cdot V_1 = \frac{\pi}{4} \times 0.3^2 \times 2.73$$

$$\therefore \quad \boxed{Q = 0.193 \text{ m}^3/\text{s}}$$

To get pressure head just before the contraction applying Bernoulli's theorem to liquid surface in the reservoir and the junction taking horizontal through junction as datum, we get

$$Z_1 + \frac{p_1}{\gamma} + \frac{V_1^2}{2g} = Z_2 + \frac{p_2}{\gamma} + \frac{V_2^2}{2g} + \text{losses} \quad [1 - \text{reservoir}, 2 - \text{junction}]$$

$$35 + 0 + 0 = 0 + \frac{p_2}{\gamma} + \frac{V_2^2}{2g} + h_{entry} + h_{f_1}$$

$$= \frac{p_2}{\gamma} + \frac{(2.73)^2}{19.62} + \frac{0.5\,(2.73)^2}{19.62} + \frac{20\,(2.73)^2}{19.62}$$

$$\frac{p_2}{\gamma} = 26.833 \text{ m}$$

∴ **Pressure before the junction = 263.231 kPa**

Pressure just after the junction = $p_2 - \gamma \cdot h_c$

$$= \left[263.231 - 9.81 \times 1.9 \frac{(2.73)^2}{2g}\right] = 256.15 \text{ kPa}$$

**Pressure just after the junction = 256.15 kPa**

**Various losses**

$h_{entry} = 0.19$ m, $h_{f_1} = 7.6$ m, $h_c = 0.72$ m, $h_{f_2} = 34.61$ m and $h_{exit} = 1.92$ m

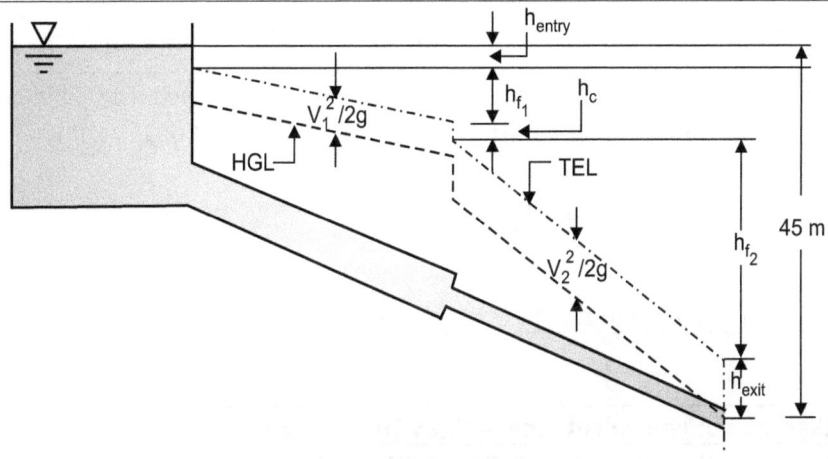

**Fig. 4.20: H.G.L. and T.E.L.**

### Example 4.11:

Three pipes 300 m long, 300 mm diameter; 150 m long, 200 mm diameter and 200 m long, 250 mm diameter are connected in series in the same order. Pipe having 300 mm diameter is connected to reservoir. Water level in the reservoir is 15 m above the pipe axis which is horizontal. The respective friction factors for three pipes are 0.018, 0.02 and 0.019. Determine:
(i) flow rate
(ii) magnitude of loss in each pipe section and
(iii) the diameter when the three pipes are replaced by a single pipe (f = 0.016) to give the same discharge. Neglect minor losses.

## Solution:

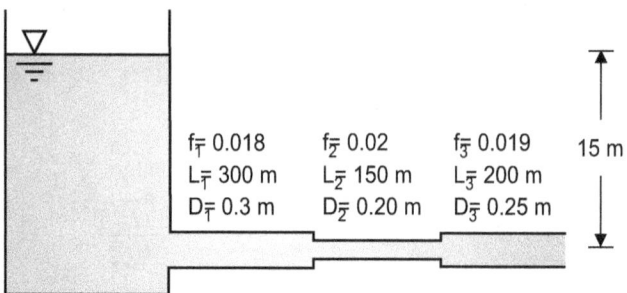

**Fig. 4.21**

Total loss of head = $15 = h_{f_1} + h_{f_2} + h_{f_3}$   For pipes in series, Q is same.

$$\therefore \quad 15 = \frac{f_1 L_1 Q^2}{12.1 D_1^5} + \frac{f_2 L_2 Q^2}{12.1 D_2^5} + \frac{f_3 L_3 Q^2}{12.1 D_3^5}$$

$$15 = \frac{0.018 \times 300 \times Q^2}{12.1 \times (0.3)^5} + \frac{0.02 \times 150 \times Q^2}{12.1 \times (0.2)^5} + \frac{0.019 \times 200 \times Q^2}{12.1 \times (0.25)^5}$$

or  $15 = (183.65 + 774.79 + 321.59) Q^2$

$\boxed{Q = 0.10825 \text{ m}^3/\text{s}}$

Now,  $\boxed{h_{f_1} = 2.152 \text{ m}, \; h_{f_2} = 9.08 \text{ m}, \; h_{f_3} = 3.77 \text{ m}, \text{ Total} = 15.00 \text{ m}}$

Now, the three pipes are to be replaced by only one uniform pipe. This pipe (equivalent pipe) must pass the discharge of 0.10825 m³/s for the loss of head of 15 m. It will have total length of 650 m, the sum of the lengths of three pipes.

$$\therefore \quad \frac{f_e L_e Q^2}{12.1 D_e^5} = 15$$

or  $$\frac{0.016 \times 650 \times (0.10825)^2}{12.1 \times D_e^5} = 15$$

$\therefore$ $\boxed{\text{Diameter of equivalent pipe} = 0.232 \text{ m or } 23.2 \text{ cm.}}$

### Example 4.12:

Pipes of 50 cm diameter, 1800 m length; 40 cm diameter, 1200 m length and 30 cm diameter, 600 m length are connected in series.

(i) If these pipes are to be replaced by an equivalent pipe of 40 cm diameter, what would be its length?

(ii) What would be the diameter of the equivalent pipe of 3600 m length?

(iii) If the three pipes are connected in parallel, what is the equivalent length of a 50 cm diameter pipe?

## Solution:

(1) The equivalent pipe must carry the same discharge as that in the compound pipe for the same loss head as in the compound pipe.

$$\therefore \quad \frac{f_e L_e Q^2}{12.1 D_e^6} = \frac{f_1 L_1 Q^2}{12.1 D_1^5} + \frac{f_2 L_2 Q^2}{12.1 D_2^5} + \frac{f_3 L_3 Q^2}{12.1 D_3^5}$$

Since friction factors are not given, they are assumed to be same for all the pipes.

$$\therefore \quad \frac{L_e}{D_e^5} = \frac{L_1}{D_1^5} + \frac{L_2}{D_2^5} + \frac{L_3}{D_3^5}$$

$$\therefore \quad \frac{L_e}{(0.4)^5} = \frac{1800}{(0.5)^5} + \frac{1200}{(0.4)^5} + \frac{600}{(0.3)^5}$$

$$\therefore \quad \boxed{L_e = 4318.22 \text{ m}}$$

(2) In the second case, $L_e = 3600$ m

$$\therefore \quad \frac{3600}{D_e^5} = \frac{1800}{(0.5)^5} + \frac{1200}{(0.4)^5} + \frac{600}{(0.3)^5}$$

$$\therefore \quad \boxed{D_e = 385.7 \text{ mm}}$$

(3) When the pipes are connected in parallel, the loss of head across each pipe is same although discharges differ.

$$\therefore \quad \frac{f_e L_e Q^2}{12.1 D_e^5} = \frac{f_1 L_1 Q_1^2}{12.1 D_1^5} = \frac{f_2 L_2 Q_2^2}{12.1 D_2^5} = \frac{f_3 L_3 Q_3^2}{12.1 D_3^5}$$

Taking first and second term and simplifying

$$Q_1 = 0.0236\, Q \sqrt{L_e}$$

Similarly $\quad Q_2 = 0.0165\, Q \sqrt{L_e}$

$$Q_3 = 0.0114\, Q \sqrt{L_e}$$

but for parallel pipes $\quad Q = Q_1 + Q_2 + Q_3 = Q \sqrt{L_e}\, (0.0236 + 0.0165 + 0.0114)$

$D_e = 0.5$ m, $D_1 = 0.5$ m, $D_2 = 0.4$ m and $D_3 = 0.3$ m

∴ Equivalent length of pipe when pipes are connected in parallel

$$\boxed{L_e = 377.04 \text{ m (377.34 if all decimals are taken)}}$$

Or The relation between the parallel pipes and their equivalent pipe can be directly used.

[see Equ. 4.29]
$$\left[\frac{D_e^5}{f_e L_e}\right]^{1/2} = \left[\frac{D_1^5}{f_1 L_1}\right]^{1/2} + \left[\frac{D_2^5}{f_2 L_2}\right]^{1/2} + \left[\frac{D_3^5}{f_3 L_3}\right]^{1/2} \quad \text{f is same}$$

$$\therefore \quad \left[\frac{(0.5)^5}{L_e}\right]^{1/2} = \left[\frac{(0.5)^5}{1800}\right]^{1/2} + \left[\frac{(0.4)^5}{1200}\right]^{1/2} + \left[\frac{(0.3)^5}{600}\right]^{1/2}$$

$$\therefore \quad \boxed{L_e = 377.37 \text{ m.}}$$

## Example 4.13:

Two reservoirs with water levels 180.00 and 150.00 are connected by a pipe line 500 mm in diameter and 2000 m long. The pipe line crosses a ridge whose summit is 15 m above the level of and 200 m distant from the higher reservoir. Find the minimum depth below the ridge, at which the pipe must be laid if separation occurs at 2 m of water absolute. Take $f = 0.04$ and atmospheric pressure 10 m of water.

**Solution:**

$$\begin{bmatrix} \text{Difference of elevation} \\ \text{between the water levels} \\ \text{in the reservoirs} \end{bmatrix} = \begin{bmatrix} \text{Loss due} \\ \text{to entry} \end{bmatrix} + \begin{bmatrix} \text{Friction} \\ \text{loss in} \\ \text{the pipe} \end{bmatrix} + \begin{bmatrix} \text{Exit} \\ \text{loss} \end{bmatrix}$$

$\therefore \quad 30 = 0.5 \dfrac{V^2}{2g} + \dfrac{fL}{D} \cdot \dfrac{V^2}{2g} + \dfrac{V^2}{2g}$, $\quad V$ = velocity of water in the pipe

$\therefore \quad 30 = \left[1.5 + \dfrac{fL}{D}\right] \cdot \dfrac{V^2}{2g}$

$\quad = \left[1.5 + \dfrac{0.04 \times 2000}{0.5}\right] \cdot \dfrac{V^2}{19.62}$

$\quad V = 1.91 \text{ m/s} \qquad\qquad Q = \dfrac{\pi}{4} D^2 \cdot V = 0.375 \text{ m}^3/\text{s}$

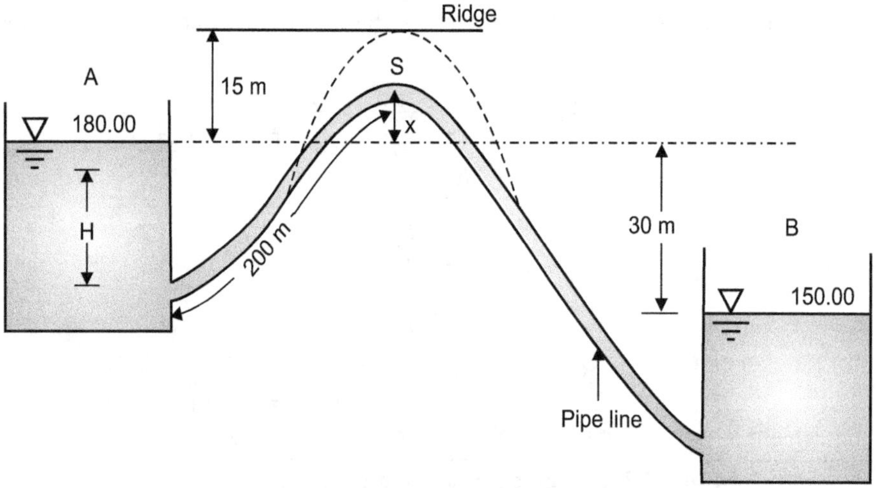

**Fig. 4.22**

Now the pressure at summit is to be restricted to 2 m of water absolute. Let the height of summit above the liquid level in upper reservoir be 'x'.

Applying Bernoulli's theorem to liquid level in upper reservoir 'A' and the summit "S" taking water level in upper reservoir as datum, we get

$$Z_A + \dfrac{p_A}{\gamma} + \dfrac{V_A^2}{2g} = Z_S + \dfrac{p_S}{\gamma} + \dfrac{V_S^2}{2g} + \begin{array}{c}\text{loss due}\\\text{to entry}\end{array} + \begin{bmatrix}\text{loss due to friction in pipe}\\\text{from A to S i.e. 200 m length}\end{bmatrix}$$

But $\qquad V_S = V$

# FLUID MECHANICS (NMU) (S.E. MECHANICAL)   DIMENSIONAL ANALYSIS AND FLOW THROUGH PIPES

$$\therefore \quad Z_A + \frac{p_A}{\gamma} + \frac{V_A^2}{2g} = Z_S + \frac{p_S}{\gamma} + \frac{V^2}{2g} + 0.5\frac{V^2}{2g} + \frac{fL_1}{D_1} \cdot \frac{V^2}{2g}$$

$Z_A = 0$, $V_A = 0$ and $D_1 = D$

$$\therefore \quad \frac{p_A}{\gamma} = x + \frac{p_S}{\gamma} + \left[1.5 + \frac{fL_1}{D}\right] \cdot \frac{V^2}{2g}$$

[Note: In the above equation there are three unknowns

(1) 'x' height of summit above liquid level in upper reservoir

(2) $\frac{p_S}{\gamma}$ pressure head at the summit

(3) $L_1$ length of inlet leg.

In the problems on siphon, two of the three unknowns are given and the third is required to be found out.

$$\therefore \quad 10 = x + 2 + \left[1.5 + \frac{0.04 \times 200}{0.5}\right] \frac{(1.91)^2}{19.62}$$

$$x = 4.75 \text{ m}$$

∴ **Minimum depth below the ridge at which pipe can be laid = 15 − 4.75 = 11.25 m**

### Example 4.14:

Two pipes of 15 cm and 30 cm diameter are laid in parallel to pass a total discharge of 100 L.P.S. Each pipe is 250 m long. Determine discharge through each pipe.

Now these pipes are connected in series to connect two tanks 500 m apart, to carry same total discharge.

Determine water level difference between the tanks.

Neglect minor losses in both cases. Take f = 0.02 for both pipes.

**Solution:**

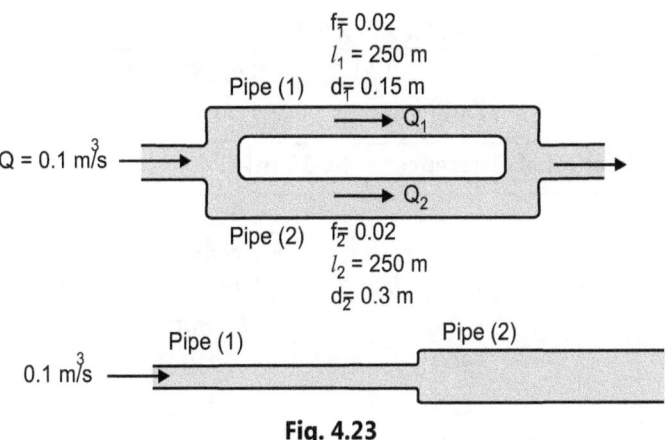

Fig. 4.23

(i) When pipes are in parallel, friction loss in each pipe is same

$$\therefore \quad h_{f_1} = h_{f_2}$$

$$\therefore \quad \frac{f_1 l_1 Q_1^2}{12.5 \, d_1^5} = \frac{f_2 l_2 Q_2^2}{12.1 \, d_2^5} \quad \text{but } f_1 = f_2, \ l_1 = l_2$$

$$\therefore \quad Q_1^2 = \left(\frac{d_1}{d_2}\right)^5 \cdot Q_2^2 = \left(\frac{0.15}{0.3}\right)^5 Q_2^2$$

$$\therefore \quad Q_1 = 0.1768 \, Q_2$$

But $Q_1 + Q_2 = Q = 0.1 \text{ m}^3/\text{s}$

$$\therefore \quad 0.1768 \, Q_2 + Q_2 = 0.1$$

$$\therefore \quad Q_2 = \frac{0.1}{1.1768}$$

$$\boxed{Q_2 = 0.08498 \text{ m}^3/\text{s}}$$

$$Q_1 = 0.1 - 0.08498 = 0.01502 \text{ m}^3/\text{s}$$

$$\therefore \quad \boxed{Q_1 = 15.02 \text{ l.p.s.}, \ Q_2 = 84.98 \text{ l.p.s.}}$$

(ii) When the same pipes are connected in series water level difference between the tanks

= Total loss of head in the two pipes.

or $\quad H = h_{f_1} + h_{f_2} \quad$ neglecting minor losses

or $\quad H = \dfrac{f_1 l_1 Q_1^2}{12.1 \, d_1^5} + \dfrac{f_2 l_2 Q_2^2}{12.1 \, d_2^5}$

but $f_1 = f_2, \ l_1 = l_2$ and $Q = 0.1 \text{ m}^3/\text{s}$

$$\therefore \quad H = \frac{f_1 l_1 Q^2}{12.1}\left[\frac{1}{d_1^5} + \frac{1}{d_2^5}\right]$$

$$= \frac{0.02 \times 250 \times (0.1)^2}{12.1}\left[\frac{1}{(0.15)^2} - \frac{1}{(0.3)^5}\right]$$

$$= 56.11 \text{ m}$$

$$\therefore \quad \boxed{\text{Water level difference} = 56.11 \text{ m}}$$

### Example 4.15:

Following details refer to system of three pipes connected in parallel. Calculate total discharge through all the pipes if the discharge through pipe 1 is 150 lit/sec.

| Pipe | L (m) | D (mm) | f |
|---|---|---|---|
| 1 | 300 | 250 | 0.02 |
| 2 | 250 | 200 | 0.025 |
| 3 | 450 | 150 | 0.03 |

## Solution:

For pipes in parallel, friction loss across each pipe is same.

∴ $\quad h_{f_1} = h_{f_2} = h_{f_3}$

$$\frac{f_1 L_1 Q_1^2}{12.1\, D_1^5} = \frac{f_2 L_2 Q_2^2}{12.1\, D_2^5} = \frac{f_3 L_3 Q_3^2}{12.1\, D_3^5}$$

∴ $\quad \dfrac{0.02 \times 300 \times (0.15)^2}{(0.25)^5} = \dfrac{0.025 \times 250 \times Q_2^2}{(0.2)^5} = \dfrac{0.03 \times 450 \times Q_3^2}{(0.15)^5}$

Solving $\quad Q_2 = 0.0841$ m³/s

$\quad\quad\quad Q_3 = 0.0279$ m³/s

∴ $\quad Q = Q_1 + Q_2 + Q_3 = 0.15 + 0.0841 + 0.0279 = 0.262$ m³/s

∴ **Discharge through all pipes $Q = 0.262$ m³/s**

## Example 4.16:

An Indian farmer wishes to connect two pipes of different lengths and diameters to a common header supplied with 0.006 m³/s of water from a pump. One pipe is 200 m long and 10 cm in diameter. The other pipe is 800 m long. Determine the diameter of the second pipe such that both pipes have same discharge. Assume that the both pipes are laid down on ground and friction coefficient for both pipes is 0.025. Also determine the head loss in metres of water in the pipes.

### Solution:

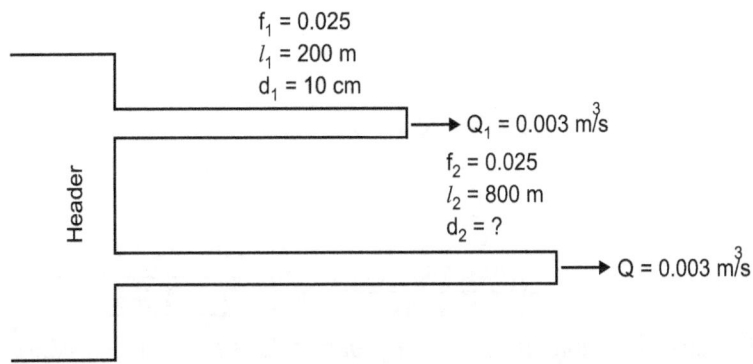

Fig. 4.24

For pipes in parallel, loss of head in each pipe is same

∴ $\quad h_{f_1} = h_{f_2}$

∴ $\quad \dfrac{f_1 l_1 Q_1^2}{12.1 \times d_1^5} = \dfrac{f_2 l_2 Q_2^2}{12.1 \times d_2^5} \quad$ but $\quad \begin{array}{l} f_1 = f_2 \\ Q_1 = Q_2 \end{array}$

∴ $\quad \dfrac{l_1}{d_1^5} = \dfrac{l_2}{d_2^5}$

$$\therefore \quad \frac{200}{(0.1)^5} = \frac{800}{d_2^5}$$

$$\therefore \quad d_2^5 = \frac{800}{200}(0.1)^5$$

$$\therefore \quad d_2^5 = 4 \times (0.1)^5$$

$$\therefore \quad d_2 = 0.13195$$

or $\quad d_2 = 13.195$ cm

**Diameter of second pipe = 13.195 cm**

Loss of head in each pipe is same

$$h_{f_1} = \frac{0.025 \times 200 \times (0.003)^2}{12.1 \times (0.1)^5} = 0.372 \text{ m}$$

$$h_{f_2} = \frac{0.025 \times 800 \times (0.003)^2}{12.1 \times (0.13195)^5} = 0.372 \text{ m}$$

**Headloss in each pipe = 0.372 m**

### Example 4.17:

A pipe line of 0.6 m diameter is 1.5 km long. In order to augment the discharge another pipe-line of same diameter is introduced parallel to the first in the second half of the length. Neglecting minor losses, find the increase in discharge if the friction factor f = 0.04 and the head at inlet 30 m.

**Solution:**

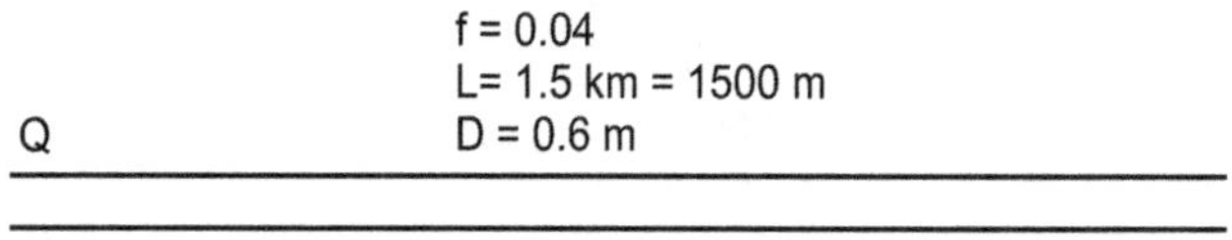

$f = 0.04$
$L = 1.5$ km $= 1500$ m
$D = 0.6$ m

Fig. 4.25

**Case I:** When there is only one pipe

$$h_f = \frac{fLQ^2}{12.1 \, D^5}$$

$$\therefore \quad 30 = \frac{0.04 \times 1500 \times Q^2}{12.1 \times (0.6)^5} \quad \therefore \quad \boxed{Q = 0.686 \text{ m}^3/\text{s}}$$

**Case II:** Pipe line with additional pipe line in parallel is as shown in Fig. 4.26.

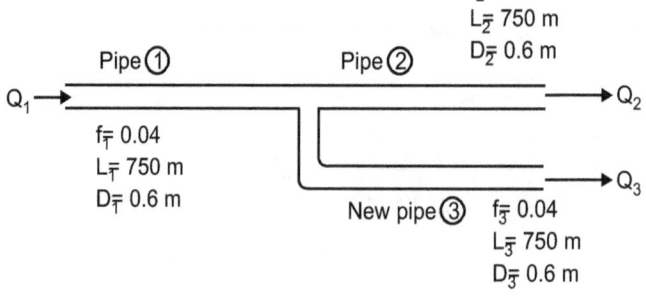

Fig. 4.26

Now, we have $Q_1 = Q_2 + Q_3$

Further for parallel pipes 2 and 3

$$h_{f_2} = h_{f_3}$$

$$\therefore \frac{f_2 L_2 Q_2^2}{12.1 \, D_2^5} = \frac{f_3 L_3 Q_3^2}{12.1 \, D_3^5} \quad f_2 = f_3, \, L_2 = L_3, \, D_2 = D_3$$

$\therefore \quad Q_2 = Q_3$, pipes 2 and 3 will carry equal discharges.

$\therefore \quad Q_1 = Q_2 + Q_3 = 2 Q_2$

Now, going via pipe 1 and pipe 2

$$30 = h_{f_1} + h_{f_2} = \frac{f_1 L_1 Q_1^2}{12.1 \, D_1^5} + \frac{f_2 L_2 Q_2^2}{12.1 \, D_2^5}$$

$$= \frac{0.04 \times 750 \times Q_1^2}{12.1 \times (0.6)^5} + \frac{0.04 \times 750 \times \left(\frac{Q_1}{2}\right)^2}{12.1 \times (0.6)^5}$$

$\therefore \quad \boxed{Q_1 = 0.868 \text{ m}^3/\text{s}}$

$\therefore \quad$ Increase in discharge $= Q_1 - Q$

$= 0.868 - 0.686$

$= 0.182 \text{ m}^3/\text{s}$

$\boxed{\text{Increase in discharge} = 0.182 \text{ m}^3/\text{s or 182 l.p.s.}}$

### Example 4.18:

The difference in levels between the catchment reservoir and the service reservoir of a town supply is 160 m and the distance between them is 50 km. The reservoirs were originally connected by a single pipe designed to carry 260 lit/s. It was later found necessary to increase the flow to 375 lit/s and it was decided to lay another pipe of 500 mm diameter along side the first over part of the length, the two pipes being cross connected. Calculate diameter of the original pipe and the length of the second pipe. Take $f = 0.028$ for all pipes. Neglect minor losses.

### Solution:

**Case I:** When there is only one pipe we have

$$160 = \frac{fLQ^2}{12.1 \, D^5}$$

$$= \frac{0.028 \times 50000 \times (0.26)^2}{12.1 \, D^5}$$

$\therefore \quad \boxed{\text{Diameter of original pipe} = D = 0.547 \text{ m}}$

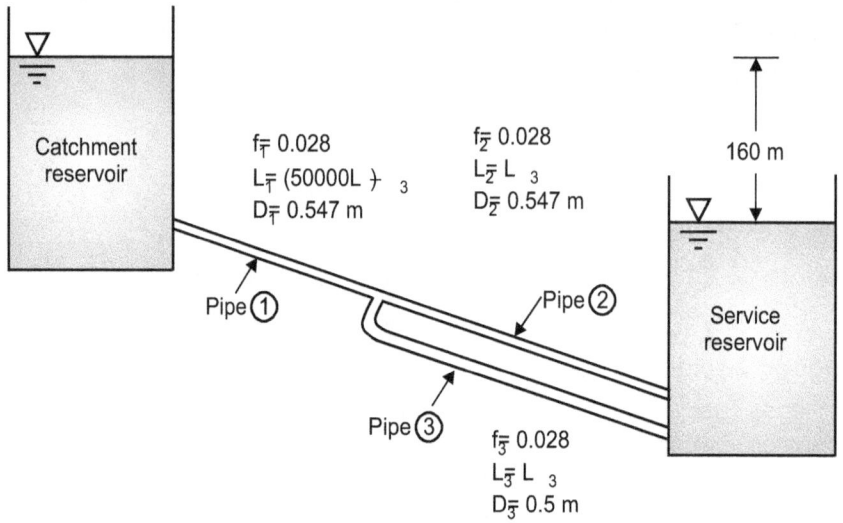

**Fig. 4.27**

**Case II:** Total discharge = 0.375 m³/s = $Q_1$

Now for parallel pipes 2 and 3

$$h_{f_2} = h_{f_3}$$

∴ $$\frac{f_2 L_2 Q_2^2}{12.1\, D_2^5} = \frac{f_3 L_3 Q_3^2}{12.1\, D_3^5} \quad \text{where } f_2 = f_3, \text{ and } L_2 = L_3$$

∴ $Q_2 = 1.252\, Q_3$

∴ $Q_1 = Q_2 + Q_3 = 1.252\, Q_3 + Q_3 = 2.252\, Q_3$

∴ $0.375 = 2.252\, Q_3$

∴ $\boxed{Q_3 = 0.167 \text{ m}^3/\text{s} \quad \text{and} \quad Q_2 = 0.208 \text{ m}^3/\text{s}}$

Loss of head along pipes 1 and 2 or along 1 and 3 must be same.

∴ $160 = h_{f_1} + h_{f_3}$

∴ $$160 = \frac{f_1 L_1 Q_1^2}{12.1\, D_1^5} + \frac{f_3 L_3 Q_3^2}{12.1\, D_3^5}$$

$$= \frac{0.028\, (50000 - L_3)\, (0.375)^2}{12.1 \times (0.547)^5} + \frac{0.028 \times L_3 \times (0.167)^2}{12.1 \times (0.5)^5}$$

$69142.86 = 2.872\,(50000 - L_3) + 0.892\, L_3$

∴ $69142.86 = 143600 - 2.872\, L_3 + 0.892\, L_3$

∴ $1.98\, L_3 = 74457.14$

$\boxed{\text{Length of new pipe, } L_3 = 37.6 \text{ km.}}$

# Example 4.19:

Two reservoirs containing water have difference of levels of 70 m, and are connected by a 250 mm diameter pipe which is 4 km long. The pipe is tapped midway between reservoirs and water is drawn at rate of 0.04 m³/sec. Assuming friction factor = 0.04, determine rate at which water enters in the lower reservoir.

**Solution:**

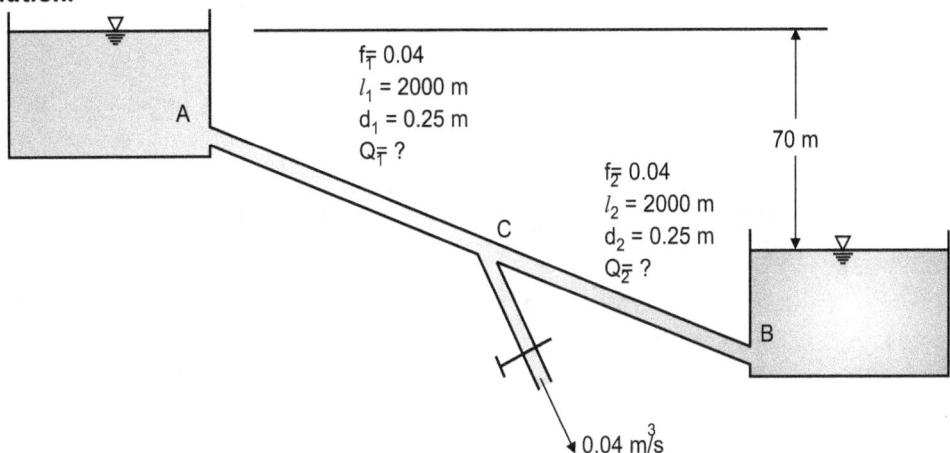

Fig. 4.28

Let  $Q_1$ = discharge through pipe AC
     $Q_2$ = discharge through pipe CB

It can be observed that
$$Q_1 = Q_2 + 0.04$$

Now sum of the loss of head in AC and CB
$$h_{f_{AC}} + h_{f_{CB}} = 70 \text{ m}$$

or
$$\frac{f_1 l_1 Q_1^2}{12.1\, d_1^5} + \frac{f_2 l_2 Q_2^2}{12.1\, d_2^5} = 70 \qquad \begin{array}{l} f_1 = f_2 = 0.04 \\ l_1 = l_2 = 2000 \text{ m} \\ d_1 = d_2 = 0.25 \text{ m} \end{array}$$

$$\therefore \quad \frac{0.04 \times 2000}{12.1 \times (0.25)^5}\left[Q_1^2 + Q_2^2\right] = 70$$

$$\therefore \quad Q_1^2 + Q_2^2 = \frac{70 \times 12.1 \times (0.25)^5}{0.04 \times 2000}$$

$$\therefore \quad Q_1^2 + Q_2^2 = 0.0103$$

but $\quad Q_1 = Q_2 + 0.04$

$$\therefore \quad (Q_2 + 0.04)^2 + Q_2^2 = 0.0103$$

$$\therefore \quad (Q_2^2 + 0.08\, Q_2 + 1.6 \times 10^{-3}) + Q_2^2 = 0.0103$$

$$\therefore \quad 2Q_2^2 + 0.08\, Q_2 - 0.0087 = 0$$

or

$$Q_2^2 + 0.04\, Q_2 - 0.00435 = 0$$

$$\therefore \quad Q_2 = \frac{-0.04 + \sqrt{(0.04)^2 - 4 \times 1 \times (-0.00435)}}{2}$$

$$\therefore \quad Q_2 = \frac{-0.04 + 0.1378}{2} \qquad \text{neglecting} - \text{ve sign}$$

$$\therefore \quad Q_2 = 0.049\ \text{m}^3/\text{s}$$

$\therefore$ **Rate at which water enters the lower reservoir = 0.049 m³/s**

## Example 4.20:

The water levels in the two reservoirs 'A' and 'B' are 104.5 m and 100 m respectively above the datum. A pipe joins each to a common point 'D' where pressure is 98.1 kN/m² gauge and height is 83.5 m above datum. Another pipe connects 'D' to another tank 'C'. What will be the height of water level in 'C' assuming same value of f for all pipes. Take friction co-efficient = 0.03. The diameters of the pipes AD, BD and CD are 300 mm, 450 mm, 600 mm respectively and their lengths are 240 m, 270 m, 300 m respectively. The arrangement is as shown in Fig. 4.29.

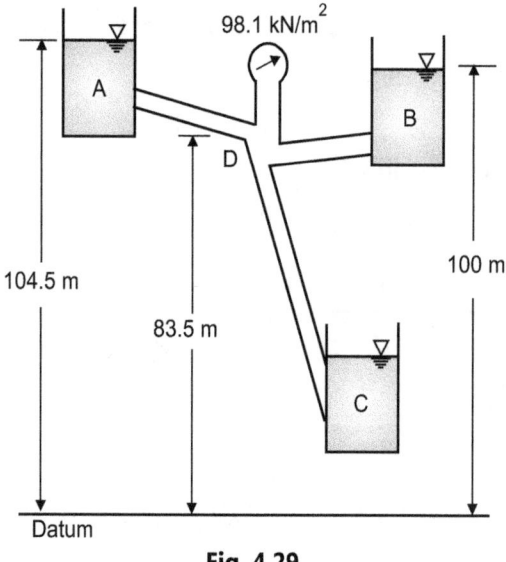

Fig. 4.29

### Solution:

Pressure head at point D is $\dfrac{98.1}{9.81} = 10$ m of water. Thus, it is as if having an imaginary 4th reservoir with free water surface at 93.5 m above datum.

## (i) Discharge through AD:

Head loss between A and D = Difference in the level of water between A and D

∴ Taking into account only major loss due to friction

$$104.5 - 93.5 = \frac{fLQ^2}{12.1\, D^5}$$

$$\therefore \quad 11 = \frac{0.03 \times 240 \times Q^2}{12.1 \times (0.3)^5}$$

∴ $\boxed{Q_{AD} = 0.21 \text{ m}^3/\text{s}}$

## (ii) Discharge through BD:

Since water level in reservoir B (100 m) is higher than that at D (93.5 m), flow is from B to D.

$$\therefore \quad 100 - 93.5 = \frac{fLQ^2}{12.5 \times D^5}$$

$$\therefore \quad 6.5 = \frac{0.03 \times 270 \times Q^2}{12.1 \times (0.45)^5}$$

∴ $\boxed{Q_{BD} = 0.42 \text{ m}^3/\text{s}}$

## (iii) Height of water level in reservoir C:

Now $\quad Q_{DC} = Q_{AD} + Q_{BD}$

∴ $\quad Q_{DC} = 0.21 + 0.42 = 0.63 \text{ m}^3/\text{s}$

∴ Loss of head due to friction in DC

$$h_{f_{DC}} = \frac{fLQ^2}{12.1 \times D^5}$$

$$= \frac{0.03 \times 300 \times (0.63)^2}{12.1 \times (0.6)^5}$$

∴ $\boxed{h_{f_{DC}} = 3.79 \text{ m}}$

∴ Water level in reservoir C

$$= 93.5 - 3.79$$
$$= 89.71 \text{ m}$$

∴ $\boxed{\text{Height of water level in reservoir C} = 89.71 \text{ m}}$

### Example 4.21:

Power is transmitted hydraulically through 100 mm diameter horizontal pipes for a distance of 4.8 km. If a pressure of 70 bar is maintained at the far end of the pipe, find the minimum number of pipes required to ensure an efficiency of transmission of 90 %, when the power delivered is 115 kW. Take $f = 0.028$.

## Solution:

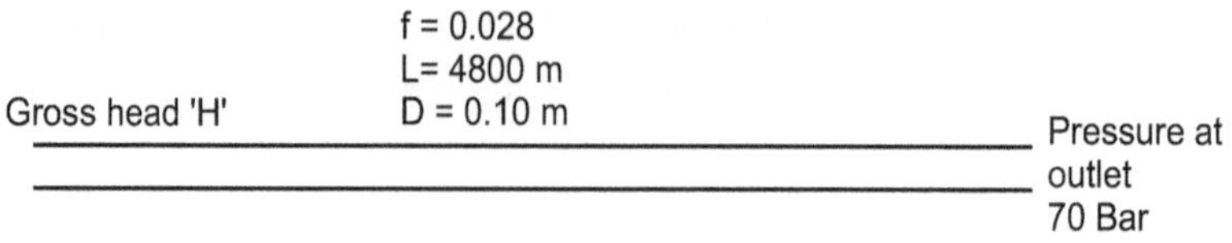

```
                    f = 0.028
                    L = 4800 m
     Gross head 'H'  D = 0.10 m
                                                    Pressure at
                                                    outlet
                                                    70 Bar
```

Fig. 4.30

$$\text{Pressure head at outlet} = \frac{70 \times 10^5}{9810} = 713.558 \text{ m of water}$$

$$\text{Efficiency of transmission} = 0.9 = \frac{H - h_f}{H}, \quad H - \text{Gross head at inlet of pipe}$$

∴ But  $H - h_f = 713.558$ m

∴ $H = \dfrac{713.558}{0.9} = 792.842$ m of water

∴ $h_f = 792.842 - 713.558 = 79.284$ m (for each pipe)

But loss of head in the pipe is

$$h_f = \frac{fLQ^2}{12.1 \, D^5} = 79.284$$

∴ $79.284 = \dfrac{0.028 \times 4800 \times Q^2}{12.1 \times (0.1)^5}$

$Q = 8.449 \times 10^{-3}$ m³/s (through each pipe)

Now, power delivered by each pipe is

$$P = \gamma \cdot Q \cdot (H - h_f) = 9.81 \times 8.449 \times 10^{-3} \times 713.558$$

∴ Power delivered by each pipe = 59.143 kW

∴ Number of pipes = $\dfrac{\text{Total power to be delivered}}{\text{Power delivered by one pipe}}$

$$= \frac{115}{59.143} = 1.944$$

∴ **Number of pipes required = 2 pipes.**

Alternatively,

∴ Total power = 115 kW
$= 9.81 \times Q \times 713.558$

∴ Total discharge required = 0.01643 m³/s

∴ Number of pipes required = $\dfrac{\text{Total discharge required}}{\text{Discharge through each pipe}}$

$$= \frac{0.01643}{8.449 \times 10^{-3}}$$

$= 1.944,$  use 2 pipes.

## Example 4.22:

Power is to be transmitted through 300 mm diameter, 500 m long pipe fitted with a nozzle at the end. The inlet is from a reservoir where water level is 90 m above the nozzle. Calculate the maximum power which can be transmitted and the diameter of nozzle required. Take $f = 0.03$.

### Solution:

For maximum power transmission

$$h_f = \frac{1}{3}H = \frac{1}{3} \times 90 = 30 \text{ m}$$

$$\therefore \quad 30 = \frac{fLQ^2}{12.1\, D^5} = \frac{0.03 \times 500}{12.1 \times (0.3)^5} \times Q^2$$

$$\therefore \quad Q = 0.2425 \text{ m}^3/\text{s}$$

$\therefore$ Max. power transmitted $P_{max} = \gamma \cdot Q \cdot (H - h_f)$

$$= 9.81 \times 0.2425 \times 60$$

$$\boxed{P_{max} = 142.74 \text{ kW}}$$

Diameter of the nozzle

$$d = \sqrt[4]{\frac{D^5}{2fL}} = \sqrt[4]{\frac{(0.3)^5}{2 \times 0.03 \times 500}}$$

$$= 0.0949 \text{ m}$$

$\therefore$ $\boxed{\text{Diameter of nozzle} = 9.5 \text{ cm}}$

Alternatively,

$$Q = a \cdot v \quad \text{but } H - h_f = \frac{v^2}{2g}$$

$$\therefore \quad v = \sqrt{60 \times 19.62} = 34.31 \text{ m/s}$$

$$\therefore \quad \text{Area of nozzle 'a'} = \frac{0.2425}{34.31} = 7.07 \times 10^{-3} \text{ m}^2$$

$\therefore$ Diameter of nozzle $= 0.0949$ m
$\therefore$ Diameter of nozzle $= 9.5$ cm.

## THEORETICAL QUESTIONS

1. What do you understand by a pipe?
2. Describe Reynold's experiment and state the significance of Reynold's Number.
3. What are the different losses taken into account in pipe flow problems and write expression for computing them.
4. Define the terms major energy losses and minor energy losses in pipe.
5. Derive Darcy - Weisbach equation for friction loss.
6. Derive Darcy-Weisbach expression for friction head loss in a pipe flow. Explain how friction factor varies with type of flow?
7. Derive an expression for the loss of head due to sudden enlargement in pipe flow.

8. What is loss due to sudden contraction? Why does it take place? Derive an expression for the same.
9. What is an equivalent pipe.
10. What is 'equivalent length of pipe for a minor loss? How is it obtained? What is the advantage of expressing minor losses in terms of their equivalent lengths?
11. What do you mean by Hydraulic Gradient line and Energy Gradient line?
12. What do you understand by pipes in series or a compound pipe? What are the characteristics of pipes in series?
13. Explain the concept of 'equivalent pipe' and derive Dupit's equation in the following form

$$\frac{L}{D^5} = \frac{L_1}{D_1^5} + \frac{L_2}{D_2^5} + \frac{L_3}{D_3^5} + \ldots$$

14. What do you understand by 'pipes in parallel'? What are the characteristics of pipes in parallel? Why are pipes used in parallel? How is the 'equivalent pipe' for a set of parallel pipes related with them?
15. What is a siphon? Where is it used? Explain its working.
16. Derive an expression for power transmission through the pipes.
17. Show that power transmitted through pipe is maximum when the head lost due to friction is equal to $\frac{1}{3}$ of total supply head.
18. Show that for maximum transmission of power through a pipe line, the ratio of area of pipe and that of the nozzle is given by

$$\frac{A}{a} = \sqrt{\frac{2fL}{D}}$$

where  A = Area of cross section of pipe connected to the reservoir
 a = Area of cross section of nozzle connected to the pipe at the end
 f = Friction factor
 L = Length of pipe
 D = Diameter of pipe

19. Prove that corresponding to the maximum power transmission through a pipe, the power transmission efficiency is 66.67%.
20. Derive an expression for nozzle diameter for maximum power transmission.
21. What is water hammer phenomenon?
22. Write a note on water hammer.
23. Explain water hammer. State its significance in fluid mechanics studies.
24. Explain the phenomenon of water hammer giving details of pressure cycle and the related sketch.

## NUMERICAL PROBLEMS

1. A 150 mm diameter pipe is attached to a 100 mm diameter pipe. If the loss of head in sudden expansion is 0.23 m, find the discharge through the pipe. Draw total energy line and hydraulic grade line or sudden expansion.

   What will be the equivalent length of 100 mm diameter pipe of this fitting, if the friction factor 'f' = 0.022?

   **(Ans. 0.03 m³/s, 1.4 m)**

2. The rate of flow of water through a horizontal pipe is 0.25 m³/s. The diameter of the pipe which is 0.2 m is suddenly enlarged to 0.4 m. The pressure intensity in the smaller pipe is $11.772 \times 10^4$ N/m².

   Determine:
   (i) Loss of head due to sudden enlargement
   (ii) Pressure intensity in the large pipe, and
   (iii) Power lost due to enlargement.

   **[Ans. 1.817 m, $12.96 \times 10^4$ N/m², 4.456 kW]**

3. A pipeline 0.225 m in diameter and 1580 m long has a slope of 1 in 200 for the first 790 m and 1 in 100 for the next 790 m. The pressure at the upper end of the pipeline is 107.91 kPa and at the lower end is 53.955 kPa. Determine the discharge through the pipe. Take f = 0.032.

   **[Hint:** Draw the sketch. Taking horizontal through lower end of the pipe line, we can write
   Total head at the upper end

   $$Z_1 + \frac{p_1}{\gamma} + \frac{V_1^2}{2g} = 11.85 + \frac{107.91 \times 10^3}{9810} + \frac{V_1^2}{2g}$$

   ∴ Total head at upper end $= \left(11.85 + 11 + \frac{V_1^2}{2g}\right)$ ... (i)

   Total head at lower end $= 0 + \frac{53.955 \times 10^3}{9810} + \frac{V_2^2}{2g}$

   Total head at lower end $= \left(5.5 + \frac{V_2^2}{2g}\right)$ ... (ii)

   Since $V_1 = V_2$, equations (i) and (ii) show that flow is from upper end to lower end.

   ∴ $Z_1 + \frac{p_1}{\gamma} + \frac{V_1^2}{2g} = Z_2 + \frac{p_2}{\gamma} + \frac{V_2^2}{2g}$ + friction loss in the pipe etc.]

   **[Ans. 0.0489 m³/s]**

4. A compound piping system consists of 1800 m of 500 mm diameter, 1200 m of 400 mm diameter and 600 m of 300 mm diameter. Convert the system to an equivalent length of 400 mm diameter pipe. Obtain an equivalent size pipe of 3600 m long.

   **(Ans. 4318.23 m, 0.385 m)**

5. A pipe of 200 mm diameter is 60 m long and carries a discharge of 100 l.p.s. Find the power lost in friction. Take Darcy–Weisbach friction factor = 0.04.

   If the central 40 m length is replaced by pipe of 300 mm diameter, the changes of sections being sudden, what will be saving in power due to this adaptation?

   **[Hint:** Find out $h_f$ = 6.198 m, power = $\gamma Q h_f$ = 6080.57 watts.

   In the second case $h_f = h_{f_1} + h_{f_2} + h_{f_3}$ = 2.61 m and Power = 2560.41 watts

   ∴ Saving of power = 3520.16 watts]

   **(Ans. 3520.16 watts)**

6. Water is to be supplied to a small town at the rate of 800 m³ per day in 8 hours of pumping. Town is 3 km away from the river where two pumps, each of 80 kW are installed. The service reservoir is 30 m higher than river water elevation. Find the suitable diameter of the pipe to be laid. Assume friction factor for pipe f = 0.2.

   **[Hint:** From power 8 kW, find out head supplied by pump by formula, Power = $\gamma Q H_p$.

   $H_p$ = 293.343 m. Then apply B. T. to river surface and water surface in the reservoir. Get $h_f$ from which get value of D. $H_f$ = 263.343 m]

   **(Ans. 0.1708 m)**

7. Water is to be supplied to the inhabitants of a college hostel through a supply main. The following data are given:

   Distance of the reservoir from the hostel = 4000 m

   Number of inhabitants = 3000

   Consumption of water per day of each inhabitant = 180 ltrs.

   Loss of head due to friction = 18 m

   Coefficient of friction for the pipe f = 0.007

   If half of the daily supply is pumped in 8 hrs, determine the size of the supply main.

   **[Hint:** Daily supply = 3000 × 0.18 = 540 m³, Supply in 8 hrs. = 270 m³

   ∴ $Q = \dfrac{270}{8 \times 3600} = 9.375 \times 10^{-3}$ m³/s, $h_f = 18 = \dfrac{fLQ^2}{12.1 D^5}$

Since the value of f = 0.007 is very low, the friction factor is taken as four times the given value i.e. it is taken as 0.028 and the example is solved]

**[Ans. 0.135 m]**

8. A 425 mm diameter pipe having 800 m length conveys water from high level tank to a point 22 m below water level in the tank. Calculate the percentage error committed in the calculation of discharge by neglecting the minor energy losses. Take f = 0.03.

   **[Hint:** Calculate discharge with all losses $22 = 0.5\dfrac{V^2}{2g} + \dfrac{fl}{d}\cdot\dfrac{V^2}{2g} + \dfrac{V^2}{2g}$

   V = 2.729 m/s, Q = 0.387 m³/s, without minor losses Q = 0.392 etc.]

   **(Ans. 1.29%)**

9. Two reservoirs, whose water levels differ by 20 m are connected with a compound pipe line consisting of three pipes in series. Pipe of 200 mm diameter is connected to upper reservoir and pipe of 300 mm diameter is connected to lower reservoir. Middle pipe is 150 mm diameter. All pipes are 100 m long with friction factors 0.023, 0.024 and 0.025 respectively. Considering all losses, find rate of flow of water and velocity in each pipe.

   **(Ans. 74.93 m³/s, 2.3857 m/s, 4.24 m/s, 1.06 m/s)**

10. Cross-section of a pipe carrying a given discharge is suddenly enlarged. What should be the ratio of diameters of the two sections of the pipe if the magnitude of the loss of head at the change of cross-section is same irrespective of direction of flow? $C_C$ = 0.66.

    **(Ans. 0.696)**

11. Two reservoirs having a difference in elevation of 15 m are connected by a 200 mm diameter syphon. The length of syphon is 400 m and the summit is 3 m above the water level in the upper reservoir. The length of pipe from upper reservoir to summit is 120 m. If coefficient of friction is 0.02, determine (neglect minor losses):
    (i) Discharge through syphon
    (ii) Pressure at the summit

    **[Ans. 0.0852 m³/s, –7.873 m]**

12. A siphon of diameter 200 mm connects two reservoirs having difference of elevation of 15 m. The total length of the siphon is 600 m and the summit is 4 m above the water level in the upper reservoir. If the separation takes place at 2.8 m of water (abs), find the maximum length of siphon from upper reservoir to the summit. Take friction factor = 0.016, atmospheric pressure = 10.3 m of water. Neglect minor losses.

    **[Hint:** Applying B. T. to upper surface level and summit, neglecting minor losses. $1.5\dfrac{V^2}{2g}$,

    $\therefore \quad 10.3 = 4 + 2.8 + \dfrac{15}{600} \times L_1, L_1 = 140\text{ m}]$

    **(Ans. 140 m)**

13. A pipe 300 mm in diameter and 1200 m long connects two reservoirs whose water surface elevations differ by 20 m. The pipe has to pass a hillock whose top is 5 m above the water surface in the upper reservoir. What should be the minimum depth of the pipe below the top of the hillock if the separation takes place at a pressure of 2.5 m of water head absolute? The length of the pipe from the upper reservoir to the top of the hillock is 300 m. Assume the friction factor f = 0.025 and the atmospheric pressure as 11.3 m of water head. Also compute the discharge through the pipe.

    **(Ans.** 2.42 m, 0.139 m$^3$/s)

14. Water from the drainage gallery of a dam under construction is to be siphoned to the downstream of the dam by means of pipe 100 mm diameter. The length of the pipe line upto summit is 30 m and the total length of the pipe is 80 m. The pipe discharges freely into the atmosphere and the downstream end is 15 m below the water surface level in the gallery. Assume f = 0.03.

    (i) What is the maximum permissible height of the summit above the water level in the gallery? Separation occurs at the absolute pressure head of 2.44 m of water.

    (ii) If the total quantity of water required to be discharged is 80 litres/sec., how many pipes are required.

    Assume atmospheric pressure head as 10 m of water.

    **(Ans.** 1.386 m, 3 pipes)

15. Three pipes of diameter d, 2d and 2d of same length and same friction factor are laid in parallel between two points. If total discharge is 20 m$^3$/s, calculate discharge through each pipe. Neglect minor losses.

    **(Ans.** 1.624 m$^3$/s, 9.188 m$^3$/s, 9.188 m$^3$/s]

16. A reservoir 'A' supplies water to reservoir 'B' by a uniform long pipe line. It is proposed to increase the supply to reservoir 'B' by 50 % by laying an additional pipe line along side the existing one of the same diameter and same frictional resistance and connecting it's lower end to reservoir 'B' and cross connecting it's upper end to the existing pipe line. Calculate the length of new pipe line in comparison with the old one.

    **[Hint:** Take new discharge $Q_1$ = 1.5 Q, $Q_2$ = $Q_3$ = 0.75 Q]

    **(Ans.** 74 %)

17. An existing 300 mm diameter pipeline of 3200 m length connects two reservoirs with 13 m difference in their water levels. Calculate the discharge $Q_1$. If a parallel pipe of 300 mm diameter is attached to last 1600 m length of existing pipeline, find the new discharge $Q_2$. Take only wall friction into account. Take f = friction factor = 0.04 m Darcy-Weisbach formula.

    **(Ans.** 0.0546 m$^3$/s, 0.0691 m$^3$/s)

18. A 150 mm diameter pipe, 800 m long connects two reservoirs whose water levels differ by 20 m. If friction factor for the pipe is 0.024, find the discharge through the pipe.

    In order to increase this discharge by 40%, it is proposed to lay another pipe of 200 mm diameter starting from upper reservoir and cross connected to old pipe. Obtain the length of new pipe. Take f = 0.02 for new pipe.

    (**Note:** Location of the parallel pipe does not matter, the problem is not affected. Refer solved example.)

    (**Ans.** 434.558 m)

19. At a sudden enlargement of a water line from 250 mm to 500 mm, the hydraulic gradient rises by 100 mm. Estimate the rate of flow.

    (**Ans.** 35.54 l.p.s.)

20. A 30 km long pipe, 1 m in diameter, supplies power to a machine. The loss of head in the pipe line is 100 m and the machine requires a head of 100 m. Find the efficiency of transmission and the power transmitted. Take f = 0.04.

    (**Ans.** 50%, 981 kW)

21. A 30 cm diameter, 600 m long pipe supplies water to a machine situated 120 m below the reservoir level. Find the diameter of the nozzle for maximum power transmission and the maximum power transmitted. Take f = 0.02.

    (**Ans.** 10 cm, 245.64 kW)

22. Pressure at the inlet of a pipe used for power transmission is 70 BAR and the pressure drop in the pipe is 7 BAR. If the pipe line is 15 km long and power transmitted over the pipe is 75 kW, find the diameter of the pipe and the efficiency of transmission. Take f = 0.025.

    (**Ans.** 90 %, 0.1438 m)

23. In a hydro electric plant, water is supplied to Pelton wheels through a 2 m diameter and 2000 m long pipe at the end of which a horizontal nozzle 20 cm in diameter is attached. The water level in the reservoir stands 200 m above the nozzle level. If the coefficient of friction is 0.04, what will be the power imparted to the wheels? Draw the hydraulic gradient.

    (**Ans.** 3838.63 kW)

24. A pipe of diameter 500 mm and length 5000 m is used for the transmission of power by water. The total head at inlet of pipe is 500 m. Find the maximum power available at outlet of pipe. Take f = 0.004.

    [**Hint:** Refer example 9.21]

    (**Ans.** 5804.58 kW)

25. A 3000 m long 30 cm diameter pipe with frictional coefficient f = 0.032 is to be used for power transmission. What should be the diameter of the nozzle to be fitted at the end of the pipeline for maximum power transmission? Prove the formula.

**(Ans.** 5.97 cm, Formula $d = \sqrt[4]{\dfrac{D^5}{2fL}}$

where d = diameter of nozzle and D and L the diameter and length of pipe)

# Unit 5

# CENTRIFUGAL AND RECIPROCATING PUMP

## (A) CENTRIFUGAL PUMP

## 5.1 Centrifugal Pumps

Centrifugal pumps are rotodynamic pumps. The wheel which converts mechanical energy into hydraulic energy is called as an *'impeller'*. The energy added by the impeller to the liquid is largely due to centrifugal effects and hence the pump is called *'Centrifugal pump'*.

## 5.2 Components of a Centrifugal Pump

A centrifugal pump has the main components as described below. They have been shown in Fig. 5.1

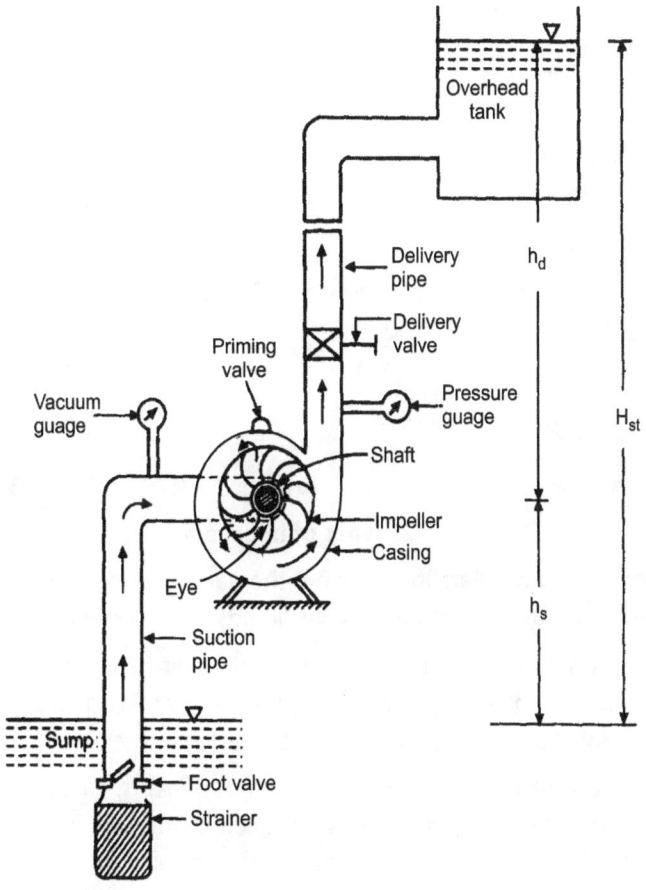

**Fig. 5.1: Components of a centrifugal pump**

1. **Impeller:** The rotating wheel of the centrifugal pump is known as impeller. It is fitted with specially designed vanes on it's periphery (similar to the rotor of a reaction turbine). The impeller is fitted on the shaft which is rotated by a diesel engine or generally an electric motor. Impeller is responsible for imparting the centrifugal head to the liquid.

The impeller may be (i) Closed type, (ii) Semi-open type or (iii) Open type of impeller. [Fig. 5.2.]

(i) **Closed type impeller:** When the vanes of the impeller are covered by plates or discs known as shroudes on both sides, it is called closed impeller. It is more efficient since it can guide the liquid in better manner. However, this impeller can be used only for clean liquids free from debris. Otherwise, there is possibility of clogging. It can be used for liquids of low viscosity e.g. water, chemicals, milk etc. Material used for impeller depends upon the liquid to be handled. For example, for non-corrosive liquids cast iron, for corrosive liquids stainless steel or gun metal, for water above 140°C, cast steel, and stainless steel for milk industry are used. [Fig. 5.2 (a)]

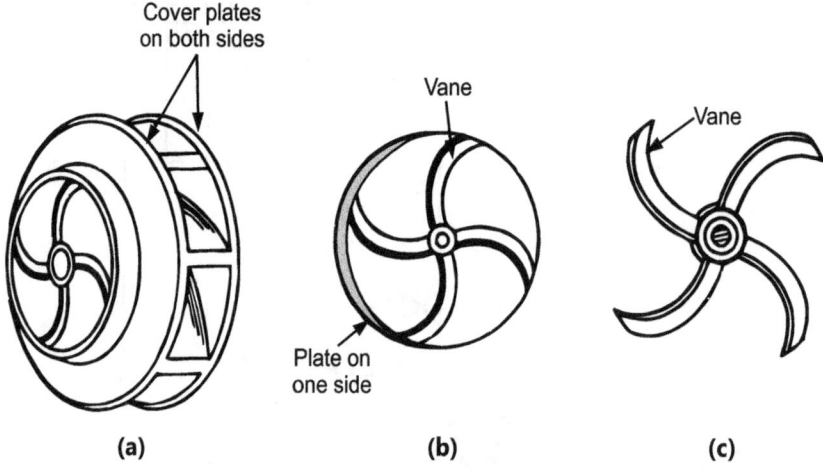

**Fig. 5.2: Types of impellers**

(ii) **Semi-open type impeller:** In this type, the vanes are covered by disc or shroud only on one side. It can be used to handle viscous liquids with some debris. [Fig. 5.2 (b)]

(iii) **Open type impeller:** It is an impeller without cover plate or shroude on both the sides. Such an impeller can be used for pumping liquids containing solid matter e.g. paper pulp, sewage water, water containing silt, clay, sand etc. [Fig. 5.2 (c)]

2. **Casing of the pump:** The impeller of the centrifugal is surrounded by an airtight passage called *'casing'*. The casing of pump is designed in such a way that large part of the kinetic energy of liquid discharged at the outlet of the impeller is converted into pressure energy before it enters the delivery pipe.

3. **Suction pipe:** It is a pipe whose one end is connected to the central inlet of the pump (which is known as **'eye'**) and the other end dips into the sump. There should be no leakage in this pipe. Usually diameter of the pipe is large so as to minimise the losses due to friction. To minimise the losses further, the pipe is kept short (as far as possible) and bends and elbows are used to minimum extent. If the diameter of pipe is larger than that of the pump at inlet, a small reducer is used between suction pipe and the inlet of the pump.

**Foot valve and strainer:** At the lower submerged end of suction pipe, a foot valve with strainer is fitted. **Strainer** is used to remove debris from the liquid. A foot valve is provided at the submerged end of suction pipe.

**Foot valve** is one-way type valve or non-return valve which opens only in the upward direction (from sump towards the pump). It is used to prevent flow of water to the sump while the pump is primed. Further, when the pump is closed, water in the pump is prevented from going back to sump so that priming is not required everytime the pump is started.

4. **Delivery pipe:** It is the pipe connecting the outlet of the pump and the place of delivery. Generally, a sluice valve is provided in this pipe, very near the outlet of the pump, to control the discharge from the pump. Initially, this valve is closed, the pump is primed and started and then the valve is gradually opened.

## 5.3 Classification of Centrifugal Pumps

Centrifugal pumps are classified according to

1. Type of casing
2. Direction of flow of liquid
3. Number of stages
4. Number of entrances
5. Disposition of shaft
6. Specific speed
7. Working head.

**1. Type of casing:** Depending upon the type of casing, centrifugal pumps are classified as (a) Volute pump, (b) Vortex pump and (c) Diffuser pump.

**(a) Volute pump:** There pumps are fitted with casing in spiral form called volute casing. The area of volute casing gradually increases from tongue towards the delivery pipe as shown in Fig. 5.3.

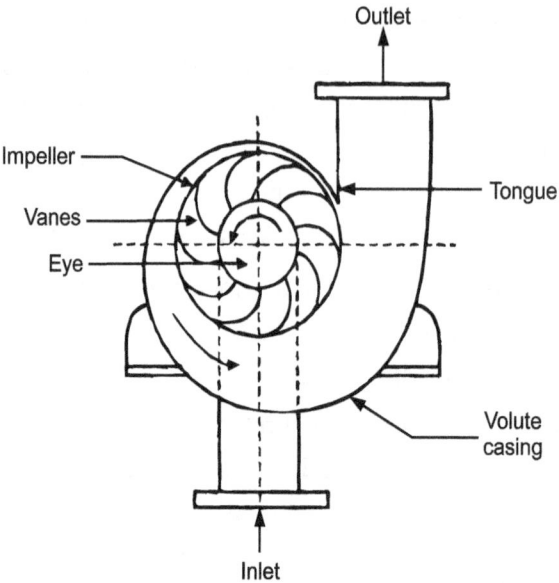

**Fig. 5.3: Volute pump**

The gradual increase in area is provided to accommodate increased flow of liquid towards the delivery pipe without changing the velocity. Further, as water flows from suction towards delivery side, the pressure increases gradually. Due to formation of eddies, heavy losses take place in the casing and the efficiency of pump is not improved much.

**(b) Vortex pump:** Professor James Thomson improved the volute chamber by providing what is called "**Vortex or Whirlpool Chamber**". Vortex chamber is a circular chamber between the impeller and the volute casting as shown in Fig. 5.4. When liquid leaves the impeller, it goes freely in the chamber and a free vortex is formed. As liquid flows radially outwards, due to increase in area, the velocity decreases and the pressure increases.

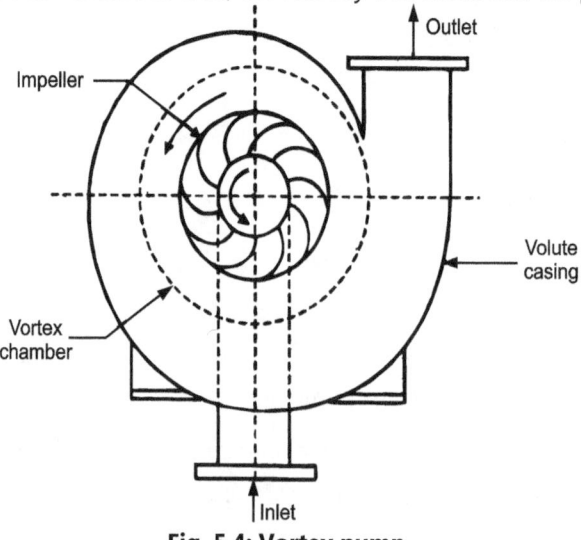

**Fig. 5.4: Vortex pump**

Liquid from the chamber is then discharged in volute casing as usual.

Vortex chamber reduces formation of eddies and hence gives better efficiency as compared to volute casing.

**(c) Diffuser pump:** In this type, the impeller is surrounded by a ring which consists of series of guide vanes [Fig. 5.5.] This ring is called **diffuser ring**. Liquid enters the guide vanes without shock. The adjoining guide vanes provide gradually enlarging passages for flow of liquid. Thus, when liquid passes between the guide vanes of diffuser, the velocity decreases and pressure increases. Guide vanes are designed in such a way that liquid leaves the vanes tangentially. Thus, losses at entry as well as at the exit are minimised. Due to all these factors, the efficiency of this type of pump is very high. These pumps are also called **turbine pumps**.

However, these pumps work efficiently only for one particular discharge at a particular speed. Due to their complex construction, these pumps are more costly as compared to other pumps.

In general, single-stage pumps are provided with volute or vortex casing while multistage pumps are provided with a diffuser ring.

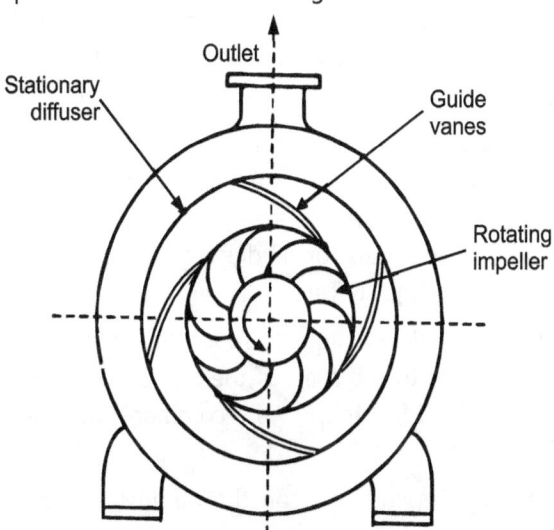

**Fig. 5.5: Diffuser pump or Turbine pump**

2. **Direction of flow of liquid:** As in the case of turbines, depending upon the direction of flow of liquid as it passes through the impeller, pumps can be classified as

(a) Radial flow pumps

(b) Mixed flow pumps

(c) Axial flow pumps.

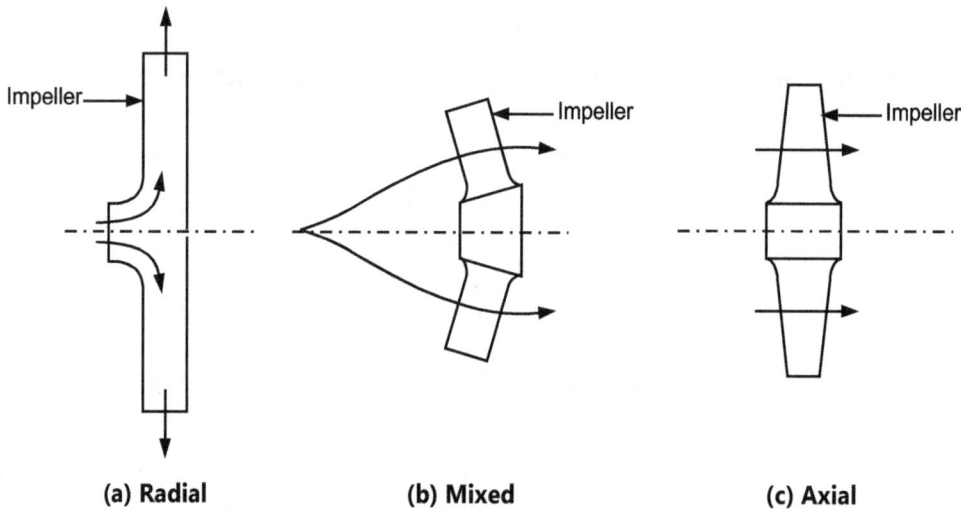

**Fig. 5.6: Types of flow in centrifugal pumps**

**(a) Radial flow pumps:** The direction of flow of liquid when it passes through the impeller is completely in radial direction, perpendicular to the shaft. Outward flow pumps are most commonly used. Due to the difficulty in starting, the inward flow pumps are not in practice. Centrifugal pumps are generally radial flow pumps. These pumps are used for high head and low discharge. [Fig. 5.6 (a)].

**(b) Mixed flow pumps:** The direction of flow of liquid in the impeller of these pumps is axial as well as radial. They are reverse of mixed flow type turbine like Francis turbine. Due to combination of axial and radial flow, the area of flow can be increased to handle more discharge. Mixed flow pumps are used for medium discharge at medium head. These are suitable for irrigation purposes. [Fig. 5.6 (b)].

**(c) Axial flow pumps:** The flow of liquid through the impeller of these pumps is purely along the axial direction parallel to the shaft of the pump. Axial flow pumps are reverse of propeller or Kaplan turbine. Axial flow pumps are commonly used to lift large quantities of liquid at low heads. [Fig. 5.6 (c)].

**3. Number of stages:** Depending upon the number of stages, the pumps can be classified as –

(a) Single-stage pumps

(b) Multistage pumps

**(a) Single-stage pumps:** In the single-stage pump, a single impeller is mounted on the shaft.

**(b) Multistage pumps:** In multistage pump, number of impellers are mounted on the shaft and are enclosed in the same casing. These pumps are used to deliver liquid against very high heads which is not possible only with single impeller.

4. **Number of entrances:** Depending upon number of entrances, pumps can be classified as (a) Single suction pumps and

(b) Double suction pumps

(a) **Single suction pumps:** In these pumps the liquid is admitted from the suction pipe only on one side of the impeller. [Fig. 5.7 (a).]

(b) **Double suction pumps:** In these pumps, the liquid is admitted from the suction pipe on both sides of the impeller. These pumps are suitable for large discharges. In addition, the axial thrust on the impeller is neutralised. [Fig. 5.7 (b).]

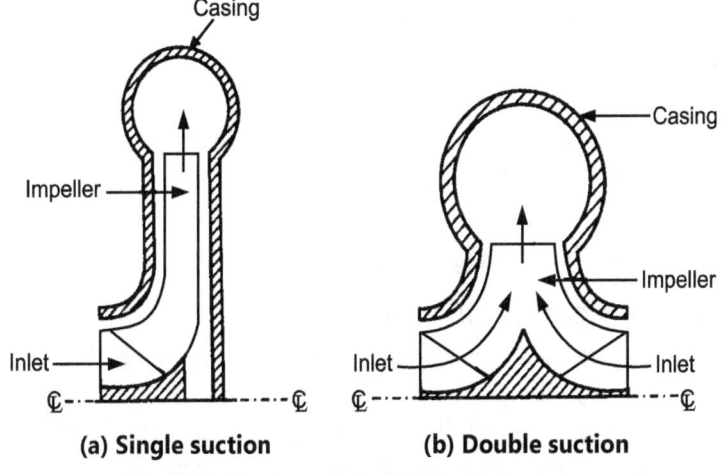

(a) Single suction  (b) Double suction

**Fig. 5.7: Single and double suction pumps**

5. **Disposition of shaft:** The shaft of the centrifugal pump may be horizontal or vertical. Generally the shafts of the pumps are horizontal. However, vertical shaft pumps are used where there is less space available e.g. deep wells, mines, etc.

6. **Specific speed:** *Specific speed of pump is the speed of a geometrically similar pump which would deliver unit discharge (1 m³/s) of liquid under unit head (1 m).*

Specific speed is given by

$$N_s = \frac{N\sqrt{Q}}{H^{3/4}}$$

Based on specific speed, the pumps are classified as given in the following table.

**Table 5.1: Classification of centrifugal pumps based on specific speed**

|   | Type of flow | Type of impeller | Specific speed |
|---|---|---|---|
| 1. | Radial flow | Slow speed | 10 – 30 |
|   |   | Medium speed | 30 – 50 |
|   |   | High speed | 50 – 75 |
| 2. | Mixed flow | High speed | 75 – 160 |
| 3. | Axial flow | High speed | 110 – 475 |

**7. Working head:** Generally lift or working head of the pump is the height through which liquid is actually lifted. Based on the lift or working head, pumps are classified as:
   (a) Low head pumps – (upto 15 m)
   (b) Medium head pumps – (between 15 m – 40 m)
   (c) High head pumps – (above 40 m)
   (a) **Low head pumps:** These pumps are employed upto head of 15 m. Volute casing is generally used for such pumps.
   (b) **Medium head pumps:** If the working head of the pumps lies between 15 m and 40 m, the pumps are called medium head pumps. They are generally single-stage pumps. Guide vanes may be or may not be provided.
   (c) **High head pumps:** If the working head of the pumps is more than 40 m, the pumps are called high head pumps. They are generally multistage pumps. They are generally provided with guide vanes.

# 5.4 Working of Centrifugal Pump
## 5.4.1 Priming of a Centrifugal Pump

Before the pump is started, it is necessary to prime the pump. Thus, the first step in operation of the pump is *'priming'*.

Priming is the operation in which the suction pipe, casing of the pump and the portion of delivery pipe upto delivery valve are competely filled with the liquid to be pumped. Purpose of priming is to remove all air, gas or vapour from these parts of the pump. Even if there is small air in these parts of the pump, the pump will not deliver liquid.

This is because the pressure developed by a pump impeller is directly proportional to the density of fluid in contact with the impeller. Thus, if the impeller is rotated in air, the head developed is proportional to density of air. This head will be very negligible in terms of head of liquid and hence no liquid will be lifted by the pump. Thus, an impeller producing 50 m of head, when rotated in air, will produce only 50 m of air which will be approximately equivalent to $\frac{50}{1000}$ = 0.05 m of water or 5 cm of water (since density of air, approximately $\frac{1}{1000}$ th the density of water) and will not be sufficient to lift water more than 5 cm. Hence, it is absolutely essential to prime the pump with water if it is to develop head of 50 m of water.

**Priming Devices:** Some of the priming devices used for priming are as follows:
1. **Pouring water:** Water is poured in the pump through the funnel provided on the top of the casing of the pump. Air escapes through the air vent which is closed by valve after the priming. Many times the air vent and the funnel are combined and a valve is provided on the same.

2. **Connection to city water main:** Sometimes the pump is connected to water supply which can be used to prime the pump.

3. **Auxiliary pump:** Sometimes a small pump is used to take water from sump and fill it in the pump for priming. After priming is done the auxiliary pump is stopped.

4. **Chamber for priming:** Sometimes a priming chamber is provided on the delivery side to store water and this water in the chamber is used to prime the pump.

5. **Devices producing vacuum:** The air in the pump can be removed with the help of a vacuum producing device. As the air in the parts of the pump (suction pipe, casing etc.) is removed the water from the sump rises due to atmospheric pressure on the liquid surface in the sump and the pump is primed. A vacuum pump, ejector using high pressure water, compressed air or steam are some of the devices used for this purpose.

6. **Self-priming pump:** In some pump special devices which automatically prime the pump after it is started are employed.

**A vacuum pump:** It is mounted on the shaft of the pump itself. When the pump is started the vacuum pump takes of air from the pump and creates vacuum in the pump. This makes the water from sump to rise and fill the parts of pump and thus the pump can be primed.

**Priming separator:** Sometimes a special separator chamber which can gradually remove the air from the suction pipe, casing etc. is provided on the delivery side of the pump. Thus the air is gradually removed from these parts, vacuum is created, the liquid rises up in these parts and the pump is automatically primed.

## 5.4.2 Working of Pump

After priming is completed, the electric motor is started keeping the delivery valve closed. Delivery valve is closed to reduce the starting torque on the motor. The delivery valve is then gradually opened. Now, the impeller rotating inside the casing full of liquid, imparts centrifugal head to the liquid and the liquid flows to the outer periphery of the impeller with increased velocity and pressure. This movement of fluid from centre of the pump towards outer periphery creates partial vacuum at 'eye' of the pump. This negative pressure at the 'eye' makes the liquid in the sump to rise upto the centre of the pump due to atmospheric pressure acting on liquid surface in the sump. This process is continued and the liquid is continuously lifted up. Since centrifugal action is used to lift liquid, these pumps are called centrifugal pumps.

## 5.5 Work Done by Centrifugal Pump

While deriving the equation for work done by a centrifugal pump, following assumptions are made.

(i) The impeller has infinite number of vanes and the liquid is smoothly guided over the vanes.

(ii) There are no losses due to friction or eddy formation.

(iii) There are no shock losses at the entry. The vane at the entry is parallel to the relative velocity vector $V_r$ at the entrance.

The expression for work done by the impeller of a centrifugal pump can be derived as follows by application of moment of momentum principle. As shown in the figure, liquid enters the impeller at the eye and leaves at the outer periphery. Fig. 5.8 shows the vane of the pump and the inlet and outlet triangles. The same notations as used in case of turbines are used.

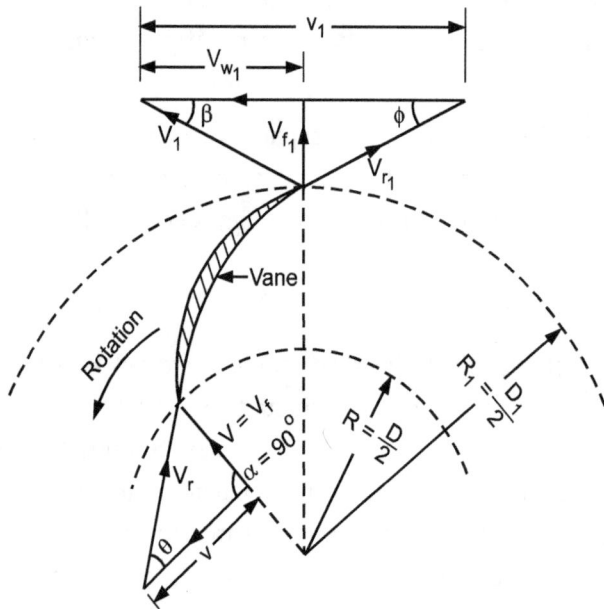

**Fig. 5.8: Velocity triangle of a centrifugal impeller**

The quantities without suffix refer to inlet while those with suffix refer to outlet of the vane.

Now let W be the weight of liquid passing through the impeller per second.

$$\text{Mass of liquid passing/sec} = \frac{W}{g}$$

$$\text{Tangential momentum of liquid at the exit} = \frac{W}{g} \cdot V_{w_1}$$

$$\text{Tangential moment of momentum or angular momentum at exit} = \frac{W}{g} \cdot V_{w_1} \cdot R_1$$

$$\text{Tangential moment of momentum or angular momentum at inlet} = \frac{W}{g} \cdot V_w \cdot R$$

∴ Torque exerted by the impeller on liquid = Rate of change of angular momentum

= Angular momentum at exit − Angular momentum at inlet

∴ Torque exerted by the impeller on the liquid $= \frac{W}{g}(V_{w_1} R_1 - V_w R)$

∴ Work done by the impeller on the liquid $= \frac{W}{g}(V_{w_1} R_1 - V_w R) \cdot \omega$

but $\omega R_1 = v_1$ and $\omega R = v$ where $v$ and $v_1$ are the tangential velocities at inlet and outlet of the impeller.

Therefore,

$$\boxed{\text{Work done by impeller on the liquid} = \frac{W}{g}(V_{w_1} v_1 - V_w v)} \qquad \text{... (5.1)}$$

In case of turbines, to achieve maximum output, absolute velocity $V_1$ at outlet is made minimum by making the flow at the exit radial. With the same argument in order to get maximum work done on liquid, the flow at the inlet is made radial.

With radial flow at inlet (i.e. when liquid enters the impeller radially) we have, $\alpha = 90°$, and hence $V_w = 0$

The equation (5.1) then becomes

$$\boxed{\text{Work done by the impeller on the liquid} = \frac{W}{g}(V_{w_1} v_1)} \qquad \text{... (5.2)}$$

Dividing by W, we get

$$\boxed{\text{Work done by the impeller per unit weight of liquid} = \left(\frac{V_{w_1} v_1}{g}\right)} \qquad \text{... (5.3)}$$

Equation (5.3) represents the head imparted to the liquid. $\dfrac{V_{w_1} v_1}{g}$ is the theoretical head imparted by impeller and is called **'Euler head'**. Further, from outlet triangle, we have

$$\boxed{V_{w_1} = v_1 - V_{f_1} \cot \phi} \qquad \text{... (5.4)}$$

As in the case of turbine, the tangential velocity '$v_1$' at outlet and the flow velocity '$V_f$' at outlet are expressed in terms of $H_m$, the manometric head as

$$\boxed{v_1 = \phi \sqrt{2g\, H_m}} \qquad \text{... (5.5)}$$

and

$$\boxed{V_{f_1} = \psi \sqrt{2g\, H_m}} \qquad \text{... (5.6)}$$

where $\phi$ (or $k_u$) and $\psi$ (or $k_f$) are the velocity ratio and flow ratio respectively.

Equation (5.1) can also be written as

$$\boxed{\text{Work done per unit weight} = \dfrac{(V_{w_1} v_1 - V_w v)}{g}} \qquad \text{... (5.7)}$$

Equation (5.7) can be transformed in the form

$$\boxed{\text{Work done per unit weight} = \left(\dfrac{v_1^2 - V^2}{2g}\right) + \left(\dfrac{v_1^2 - v^2}{2g}\right) + \left(\dfrac{V_r^2 - V_{r_1}^2}{2g}\right)} \qquad \text{... (5.8)}$$

as follows.

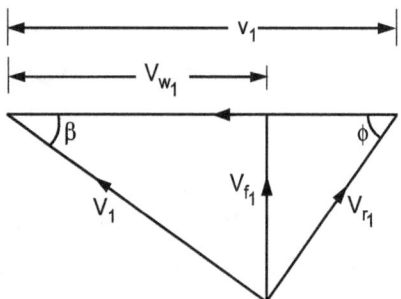

**Fig. 5.9 (a): Outlet triangle**

From output triangle, we have

$$V_{r_1}^2 = V_{f_1}^2 + (v_1 - V_{w_1})^2$$
$$= V_{f_1}^2 + v_1^2 - 2V_{w_1} v_1 + V_{w_1}^2$$
$$= \left(V_{f_1}^2 + V_{w_1}^2\right) + v_1^2 - 2V_{w_1} v_1$$
$$= V_1^2 + v_1^2 - 2V_{w_1} v_1 \qquad \therefore V_{f_1}^2 + V_{w_1}^2 = V_1^2$$

Therefore,
$$V_{w_1} v_1 = \frac{1}{2}\left[V_1^2 + v_1^2 - V_{r_1}^2\right] \quad \ldots (i)$$

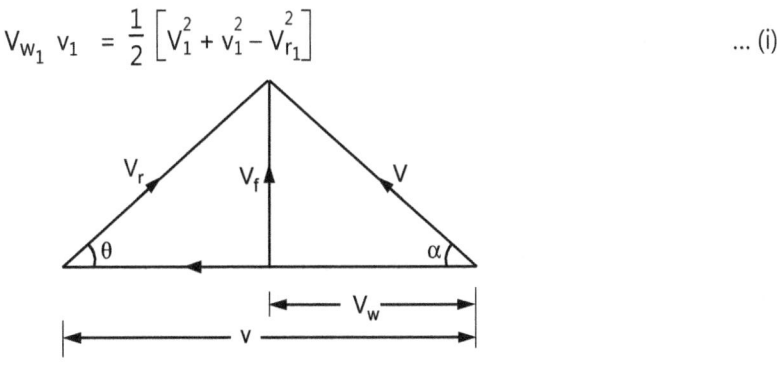

Fig. 5.9 (b): Inlet triangle

From the inlet triangle
(Please note that the inlet triangle shown in Fig. 5.8 is a typical case of this general triangle with $\alpha = 90°$ and $V_w = 0$)

$$V_r^2 = V_f^2 + (v - V_w)^2$$
$$= V_f^2 + v^2 - 2 V_w v + V_w^2$$
$$= \left(V_f^2 + V_w^2\right) + v^2 - 2 V_w v$$
$$= V^2 + v^2 - 2 V_w v \qquad \therefore V_f^2 + V_w^2 = V^2$$

Therefore, $\quad V_w v = \frac{1}{2}\left[V^2 + v^2 - V_r^2\right] \quad \ldots (ii)$

Substituting these values in equation (5.7), we get

Work done per unit weight
$$= \frac{V_{w_1} v_1}{g} - \frac{V_w v}{g}$$
$$= \frac{V_1^2 + v_1^2 - V_{r_1}^2}{2g} - \frac{V^2 + v^2 - V_r^2}{2g}$$

or  Work done per unit weight
$$= \left[\frac{V_1^2 - V^2}{2g}\right] + \left[\frac{v_1^2 - v^2}{2g}\right] + \left[\frac{V_r^2 - V_{r_1}^2}{2g}\right]$$

The first term in the above equation represents the change in kinetic energy of the liquid. The second term represents the pressure change due to centrifugal effects while the third term represents the static pressure change due to relative kinetic energy.

Equation (5.8) is the fundamental equation for centrifugal pumps and is known as **'Euler's energy transfer equation'**.

## 5.6 Heads of a Pump

1. **Static head:**

   The vertical distance between the liquid level in the sump and the level to which the liquid is lifted (liquid level in the overhead tank in case of Fig. 5.1) is called 'static head' $H_s$.

   **Suction lift:** The vertical distance between the liquid level in the sump and the centreline of the pump is called suction lift or suction head '$h_s$'.

   **Delivery lift:** The vertical distance, through which the liquid is lifted above the centre-line of the pump is called 'delivery lift' or 'delivery head' '$h_d$'.

   Therefore, $\boxed{H_s = h_s + h_d}$

2. **Manometric head:**

   Manometric head is defined in any of the following ways.

   (i) It is the actual head against which the pump has to work.

   (ii) From the above definition it can be seen that

   $$H_m = \text{Suction head} + \text{Delivery head} + \text{All the losses}$$

   or  $\boxed{H_m = h_s + h_d + h_{fs} + h_{fd} + \dfrac{V_d^2}{2g}}$ ... (5.9)

   where  $h_{fs}$ – loss of head due to friction in suction pipe

   $h_{fd}$ – loss of head due to friction in delivery pipe.

   $\dfrac{V_d^2}{2g}$ – Velocity head in delivery pipe

   (It may be noted that other losses e.g. loss at entry, losses in the impeller and casing and velocity head in suction pipe are not considered.)

   (iii) $\qquad H_m = $ Work done per unit weight of liquid – Losses in the impeller

   $\therefore$ $\boxed{H_m = \dfrac{V_{w_1} v_1}{g} - \text{Impeller losses}}$ ... (5.10)

   (iv) $\qquad H_m = $ Total energy of liquid at the exit of the pump (Impeller)

   – Total energy of liquid at the inlet of the pump.

   $\boxed{H_m = \left(z_d + \dfrac{p_d}{\gamma} + \dfrac{V_d^2}{2g}\right) - \left(z_s + \dfrac{p_s}{\gamma} + \dfrac{V_s^2}{2g}\right)}$ ... (5.11)

Subscript 's' is for the suction side of the pump (inlet) and subscript 'd' is for the delivery side of the pump.

If further, $z_s = z_d$ and the suction and delivery pipes have same diameter, i.e. $V_s = V_d$,

$$\boxed{H_m = \frac{p_d}{\gamma} - \frac{p_s}{\gamma}} \qquad \ldots (5.12)$$

Thus, if two gauges (vacuum gauge on suction side and pressure gauge on delivery side) are installed at the same level one on suction side and other on delivery side very near the pump,

$H_m$ = Arithmetical addition of the readings of pressure gauge and the vacuum gauge.

**Manometric head is also called 'Gross head' (actual) or 'total head' 'effective head' or 'dynamic head'.**

## 5.7 Efficiencies of a Centrifugal Pump

The pump gets it's power from a prime mover and ultimately transfers it to the liquid which goes out at the exit of pump. During this course of power transfer, different losses take place and the energy goes decreasing as it passes from prime mover to exit of pump. Taking into account the various losses, the efficiencies of the pump are defined as follows:

(a) Manometric efficiency

(b) Mechanical efficiency

(c) Volumetric efficiency

(d) Overall efficiency.

**(a) Manometric efficiency:** Manometric efficiency is defined as the ratio of manometric head developed by the pump to the head imparted by the impeller to the liquid. This is denoted by $\eta_{mano}$.

Thus,
$$\eta_{mano} = \frac{\text{Manometric head}}{\text{Head imparted by impeller to liquid}}$$

$$= \frac{H_m}{\left(\frac{V_{w_1} v_1}{g}\right)}$$

or
$$\boxed{\eta_{mano} = \frac{g\, H_m}{V_{w_1} v_1}} \qquad \ldots (5.13)$$

but, $\dfrac{V_{w_1} v_1}{g} = H_m + $ losses in the pump

∴ $$\eta_{mano} = \dfrac{H_m}{H_m + \text{losses in the pump}} \qquad \text{... (5.14)}$$

If Q is the quantity of liquid delivered by pump per second

$$\eta_{mano} = \dfrac{\gamma Q H_m}{\gamma Q \left(\dfrac{V_{w_1} v_1}{g}\right)} \qquad \text{... (5.15)}$$

or $$\eta_{mano} = \dfrac{\text{Output power of pump}}{\text{Power imparted to the impeller}} \qquad \text{... (5.16)}$$

This efficiency accounts for the hydraulic losses in the pump. **Hydraulic losses** may be due to (i) shock losses at the entry to the vanes, (ii) friction in the impeller, (iii) friction and eddy losses in the diffuser and (iv) friction and other losses in the suction and delivery pipes etc.

It is also called **'Hydraulic efficiency'**.

Manometric efficiency ranges between 60 to 90 %.

**(b) Volumetric efficiency:** It is the ratio of the actual discharge at the outlet of the pump to the discharge flowing through the impeller. This is denoted by $\eta_v$.

Thus, $\eta_v = \dfrac{\text{Actual discharge}}{\text{Discharge passing through the impeller}}$

or $$\eta_v = \dfrac{Q}{Q + \Delta Q} \qquad \text{... (5.17)}$$

where, $Q$ = Actual discharge

$\Delta Q$ = Amount of leakage

This efficiency accounts for leakage losses. **Leakage losses** are due to the quantity of liquid which leaks back from impeller to eye through the clearance (small gap) between impeller and casing.

Volumetric efficiency ranges between 96 to 98 %.

**(c) Mechanical efficiency:** It is the ratio of power actually supplied to liquid by the impeller to the power supplied to the shaft of the pump by the prime mover. This is denoted by $\eta_m$.

Thus, $\eta_m = \dfrac{\text{Power delivered by the impeller to the liquid}}{\text{Power supplied to the shaft}}$

∴ $$\boxed{\eta_m = \dfrac{\gamma(Q + \Delta Q)\left(\dfrac{V_{w_1} V_1}{g}\right)}{\text{Shaft power}}} \qquad \ldots (5.18)$$

This efficiency accounts for the mechanical losses. **Mechanical losses** may be due to (i) losses in bearings and glands and (ii) disc friction between the impeller and the liquid.

Mechanical efficiency ranges between 95 to 98 %.

**(d) Overall efficiency:** It is the ratio of output power of the pump to the input power of the pump.

Thus, $\eta_o = \dfrac{\text{Output power of pump}}{\text{Input power to pump}}$

or $$\boxed{\eta_o = \dfrac{\gamma Q H_m}{\text{Shaft power}}} \qquad \ldots (5.19)$$

Overall efficiency varies from 70 to 85 %.

Further, we can write

$$\eta_o = \left[\dfrac{\gamma Q H_m}{\gamma Q \left(\dfrac{V_{w_1} V_1}{g}\right)}\right] \times \left[\dfrac{Q}{(Q + \Delta Q)}\right] \times \left[\dfrac{\gamma(Q + \Delta Q)\left(\dfrac{V_{w_1} V_1}{g}\right)}{\text{Shaft power}}\right]$$

∴ $\boxed{\eta_o = \eta_{mano} \times \eta_v \times \eta_m}$ ... (5.20)

If $\eta_v = 1$ or 100 %, $\boxed{\eta_o = \eta_{mano} \times \eta_m}$ ... (5.20 (a))

## 5.8 Minimum Starting Speed of a Centrifugal Pump

When the pump is started, it will not deliver liquid until head developed by pump is sufficient to overcome the head against which the pump is to work. i.e. manometric head.

Till the pump starts delivering liquid, there is no flow and hence all velocities (V, $V_r$, $V_1$, $V_{r_1}$ etc.) are zero. Only head which is impressed on liquid is the centrifugal head. Thus, flow will start when this centrifugal head is equal to the manometric head.

Centrifugal head = $\dfrac{v_1^2 - v^2}{2g}$ = $H_m$

But $v_1 = \omega R_1 = \dfrac{\pi D_1 N}{60}$, $v = \dfrac{\pi D N}{60}$

where N is the minimum starting speed of the pump.
Substituting values of $v_1$ and $v$ we get,

$$\left[\left(\dfrac{\pi D_1 N}{60}\right)^2 - \left(\dfrac{\pi D N}{60}\right)^2\right] = 2g H_m$$

or $\left(\dfrac{\pi N}{60}\right)^2 \left[D_1^2 - D^2\right] = 2g H_m$

∴ Minimum starting speed of the pump is given by

$$\boxed{N = \dfrac{60}{\pi} \sqrt{\dfrac{2g H_m}{(D_1^2 - D^2)}}} \qquad \ldots (5.21)$$

But $\eta_{mano} = \dfrac{H_m}{\dfrac{V_{w_1} v_1}{g}}$ or $H_m = \eta_{mano} \dfrac{V_{w_1} v_1}{g}$

∴ Minimum starting speed of the pump can also be written as

$$N = \dfrac{60}{\pi} \sqrt{\dfrac{\eta_{mano} \times 2g}{(D_1^2 - D^2)} \times \dfrac{V_{w_1} \cdot v_1}{g}}$$

$$\boxed{N = \dfrac{60}{\pi} \sqrt{\dfrac{2\, \eta_{mano} \cdot V_{w_1} \cdot v_1}{(D_1^2 - D^2)}}} \qquad \ldots (5.22)$$

Further substituting $v_1 = \dfrac{\pi D_1 N}{60}$ in the above equation, the expression for minimum starting speed can be written as

$$\boxed{N = \dfrac{120 \times \eta_{mano} \times V_{w_1} \times D_1}{\pi (D_1^2 - D^2)}} \qquad \ldots (5.23)$$

## 5.8.1 Least Diameter of the Impeller

For the pump to start pumping, the centrifugal head must be equal to the total head '$H_m$'. On the basis of this fact, an expression for least (minimum) diameter of the impeller can be obtained as follows.

$$\frac{v_1^2 - v^2}{2g} = H_m$$

or

$$\left[\frac{\pi D_1 N}{60}\right]^2 - \left[\frac{\pi D N}{60}\right]^2 = 2g\, H_m$$

or

$$D_1^2 - D^2 = \left(\frac{60}{\pi N}\right)^2 \times (2g\, H_m)$$

Generally,

$$D = \frac{1}{2} D_1$$

$$D_1^2 - \left(\frac{D_1}{2}\right)^2 = \left(\frac{60}{\pi N}\right)^2 \times (2g\, H_m)$$

Solving, we get

$$\boxed{D_1 = \frac{(97.68)\left(\sqrt{H_m}\right)}{N}} \qquad \ldots (5.24)$$

## 5.9 Multistage Centrifugal Pump

**Multistage Pumps**

A multistage pump is the one in which more than one impellers are mounted on the same shaft enclosed in the same casing. All the impellers work in series so that liquid discharged with increased pressure from one impeller passes to the inlet of the other impeller and the liquid delivered from the second impeller passes to the inlet of the third impeller and so on till the liquid from the last impeller passes in the delivery pipe. Each impeller runs at the same speed, has the same diameter, passes the same discharge and develops the same head. Specific speed of such a pump is the same as that of one impeller. See Fig. 5.10 (a).

**Necessity of using a multistage pump**

To develop a high head the rim speed of the impeller has to be increased. This can be done either by increasing the diameter of the runner or by increasing the speed of the impeller or both. Both these have the following disadvantages.

(a) It may lower the efficiency due to increased losses due to friction and turbulence.
(b) The centrifugal stresses on the impeller are increased.
(c) It increases the possibility of cavitation.

**Advantages of multistage pump**

1. Centrifugal stresses on the impeller can be reduced by choosing smaller diameter of the impeller and hence no special materials are required to be used for impellers.
2. Due to reduced speed, disc friction losses and turbulence losses are reduced and hence better efficiency can be obtained.
3. Leakage losses are reduced due to lesser head developed by each impeller.
4. Pump can be adapted to suit the speed of the drive.
5. Lower specific speed permits a large suction lift.
6. Lower cost of equipment.

Number of stages required depend upon r.p.m. of motor, discharge required and the head to be developed. Normally head per stage is limited to about 50 m to 60 m and the specific speed of about 40 to 50, but never below 20 m. Total head developed is $H = n H_s$, $H_s$ = head developed per stage and n = number of stages.

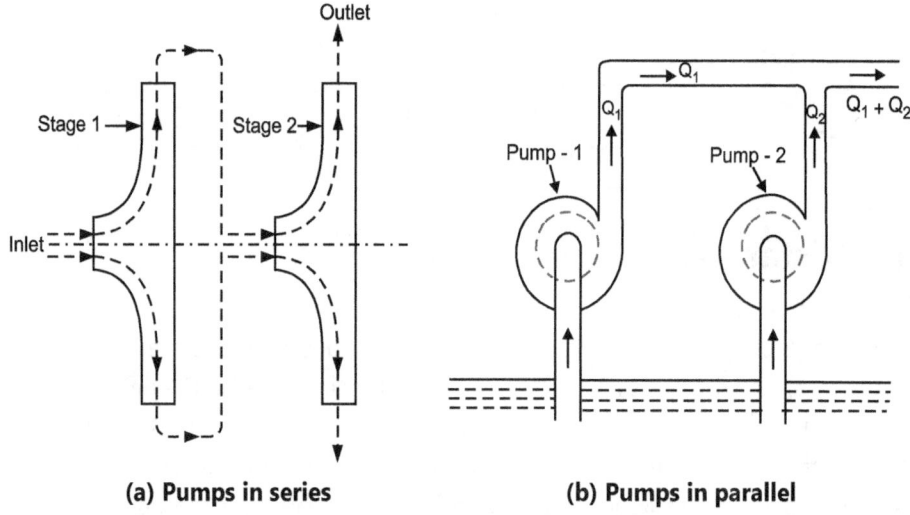

(a) Pumps in series  (b) Pumps in parallel

**Fig. 5.10**

# 5.10 Principles of Similarity Applied to Centrifugal Pump

Similar to other hydraulic structures or machines etc., tests are conducted on small-scale model of centrifugal pumps. Tests are done to know the likely performance of the large size pump (prototype), well in advance, before the pump is manufactured and installed. Most efficient designs can be arrived at saving money, time and labour. In order that the results from model can be translated in terms of the results which can be applied to prototype, there should be complete similarity between model and the prototype.

1. Geometric similarity is achieved by keeping the ratios of the corresponding dimensions in the model and prototype constant.

2. Kinematic similarity can be obtained by making the velocity triangles in the model similar to velocity triangles in prototype.

3. Conditions for dynamic similarity can be found out by use of dimensional analysis as explained below.

Various variables involved in case of a pump are discharge – Q, head – H, speed – N, diameter of the impeller – D, power – P, mass density – ρ and viscosity – μ of the liquid and gravitational acceleration – g.

Considering 'gH' as one variable as in case of turbines, we can write

$$f(Q, gH, N, D, P, \rho, \mu) = 0 \text{ or constant}$$

Taking ρ, N and D as repeating variables, following dimensionless parameters can be obtained.

(a) $\left(\dfrac{Q}{ND^3}\right)$ – Discharge Number

(b) $\left(\dfrac{gH}{N^2D^2}\right)$ – Head Number

(c) $\dfrac{P}{\rho g H N D^3}$ – Power Number and

(d) $\dfrac{\mu}{\rho N D^2}$ – Reynold's Number

Another term which is very important in the study of hydraulic machines is the specific speed which can be derived from discharge number and head number as follows.

$$\dfrac{\sqrt{\text{Discharge number}}}{(\text{Head number})^{3/4}} = \dfrac{\sqrt{Q}}{\sqrt{ND^3}} \cdot \left(\dfrac{N^2 D^2}{gH}\right)^{3/4}$$

$$= \dfrac{N\sqrt{Q}}{(gH)^{3/4}}$$

which is nothing but non-dimensional form of specific speed or shape number of the pump.

Thus, for complete similarity in model and prototype pumps, the necessary conditions are as follows.

(i) $\left(\dfrac{Q}{ND^3}\right)_m = \left(\dfrac{Q}{ND^3}\right)_p$

(ii) $\left(\dfrac{gH}{N^2D^2}\right)_m = \left(\dfrac{gH}{N^2D^2}\right)_p$

(iii) $\left(\dfrac{P}{\rho g H N D^3}\right)_m = \left(\dfrac{P}{\rho g H N D^3}\right)_p$

(iv) $\left[\dfrac{N\sqrt{Q}}{(gH)^{3/4}}\right]_m = \left[\dfrac{N\sqrt{Q}}{(gH)^{3/4}}\right]_p$

In practice, keeping the same Reynold's number in model and prototype is not possible. However, it is found that Reynold's number does not influence the similarly if the flow in both model and prototype is turbulent and hence it is not considered.

Further, the efficiencies in model and prototype are different. Model efficiency is generally lower than that in the prototype. This is due to the fact that under corresponding conditions, the losses in the model are more than losses in the prototype. By applying a suitable correction to the model efficiency, the correct efficiency for prototype can be obtained. Following expression by G.F. Wislicenus can be used for such correction.

$$\dfrac{0.95 - \eta_m}{0.95 - \eta_p} = \left[\dfrac{0.658 + \log_{10} Q_p}{0.658 + \log_{10} Q_m}\right]^2$$

$Q_m$ and $Q_p$ are in litres per minute.

## 5.11 Specific Speed of a Centrifugal Pump

Centrifugal pumps are available in different varieties handling different discharges under different heads. In order to compare one class with the other, it is necessary to have some common basis. The concept of "specific speed" is used as the common basis for such comparison.

*"Specific speed of a pump is defined as the speed of a geometrically similar pump (specific pump) when delivering one m³/s against a head of one metre".*

An expression for specific speed can be derived as follows:

We know that

$$V_1 = \phi\sqrt{2g H_m}, \quad \phi \text{ (or } K_u) = \text{Speed ratio}$$

∴ $V_1 \propto \sqrt{H_m}$

Also $V_1 = \dfrac{\pi D_1 N}{60}$

or $D_1 N \propto V_1$

∴ $D_1 N \propto \sqrt{H_m}$

∴ $D_1 \propto \dfrac{\sqrt{H_m}}{N}$ ... (i)

or $\dfrac{\sqrt{H_m}}{D_1 N} = \text{Constant}$

Now the discharge through the pump

$$Q = \text{Area of flow at outlet} \times \text{velocity of flow at outlet}$$
$$Q = K_1 \pi B_1 D_1 V_{f_1}$$
∴ $Q \propto B_1 D_1 V_{f_1}$

But $B_1 \propto D_1$ and $V_{f_1} \propto \sqrt{H_m}$

∴ $Q \propto D_1^2 \sqrt{H_m}$

But from (i), $D_1 \propto \dfrac{\sqrt{H_m}}{N}$

∴ $Q \propto \dfrac{H_m}{N^2} \cdot \sqrt{H_m}$ ... (ii)

or $Q \propto \dfrac{H_m^{3/2}}{N^2}$

or $N^2 \propto \dfrac{H_m^{3/2}}{Q}$

or $N = C \dfrac{H_m^{3/4}}{\sqrt{Q}}$

But when $H_m = 1$ m, $Q = 1$ m³/s and $N = N_s$

∴ $N_s = C$

or $N = N_s \cdot \dfrac{H_m^{3/4}}{\sqrt{Q}}$

or $\boxed{N_s = \dfrac{N\sqrt{Q}}{H_m^{3/4}}}$ ... (5.25)

Equation (5.25) represents the equation for specific speed of a centrifugal pump. Classification of pumps based on specific speed is given in Table 5.2.

## 5.12 Net Positive Suction Head (NPSH)

Another way of specifying the suction head is the concept of net positive suction head or (NPSH). The quantity $\left(\dfrac{p_s}{\gamma} + \dfrac{V_s^2}{2g}\right)$ is called **'total suction head'** at the inlet of the pump. This total head minus the vapour pressure head of liquid corresponding to the temperature of liquid is called **"Net positive suction head"** or **"NPSH"**.

*"Thus, NPSH is the amount by which the total head at the inlet of the pump is more than the vapour pressure head of liquid".*

Thus, $\quad\quad\quad\quad \text{NPSH} = \left(\dfrac{p_s}{\gamma} + \dfrac{V_s^2}{2g}\right) - \dfrac{p_v}{\gamma} \quad\quad\quad\quad$ ... (i)

where $\dfrac{p_v}{\gamma}$ is the vapour pressure head corresponding to the temperature of the liquid.

Now applying Bernoulli's theorem to the liquid level in the sump and the inlet of the pump we get

$$\left(\dfrac{p_a}{\gamma}\right) = \left(\dfrac{p_s}{\gamma}\right) + \dfrac{V_s^2}{2g} + h_s + h_{fs}$$

or $$\left(\dfrac{p_s}{\gamma} + \dfrac{V_s^2}{2g}\right) = \left(\dfrac{p_a}{\gamma}\right) - h_s - h_{fs}$$

or $$\text{NPSH} = \left(\dfrac{p_a}{\gamma}\right) - h_s - h_{fs} - \dfrac{p_v}{\gamma}$$

or $\quad\boxed{\text{NPSH} = \left(\dfrac{p_a}{\gamma} - \dfrac{p_v}{\gamma}\right) - h_s - h_{fs}}\quad$ ... (5.26)

Following diagram will illustrate the concept of NPSH.

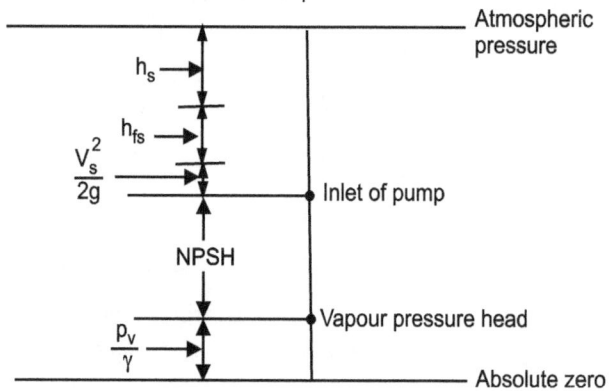

Fig. 5.11

The concept of NPSH is very important in the installation of a pump. NPSH calculated by the above formula is called **"available NPSH"**. The pump manufacturers specify the amount of NPSH required for the installation of the pump (so that it works without the possibility of cavitation). The NPSH specified by the manufacturer is called **"required NPSH"**.

*"The available NPSH should be always greater than or equal to the required NPSH".*

## 5.13 Cavitation in Centrifugal Pumps

If the pressure at any point inside the pumps falls below vapour pressure of the liquid, the dissolved gases are liberated and the liquid vapourises and bubble or cavities are formed. These bubbles travel with the flow and when they reach a region of high pressure they collapse. The phenomenon of the formation, travel and collapse of the vapour bubbles is called 'cavitation'. Since the pressure on the suction side of the pump is lower, cavitation is more likely to occur near to suction end of the pump and the blade passages nearby.

Noise, vibrations, sudden reduction in head and efficiency are the indications of inception of cavitation.

**Some bad effects of cavitation:**
1. The material of the impeller and nearby parts is worn out or erroded (removed) resulting in what is called 'pitting'.
2. Efficiency of pump is reduced to great extent.
3. Pump is subjected to serious vibration and lot of noise is produced.

Due to the bad effects of cavitation, as seen above, attempts should be made to avoid cavitation as far as possible.

Some of the methods to prevent or at least reduce the possibility of cavitation are as follows:
1. The pump should be properly designed to prevent separation of flow. Sharp corners and curvatures which produce separation of flow should be avoided.
2. Extensive model testing should be done before finalising the design.
3. For a given head and capacity, a pump of low specific speed should be chosen.
4. Suction lift should be restricted to safe limit by installing the pump as near to sump level as possible. Sometimes the pump is even installed below the liquid level in the sump.
5. Cavitation resistant materials like stellite, chromium-nickel stainless steel, nickel-aluminium bronze etc. should be used for construction of the pump.

6. The surface parts of the pump should be highly finished.

7. The temperature of the liquid pumped should be low.

A cavitation parameter '$\sigma$' called **'Thoma's Number'** is the criterion to decide whether the cavitation is possible or not.

Thoma's number for centrifugal pumps is given by

$$\sigma = \frac{\left(\frac{p_a}{\gamma} - \frac{p_v}{\gamma}\right) - h_s - h_{fs}}{H} \quad \ldots (5.27)$$

But as seen in Art (5.17)

$$\left(\frac{p_a}{\gamma} - \frac{p_v}{\gamma}\right) - h_s - h_{fs} = NPSH$$

Therefore, Thoma's number for pumps

$$\sigma = \frac{NPSH}{H} \quad \ldots (5.28)$$

Critical value of Thoma's number '$\sigma_c$' is the one when cavitation takes place. For pump to operate without cavitation, '$\sigma$' should be greater than or at the most equal to '$\sigma_c$'.

or
$$\sigma \geq \sigma_c \quad \ldots (5.29)$$

or
$$NPSH \geq \sigma_c H \quad \ldots (5.30)$$

From the above value, minimum value of NPSH can be obtained as

$$\text{minimum (NPSH)} = \sigma_c H \quad \ldots (5.31)$$

Value of $\sigma_c$ can be obtained experimentally, or from the standard tables relating specific speed ($N_s$) and $\sigma_c$ or by the following formula

$$\sigma_c = (1.042 \times 10^{-3}) (N_s)^{4/3} \quad \ldots (5.32)$$

## (B) RECIPROCATING PUMPS

# 5.14 Reciprocating Pumps

Reciprocating pump is a positive displacement in which the fluid is physically pushed or displaced from a closed space. Initially, a small quantity of liquid is taken into a chamber and then it is physically pushed or displaced with the help of some moving mechanism like rotating gear or a piston. The most common example of positive displacement pump is the reciprocating pump in which forward and backward motion of a piston is used to push the liquid.

The use of reciprocating pump is limited now a days, due to many of it's shortcomings. They are replaced by centrifugal pumps. Still for small requirements like light oil pumping, feeding small boilers, lifting water from well etc. they are sometimes used.

# 5.15 Parts of Reciprocating Pump

Following are the main parts of a reciprocating pump. [See Fig. 5.12]

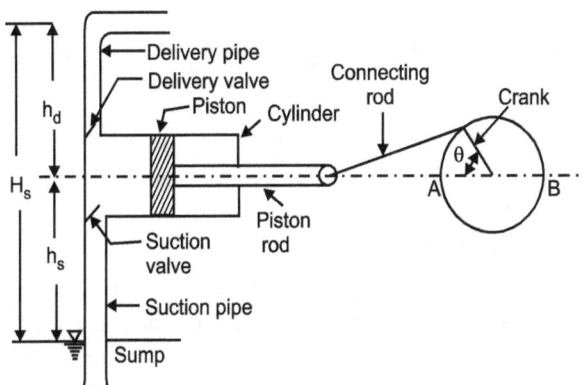

**Fig. 5.12: Single acting reciprocating pump**

1. Pump cylinder
2. Piston
3. Piston rod, crank and connecting rod
4. Suction and delivery pipes
5. Suction and delivery valves.

The piston or plunger of the pump is moved forward and backward with the help of a connecting rod and a crank shaft. The crank is connected to the external power source like diesel engine or an electric motor. The suction pipe connects the sump and the pump and the delivery pipe connects the pump and the outlet. At the junction where suction and delivery pipes meet the cylinder, suction and delivery valves are provided. These valves are non-return type of valves and allow the liquid to flow only in one direction. Suction valve allows the liquid to flow from suction pipe to cylinder only and the delivery valve allows the liquid to flow from cylinder to delivery pipe only.

## 5.16 Working of a Reciprocating Pump

When the crank moves from A to B i.e. crank moves from $\theta = 0°$ to $\theta = 180°$, the piston moves from left to right and the **suction stroke** is completed. When the crank moves from B back to A i.e. crank moves from $\theta = 180°$ to $\theta = 360°$, the piston moves from right to left completing the **delivery stroke**. The suction stroke and delivery strokes (i.e. two strokes) complete one cycle of the crank. During the suction stroke, a negative pressure (vacuum) is created in the cylinder, the delivery valve closes, the suction valve opens, and the liquid is sucked up and taken to the cylinder, the pressure on the liquid surface in the sump being atmospheric. During the delivery stroke, due to high pressure in the cylinder, the suction valve closes, the delivery valve opens and the liquid is taken to higher level through the delivery pipe.

## 5.17 Classification of Reciprocating Pumps

A broad classification of reciprocating pump can be done as follows:
1. **According to the use of number of sides of the piston:**
   (a) Single acting pump
   (b) Double acting pump
   
   **(a) Single acting pump:** When the liquid comes in contact with only one side of the piston, the pump is called single acting pump. The liquid fills only one side of the piston. This has only one suction and one delivery pipe. There is only one delivery stroke in one cycle and hence the discharge is intermittent. [Fig. 5.13 (a)]
   
   **(b) Double acting pump:** Liquid comes in contact with both the sides of the piston. There are two suction and two delivery pipes attached on either side of the piston. Thus, in one cycle of crank, there are two suction and two delivery strokes. Due to two delivery strokes in one cycle of the crank, the discharge of double acting pump is more uniform as compared to single acting pump. [See Fig. 5.13 (b).]

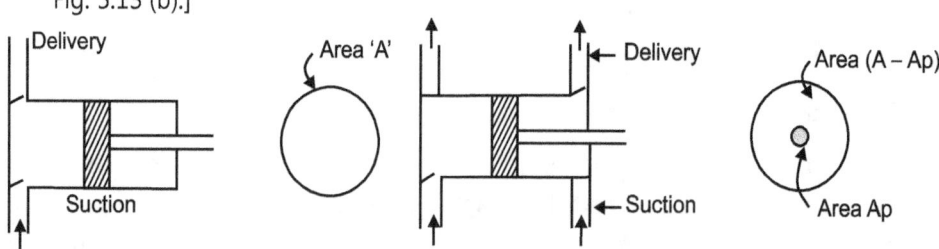

(a) Single acting pump  (b) Double acting pump
Fig. 5.13: Single and double acting pump

2. **According to the number of cylinders:** According to the number of cylinders used in the pump, reciprocating pumps are classified as:
   (a) Single cylinder pump
   (b) Double cylinder pump
   (c) Triple cylinder pump.

   (a) **Single cylinder pump:** If only one cylinder is used, the pump is a single cylinder pump. It may be single acting or double acting.
   (b) **Double cylinder pump:** Double cylinder or two throw pump has two cylinders connected to same shaft. The cranks of the two pistons are simultaneously driven by cranks set at 180° to each other. Thus, when one pump undergoes suction stroke, the other undergoes a delivery stroke. Thus, the discharge is more uniform as compared to a single cylinder pump.
   (c) **Triple cylinder pump:** This pump has three single acting cylinders with cranks set at 120° to one another. Each pump has it's own piston, suction and delivery pipes. The discharge is further more uniform.

Like this many number of cylinders can be used. Pumps having more than one cylinder are generally called "multi-cylinder pumps".

## 5.18 Discharge Through a Reciprocating Pump

(a) **Discharge through a single acting pump**

Consider a single acting pump as shown in Fig. 5.13 (a).
Let,
$A$ = Area of cross section of the piston or cylinder
$L$ = Length of stroke = 2 × radius of crank
$N$ = r.p.m. at crank

Now the volume of liquid pumped by the pump in one revolution
= Area × Length of stroke
= $A \times L$

Now the number of revolutions per second
$$= \frac{N}{60}$$

∴ The theoretical discharge of pump per second
$$= \frac{ALN}{60}$$

or
$$\boxed{Q_{th} = \frac{ALN}{60}} \qquad \ldots (5.33)$$

Work done by a single acting reciprocating pump is given by

Work done/sec = Weight of liquid lifted per second
× Total height through which liquid is lifted

∴ $\boxed{\text{Work done/sec} = \gamma \cdot \left(\dfrac{ALN}{60}\right) \times (h_s + h_d)}$ ... (5.34)

∴ Theoretical power required to drive the pump

$$\boxed{P = \dfrac{\gamma (ALN)(h_s + h_d)}{60}}$$ ... (5.35)

where
- $\gamma$ = Unit weight of liquid
- $h_s$ = Height of axis of cylinder above the liquid surface in the sump below – suction head
- $h_d$ = Height to which liquid is lifted above the centre-line of cylinder – delivery head.

However, actual power required by the pump is more than this due to frictional losses, leakage losses etc.

**(b) Discharge through a double acting pump**

Consider a double acting pump as shown in Fig. 5.14.

In case of double acting pump, there are two delivery strokes per revolution of crank. It can be understood from the figure that full area 'A' of piston is utilized on one side (left side) but on the other side the area is reduced due to the presence of piston rod.

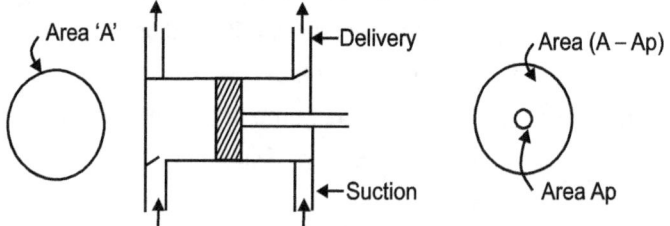

**Fig. 5.14: Double acting pump**

In case of double acting pump, the discharge is given by

$$Q_{th} = \dfrac{ALN}{60} + \dfrac{(A - A_p)LN}{60}, \text{ where } A_p \text{ is the area of piston rod.}$$

or

$$\boxed{Q_{th} = \dfrac{(2A - A_p)LN}{60}}$$ ... (5.36)

If area of piston rod is neglected,

$$Q_{th} = \frac{2ALN}{60} \qquad \ldots (5.37)$$

The discharge of double acting pump is twice the discharge of single acting pump. Work done by a double acting pump is given by

$$\text{Work done/sec} = \frac{\gamma (2A - A_p) LN}{60} (h_s + h_d) \qquad \ldots (5.38)$$

If area of piston rod is neglected

$$\text{Work/sec} = \frac{2\gamma ALN (h_s + h_d)}{60} \qquad \ldots (5.39)$$

Power required (theoretical) to run the pump

$$P = \frac{\gamma (2A - A_p) LN (h_s + h_d)}{60} \qquad \ldots (5.40)$$

If area of piston is neglected,

$$P = \frac{2\gamma ALN (h_s + h_d)}{60} \qquad \ldots (5.41)$$

## 5.19 Slip of Reciprocating Pump

**(a) Slip:** "Slip" of the pump is the difference between the theoretical discharge of the pump and the actual discharge of the pump.

Due to the leakage losses and improper operation of the valves, the actual discharge through the pump is always different from the theoretical discharge.

Thus,

$$\text{Slip} = \text{Theoretical discharge} - \text{Actual discharge}$$

$$\boxed{\text{Slip} = Q_t - Q_a} \qquad \ldots (5.42)$$

Sometimes, slip is also expressed as percentage.

$$\text{Percentage slip} = \left(\frac{Q_t - Q_a}{Q_t}\right) \times 100 \qquad \ldots (5.43)$$

$$\text{Percentage slip} = \left(1 - \frac{Q_a}{Q_t}\right) \times 100$$

$$\boxed{\text{Percentage slip} = (1 - C_d) \times 100} \qquad \ldots (5.44)$$

where $C_d$ is known as coefficient of discharge and is defined as ratio of actual discharge to the theoretical discharge.

$$\boxed{\text{Coefficient of discharge, } C_d = \frac{Q_a}{Q_t}} \qquad \ldots (5.45)$$

% slip of nicely maintained pump is about 2 %.

**(b) Negative slip:** Generally, actual discharge is less than the theoretical discharge. However, it sometimes happens that the actual discharge is more than the theoretical discharge. If the suction pipe is very long while delivery pipe short, and the pump runs at high speed, the inertial forces in the suction pipe become very large. Due to this, the delivery valve opens even before the suction stroke is completed. Thus, some liquid goes directly into the delivery pipe before the delivery stroke starts. Thus, the actual discharge is more than the theoretical discharge. The slip is negative, and $C_d$ is greater than one.

## 5.20 Air Vessels

As has been shown already that due to the acceleration head, the maximum speed of the pump and hence the maximum discharge through the pump or the capacity of the pump is restricted.

If the acceleration head is reduced, the pump can be run at higher speed and can give higher discharge.

Due to reduction in acceleration, the velocity in suction and delivery pipes becomes more uniform. Due to this the flow becomes more uniform.

An air vessel is a closed chamber containing compressed air in the top portion and liquid at the bottom of the chamber. At the base there is an opening through which the liquid can flow into the vessel or out of vessel. When liquid enters the vessel, air gets compressed and vice versa.

**Advantages of Air Vessel**

1. Uniform and continuous discharge can be obtained.
2. Considerable amount of work in overcoming the friction in suction and delivery pipe can be saved.
3. The pump can be run at higher speed to give more discharge without the danger of cavitation.

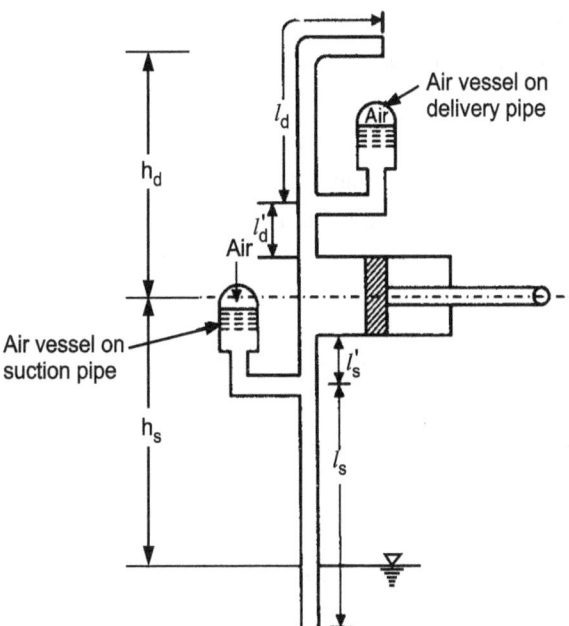

**Fig. 5.15: Reciprocating pump with air vessels**

## 5.20.1 Working of Air Vessel

**(a) Vessel on the suction pipe:** During the first half of the suction stroke, the piston moves with acceleration. Due to this, the velocity of liquid in the suction pipe is more than the average velocity of flow. Therefore, the discharge entering the cylinder is more than the average discharge. This quantity of liquid in excess of average discharge is supplied by the air vessel to the cylinder in such a way that the velocity of liquid in the suction pipe below air vessel is equal to mean velocity of flow in the suction pipe.

During the second half of suction stroke, piston moves with retardation and hence the velocity of liquid in suction pipe is less than the average velocity of flow in the suction pipe. Due to this the discharge entering the cylinder is less than the mean discharge. But due to air vessel, the discharge in the suction pipe below air vessel is average discharge. The discharge, in excess of the discharge required by the cylinder is stored in the air vessel and compresses the air in air vessel. This stored liquid is again supplied during the first half of the next stroke.

**(b) Air vessel on the delivery pipe:** During the first half of delivery stroke, the piston moves with acceleration and forces liquid with velocity more than the average velocity in the delivery pipe. The quantity of liquid which is in excess of the average discharge is stored in the air vessel.

During the second half of delivery stroke, the piston retards and the velocity of liquid in the delivery pipe is less than the average velocity. The liquid, which is already stored in the air vessel, starts flowing out in the delivery pipe, thus maintaining average discharge in the delivery pipe.

Thus, due to air vessels, the velocity of liquid in the suction pipe before the air vessel and in the delivery pipe after the air vessel is uniform and hence the discharge also is more uniform.

However, it may be remembered that the liquid in the suction pipe between the air vessel and the cylinder as well as the liquid in the delivery pipe between the cylinder and the air vessel is subjected to acceleration effects due to changing velocity in these portions of the pipes.

Let
- $A$ = Area of cylinder
- $a$ = Area of suction or delivery pipe
- $L$ = Length of stroke
- $l_d$ = Length of delivery pipe beyond air vessel
- $l'_d$ = Length of delivery pipe between cylinder and air vessel
- $l_s$ = Length of suction pipe below air vessel
- $l'_s$ = Length of suction pipe between air vessel and cylinder
- $h'_{ad}$ = Pressure head due to acceleration in the delivery pipe ($l'_d$)
- $h'_{as}$ = Pressure head due to acceleration in the suction pipe ($l'_s$)
- $h_{fd}$ = Loss of head due to friction in delivery pipe beyond air vessel
- $h'_{fd}$ = Loss of head due to friction in delivery pipe before air vessel
- $h_{fs}$ = Loss of head due to friction in suction pipe before air vessel
- $h'_{fs}$ = Loss of head due to friction in suction pipe beyond air vessel
- $h_{vs}$ = Mean velocity head in the suction pipe
- $h_{v_d}$ = Mean velocity head in delivery pipe.

## 5.20.2 Rate of Flow from and into the Air Vessel

Now for a single acting pump

$$Q = \frac{ALN}{60}$$

Mean velocity of flow in pipe

$$V_m = \frac{Q}{\text{area of pipe}}$$

∴ $V_m = \dfrac{ALN}{60} \cdot \dfrac{1}{a}$

∴ $V_m = \left(\dfrac{AL}{60\,a}\right) \cdot N$      But $\omega = \dfrac{2\pi N}{60}$    ∴ $N = \dfrac{60\,\omega}{2\pi}$

∴ $V_m = \left(\dfrac{AL}{60\,a}\right) \cdot \left(\dfrac{60\,\omega}{2\pi}\right)$      But $L = 2r$

or    $V_m = \dfrac{A}{a} \cdot 2r \cdot \dfrac{\omega}{2\pi}$

or    $\boxed{V_m = \dfrac{A}{a} \cdot \dfrac{\omega r}{\pi}}$      ... (5.46)

However, the instantaneous velocity of liquid in the pipe is given by

$$\boxed{v = \dfrac{A}{a} \cdot \omega r \cdot \sin\theta}$$

The velocity in the pipe will be maximum when $\theta = 90°$, $\sin\theta = 1$ and can be written as

$$\boxed{V_{max} = \dfrac{A}{a} \cdot \omega r} \qquad ... (5.47)$$

∴ From equations (5.46) and (5.47), we get

$$\boxed{V_m = \dfrac{V_{max}}{\pi}} \qquad ... (5.48)$$

or    $\boxed{\dfrac{V_m}{V_{max}} = \dfrac{1}{\pi}}$      ... (5.49)

For double acting pump

$$\boxed{\dfrac{V_m}{V_{max}} = \dfrac{2}{\pi}} \qquad ... (5.50)$$

and so on.

Now, although the discharge from the cylinder into the delivery pipe will vary as the velocity of piston varies, the discharge in the delivery pipe beyond air vessel will be the mean discharge.

Now

Rate of flow from the cylinder

     = Area of piston × velocity of piston

     = $A \times \omega r \sin\theta$      ∵ Velocity of piston = $\omega r \sin\theta$

     = $\boxed{A\omega r \sin\theta}$

Rate of flow in delivery pipe beyond air vessel or in suction pipe before air vessel
= Area of pipe × mean velocity

$$= a \times \left(\frac{A}{a} \cdot \frac{\omega r}{\pi}\right) = \boxed{\frac{A\omega r}{\pi}}$$

Now, Rate of flow of liquid in the air vessel
= Rate of flow from the cylinder − Rate of flow in the delivery pipe beyond air vessel or in suction pipe before air vessel

$$= A\omega r \sin\theta - \frac{A\omega r}{\pi}$$

∴ $\boxed{\text{Rate of flow of liquid in the air vessel} = A\omega r \left(\sin\theta - \frac{1}{\pi}\right)}$ ... (5.51)

If the value of the above equation is positive, the flow is flowing into the air vessel fitted on the delivery pipe. If the value is negative, the flow is from air vessel into the delivery pipe. Exactly reverse is the case for air vessel on suction pipe.

Further it can be seen that, when $\sin\theta = \frac{1}{\pi}$ or $\theta = 18°\ 34'$ or $161°\ 26'$, the right hand side of above equation becomes zero. This means that there will be no flow into or from air vessel.

For double acting pump, we can similarly write

$$\boxed{\text{Rate of flow into the air vessel} = A\omega r \left(\sin\theta - \frac{2}{\pi}\right)} \quad \text{... (5.52)}$$

Again for positive value of above equation, flow is into the air vessel and for negative value flow is out from air vessel for delivery stroke.
Exactly reverse is the case for air vessel on the suction side.
For condition of no flow either into or from air vessel,

$$\theta = \frac{2}{\pi}, \text{ or } \theta = 39°\ 32' \text{ or } 140°\ 27'$$

## 5.20.3 Pressure Head in the Cylinder with Air Vessel

**(a) During suction stroke:** The total head $H_s$ developed during suction stroke for any angle '$\theta$' of the crank is the sum of the following heads.

1. The static head − $\boxed{h_s}$

2. The acceleration head in pipe of length $l_s'$ between the air vessel and the cylinder

$$\boxed{h_{as}' = \frac{l_s'}{g} \cdot \frac{A}{a_s} \cdot \omega^2 r \cos\theta}$$

3. The loss of head due to friction in pipe of length $l_s'$

$$h_{fs}' = \frac{fl_s'}{2g\, d_s}\left(\frac{A}{a}\cdot \omega r \sin\theta\right)^2$$

4. The loss of head due to friction in the suction pipe of length $l_s$ due to uniform velocity $V_{ms}$ in suction pipe below air vessel.

$$h_{fs} = \frac{fl_s}{2g\, d_s}\cdot \frac{V_{ms}^2}{2g}$$

5. The mean velocity head in the suction pipe

$$h_{vs} = \frac{V_{ms}^2}{2g}$$

Therefore, the total head developed during suction stroke can be written as

$$H_s = h_s + h_{as}' + h_{fs}' + h_{fs} + \frac{V_{ms}^2}{2g} \qquad \text{... (5.53)}$$

$$H_s = h_s + \frac{l_s'}{g}\cdot\frac{A}{a_s}\cdot \omega^2 r \cos\theta + \frac{fl_s'}{2g\, d_s}\left(\frac{A}{a}\cdot \omega r \sin\theta\right)^2 + \frac{fl_s}{2g\, d_s}\cdot\frac{V_{ms}^2}{2g} + \frac{V_{ms}^2}{2g} \qquad \text{... (5.54)}$$

Values of $H_s$ at the beginning of the stroke, middle of the stroke and at the end of the stroke can be obtained by putting $\theta = 0°$, $\theta = 90°$ and $\theta = 180°$ respectively.

However, if $l_s'$ is very small, second term $\left(h_{as}'\right)$ and third term $\left(h_{fs}'\right)$ can be neglected.

Many times the last term $\dfrac{V_{ms}^2}{2g}$ is also neglected. Then

$$H_s = h_s + h_{fs} \qquad \text{... (5.55)}$$

The above equation gives the pressure head in the cylinder below atmospheric pressure (or vacuum).

The pressure head in the cylinder can be expressed in terms of absolute pressure as:

$$(H_s)_{absolute} = H_{atmos} - H_s \qquad \text{... (5.56)}$$

**(b) During delivery stroke:** With similar analysis, the pressure head during the delivery stroke with proper subscripts can be written as

$$H_d = h_d + h_{ad}' + h_{fd}' + h_{fd} + \frac{V_{md}^2}{2g} \qquad \text{... (5.57)}$$

or $$H_d = h_d + \frac{l'_d}{g} \cdot \frac{A}{a_d} \cdot \omega^2 r \cos\theta + \frac{fl_d}{2g\, d_d} \cdot \left(\frac{A}{a} \cdot \omega r \sin\theta\right)^2 + \frac{fl_d}{2g\, d_d} \cdot \frac{V_{md}^2}{2g} + \frac{V_{md}^2}{2g} \quad \ldots (5.58)$$

In this case also the values of $H_d$ at the beginning, middle and end of the stroke can be obtained by putting $\theta = 0°$, $\theta = 90°$ and $\theta = 180°$ respectively. If $l'_d$ is small, neglecting minor terms [(2), (3), (5)], we get

$$H_d = h_d + h_{fd} \quad \ldots (5.59)$$

Above equation gives the pressure in the cylinder above atmospheric pressure. If it is expressed as absolute pressure, we get

$$(H_d)_{absolute} = H_{atmos} + H_d \quad \ldots (5.60)$$

# 5.21 Comparison between Centrifugal Pump and Reciprocating Pump

Some of the very important points of comparison between the centrifugal pumps and reciprocating pumps are as follows.

| Centrifugal Pump | Reciprocating Pump |
|---|---|
| 1. For the same capacity, it is more compact in size. | 1. It is more bulky. |
| 2. It is very simple in construction. It has less number of parts. | 2. It is more complicated in construction. It has more number of parts. |
| 3. It is free from valves, glands etc. | 3. Valves, glands etc. require more attention. |
| 4. Discharge is more even and hence freedom from shocks. | 4. Discharge is uneven and hence more shocks on the system. |
| 5. It has high efficiency for wide range of head. | 5. Efficiency falls rapidly under low heads. |
| 6. It is easily adaptable to high speed and hence can be directly coupled to the prime mover. | 6. Not suitable for high speeds and hence has to be coupled through reduction gears. |
| 7. It can be used for viscous oils, sewage water, paper pulp, sugar molasses, chemicals etc. (wide range of fluids) | 7. It can be used only for pure water or clean liquids of low density. |
| 8. It requires low maintenance. Only periodic check is required. | 8. High maintenance cost. Frequent changes of parts is required. |

## ILLUSTRATIVE EXAMPLES

**Example 5.1:**

A centrifugal pump delivers water against a net head of 14.5 m and at a design speed of 1000 rpm. The vanes are curved back at an angle of 30° with the periphery. The impeller diameter is 300 mm and the outlet width is 50 mm. Determine the discharge of the pump if the manometric efficiency is 95%.

**Solution:**

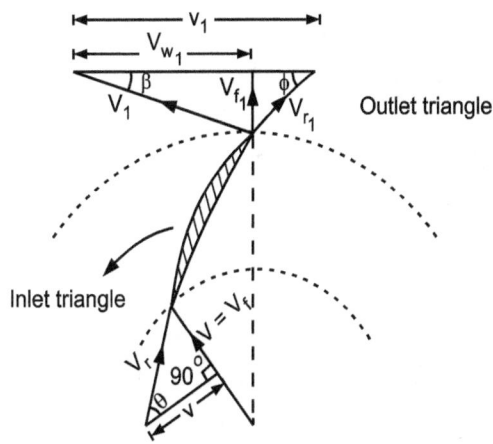

**Fig. 5.16: Inlet and outlet triangle**

The peripheral velocity at exit of the pump,

$$V_1 = \frac{\pi D_1 N}{60} = \frac{\pi \times 0.3 \times 1000}{60}$$

or  $\boxed{V_1 = 15.70 \text{ m/s}}$

Now, manometric efficiency

$$\eta_{mano} = \frac{gH}{V_{w_1} V_1}$$

or $$V_{w_1} = \frac{gH}{\eta_{mano} \times V_1} = \frac{9.81 \times 14.5}{0.95 \times 15.70}$$

or  $\boxed{V_{w_1} = 9.54 \text{ m/s}}$

From outlet triangle, we have

$$V_{f_1} = (V_1 - V_{w_1}) \cdot \tan\phi$$
$$= (15.70 - 9.54) \cdot \tan 30°$$

or  $\boxed{V_{f_1} = 3.556 \text{ m/s}}$

Now, discharge of the pump

$$Q = K_1 \cdot \pi B_1 D_1 V_{f_1}$$
$$= 1 \times \pi \times 0.05 \times 0.3 \times 3.556$$
$$= 0.1676 \text{ m}^3/\text{s}$$

∴ **Discharge of the pump = 167.6 l.p.s.**

### Example 5.2:

The impeller of a centrifugal pump runs at 1440 r.p.m. and has vane curved back at 30°. The radial velocity of flow is constant at 3 m/s. If the manometric efficiency is 80% and the manometric head is 25 m, determine
(i) the vane angle at inlet
(ii) the diameters of the impeller at inlet and exit.
Assume the ratio of outlet diameter of runner to inlet diameter as 2.
Draw the triangles.

**Solution:**

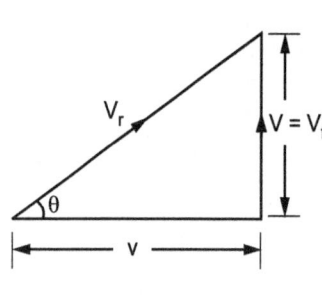
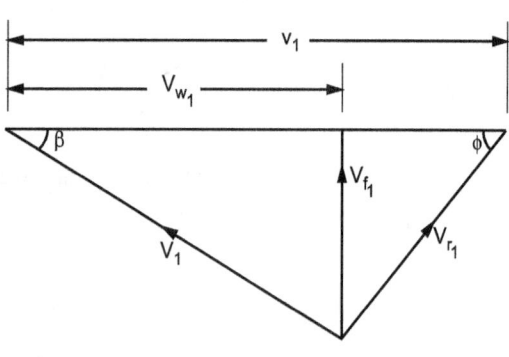

(a) Inlet triangle                    (b) Outlet triangle

**Fig. 5.17**

We have,
$$\eta_{mano} = \frac{gH_m}{V_{w_1} V_1}$$

∴ $$0.8 = \frac{9.81 \times 25}{V_w V_1}$$

∴ $$\boxed{V_{w_1} V_1 = 306.56}$$ ... (i)

Further, from outlet triangle,

$$V_{w_1} = V_1 - \frac{V_{f_1}}{\tan \phi} = V_1 - \frac{3}{\tan 30°}$$

or $$\boxed{V_{w_1} = V_1 - 5.2}$$ ... (ii)

Substituting value of $V_{w_1}$ from (ii) in (i), we get

$$(v_1 - 5.2) \cdot v_1 = 306.56$$

Solving, we get, $\boxed{v_1 = 20.3 \text{ m/s}}$

Tangential velocity at inlet, $v = \dfrac{V_1}{2} = 10.15$ m/s $\qquad \left(\because D = \dfrac{D_1}{2}\right)$

Now from inlet triangle,

$$\theta = \tan^{-1}\dfrac{V_f}{v} = \tan^{-1}\dfrac{3}{10.15} = 16.466° \text{ or } 16° - 27' - 57''$$

∴ $\boxed{\text{Vane angle at inlet, } \theta = 16° - 27' - 57''}$

Diameters at inlet and exit

$$V_1 = \dfrac{\pi D_1 N}{60}$$

∴ $\qquad 20.3 = \dfrac{\pi \times D_1 \times 1440}{60}$

or $\qquad D_1 = 0.269$ m

∴ $\boxed{\text{Diameter at exit, } D_1 = 0.269 \text{ m}}$

$\boxed{\text{Diameter at inlet, } D = \dfrac{D_1}{2} = 0.1345 \text{ m}}$

## Example 5.3:

*The static lift of a centrifugal pump is 40 m. Water level in the sump is 4 m below the axis of the pump. The diameter of suction and delivery pipes is 150 m and the losses of energy head in these pipes are respectively 1.2 m and 8 m of water. The diameter of the impeller is 400 mm and width at outlet is 25 mm. The vanes of impeller are curved backwards at 30° to the tangent. 5 % area of flow is blocked by vane thickness. The manometric efficiency of the pump is 82 %. If the pump runs at 1200 r.p.m., determine:*

*(i) discharge through the pump*

*(ii) pressure head on suction side of pump*

*(iii) pressure head on delivery side of pump.*

**Solution:**

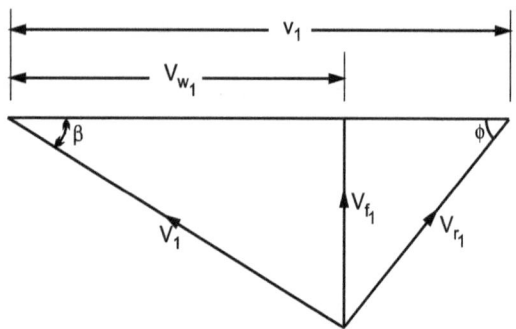

**Fig. 5.18: Outlet triangle**

We have,

$$v_1 = \frac{\pi D_1 N}{60} = \frac{\pi \times 0.4 \times 1200}{60} = 25.13 \text{ m/s}$$

The manometric head

$$H_m = \text{Static lift + friction head loss in suction pipe} + \text{friction head loss in delivery pipe} + \text{velocity head in delivery pipe}$$

or

$$H_m = (h_s + h_d) + h_{fs} + h_{fd} + \frac{V_d^2}{2g}$$

$$= 40 + 1.2 + 8 \qquad \left(\text{neglecting } \frac{V_d^2}{2g}\right)$$

or

$$\boxed{H_m = 49.2 \text{ m}}$$

Now,

$$\eta_{mano} = \frac{gH_m}{V_{w_1} v_1}$$

or

$$V_{w_1} = \frac{gH_m}{\eta_{mano} \cdot v_1} = \frac{9.81 \times 49.2}{0.82 \times 25.13}$$

∴

$$\boxed{V_{w_1} = 23.42 \text{ m/s}}$$

Further,

$$V_{w_1} = v_1 - \frac{V_{f_1}}{\tan \phi}$$

or

$$V_{f_1} = (v_1 - V_{w_1}) \tan \phi$$

$$= (25.13 - 23.42) \cdot \tan 30°$$

∴

$$\boxed{V_{f_1} = 0.99 \text{ m/s}}$$

(i) Discharge, $Q = K_1 \pi B_1 D_1 V_{f_1}$

$= 0.95 \times \pi \times 0.025 \times 0.4 \times 0.99$

$= 0.0295 \text{ m}^3/\text{s}$

∴ **Discharge = 0.0295 m³/s**

Let $V_s$ and $V_d$ be the velocities in suction and delivery pipes respectively.

∴ $V_s = V_d = \dfrac{Q}{\frac{\pi}{4} \cdot d^2} = \dfrac{0.0295}{\frac{\pi}{4} \times (0.15)^2} = 1.67 \text{ m/s}$

∴ $\dfrac{V_s^2}{2g} = \dfrac{V_d^2}{2g} = \dfrac{(1.67)^2}{19.62} = 0.14 \text{ m}$

(ii) Let $p_s$ be the pressure on suction side.

$\dfrac{p_s}{\gamma} = h_s + h_{fs} + \dfrac{V_s^2}{2g}$

$= 4 + 1.2 + 0.14$

$= 5.34 \text{ m (Vacuum)}$

∴ **Pressure head on the suction side = 5.34 m (Vacuum)**

(iii) Let $p_d$ be the pressure on delivery side.

$\dfrac{p_d}{\gamma} = h_d + h_{fd} + \dfrac{V_d^2}{2g}$

$= 36 + 8 + 0.14$

$= 44.14 \text{ m}$

∴ **Pressure head on the delivery side = 44.14 m**

### Example 5.4:

Show that, pressure rise in the impeller of a centrifugal pump having radial entry is given by the expression

$$\dfrac{V_f^2 + v_1^2 \, V_{f_1}^2 \cosec^2 \phi}{2g}$$

provided the frictional and other losses in the impeller are neglected.

**Solution:**

Let $p$ and $p_1$ be the pressure intensities at inlet and outlet of the impeller of the pump.
Applying Bernoulli's equation to inlet and outlet of the impeller neglecting losses,

$\dfrac{p}{\gamma} + \dfrac{V^2}{2g} + \dfrac{V_{w_1} V_1}{g} = \dfrac{p_1}{\gamma} + \dfrac{V_1^2}{2g}$

$$\therefore \quad \frac{p_1}{\gamma} - \frac{p}{\gamma} = \frac{V^2}{2g} + \frac{V_{w_1} v_1}{g} - \frac{v_1^2}{2g}$$

But $\quad \dfrac{p_1}{\gamma} - \dfrac{p}{\gamma} =$ pressure rise in the impeller

$\therefore \quad$ Pressure rise in the impeller $= \dfrac{V^2}{2g} + \dfrac{V_{w_1} v_1}{g} - \dfrac{v_1^2}{2g}$

Since the entry is radial, $V = V_f$. (See any inlet triangle of centrifugal pump)

$$\therefore \quad \boxed{\frac{p_1}{\gamma} - \frac{p}{\gamma} = \frac{V_f^2}{2g} + \frac{V_{w_1} v_1}{g} - \frac{v_1^2}{2g}} \quad \ldots \text{(i)}$$

Now, from outlet triangle,

$$\boxed{V_{w_1} = v_1 - V_{f_1} \cot\phi} \quad \ldots \text{(ii)}$$

and $\quad v_1^2 = V_{f_1}^2 + V_{w_1}^2 = \left[V_{f_1}^2 + (v_1 - V_{f_1}\cot\phi)^2\right]$

or $\quad v_1^2 = V_{f_1}^2 + v_1^2 - 2v_1 V_{f_1}\cot\phi + V_{f_1}^2 \cot^2\phi$

or $\quad v_1^2 = V_{f_1}^2 (1 + \cot^2\phi) + v_1^2 - 2v_1 V_{f_1}\cot\phi$

or $\quad \boxed{v_1^2 = V_{f_1}^2 \csc^2\phi + v_1^2 - 2v_1 V_{f_1}\cot\phi} \quad \ldots \text{(iii)}$

Substituting values of $V_{w_1}$ and $V_1$ in the expression for pressure rise (i), we get

$$\frac{p_1}{\gamma} - \frac{p}{\gamma} = \frac{V_f^2}{2g} + \frac{v_1(v_1 - V_{f_1}\cot\phi)}{g} - \frac{V_{f_1}^2 \csc^2\phi + v_1^2 - 2v_1 V_{f_1}\cot\phi}{2g}$$

$$= \frac{V_f^2}{2g} + \frac{2v_1^2}{2g} - \frac{2v_1 V_{f_1}\cot\phi}{2g} - \frac{V_{f_1}^2 \csc^2\phi}{2g} - \frac{v_1^2}{2g} + \frac{2v_1 V_{f_1}\cot\phi}{2g}$$

$$= \frac{V_f^2}{2g} + \frac{v_1^2}{2g} - \frac{V_{f_1}^2 \csc^2\phi}{2g}$$

$$= \frac{1}{2g}\left[V_f^2 + v_1^2 - V_{f_1}^2 \csc^2\phi\right]$$

or $\quad \boxed{\text{Pressure rise in the impeller} = \dfrac{1}{2g}\left[V_f^2 + v_1^2 - V_{f_1}^2 \csc^2\phi\right]}$

## Example 5.5:

Show that manometric head of a centrifugal pump running at speed N and giving discharge Q may be written as

$$H_{mano} = AN^2 + BNQ + CQ^2$$

where A, B and C are constants.

### Solution:

We know that the manometric head

$$H_m = \frac{V_{w_1} v_1}{g} - \frac{v_1^2}{2g}$$

provided nothing of $V_1$ is converted into pressure head.

But we have from outlet triangle,

$$V_{w_1} = (v_1 - V_{f_1} \cot \phi)$$

and

$$v_1^2 = V_{f_1}^2 + V_{w_1}^2$$

Substituting,

$$H_m = \frac{(v_1 - V_{f_1} \cot \phi) v_1}{g} - \frac{V_{f_1}^2 + (v_1 - V_{f_1} \cot \phi)^2}{2g}$$

$$= \frac{2v_1^2}{2g} - \frac{2v_1 V_{f_1} \cot \phi}{2g} - \frac{V_{f_1}^2}{2g} - \frac{v_1^2}{2g} + \frac{2v_1 V_{f_1} \cot \phi}{2g} - \frac{V_{f_1}^2 \cot^2 \phi}{2g}$$

$$= \frac{v_1^2}{2g} - \frac{V_{f_1}^2}{2g} (1 + \cot^2 \phi)$$

or

$$\boxed{H_m = \frac{1}{2g} \left( v_1^2 - V_{f_1}^2 \operatorname{cosec}^2 \phi \right)} \quad \ldots (i)$$

This expression is true if there is no device provided in pump to convert the kinetic energy of water on leaving the impeller. If any device like volute chamber, or a vortex chamber is used, part of the kinetic energy $\frac{v_1^2}{2g}$ can be converted into pressure head. Let the portion of kinetic energy converted into pressure head be $K \frac{v_1^2}{2g}$. Then,

$$H_m = \frac{1}{2g} \left( v_1^2 - V_{f_1}^2 \operatorname{cosec}^2 \phi \right) + K \frac{v_1^2}{2g}$$

or
$$H_m = \frac{1}{2g}\left(v_1^2 - V_{f_1}^2 \cosec^2\phi\right) + K\frac{\left(V_{w_1}^2 + V_{f_1}^2\right)}{2g}$$

$$= \frac{1}{2g}\left(v_1^2 - V_{f_1}^2 \cosec^2\phi\right) + \frac{K}{2g}\left[(v_1 - V_{f_1} \cot\phi)^2 + V_{f_1}^2\right]$$

or
$$H_m = \frac{(1+K)}{2g}v_1^2 - \frac{2K\cot\phi}{2g}v_1 V_{f_1} - \frac{(1-K)\cosec^2\phi}{2g}V_{f_1}^2$$

But
$$v_1 = \frac{\pi D_1 N}{60} \quad \text{or } v_1 \propto N$$

and
$$Q = K_1 \pi B_1 D_1 V_{f_1} \quad \text{or } V_{f_1} \propto Q$$

∴
$$\boxed{H_m = AN^2 + BNQ + CQ^2}$$

### Example 5.6:

A four stage centrifugal pump has four identical impellers, keyed to the same shaft. The shaft is running at a speed of 400 r.p.m. and the total manometric head developed by the multistage pump is 40 m. The discharge through the pump is 0.2 m³/s. The vanes of each impeller are having outlet angle of 45°. If the width and diameter of each impeller at outlet is 5 cm and 60 cm respectively, determine manometric efficiency.

**Solution:**

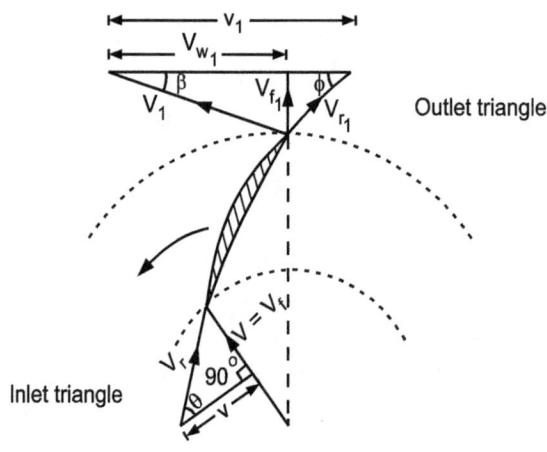

**Fig. 5.19**

The manometric head per stage $= \frac{40}{4} = 10$ m

The peripheral velocity at outlet, $v_1 = \frac{\pi D_1 N}{60} = \frac{\pi \times 0.6 \times 400}{60}$

or
$$\boxed{v_1 = 12.56 \text{ m/s}}$$

Now, we have, $Q = K_1 \pi B_1 D_1 V_{f_1}$

or $\quad 0.2 = 1 \times \pi \times 0.05 \times 0.6 \times V_{f_1}$

or the velocity of flow at outlet, $\boxed{V_{f_1} = 2.122 \text{ m/s}}$

From velocity triangle at outlet, the velocity of whirl at outlet is

$$V_{w_1} = v_1 - \frac{V_{f_1}}{\tan \phi}$$

$$= 12.56 - \frac{2.122}{\tan 45°}$$

$$= 12.56 - 2.122$$

or $\quad \boxed{V_{w_1} = 10.438 \text{ m/s}}$

∴ Manometric efficiency

$$\eta_m = \frac{gH_m}{V_{w_1} v_1}$$

$$= \frac{9.81 \times 10.0}{10.438 \times 12.56}$$

$$= 0.7482 \text{ or } 74.82\%$$

∴ $\boxed{\text{Manometric efficiency} = 74.82\%}$

## Example 5.7:

A three stage centrifugal pump has impeller 425 mm diameter and 20 mm wide at the outlet. The vanes are curved back and the outlet vane angle is 30°. The vanes occupy 5% of the outlet area. The manometric efficiency is 87% and overall efficiency is 77%. What head will the pump generate when running at 850 r.p.m. discharging 3800 lit./min.? What is the input power required by the pump?

**Solution:**

We have,

$$v_1 = \frac{\pi D_1 N}{60} = \frac{\pi \times 0.425 \times 850}{60}$$

or $\quad \boxed{v_1 = 18.915 \text{ m/s}}$

Further, $\quad Q = K_1 \pi B_1 D_1 V_{f_1} \quad \left[ \text{where } Q = \frac{3800}{1000 \times 60} = 0.0633 \text{ m}^3/\text{s} \right]$

∴ $\quad 0.0633 = 0.95 \times \pi \times 0.02 \times 0.425 \times V_{f_1}$

or $\quad \boxed{V_{f_1} = 2.5 \text{ m/s}}$

Now from outlet triangle,

$$V_{w_1} = V_1 - \frac{V_{f_1}}{\tan \phi} = 18.915 - \frac{2.5}{\tan 30°}$$

or $\boxed{V_{w_1} = 14.59 \text{ m/s}}$

Therefore, the manometric head per stage of the pump is,

$$\eta_{mano} = \frac{gH_{m_1}}{V_{w_1} V_1}$$

$$\therefore \quad H_{m_1} = \frac{\eta_{mano} \cdot V_{w_1} \cdot V_1}{g}$$

$$= \frac{0.87 \times 14.59 \times 18.915}{9.81} = 24.47 \text{ m}$$

Hence, the total manometric head developed by three stages

$$H_m = 3 \times 24.47$$

or $\boxed{H_m = 73.42 \text{ m}}$

Power required by pump is given by

$$\text{Power} = \frac{\gamma \cdot Q \cdot H_m}{\eta_o} = \frac{9.81 \times 0.0633 \times 73.42}{0.77}$$

$$\boxed{\text{Power} = 59.21 \text{ kW}}$$

### Example 5.8:

Impellers of a 3 stage pump have their external diameter and width as 350 mm and 50 mm respectively. The pump runs at 1000 r.p.m. against a total head of 45 m. If the vane angle at outlet is $35°$ and manometric efficiency is 80%, determine (i) the velocity of water leaving the vane and it's direction and (ii) the discharge if 10% of the area at outlet is blocked by vane thickness. Draw velocity triangles.

**Solution:**

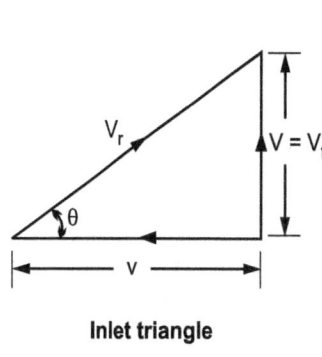

Inlet triangle

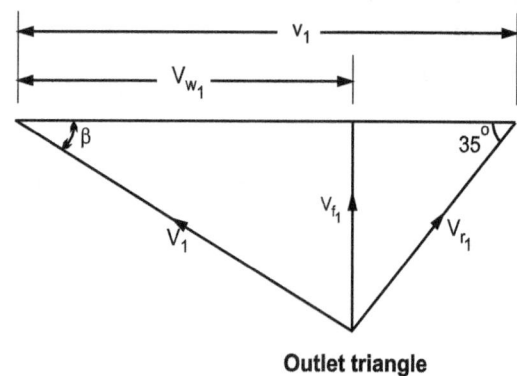

Outlet triangle

Fig. 5.20

The manometric head per stage of pump

$$H_m = \frac{45}{3} = 15 \text{ m}$$

The tangential velocity at the exit of pump

$$v_1 = \frac{\pi D_1 N}{60} = \frac{\pi \times 0.35 \times 1000}{60}$$

or $\boxed{v_1 = 18.33 \text{ m/s}}$

Now we have,

$$\eta_{mano} = \frac{gH_m}{V_{w_1} v_1}$$

or

$$V_{w_1} = \frac{gH_m}{v_1 \cdot \eta_{mano}}$$

$$= \frac{9.81 \times 15}{18.33 \times 0.8}$$

or $\boxed{V_{w_1} = 10.04 \text{ m/s}}$

Further, we have, from outlet triangle,

$$V_{w_1} = v_1 - \frac{V_{f_1}}{\tan \phi}$$

or $V_{f_1} = (v_1 - V_{w_1}) \cdot \tan \phi$

$$= (18.33 - 10.04) \cdot \tan 35°$$

or $\boxed{V_{f_1} = 5.8 \text{ m/s}}$

Therefore, the velocity of water leaving the vane, from outlet triangle is

$$V_1 = \sqrt{V_{f_1}^2 + V_{w_1}^2}$$

$$= \sqrt{(5.8)^2 + (10.04)^2}$$

$$= 11.6 \text{ m/s}$$

∴ $\boxed{\text{Velocity of water leaving the vane, } V_1 = 11.6 \text{ m/s}}$

Further,

$$\tan \beta = \frac{V_{f_1}}{V_{w_1}}$$

$$= \frac{5.8}{10.04}$$

$$= 0.577$$

∴ $\boxed{\beta = 30.01°}$

Discharge, $Q = K_1 \pi B_1 D_1 V_{f_1}$
$= 0.9 \times \pi \times 0.05 \times 0.35 \times 5.8$
$= 0.287 \text{ m}^3/\text{s}$

∴ **Discharge, $Q = 0.287 \text{ m}^3/\text{s}$**

## Example 5.9:

A centrifugal pump with external diameter 600 mm and internal diameter 200 mm delivers 500 lps of water against a head of 15 m.

The speed of the pump is 600 r.p.m. The vanes of impeller are curved backwards at an angle of 30° to the wheel tangent at outlet. The velocity of flow is constant at 2 m/s. If the entry to the pump is radial, determine

(i) Power required

(ii) Efficiency and

(iii) Minimum starting speed.

**Solution:**

Refer to Fig. 5.16.

We have, $V_1 = \dfrac{\pi D_1 N}{60} = \dfrac{\pi \times 0.6 \times 600}{60}$

$\boxed{V_1 = 18.85 \text{ m/s}}$

Now from outlet triangle

$V_{w_1} = V_1 - V_{f_1} \cot \phi$

$= 18.85 - 2 \times \cot 30°$

$= 18.85 - 3.464$

or $\boxed{V_{w_1} = 15.386 \text{ m/s}}$

(i) Power required

$P = \gamma.Q. \dfrac{V_{w_1} V_1}{g}$

$= 9.81 \times 0.5 \times \dfrac{15.386 \times 18.85}{9.81}$

or $P = 145.01 \text{ kW}$

or **Power required $= 145.01 \text{ kW}$**

## (ii) Efficiency

$$\eta_{mano} = \frac{gH}{V_{w_1} V_1} = \frac{9.81 \times 15}{15.386 \times 18.85}$$

$$= 0.507 \text{ or } 50.7\%$$

$$\therefore \boxed{\eta_{mano} = 50.7\%}$$

(iii) Minimum starting speed. For minimum speed,

$$\frac{V_1^2}{2g} - \frac{v^2}{2g} = H_m$$

Now, $\dfrac{V_1}{D_1} = \dfrac{V}{D}$

$$V_1 = \frac{D_1}{D} V = \frac{600}{200} \cdot V$$

or $V_1 = 3v$

$\therefore (3v)^2 - (v)^2 = 2g\, H_m$

$\therefore \quad 8v^2 = 19.62 \times 15$

$\therefore \quad v = 6.0653$ m/s

But, $V = \dfrac{\pi DN}{60}$

or $\dfrac{\pi \times 0.2 \times N}{60} = 6.0653$

or $N = \dfrac{6.0653 \times 60}{\pi \times 0.2}$

or $N = 579.19$ r.p.m.

$\therefore$ $\boxed{\text{Minimum starting speed} = 579.19 \text{ rpm}}$

## Example 5.10:

A centrifugal pump discharges 200 lps of water against a head of 15 m. The pump runs at 600 rpm. The outer and inner diameters of the impeller are 50 cm and 25 cm respectively and the vanes are setback at 45° to the tangent at the exit. If the area of flow remains 0.08 m² from inlet to outlet, calculate

(i) Manometric efficiency of the pump,
(ii) Vane angle at inlet, and
(iii) Loss of head at inlet to the impeller if the discharge is reduced by 40% without changing the speed.

**Solution:**

Since the area of flow is constant at inlet and outlet, velocity of flow at inlet and outlet will be the same, given by

$$V_f = V_{f_1} = \frac{Q}{\text{Area of flow}} = \frac{0.2}{0.08} = 2.5 \text{ m/s}$$

or $\boxed{V_f = V_{f_1} = 2.5 \text{ m/s}}$

The tangential velocities at outlet and inlet are

$$V_1 = \frac{\pi D_1 N}{60} = \frac{\pi \times 0.5 \times 600}{60} = 15.70 \text{ m/s}$$

$$V = \frac{\pi D N}{60} = \frac{\pi \times 0.25 \times 600}{60} = 7.85 \text{ m/s}$$

∴ $\boxed{V_1 = 15.70 \text{ m/s}}$ and $\boxed{v = 7.85 \text{ m/s}}$

Now, from outlet triangle,

$$V_{w_1} = V_1 - V_{f_1} \cot \phi = 15.70 - 2.5 \times 1$$

$$\boxed{V_{w_1} = 13.20 \text{ m/s}}$$

**(i) Manometric efficiency**

$$\eta_{mano} = \frac{gH}{V_{w_1} V_1} = \frac{9.81 \times 15}{13.2 \times 15.70} = 0.71$$

∴ $\boxed{\eta_{mano} = 71\%}$

**(ii) Vane angle at inlet**

$$\tan \theta = \frac{V_f}{V} = \frac{2.5}{7.85} = 0.3185$$

$$\theta = 17.677° \text{ or } \theta = 17° - 40'$$

∴ $\boxed{\text{Vane angle at inlet} = 17° - 40'}$

**(iii) Loss of head at inlet**

Now discharge $= 0.6 \times 0.2 = 0.12 \text{ m}^3/\text{s}$

∴ New velocity of flow,

$$V_f = \frac{0.12}{0.08} = 1.5 \text{ m/s}$$

∴ Loss due to change in discharge,

$$h_L = \frac{(v - V_f \cot\theta)^2}{2g}$$

$$= \frac{[7.85 - 1.5 \times \cot(17.667)]^2}{19.62}$$

$$= 0.503 \text{ m}$$

∴ **Loss of head due to reduction in discharge = 0.503 m**

## Example 5.11:

During a test on a centrifugal pump, following observations were made:

1. Vacuum gauge reading on suction side — 295 mm of mercury
2. Pressure gauge reading on delivery side — 18 m of water
3. Distance between the gauges (delivery above suction) — 0.5 m
4. Power required by pump — 70 kW
5. Discharge of pump — 200 l.p.s.
6. Diameter of suction pipe — 30 cm
7. Diameter of delivery pipe — 25 cm

Find the manometric head and overall efficiency of the pump.

**Solution:**

Pressure head on suction side

$$\frac{p_s}{\gamma} = -\left(\frac{295}{1000} \times 13.6\right) = -(4.0) \text{ m}$$

∴ $\boxed{\dfrac{p_s}{\gamma} = -4.0 \text{ m}}$

Pressure head on delivery side

$$\boxed{\frac{p_d}{\gamma} = 18.0 \text{ m}}$$

Velocity in suction pipe,

$$V_s = \frac{4Q}{\pi \times (0.3)^2}$$

$$= \frac{4 \times 0.2}{\pi \times (0.3)^2} = 2.83 \text{ m/s}$$

∴ $\boxed{\dfrac{V_s^2}{2g} = 0.408 \text{ m}}$

Velocity in delivery pipe

$$V_d = \frac{4Q}{\pi \times (0.25)^2}$$

$$= \frac{4 \times 0.2}{\pi \times (0.25)^2} = 4.07 \text{ m/s}$$

∴ $\boxed{\dfrac{V_d^2}{2g} = 0.844 \text{ m}}$

Applying Bernoulli's equation to suction and delivery side

$$Z_s + \frac{P_s}{\gamma} + \frac{V_s^2}{2g} + H_m = Z_d + \frac{P_d}{\gamma} + \frac{V_d^2}{2g}$$

$$0 + (-4) + 0.408 + H_m = 0.5 + 18 + 0.844$$

∴ $\boxed{H_m = 22.94 \text{ m}}$

Manometric efficiency,

$$\eta_o = \frac{\text{Power developed by pump}}{\text{Input power}}$$

$$= \frac{\gamma Q H_m}{\text{Input power}}$$

$$= \frac{9.81 \times 0.2 \times 22.94}{70}$$

$$= 0.643 \text{ or } 64.3\%$$

∴ $\boxed{\text{Overall efficiency} = 64.3\%}$

## Example 5.12:

Two geometrically similar pumps are run at the same speed of 1000 r.p.m. One pump has an impeller diameter of 0.25 m and lifts water at the rate of 20 lit./sec. against a head of 15 m. Determine the head and impeller diameter of other pump to deliver half the discharge.

**Solution:**

| Pump 1 | Pump 2 |
|---|---|
| $N_1$ = 1000 r.p.m. | $N_2$ = 1000 r.p.m. |
| $D_1$ = 0.25 m | $D_2$ = ? |
| $Q_1$ = 0.02 m³/s | $Q_2$ = 0.01 m³/s |
| $H_1$ = 15 m | $H_2$ = ? |

(i) We have
$$\left[\frac{N\sqrt{Q}}{H^{3/4}}\right]_1 = \left[\frac{N\sqrt{Q}}{H^{3/4}}\right]_2$$

$$\therefore \frac{1000 \times \sqrt{0.02}}{(15)^{3/4}} = \frac{1000 \times \sqrt{0.01}}{H_2^{3/4}}$$

$$\therefore H_2 = 9.45 \text{ m}$$

**Head of the second pump = 9.45 m**

(ii) Now,
$$\left[\frac{Q}{ND^3}\right]_1 = \left[\frac{Q}{ND^3}\right]_2$$

$$\therefore \frac{0.02}{1000 \times (0.25)^3} = \frac{0.01}{1000 \times D_2^3}$$

$$\therefore D_2 = 0.198 \text{ m or } 19.8 \text{ cm}$$

**Diameter of the second pump = 19.8 cm**

### Example 5.13:

A centrifugal pump supplies water to an head of 38.5 m. However, later it was required to supply water against head of 35 m. Find the necessary reduction in impeller diameter if it is required to reduce the original diameter of 500 mm without reducing the speed of impeller.

**Solution:**

We have,
$$\left[\frac{H}{N^2 D^2}\right]_1 = \left[\frac{H}{N^2 D^2}\right]_2$$

$$\therefore \frac{38.5}{N_1^2 \times (0.5)^2} = \frac{35}{N_2^2 \times (D_2)^2} \quad \text{But } N_1 = N_2$$

$$\therefore D_2^2 = \frac{35}{38.5} \times (0.5)^2$$

$$\therefore D_2 = 0.477 \text{ m or } 477 \text{ mm}$$

$$\therefore \boxed{\text{Reduction in diameter} = 23 \text{ mm}}$$

### Example 5.14:

The diameter of a centrifugal pump which is discharging 0.03 m³/s of water against a head of 20 m is 0.4 m. The pump is running at 1500 r.p.m. Find the head, discharge and ratio of power of a geometrically similar pump of diameter 0.25 m when it is running at 3000 r.p.m. What will be specific speed for the second pump?

## Solution:

We have,

**Head:**
$$\left[\frac{\sqrt{H_m}}{DN}\right]_1 = \left[\frac{\sqrt{H_m}}{DN}\right]_2$$

$$\left[\frac{\sqrt{20}}{0.4 \times 1500}\right] = \left[\frac{\sqrt{H_m}}{0.25 \times 3000}\right]$$

∴ **Head of second pump = 31.25 m**

**Discharge:**
$$\left[\frac{Q}{ND^3}\right]_1 = \left[\frac{Q}{ND^3}\right]_2$$

∴ $$\left[\frac{0.03}{1500 \times (0.4)^3}\right] = \left[\frac{Q}{3000 \times (0.25)^3}\right]$$

∴ **Discharge of second pump = 0.01465 m³/s**

**Power ratio:**
$$\left[\frac{P}{D^5 N^3}\right]_1 = \left[\frac{P}{D^5 N^3}\right]_2$$

∴ $$\frac{P_1}{P_2} = \frac{[D^5 N^3]_1}{[D^5 N^3]_2}$$

$$= \frac{(0.4)^5 (1500)^3}{(0.25)^5 (3000)^3}$$

$$= 1.31$$

∴ **Power ratio = 1.31**

**Specific speed:** $N_{s1} = N_{s2} = \dfrac{N\sqrt{Q}}{H^{3/4}} = \dfrac{3000\sqrt{0.01465}}{(31.25)^{0.75}}$

**$N_s$ = 27.47**

## Example 5.15:

Determine the least number of stages for a multistage pump for following data:
1. Discharge = 60 l.p.s.
2. Head = 175 m
3. Speed = 1440 r.p.m.

The specific speed per stage should not exceed 20.

**Solution:**

Specific speed per stage is limited to 20. Therefore, the maximum head per stage is given by,

$$N_s = \frac{N\sqrt{Q}}{H^{3/4}}$$

$$H^{3/4} = \frac{1440 \times \sqrt{0.06}}{20}$$

Head per stage, $H = 45.9$ m

∴ Number of stages $= \dfrac{\text{Total head}}{\text{Head per stage}}$

$$= \frac{175}{45.9}$$

$$= 3.81 \approx 4$$

∴ use 4 stages

## THEORETICAL QUESTIONS

1. What do you understand by centrifugal pump?
2. Compare centrifugal pump with reciprocating pump.
3. Explain classification of centrifugal pump.
4. What are different component parts of a centrifugal pump? Explain their function with a neat sketch.
5. Explain with neat sketch the three types of impeller for a centrifugal pump.
6. Give classification of centrifugal pump based on various factors. Sketch centrifugal pump and show all its component parts.
7. How are centrifugal pumps classified based on specific speed?
8. Draw centrifugal pump and explain its working.
9. Write a short note on priming of a centrifugal pump.
10. Why priming is necessary for a centrifugal pump? What are the various methods of priming?
11. Define: (a) Static head
    (b) Manometric head
    (c) Specific speed
    (d) Delivery head
    (e) Gross head
    (f) Suction head

12. What do you mean by manometric efficiency, mechanical efficiency, volumetric efficiency, hydraulic efficiency and overall efficiency of a centrifugal pump and state their formulae?
13. Write a short note on efficiency of centrifugal pump.
14. Write a short note on minimum starting speed.
15. Derive an expression for minimum speed of starting a centrifugal pump.
16. Derive an expression for the loss of head in case of a centrifugal pump, when the discharge flowing is either greater or less than the design discharge.
17. Write short note on: NPSH – Centrifugal pump.
18. List out any four factors affecting value of NPSH of a centrifugal pump.
19. What is the NPSH of centrifugal pump? Distinguish between available NPSH and required NPSH.
20. Write a short note on: Cavitation in centrifugal pump.
21. Write a note on cavitation in centrifugal pump and it's effects and remedies to reduce these effects.
22. What is specific speed of centrifugal pump? How does it differ from specific speed of turbine?
23. Derive an expression for specific speed of a centrifugal pump.
24. Write a short note on: Characteristic curves of a centrifugal pump.
25. Write a note on model testing of pumps.
26. Write short notes on:
    (1) Multistaging for high heads.
    (2) Multistaging for high discharges.
27. Differentiate between a single stage and multistage centrifugal pump. Describe multi-stage pumps with impellers in (i) series and (ii) parallel.
28. Write a short note on selection of pump.
29. Name the type of pump in the following cases:
    (i) Pumping paper pulp and sewage water.
    (ii) Pumping large quantity of water under small head.
30. What is the use of foot valve in centrifugal pump?
31. Write a note on self-priming pump.
32. Write a note on different impellers used in a centrifugal pump.
33. Write merits and demerits of a centrifugal pump.
34. On starting the centrifugal pump, if no water is delivered, what is the probable reason? What corrective measures should be taken?

## NUMERICAL PROBLEMS

1. A centrifugal pump running at a speed of 1440 r.p.m. gives 63 lps under a static head of 37 m. If the delivery pipe diameter is 150 mm and the loss in the pipe system is 9.27 m, determine the specific speed of the pump. Which type of pump is it?
   [**Ans.** 20.158, radial flow pump]

2. The impeller of a centrifugal pump runs at 750 r.p.m. and has the vanes inclined at 150° to the direction of motion at exit. The manometric head of the pump is 35 m and the manometric efficiency is 84%. Assuming velocity of flow to be constant at 3.2 m/s and the diameter of the impeller at exit as twice that at inlet, calculate:
   (i) The diameter of impeller at exit and
   (ii) The vane angle at inlet.
   [**Ans.** 0.59 m, 15° – 26′]

3. A centrifugal pump with inner and outer impeller diameters of 200 mm and 400 mm respectively, runs at 1440 r.p.m. Radial velocity of water through the pump is constant at 2.7 m/s. If the vanes are set back at 30° to outlet, determine the angle of vanes at inlet and velocity and direction of flow at outlet.
   [**Ans.** 10.15°, 25.622 m/s, 6.05°]

4. A centrifugal pump with external diameter 600 mm and internal diameter 200 mm delivers 500 lps of water against a head of 15 m. The speed of the pump is 600 r.p.m. The vanes of impeller are curved backwards at an angle of 30° to the wheel tangent at outlet. The velocity of flow is constant at 2 m/s. If the entry to the pump is radial, determine
   (i) Power required
   (ii) Efficiency.
   (iii) Minimum starting speed.
   [**Ans.** 145 kW, 51%, 570.19 r.p.m.]

5. The outer diameter and outlet width of a centrifugal pump is 50 cm and 5 cm respectively. The pump develops total head of 25 m, when running under 1000 r.p.m. If the vane angle at outlet is 40° and manometric efficiency is 80%, find
   (i) Velocity of flow at outlet.
   (ii) Velocity of water leaving the vane.
   (iii) Angle made by absolute velocity at outlet.
   (iv) Discharge.
   [**Hint:** Refer Illustrative example 5.8]
   [**Ans.:** 12.14 m/s, 16.86 m/s, 134°, 0.953 m$^3$/s]

6. A centrifugal pump operating against a total head of 55 m discharges 0.03 m$^3$/s of water when running at 1440 r.p.m. The velocity of flow is constant at 2 m/s and the vanes are curved back at 45° to the tangent at exit. Impeller diameters at inlet and outlet are 45 cm and 90 cm respectively. If the manometric efficiency is 80%, find
   (i) Blade angle at the inlet and
   (ii) Power required to drive the pump.
   [**Ans.** 8.43°, 20.233 kW]

7. With the following data in respect of centrifugal pump, determine the discharge and pressure at suction and delivery side of the pump.
   (i) Total static head = 35 m
   (ii) Speed of rotation = 1200 r.p.m..
   (iii) Suction head 4 m, loss in suction 1.5, suction pipe diameter – 150 mm.
   (iv) Delivery head loss 7 m, delivery pipe diameter 150 mm
   (v) Impeller outer diameter 380 mm, width at outlet 25 mm
   (vi) Exit blade angle 38°, vanes occupy 5% of outlet area.
   (vii) Manometric efficiency 80%.
   Assume radial inlet.
   [**Ans.** 0.0323 m³/s, 55.62 kPa (vacuum), 372.78 kPa]

8. A centrifugal pump lifts water under static head of 36 m of which suction head is 4 m. Suction and delivery pipes are 150 mm diameter and having their lengths such that they cause head loss of 1.5 m and 7 m in suction and delivery pipe respectively. Impeller outer dia = 0.38 m, width at outlet = 25 mm, N = 1200 r.p.m. Exit blade has an angle of 38°. The vanes occupy 5% of the total area, manometric efficiency = 80%. Assume radial inlet entry. Determine discharge, suction pressure and delivery pressure.
   [**Hint:** Refer Illustrative Example 5.3]
   [**Ans.** 22.8 lps, 54.79 kPa (Vacuum), 383.42 kPa].

9. The diameters of an impeller of centrifugal pump at inlet and outlet are 30 cm and 60 cm respectively. The velocity of flow at outlet is 2.5 m/s and the vanes are set back at an angle of 45° at the outlet. Determine the starting speed of the pump if the manometric efficiency is 80%.

   **Hint:** 
   $$v_1 = \frac{\pi \times 0.6}{60} \times N = 0.03141 \, N - m/s.$$
   $$V_{w_1} = (0.03141 \, N - 2.5) \, m$$
   $$N = \frac{120 \times \eta_{mano} \times (V_{w_1}) \times D_1}{\pi \left(D_1^2 - D^2\right)} \text{ etc.}$$

   [**Ans.** 149.84 ppm say 150 r.p.m.]

10. A three stage centrifugal pump has impellers 600 mm in diameter and 30 mm wide at outlet. The vanes are curved back and the outlet vane angle is 30°. The vanes occupy 5% of the outlet area. The manometric efficiency is 85% and the overall efficiency is 75%. What head will the pump generate when running at 1200 r.p.m. and discharging 4200 lpm? What is the input power required? What is the specific speed of the pump?
    [**Ans.** 347.31 m, 318 kW, 3.95 for all stages, 8.996 for single stage]

■■■

www.ingramcontent.com/pod-product-compliance
Lightning Source LLC
Chambersburg PA
CBHW080540230426
43663CB00015B/2660